P9-BZR-792

OUR GLORIOUS CENTURY

READER'S DIGEST

OUR GLORIOUS CENTURY

Reader's Digest

THE READER'S DIGEST ASSOCIATION, INC.　　PLEASANTVILLE, NEW YORK / MONTREAL

McLean County Unit #5

OUR GLORIOUS CENTURY

STAFF

Editorial

Editor
Edmund H. Harvey, Jr.

Senior Editor
David G. Rattray

Senior Associate Editors
Kathryn Bonomi
Thomas A. Ranieri

Associate Editor
Audrey Peterson

Art

Group Art Editor
Joel Musler

Project Art Editor
Sandra Berinstein

Senior Art Associate
Nancy Mace

Art Associate
Bruce R. McKillip

Research

Research Editors
Sandra Streepey
Susan Biederman

Research Associate
Kathleen Derzipilski

Research Librarian
Nettie Seaberry

CONTRIBUTORS

Editor-Writers
Bryce Walker (Chief), John L. Cobbs,
Anne Moffat, George Walsh,
Henry Wiencek

Writers
Robert Brown, Terry Brown,
Tom Callahan, Rita Christopher,
Justin Cronin, Joseph Durso,
Martha Fay, Thomas J. Fleming,
Marjorie Flory, Annette Foglino,
Mark Gasper, Kevin Gillespie,
Roger E. Hernandez, Eileen Hughes,
William C. Nowels, Josh Ozersky,
Donald Pfarrer, Karla K. Powell,
Curtis W. Prendergast,
Susan Harrington Preston,
Carl Proujan, Thomas L. Robinson,
Gerry Schremp, Charles A. Silliman,
Jozefa Stuart, Evelyn Toynton,
Daniel Weiss

Designers
Richard Boddy, Ed Jacobus (Maps),
Design Five (Charts),
Steve Karp (Computer Graphics)

Copy Editor
Joan Wilkinson

Researchers
Mary Hart (Chief), Pamela Kladzyk,
Willard Lubka, Marlene McCampbell,
Joan Walsh

Picture Researchers
Mary Leverty (Chief), Mary Burns,
Romy Charlesworth, Richard Fox,
Sue Israel, Jerry Kearns,
Sybille Millard, Sabra Moore,
Marion Paone, Richard Seidel,
Yvonne Silver

Indexer
Sydney Wolfe Cohen

Principal Consultants
Col. John R. Elting
  U. S. Army (Retired)

Irwin Unger, Ph.D.
  Professor of American History
  New York University

Consultants
Alan C. Aimone
  *Assistant Librarian for Special
  Collections*
  U.S. Military Academy Library

Claudia Anderson
  Senior Archivist
  Lyndon Baines Johnson Library

Frank Aucella
  Assistant Director
  Woodrow Wilson House
  A Museum Property of the National
  Trust for Historic Preservation

Consultants *(continued)*

David Bafumo
Researcher
National Archives

Paul Boyer
Merle Curtis Professor of History
University of Wisconsin – Madison

Bruce Conforth, Ph.D.
Curator
Rock and Roll Hall of Fame and
Museum

Vincent Demma
Historian
U. S. Army Center of Military History

Amy Devone
Curator
Sagamore Hill National
Historic Site

John A. Gable, Ph.D.
Executive Director
Theodore Roosevelt Association

Ron Grantz
Curator
National Automotive History
Collection of the Detroit Public
Library

Henry Guzda
Industrial Relations Specialist
U.S. Department of Labor

Elaine Tyler May
*Professor of American Studies
and History*
University of Minnesota

J. Kenneth McDonald
Chief Historian
Central Intelligence Agency

Valerie Neal
Space History Curator
National Air and Space Museum

Mary Nolan
Professor of History
New York University

Sam Tanenhaus
Author and Editor

Bernard Weisberger
Historian

Warren W. Wrenn
Supervisory Park Ranger
Wright Brothers National Monument

READER'S DIGEST GENERAL BOOKS

Editor in Chief
John A. Pope, Jr.

Managing Editor
Jane Polley

Executive Editor
Susan J. Wernert

Art Director
David Trooper

Group Editors
Will Bradbury
Sally French
Norman B. Mack
Kaari Ward

Group Art Editors
Evelyn Bauer
Robert M. Grant
Joel Musler

Chief of Research
Laurel A. Gilbride

Copy Chief
Edward W. Atkinson

Picture Editor
Richard Pasqual

Head Librarian
Jo Manning

The credits and acknowledgments that appear on pages 502–504 are hereby made a part of this copyright page.

Copyright © 1994 The Reader's Digest Association, Inc.
Copyright © 1994 The Reader's Digest Association (Canada) Ltd.
Copyright © Reader's Digest Association Far East Ltd.
Philippine Copyright 1994 Reader's Digest Association
   Far East Ltd.

All rights reserved. Unauthorized reproduction, in any manner, is prohibited.

Reader's Digest and the Pegasus logo are registered trademarks of The Reader's Digest Association, Inc.

Library of Congress Cataloging in Publication Data

Our glorious century.
        p.   cm.
    Includes index.
    ISBN 0-89577-616-2
    1. United States—History—20th century. 2. United States—
Civilization—20th century.   I. Reader's Digest Association.
E741.096 1994
973.92—dc20   94-14328

Printed in the United States of America
Third Printing, June 1995

About this book

OUR GLORIOUS CENTURY is an affectionate look back at America as it traveled through the 20th century. It begins at the beginning, with those tumultuous years that saw the first stirrings of American world power, President McKinley assassinated, and Teddy Roosevelt bursting into the White House. Then it moves forward through the century, ending with America standing at the head of nations, mindful of its key role in shaping the next 100 years.

Although OUR GLORIOUS CENTURY takes a historical tour of the 20th century, it covers history in a special way. For interwoven with the great events — wars, economic upheavals, social movements, presidential elections — is the stuff that made us sing and dance, cheer and boo, laugh and cry. It is a frankly, unashamedly nostalgic book.

Far more than any previous era, ours has been a century of images, millions and millions of them in ever more visual and colorful publications, in films of stunning technical virtuosity, and in television, the communications phenomenon of our age. Addressing this visual profusion, OUR GLORIOUS CENTURY has selected, from among tens of thousands, more than 1,600 of the most revealing and memorable images of the century. The variety and range are remarkable: rare old black-and-whites, gorgeous new color photos, family snapshots, patriotic posters, song sheets, mementos, book and magazine covers, advertisements, postcards; the list goes on.

About 200 lively narratives, beginning with "Roaring Into A New Era" and ending with "Eyes on the Future," form the heart of OUR GLORIOUS CENTURY. Within many of these text pieces, you'll find boxes on specific topics as diverse as the air aces of World War I (page 95), African-American contralto Marian Anderson (page 177), baby doctor Benjamin Spock (page 249), Three Mile Island (page 363), and rap music (page 409).

In addition, there are detailed maps of the century's world wars and these two major special features:

Century Spanners, spaced throughout the book, explore subjects dear to America's heart from the perspective of the whole century. Our favorite cars, favorite foods, favorite board games, and so on, from their earliest appearance in the century right up to the present.

Facts at Your Fingertips is a 64-page 20th-century chronology and almanac. It starts on page 438 following the main text. In addition to thousands of facts and dates, this section includes memorable quotations, illustrated charts, photos, and decade-by-decade price lists of selected consumer items, all providing intriguing nuggets of information in seven categories: U.S. History & Politics, Everyday Life, Arts & Letters, Entertainment & Sports, Business & Economics, Science & Medicine, World Political Events.

Whether you start at the beginning and read straight through or jump in at a favorite decade, OUR GLORIOUS CENTURY makes it easy to find your way through the latest 100 years of the American experience. Beginning on the next page is a detailed table of contents listing the title of every one of the book's 2- to 4-page narrative pieces. Moreover, every other page of the text is headed by an identifying chapter phrase, and the text itself contains numerous cross-references to related events recounted elsewhere in the book. An extensive index, starting on page 505, rounds out the list of aids for the serious reader.

Not only is a new century now upon us, but a new millennium. The story of where the nation has come from, what it has won and lost, celebrated and endured, is rich with lessons that can inspire and guide America in the 21st century.

— The Editors

C O N T E N T S

Chapter 1 🐘 *1900–1913*

Dawn of the 20th Century

**Ellis Island immigrants
pp. 12–13**

Chapter 2 ✠ *1914–1919*

WORLD WAR I: THE WAR TO END ALL WARS

**Victorious doughboys
pp. 62–63**

Chapter 3 ◆ *1919–1929*

THE UNRULY DECADE

Jazz and the blues
pp. 100–101

Chapter 4 ◑ *1930–1939*

The Down-and-Up 1930's

Surviving the bad times
pp. 146–147

Chapter 5 ★ 1939–1945

WORLD WAR II: HOME FRONT & BATTLEFIELD

**Hard-won triumphs
pp. 188–189**

Chapter 6 ● 1945–1959

POSTWAR CHALLENGE AND CHANGE

**Peace, promise, and peril
pp. 244–245**

Chapter 7 ✿ 1960–1969

The Clamorous 1960's

Dreamers and marchers
pp. 302–303

Chapter 8 🕊 1970–1979

The Seesaw 1970's

America at 200
pp. 352–353

Prelude to 2001
pp. 386-387

Chapter 9 ❸ *1980–1990's*

THE CLOSING YEARS

FACTS AT YOUR FINGERTIPS

Chapter 1

Dawn of the 20th Century

Bursting with energy, America vaults

onto the world stage, led by the irrepressible

Teddy Roosevelt and a host of dreamers, explorers,

crusaders, inventors, and tycoons.

Immigrants at Ellis Island await a ferry that will take them across the bay to New York City and a new world.

ROARING INTO A NEW ERA

Never had Americans felt more confident, more vigorous, or more eager to assert themselves. With prosperity at home and newly won prominence in world affairs, the nation had good reason to feel proud of itself.

On December 31, 1899, *The New York Times* ran an editorial reviewing the past century and looking forward to the prospects ahead. "We step upon the threshold of 1900 . . . facing a still brighter dawn for human civilization," the editors declared. Everywhere the outlook seemed to shine. Factories were humming and incomes were on the rise. Remarkable new inventions — the automobile, the electric light bulb, the telephone, to name just three — were transforming the way people lived. "Laws are becoming more just, rulers humane," declared a Brooklyn pastor; "music is becoming sweeter and books wiser." It seemed obvious to everyone.

▲ *Prosperous and secure, an American family of 1900 poses in its Sunday best.*

Already the United States was the world's largest industrial power. After a severe economic slump in the early 1890's, its annual output of goods and services was pushing toward a record $19 billion. The nation had nearly half the world's railroad mileage, shipped half its freight, pumped half its oil, forged a third of its steel, and mined a third of its gold. In just 30 years the number of Americans had doubled and now stood at 76 million. Three new states had been added to the union in the past decade alone, for a total of 45; by 1912 there would be 48. The entire country was getting bigger, stronger, and seemingly more wonderful.

Many aspects of the old century lingered on, to be sure. Fully 60 percent of all Americans lived in rural communities of less than 2,500 people. The largest occupation was farming. Nearly one person out of every two belonged to a church congregation, and almost nobody got divorced. Many families still made their own clothes. Many used a

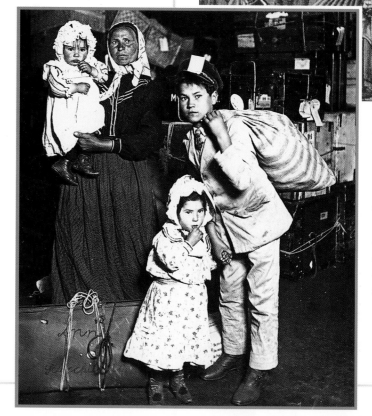

◄ *Newcomers from Italy — weary, apprehensive, determined to make good — move through the reception area at Ellis Island. By 1910 nearly one out of every seven Americans was foreign-born.*

A 1909 railroad poster celebrates American progress and material wealth. The map shows 48 states, even though Arizona and New Mexico were still territories. Oklahoma, the newest state, was added in 1907.

▼ Confined to a reservation in northern Montana, Chief Moise of the Salish Indian tribe poses with his family in front of their wigwam.

horse and buggy for transportation. Sugar cost 4 cents a pound, corned beef 8 cents, and $2.50 bought a handsome pair of men's shoes. The term *radio* did not exist in 1900, nor did *vacuum cleaner* or *electric toaster*. Hollywood was still an orange grove. There was not a single traffic light, and no one had to pay an income tax.

Massive changes were under way, however. The great American frontier — the vast stretch of untamed land that ever since colonial days had been a source of both lurking dread and unbounded opportunity — had largely disappeared. The last major Indian battle, at Wounded Knee, South Dakota, was a decade old; the former Indian territory of Oklahoma swarmed with thousands of new settlers. Other Western lands were filling fast. Only in Alaska, gateway for a rush of fortune seekers heading for the Klondike goldfields, did the wide-open frontier spirit still flourish.

For all the nation's agricultural wealth (it produced more than half the world's cotton, 50 percent of its corn, and most of its tobacco), the United States was becoming increasingly urbanized. Its three largest cities — New York, Chicago, and Philadelphia — each boasted a million or more inhabitants. Small farmers, many of them Southern blacks, were beginning to move to Northern cities looking for jobs. At the same time, a massive influx of foreign immigrants arrived from overseas, all searching for a better life under an American sky.

Some 9 million newcomers poured into the United States between 1900 and 1910, moving through processing centers, such as Ellis Island in New York, with their bundled belongings, odd foreign garb, and hopeful, bewildered faces. Most came from southern or eastern Europe — Italy, Russia's western regions, the multiethnic lands of the Austro-Hungarian Empire — and very few spoke English. Many were Roman Catholic, many Jewish, at a time when the nation was overwhelmingly Protestant. They crowded into cold-water tenements, took what work they could find, and endured the scorn of some native-born Americans. ("The scum of creation has been dumped on us," lamented one such irate citizen.) Yet the newcomers hung on, caught up in the golden American promise and confident, like most Americans in that exuberant moment of the century's turn, that things would surely get better.

◄

African-American schoolgirls, some perhaps daughters of Southern sharecroppers who had left the farm, pore over their studies at a public school in Washington, D.C.

Make way for Manifest Destiny

Urged on by patriotic drumbeating in the newspapers and prompted by a deadly explosion in Havana Harbor, the country went to war with Spain. Six months later, with surprisingly little effort or loss of blood, it had won itself an overseas empire.

The 7,000-ton U.S.S. *Maine,* the navy's newest battleship, rode quietly at anchor in Havana, Cuba, on February 15, 1898, its white hull gleaming in the tropical night. It had come to pay a courtesy call on the island's Spanish colonial government. Suddenly a deafening explosion tore through the vessel. The hull lifted, split into two sections, and then settled to the bottom; 250 American sailors lost their lives. The cause of the blast was never fully determined, but most Americans took a quick guess. "Spanish Treachery," screamed William Randolph Hearst's New York *Journal,* and the country agreed.

Trouble with Spain had been brewing for more than a decade. A guerrilla insurrection was devastating Cuba, and some $50 million of U.S. investment in Cuban sugar and tobacco lay at peril. Press reports of atrocities by Spanish soldiers further inflamed public opinion. And now this. President William McKinley, elected to office in 1896, had promised "no jingo nonsense," such as sending U.S. troops overseas. His position quickly changed. "Remember the *Maine* and the hell with Spain!" became the national battle cry, and on April 25 the Congress declared war.

The first guns sounded halfway round the world in the Spanish-controlled Philippines. A naval task force under Commodore George Dewey steamed into Manila Bay on May 1, swung broadside, and trained its formidable big guns on the local Spanish squadron. "You may fire when ready, Gridley," Dewey told the commander of his flagship. The Spanish fleet, undergunned and badly trained, stood little chance; all 10 ships were captured or destroyed. Total U.S. casualties: eight men wounded.

In Cuba a U.S. invasion force arrived from Tampa with orders to knock out the harbor defenses guarding Santiago, a seaport on

A gruesome lithograph (top, left) of the Maine *disaster helped fuel the outcry for war with Spain.*

▼ *The U.S. Navy's mighty Asiatic Squadron — four cruisers and two gunboats led by Commodore George Dewey (inset) — sweeps toward a decisive victory at the Battle of Manila Bay.*

U.S. marines raise the Stars and Stripes on Cuban soil near Santiago (below). In the Philippines (right), U.S. troops fought on through 1902 to subdue a revolt by local guerrillas.

President McKinley

"I love McKinley. He is the best man I ever knew," declared Republican Party strategist Mark Hanna, who was the president's closest friend and adviser. Most Americans agreed, whatever their politics. No kinder, wiser man seemed ever to have occupied the White House. A masterful reader of the public mood, he loved meeting his fellow countrymen. He could greet voters at the astonishing rate of 50 handshakes a minute.

In his first run for president, in 1896, McKinley urged a policy of sound money while his opponent, the charismatic Nebraska orator William Jennings Bryan, championed the free coinage of silver. Four years later, after a dramatic rise in national prosperity, McKinley pointed out that his administration had given "a full dinner pail" to all Americans — besides, of course, bequeathing them an empire. He handily won reelection.

THE FULL DINNER PAIL

▶ *An American relief force sent to help quell China's Boxer Rebellion battles insurgents at the gates of Peking.*

the south coast. The soldiers landed 17,000 strong; they were eager but ill-prepared. Some wore heavy winter uniforms and carried outmoded rifles. Cavalry units arrived without their horses. Despite these problems, on July 1 assault regiments stormed the defense batteries, located on San Juan Heights, and by evening the Spanish guns were silent. Two days later the U.S. Navy caught the Spanish Fleet and blew it out of the water, at a cost to itself of one man killed and one wounded.

This action effectively ended what Secretary of State John Hay would call a "splendid little war." In December 1898 Spain officially ceded Cuba, Puerto Rico, the Philippines, and Guam. The United States, in return, agreed to pay Spain $20 million. Meanwhile, the nation acquired still another possession, Hawaii, where pro-American businessmen had already deposed the local Polynesian monarch and declared a republic. "We need Hawaii just as much . . . as we did California," McKinley remarked. "It is manifest destiny."

All the great powers of Europe had overseas empires, and now the United States had one too. But what to do next? In the Philippines a powerful independence movement gave rise to armed rebellion. McKinley, resolving to "civilize and Christianize" the Filipinos, sent more troops. His intentions may have been good, but his facts were confused. Of the islands' 7.5 million inhabitants, 6 million were already baptized into the Christian faith. It would take nearly four years of bloodshed to end the revolt.

But the nation was now committed to global reach. America did not want any nation to corner the China market, and in 1900 it declared the Open Door policy for trading with the Chinese. Then, when Chinese fanatics known as Boxers, intent on expelling "foreign devils," began killing Western residents, the United States joined European nations in sending troops to restore order. A still-innocent country was learning the burdens of policing the world.

Hawaii's last monarch, Queen Liliuokalani (left), stepped down in 1893 to make way for a republic. Five years later the United States took possession in a flag-raising ceremony at the royal palace.

Death of an Empress, End of an Era

No single event more clearly marked the passing of the old century than the death — on January 22, 1901 — of England's Queen Victoria. She had come to the throne in 1837, at age 18, and she presided with unshakable dignity and distinction for the next 63 years. Tiny, soft-spoken, Victoria gave her name to a dozen cities and provinces around the globe, to a carriage and a furniture style, to Africa's largest lake, to one of the earth's mightiest cataracts (Victoria Falls on the Zambezi River in Africa), and to a pivotal period of world history.

During her reign Great Britain grew into the strongest nation on earth, with trade routes that crisscrossed every ocean and with colonies on every habitable continent. The world counted time from the prime meridian in Greenwich, and the British pound was the international monetary standard. Other nations boasted overseas possessions, but upon Victoria's empire — stretching from Sydney to New Delhi, from Toronto to Cape Town — the sun was said never to set. And her power extended well beyond British soil — through family ties. With 9 children and 40 grandchildren, she was matriarch to most of the royal families of Europe. The world has yet to see her equal.

THE WORLD'S CONSTABLE.

For all his bluster, Roosevelt pursued a foreign policy of sober arbitration, backed up by a strong navy. So great was his reputation for solid dealing that nations from Latin America to the Far East turned to him, as this 1904 cartoon suggests.

TEDDY WIELDS THE BIG STICK

When an assassin's bullet claimed the life of President McKinley, all America wept. His successor charged in with a program of brash, high-pitched activism that took the breath away — and projected America's might abroad.

It was over in seconds. On the afternoon of September 6, 1901, President William McKinley stood shaking hands in an ornate pavilion at the Pan-American Exposition, an international fair in Buffalo, New York. Up to the receiving line stepped a nervous young man, Leon Czolgosz, an avowed anarchist. Czolgosz raised a pistol and pumped off two quick shots. One bullet glanced harmlessly off a presidential vest button; the other pierced McKinley's stomach. Eight days later the president lay dead, his body ravaged by internal infection. Just a few houses away, in the formal library of a Buffalo mansion, Vice President Theodore Roosevelt was sworn in as the new president.

Roosevelt spoke the oath of office in a rapid-fire, high-pitched bark that gathered strength as he went along. The final "And so I swear!" rang out like an artillery salvo, an observer noted. He promised to follow McKinley's policies for prosperity at home and honor abroad. Then the new president rolled up his sleeves and went to work.

"Speak softly and carry a big stick; you will go far" was his political motto. And while he seldom spoke softly, he wielded the stick like a master. In 1902, when Germany blockaded Venezuela to collect unpaid debts, Roosevelt called in the German ambassador and suggested the matter go to arbitration. When the ambassador demurred, Roosevelt threatened to send in U.S. battleships. Germany agreed to arbitration. Two years later, when European governments moved against the Dominican Republic, also for overdue debts, the president unilaterally announced the Roosevelt Corollary to the Monroe Doctrine. Henceforth, he said, the United States alone would police all such disputes in the Western Hemisphere.

With similar directness, the president launched a project many people deemed impossible: a canal across the Isthmus of Panama. Everybody wanted one, for a canal would trim travel time between New York and San Francisco by 8,000 miles and drastically shorten other world trade

Roosevelt poses with members of the Russian and
Japanese delegations during his negotiations to mediate a
peaceful settlement of the Russo-Japanese War.

routes. The French had made an attempt, starting in 1881; but after eight years they gave up, having lost $260 million and the lives of 20,000 laborers to malaria and yellow fever. Roosevelt persisted. When Colombia, which governed Panama, refused to allow in U.S. engineers, despite a $10-million offer for digging rights, the Panamanians were inspired to declare their independence. They then signed with Roosevelt, and in 1904 the United States started digging.

In the Pacific, where war had broken out between Russia and Japan, Roosevelt found another way to spread American prestige. The squabble had arisen over control of Port Arthur, Manchuria, which Russia had leased in hopes of obtaining a warm-water anchorage. Japan also had claims in Manchuria, and it attacked. In the course of battle the Japanese ambushed Russia's main fleet — 42 ships sent all the way from the Baltic, 18,000 miles away — and utterly destroyed it. Not in modern memory had an Eastern power so humiliated a Western one. Roosevelt, invited to mediate a peace agreement, brought the parties together with such statesmanly skill that he earned the 1906 Nobel Peace Prize.

Riding high, the president next treated the world to a dramatic show of American naval strength. In December 1907, 16 white-hulled battleships and their supporting craft set off, bands playing and pennants flying, on a 14-month round-the-world cruise. The Great White Fleet was part training exercise, part publicity stunt — and a total success. (When Congress, balking at the expense, had threatened to withhold funds for fuel, Roosevelt said he had enough to get the fleet halfway and would let Congress bring it back.) At every country where the fleet dropped anchor — Brazil, Argentina, Peru, out across the Pacific — it met with a thunderous welcome. The only questionable destination was Japan, where relations had abruptly turned sour. But even there the reception was overwhelming. Ten thousand Japanese children sang "Hail, Columbia" in English. At one imperial gala, Japanese naval cadets picked up the U.S. fleet commander and tossed him into the air with lusty shouts of "Banzai." It was the ultimate accolade to America's growing power.

Patriotic songs, like this one from 1908, proclaimed America's new spirit of energetic nationalism and its willingness to send its troops on overseas missions.

Teddy rides in the cab of a giant steam shovel on an inspection tour of construction at the Panama Canal.

Topsides gleaming, the Great White Fleet steams out of Hampton Roads, Virginia, on its 44,000-mile globe-girdling voyage to proclaim America's status as a world power.

THAT COWBOY IN THE WHITE HOUSE

"I am only an average man, by George," he liked to say, but most people knew better. The new president was a bundle of nonstop energy and intellect who charmed some, alarmed others, and fascinated everyone.

Teddy Roosevelt moved into the White House at age 42, the youngest president ever, bringing a pretty young wife, six rambunctious children, and boundless self-confidence and zest. "In life, as in a football game," he once advised, "the principle to follow is: Hit the line hard." He was everywhere at once — meeting voters, shaping policy, writing books, galloping horses, roughhousing with his children — all the while barking orders and delivering opinions on every imaginable topic. He loved the spotlight. "Whenever he is in the neighborhood," said a friend, "the public can no more look the other way than a small boy can turn his head from a circus parade."

From Sickly Child to National Hero

All his life Roosevelt surprised people. Son of a patrician New York family, he had been a timid, nearsighted youth plagued by asthma attacks. To build his strength, he took up boxing. Later, entering politics as a crusading Republican, he applied the same fierce energy to cleaning up political abuses. As the New York City police commissioner, he strapped on a pistol and led his policemen on street patrols. When the Spanish-American War broke out, Roosevelt was in Washington as assistant secretary of the navy. He quit his desk and headed for Cuba. Organizing a volunteer cavalry regiment, the self-styled Rough Riders, he led a gallant, and highly publicized, charge under fire against enemy positions flanking San Juan Hill.

Teddy came home a hero, his toothy grin and steel-rimmed spectacles splashed across the nation's press. From San Juan Hill it was a quick gallop to the governorship of New York, and from there to the 1900 Republican national ticket as McKinley's running mate. Some old-guard party

◄ *TR's work clothes at Maltese Cross Ranch, in the Dakota Badlands, included a Western sombrero and chaps.*

► *Always firm in the saddle, the president smoothly clears a fence at a country club outside Washington.*

▼ *Outdoorsman and aristocrat both, the president goes over papers wearing white tie and riding puttees.*

All spiffed up for the photographer, the Roosevelts sit still for a First Family portrait in 1903. Along with the president and Mrs. Roosevelt, they are (from left) Ethel, 11; young Ted, 15; Archie, 9; Alice, 19; Kermit, 13; and Quentin, 5.

leaders questioned the choice. "Don't any of you realize," cautioned Ohio's powerful Senator Mark Hanna, "that there's only one life between that madman and the presidency?" No matter: Teddy would win votes, and as vice president he would be relatively powerless. Then, with McKinley's assassination in 1901, everything changed. "Now look," Hanna exclaimed, "that damned cowboy is president of the United States."

And cowboy he truly was, for he had ridden the range with the best of them. Years earlier, as a young man not long out of Harvard, he had gone west to recover from the deaths, on a single devastating day in 1884, of both his mother and his wife, Alice. (His mother died of typhoid, Alice after giving birth to his oldest daughter.) The grieving Roosevelt took refuge at a ranch he had purchased in the Dakota Territory. For two years he roped cattle, hunted buffalo, and tracked outlaws, often spending 14 to 16 hours a day in the saddle. Ever after he would preach the recuperative joys of "the strenuous life." As president, he would lead perspiring diplomats on hikes through Washington's Rock Creek Park, and more than once he swam the Potomac River in winter, through chunks of floating ice.

For all his physical vigor, the president was also a man of prodigious intellect. He devoured books at the rate of 2 or

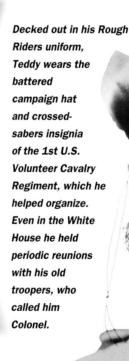

Teddy's military exploits and his reputation for gallantry inspired a number of admiring popular songs, like these.

3 a day, and he wrote 30 himself, on an astonishing range of subjects: history, biography, personal accounts of cattle ranching and wilderness travel, political writings, and scholarly works on natural science. He was such an authority on American wildlife that the Smithsonian, unable to name a rare species of mammal in its collection, called the White House to obtain positive identification.

Above all, he was a wonderful father. After his first wife's death, he married a childhood sweetheart, Edith Carow, who gave him five more children. They swarmed into the White House with a menagerie of pets — dogs, horses, birds, flying squirrels, a badger, a small black bear — and an abundance of high spirits. There were baseball games on the front lawn, tag in the front hall, and sledding competitions down the grand front staircase. Alice, the oldest daughter, stayed aloof from these frolics; the press corps dubbed her Princess Alice. But the president loved it all. "A household of children," he declared, "certainly makes all other forms of success and achievement lose their importance by comparison."

Decked out in his Rough Riders uniform, Teddy wears the battered campaign hat and crossed-sabers insignia of the 1st U.S. Volunteer Cavalry Regiment, which he helped organize. Even in the White House he held periodic reunions with his old troopers, who called him Colonel.

VOL. LXII. No. 1593. PUCK BUILDING, New York, September 4th, 1907. PRICE TEN CENTS.

"What Fools these Mortals be!"

Puck

"YOU DIRTY BOY!"

▲ **In his role as trustbuster, a matronly TR gives a no-nonsense scrubbing to a shady financier in this cover cartoon from the magazine Puck.**

SQUARE DEAL, BULL MOOSE

A born crusader, Teddy took on corruption and greed at every level. Then he quit politics to go on safari and soon regretted his decision.

Shortly after taking office as president, Teddy Roosevelt issued a message designed to reassure conservative Republicans. "I shall go slow," he promised party leader Mark Hanna. But going slow was not in the president's nature. His driving instinct was to reform the world, and he was not about to stop now.

His first target was the growing wealth and power of big business. Giant holding companies, which enjoyed an almost unlimited power to set prices and squelch competition, had come to dominate the nation's basic industries. Tobacco, sugar, petroleum, copper — all were virtual monopolies. So, too, were many of the nation's railroads, and here it was that Roosevelt stepped in. In 1902 he brought legal action against the Northern Securities Company, a railroad trust that had gained a hammerlock on rail transportation from Chicago west to Seattle.

Teddy shares the podium with his friend, and occasional White House dinner guest, black educator Booker T. Washington.

In attacking Northern Securities, TR took on four of the world's most powerful men: oilman John D. Rockefeller, railroad tycoons James J. Hill and E. H. Harriman, and investment banker J. Pierpont Morgan. As Wall Street's leading financier, Morgan was used to settling differences quietly. The indictment shocked him. He hurried to Washington. "If we have done anything wrong," he told Roosevelt, "send your man to my man and they can fix it up."

"That can't be done," the president replied. The attorney general, Philander C. Knox, explained further: "We don't want to fix it up; we want to stop it."

Roosevelt relied on a little-used statute, the 1890 Sherman Antitrust Act, to force the breakup of Northern Securities. He then went gunning for Rockefeller's Standard Oil monopoly, American Tobacco, Du Pont, the Chicago meat packers, and some 40 other major trusts. He won every case. Faced with his reformist zeal, the "malefactors of great wealth," as he called them, stood no chance at all.

The public loved it. That same year, 1902, a strike broke out in the coalfields. Supplies ran short, schools had to close, and prices shot from $5 to $35 a ton. Roosevelt summoned the coal producers and the head of the United Mine Workers of America (UMW) to Washington and told them to negotiate. The union was willing, but the producers refused. Most people sided with the miners (who were laboring in deplorable conditions for wages of $2 a day), and eventually the producers gave in. Roosevelt came out glowing. He had given the miners, he boasted, "a square deal."

He had done much more. Never before had a chief executive intervened to referee a labor dispute. In doing so, Roosevelt carved out a new sphere of presidential power, and he established a new principle of government responsi-

◀

On a campaign speaking tour, Roosevelt drives home his point with characteristic vehemence. He liked to refer to the White House as "a bully pulpit."

bility. Henceforth, Uncle Sam would be seen as the main guardian of the public interest.

Promising a "square deal for all Americans," Roosevelt was swept back into office in 1904. The crusade continued. Congress, at his urging, passed laws to clear slums, to make factories safer, to regulate commerce, to prevent kickbacks in the railroad industry. The U.S. Forest Service came into being, as did the Food and Drug Administration (FDA). Then, after seven spectacular years, just before the 1908 election, Teddy decided to quit Washington. Turning over the nation's destiny to fellow Republican William Howard Taft, he sailed to Africa to hunt big game. On his last day in office, sage old Henry Adams, dean of American historians, stopped by to shake his hand. "I shall miss you very much," Adams said. Many Americans agreed.

They agreed so wholeheartedly that soon there were clamorous cries for his return. So in 1912 Roosevelt decided to run again for president. With President Taft as the Republican candidate, Teddy formed his own Progressive Party, known also as the Bull Moose Party. He stormed onto the campaign trail with a radical prolabor platform that urged woman suffrage and an inheritance tax. But too few voters bought it. When the ballots were counted, a less strident reformer emerged as the new president: Democrat Woodrow Wilson.

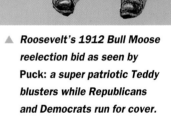

▲ *Roosevelt's 1912 Bull Moose reelection bid as seen by Puck: a super patriotic Teddy blusters while Republicans and Democrats run for cover.*

▼ *Teddy's hand-picked successor, William Howard Taft (right), poses with Woodrow Wilson, presidential victor of 1912.*

ECONOMIC COLOSSUS

Driven by the powerful twin engines of high finance and low-cost labor — and fueled by vast natural resources — America grew into the richest, most productive nation in history.

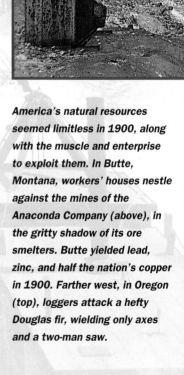

Pennsylvania wildcatters open up an oil well with a shot of nitroglycerin. Price wars in the industry's early days opened the way for Standard Oil's near-total monopoly by 1900.

The quantities seemed almost unimaginable. Fourteen million tons of steel. Over 200 million tons of coal. Nine and a half million tons of petroleum. Plus 10.6 million bales of cotton, 763 million bushels of wheat, 822 million pounds of tobacco, and enough finished lumber to build a small summer cottage for every family in America. Such were the riches served up each year by the nation's economy in the early 1900's, and each year the numbers grew bigger. From 1900 to 1914 the nation's total output of goods and services would more than double, swelling to a staggering $38.6 billion. Much of this wealth poured into the hands of a few top industrialists, who simply could not build enough new marble palaces or steam yachts to spend it all. Far less filtered down to the nation's industrial rank and file: to the mill hands, mine workers, roustabouts, and office clerks, who helped make it happen. Even so, most Americans found themselves better off than their grandparents.

A Golden Age for American Tycoons

Right from the start it was clear that big things were happening. Around Christmas of 1900 Andrew Carnegie, the white-bearded, twinkly-eyed entrepreneur who had parlayed a small Pittsburgh steel company into an industrial empire, stepped from the golf course and scribbled a figure on a scrap of paper: $480 million. Carnegie had decided to sell out, and this was his price. The buyer was John Pierpont Morgan, Sr., the Napoleon of Wall Street and America's most powerful financier. By combining Carnegie's steel holdings with his own and persuading other producers to join in, Morgan created the United States Steel Corporation.

The new company had assets valued at $1.4 billion, a sum so large it exceeded the entire U.S. national debt. It owned iron mines, ore smelters, shipping lines, and fabricating plants, and it dominated fully 60 percent of the national steel market. This degree of economic clout made some people extremely nervous. "The world has ceased to be ruled by statesmen," fretted *Cosmopolitan Magazine*,

America's natural resources seemed limitless in 1900, along with the muscle and enterprise to exploit them. In Butte, Montana, workers' houses nestle against the mines of the Anaconda Company (above), in the gritty shadow of its ore smelters. Butte yielded lead, zinc, and half the nation's copper in 1900. Farther west, in Oregon (top), loggers attack a hefty Douglas fir, wielding only axes and a two-man saw.

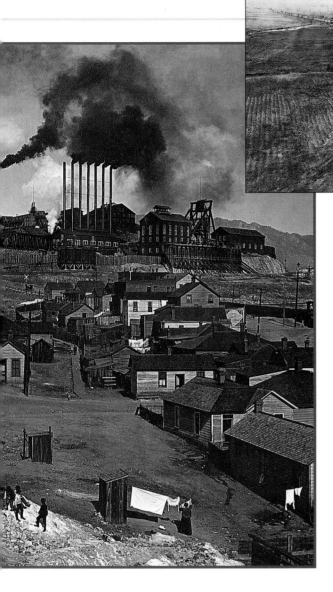

On the Illinois Central line, one of the nation's 65,000 locomotives hauls a freight train so long its cars vanish on the horizon.

If they refused, he slashed prices and bought them out. His methods were often brutal, and some would later be deemed illegal. But as Rockefeller's domain expanded, the oil market stabilized. Profits soared. Then in 1882 he delivered his master stroke: a giant compendium of former rivals whom he cajoled into forming the Standard Oil Trust, with himself as chairman. As far back as 1879 Standard Oil company had controlled 90 percent of the nation's refining capacity and most of the world's oil trade. Not even oil strikes at Spindletop, Texas, in 1901, and in Oklahoma in 1905, could topple the trust's preeminence. Every one of its officers grew rich.

In each major industry, similar corporate Goliaths appeared. National Biscuit, American Sugar, American Tobacco, United States Rubber, American Can, United Fruit, International Harvester — the list grew steadily. And much as these giant companies alarmed their critics, there was no going back. For where the trusts took over, markets steadied and prosperity tended to follow. Even Teddy Roosevelt,

and some observers prophesied dangerous social upheavals.

Vast concentrations of power and capital are the hallmark of an industrial age, however. The trend had been building since the 1870's, and it began on the freewheeling frontier of American enterprise: the Pennsylvania oil fields. The first gusher, at Titusville, had brought a stampede of drillers and refiners eager to light up the nation's households. (In those preautomobile days, kerosene for lamps was the main use of petroleum.) Wildcat drilling caused devastating cycles of overproduction, which in turn left a litter of bankruptcies. Then came John D. Rockefeller.

A young commodity broker in nearby Cleveland, Ohio, Rockefeller saw the chaos in the oil patch and also the cure for it. "Idiotic, senseless" competition, he felt, was destroying the industry. So Rockefeller built his own, highly efficient refinery and urged his competitors to join him.

San Francisco Rises From Its Ashes

First came the earthquake: a bone-jarring convulsion that roared through San Francisco shortly before sunrise on April 18, 1906, smashing buildings, heaving up streets, shattering gas lines and water mains. Then came the fire. It blazed up south of Market Street, the main business thoroughfare, and swept across the city. Banks, skyscrapers, the magnificent opera house, the teeming immigrant districts of North Beach and Chinatown, the mansions on Nob Hill — all were consumed. Three days later, when the flames died out, some 500 people had lost their lives and 225,000 more were left homeless. But the city refused to die.

Even before the embers stopped glowing, orders went out for steel to rebuild. The entire nation pitched in. Washington sent $2.5 million in aid. Rockefeller donated $100,000, and press lord William Randolph Hearst arrived in person with $200,000. Los Angeles bakers contributed free bread, and the Philadelphia Athletics handed over a day's gate receipts. But no one did more to speed the city's recovery than A. P. Giannini, president of the local Bank of Italy. As the flames engulfed his offices, Giannini carted off the bank's assets — $80,000 in gold — under orange crates in a fruit wagon. Days later he was back in business, handing out construction loans from a makeshift desk on the waterfront. This display of civic confidence did wonders to restore San Francisco's natural energy and optimism. And Giannini's company, renamed the Bank of America, would grow into one of the world's largest financial institutions.

Refugees on Russian Hill watch the city burn while soldiers (inset) patrol a devastated Market Street.

The Imperious Titans of Big Business

In the era of giant trusts and the first billion-dollar deals, America's top capitalists loomed larger than life. Immensely rich, ruthlessly ambitious, and mostly free from government regulation, they made decisions that affected the pocketbook of every citizen. Yet many started out poor.

Andrew Carnegie began working at age 13 in a Pittsburgh cotton mill for $1.20 a week. John D. Rockefeller's first job, as an office clerk in Cleveland, earned him $25 per month; by 1910 he had amassed a personal fortune of $1 billion. "God gave me my money," he once declared in an apparent attempt at modesty.

To be sure, some of the period's plutocrats were born rich. Railroad magnate Edward H. Harriman was the son of a Wall Street stockbroker. And no one projected more frock-coated patrician grandeur than J. Pierpont Morgan, Sr., scion of a well-established banking clan. With his imposing presence and piercing hazel eyes — likened by an associate to "the lights of an oncoming express train" — he seemed the living embodiment of power and purpose. Through a system of interlocking directorships, he controlled the destiny of 112 major corporations, and he commanded more respect than the president. During the economic depression of 1895, he bailed out the U.S. government with a timely loan of $60 million in gold. And when a financial panic hit Wall Street in 1907, he saved the nation once again by calling New York's top money men to a meeting in his sumptuous private library on Madison Avenue and forcing them to ante up the needed capital.

Andrew Carnegie made $23 million tax free in 1900.

J. Pierpont Morgan ruled over American finance.

E. H. Harriman operated 64,000 miles of railroad.

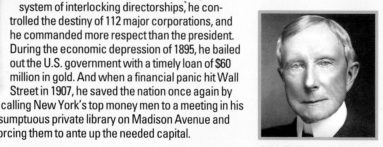

John D. Rockefeller was the world's richest man.

Making his bid to join the nation's growing middle class, an African-American jeweler plies his trade in Knoxville, Tennessee, about 1900.

for all his trust-busting zeal (see pp.22–23), had no objection to size alone. Only "bad" trusts — those engaged in price-fixing, for example — aroused his ire.

The railroads were among the nation's largest enterprises. A rash of consolidations in the 1880's and 1890's, many of them engineered by Morgan, had created sprawling regional systems. In 1900, some 193,000 miles of track crisscrossed the country, more than half the railroad mileage in the world, and each year the tracks reached farther. They became prosperity's vanguard: new towns sprang up in their wake, new acres of prairie land were laid open to farming. Railroads gave access to the mining camps of

These bright young Massachusetts office workers belonged to an army of "lady typewriters" who had joined the labor force by 1900. A female threshing crew (far right) helps tend a steam tractor on a Minnesota farm.

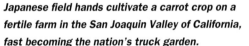

▲ *Japanese field hands cultivate a carrot crop on a fertile farm in the San Joaquin Valley of California, fast becoming the nation's truck garden.*

Proud and tough, lignite coal workers stand at a mine shaft in Rockdale, Texas. Productivity in mining rose dramatically during the century's first decade.

Nevada and Montana, and they knit the forests and fisheries of the Pacific Northwest to the rest of the nation. By 1910 more Americans worked for the railroads than for any other employer.

Even in agriculture, changes were occurring on a massive scale. Mechanized farming brought wonders of efficiency to the business of growing food, but large capital investments were required. No longer could a farmer get by with 40 acres and a mule; he needed chemical fertilizers, barbed-wire fencing, a reaper-thresher combine, perhaps a steam-driven tractor, and a broad sweep of land to work them on. As a result, traditional family farms gave way to large commercial spreads funded by Eastern bankers and run by professional managers. One so-called bonanza farm in Minnesota's Red River valley covered 34 million acres, employed thousands of workers, and had a wheat field larger than Manhattan. In California enormous tracts of vegetables and fruit were planted and picked by armies of part-time immigrant workers.

Long Hours, Low Pay

The revenues generated by these giant enterprises went mostly to the owners and their bankers. Employee wages remained adequate at best, with the average yearly pay ranging between $418 and $575. In exchange, most workers, whether in agriculture or industry, put in 10 hours a day, 6 days a week, often in punishing heat or cold, or in airless, ill-lighted factory lofts. Industrial accidents took a terrible toll. In the single year of 1901, one out of every 399 railroad employees died from on-the-job injuries, and the fatality rate for engineers and brakemen was even higher.

Yet some workers made out surprisingly well. Near the top of the scale were Boston's unionized cigar makers, who in 1902 took home between $15 and $25 a week. In a time of 20-cent dinners, $6 overcoats, $1.50 women's shoes, 75-cent bottles of gin, and almost no inflation — and when public school teachers made less than $500 a year — the cigar maker lived quite comfortably indeed.

GOOD-BYE HORSES, HELLO MODEL T

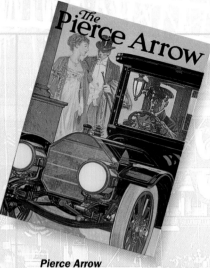

"The horse will continue indispensable for a long time," wrote a reporter after viewing the battery-, steam-, and gas-powered cars at the National Auto Show of 1900 (background photo). Then along came Henry Ford.

Now, finally, there was heard in the streets of Detroit the murmur of this newest and most perfect of forces, the automobile, rushing along at the rate of 25 miles an hour." So rhapsodized a feature writer for the city's *News-Tribune* in early 1900, after his first ride in the latest, most glamorous mechanical marvel.

Just seven years had passed since the American prototype, a one-cylinder Duryea, had chugged noisily forth from a bicycle shop in Springfield, Massachusetts, and already the nation was going car crazy. More than 40 companies were turning out horseless carriages. Some 8,000 Americans had purchased their first car.

Autos were so new that no one quite knew what to call them. Suggestions ranged from "autobat" to "viamote," from "mocle" to "motorfly." Most resembled tricycles or horse carts, and a few came complete with a socket for a buggy whip. Steering was by tiller. Maximum speed seldom topped 30 miles per hour.

Even that was enough to terrorize most bystanders. Minneapolis car owner T. H. Shevlin received the city's first speeding ticket, in 1902: a $10 fine for driving at a breakneck speed of 10 miles per hour. A 1902 Vermont law required that autos be preceded by an attendant waving a red flag.

As engines grew more efficient and control

devices improved, these strictures gave way. Car manufacturers continued to test power systems. The early favorites were electric automobiles, such as Woods and Bakers, which proved easy to start, smooth driving, and free of the sputtering noise and fumes of gasoline buggies. If slow compared to gas-driven autos, the electrics also seemed safer. As one manufacturer of electrics, Albert Pope, pointed out, "You can't get people to sit over an explosion." Steam-driven cars were the era's true speedsters. But steamers were a rich man's toy.

Any automobile meant a substantial cash outlay, to be sure. Millionaires paid $4,000 and more for Pierce Arrows and Panhards fitted with brass ornamentation and padded leather seats. The average list price of a 1900 vehicle topped $1,000, far too much for the typical American family.

But that was about to change. In 1901 a small Detroit automobile factory burned down with all its inventory, except for a single car, a one-cylinder runabout with a rakishly turned-up front end. It seemed little enough to restart the business, but once back in production, the Olds Motor Works could scarcely meet the demand. So popular was the trim $650 runabout that it inspired one of the decade's biggest song hits: "Come away with me Lucille/ In my merry Oldsmobile...."

Detroit was a city of machine shops and skilled mechanics, and it attracted other automakers. The Packard Motor Com-

Pierce Arrow ads (above) emphasized the status of the luxury vehicle's owner, not practical matters. As a five-time winner of the 12-day, 857-mile Glidden Tour, the Pierce Arrow had little need to toot its own horn.

Fred Marriot (left) rocketed his Stanley Steamer to a 1906 record of 127.66 m.p.h. on the hard sands at Daytona Beach, Florida.

For protection from insects, dirt, and noxious fumes, the well-dressed motorist swathed herself in a duster, a bonnet, gloves, and, customarily, goggles and a mask.

pany arrived from Ohio. David Buick, a local plumbing magnate, began turning out cars. The Dodge brothers built auto parts. Carriage maker W. C. Durant, from nearby Flint, bought up a number of Detroit producers, and in 1908 he launched the world's first auto conglomerate: the General Motors Corporations.

Mechanical Whiz, National Hero

Detroit's true pioneer — and the man who would transform the automobile from a passing fancy into one of life's necessities — was Henry Ford. A farmer's son with a genius for making things work, Ford built his first car, a gas-powered quadricycle with no brakes, in 1896. A parade of improved models followed, each designated by a letter of the alphabet. By 1907 Ford had reached *T*. "I will build a motor car for the great multitude . . . so low in price that no man making a good salary will be unable to own one."

The Model T was all that and much more. Wonderfully rugged, it bounded along dirt roads at speeds up to 35 miles per hour. Repairs were easy. And each year the price dropped, from $850 in 1908 to $490 in 1914 and then lower. Soon more than half the cars in America were Model T's, all of them identical down to color. "They can have any color they want," explained Ford, "so long as it's black." The cars rattled, spat oil, and were generally so uncomfortable that people joked about them. (Question: What shock absorbers does your Ford use? An-

Auto industry pioneer Henry Ford poses in his first motor vehicle, the 2-cylinder, 4-horsepower quadricycle. On June 4, 1896, he took the 500-pound car for a spin down a Detroit street.

swer: The passengers.) Nevertheless, everyone loved the Tin Lizzie. "Your car lifted us out of the mud," said one owner.

So great was the demand for the Model T that to boost output, Ford began tinkering with the production process. The world's first automobile assembly line rolled into action in 1914 at his new Detroit plant. Quickly adopted by other carmakers, assembly-line production revolutionized American industry . A second innovation was equally far-reaching. Ford doubled his workers' salaries, to an unheard-of $5 a day, and initiated a profit-sharing plan, moves that made him a hero to just about all of America.

▼ *Mom looks on as Dad and the kids hop aboard the Model T for an outing. In 1914, a year after this photo was shot, every other new car bought was a Tin Lizzie.*

ORVILLE AND WILBUR GET UP FIRST

Americans had tried to take wing and failed; Europeans had flown airships and gliders, but powered heavier-than-air flight had eluded them. Only the combined genius of two persevering brothers from Dayton, Ohio, would loft the first true airplane into the sky.

Poised on the brink, Otto Lilienthal surveys the land below before taking off in one of his bat-winged gliders.

An eager crowd of reporters and government officials gathered in boats on Washington's Potomac River to witness a science spectacular: the launch of Samuel P. Langley's flying machine. For more than a decade, inventors had attempted to break the barrier to manned mechanized air travel. Finally, on October 7, 1903, it looked as though someone might actually do it.

As secretary of the Smithsonian Institution, Langley had spent five years and $50,000 to develop his tandem-winged "aerodromes." One of them now perched above the river atop a houseboat. The twin propellers whirred, the pilot braced himself, and then fiasco. "There was a roaring, grinding noise," reported *The Washington Post*, "and the Langley airship tumbled . . . into the water like a handful of mortar." Two months later Langley tried again, with the same result. Perhaps astronomer Simon Newcomb, Langley's contemporary, was right: "Aerial flight is one of that class of problems with which man can never cope."

Yet, at that moment, on a remote North Carolina beachfront, two lone geniuses were rapidly approaching that goal. For the past several years, brothers Orville and Wilbur Wright, young bicycle manufacturers from Dayton, Ohio, had been testing kites and gliders at Kitty Hawk. They had studied the dynamics of wind forces on airfoils, tried more than 200 wing shapes in their own wind tunnel, and

Orville Wright

Wilbur Wright

developed just what Langley's aerodromes could have used: a system for maintaining stability in flight. Now they were ready to fly their first true airplane, a biplane of spruce and muslin, powered by a lightweight gasoline engine built in their shop. It was christened the *Flyer*. On the chilly morning of December 17, 1903, nine days after Langley's second attempt, they hauled the *Flyer* to its launching rail.

The toss of a coin three days earlier put Orville at the controls. As Wilbur trotted alongside, the *Flyer* rose from its track, wobbled briefly forward, and then settled back on the sand. The next flight went better, and the longest lasted 59 seconds and extended 852 feet. "SUCCESS FOUR FLIGHTS . . ." Orville telegraphed, "INFORM PRESS HOME CHRISTMAS."

Only six papers carried the news; *The New York Tribune* ran it on the sports page. Indeed, even as, in 1904 and 1905, the Wrights were clocking ever-longer flights, only buffs paid much attention. The U.S. War Department, invited on numerous occasions to watch a demonstration, twice sent nearly identical letters of refusal.

With the order "Let go the lines," Prussian Count Ferdinand von Zeppelin sent the first of his giant hydrogen-filled airships on its maiden voyage, over a lake in southern Germany.

Across the Atlantic, however, people had begun to take notice. Since the 1780's Europeans had sailed aloft in balloons; German aeronautical engineer Otto Lilienthal completed over 2,000 glider flights before crashing to his death in 1896; and, in 1900, Count Ferdinand von Zeppelin, a retired cavalry officer, ascended in the first of his giant dirigibles. Surely, in the race to propel a machine into the air, the Europeans should have come in first. But not until 1906 did Europe accomplish true mechanized flight. The pilot was a dapper expatriate Brazilian named Alberto Santos-Dumont, who that year skimmed over Paris in a gawky aircraft dubbed *Canard* for its resemblance to a duck. Frenchmen Henri Farman and Gabriel Voisin took to the air next, followed by their countryman Louis Bleriot, who became the first to fly across the English Channel, in 1909. By then the excitement of airborne travel had filtered across the ocean. The U.S. War Department consented to look at a Wright *Flyer* and, in February 1908, ordered one for $25,000.

But if the Wrights had finally won their due, it was another backyard aviator who captured America's imagination. Glenn Curtiss, an engine maker in upstate New York, was first interested in designing motorcycles. Then, when "aviation cranks" began pestering him for his light, efficient motors, he caught the fever himself. On July 4, 1908, he flew his first airplane, *June Bug,* in a competition sponsored by *Scientific American*. As a crowd of dignitaries looked on, Curtiss lifted into the air. "We all lost our heads," recalled his daughter, "and everyone cheered . . . and engines tooted." Her husband chimed in: "Man flies!"

Curtiss never looked back. He designed the first successful seaplane and the first aircraft to take off from a warship. In a clash of geniuses, he lost a patent suit to the Wrights involving a wing design. But legal wrangles hardly mattered in the long run. The real message was that flying machines — for sport, for travel, for defense — had flown in to stay.

Aviatrix Harriet Quimby's 1912 hop across the English Channel made her the first lady of the air.

A major rival of the Wrights, Glenn Curtiss, soars above his hometown of Hammondsport, New York for the first recorded flight of one kilometer.

The first American air meet attracted a daily crowd of more than 20,000 spectators, who cheered intrepid French pilot Louis Paulhan on to collect some $19,000 in winnings.

With Orville Wright lying prone on the lower wing and his brother Wilbur running alongside, the Flyer rises 2 feet above the track on its 100-foot-long initial flight, the first one by a power-driven, man-carrying machine. The Wrights chose Kitty Hawk, a lonely stretch of sand on North Carolina's Outer Banks, as the site of their experiments because of the strong winds that prevail there.

"HELLO CENTRAL" AND THE WONDROUS WIRELESS

Suddenly telephones were in demand: businessmen traded stocks and farmers got prices by phone, the party line provided entertainment, and Central became a trusted friend. Meanwhile, radio waves were about to be news.

For a nation in love with speed, no pleasure seemed more custom-tailored to the popular mood than the joy of instant communication. Telephones were coming into more widespread use. Some 1.3 million were in service when the century began; by 1907 the number would increase fivefold.

When first shown to the public at the Philadelphia Centennial Exposition of 1876, the telephone had seemed little more than an ingenious toy. "My God! It talks!" exclaimed the visiting emperor of Brazil, who went on to view the other exhibits. The following year Massachusetts resident Charles Williams installed the country's first private home phone. He put another set in his Boston office in order to have some place to call. The device spread rapidly, however, with energetic promotion by its inventor, Alexander Graham Bell. The first central exchange started operation in New Haven, Connecticut, in 1878. The White House installed its first set — in a phone booth. And while the Bell

A popular 1901 tune has a tearful child phone her prayers into Central: "Hello Central, Give me Heaven, for my mama's there!"

This demure young lady pays a "telephone visit" over her candlestick-style desk set.

A farmer uses the reliable wooden-box, wall-mounted type of telephone, still offered by manufacturers as late as 1940.

System controlled the lion's share of the service, around 855,900 telephones in 1900, challengers were springing up on every hand — some 6,000 independents fielded phone calls throughout the nation.

In rural areas, the local exchange was often a do-it-yourself venture. Farmers would cut wood for poles, string wire, and set up a switchboard, perhaps in someone's kitchen. Often the entire community shared a single circuit, with all the hazards of party-line calling. One farm wife, asked what she thought of her new phone, replied: "Well, we liked it a lot at first . . . only spring work is coming on so heavy that we don't hardly have time to listen now."

As phone lines proliferated, instruments took on a wonderful variety of sizes and styles. Besides the ordinary table phones and wall phones, there were elaborately carved cabinet phones and carpeted, oak-paneled phone booths. Callers lacking home telephones could walk to a nearby pay phone; some 81,000 were in service by 1902.

The key figure in these largely pre-dial days was the central exchange operator. Soft-spoken young women had long since replaced the ill-mannered boys who first manned the switchboards. "The Voice With a Smile" is how the New York Telephone Company described its operators in 1912.

Operators could be counted on to perform all kinds of tasks. A typical request, according to a 1905 magazine story, ran: "Oh, Central! Ring me up in 15 minutes so I won't forget to take the bread out of the oven." Small-town operators were known to babysit by wire: a busy parent would leave the receiver off the hook at cradle side. Railroad baron E. H. Harriman depended on the telephone to an extraordinary extent: his country estate alone boasted 100 sets. Accused of being a slave to the instrument, he replied for all heavy phone users, "Nonsense. It is a slave to me."

At this exchange in Hamburg, New York, two operators work the switchboard while their supervisors look on. "Hello girls" followed strict rules: enter chairs from the left, place feet on the floor, and look straight ahead.

Marconi's Marvel

While the telephone wove itself into the fabric of American culture, radio, or "wireless," was still an exotic device used mainly by ships at sea and a few ham operators. It made its first public U.S. appearance in 1899 at the America's Cup yacht race. Sailing alongside to report the outcome was none other than Guglielmo Marconi, age 25, radio's most notable pioneer. Four years earlier, in his native Italy, Marconi had invented the first practical system for wireless transmission. He had come to peddle the device in the United States.

Marconi's reports, in Morse code, came in garbled, but the spark caught fire. Two years later Marconi sent the first transatlantic wireless signal, the letter S. Before long, radio waves were humming through the air, ship to shore and across the ocean. In 1903 Theodore Roosevelt exchanged wireless greetings with Britain's Edward VII. And in 1907 the first regular intercontinental service began transmitting news reports and private messages between New York and London.

During crises on the high seas, the wireless proved itself a thousand times over. Some 300 vessels were equipped with wireless devices by 1909. That year an operator on the *Republic* coordinated the rescue of 1,700 survivors of a collision between his ship and the *Florida*. In 1910 radio would be used for the first time in the apprehension of a criminal. Aboard the liner *Montrose* as it steamed from Belgium to Canada were wife-murderer Hawley Harvey Crippen and his mistress, disguised as father and son. The sharp-eyed captain spotted the pair partway into the journey and wired the police, who arrested them as they disembarked. The capture of Crippen, along with a growing number of radioed rescues at sea, secured the place of wireless in the world of communications.

Greeting cards promoted the new vogue for telephony, but the magazine Lippincott's Monthly cautioned readers that "telephoning from habit finally becomes a vice."

HERE COME THE CONSUMERS

A thrilling new sound, music to merchants' ears,

echoed through the land: the jingle of cash registers.

Almost everyone, it seemed, wanted to spend money on

something, and retailers were all too happy to oblige.

Every era has its folktales, but the story of a turn-of-the-century Idaho farm boy stands out as particularly apt. Asked by his Sunday school teacher where the Ten Commandments came from, the lad did not hesitate: "Why, from Sears, Roebuck, where else?" Indeed. At a time of ever-increasing national prosperity, the giant Chicago mail-order house stood ready to supply every need, from age-old words of wisdom to the latest gadgets for home and workplace. If Sears was out of stock, the mail-order customer could try its rival, Montgomery Ward. In cities shoppers flocked to the local department stores, which by 1900 had grown into glorious cathedrals of commerce, complete with art galleries, fashion shows, and retail areas offering everything from Parisian dresses to Persian rugs. Throughout America people were awakening to an age of breathless mass consumption, when it seemed that everything, even happiness itself, was up for sale.

Happiness may have been the only item not listed in the nation's two great retail wish books, the Sears and Montgomery Ward catalogs. Running many hundreds of pages — they were as thick as the Bible and almost as popular — the catalogs reached 10 million households by 1910, thanks to parcel post and rural free delivery. For readers in remote farm country, they opened the door to a wondrous world of travel, art, information, and material enchantment.

Ladies learned about the latest fashions in dresses, kitchenware, and home furnishings; a section on patent nostrums touted "La Dore's famous bust food" for building "a plump, full, rounded bosom." Men browsed through ads for guns, farm tools, haberdashery, and grooming aids.

Out of young Frank W. Woolworth's idea of cutting prices on slow-selling merchandise grew a chain for thrifty shoppers.

The cover of the Sears, Roebuck catalog gave a taste of the riches within, just a postage stamp away.

▶ *A Kansas housewife shows she needs just one hand to operate a washing machine bought from a mail-order catalog. It was still manual labor, but less work than a scrub board.*

As electrification spread, demand rose for appliances like the General Electric range (1913) and the Model C Hoover cleaner (1908). The Kodak Brownie camera sold for $1.00.

Crammed to overflowing, a Montgomery Ward truck delivers a load of mail-order goods. For decades "Monty Ward" and Sears, Roebuck vied for mail-order customers, and both opened retail outlets. For city dwellers, department stores, like R. H. Macy's in New York City (right), offered all the delights that catalogs could only picture.

Richard W. Sears boasted that his catalog sold a watch every minute. Children, now a distinct consumer group, were bedazzled by pictures of Daisy air rifles, doll houses, stereopticons, and even live pets. More than one lonely farmer wrote the retailers to ask about buying a wife.

Urban husbands, meanwhile, were losing their wives to Wanamaker's in Philadelphia, Marshall Field's in Chicago, and Macy's in New York City. When shoppers crossed the threshold to one of these magnificent iron-and-plate-glass emporiums, they entered a consumer's fantasyland, where sales floors spread across acres. Once inside, they had little reason to leave. The stores offered amenities ranging from libraries to nurseries, and entertainments from tearooms to theaters, from botanical gardens to miniature zoos. Who could resist them?

Bargain Prices and Electrical Appliances

What department stores provided in luxury and comfort, cash-and-carry vendors, such as Grand Union, F. W. Woolworth, and The Great Atlantic and Pacific Tea Company (better known as the A&P), delivered in savings. Woolworth's five-and-tens peddled tin cookware, sewing notions, and other inexpensive items; by 1910 Woolworth had more than 200 stores. Discount grocers, forerunners of today's supermarkets, lined their shelves with low-cost staples.

The upsurge in consumer goods worked a miraculous transformation on the American home. As the nation became wired for electricity, a steady flow of labor-saving appliances came on the market. Housewives no longer had to stand over the heat of a coal-burning stove; an electric range with automatic timer promised to "do oven watching" for them. Hoover vacuum cleaners made short work of the soot from open fireplaces. Electric irons appeared in 1908, followed by toasters, coffee percolators, and hot plates. For men, the Gillette safey razor, patented in 1895, meant no further need for daily trips to the barbershop at 30 minutes per shave. Now a man could be "master of his own time and appearance," just as the ads suggested.

Fanning the national rage for consumer goods, advertising and packaging gained unprecedented importance in the plans of businessmen. The signature label of the Campbell's tomato soup can made its debut in 1899. Eastman Kodak plugged the Brownie in 1900 as a camera "so simple a child can use it." The Woodbury soap ads of 1911 pictured a man and a woman locked in an embrace, together with the words "the skin you love to touch." Though the Woodbury advertising scandalized readers of *The Ladies' Home Journal*, causing some to cancel their subscriptions, even more subscribers signed on because of the ads. And the admen discovered a fundamental lesson for the new consumer age: sex can sell a lot of soap.

An Age of Artful Advertising

His Master's Voice ✦ 1904
A loyal if somewhat baffled dog vouches for the audio fidelity of the Victor Talking Machine, or Victrola.

Flexible Flyer ✦ 1905
Kids sped downhill on the sturdy, steel-runnered wooden sleds that bore an inflexibly patriotic eagle.

Gold Medal ✦ 1906
Until 1928 the Washburn Crosby Company made Gold Medal flour, then the company merged with several others to form General Mills. But the Gold Medal emblem has endured to this day.

Morton Salt ✦ 1933
The girl has been "modernized" over the years, but the basic image and "When It Rains It Pours" date from 1914.

Breck ✦ 1937
Idealized "Breck girls" sold a lot of shampoo. This painting of 17-year-old Roma Whitney later became a Breck trademark.

About the time America was discovering it was an economic powerhouse, capable of producing a vast volume and variety of almost everything, advertising became a surging growth industry. By 1900 companies regularly used talented artists and writers to create pitches for their wares. Some companies had their own creative advertising teams; others hired one of a swelling number of ad agencies to create the words and pictures that would sell their products, services, or ideas. By 1950 advertising expenditures in America were $5.7 billion a year; in the 1990's the annual figure reached $100 billion. On these two pages are 20 ad images that caught our attention in the 20th century.

Fisk Tires ✦ 1914
A memorable ad for replacement tires, the idea hit 18-year-old advertising artist Burr E. Giffen as he lay abed one night in 1907. He leaped up and illustrated the pun "Time to Re-Tire?" with a tyke, a candle, and a Fisk.

Bon Ami ✦ 1918
A chick and the slogan "Hasn't Scratched Yet" pitched the gentler scouring power of Bon Ami.

Cracker Jack ✦ late 1920's
Immortalized in the 1908 song "Take me out to the ball game," the crunchy confection added in-box prizes in 1912.

America's Answer ✦ 1942
When the nation has gone to war, so have ad agencies and their creative talent, as in this World War II poster.

Howard Johnson's Restaurants 🍦 **1942**
By the 1940's, this "Simple Simon Met a Pieman" logo was becoming a familiar sight up and down the East Coast.

Motorola TV 🍦 **1950**
When TV was new, consumers wondered how the sets would fit in their homes. Makers responded with stylish cabinets.

Coca-Cola 🍦 **1953**
Ads for the soft drink have long linked it to good feelings and happy times.

Coppertone 🍦 **1960's**
"Little Miss Coppertone," in magazines and on billboards, was such a hit in the 1960's that 9 out of 10 Americans recognized her suntan lotion's name.

Clairol 🍦 **1968**
The ambiguity of "Does she or doesn't she [use hair coloring]?" offended some but did wonders for Clairol sales.

American Cancer Society 🍦 **1972**
Peter Max's anti-smoking poster "Life Is So Beautiful" was aimed at the young.

Revlon 🍦 **1980's**
The ads left no doubt that Charlie fragrance was for confident career women.

Fruit of the Loom 🍦 **1987**
Until their retirement in 1992 after years of service, these happy fellows in fruit costumes promoted the goods of "America's No. 1 manufacturer of men's underwear."

Xerox 🍦 **1977**
The leader in office copiers in the 1960's, Xerox used inspired advertising to try to hold its market share.

Energizer 🍦 **1992**
One brand of battery looks much like another, but the tireless bunny gave Energizer batteries a winning personality all their own.

Smokey Bear 🍦 **1987**
Forest-fire prevention and Smokey teamed up in the 1940's, when the Foot, Cone & Belding ad agency paired them for the U.S. Forest Service.

▼ Newspaper baron and future lord of San Simeon castle in California, William Randolph Hearst, with his wife and son.

HIGH SOCIETY HIGHS AND LOWS

In the days before movie stars, the nobs and swells of high society were the nation's celebrities, and their every move, from the staging of silly costume balls to wilder misadventures, riveted the public.

The Potter Palmer château in Chicago.

Every year society parties got curiouser and curiouser. In 1899 Rudolf Guggenheimer feted 40 guests at the Waldorf-Astoria, its Myrtle Room transformed for the occasion into a lush garden overgrown with roses, hyacinths, and tulips, and populated by a chorus of blackbirds, canaries, and nightingales. In 1902 the Cornelius Vanderbilts transported the cast of the Broadway musical *The Wild Rose* to their Newport estate for an evening's diversion. Mrs. Stuyvesant Fish once coaxed a baby elephant to pass out peanuts to the company gathered at her home, and Harry Lehr served a bone-and-biscuit feast to 100 dogs. Mrs. Fish and Mr. Lehr teamed up to honor mystery guest Prince del Drago of Corsica, who turned out to be a monkey dressed in formal evening wear.

It was a great time to be rich. Maintaining a household staff was inexpensive, and no federal income tax would be imposed until 1913.

James Hazen Hyde, heir to the vast Equitable Life

▼ Echo Camp, the Adirondack "lodge" of Phineas C. Lounsbury, Connecticut governor and president of the Merchants Bank, was typical of the mountain hideaways favored by the Eastern elite.

During the summer and winter seasons wealthy enclaves from Newport, Rhode Island to Palm Beach, Florida saw the rich participate in a dizzying rush of activities including debuts, balls, and fêtes such as this garden party.

Dressed for a ball at Albert Hall, London, the duchess of Roxburghe (seated), née May Goelet, the American heiress, poses with her husband and two high-class friends.

Insurance fortune, took full advantage of his privileged station when he threw a fancy dress ball in 1905. Hyde chose as his theme the court of Louis XV. Everyone was there — the Astors, the Goulds, the Belmonts — the list included 350 names. The ladies, costumed as Madame de Pompadours and Marie Antoinettes, layered themselves in silks and satins, hauled ermine-lined trains, carried aloft scepters, and draped precious jewels about their necks and wrists. Mrs. Potter Palmer, wife of the Chicago department store magnate, scintillated in a diamond dog collar, a tiara, and breastplates. The gentlemen sported frock coats, silk stockings, and pumps. Trumpets blared, an orchestra played, the corps de ballet danced, a French actress performed a farce, and the guests indulged in three suppers and a breakfast. When it was all over, the bill for the evening (footed by unwitting Equitable stockholders) reached a reported $200,000.

Pursuing Comfort, Nobility, and Virtue

The wealthy spared no expense in the pursuit of leisure. Their second homes, which they called "cottages," were lavish estates in resorts from Palm Beach, Florida, to Pebble Beach, California. In Newport, Rhode Island, playground of the great New York families, William K. Vanderbilt's Marble House, an $11-million edifice in Louis XIV style, came complete with a portrait of the Sun King gazing regally over the dining room. Willie K.'s brother, Cornelius, summered at The Breakers, a 70-room villa staffed with 33 servants and 16 bewigged footmen. The opulence of Newport proved overwhelming for one French visitor: "There are too many tapestries, too many paintings on the walls . . . too many plants, too much crystal, too much silver."

Newport days and nights were filled with horseback riding, yachting, tennis and polo matches, soirees, and balls.

But though they lived the lives of kings, the doyens of high society aspired to something more: a noble title. Even that could be bought. It wasn't hard to find a European noble willing to exchange his title for a handsome dowry and a carefree existence. John Graham Hope Horsley-Beresford (fifth lord Decies and major of His Majesty's 7th Hussars) made Vivien Gould a lady and, with the wedding, got the first taste of his own newly acquired status. Over 200 seamstresses assembled the bride's trousseau, and the wedding cake was a $1,000 confection topped by cupids bearing the groom's coat of arms.

The antics of America's wealthy provided fodder for the gossip pages, and newspapers found no better source of rumors than Harry K. Thaw, scion of a Pittsburgh steel and mining family. Thaw's escapades — he tore apart cafés and once rode horseback up the stairs of the Union League Club — turned deadly on June 25, 1906, the evening he and his wife, Evelyn Nesbit, attended opening night of a musical at Madison Square Garden. Just as the final strains of "I Could Love a Million Girls" lilted from the stage, Thaw rose from his chair, walked up to architect Stanford White, seated nearby, and muttering, "You ruined my wife," shot him. It seems White had carried on an affair with Evelyn when she was 16. Two murder trials ensued, and Thaw, found "not guilty because insane," was institutionalized. His defense team had portrayed their client as a man who had "struck for the purity of the wives and homes of America."

Chorus girl and artist's model Evelyn Nesbit formed one corner of the love triangle conjoining her hot-tempered husband, Harry K. Thaw, and her lover, the eminent architect Stanford White. White designed Madison Square Garden, New York City, the site of his murder at the hands of Thaw.

A Grim Night on the North Atlantic

The *Titanic,* "the world's safest liner," had a pool, a Parisian café, luxury rooms for its first-class passengers — and too few lifeboats: only 1,178 lifeboat spaces for 2,207 passengers and crew. When the ship hit an iceberg, the captain, Edward Smith, ordered "women and children first" into the lifeboats, but many first-class male passengers got into the boats anyway. Meanwhile, women and children farther below in second and third classes failed to reach the boats in the confusion, and were doomed. Some of the wealthy men who survived were branded cowards, but high society had its heroes too. Financier John Jacob Astor put his new bride in a lifeboat and went down with the ship. Macy's owner, Isidore Strauss, also perished, with his wife, Ida, who chose to stay with him.

More than 1,500 died that morning of April 15, 1912. For some, the sinking was a symbol of the weakness and decay of high society. Others saw it as simply an avoidable tragedy.

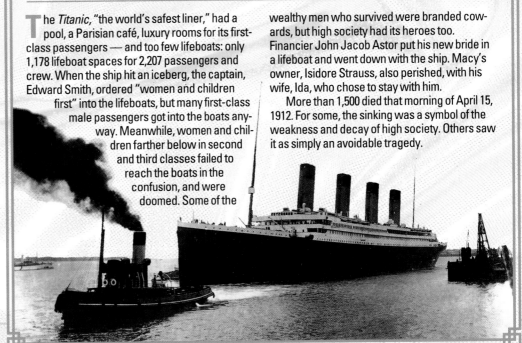

AMERICA DISCOVERS ITS NERVES

Nervous conditions certainly existed before 1900, but when psychologists theorized that overuse of the intellect was the cause, neurosis took on a certain glamour. Sigmund Freud proposed a radically different source of neurological disorders: the unconscious mind.

As the United States entered the 20th century, it was suffering a nationwide attack of nerves. The bustle and strain of the modern industrial era, according to medical experts of the time, had jangled America's nerves — so much so that the very word *nerves* took on a new meaning. Formerly, having "nerves" meant that a person was blessed with coolness under pressure, but by the turn of the century, *nerves* had become synonymous with *jittery*, *jumpy*, and *irritable*. Annoyances were things that "got on one's nerves." Doctors theorized that each person had a limited reservoir of "nerve force" and that when the supply was used up, mental illness resulted. Whatever the cause, doctors called the new malady American nervousness.

One of the most prominent neurologists of the era, George M. Beard, attributed the nation's mental woes to the ever-accelerating pace of life brought on by the steam engine, the telegraph, the printing press, and other modern contrivances. Cities, in which such baleful influences multiplied, were portrayed as modern versions of the primeval jungle, where the workingman used "nerve power" instead of physical strength in the struggle to survive. Fitness experts worried that the shift from rural to city jobs represented an unnatural trend. "Is it not shameful," wrote one doctor, "to think of a big, well-built man, brought up on the farm . . . spending his

The founders of modern psychology met at Clark University in Worcester, Massachusetts, in 1909. Left to right: (standing) A. A. Brill, Ernest Jones, Sandor Ferenczi; (sitting) Sigmund Freud, G. Stanley Hall, and Carl G. Jung. Inset: the American philosopher, psychologist, and theologian William James.

An illustration from an advertisement depicts a man in the throes of an attack by vicious demons representing catarrh (sinusitis), neuralgia, headache, toothache, and "weak nerves." The recommended cure? Wolcott's Instant Pain Annihilator, of course.

At right is a sampling of treatments and cures for nervous conditions (clockwise from upper left): the Heidelberg Electric Belt was guaranteed to restore manly vigor by means of a mild electrical current; Warburg's Tincture contained pure opium; Dr. Shoop's Headache Tablets promised relief in 20 minutes; Iron Bitters were touted as a panacea for nervous ailments and indigestion.

▼ In the privacy of her boudoir, a woman with "weakness of the nerves" could indulge in a soothing electric head bath.

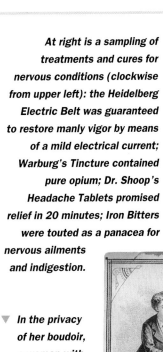

days . . . whispering into a Dictaphone?"

To describe the malady he diagnosed with increasing frequency, Dr. Beard used the word *neurasthenia*, meaning weakness of the nerves. Oddly enough, it was chic to be diagnosed as neurasthenic. The intelligent were considered especially prone to the condition, their brains being susceptible to exhaustion from thinking too much. Before long, *neurasthenia* became a catchall term for any inexplicable ailment. Complaints as varied as insomnia, asthma, headache, skin rash, hay fever, and even baldness were all attributed to nervousness.

Charlatans promoted all manner of nerve medications, guaranteed to bring relief from "brain fatigue." In the Sears, Roebuck and Company catalog, tucked among the ads for bicycles and sewing machines, one could find the Heidelberg Electric Belt, an apparatus that, when strapped about the waist, sent electric impulses coursing through the body. The official cure called for treatments that differed according to gender: men were advised to head out west for a dose of fresh air and exercise; women were told to stay indoors and avoid all stimulation.

America Welcomes Freud

America's penchant for looking at itself made this country fertile ground for the revolutionary theories of Viennese neurologist Sigmund Freud. Using dream interpretation to delve into the unconscious mind, Freud theorized that the repression of impulses and experiences, including those of a sexual nature, underlay many mental abnormalities. In 1909 Freud made a triumphant visit to the United States, giving a series of lectures at Clark University, in Worcester, Massachusetts. He was surprised and delighted at his warm reception. William James, whose *Principles of Psychology* had been published in 1890, assured his colleague that the "future of psychology belongs to your work." Freud's host in Worcester, having heard of his guest's fondness for cigars, placed a box in every room of the house.

Freud had expected his theories to offend "prudish America." "Won't they get a surprise when they hear what we have to say to them!" he exclaimed upon his arrival. But America's enthusiasm for psychoanalysis was proof of this nation's hunger for fresh ideas.

Russian physiologist Ivan P. Pavlov used dogs in a series of experiments to prove his conditioned-reflex theory by demonstrating that neurotic behavior can be learned.

MEDICINE GETS A DOSE OF SCIENCE

The patent-medicine industry was exposed as a hoax, and health officials, armed with scientific know-how and training, waged a winning battle against illness and filth.

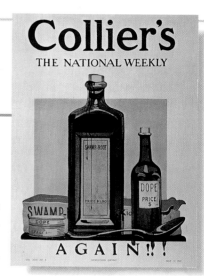

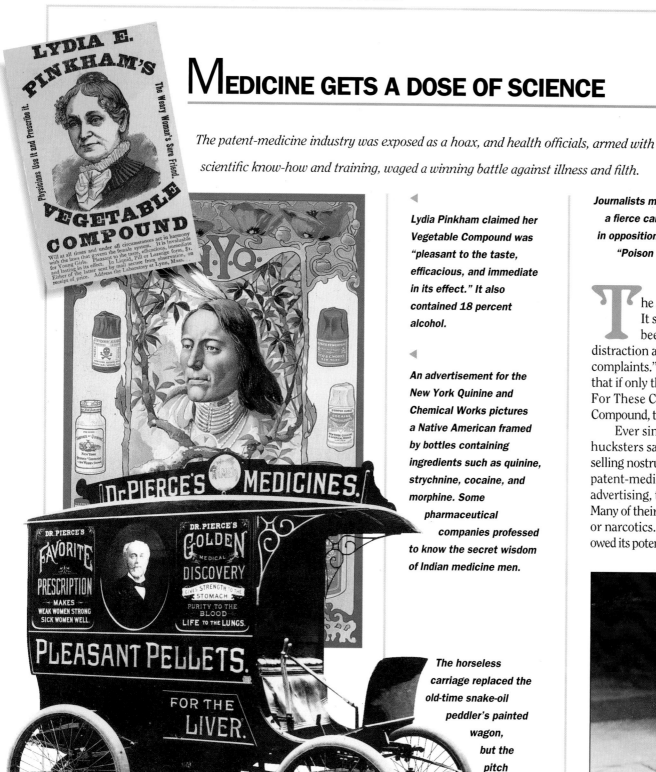

◄ **Lydia Pinkham claimed her Vegetable Compound was "pleasant to the taste, efficacious, and immediate in its effect." It also contained 18 percent alcohol.**

◄ **An advertisement for the New York Quinine and Chemical Works pictures a Native American framed by bottles containing ingredients such as quinine, strychnine, cocaine, and morphine. Some pharmaceutical companies professed to know the secret wisdom of Indian medicine men.**

The horseless carriage replaced the old-time snake-oil peddler's painted wagon, but the pitch remained pretty much the same.

Journalists mounted a fierce campaign in opposition to the "Poison Trust."

The advertisement recounted "A Fearful Tragedy." It seems a gentle Massachusetts clergyman had been murdered by his wife, a woman driven to distraction after suffering for 16 long years with "female complaints." The sad tale concluded with the observation that if only the afflicted woman had used "The Sure Cure For These Complaints," Lydia E. Pinkham's Vegetable Compound, the "direful deed" might have been averted.

Ever since the days of the traveling medicine show, hucksters saw a way to make money by concocting and selling nostrums promising cure-all benefits. It didn't take patent-medicine hawkers long to discover that through advertising, their products reached a far wider audience. Many of their secret compounds consisted largely of liquor or narcotics. Dr. King's New Discovery for Consumption owed its potency to both opium and chloroform.

With the new century, the medical tide began to turn. Crusading physicians and muckrakers challenged the leaders of the patent-medicine industry (the "Poison Trust") and, in 1906, forced passage of the Pure Food and Drug Act, requiring drug manufacturers to list contents on labels. The profits of the Poison Trust fell off markedly once customers were able to read what they had so blithely been consuming.

The era of modern medicine had begun. Doctors and public health officials made inroads against the appalling urban squalor that bred diseases, including cholera, diphtheria, and typhoid. Sanitation and nutrition standards in late-19th-century New Orleans had been so poor that the life expectancy for a white person was 38.1 years and for a black person, 25.5 years. The mortality rate at a New York orphanage in 1897 was just under 100 percent. But by the turn of the century, almost every major city and most states had established a health department, and the fight was on for proper sanitation, a reduction of air and water pollution, and a healthy food supply.

With each new advance, physicians pondered the many medical marvels that lay ahead. Under the headline "May Transplant the Human Heart," *The New York Times* reported in 1908 that pathologist Simon Flexner had predicted the transplanting of hearts, kidneys, and other organs in

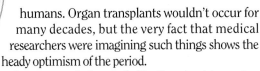

▶ A French physician in 1895 examines his patient with an early X-ray device. X-rays were first used in diagnosis and later for therapy.

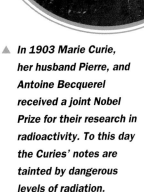

▲ In 1903 Marie Curie, her husband Pierre, and Antoine Becquerel received a joint Nobel Prize for their research in radioactivity. To this day the Curies' notes are tainted by dangerous levels of radiation.

humans. Organ transplants wouldn't occur for many decades, but the very fact that medical researchers were imagining such things shows the heady optimism of the period.

It was an optimism fueled by the promising union of science and medicine. In 1895 German physicist Wilhelm Roentgen had discovered the X-ray, a form of radiation. Shortly thereafter, French scientist Antoine Henri Becquerel noted the phenomenon of naturally occurring radiation, and Marie and Pierre Curie embarked on research that would lead to the isolation of two radioactive elements. The uses for radiation in cancer treatment would become evident over time, but medical applications for the X-ray were immediately apparent: for the first time doctors could look inside the human body without performing invasive surgery. During the Spanish-American War, U.S. military surgeons took X-ray machines into the field. By 1903 an American doctor was using X-rays to treat leukemia.

But the era's most dramatic feat was the conquest of yellow fever. To test the theory that mosquitoes were the agents of the disease, American doctors and soldiers and Cuban civilians volunteered to subject themselves to the bites of mosquitoes that had already bitten yellow-fever victims. When several volunteers contracted the disease and died, the experts had the dreadful evidence they needed to prove that mosquitoes were indeed the culprits. Medical teams set about exterminating the insects in Cuba, Panama, and the American South. The mainland United States saw its last major epidemic in 1905.

A nurse for the Board of Health weighs a baby. By 1915 pediatrics would become a specialty.

◀ Children play in an open gutter on New York's Lower East Side. Citizens' groups, largely made up of women, sought to clean city streets of litter, sewage, and spoiled produce.

The grim visage of yellow fever looms over the Panama Canal Zone in this 1904 cartoon. That year saw a fresh outbreak of the disease.

CONQUERING EARTH'S FROZEN FRONTIERS

Most of the world's wild places — the jungles of Africa, the deserts of Arabia — had by now been explored. But the earth's two polar regions were still blanks on the map. The challenge of reaching them brought triumph to some, tragedy to others.

Hundreds of artifacts celebrated Robert Peary's Arctic achievements, including this portrait from a 1910 souvenir dinner menu. More than a decade earlier, artist F. W. Stokes had painted the explorer's ship (far left) under a shimmering aurora borealis on an expedition to Greenland. A 1909 photo (inset) shows a group of Peary's sled dogs and Eskimo guides.

Dr. Frederick Cook, who claimed he reached the North Pole first, takes a breather during his 1908 Arctic venture. He delayed his announcement, he said, because he got lost on the way home.

ore than 400 miles beyond remotest Greenland, amid the constantly shifting pack ice of the Arctic Ocean, lies the planet's northernmost point. No landmark indicates the North Pole; only readings from a sextant or other navigational device will show its exact position. Yet by the turn of the century, the desire to reach it had become an obsession. For around it — and around the South Pole in Antarctica 180 degrees to the south — spread the last unexplored regions of planet Earth. To some their call was irresistible.

Robert E. Peary first journeyed to the Arctic in the 1880's as a surveyor for the U.S. Navy. He trekked through Greenland, mapped its north coast, and brought back valuable data for science. And all the while his attention drifted north toward the pole — "the goal of the world's desire," as he put it. He made his first attempt to reach the pole in 1893

but was forced back. In 1905–06 he came within 174 nautical miles, farther north than anyone before him. And in 1908, at age 52, he ventured forth once again.

He took six companions, including a black assistant, Matthew Henson, who shared all his exploits. His ship, the *Roosevelt*, was a steamer he had designed himself. In Greenland they picked up dogs, sledges, Eskimo guides, and, for food, 70 tons of whale meat and walrus blubber. Then, in the deepening twilight of Arctic summer, they plowed through the ice floes toward Cape Sheridan, on the north coast of Ellesmere Island. There Peary and his men hunkered down in the round-the-clock darkness of polar winter.

The pole lay 413 miles across the ice pack from Ellesmere. On February 28, 1909, they set out: 7 Americans, 17 Eskimos, and 133 dogs pulling 19 sturdy sledges. Behind them the returning sun cast a pale yellow

This photograph of the doomed Capt. Scott (center) and his party at the South Pole was developed from film found with their bodies. Lt. Bowers (bottom, left) had snapped the shutter with a piece of string.

graciously penned a welcome note to Scott, and headed for home. The trip had run as smoothly as silk over glass.

With Scott, meanwhile, everything went wrong. Instead of sledge dogs he used Mongolian ponies, a disastrous choice. The ponies died off in the cold, and his men had to pull the sledges. Food ran low, and exhaustion set in. Grimly Scott drove on with four companions. They reached the pole on January 17, 1912 — only to find Amundsen's note. The trip back was worse. Weakened by malnutrition and exposure, they perished in a blizzard only 11 miles from a food cache. Even so, Scott died a hero. A relief expedition found his diary, with a final entry that seemed to represent the ultimate triumph of grace over adversity. "We shall stick it out to the end . . ." it said, "and the end cannot be far." And then a postscript: "For God's sake, look after our people."

glow; temperatures hovered at 50 degrees below zero, cold enough to freeze a flask of brandy Peary carried under his parka. Ahead stretched a frozen, gale-swept chaos of ice ridges and flats cut by ominous black leads (channels) of open water. Advance teams, moving in relays, set up camps and food caches. Finally, Peary, Henson, and four Eskimos made a final dash for the pole. They sped the last 133 miles in just four days, and on April 6, 1909, they were there. Crisscrossing the ice to make sure of his position, Peary chose a low ice mound and marked it with the American flag. Then, reaching Labrador on his return trip, he cabled his wife: "Have made good at last. I have the old Pole."

But had he? Only days earlier a rival explorer, Dr. Frederick A. Cook, had turned up in Denmark claiming to have reached the North Pole the previous summer. The newspapers labeled Cook a hero. Then over the next months it became clear that the doctor was lying; according to his Eskimo guides, he had never gone beyond sight of land. But for a while, a cloud hung over Peary's triumph.

South in Antarctica, two nations were in a race to the planet's other pole. Capt. Robert Scott of the British Royal Navy landed at McMurdo Sound in early 1911 on his second trip to the frozen continent. At almost the same time, a rival expedition, led by Roald Amundsen of Norway, disembarked on the Ross Ice Shelf, some 400 miles to the east.

Amundsen had already scored some notable firsts in the Far North, including his discovery of the long-sought Northwest Passage between Greenland and Alaska. Relying on his years of Arctic experience, he equipped himself with skis, dog sledges, Eskimo parkas, and seal meat to ward off scurvy. In mid-October he led his men across the ice shelf, then worked his way over the 12,000-foot-high glaciers of the Queen Maud Mountains. On December 15 he reached the world's basement. He raised the Norwegian flag,

Roald Amundsen, clad in Eskimo furs, scans the Antarctic horizon. Here the Norwegian carries snowshoes and an alpenstock, but usually he traveled on cross-country skis.

"He Was the Greatest Leader"

Sir Ernest Shackleton's attempt to cross Antarctica in 1915 ended before it began. Pack ice imprisoned his ship, then crushed it, and the British explorer and his 28-man crew found themselves and their small lifeboats adrift on an ice floe. After five months, the floe carried the men to within sight of a rock called Elephant Island, where they managed to land. Knowing no one would look for them there, Shackleton and five others set out in a lifeboat for a whaling station on South Georgia Island, 800 miles away. Dehydrated, frozen, and fighting delirium, they made it in 16 days. Then Shackleton and two crewmen hiked 36 hours over a mountain range to find help. He personally led rescuers to Elephant Island, saving his entire crew. As one later said, "He was the greatest leader that ever came on God's earth, bar none."

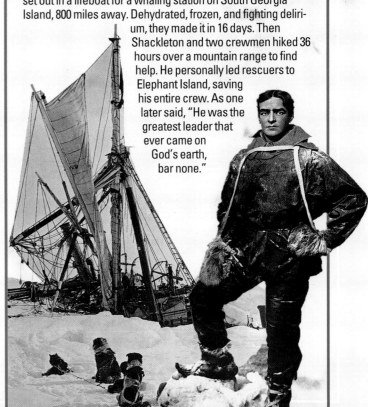

CRUSADERS FOR A BETTER WORLD

Its conscience stung by muckraking reports of widespread poverty and corruption, the nation embarked on a series of needed reforms. Private charities, government legislatures, and individual citizens all pitched in.

In the fall of 1902 wealthy socialite J. G. Phelps Stokes made front-page headlines in *The New York Times* with a shocking announcement: he would leave the family mansion on Madison Avenue and live permanently at the University Settlement on Eldridge Street, in the heart of the slums, where he would spend the rest of his life working with the poor. His parents must have been astonished. Yet, from patrician drawing rooms to middle-class parlors, from church socials to the loftiest corridors of political power, an awareness was growing that large segments of American life were in need of major repair. The result was a national groundswell of social activism, which ranged from simple charity to business and labor reform to improved housing and health care to such radical programs as woman suffrage, socialism, birth control, and the prohibition of strong drink.

Champions of "the Other Half"

The most glaring social flaw was poverty. In 1890 a Danish-born journalist, Jacob Riis, working the police beat for a New York City newspaper, published a book of photographs he had taken in the immigrant tenements of the city's Lower East Side. *How the Other Half Lives,* with its heartrending images of ragged children, decrepit rooming houses, and sweatshop working conditions, stung the national conscience. At a time when most Americans were enjoying the liveliest economic boom in decades, it was clear that millions of their countrymen were leading lives of appalling deprivation. Boston, Chicago, Baltimore, Philadelphia — almost every major city contained a squalid ghetto neighborhood characterized by shoddy housing, poor sanitation, high unemploy-

Upton Sinclair's savage indictment of America's ▲
meatpacking industry told of tubercular hogs, foul working conditions, and mistreatment of employees.

ment, and rampant disease. In these dark precincts, crime flourished and drunkenness prevailed.

Some people were quick to blame the victims, many of whom were immigrants from eastern and southern Europe. "The vice and crime which they have planted in our midst are sickening and terrifying," lamented one observer. Others took a more reasoned look. Beginning in 1902, Lincoln Steffens, an editor for *McClure's Magazine,* wrote a series of articles entitled "The Shame of the Cities," which pointed an accusing finger at flagrant corruption by local politicians. Illiteracy, low wages, and exploitive business practices were also blamed.

Even as journalists were alerting the public, individual citizens rolled up their sleeves to make things better. The remarkable Jane Addams, a former medical student, moved to the Chicago slums and opened Hull House as a center of relief, comfort, education, and settlement for the city's needy. Saint Jane, as her grateful clients dubbed her, taught sewing and reading, ran a kindergarten, organized boys' clubs, offered baths to families with no running water, and badgered municipal authorities for better schools, sewers, and other services. For a time she tailed the city garbage truck to make sure it picked up trash. The local ward boss fought her tooth and nail — "no petticoats in politics," he grumbled — but Addams remained at Hull House for 40 years, and in 1931 she won a Nobel Peace Prize. Similar settlement houses sprang up in dozens of other cities, and together they gave respectability to a newly developing profession: social work.

Some reformers sprang from the ranks of the victims themselves. Seamstresses in New York City sweatshops regularly worked 10-hour days, 6 days a week, and earned as little as 30 cents a day. In 1900 they banded together in the International Ladies' Garment Workers' Union (ILGWU) and pushed for higher pay. The American Federation of

Anarchist Emma Goldman fought for labor and cried out against government in any form. She was deported to Russia in 1919.

Journalist Ida Tarbell set the era's muckraking style with her exposé of Standard Oil, which caused the monopoly's breakup.

Volunteer nurses report for duty at the Henry Street Settlement, on New York City's Lower East Side. Nearly 100 settlement houses were already ministering to immigrants' needs in the nation's slums when the century opened, and most of them took their cue from Chicago's Hull House, founded by social pioneer Jane Addams (inset) in 1889.

A crew of teenage "breaker" boys at a Pennsylvania coal mine poses for the camera of muckraking journalist Lewis Hine. Miners' sons normally went full-time to the pits at age 10; they sorted coal from other rock as it emerged from a crushing machine, or breaker. Starting pay for children at the mines was 35 cents a day.

Immigrants in a New York City tenement building might have lived as many as seven to a room, as in this 1910 family portrait by Jacob Riis. There was no fire escape, no central heat, no hot water, and sanitation facilities were a privy in the backyard.

Ladies on the March

Most Americans in 1900 knew very well where women belonged: at home, tending the children, and certainly not in the voting booth. Only four states gave ballot privileges to females: Wyoming, Colorado, Idaho, and Utah. "Sensible and responsible women do not want to vote," declared former President Grover Cleveland, who smugly explained that God himself had worked out a social and political hierarchy with men on top. Astonishingly, many wives and daughters dutifully agreed.

Yet the status of women was changing with blurring rapidity. As many as 700,000 young ladies had left their family kitchens by 1900 to work as teachers, salesclerks, or office assistants. A battery of newly

As women paraded for the vote draped in patriotic glory (left), men reacted first with scorn, then alarm. The male readers at right scan bulletins posted by a Washington, D.C., anti-suffragette lobby.

HEADQUARTERS NATIONAL ASSOCIATION
OPPOSED TO WOMAN SUFFRAGE

founded women's colleges was spewing out alumnae — more than 8,000 a year by 1910. Women were learning to swim, to drive cars, to run businesses, to play tennis and golf. In 1902 a Texas schoolteacher, Anna Taylor, shot Niagara Falls in a barrel. Mrs. Thomas Hitchcock, a Long Island socialite, was seen to ride her horse cross-saddle, just like a man. Alice

VOTES FOR WOMEN 1915

VOTES FOR WOMEN PATRIOTISM

Suffragette campaign buttons promised a glorious new dawn in American politics, in which votes for women would end corruption, graft, and other evils.

Roosevelt, the president's beautiful, high-stepping daughter, shocked her elders by playing poker and puffing cigarettes, and nonetheless became a national idol of liberated womanhood.

Terrible inequality still existed, to be sure. Many states denied married women the right to own property. In Pennsylvania a wife could not sign a business contract without her husband's consent, and in Georgia she was constrained by law to give her husband all her earnings. Even in New York City she could be arrested for smoking in public.

The political clout of the ballot box would go far toward correcting the balance. A movement backing woman suffrage had existed for decades, but the death of its two most prominent leaders, Susan B. Anthony and Elizabeth Cady Stanton, was causing it to languish. Then new inspiration swept in from England, where ardent campaigners, like Emmeline Pankhurst, were storming Parliament and getting themselves jailed in pursuit of the right to vote. American women were less violent, but no less determined. Venerable organizations, like the National American Woman Suffrage Association, launched rallies and sent out petitions. Rival society matrons Mrs. O.H.P. Belmont and Mrs. Clarence Mackay formed their own mutually exclusive groups. Male opposition was strong at first; a suffragette, scoffed an unknown wit, was "one who has ceased to be a lady and not yet become a gentleman." But the momentum grew until there was no stopping it. Some 15,000 women and a gentlemen's brigade of male supporters, cheered on by an estimated 500,000 spectators, marched down Fifth Avenue in New York in May of 1912 in a parade that *The New York Tribune* called "the greatest demonstration of women in American history." By the time America entered World War I, it was obvious to all that the 19th Amendment was just around the corner.

W.E.B. Du Bois — proud, passionate, and brilliant — spent a lifetime battling for the rights of black people. The first African-American to win a doctorate from Harvard, he became America's most outspoken black intellectual. In 1909 he joined other activists, both white and black, to found the National Association for the Advancement of Colored People (NAACP). He thrived on controversy. Demanding government action to bring about full racial equality, Du Bois clashed with the highly respected Booker T. Washington, president of all-black Tuskegee Institute, who took a more accommodating line. As editor of **The Crisis,** the era's leading black publication, he backed an early form of black separatism, vowing "to disdain and forget . . . that outer, whiter world." He urged his readers to see "beauty in black."

Labor (AFL), founded in 1886 and headed by New York cigar maker Samuel Gompers, already boasted more than 500,000 members in 1900, and it was growing. Slowly, wages and working conditions would begin to improve.

One section of the labor force remained shockingly unrepresented, however. According to the 1900 census, more than 1.7 million children, including 26 percent of all American boys between ages 10 and 15, were "gainfully employed." Most worked on family farms. But an estimated 284,000 boys and girls toiled in coal mines, textile factories, and the like, where conditions were hazardous, injuries frequent, and where the workday might last 12 hours. One of the most poignant verses of the time did not exaggerate:

The golf links lie so near the mill
That almost every day
The laboring children can look out
And see the men at play.

Legislation to prohibit child labor did not pass the U.S. Congress until 1916, and even then the Supreme Court struck it down. (It would be 1938 before the nation acquired its first child labor law.) But in other areas, government moved firmly to curtail abuses. New York City, responding to Riis's slum photos, passed a series of landmark housing laws. In Chicago, at Jane Addams's urging, officials opened the first juvenile court. Reformist mayors swept away political skulduggery in Cleveland, Toledo, and other cities. And in Wisconsin, Robert La Follette, elected governor in 1900, launched a far-reaching program that included election reform, business regulation, banking laws, a civil service act, and the first state income tax.

No sector of American life seemed immune from the crusaders' zeal. Cutthroat practices in the oil business came under attack in Ida Tarbell's profile of Standard Oil, published in *McClure's Magazine;* the series turned John D. Rockefeller into everyone's favorite villain and led to the eventual breakup of his oil monopoly. Young Upton Sinclair, researching a novel about the hard life of Chicago meat-packing workers, discovered that much of the nation's output of breakfast sausages contained tainted pork. Sinclair's *The Jungle* caused such a furor that it spurred passage of the 1906 Pure Food and Drug Act. No one was more astonished than the novelist himself. "I aimed at the public's heart," he said, "and by accident I hit in the stomach."

Some 2,000 journalistic exposés appeared during the decade in the popular magazines, like *McClure's, Collier's,* and *The Ladies' Home Journal,* and so strident did their tone become that even Teddy Roosevelt, surely one of the era's most outspoken crusaders (see pages 22–23), grew

tired of them. The authors were muckrakers, the president declared. But the muckrakers wore their title proudly and continued to attack the nation's ills.

Roosevelt had another name for radical extremists in any reform movement: the lunatic fringe. The group included labor agitators, such as William D. (Big Bill) Haywood, a founder of the Industrial Workers of the World (IWW), and all others who urged violence to bring about change. The twice-jailed Eugene V. Debs, who co-founded the Socialist Party and ran five times for president between 1900 and 1920, presumably qualified. Emma Goldman, editor of the anarchist *Mother Earth* magazine, surely did; she preached birth control, practiced free love, and spent time in jail for telling unemployed workers to steal bread.

And there were the formidable ladies of the Woman's Christian Temperance Union (WCTU). Convinced that demon rum was the cause of society's ills, these advocates of a dry America joined the militant Anti-Saloon League to take arms against the nation's 200,000 liquor dealers. With rallies, revival meetings, and temperance marches as their weapons, they forced county after county to pass ordinances closing bars and liquor stores. And woe to the neighborhood that chose to remain wet. It invited assault by a fearsome phalanx of hymn-singing temperance vigilantes, led perhaps by the imposing Carry Nation. Nearly six feet tall, Carry would stride majestically into saloons in Kansas with her trademark hatchet, chop up the bar, smash bottles, and terrorize drinkers. "I tell you, ladies," she exhorted her followers, "you don't know how much joy you will have until you begin to smash, smash, smash." She knew she was on the side of the angels, and of the electorate: in 1920 the 18th Amendment to the Constitution made Prohibition the law of the land.

Temperance warrior Carry Nation went after booze, tobacco, and foreign food. She financed her crusade by selling souvenir hatchet pins like the one shown here.

LOVING THE GREAT OUTDOORS

"Thousands of tired, nerve-shaken, over-civilized people are beginning to find out that . . . wildness is a necessity," observed American naturalist John Muir, a tireless battler for unspoiled areas.

As the nation got more crowded, places like Yosemite Valley (above left) and Yellowstone National Park, established in 1872, drew increasing public attention.

In the midst of his controversial first term, in mid-May of 1903, as the nation eagerly awaited decisions on matters such as trust-busting and labor strife, Theodore Roosevelt decided to go camping. He asked renowned naturalist and a founder of the Sierra Club, John Muir, to be his personal guide for a tour of California's Yosemite Valley: "I want to drop politics absolutely for four days and just be out in the open with you." His intent was far from frivolous, however. Deeply disturbed at the prospect of Western lands being chewed up by timber barons, cattle kings, and dam builders, he wanted to see for himself the glories of Yosemite Valley. He brushed aside offers of comfortable accommodations and slept under the open sky. Indeed, he was thrilled one morning to awaken and find himself covered with four inches of fresh snow. "This is bullier yet!" he exclaimed.

Roosevelt could not have chosen a better guide. John Muir, then 65, had long called for the preservation of the wilderness. At last the country had begun to heed his pleas and respond to the lyrical prose of naturalist John Burroughs of New York, whose writings on life in the Catskills were among the most popular of the era. Facing staunch opposition from would-be developers, Muir helped set the stage for Roosevelt's campaign to save as much wilderness as he could. "I hate the man who would skin the land!" Roosevelt thundered, and during his term of office he set aside some 230 million acres of land for preservation.

Roosevelt signed laws to withdraw important watersheds from settlement and to protect Alaskan fisheries; he appointed the National Conservation Commission to undertake a survey of natural resources, established the first federal wildlife refuges, and doubled the number of national parks. Among his strongest supporters was the railroad industry, one of the great engines of development. But the railroad barons recognized that the creation of national parks would give a tremendous boost to tourism and that the railroads, in turn, would profit.

Legacy of the Lost Hetch Hetchy

John Muir crusaded valiantly to preserve a spectacular valley, called Hetch Hetchy, to the north of Yosemite. He praised the valley as "one of Nature's rarest and most precious mountain temples." The city of San Francisco wanted to dam the waters of the valley and turn it into a reservoir system. "Dam Hetch Hetchy?" Muir spluttered. "As well dam for water-tanks the people's cathedrals and churches, for no holier temple has ever been consecrated by the heart of man." He was able to hold off the dam builders for several years, but in 1913 Woodrow Wilson's secretary of the interior engineered the removal of the valley from federal protection. Muir died the next year, defeated in his last major battle. A fresh army was forming to fight for future Hetch Hetchys, however, an army of youngsters who would learn first-hand a reverence for nature.

Nowhere was the yearning for the outdoor life more evident than in the explosive growth of the Boy Scout movement. Scouting had been founded in Great Britain in 1908 by Lt. Gen. Robert Baden-Powell, a

Robert Baden-Powell in the "practical, cheap, and comfortable" uniform he designed for the Boy Scouts.

Half Dome rises above John Muir and Theodore Roosevelt on their 1903 Yosemite trip. When Muir (inset left) and John Burroughs (inset far left) visited the park together in 1909, Burroughs quietly contemplated its wonders as Muir exuberantly hailed waterfalls and rock formations.

Ruffling Some Feathers

In the early years of the 20th century, millinery fashions reached their height — literally. Hatmakers piled their creations high with ostrich and egret plumes and jaunty sprays of bird-of-paradise and parrot feathers. Some hats were taxidermic still lifes that featured a stuffed oriole, wren, skylark, even a sea gull or owl, as the centerpiece.

But such fashions came at a price: the loss of native birds by the thousands each year. In 1903 Roosevelt took steps to end the devastation by establishing the first federal wildlife refuge, on Pelican Island, Florida, a nesting place for the besieged waterfowl of the area. This action, along with a shift in taste toward smaller, less downy headdress, marked the beginning of a comeback for many birds.

renowned tracker and a hero of the Boer War. A chance encounter brought Scouting to the United States. On a visit to London in 1909, an American businessman named William D. Boyce became disoriented by a thick fog and was aided by a boy in a strange uniform. The boy turned down a tip, with the explanation that as a Scout he was sworn to do a good deed every day. Boyce was so impressed by the Good Samaritan that he arranged to meet Baden-Powell and then imported Scouting to the United States.

The Boy Scouts of America movement spread like wildfire: within two years more than 125,000 members had joined up. Former President Theodore Roosevelt lent his name and prestige to the group and became its honorary vice president. The lack of a similar outdoor group for girls led quickly to the formation of the Camp Fire Girls. In a statement of purpose, the founders wrote: "What we are trying to do . . . is to brush away . . . the oil and smoke of this machine age . . . to reveal the beauty, romance, and adventure of the common things of life."

The nation was gripped by an immense enthusiasm for the outdoors early in the century. As America moved headlong toward becoming an urban society, many of its citizens came to recognize the value of wilderness lands as places of sanctuary and moral uplift. "It is blessed to lean fully and trustfully on Nature," wrote Muir, "to experience the infinite tenderness and power of her love."

From 1907 to 1919, Ty Cobb (right) of the Detroit Tigers led the American League in batting 12 times, won 4 RBI titles, and stole the most bases 6 times.

THE CENTURY'S GAMES BEGIN

Modern sports took the field in the century's opening decade. Firsts included baseball's World Series, college football's Rose Bowl, tennis's Davis Cup, and Olympic Games held in America.

"Take me out to the ball game," implored Katie Casey in the 1908 song, and America's fans with their peanuts and Cracker Jacks heeded her call. Just after the turn of the century, they had made professional baseball the country's dominant sport. The upstart American League persuaded the standoffish National League to compete, and in 1903 they met for the first World Series. In the best-of-nine contest, the American League's Boston Red Sox, with superb pitching by Bill Dineen and Cy Young, beat the National League's Pittsburgh Pirates five games to three.

From 1903 to 1914 the Chicago Cubs, New York Giants, and Pittsburgh Pirates dominated the National League. The Cubs boasted a feisty double-play infield of Johnny Evers, Joe Tinker, and Frank Chance, whose acroba-

tics moved columnist and Giant rooter Franklin P. Adams to lament, "Words that are weighty with nothing but trouble, 'Tinker to Evers to Chance.'" New York countered with short, stout, combustible John McGraw, a manager who made umpires tremble. Pittsburgh's Honus Wagner led the league in batting eight times and fielded his shortstop position beautifully. In the American League, the Philadelphia Athletics and Detroit Tigers held sway. Connie Mack, born Cornelius McGillicuddy, managed the Athletics with an austere hand. He ruled the dugout in a three-piece suit, celluloid collar, and tie, directing his minions with a rolled-up scorecard. Center fielder Ty Cobb, arguably the best player ever, roamed the base paths for Detroit with a single-minded intensity that bordered on pathological aggression.

Professional boxing, though outlawed in many states, captured the nation's headlines in 1910. Undefeated heavy-

New York Giants' manager John McGraw (left) greets the Philadelphia Athletics' Connie Mack before the 1911 World Series. McGraw managed for 33 years, Mack for 53.

OFFICIAL SCORE CARD
WORLD'S CHAMPIONSHIP SERIES
NEW YORK GIANTS
CHAMPIONS OF THE
NATIONAL LEAGUE
VS
PHILA. ATHLETICS
CHAMPIONS OF THE
AMERICAN LEAGUE

JOHN T. BRUSH

BRUSH STADIUM
1·9·1·1
PRICE 10 CENTS

Infield stars Johnny Evers, Joe Tinker, and Frank Chance (from left to right) kept the Chicago Cubs at or near the top of the National League.

Football rules changes after 1906 — designed to reduce the brutal, bone-crushing tactics that too often led to fatalities — also legalized the forward pass and made the game more exciting for fans.

weight champion Jim Jeffries, after six years of retirement, was coaxed back into the ring in Reno, Nevada, to dethrone Jack Johnson, a Texan who in 1908 had become the first black champion. Johnson's marriages to white women and his defiant attitude had released a torrent of racism: Jeffries was billed as the Great White Hope. Instead, Johnson toyed with the overweight Jeffries, dispatching him in the 15th round. Three years later, a dubious morals charge forced the champion to flee the country.

College football flourished. The first Rose Bowl contest took place on January 1, 1902, when Michigan walloped Stanford 49–0. But three years later football had to face a crisis. In the 1905 season, 18 players died from injuries received while playing the game. That same year President Theodore Roosevelt, an ardent fan, called together officials from Yale, Harvard, and Princeton to demand that they take the lead in reducing the mayhem. They created the forerunner of the National Collegiate Athletic Association (NCAA) to monitor competition, and wrote rules to make football safer. Coaches added innovative offenses: at the University of Chicago Amos Alonzo Stagg dreamed up the backfield shift, and at the Carlisle Indian School, Pop Warner introduced the single wing. By 1913 a little-known school named Notre Dame, with a sticky-fingered end named Knute Rockne, came east with a forward passing game and upset mighty Army 35–13.

In the first Davis Cup match, Malcolm Whitman, Dwight Davis, and Holcombe Ward beat the British 5–0.

Even country-club tennis and golf were producing world-class athletes. In 1900 Harvard student Dwight Davis initiated the Davis Cup to spur competition with England and stimulate U.S. interest in tennis. The U.S. Open golf tournament, begun in 1895, finally crowned its first American champion in 1911, when New Jersey's Johnny McDermott turned the trick.

But American golf had an even greater day in 1913, when Francis Ouimet, a local amateur, went up against England's foremost pros, Harry Vardon and Ted Ray, at the U.S. Open in Brookline, Massachusetts. Ouimet tied them at the end of regulation play and, the next day, in a pressure-filled 18-hole play-off, defeated them.

Although 1904 saw the first Olympics ever held in America, in St. Louis, the 1912 Stockholm Olympics capped the era. It spotlighted the triumph, and tragedy, of Jim Thorpe, an Oklahoma-born American Indian whose athletic feats had helped tiny Carlisle Indian School reach top status in football and track. Thorpe's incredible versatility enabled him to take gold medals in the pentathlon and the decathlon (setting a record for total points). Everyone from kings to presidents toasted him. Then tragedy struck: when the Olympic panjandrums learned that Thorpe had earned $60 a month to play minor league baseball, they stripped him of his medals. Thorpe's medals were not returned until 1982, nearly 30 years after his death.

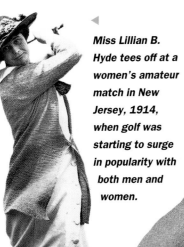

Miss Lillian B. Hyde tees off at a women's amateur match in New Jersey, 1914, when golf was starting to surge in popularity with both men and women.

Jim Thorpe hurls the shot put, one of four events he won on his way to first place in the decathlon at the 1912 Stockholm Olympics.

On July 4, 1910, Jim Jeffries (left) proved no match for heavyweight champion Jack Johnson.

This 1894 kinetoscope of the mighty sneeze of Edison lab worker Fred Ott was a runaway hit.

FRED'S SNEEZE, NICKELODEONS, AND HOLLYWOOD

Within 15 years what had begun as turn-of-the-century tinkering with awkwardly moving images evolved into a multimillion-dollar industry that shed glamour on a patch of California sagebrush.

For years photographers and inventors had demonstrated to fascinated Victorians that images could seem to move in "trick" machines with weird names like Projecting Phenakistiscope and the Wheel of Life. In 1891 Thomas A. Edison, already world famous for the light bulb and the phonograph, exhibited the kinetoscope, a box with a peephole and a crank that rolled a few seconds of "moving" images past a viewer (above, left). Soon kinetoscope parlors with rows of boxes enthralled viewers, who paid pennies to see "Fred Ott's Sneeze" or a clown juggle.

Across the Atlantic, pioneer French filmmakers had thrown a kinetoscope image onto a large screen for a Paris audience, creating arguably the first picture show. (Edison's attempts to project kinetoscope images onto a larger screen were not so successful.) Another Parisian, the magician Georges Méliès, discovered something else when his camera jammed shooting a Paris street scene: a hearse "magically" replaced a bus, and special effects were born. Méliès pushed on with "magic" films, like *Christ Walking on the Waters* (1899), *The India Rubber Head* (1901), *A Trip to the Moon* (1902) with frilly "moon girls" and a rocket ship, and, later, *Conquest of the Pole* (1912).

Edison, too, was busy. Creating interior scenes on a Manhattan rooftop set and outdoor scenes on location in New Jersey, he produced the first western. Filmed by Edwin S. Porter, *The Great Train Robbery* (1903) electrified viewers. Into 12 minutes it packed a train robbery, a horseback chase, a running gunfight, and the villains' deaths. The public clamored for more movies, and for places to see them.

The first nickelodeon opened in 1905, a tiny, dark room where customers paid a nickel for a few minutes of a melodrama featuring endangered maidens and infants, gallant rescuers, or leering mustachioed scoundrels. Within a year

Filmmaker Georges Méliès works on a painting of a rocket rammed into the moon's right eye for A Trip to the Moon.

▲ *At Edison's New Jersey "Black Maria" studio (above), some 300 movies were shot from 1893 to 1903. The building rotated on a center pivot and was pushed to follow the sun. In The Great Train Robbery, Justus T. Barnes (top) fires his six-gun directly at the audience. Many nickelodeon owners used this sensational scene both to begin and to end a showing.*

Men made up three-fourths of the nickelodeon audience. As better movie theaters opened, they attracted more women and children.

The Keystone Kops head out on a chase, one of 500 shorts made by Mack Sennett between 1912 and 1917.

there were 1,000 nickelodeons, and the number reached 10,000 by the decade's end, when people were spending nearly $100 million in nickelodeons and more than 25 percent of the population of New York City went to a nickelodeon once a week. By 1914 the first "picture palace" opened on Broadway, with crystal chandeliers and a live orchestra.

Early films made no claim to sophistication. Sometimes called Democracy's Theater, nickelodeons coupled movies with sing-alongs, vaudeville comics, dog acts, and illustrated lectures. The audiences were mainly workingmen (a blue collar city like Pittsburgh had a hundred theaters). The titles often gave away the plot: *The Perils of Pauline*, *Rescued From an Eagle's Nest*, and *What Drink Did*. Every scene seemed to end with an explosion or a beating.

Most movies came from three producers: Edison, Biograph, and Vitagraph. Using natural light, they filmed in open-air studios on rooftops in New York City, across the river in New Jersey, and in Philadelphia. Rain, cold, and passing pigeons often interrupted production. Soon costly labor, long winters, and Edison's ironfisted lock on some key movie-technology patents were too much for many moviemakers. California beckoned. The Los Angeles Chamber of Commerce guaranteed sunshine 350 days a year. Actors were cheap, there were no unions, and the wide-open spaces made Edison's patent sleuths easier to avoid.

In Hollywood the first studio was a roadhouse leased to movie people because local prohibition laws had doomed it to bankruptcy. Agnes de Mille, the great dancer and choreographer, later remembered "wild, wild hills. Sagebrush, and rattlesnakes, and coyotes. . . ." Sunset Boulevard, mostly dirt, followed an old cattle trail; early studios provided hitching rails; and a sign on the back of a streetcar warned, "Don't shoot rabbits from the rear platform."

Everywhere new directors and stars flourished. At Biograph, D. W. Griffith invented the language of film in one-reelers, developing techniques of pacing, editing, crosscutting, and close-ups. After his first movie, *The Adventures of Dollie,* in 1908, Griffith directed some 400 movies over the next five years. He never abandoned the melodrama of cliff-hangers like *Her Terrible Ordeal* (1910), a one-reel thriller about a secretary locked in the company safe. But his camera technique was an inspiration to other directors.

At Keystone Studios, Griffith protégé Mack Sennett gave the frenetic Griffith chase scene a comic turn. In 1912 he directed the first of the roller-coaster Keystone Kops shorts. They were dazzling orgies of action, with actors racing, sliding, falling, and driving, always wildly out of control and endlessly colliding with cars, animals, pies, and each other.

Two years later Sennett's Keystone Kops romped in America's first feature-length comic film, *Tillie's Punctured Romance,* starring Marie Dressler as a farm girl deceived into marriage by a dastardly smoothy. Her costar was a wispy British music hall comedian who had just joined Keystone Studios at $150 a week: Charlie Chaplin.

McLean County Unit #5
105 - Carlock

MODERNISM HITS THE ARTS

New ideas threatened some, but they stimulated others to rethink their views of what art could be. One critic wrote: "We are in the midst of . . . a new Renaissance in art — an epoch whose means and discoveries have opened . . . an infinitude of possibilities."

Marcel Duchamp's "Nude Descending a Staircase," dismissed by one critic as "an explosion in a shingle factory," created a stir at the New York Armory Show.

display of 58 drawings by Auguste Rodin. He followed that exhibit with the first American showing of Henri Matisse, then with Toulouse-Lautrec, Rousseau, and a major exhibit of Picasso's works in 1911. Among the innovative American painters Stieglitz introduced were Max Weber, Alfred Maurer, and Georgia O'Keeffe, who married Stieglitz in 1924.

The movement that began in Stieglitz's tiny studio burst into a larger American consciousness in 1913 with the New York Armory Show. There were an estimated 1,300 art works in the Armory Show, one-third by European artists and two-thirds by Americans. Europe was represented by some of the reigning giants of modern art, among them Picasso, Matisse, Braque, and

▲ **Edward Steichen, Heinrich Kuehn, Alfred Stieglitz, and Frank Eugene (left to right) critique artwork.**

In the tiny attic of a brownstone at 291 Fifth Avenue in New York City, an intense dark-haired man who sported rimless glasses and a graying mustache plotted a revolution. As a young man he had gone to Berlin to study mechanical engineering, but chance led him to a career in photography. Soon the brilliant Alfred Stieglitz gained an international reputation. "He pushed himself and the medium to the utmost," said one critic. Photography itself was still suspect in most artistic circles. Many doubted that a machine could produce a work of art. Stieglitz devoted himself to a new movement he called Photo Secession, a name to signal his intention to "secede" from the accepted view of what constituted photography.

With the help of the photographer and painter Edward Steichen, Stieglitz's attic became a gallery, known simply as "291," where he displayed works by artists destined to become some of the greatest names in photography: Gertrude Kasebier, Clarence H. White, and Alvin Langdon Coburn. Not content with breaking new ground in photography, Stieglitz began to show paintings as well. In January 1908 he put up the first modern art exhibit in America: a

▶ **Edward Steichen used pigment with gum dichromate to achieve a color effect in this 1904 photo of New York's Flatiron Building.**

Vaslav Nijinsky, star of the Ballets Russes, dances the ballet Giselle.

Impresario Sergei Diaghilev woke up the world of ballet.

Cézanne. Traditional critics lost little time in skewering the Armory Show. *The New York Times* worried about modern artists being "cousins to the anarchists in politics," and former President Theodore Roosevelt labeled some of the Armory artists "the lunatic fringe."

Stirrings in the Staid World of Dance

The trend in the performing arts, too, was away from the forms of the past and toward more vitality of expression. The Ballets Russes, launched in 1909 in Paris by impresario Sergei Diaghilev, amazed and sometimes outraged audiences accustomed to the narrowly prescribed movements and conservative themes of traditional ballet. The sweep of Diaghilev's vision was matched only by the talent of his company, which included prima ballerinas Anna Pavlova and Tamara Karsavina, as well as the great Vaslav Nijinsky. As a dancer, Nijinsky brought to the stage a sexual magnetism and athletic ability that set new standards and exploded ballet goers' sense of what was possible.

Still, for creating sheer excitement, Nijinsky was surpassed by an American dancer, Isadora Duncan. Her dancing was something completely new. She had no formal training, for one thing, and danced alone, without the set steps or the tutus and box-toed shoes of the ballet. Dressed in a daring Greek-style tunic, her bare arms and legs visible to all, the dark-eyed melancholy beauty seemed to let the music itself control her, as if she weren't dancing to music but inside it.

Audiences around the world were electrified. "Her body is as though bewitched by the music," wrote one reviewer of her first performance in St. Petersburg in 1904. "Here *everything* dances: waist, arms, neck, head — *and* legs.

Duncan's bare legs and bare feet are like those of a rustic vagabond; they are innocent. . . ." Others were not so enraptured. Like her dancing, Isadora's ideas on nearly every subject were ahead of her time, and her lifestyle was unorthodox. She kept many lovers, bore children out of wedlock, and finally married a man 17 years her junior, the Russian poet Sergei Esenin. That he was so much younger and a confirmed alcoholic contributed to her reputation for moral looseness; that he was Russian awakened something akin to panic in the American press. Never one to steer clear of controversy, Duncan scandalized audiences on an American tour in 1922, delivering revolutionary speeches between dances and baring her breasts to an audience of staid Bostonians. City after city canceled her performances in the interests of public safety.

Finally, Isadora proved too much for America. She returned to Europe, where she died in a freak accident in 1927. The nation was hungry for all things new — but not as new as Isadora Duncan.

As free-spirited in life as in her dancing, Isadora Duncan here strikes a classical pose.

RAGTIME AND RAZZLE-DAZZLE

Heralding the decades to come, a new breed of entertainers shook off fusty traditions and wowed America with a bubbly blend of originality, innocence, confidence, and rebellion.

Dancers did the bunny hug. They also did the camel walk, the buzzard lope, the monkey glide, and the kangaroo dip. And if Americans looked a little silly bouncing on the balls of their feet like turkeys or scratching the dance floor like chickens, who cared? A new century called for a whole new rhythm.

The new rhythm was ragtime. From the start, rag was played mostly on the piano, and its origins were too many to count. In its syncopated rhythms and catchy melodies, there were echoes of everything from European marches to plantation spirituals. The original rag musicians drifted through the South and along the eastern seaboard playing honky-tonks and saloons; most could not read music, so few of their rags were recorded, except as piano rolls.

The recognized king of ragtime was Scott Joplin, the son of a black railroad laborer from Texarkana, Texas. As a teenager Joplin joined the itinerant ranks of piano thumpers in bawdy saloons up and down the Mississippi River. After a long sojourn in the tenderloin districts of St. Louis, he settled in Sedalia, Missouri, where in 1899 music publisher John Stark heard him playing at the Maple Leaf Club. Stark bought the piece then and there, and before long, sheet music sales had made Joplin and "The Maple Leaf Rag" household names.

Joplin created many of the classic rags of the decade, but there were others who were nearly as important: Eubie Blake, whose lightning-quick tempos and hard-rolling base lines made him the unofficial dean of the Eastern school of rag; New Orleans-based Ferdinand (Jelly Roll) Morton, who pioneered the music called jazz; and, of course, Irving Berlin, whose "Alexander's Ragtime Band" was on the lips of nearly every American in 1911. The explosive growth of ragtime — as well as of blues, jazz, and dance steps — was part of a general freedom sweeping the popular arts.

▲ *"Animal dances," such as those featured in the song sheets above, exuberantly pronounced that formality was out, abandon was in.*

▶ *In 1912 Irene and Vernon Castle returned to America from Paris and sparked a nationwide ballroom dancing craze, especially for their Castle Walk.*

"The Vaudeville Theatre is an American invention," wrote *Scribner's Magazine* in 1899. "There is nothing like it anywhere in the world." Some theaters ran almost non-stop: a dozen shows a day, each with 20 or more acts. Providing sheer unpretentious enjoyment, vaudeville had become respectable, and entertainers of every stripe — Broadway and classical artists, too — appeared to try out new acts or to earn what were sometimes huge appearance fees. Those artists included Will Rogers, the Marx Brothers, Anna Pavlova, Joe E. Brown, Sarah Bernhardt, and Ethel Barrymore.

Vaudevillians who became famous could forgo, at least for many months, the grueling tours of theaters across the country. The stars' milieu was New York City, especially the Palace Theatre, which opened in 1913. The main rival for the Palace's vaudeville acts was *The Ziegfeld Follies*, an annual show that producer Florenz Ziegfeld had created in 1907. Using the slogan "Glorifying the American Girl," the wildly successful *Follies* featured chorus-line beauties in lavish costumes. Between the chorus lines, Ziegfeld introduced many major

Sophie Tucker (top) debuted in the 1909 Follies. Later, she sang the first tune by Noble Sissle (left) and Eubie Blake.

stars: Nora Bayes, Fanny Brice, Sophie Tucker, and Bert Williams, to name just a few.

Meanwhile, all of Broadway was thriving. In 1901 New York had more legitimate theaters, 33 to be exact, than any other city in the world. That same year George M. Cohan debuted in his play *The Governor's Son*. The talented Cohan — he sang, danced, acted, directed, produced, composed music and lyrics, and wrote plays and musicals — would light up Broadway for 40 years.

If Broadway produced little serious or innovative drama in the first decade of the new century, audiences were seldom bored. A flock of soon-to-be-major stars began their careers in this high-spirited era: the Barrymore family, Katharine Cornell, Helen Hayes, Peggy Wood, Eddie Foy, Al Jolson. Plays like *Peter Pan* (opening in 1905) were enchanting audiences, and everywhere there were signs of a new openness and vitality, a breaking free from the restrictive forms of the past.

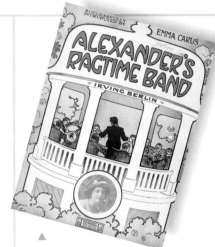

Irving Berlin, born Israel Baline in Siberia, made ragtime more popular than ever with his 1911 hit; his career would span more than 50 years.

▼ *In* The Ziegfeld Follies of 1910, *Billy Reeves (left, as Jim Jeffries) and Bert Williams (as Jack Johnson) restage the era's most famous boxing fight.*

NEW LITERATURE, NEW LIBRARIES

The nascent century saw a widening of literary tastes. While romantic tales of virtue triumphant never really went out of style, American publishers began to bring out books that probed darker aspects of the human experience.

Publisher Frank Doubleday's wife took one look at Theodore Dreiser's *Sister Carrie*, which her husband's company had agreed to publish in 1900, and was horrified. The novel's "heroine" is a working girl who escapes poverty by becoming the mistress of a wealthy man. Siding with his wife, Doubleday told Dreiser, "It's an immoral book," and refused to advertise it. The novel languished, almost unsold, and Dreiser, in despair, contemplated suicide. "My power to write was taken away," he said, and wrote no more fiction for nearly a decade.

For Mrs. Doubleday and many American readers, happy endings and moral rectitude were just fine. The first bestseller of the new century was *To Have and To Hold,* about an English noblewoman who escapes the lustful clutches of Lord Carnal and finds bliss in the arms of a hardworking American. Other big successes in the romantic genre included *Mrs. Wiggs of the Cabbage Patch* (1902), *Rebecca of Sunnybrook Farm* (1904), and *Pollyanna* (1913).

Of course, Americans were reading more than just sentimental romanticism. From the "Editor's Study" at *Harper's Monthly,* William Dean Howells championed the work of his friends Mark Twain and Henry James. By 1900 Twain was world famous, but at 65 he had his best work behind him. He continued to write for magazines (at the princely sum of 20 cents a word) and to lecture extensively until his death in 1910. Henry James, who had forsaken America for England, published *The Wings of the Dove, The Ambassadors,* and *The Golden Bowl* in the first four years of the century. He returned to America for a visit in 1904 and met President Roosevelt, who thought him "effete" and "a miserable little snob." James referred to TR as "the mere monstrous embodiment of unprecedented resounding Noise."

The finely tuned moral and social sensibilities of Henry James's upper-middle-class world were not of great interest to a group of young writers who called themselves naturalists. Characters in their novels battled to survive in a cruel environment; they often were destroyed by weakness or fate, but sometimes prevailed through strength and courage. Naturalists set their fiction in the raw world — in the slums, mills, and jails of industrial America or in the

This caricature of American expatriate Henry James, who lived most of his life in England, conveys the novelist's elitism, which antagonized Teddy Roosevelt when he met James in 1904.

James Montgomery Flagg's sketch of Jack London captured the tough, adventurous spirit of the author, whose first bestseller, The Call of the Wild, featured a dog named Buck and stressed London's view that one needed to adapt to survive.

Theodore Dreiser was just 29 when Doubleday balked at promoting his first novel because it dealt with "offensive" issues.

Sister Carrie
By
Theodore Dreiser

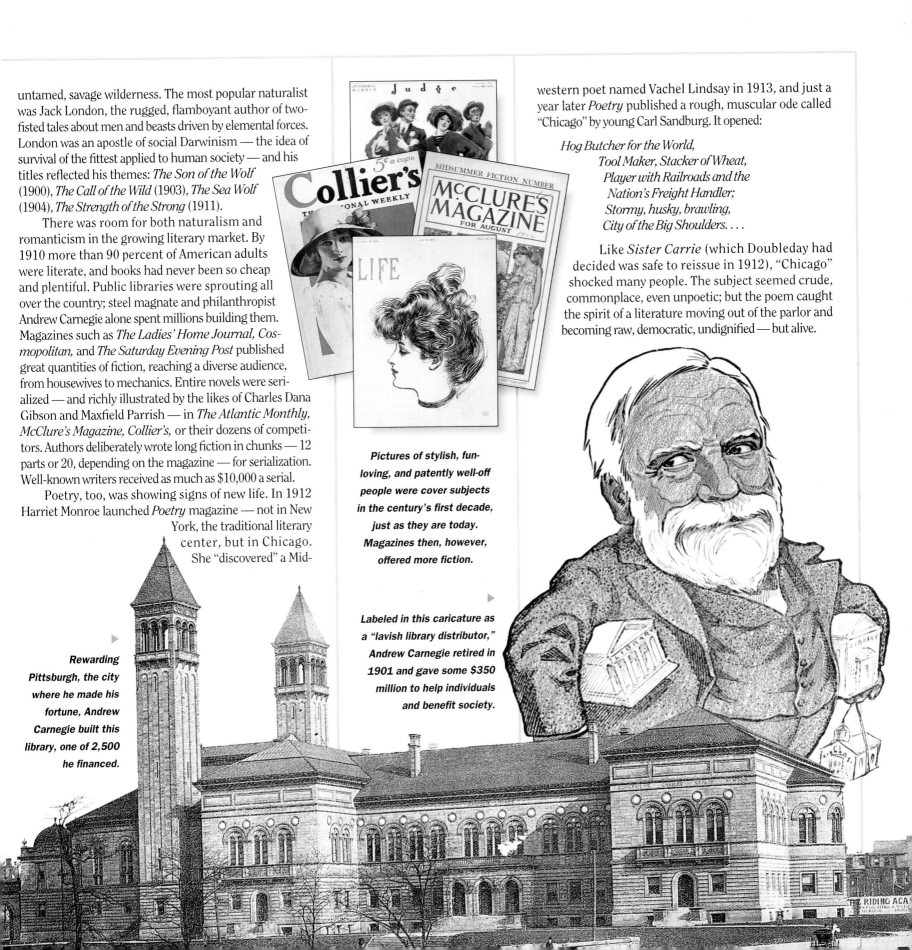

untamed, savage wilderness. The most popular naturalist was Jack London, the rugged, flamboyant author of two-fisted tales about men and beasts driven by elemental forces. London was an apostle of social Darwinism — the idea of survival of the fittest applied to human society — and his titles reflected his themes: *The Son of the Wolf* (1900), *The Call of the Wild* (1903), *The Sea Wolf* (1904), *The Strength of the Strong* (1911).

There was room for both naturalism and romanticism in the growing literary market. By 1910 more than 90 percent of American adults were literate, and books had never been so cheap and plentiful. Public libraries were sprouting all over the country; steel magnate and philanthropist Andrew Carnegie alone spent millions building them. Magazines such as *The Ladies' Home Journal, Cosmopolitan,* and *The Saturday Evening Post* published great quantities of fiction, reaching a diverse audience, from housewives to mechanics. Entire novels were serialized — and richly illustrated by the likes of Charles Dana Gibson and Maxfield Parrish — in *The Atlantic Monthly, McClure's Magazine, Collier's,* or their dozens of competitors. Authors deliberately wrote long fiction in chunks — 12 parts or 20, depending on the magazine — for serialization. Well-known writers received as much as $10,000 a serial.

Poetry, too, was showing signs of new life. In 1912 Harriet Monroe launched *Poetry* magazine — not in New York, the traditional literary center, but in Chicago. She "discovered" a Mid-

western poet named Vachel Lindsay in 1913, and just a year later *Poetry* published a rough, muscular ode called "Chicago" by young Carl Sandburg. It opened:

> *Hog Butcher for the World,*
> *Tool Maker, Stacker of Wheat,*
> *Player with Railroads and the*
> *Nation's Freight Handler;*
> *Stormy, husky, brawling,*
> *City of the Big Shoulders. . . .*

Like *Sister Carrie* (which Doubleday had decided was safe to reissue in 1912), "Chicago" shocked many people. The subject seemed crude, commonplace, even unpoetic; but the poem caught the spirit of a literature moving out of the parlor and becoming raw, democratic, undignified — but alive.

Pictures of stylish, fun-loving, and patently well-off people were cover subjects in the century's first decade, just as they are today. Magazines then, however, offered more fiction.

Labeled in this caricature as a "lavish library distributor," Andrew Carnegie retired in 1901 and gave some $350 million to help individuals and benefit society.

Rewarding Pittsburgh, the city where he made his fortune, Andrew Carnegie built this library, one of 2,500 he financed.

Chapter 2

WORLD WAR I
THE WAR TO END ALL WARS

It begins with hopes of quick victory on

both sides, descends into the hell of

trench warfare, and ends after fresh American

doughboys finally arrive "Over There."

A pint-sized Uncle Sam keeps a firm grip on his hat as he watches America's victorious doughboys march by.

On the eve of World War I, Britain led the world's powers with heavily armored, big-gunned battleships like **Dreadnought** (below), launched in 1906, and **Iron Duke** (above), in 1912.

STORM CLOUDS GATHER

Oddly, national anxieties about who would control the seas were a major theme in the prelude to the most devastating land battles in history. Neither Germany nor Great Britain was inclined to play peacemaker.

The letter on President Wilson's desk contained troubling news. "The whole of Germany is charged with electricity," wrote Wilson's friend and confidant Edward Mandell House. "Everybody's nerves are tense. It only requires a spark to set the whole thing off."

Colonel House was correct. All of Europe was jittery in the spring of 1914. Many Americans, however, chose to ignore the clouds gathering over Europe. They clung to the belief that the New World was safe from strife that might break out in the Old World, and the official policy of the United States remained one of noninvolvement in European affairs. But the Spanish-American War had, for better or worse, given America overseas possessions that required a global outlook. American policymakers were nervous about the possibility of a war that might leave Germany the master of Europe, poised to expand its influence across the oceans.

▲ *Edward M. House, an honorary Texas colonel and President Wilson's trusted aide, made fact-finding trips to Berlin, London, and Paris.*

Great Britain's policy was to keep the European nations divided so that no one nation could dominate the continent by controlling the balance of power. That delicate balance was threatened by rising German power. Since the late 1800's Germany had enjoyed a steady growth in population, foreign trade, and industrial might. Many Germans believed that they had reached a pivotal point in their history. It was time, these patriotic Germans thought, for their country to assume a more active role in world affairs. "In the coming century," one of them said, "the German nation will be either the hammer or the anvil."

Great Britain feared that Germany's increasing share of world trade would inevitably hurt British interests. The British home islands depended on overseas colonies as sources of raw materials and as markets for manufactured goods. When Germany began to build up its navy to protect its own foreign trade, many British leaders were thoroughly alarmed. They saw a more powerful German navy as a serious threat to Britain's economic lifelines.

As early as 1907, American diplomat Henry White expressed dismay at the offhand way that Arthur James Balfour, then the British Conservative Party leader, talked of going to war with Germany to preserve Britain's commercial and naval supremacy. White told Balfour it would be immoral for England to sacrifice human lives to fight a nation "which has as good a right to a navy as you have." The American further suggested, with admirable directness: "If you wish to compete with German trade, work harder." To that remark Balfour replied: "It would be simpler for us to have a war." Balfour was not alone in contemplating the benefit of a war. In Germany the writer Thomas Mann wondered if war might be good for humankind: might it not sweep away the cobwebs of the old order and prove to be "a purification, a liberation, an enormous hope?"

A fragile web of pacts and understandings held Europe together. The English and the French had put aside their long-standing enmity — their "snarling and scratching," as one diplomat put it — and signed a treaty of friendship. On the other side of Europe, Russia bristled at the growth of German ambition, especially because Russian pride and power had suffered a grievous blow in the Russo-Japanese War. With a jaundiced eye on the Germans, Russia entered into alliances with England and France, and offered its protection to Serbia, which was in danger of being swallowed up by Germany's ally, the Austro-Hungarian Empire.

▲ *The future Lord Balfour of Great Britain believed that German ambitions had to be checked, by war if necessary.*

Powerful nations pushed their great fleets around the globe like pieces on a chessboard. The British made a pact with the Japanese, who agreed to look after British stakes in the Far East, freeing British ships to return to the Atlantic. The French agreed to guard Britain's interests in the Mediterranean in exchange for British naval protection of France's Atlantic coast. This gave Britain an excuse to beef up its navy in the North Sea. In 1905 the British began building the first modern Dreadnought battleship, designed to make all previous big warships obsolete. Because the kaiser had assembled an army that dwarfed British ground forces, Britain saw its navy as the empire's best shield.

Hot Air Feeds the Flames

Against the backdrop of these grand strategic ploys, politicians in both England and Germany whipped up public hysteria over the threat of imminent attacks. Bedeviled by England, France, and Russia, Germany felt a naval and diplomatic noose tightening around its neck. Kaiser Wilhelm II, a master at saber rattling, let loose a stream of threats, hoping to frighten Europe into granting him greater power, prestige, and influence, but he did not really want to fight. In the words of one historian: "He wanted the gladiator's rewards without the battle." The kaiser may well have believed that war was avoidable, that the ambassadors in their dapper clothing and the monarchs in their impressive uniforms were mere actors in a diplomatic drama. But as the threats and counterthreats multiplied, the atmosphere grew ever more heated, and as Colonel House advised President Wilson, not much was needed to ignite it.

▲ *Flanked by his six sons, all resplendent in military finery, Kaiser Wilhelm II of Germany (top) parades in Berlin, in a photo dated circa 1914. Though much of the world blamed "Kaiser Bill" for plunging Europe into chaos, most Germans backed his bellicose actions. Germany's first and second battleship squadrons (above), at Kiel before the war, showed the kaiser's resolve to make his navy second to none.*

Berliners cheer their soldiers marching off "on the first mile to Paris" after the kaiser's order for mobilization, here being read by a German officer (inset) on August 1, 1914.

Lord Kitchener calls Britons to arms in the poster that inspired America's famous Uncle Sam recruiting image.

▼ Archduke Francis Ferdinand and his wife, Sophie (both seated at right), set out on the fateful ride in Sarajevo.

"THE LAMPS ARE GOING OUT"

When Austria-Hungary picked a fight with Serbia after Archduke Ferdinand's assassination, it all seemed too irrational to lead very far, but then Russia and Germany jumped in, and Europe began tumbling into chaos.

It was a narrow escape. As their motorcade wound through the town of Sarajevo, Archduke Francis Ferdinand and his wife, Sophie, watched in horror as a man emerged from the crowd and tossed a bomb at their car. The bomb thudded onto the hood, skidded off, and detonated on the street, injuring a number of bystanders.

Ferdinand, the heir apparent of the Austro-Hungarian Empire, had been warned not to go to Sarajevo, capital of the provinces of Bosnia-Herzegovina. These provinces, once part of the Ottoman Empire, had been formally annexed in 1908 by Austria-Hungary, a power grab that deeply rankled neighboring Serbia. Serbian extremists were known to be plotting Ferdinand's assassination, perhaps with the aid of Russian agents intent upon weakening Austria-Hungary and its ally, Germany.

Leaving Sarajevo, Ferdinand and Sophie abruptly ordered their driver to take them to see the victims of the bomb attack, an act of both charity and bravery. As the car came to a halt, a young Serbian named Gavrilo Princip stepped from the curb and fired several pistol shots point-blank at the royal couple. Both were dead within minutes. No one realized it at the time, but those shots of June 28, 1914, would ignite all Europe.

Although the Serbian government disclaimed involvement in the assassination, Austria-Hungary used the murders to demand powers over Serbia's internal affairs. To everyone's surprise, on July 25 Serbia agreed to many of the demands, but to everyone's greater surprise, Austria-Hungary began bombarding Serbia anyway. Dominoes began to fall. Germany's kaiser, Russia's czar, and diplomats on both sides sought to defuse the situation, but Germany and Russia ordered full mobilizations of their armies. The military machines of the Continent began to roll into action, and the delicate web of defensive alliances became an iron net that dragged nations into war.

In the first days of August, Germany declared war on Russia, France, and Belgium; Britain declared war on Germany, after the German Army surged into Belgium in the first offensive of the war. Eventually the belligerents would arrange themselves into the Central Powers (Austria-Hungary, Germany, Turkey, and Bulgaria in 1915) fighting the Allies (Britain, France, Russia, Belgium, and Italy in 1915, joined by the United States in 1917).

President Wilson proclaimed on August 4, 1914, that America would be neutral. He envisioned a great role for the United States: to serve humanity as the arbiter of conflict. He decided to allow loans and shipments of food and war supplies to both sides. He admitted that American interests might best be served by an Allied victory, but he was careful not to offend Germany.

Britons marched off to war full of high spirits, convinced that the conflict would soon be over. Although Britain's army was a small one, the English took comfort from the fact that their worldwide empire, from Africa to Australia to Canada to India, was joining the rush to arms.

The Germans were also optimistic. More than a decade earlier Germany had devised a strategy to achieve a quick, decisive victory over France. The plan called for a massive semicircular maneuver through Belgium to outflank French defenses. Called the Schlieffen Plan after its author, Count Alfred von Schlieffen, chief of the general staff, it depended upon speed of execution to knock out France before the Russians and British could finish mobilizing.

But the Schlieffen Plan worked better on paper than it did in the field. Scheduled to take just 42 days, the plan called for advances of 20 to 25 miles a day, a timetable that was just too ambitious for the soldiers and their supply lines to sustain.

The British Expeditionary Force (BEF) crossed the Channel and met the Germans at the town of Mons, Belgium. The Battle of Mons, hailed as a British victory, in fact ended with a British retreat. Though slowed briefly, the German war machine pushed relentlessly onward. In some minds there arose the ugly thought that this war might not be the short and glorious outing that the generals had promised. That possibility haunted Sir Edward Grey, the British foreign secretary, who had written on the night before war erupted: "The lamps are going out all over Europe; we shall not see them lit again in our lifetime."

▶

Outgunned by the Germans, Belgian soldiers and their dog-drawn machine guns retreat to Antwerp, August 20, 1914.

▼ **Britain expected its far-flung colonials to join its fight in Europe, as this Australian recruiting poster makes very clear.**

Fall-in!

The British historian John Keegan, seeking later to understand how the world fell into the first "total war," noted that no group of countries in history had ever fielded so many soldiers, as a percentage of population, as did Europe in August 1914. In the first two weeks of the war, the belligerent nations put some 20 million men in uniform, or nearly 10 percent of the total population.

As the soldiers marched away, their leaders said they'd be home before the leaves fell, or by Christmas at the latest. The trouble was that though the nations knew how to raise armies, they no longer knew how to use them. Machine guns, massed artillery, and other new tactics and weapons had changed the realities of battle. Never before had head-on assaults faced such devastating firepower.

A GHASTLY KIND OF WARFARE

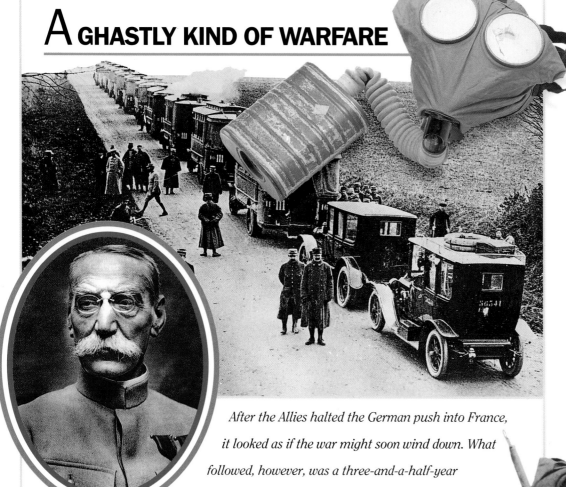

After the Allies halted the German push into France, it looked as if the war might soon wind down. What followed, however, was a three-and-a-half-year deadlock, which reached new depths of agony and slaughter.

In the final days of August 1914, seven German armies were driving like knives toward the heart of France. Their plan was to take Paris, demoralizing the French, and bring all of Western Europe to its knees. Along a 300-mile front, from northeastern France to central Belgium, the French and their allies in the Belgian Army and the British Expeditionary Force were fighting valiantly, but they were giving ground almost everywhere.

As the Germans surged southwest, the commander of the French armies, Gen. Joseph-Jacques-Césaire Joffre, was doing everything he could to halt the German advance. He had ordered the military governor of Paris, Gen. Joseph-Simon Gallieni, to forge the French Sixth Army into a force that could join in an effective counterattack. Gallieni, a renowned old soldier called out of retirement in his country's hour of peril, threw himself into the task while at the same

Rushing troops to stop the German thrust at Paris, General Gallieni (above) drafted 1,200 taxis (above). Six months later, an ugly war got uglier when the Germans used poison gas, making gas masks (top) vital for survival.

The French foot soldier, or poilu (right), was Verdun's real hero.

time solidifying plans for the defense of Paris. Short of men, he appealed to the French high command: "What do we have in troops to defend this heart and brain of France? A drop in the bucket." Joffre responded by calling up more reservists and daringly transferring troops from sectors where the German offensive had slowed.

But almost everywhere the Germans kept coming. Early in September, their advance scouts were less than 25 miles from Paris. By then the French government had fled the city, but Gallieni and his men stayed. On September 5, near Monthyon, about 30 miles from Paris, a German corps pounced on a unit of the French Sixth Army that was

"THEY SHALL NOT PASS!"

On February 21, 1916, in the gray light of a winter's dawn, the kaiser's artillery opened up the most intensive barrage of the war so far: as many as 1,400 heavy guns, including 13 giant 420-mm howitzers, lobbing 100,000 shells an hour for 12 excruciating hours. "We were lifted and tossed about," recalled a French survivor. "Our blinded, wounded, crawling, and shouting soldiers kept falling on top of us and died while splashing us with their blood. . . ." It seemed that nothing could live.

Finally the savage pounding stopped, but the French had little time to enjoy the silence. Toward them came the forward battalions of the German Fifth Army, 140,000 strong.

The German objective was to draw the French into an all-out defense of the city of Verdun, which the French high command regarded as a key strategic link in protecting France's interior. The French would attempt to hold Verdun at any cost, the Germans reasoned. And if forced out, they would pay any price to win it back. "If we plan properly at Verdun," declared Gen.

moving up to counterattack. It was the beginning of the First Battle of the Marne, the "miracle on the Marne" that shattered the kaiser's hope of quick conquest.

To strengthen the Sixth Army, Gallieni commandeered 1,200 Paris taxicabs. Each cab, carrying up to five soldiers per trip, made one or more trips to the front, bringing a total of 6,000 fresh troops to fight the Germans.

Meanwhile, in an unaccountable blunder, the attacking German First and Second Armies had split too far apart, opening a gap between them. As the French Fifth Army hit the flank of the German Second Army, the BEF crept slowly into the gap. Hundreds of fierce little engagements led to

For holding Verdun, Henri Pétain won France's adoration, but his World War II collaboration with Germany disgraced him.

British Field Marshal Haig kept pouring men into the hell of German guns.

widespread confusion, but gradually there came a realization that the Allies had at last halted the German advance.

The Germans withdrew 40 to 50 miles north and dug deeply into positions north of the Aisne River. Hoping to outflank the Allies, they sent some of their forces westward toward the English Channel. In a series of battles called the Race to the Sea — along the Aisne and Yser rivers, through Flanders, Picardy, and Artois — the Allies fought the Germans to a draw and kept them from taking key ports.

In the first three weeks of the war, as later calculated, each side had lost half a million men to death, wounds, or capture. But worse was to come. The fall of 1914 marked the beginning of a three-and-a-half-year standoff that made the word *trenches* a synonym for the horrors of war.

Hundreds of miles of battlefront in Western Europe stabilized into two opposing and roughly parallel trench networks with a belt of no-man's-land in between. Beneath the surface trenches often lay increasingly elaborate subterranean shelters, sometimes connected by minirailways, to protect troops and supplies against artillery bombardments. And beneath no-man's-land, sappers from each side tried to

Erich von Falkenhayn, the German chief of staff, "we can bleed the enemy white."

In the months that followed, it seemed that Germany would do just that. When the Germans quickly took Fort Douaumont, one of Verdun's protective bastions, France began pouring in men to save the city. Gen. Henri Philippe Pétain, summoned to assume command, demanded nothing less than his men's utmost heroism. With casualties running at some 16,000 men a week, he established a roadway, La Voie Sacrée, over which shuttled a continuous stream of fresh troops and munitions. And an order rang out — *"Ils ne passeront pas!"* ("They shall not pass!") — that became the rallying cry of the French defense of Verdun.

And hold the French soldiers did, through explosive hailstorms of enemy artillery, against repeated German infantry assaults, amid clouds of choking phosgene gas, and in defiance of a terrifying new weapon, the flamethrower (painting below). By the year's end the French had retaken some of the ground they had lost, and stood poised to gain a bit more. But at what cost! France had lost more than half a million men at Verdun in dead, wounded, and missing. The Germans, in their effort to "bleed the enemy white," had depleted their own forces by more than 400,000 troops.

Heeding Britain's call, Canadians soon had some tough battles under their belt (poster, right); West Indian (inset) and Anzac (Australian–New Zealand) forces (below) fought at the Somme.

New names in Canadian history. More are coming — Will you be there?

ENLIST!

burrow under the other's positions to set off huge explosions that sometimes lifted acres of earth into the air. No-man's-land became a nightmare landscape of blasted trees, sucking mud, water-filled shell craters where men could drown, and flesh-and-bone-ripping shrapnel and bullets.

On paper, the trenches formed a splendid defense line, but no diagram showed the rats, mud, stench, cold, filth, sleeplessness, boredom, fear, blood, deafening bombardments, endless nights, and cries of the wounded and dying. Sometimes there wasn't a safe interval in which to bury the dead, either one's own or the enemy's, fallen in a futile assault. And when the dead did get buried, they were often exhumed whole or in pieces by exploding artillery shells.

If life in the trenches was hell, hell was usually safer than "going over the top" — charging up out of the trenches to face the machine guns. Time and again Allied divisions scrambled over their earthen parapets to

When enemy shells cut the wires connecting field telephones, carrier pigeons, and sometimes dogs, carried messages along the front lines.

A German machine-gun crew awaits an Allied infantry attack on the western front.

Soldiers of the 2nd Canadian Division (bottom of page) trudge across a rain-soaked landscape beaten to muddy mush by artillery in the Allies' Passchendaele offensive near Ypres, Flanders, in the summer and fall of 1917.

assault the German lines. Time and again they were driven back, with appalling loss of life.

Combined with the power of massed artillery, the machine gun became a machine to consume men. At the First Battle of the Somme, in the summer of 1916, British big guns blasted the German trenches for a solid week, sending some 1.5 million artillery shells into the enemy positions.

On the morning of July 1, the bombardment ceased, giving way to an eerie silence. One British soldier heard a lark singing; another, music from a German gramophone. Then came the attack. Seventeen British divisions and five French divisions went over the top and into no-man's-land. The Germans, in dugouts 30 to 40 feet deep, had waited out the rolling barrage. As it stopped, they emerged from their shelters. When the Allied infantry reached the barbed wire in front of the German trenches, the machine guns mowed down British and French by the thousands. Wrote poet Siegfried Sassoon, stationed behind the British trenches, "I am staring at a sunlit picture of Hell." In four months at the Somme, the British suffered 410,000 casualties, the French 195,000, and the Germans 500,000.

Facing such carnage, each side desperately sought any advantage. The tank could breach barbed wire and crush machine-gun nests; the flamethrower could incinerate dug-in defenders. Thus the Great War became the proving ground for tanks and flamethrowers. The same was true of airplanes, which first saw action as flying observation posts, then quickly evolved into offensive weapons (see page 95).

The Germans loosed one of the most terrifying

British medics tend to a wounded, thirsty Tommy in a trench near Thiepval, on the Somme battlefield, in September 1916.

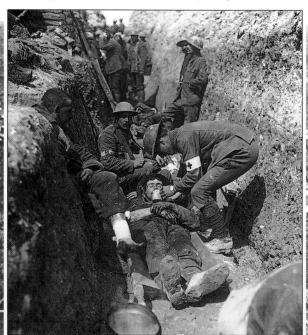

In his sixties and famous, American artist John Singer Sargent went to the front and witnessed a gas attack's grim aftermath.

weapons of all, lethal gas, near Ypres, Belgium, around dawn on April 22, 1915. French colonial troops heard a hissing from the German lines and saw a strange, some said an almost beautiful, green cloud wafting toward them. It was chlorine gas, and it soon settled into the trenches, bringing terror and death. When troop concentrations and weather conditions were right, both sides used gas, which, if it did not kill, destroyed eyes, lungs, skin, and other tissues, leaving its victims blinded, crippled, and scarred. It might have been used more frequently, but it was hard to control and likely to be blown back on the user by a shift of wind.

A year after the terrible losses at the Somme, the British commander Field Marshal Douglas Haig set his Scottish jaw and launched a new offensive, in Flanders. Starting on July 31, 1917, he pushed into the lowlands east of Ypres, heading for the heavily fortified 150-foot height of

British and French tanks, some manned by Yanks, became attack weapons.

Passchendaele Ridge. His tactics were the same as ever: massive artillery barrages followed by waves of infantry. But Haig's artillery so demolished the marshy region's drainage system that Flanders's fields became a virtual lake — "a porrage of mud," as one observer put it. It took four months, and 300,000 British casualties, to advance five miles to the top of Passchendaele. The campaign's only real success occurred at the town of Cambrai. Here a force of 324 British tanks, with no advance bombardment to alert the enemy, led a charge against two German divisions and in six hours gained more ground than had been won by all the bloodshed in Flanders. But even this was an exercise in futility, for the Germans soon won back the lost ground.

Late in 1914 the front lines ran a ragged arc from Flanders to the Swiss border. Three years later, when American troops began to arrive in force, the lines had shifted by no more than a few dozen miles. More than 2 million men had given up their lives to maintain this stalemate.

What Bill Mauldin would later do for the American GI in World War II (see page 211), Bruce Bairnsfather (below) did for British Tommies in World War I. As a 27-year-old British officer on combat duty in France, Bairnsfather began publishing cartoons of life at the front in July 1915. They were a hit with both soldiers and civilians. His anything-but-professional soldiers are fed up, but they will never give up, and they can laugh at trench life. Two of his regulars were Old Bill, a middle-aged cockney with a walrus mustache and a pipe, and his buddy Bert, a callow youth with a cigarette forever dangling from his lips. Reproduced below is his famous 1916 cartoon, whose caustic caption became one of the most quoted phrases of the Great War.

Well, if you knows of a better 'ole, go to it!

Travelers packed the Lusitania (below) on her fateful voyage despite warnings by the German Embassy published with Cunard schedules (right).

ON PERILOUS SEAS

The sinking of the British luxury liner Lusitania *showed the world the horrifying work that submarines could do. But Germany exulted in a weapon that undercut Britain's naval superiority.*

Losses like that of the cruiser Blücher (below), sunk by the British in 1915, led Germany to rely on its submarines. But U-boats could not break the blockade that, with poor harvests, eventually reduced Germans to eating potato peels (right).

The great Cunard liner *Lusitania*, queen of the British passenger fleet, steamed majestically eastward past the Irish coast en route to Liverpool from New York. It was May 7, 1915, and so far the crossing had been as smooth as anyone could have wished. But now, as the vessel entered British waters, a certain tension gripped her nearly 2,000 passengers and crew. German submarines had been reported lurking nearby. Shortly after 2 P.M., as the first-class ticket holders were stepping onto the promenade deck for an after-luncheon stroll, a U-boat's periscope broke the ocean's surface. One passenger, leaning against the starboard rail, noticed "a long, white streak of foam," a "frothy fizzing," moving rapidly toward him. Then came a heavy thud, followed by a thunderous explosion. The unthinkable had happened. A German torpedo had struck the *Lusitania*.

The liner heeled violently to starboard, then began to settle. Another torpedo hit, shattering the hull and sending up a gusher of flame and hot metal. Passengers crowded into lifeboats, but the stricken ship's steeply pitching decks prevented many boats from being lowered. Within just 18 minutes the great vessel slid under, leaving a ghastly flotsam of over-loaded boats, thrashing swimmers, and charred and mangled bodies. Of the 1,198 souls lost, 128 were Americans, including a number of celebrities, such as millionaire-sportsman Alfred Vanderbilt and Broadway producer Charles Frohman.

The United States was outraged. President Woodrow Wilson threatened to sever relations with Germany and even to intervene on the Allied side. The Germans replied that they had done no wrong and in fact had issued a warning, a notice in *The New York Times* that the *Lusitania* risked attack. They claimed, with justification, that passenger ships could also carry ammunition and war goods.

Why the Kaiser Liked His U-boats

Until the submarine demonstrated its lethal effectiveness, military strategists had measured naval might by the firepower of large surface ships: battleships and battle cruisers, which could range far and wide and pummel the enemy with their batteries of 11-inch to 15-inch guns. To the British, who chose to use their subs mostly for shore patrol, the submarine seemed a marginal weapon, even a bit unsportsmanlike: "underhanded, unfair, and un-English" is how one British Admiralty official put it.

But the Germans disagreed. At the war's outset, the kaiser had 33 U-boats — short for German *Unterseeboots* — of which 28 were fitted for long-range missions. Packed with a dozen torpedoes each, they could harass enemy warships and merchant vessels alike. And as a naval underdog, the kaiser saw his U-boats as critical to victory. His surface fleet was only half the size of Britain's Grand Fleet. With increasing German U-boat activity, certain broad conven-

Attacking an
unarmed
merchant ship,
a U-boat could
surface and
launch a
torpedo, but
armed prey
required a
submerged
approach.

tions governing naval attacks, designed to protect the lives of civilians and the rights of neutral nations, began to fray. Customarily, for example, a merchant ship suspected of carrying military supplies to the enemy could be stopped and searched, and its goods confiscated, but even if it flew an enemy flag, its seamen were given a chance to escape. German surface raiders in the Pacific followed these rules to the letter. One famous marauder, the cruiser *Emden*, managed to bag 24 Allied ships with virtually no loss of life.

But such chivalrous niceties did not survive in the North Atlantic. Any U-boat that surfaced to halt a potential prize might have found itself rammed or sent to the bottom in a hail of fire. To combat the submarine menace, the British launched decoy vessels, Q-ships, which looked like tramp steamers but carried hidden guns. Furthermore, many British ships flew the flags of neutral nations. So the U-boats continued to attack in stealth, though the kaiser, fearful of pushing the United States too far, ordered his commanders to spare American ships.

In the first month of the war, British cruisers had swept Germany's North Sea coast and sunk four ships in the Battle of Heligoland Bight. Less than four weeks later, a lone U-boat retaliated by sinking three British cruisers within an hour. Sharp, bloody exchanges flared up when enemy squadrons met in the Southern Hemisphere, off Chile and the Falkland Islands. But only once did the world's two great navies, Britain's Grand Fleet and Germany's High Seas Fleet, slug it out ship to ship: at the Battle of Jutland in May of 1916. Both sides suffered heavy losses of ships and men, but the result was a tactical draw.

After the stand-off at Jutland, the kaiser did not choose to risk his surface fleet again in battle on the high seas. Most of Germany's ships stayed in port, safe from British guns. By default, Great Britain won control of the North Sea, cutting off supplies to Germany from the outside world. As Britain tightened its blockade, poor harvests compounded Germany's predicament. Food ran low, and thousands of Germans died of starvation and disease in the "Turnip Winter" of 1916–17.

Only the U-boats managed to slip through, evading the mines and submarine nets that the British strung along the German coast. Desperate, Germany abandoned its policy of sparing U.S. ships and resumed unrestricted submarine warfare, ordering the sinking of any vessels that might aid the Allies.

In the first four months of 1917, German subs sank an average of 10 ships a day. At that rate England, too, would starve. Only by grouping the transports in heavily guarded convoys — the tactic adopted to send American troops to Europe — would the lifeline of food and munitions to the Allies remain open.

On their flimsy perch attached to a bomb-carrying dirigible, British airmen search for U-boats in the North Sea below them. The Lewis machine gun gave some defense against attacking German fighters while other crewmen looked for signs of subs lurking along convoy routes.

"HE KEPT US OUT OF WAR"

Woodrow Wilson wanted to lead his country in peace, but before his first term was over, he found himself relentlessly drawn into the maelstrom of Europe. And war with Mexico was a blink away.

To most Americans, the complex alliances that had plunged Europe into full-scale bloodshed were confusing and obscure. President Woodrow Wilson himself remarked that the war had been caused "by nothing in particular." It was even less clear what side America should take, if any. Ten percent of the United States' 100 million people claimed German descent. A greater percentage had British ties, but there were also 4 to 5 million Irish-Americans, many of whom held Britain in disdain. And the migrations of the 19th and early 20th centuries had carried to American shores huge numbers of other nationalities with various stakes in the conflict.

Perhaps no one was more vexed by the eruption of war than was Wilson. Elected in 1912 on a wave of progressive reform, Wilson had a mandate that was primarily domestic, and negotiating the currents of global war was a prospect he hardly relished. Already he was dealing with an explosive situation in Mexico (see box, next page). And he was in the midst of a personal tragedy, keeping watch at the bedside of his ailing wife, Ellen Axson Wilson, who died without knowing war had come.

Privately Wilson disdained German militarism and sided with the Allies. But above all, he feared that going to war could rip the multiethnic fabric of American life. "The United States must be neutral in fact as well as in name during these days that are to try men's souls," he told the nation. "We must be impartial in thought as well as in action."

Americans as a whole were inclined to follow Wilson's advice and wait out the storm. They believed that the war, horrible though it was, would end soon. Most were content to watch from the sidelines, rooting in a general way for the Allies. The most popular song of 1915 was "I Didn't Raise My Boy to Be a Soldier" (top of page).

But if neutrality was, in theory, the wisest course for America, in practice it proved nearly impossible. The European Allies looked to American industry for strategic materials, and soon American banks were financing Allied war purchases. American businessmen, exercising their neutral rights, were traveling into war zones on foreign vessels. On such issues, Wilson walked a diplomatic tightrope, angering nearly all the belligerents at one time or another. Brokering a settlement

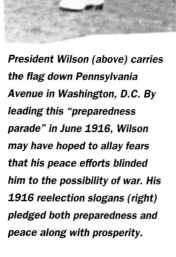

President Wilson (above) carries the flag down Pennsylvania Avenue in Washington, D.C. By leading this "preparedness parade" in June 1916, Wilson may have hoped to allay fears that his peace efforts blinded him to the possibility of war. His 1916 reelection slogans (right) pledged both preparedness and peace along with prosperity.

NEAR WAR WITH MEXICO

National Guard on the Mexican Border.

Gen. ? ? and Staff

Bodies of the Victims of the Battle of Carrizal, Mex. arriving at El Paso, Texas

Six days after raiders under the rebel Mexican general Pancho Villa (below) killed more than 15 Americans in Columbus, New Mexico, on March 9, 1916, Gen. John J. Pershing (front and center, middle photo above) rode into Mexico with 6,000 U.S. troops. Thereafter Villa and his men never crossed the U.S. border. However, in June Mexican government troops tangled with a U.S. force at Carrizal, killing some of Pershing's soldiers (bottom photo, above). This nearly provoked President Wilson to occupy northern Mexico, but he and Mexican President Venustiano Carranza agreed on the need for talks, averting what might have been a full-scale war. Pershing's Mexican campaign led Wilson to name him head of the American Expeditionary Forces (AEF) in World War I.

in Europe was his fondest hope. During the 32 months between Germany's invasion of Belgium and America's declaration of war, Wilson launched three separate initiatives to bring the warring nations to the table and negotiate a "peace without victory." All his efforts failed.

As the war news grew grimmer, more and more Americans, led by former President Theodore Roosevelt and Gen. Leonard Wood, disparaged the woeful state of the armed forces. The idea of preparing for war, however, disturbed many Americans, who thought that military preparedness was inconsistent with neutrality. Both the Allies and the Central Powers waged propaganda campaigns, hoping to sway American opinion, though the Germans were hampered by the frightening effectiveness of their U-boat campaign, reports of German atrocities in Belgium, British control of overseas cables, and a faulty grasp of American values.

Meanwhile, Germany had mounted a secret war in the United States. German agents incited labor unrest in war-related industries, bought up war supplies to keep them out of Allied hands, and planted time bombs aboard munitions-laden ships bound for Britain and France. The extent of German activities came to light stunningly when, in July 1915, an attaché to the German Embassy in Washington, Dr. Heinrich Albert, left his briefcase on a train. The briefcase, recovered by a Secret Service agent, contained plans for a German espionage campaign costing an estimated $2 million a week. When these documents were serialized in a New York newspaper, they ignited a storm of anti-German sentiment.

A year later, New York Harbor was rocked by a colossal explosion. In Jersey City, New Jersey, across the harbor from New York City, over 2 million pounds of munitions stored on Black Tom Island went up in a fireball. For six hours shells detonated, shooting hot fragments into the air and cutting deep dents into the Statue of Liberty. Not a window in Jersey City went unshattered; the thunder echoed as far away as Pennsylvania. A trail of evidence led to German saboteurs, but Germany never admitted its complicity.

In steering a neutral course, Wilson had assumed both the goodwill of the warring nations and the impartiality of the majority of Americans. In fact, the goodwill and impartiality were running out, and neutrality was doomed. When Wilson ran for reelection against Charles Evans Hughes in 1916 (and won by the slimmest of margins), his backers used the slogan "He kept us out of war."

Five months later Wilson led the country into war.

▼ *German-American women in San Francisco in 1915 hammer nails into an "Iron Cross." Each nail stood for a donor's contribution to the German relief fund.*

▲ *Caught in New Jersey in October 1915, German saboteur Robert Fay had a forged passport, a wig, and a fake mustache — and knew how to plant bombs on ships.*

RUSSIA COLLAPSES INTO COMMUNISM

The war began splendidly for Russia and then descended into a series of humiliating bloodbaths that drained away the power of the czarist regime and left the way open for revolutionaries to stoke the flames of the people's long-smoldering anger.

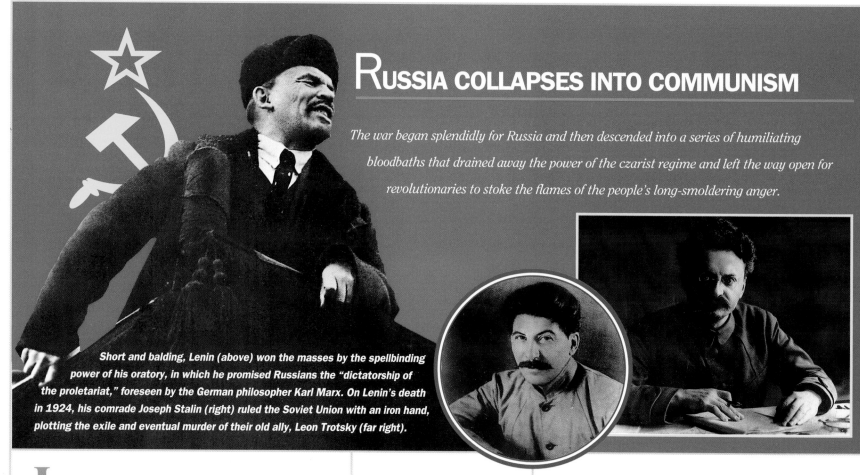

Short and balding, Lenin (above) won the masses by the spellbinding power of his oratory, in which he promised Russians the "dictatorship of the proletariat," foreseen by the German philosopher Karl Marx. On Lenin's death in 1924, his comrade Joseph Stalin (right) ruled the Soviet Union with an iron hand, plotting the exile and eventual murder of their old ally, Leon Trotsky (far right).

I f the war had continued to go as well for Russia as it did in the first three weeks, there might never have been a Communist revolution. The Russians pushed the Germans back in East Prussia, trouncing them at the Battle of Gumbinnen on August 20, 1914.

That was enough for Kaiser Wilhelm. He quickly gave responsibility for the war against Russia, the so-called eastern front, to two generals whose names would soon inspire their whole nation: Paul von Hindenburg and Erich Ludendorff. Within days the Germans had lured the Russians into an inferno called the Battle of Tannenberg.

Less a battle than a systematic slaughter of encircled Russians trying to flee the German troops, Tannenberg cost the Russian Army 125,000 men and 500 guns. And it set the pattern of Russia's military fortunes in World War I. A poorly armed and badly led army, ill-clothed and hungry, would gain a victory by sheer guts, then suffer a strategic defeat with appalling casualties. By the end of 1915, the Russians had given up all the land they had taken from the Germans and had lost 2 million men killed, wounded, or captured.

▼ **The kaiser maps strategy with Generals Hindenburg (left) and Ludendorff (right).**

Captured at Tannenberg, columns of Russian soldiers await their captors' orders. ▶

Then in his spectacular offensive of June 1916, the Russian general Alexei Brusilov thrashed the Austro-Hungarian Army and recovered considerable territory, but lost a million men. Such a drain of blood washed through Russia, weakening the pillars of traditional society and eroding loyalties to the czarist regime.

December 1916 began one of the worst winters in Russian memory. With no coal or bread, hunger and disease stalked the cities. More than two years

President Wilson first hailed the czar's overthrow, then sent U.S. troops to Archangel in northern Russia (above) to help an Allied army keep Russian war materials out of German hands. Meanwhile, in Moscow, American journalist John Reed (above, right) championed the Reds' cause.

of war had left over 300,000 dead, and the wounded and the starving choked the streets. The people cried for relief.

But "the people" terrified Czar Nicholas II, who had stood by the shattered body of his dying grandfather Alexander II, victim of a bomb hurled by "the people." His wife, Alexandra, German-born granddaughter of Queen Victoria, was autocratic to the core: "Russia loves to feel the whip," she wrote. "We have been placed on the throne by God."

Surrounding the royal couple was a sordid lot. The worst was Rasputin. A diabolical "monk" with hypnotic eyes and coils of dirty hair, he convinced the czarina that he could cure her son of hemophilia. A semiliterate drunkard and a sexual degenerate, he advised the royal family for years until he was murdered with fitting gruesomeness in 1916.

Too late the czar realized that he needed his people. In Petrograd angry mobs sang "The Internationale," the anthem of world revolution. After the city's army garrison joined the protests, Nicholas, who had taken command

of the troops at the front in 1915, finally gave up his throne on March 15, 1917. A provisional government, led by Alexander Kerensky, took over. He called for moderate socialist reform and continuation of the war.

But what the Russian people really wanted was "Peace, Land, and Bread." That was the cry of the radical Communists — the Bol-

sheviks, led by Vladimir Ilyich Lenin, Leon Trotsky, and Joseph Stalin. Outside the Petrograd railway station on April 16, 1917, Lenin proclaimed: "I greet you as the vanguard of the worldwide proletarian army." Arriving at Bolshevik headquarters, he demanded a second revolution to overthrow Kerensky's government and end the war.

Four months later, the "Kerensky offensive" on the eastern front floundered, the death knell for the provisional government. By mid-November, 1917, Lenin and the Bolsheviks had engineered and won their second revolution, known as the October Revolution. The new Soviet leadership ordered troops on the eastern front to stop fighting and opened peace talks with Germany.

Back in America, President Woodrow Wilson, who had at first called the end of Russian tyranny "wonderful and heartening," now became alarmed at the Soviets' quick peace dealing with the Germans. Fearing that the Soviets would hand over vast military stockpiles to the Germans, he joined other Allied leaders, in supporting the "White" Russian armies against Lenin's "Red" forces in the bloody civil war that convulsed Russia until 1920, when the Reds finally won. Though the Allied intervention achieved little militarily, it gave Soviet leaders a grudge against America and its western European allies for most of the rest of the century.

◀

In December 1915 Nicholas II, son Alexei, and daughter Tatyana pause in a snowy field. Two and a half years later, Lenin ordered the czar, his wife, and their five children shot.

▼ Rebellious soldiers fire on police in Petrograd in February 1917.

DISTANT GUNS

With Britain, France, and Germany all possessing colonies around the globe, the war could hardly be contained on European soil. Then Turkey got into the act, spreading the conflict to vast reaches east of the Mediterranean. And a third front in Europe became inevitable when Italy joined the Allies.

Indian Lewis gunners, part of the British force in Mesopotamia (present-day Iraq), fire at attacking aircraft, which Turkey used skillfully to harass Allied movements.

As the world focused on the collision of mighty armies on Europe's eastern and western fronts, fighting broke out in the Italian Alps and along the Aegean's sunny coast. It spilled across the deserts of Egypt and Arabia, erupted on the sands of today's Iraq, and rolled through the plains and jungles of Africa.

In the Pacific, Japan joined the Allies and plucked off German holdings on the coast of China and in the Marianas, the Marshalls, and the Carolines. Western Samoa fell to a New Zealand force without a single casualty. Australians took just a week to subdue German New Guinea.

In Africa the Allies seized chunks of Germany's colonial empire. French and British troops overran Togo in the first month of war, then moved into the Cameroons. But in East Africa, a wily Prussian, Col. Paul von Lettow-Vorbeck, and his 12,000 askari troops resisted an Allied army 10 times their size. Lettow-Vorbeck's depleted forces finally gave up on November 25, 1918, two weeks after the armistice.

Mauled by murderous Turkish fire on the beaches of the Gallipoli Peninsula, Anzac and British units held on valiantly for over eight months, but finally evacuated in January 1916.

From the outset of the war, Serbia's small army had held off assaults by Austria-Hungary. Then in October 1915, the armies of Germany and Austria, joined by their new ally, Bulgaria, swooped down 300,000 strong. Outnumbered two to one, the Serbs retreated toward the Adriatic coast, battling enemy shells, winter snows, raids by Albanian tribesmen, and a raging typhus epidemic. Entire families joined the exodus: wives, grandfathers, 12-year-olds carrying rifles and ammunition belts. Tens of thousands died.

By this time Austria-Hungary had another enemy: Italy. The two nations faced off on a 600-mile front snaking from the Swiss Alps to the Adriatic Sea. The Italian chief of staff, Gen. Luigi Cadorna, planned to advance his 875,000-man army through the Isonzo River valley and on to Vienna, the Austrian capital. Italy's morale sagged when Cadorna's first four assaults cost 170,000 Italian casualties (to his enemy's 117,000). Yet by September 1917, it was the Austrians, being battered simultaneously on the Russian front, who seemed about to crack.

That possibility alarmed Kaiser Wilhelm, and he sent six German divisions to the Italian front. The Germans joined nine Austrian divisions in a drive toward the town of Caporetto, a weak point in Cadorna's lines. Under devastating artillery bombardment and gas attacks, climaxed by the appearance of fearsome

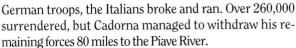

Winching cannons over icy passes was picturesque (left), but ambulance driver Ernest Hemingway (above) later wrote of the despair and hardship on the Italian front in A Farewell to Arms. *The Italian Crown Medal (left) recognized valor in the bitter campaign.*

In the Palestine campaign, T. E. Lawrence (below, left) gave the British some successes against the hard-fighting Turks. With him is American journalist Lowell Thomas, whose reports helped create the legend of Lawrence of Arabia.

German troops, the Italians broke and ran. Over 260,000 surrendered, but Cadorna managed to withdraw his remaining forces 80 miles to the Piave River.

A year later, under the popular Gen. Armando Diaz, the Italians revenged their defeat at Caporetto. On October 24, 1918, seven Italian armies, spearheaded by British and French units and joined by an American infantry regiment, stormed Austrian positions north of the Piave, around the resort town of Vittorio Veneto. In just over a week, Austrian resistance collapsed, and on November 3 a truce ended the fighting on the Italian front.

When the Turks, keepers of the declining but still formidable Ottoman Empire, entered World War I on the side of the Central Powers in October 1914, the geographical scope of the war vastly enlarged. One key Turkish possession was the Dardanelles, the strait connecting the Black Sea with the Mediterranean, which was the sole warm-water supply route to the armies of Russia. Aiming to control this vital passage, the British sent a large force to the Gallipoli Peninsula, at the head of the strait. On April 25, 1915, some 7,000 troops waded ashore. But the main body of Anzacs — Australians and New Zealanders — met murderous Turkish fire from the cliffs above their narrow beachhead. Further landings brought only more carnage. Finally, decimated by fighting, sunstroke, and dysentery, the Allies withdrew. Of 480,000 Allied soldiers who served at Gallipoli, more than half fell victim to disease and enemy guns.

In Mesopotamia, too, Britain faltered. Early in the war the British seized Basra, Turkey's Persian Gulf oil port. Then a 9,000-man British division advanced up the Tigris River toward Baghdad, outran its supplies, and had to surrender.

The British did better in Egypt. Gen. Edmund Allenby, a cavalryman with a genius for speed and deception, pushed through Gaza and on December 9, 1917, took Jerusalem, calling it a Christmas present for England. From there he marched north toward Damascus.

If the victories went to Allenby, world attention came to focus on a young British intelligence officer T. E. Lawrence. In Arabia, where the Turks maintained garrisons in important cities, he helped incite an Arab revolt. He and other Allied officers led daring guerrilla actions against the Turks.

After the war Lawrence chose to serve quietly in the Royal Air Force and drop into obscurity. But Lawrence of Arabia lived on in all his luster and romance. Of him, Winston Churchill said: "One of the greatest beings alive in our time; I do not see his like elsewhere."

PARLOR GAMES

Favorite PARLOR GAMES

Lotto
Bingo, housy-housy, keno, and screeno (played in U.S. movie theaters during the Depression) are names for variants of this ever popular game of chance.

Dominoes
Millennia ago, the Chinese played a game using pieces much like today's "bones."

Nancy Drew
Fans of the popular young fictional detective, created in 1930, applied their own sleuthing powers to solve mysteries in this 1958 game.

It has a quaint ring — parlor games. It calls up tree-lined streets with comfortable houses, in which the parlor was the room for entertaining guests and playing games around a table. Later it became the room where the radio went, and then the television set. Whist and bridge, pinochle and rummy, cribbage and checkers, backgammon and chess, Parcheesi, lotto, and dominoes were old standbys in the parlor. Then, reflecting the country's surging entrepreneurial spirit, manufacturers began turning out board games with topical tie-ins and dressing up old games of luck and skill in fancy new packages, often adding clever twists. It was only a matter of time before games and electronics teamed up. And despite the tube and all the other enticements and distractions at the end of the 20th century, kids of all ages keep sitting down to play parlor games, with or without a parlor.

Train for Boston
Steam locomotives were glamorous in the early 1900's, when parlor travelers twirled a spinner to try to reach Beantown by rail from one of four cities.

Monopoly
The classic real-estate game, with property names derived from Atlantic City, took off after Parker Brothers issued an edition in 1935.

Jackie Gleason's TV Fun Game
In 1956 the comic's popularity spawned a game in which the most "Laffs" won.

World Flyers
Taking off from New York, players tried to win a round-the-world "international air race" by dirigible. The game appeared in 1926, the year before Charles Lindbergh's solo transatlantic hop by airplane.

War of Nations
The tactics and the uniforms on the cover of this 1918 game are a far cry from the reality of World War I, but the airplane and the artillery get closer to the truth.

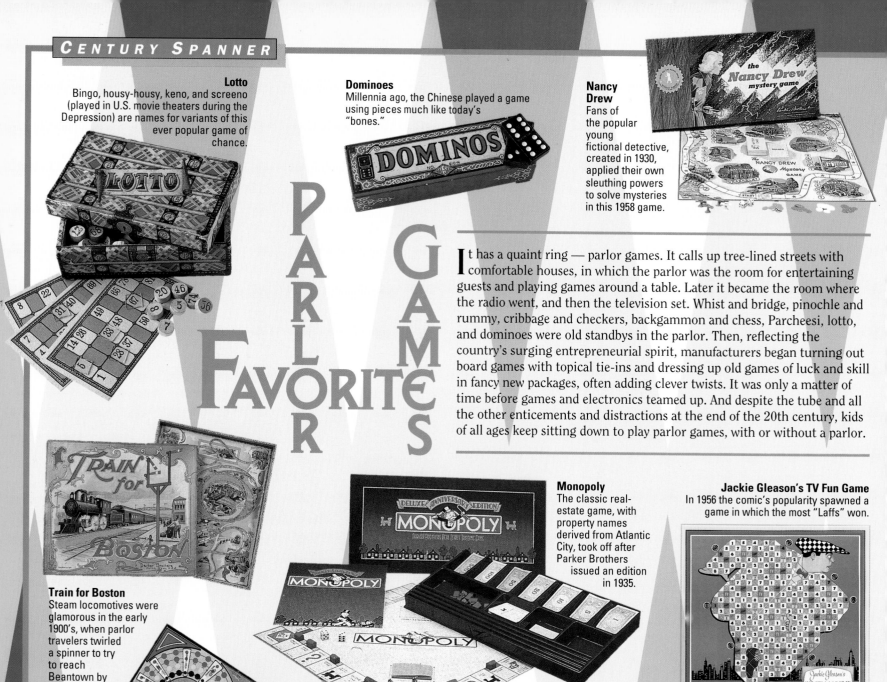

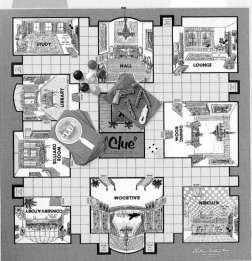

Sorry!
Getting home is not easy when a roll of the dice can mean forward or backward moves, slides, or picking a card that sends you back to Start — Sorry!

Chutes and Ladders
Preschoolers often graduate from Candy Land to this slightly more difficult game. A lucky spin sends a player up a ladder; an unlucky one, down a chute.

Trivial Pursuit
Riding in with the information explosion of the 1980's came a game that tested factual knowledge and caught on particularly with young professionals.

Candy Land
The first board game many children play, it requires neither reading nor number skills, just a knowledge of basic colors to move gingerbread men around the board to the Candy Castle.

Scrabble
Crossword puzzlers and anagram buffs find this game right up their alley. Each letter used in a word builds up points.

Simon
Computer-varied sequences of color and sound challenge players to remember and repeat as many sequences as they can exactly.

Clue
A murder has been committed and players vie to solve it with the clues provided as they move around the board. Who did it? Where? With what weapon?

Nintendo
A prince of video games in the 1990's was Nintendo's little plumber with the mustache, Mario (below). In 1993 a third of U.S homes had Nintendo ware (left), which hooks into TV sets.

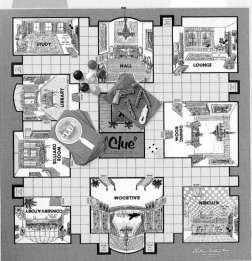

Battle at Sarlaac's Pit
Return of the Jedi, last in the *Star Wars* trilogy, inspired this 1980's cliffhanger.

"WE'RE COMING . . . OVER THERE"

After Germany launched unrestricted U-boat warfare and its diplomats plotted with Mexico against the United States, neutrality was dead. Most Americans were eager to join the battle, and a number of Yanks were already fighting under Allied flags.

Pvt. T. P. Loughlin, Rainbow Division, bids good-bye to his family before shipping out.

Congress (below) hears President Wilson ask for war, and four days later, April 6, 1917, he signed the formal declaration. Arthur Zimmermann (inset) and his infamous telegram had outraged Americans.

President Wilson was still valiantly trying to negotiate peace in Europe when the German ambassador, late on the afternoon of January 31, 1917, delivered a note to him. With a look of blank amazement, as the president's secretary later recalled, Wilson read Germany's total rebuff of his mediation efforts. Far from pursuing peace, Germany was about to escalate the war, according to the note. Starting February 1, only eight hours away, Germany would attack all shipping to Britain "with every available weapon and without further notice"; in other words, the dreaded U-boats aimed to take control of the North Atlantic and would no longer spare American ships. Three days later the United States broke

At a National Guard tent camp in a New York City park, recruits get their first lesson in saluting.

J. M. Flagg's Uncle Sam is famous, but other World War I recruiting posters were just as pointed.

A phonograph cranks out state-of-the-art French lessons to officers who may soon be on their way to France.

relations with Berlin. On March 12 the renewed U-boat fury took its first American victims: two women passengers who died aboard the torpedoed Cunard liner *Laconia*. On a single day, March 18, German subs sank three U.S. ships.

The German high command was gambling, and the stakes were ultimate victory or defeat. Although the kaiser and his top brass knew that winning the trench war on the western front was at best uncertain, they believed that if their U-boats were successful in stopping the flow of aid to Britain, Germany could concentrate on polishing off its enemies on the eastern front. Then the Germans could throw almost all their forces at Britain and the Allies on the western front, before America could mobilize. It was clear that the United States was many months away from mounting a serious military threat; and the Germans took heart from their reading of U.S. public opinion, which seemed to be running strongly against mobilization, a step many Americans felt would inevitably plunge their country into war.

But then German diplomats committed a blunder that would turn U.S. public opinion against Germany and bring America roaring into the war.

At Camp Bowie, Texas, recruits learn how to use the bayonet.

Arthur Zimmermann, the kaiser's foreign minister, was caught red-handed trying to foment trouble between the United States and Mexico.

Lacking transatlantic telegraph links (since the British had cut Germany's undersea cables in 1914), Zimmermann, in Berlin, was communicating with the German ambassador in Washington over U.S. State Department wires, a privilege granted to Germany to aid Wilson's peace efforts. But the American circuit from Europe came through England, and there, in mid-January 1917, British intelligence picked off a message being relayed via Washington to the German ambassador in Mexico. Zimmermann had sent it in the mistaken belief that Germany's diplomatic code was unbreakable. British agents quickly deciphered the message, but delayed divulging their coup to avoid alerting Berlin that they had broken the German code.

Then, in early March, the British slipped the Zimmermann telegram to the American embassy in London, and within hours its contents exploded in Washington. The telegram said that the kaiser welcomed an alliance with Mexico if the U.S. went to war against Germany. In return, Germany would condone Mexico's retaking of the land in Texas, New Mexico, and Arizona that Mexico had lost following the Mex-

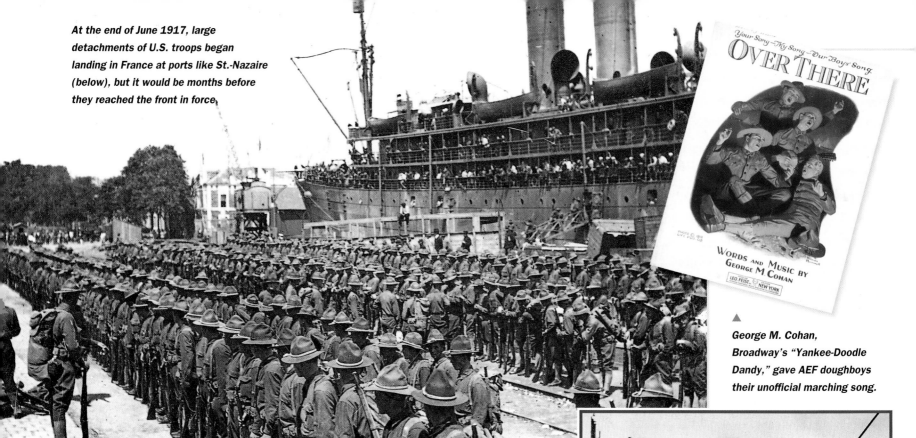

At the end of June 1917, large detachments of U.S. troops began landing in France at ports like St.-Nazaire (below), but it would be months before they reached the front in force.

George M. Cohan, Broadway's "Yankee-Doodle Dandy," gave AEF doughboys their unofficial marching song.

ican War of 1846–48. Clearly this was more than a threat to America's right to freedom of the seas. The Zimmermann telegram raised the specter of renewed warfare on the Mexican frontier and brought the war to the heart of America.

It was a cheering, foot-stamping, flag-waving Congress that heard Wilson, on April 2, excoriate the Imperial German Government for its submarine "warfare against mankind" and for its attempts "to stir up enemies against us at our very doors." After Wilson's ringing call, "the world must be made safe for democracy," the Senate voted 86 to 2, the House 373 to 50, for war on Germany. The formal declaration of war came on April 6.

"Fighting for Liberty, Justice, Civilization"

In June the first military draft since the Civil War began, and nearly 10 million men registered almost festively. "Thanks for drawing 258 — that's me," a young Mississippian wired the secretary of war, who had reached blindfolded into a fishbowl to draw the first draft number. Patriotism soared. A navy recruiting poster showed a young woman in a sailor uniform sighing, "Gee! I Wish I Were a Man." Songs like "Johnny Get Your Gun" and "Over There" — the latter

promising "the Yanks are coming. . . . And we won't come back till it's over, over there" — whipped up the nation's fighting spirit.

In fact, thousands of Americans were already "over there," and many had been wounded or killed. Ever since the war broke out in the summer of 1914, Americans had volunteered for the Allied cause. Some had relatives or friends in Canada, the British Isles, or France and went out of loyalty. Others went because they believed the Central Powers had to be defeated; still others, because they thought the war would be a grand adventure. Volunteer ambulance groups, like the American Ambulance Field Service, drew hundreds of idealistic Americans to war-torn Europe, where they risked their lives to save the wounded. One volunteer was a Philadelphian named Dillwyn Starr, who began driving an ambulance on the western front in October 1914. Then, as his father later

Gen. John J. Pershing (front) pays a visit to the port of Boulogne, France, on June 13, 1917, to check preparations for the arrival of the American Expeditionary Forces.

wrote, Starr found that he "disliked the idea of being protected by a red cross on his sleeve. . . . the conviction grew strong within him that the place for a free man was on the side of the Allies fighting for liberty, justice, civilization — the world's cause." Starr joined a British motorized unit, fought in France, and went to Gallipoli on the ill-fated Dardanelles expedition. He returned to France as an officer in the Coldstream Guards and was killed on September 15, 1916, leading a charge at Ginchy during the Battle of the Somme, in the same assault in which British tanks made their clanking debut in World War I.

Like Starr, many young Americans died fighting under foreign flags. The French Foreign Legion had a sizable contingent of Yanks, as did Canadian combat units. Perhaps the most famous American volunteers were the airmen who flew with the French in the Lafayette Escadrille. Among them were the future authors of *Mutiny on the Bounty*, Charles Nordhoff and James Hall.

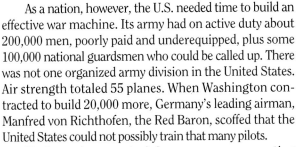

▼ *A lot of wishful thinking inspired this song, which saw Parisian revelries awaiting American soldiers in France.*

As a nation, however, the U.S. needed time to build an effective war machine. Its army had on active duty about 200,000 men, poorly paid and underequipped, plus some 100,000 national guardsmen who could be called up. There was not one organized army division in the United States. Air strength totaled 55 planes. When Washington contracted to build 20,000 more, Germany's leading airman, Manfred von Richthofen, the Red Baron, scoffed that the United States could not possibly train that many pilots.

Yet in weeks, army training camps were sprouting up across the country. On Wilson's orders, Gen. John J. Pershing hurried back from the Mexican border to get the American Expeditionary Forces (AEF), ready to ship out for Europe. The first draft swept half a million men into uniform; by war's end, over 4 million would serve.

The U.S. Navy, while augmenting its antisubmarine patrols with converted yachts and revenue cutters, had destroyers in the British Isles for convoy duty by May 1917, and on July 4, advance troops of Pershing's AEF paraded through Paris to ecstatic cheers. That day, at the tomb of the Marquis de Lafayette, the French hero of America's Revolutionary War, an aide to Pershing, Col. Charles E. Stanton, spoke the words that gave a weary France, and all the Allies, new hope: "Lafayette, we are here."

◄

In London, crowds cheer an AEF column on August 15, 1917. By midsummer of 1917, convoys of troopships holding up to 15,000 Yanks each were landing in France and England.

▼ *At Lafayette's tomb in Paris, three of Pershing's officers pay their respects to the gallant Frenchman who helped America win independence. The date was July 4, 1917.*

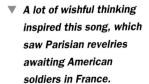

FIGHTING ON THREE CONTINENTS

The terrible battles on the western front — such as the Marne, the Somme, Ypres, Meuse-Argonne — were only part of the conflagration that consumed most of Europe and set off secondary explosions in Africa and Asia.

Rivalrous tyrants had made Europe and the Middle East a battleground for thousands of years, but nothing had prepared the people of these lands for the wholesale devastation and carnage of World War I. From Arabia and Africa to Scandinavia, armies using new weapons and tactics squared off, and always both sides paid dearly in blood. Nowhere was the fighting more vicious, or the opposing forces more stubbornly heroic, than on the western front, where hundreds of thousands died. At war's end, the map of Europe was redrawn to suit the victors, but many of the new boundaries would last less than a generation. World War II was just over the horizon.

▶

EUROPE AFTER WORLD WAR I: *Nine new nations (right) sprang from prewar empires (below). Gone was Austria-Hungary, most of it split into Austria, Hungary, Czechoslovakia, and Yugoslavia. And Russia, which had left the Allied cause after the czar abdicated, lost vast western borderlands, which became independent Poland, Lithuania, Estonia, Latvia, and Finland. Parts of Germany went to France, Belgium, and Poland.*

MAJOR BATTLEFIELDS, EUROPE AND THE MIDDLE EAST

Key
Allied Powers
Central Powers
Neutral countries

In Treaty of Brest-Litovsk, Mar.1918, Germany forces Russia to give up lands west of this line.

Areas where fighting occurred are shown in contrasting shades within red lines.

Allied land
Central Powers land

1914

Austria-Hungary attacks Serbia, July 29.

Germany invades Belgium, Aug. 4.

Battle of Tannenberg (Stebark), eastern front, Germans defeat Russians, Aug. 26–30.

Battle of Lemberg (Gnila Lipa), eastern front, Russians defeat Austrians, Aug. 26–Sept.1.

First Battle of the Marne, western front, Allies block German advance, Sept. 6–9.

First Battle of Ypres, western front, Germans attempt to break Allied line, Oct. 19–Nov. 11.

1915

German U-boats and surface ships start attempt to blockade Britain, Feb.

Second Battle of Ypres, Allies beat back Germans, who use poison gas, Apr. 22–May 25.

Battle of Gallipoli, Dardanelles campaign, Turks repel Allied force, Apr. 25, 1915–Jan. 9, 1916.

German U-boat sinks British passenger liner *Lusitania,* May 7.

1916

Battle of Verdun, western front, French block repeated German attacks, Feb.–Dec.

Siege of Kut, Mesopotamia campaign, Turks capture 10,000 British after a nearly 4-month siege, Apr. 29.

Battle of Jutland, North Sea, British and German fleets fight to a costly draw, May 31–June1.

First Battle of the Somme, western front, Allies gain little against dug-in Germans, over 1 million casualties on all sides, July 1–Nov. 18.

1917

German U-boats, after more than 16 months of restraint, resume unrestricted attacks, Feb. 1.

Battle of Arras, western front, Apr. 9 – May 3; British score only limited gains after heroic Canadian capture of Vimy Ridge, Apr. 9.

French offensive, western front, Germans yield little ground north of Aisne River, Apr.–May.

Russian offensive, eastern front, after Nicholas II abdicates, armies under Russia's new government stopped by Germans, June–Sept.

Third Battle of Ypres, Germans stop large Allied offensive, which gains only a few miles to Passchendaele, Belgium, July–Nov.

Battle of Caporetto (Kobarid, Karfreit), Italian front, Austro-Hungarian and German forces defeat Italians, Oct. 24–Nov. 12.

Fall of Jerusalem, Palestine campaign, British enter the holy city as Turks retreat, Dec. 9.

1918

German offensives, western front, three attacks — at the Somme River (beginning Mar. 21), at the Lys River near Ypres (beginning Apr. 9), and at the Aisne River (May 27) — have early success, then stall as Allies stiffen.

Battle of Cantigny, western front, in their first major engagement, U.S. troops help French advance against Germans' Somme offensive, May 28.

Battle of Château-Thierry, western front, U.S. troops help French stop Germans' Aisne offensive, June–July.

Battle of Belleau Wood, western front, U.S. soldiers and marines drive back prong of Germans' Aisne offensive, June 6–25.

Second Battle of the Marne, in the turning point of World War I, Allies halt last major German offensive on western front, July 15–Aug. 6.

Battle of Amiens, western front, British and French launch successful offensive, Aug. 8.

Battle of St.-Mihiel, western front, first major American offensive succeeds, Sept. 12–14.

Meuse-Argonne offensive, western front, U.S. troops, nearly a million strong, advance on a wide front west of the Meuse River, Sept. 26–Nov. 11.

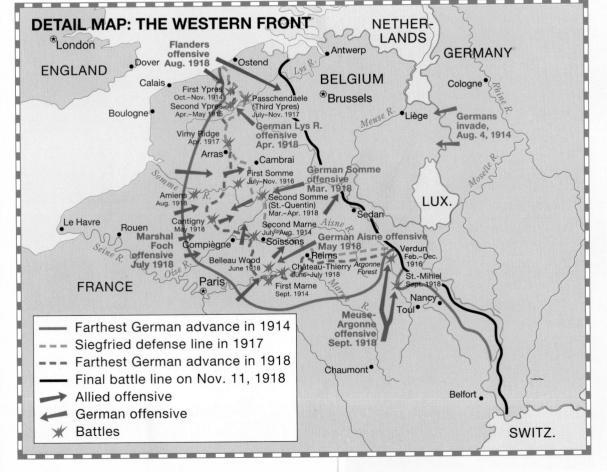

DETAIL MAP: THE WESTERN FRONT

Legend:
- Farthest German advance in 1914
- Siegfried defense line in 1917
- Farthest German advance in 1918
- Final battle line on Nov. 11, 1918
- Allied offensive
- German offensive
- Battles

A RUSH OF PATRIOTISM

Suddenly it was no longer acceptable to debate whether or not the United States should fight.

America was at war, and anybody even suspected of opposition risked being called a traitor.

After nearly three years on the sidelines of the Great War, American industry stood firmly on a civilian footing, more accustomed to producing automobiles than tanks, suits than bandages. Raising, training, feeding, equipping, and transporting an army of a million men overseas called for unprecedented planning and unity of purpose. And, in the colloquial phrase, "it had to be done yesterday."

President Woodrow Wilson went to work. "It is not an army that we must shape and train for the war," he said, "it is a nation." To mobilize the economy, he named a Wall Street financier, millionaire Bernard Baruch, to head the War Industries Board. The WIB was the mightiest of half a dozen major new wartime agencies. With czarlike authority,

Baruch steered business, labor, and the military into partnership, streamlining the entire industrial output of a nation. Under Baruch, government and industry learned to cooperate as never before in America.

To manage agriculture, Wilson chose Herbert Hoover to head the Food Administration. Hoover had impressed the president with his leadership of relief efforts for the people of war-torn Belgium and northern France after the German invasion of 1914. Very quickly Hoover spurred farmers to increase food production, took control of prices, and improved distribution of farm products. He also championed programs that stressed every citizen's duty to conserve food, and American households learned new eating habits,

Boy Scouts on Fifth Avenue in New York City (below) show their enthusiastic, if somewhat undisciplined, support for the war in April 1917, when America decided to join the fight.

One flag is not enough for Ike Sims of Atlanta, Georgia, to show the 11 stars that stand for his 11 sons in the service. On such flags, stars were usually blue, but a gold star meant the serviceman had died.

FIGHT OR BUY BONDS
THIRD LIBERTY LOAN

Beat back the HUN with LIBERTY BONDS

enduring "Meatless Tuesdays" and "Wheatless Wednesdays" and dining according the "Gospel of the clean plate."

As the war effort escalated, Wilson imposed controls that in peacetime would likely have been declared unconstitutional. Wherever there was trouble, or even the threat of it, the government stepped in. When a log-jam all but halted the overworked and financially shaky railroads in December 1917, the government pushed aside competing private owners and got the troops and war freight moving again. When a jump in demand snarled communication by telephone and telegraph, they, too, were taken over by federal authorities.

All Out to Lick the Kaiser

To finance the war, Wilson went directly to the American people. In four separate Liberty Bond drives, the government raised $21 billion, roughly 65 percent of the total cost of the war. Celebrities, such as Charlie Chaplin and Mary Pickford, whipped up the crowds, hawking bonds on busy street corners. Screen idol Douglas Fairbanks, wearing gloves marked "Victory" and "Liberty Bonds," staged a mock boxing match with the kaiser on Wall Street. Children were urged to fill books of 25-cent war stamps — to "lick a stamp and lick the kaiser." By the war's end, it was estimated that fully half of the American adult population had purchased bonds. In addition to meatless and wheatless days to conserve food, there were heatless Mondays to save coal. Adver-

tisers switched off lighted signs to save electricity.

With an eventual total of 4.8 million men serving in the armed forces, the war touched almost every household in America. Deep labor shortages occurred just when industries were trying to accelerate production. To fill the gaps in the civilian work force, women donned overalls and went to work outside the home in numbers never before seen. Women also served as nurses with the American Expeditionary Forces, as shoreside yeomenettes with the navy, and with the Red Cross both overseas and at home. Though many men grumbled — perhaps because the women proved to be no less efficient workers than men were — no one could deny women's contribution to the war effort, and suffrage leaders capitalized on these highly visible accomplishments. Eleven states had granted full suffrage by 1917, but a proposed constitutional amend-

George Creel (above, far left) headed the Committee on Public Information, responsible for keeping up the nation's patriotic spirit. To sell Liberty Bonds, he hired artists to create posters (left and above, left) that showed the glory of America's cause and the enemy's depravity. Stage and screen stars also pitched for Uncle Sam. Douglas Fairbanks (left) launches a bond drive on Wall Street.

Striking a patriotic pose, volunteers attack a pile of peach pits, which they will pack off to a maker of gas masks. Seven pounds of crushed pits made one gas mask filter that kept poison gas from the lungs.

◀ As on this locomotive crew on the Great Northern Railway at Great Falls, Montana, women filled men's shoes capably.

Whether setting the clock an hour ahead actually helped win the war has never been conclusively determined, but the patriotic enthusiasm of this poster is undeniable. Great Britain hit upon "daylight saving" during World War I as a way of saving electricity, since the extra hour of daylight at day's end meant that people did not have to turn on their lights so early at night. The idea spread to America during the war. In effect, it made nightfall come an hour later on the clock.

ment to guarantee women the vote had fallen short of the required two-thirds majority in the House. By the war's end, the balance had shifted; the 19th Amendment passed Congress in June of 1919 and was ratified by the states the following year.

A task no less formidable than bringing industry under control was galvanizing public opinion. "Woe be to the man who seeks to stand in our way in this day of high resolution," Wilson warned, and in the coming months his administration made sure no one did. The Espionage Act, Trading With the Enemy Act, Sabotage Act, and Sedition Act all contributed to an atmosphere of intolerance and placed controls on free expression, outlawing "disloyal, profane, scurrilous, or abusive" speech against the government.

George Creel Sells the War

To marshal popular sentiment for the Allied cause, Wilson turned to newspaper editor and public relations executive George Creel to head the Committee on Public Information. The CPI was in fact the United States' propaganda agency. Its task, described later by Secretary of War Newton Baker, was "the whole business of mobilizing the mind of the world." The practical Creel saw his job more simply:

"a vast enterprise in salesmanship." He called it "the world's greatest adventure in advertising." Creel's job was to sell the war, and sell it he did. In a year and a half, his agency disseminated 60 million red-white-and-blue pamphlets extolling the righteousness of the Allied cause and of Wilson's proposed Fourteen Points for a peace settlement. Some 75,000 agency speakers — called four-minute men because of the length of their prepared speeches — stirred crowds at movie theaters, schools, and churches on such topics as "Why We Are Fighting" and "Maintaining Morals and Morale." Meanwhile, the CPI's Division of Pictorial Publicity harnessed the skills of the nation's most talented artists and illustrators, whose colorful posters exhorted Americans to "Halt the Hun" and "Kill the Kaiser," reminded them to "Remember Belgium," and urged them to "Enlist."

Creel did his job exceptionally well. Two years earlier Wilson had warned: "Once lead this people into war, and they'll forget there was ever such a thing as tolerance. To fight you must be brutal and ruthless, and the spirit of ruthless brutality will enter into the very fiber of our national life." Wilson's words were prophetic.

SAVING DAYLIGHT!

"SET THE CLOCK AHEAD ONE HOUR AND WIN THE WAR!"

UNCLE SAM, YOUR ENEMIES HAVE BEEN UP AND ARE AT WORK ON THE EXTRA HOUR OF DAYLIGHT — WHEN WILL YOU WAKE UP?

United Cigar Stores Company

Bombarded with CPI warnings to be on the alert for lapses in patriotism and to "report the man who spreads pessimistic stories," many otherwise reasonable Americans confused vigilantism with love of country, bigotry with common sense. Anything German was flushed out, pulled down, or renamed. Sauerkraut became liberty cabbage, the humble hamburger turned to Salisbury steak, and dachshunds were chased off the streets. In Cincinnati a public ordinance forbade the vending of pretzels, a favorite tavern snack. Orchestras were forbidden to play Bach or Beethoven, and Dr. Karl Muck, the German conductor of the Boston Symphony, was fired and interned as an enemy alien. Teachers were required to swear loyalty oaths to the Constitution, German literature was pulled from library shelves, and in many states the teaching of German was banned altogether.

Spy fever spread like a contagious disease. In Congress and statehouses, legislators who had opposed the war were denounced as traitors. The Sedition Slammers, the American Protective League, and other self-appointed vigilante groups harassed Socialists, pacifists, resident aliens, and anyone they suspected of sympathiz-

In Baraboo, Wisconsin, zeal turns to zealotry as the townspeople burn books by German authors in the belief that anything German must be seditious. Bucking the chauvinistic tide, Berlin, New Hampshire, chose not to rename itself.

ing with the enemy, including the First Lady, President Wilson's second wife, Edith Bolling Galt Wilson, and publisher William Randolph Hearst, whose New York town-house lights were rumored to be signaling to German U-boats that were slinking beneath the Hudson River. Even the usually restrained editors of *The Wall Street Journal* suggested that hanging was a fit punishment for pacifism: "We are now at war, and militant pacifists are earnestly reminded that there is no shortage of hemp or lampposts."

It was a time of great feeling, noble and ignoble. It was also a time when Americans worried passionately about the troops overseas. In a thousand small ways — from saving peach pits for gas masks to knitting bandages and buying Liberty Bonds — Americans pitched in. Perhaps most revealing of all, during the 19 months of direct American engagement in the Great War, a craze for fortune-telling swept the nation; in 1918 alone, over 1 million Ouija boards were sold. In parlors across America, fathers and mothers, sisters and brothers, their fingers trembling over the board's magic pointer, asked the same two questions: How are our boys? When are they coming home?

The drain of men into the armed services raised serious concerns about whether there would be sufficient labor for the harvests of 1917 and 1918. These women of the Newtown Square, Pennsylvania, unit of the Women's Land Army of America helped avert the crisis.

STAR-SPANGLED ENTERTAINMENT

As the clouds of war grew more ominous and finally broke in fury over America, entertainers of every stripe did their utmost to banish glumness.

Theodosia Goodman (far left) renamed herself Theda Bara (an anagram for "Arab death") and made more than 40 silent films before her vamp appeal waned after the war. Elsie Janis (left) cheered the boys with her songs of hope and love.

In his first appearance as a featured player in The Ziegfeld Follies, in 1917, Will Rogers, with his trademark lasso, gets some help from Ziegfeld beauties.

George M. Cohan reached his peak in World War I. Here he acts in The Little Millionaire, which he also wrote, directed, and produced.

When the doughboys went off to war, they took with them tunes like "When You Wore a Tulip," "The Darktown Strutters' Ball," and "Waiting for the Robert E. Lee," favorites often sung for them at the front by tireless troupers like the dynamic Al Jolson or Elsie Janis, the Sweetheart of the AEF, who sang for the troops while shells fell around her. Back home, Broadway and Tin Pan Alley songwriters seemed to take it as their patriotic duty to keep the nation's spirits up. And from the glittering theaters of New York's Great White Way to improvised stages in small towns, headliners like Jolson and Sophie Tucker, the Last of the Red-Hot Mamas, belted out the tunes audiences loved to hear.

Nobody gave them more songs than Irving Berlin, who never learned to write music and could play the piano only in the key of F. Russian immigrant at 4, teenage singing waiter in Chinatown, Berlin was not yet 25 when "Alexander's Ragtime Band" made him famous. Drafted in 1917, he put together a show called *Yip, Yip Yaphank* at Camp Upton. In it he sang his theme song of the common soldier: "Oh, How I Hate to Get Up in the Morning." The show was light; so Berlin pulled out the song "God Bless America" as "too patriotic," and it sat on his shelf for 20 years.

On Broadway, the Barrymores — John, Ethel, and Lionel — were already big and starred in several dramas during the war years, but the musical reigned supreme. In 1916 only three of the dozens of show openings were serious dramas. Musicals, comedies, and revues made up the rest.

A self-proclaimed Yankee-Doodle optimist whose only regret was being born a day too soon, on the third of July, George M. Cohan, a five-foot-six bundle of Irish energy, touched America's heart again and again. In a dozen musical comedies and revues before 1917, he wrote and performed unforgettable numbers, like "Give My Regards to Broadway" and "You're a Grand Old Flag." Then three bugle notes inspired him to write "Over There." It became the American anthem of the war.

Cohan knew America's heart, but impresario Florenz (Flo) Ziegfeld knew its libido. He kept right on producing

▶ Enrico Caruso sings the Don José role in Carmen. A hugely popular entertainer, Caruso visited troops and led Liberty Bond drives.

his annual *Follies* during the war. Ziegfeld interviewed 15,000 chorus-line hopefuls a year to find a hundred or so who fit his ideal: "36, 26, 38, with the emphasis on the hips." He then had 50 at a time gambol on ornate ladders, spring up as flowers from trap doors, and perform scores of other such showstoppers. For comic relief, the highest-paid jokesters in the world spun their patter: Will Rogers, W. C. Fields, Eddie Cantor, and Fanny Brice were all Ziegfeld regulars.

The master of ragtime, Scott Joplin, died the year America entered the war, but his music lived on everywhere. There was another new sound, too, something between ragtime and blues. It traveled up the Mississippi from New Orleans with musicians like W. C. Handy, who wrote the immortal "St. Louis Blues" in 1914, Jelly Roll Morton, and Blind Lemon Jefferson. "Spell it Jass, Jas, Jaz, or Jazz," announced the bulletin of the Victor Talking Machine Company when it released the world's first jazz recording in 1917.

By 1915 five million people a day went to the movies. The public's thirst for vicarious adventure made stars of swashbuckling Douglas Fairbanks and strong and silent cowboy W. S. Hart. A middle-class girl from Cincinnati, Theodosia Goodman, renamed herself Theda Bara, told fan magazines she was an Arab born in the Sahara, and with sultry stares, raven hair, and fleecy bras, created the screen's first sex symbol. As the "vampire of love" (shortened to "vamp"), Theda was a far cry from Mary Pickford, America's Sweetheart, who started as a $5-a-day, uncredited, curly-topped extra. After a string of lucrative tearjerkers, like *Tess of the Storm Country,* Pickford bargained herself up to $2 million a year before the armistice.

Although controversial even then for its stereotyping of black people, director D. W. Griffith's 1915 *Birth of a Nation* proved once and for all the power of film to tell a story and move an audience. After it became the first movie shown in the White House, President Woodrow Wilson said, "It is like writing history with lightning."

Opera stars Madame Ernestine Schumann-Heink and Enrico Caruso split their time between paid performances, entertaining troops, and selling Liberty Bonds. But the most heroic star may have been actress Sarah Bernhardt, dubbed the Divine Sarah by Oscar Wilde. She wowed Americans on several farewell tours, playing roles from Cleopatra to Juliet; she was past 70 and had a wooden leg.

▶ The Ziegfeld Follies of 1915 *perfectly illustrates Flo Ziegfeld's recipe for show-business success: attractive women in expensive costumes.*

▲ Comedians Eddie Cantor and Fanny Brice ham it up in The Ziegeld Follies of 1917, *the show that also starred W. C. Fields and Will Rogers.*

Up FROM THE TRENCHES AT LAST

In the spring of 1918, the German high command believed they had every chance of executing a plan of mighty multiple offensives that would force the Allies to seek peace on Germany's terms. But rebounding Allied spirit — and a million Yanks — turned the war around.

Germany's moment had arrived, the general staff's chief strategist, Gen. Erich Ludendorff, told the kaiser in late 1917. The Allies' failed offensives in Italy and on the western front, the collapse of Romanian resistance, and revolution in Russia, ending the threat on the eastern front, "make it possible to deliver a blow on the western front," Ludendorff wrote. "We should strike . . . before the Americans can throw strong forces into the scale."

For the Allies, dispirited by three years of warfare, the Americans were arriving much too slowly — "in dribbling fashion," Britain's prime minister, David Lloyd George, complained. Of the million men Gen. John J. Pershing had requested, only 175,000 were in France by January 1918.

From the Hindenburg Line — the Allies' name for the German defenses angling southeast from Belgium across France — five German armies emerged on March 21, 1918. It was the opening of the Germans' Somme offensive, aimed at splitting the British and French armies, then swinging north to push the British to the sea. Simultaneously German guns with 117-foot barrels and a 75-mile range began shelling Paris. Damage was light, but the shock was great.

▲ *Backed by a 37-mm gun, men of the U.S. 23rd Infantry, 2nd Division (of Belleau Wood fame), move forward. Side by side (above, left) are a German leather helmet, used until 1916, and a U.S. metal helmet.*

▶

A spent shell casing flies as an artillery crew fires a 75-mm cannon at the Battle of St.-Mihiel, where the newly formed U.S. First Army mounted its first offensive.

In France in 1918, artillery captain Harry S. Truman (right) had a reputation for cussing. Future general George S. Patton (below) became a tank advocate.

In this emergency, and to preserve the shaky Allied coalition, Britain's Field Marshal Douglas Haig agreed to subordinate his forces to French command, under Marshal Ferdinand Foch. Pershing, now with eight American divisions, declared it would be a "great honor" to do likewise.

The bloodletting was frightful — 340,000 British and French casualties — but Ludendorff's Somme offensive was checked in April after initial gains. U.S. troops did not see action. But on April 20, two companies of the 26th (Yankee) Division, got a thrashing in the St.-Mihiel sector when German raiders captured and held the village of Seicheprey for 12 hours, then pulled back. It was a bitter blow to the Americans, who suffered 482 casualties. The Germans captured 179 men and 24 machine guns.

Ludendorff kept pushing. In late May he swept across the Aisne River. In three days his forces advanced 45 miles, reaching the Marne River at Château-Thierry, 30 miles from Paris. Now the Yanks were in the thick of it, and at Château-Thierry the U.S. 3rd Division repelled German attempts to cross the Marne.

With the U.S. 3rd Division holding fast, the Allied command trucked the U.S. 2nd Division, under cover of darkness, to help block a German advance toward Paris. That done, the Yanks were ready to counterattack. They struck at Belleau Wood, a mile-square boulder-strewn patch of trees. Attacking through interlocking machine-gun fire, pausing in shallow foxholes dug with bayonets and mess kits, a marine brigade led the way. On June 14 two army regiments joined the battle, and by June 25 Belleau Wood was secure.

ACES, PORTENTS, AND A SHORT LIFE EXPECTANCY

"Closing Up," by G. H. Davis, shows British DH-9A bombers (left) pulling into tight formation to focus a hail of gunfire on a Jagdstaffel ("hunting pack") *of German Fokker triplanes and D-VII's.*

World War I broke out less than 11 years after the Wright brothers made their historic flight. Before hostilities ended, airplanes added a new dimension to warfare and created a new species of hero, the air ace. At first, both sides used aircraft for reconnaissance and scouting only. Then a British pilot swooped on a German's plane, aimed his revolver, and fired. Hit or not, the German landed and became the first pilot ever forced down in such a way.

Capt. Edward V. (Eddie) Rickenbacker

In 1915 a French pilot, Roland Garros, clamped protective plates on his propeller, mounted a gun in his cockpit, and firing through his whirling prop, felled five enemy planes. Then, working for Germany, the Dutch aviation pioneer Anthony Fokker invented a device that timed a machine gun to fire between prop strokes. The fighter plane was born.

A fighter pilot's life, however gallant and thrilling, had exhaustion and death as constant companions. One-third — 50,000 — of the war's airmen died. Their average life span at the front was three weeks. Against such odds, it is surprising that any pilot survived long enough to down the five enemy aircraft that made him an ace. But Germany's "Red Baron" (below) got 80; Frenchman Réné Fonck, 75; Edward Mannock of Britain, 73; and Canadian Billy Bishop, 72. The leading American, Rickenbacker (left), had 26, followed by Frank Luke with 18, some of which were heavily protected German observation balloons. Of these six aces, only Bishop, Fonck, and Rickenbacker lived to see the armistice.

As the war progressed, fighters improved dramatically. Such improvements were a matter of life or death. The Germans' Zeppelin airships, which could fly long ranges well above the ceiling of the defenders' fighters, dropped 220 tons of bombs on England. But their raids stopped in 1916, when the British built fighters that could reach them.

The Germans then briefly sent twin-engine Gotha bombers over England. The Gotha and its Allied counterparts did relatively little damage, but they portended the massive bombing assaults of World War II.

The Red Baron, Manfred von Richthofen

During the Argonne offensive, in a battle-scarred church in Exermont, France, a squad of doughboys pauses for a song around the still-serviceable organ on October 11, 1918.

DULCE ET DECORUM EST . . .

American Alan Seeger joined the French Foreign Legion in 1914 and died in 1916.

In the voices of the poets and writers of the Great War echo all the complex passions aroused by the worst man-made catastrophe known up to that time. No war has inspired so large, so distinctive, and so fine a body of literary work.

Rupert Brooke caught his fellow Englishmen's swelling patriotism in 1914 with the lines: "If I should die, think only this of me:/ That there's some corner of a foreign field/ That is forever England." The next year, on a troopship bound for Gallipoli, Brooke died of disease. The war killed many other soldier-poets, including Britain's Wilfred Owen, Isaac Rosenberg, and Edward Thomas and America's Alan Seeger (who

wrote prophetically: "I have a rendezvous with Death") and Joyce Kilmer, author of the familiar "Trees." One of the greatest modern French poets, Guillaume Apollinaire, died of influenza in 1918 after suffering a head wound.

Owen began the war with the patriotic zeal of Brooke, but the bloodshed soon changed him. In 1918, the year he fell in action, in a poem about a gassed comrade, he used the Latin epitaph *Dulce et decorum est pro patria mori* ("Sweet and fitting it is to die for one's country") and called it "the old Lie." His friend, the twice-wounded Siegfried Sassoon, turned more savagely bitter; in one poem he calls staff officers "incompetent swine."

Of the many novels by soldiers, two that have stood the test of time are *All Quiet on the Western Front,* by the German writer Erich Maria Remarque, and the openly antiwar *Under Fire,* by Henri Barbusse, a French poet who, past 40, volunteered for the infantry and was discharged in 1917 after being badly wounded.

Wilfred Owen

Rupert Brooke

More than 1 million American troops were now in France, arriving at the rate of 300,000 a month. A vast supply network, manned by black stevedore and construction units, backed the AEF. A thousand miles of railway lines had been laid. Ordnance, however, remained a problem. Lacking their own artillery, U.S. troops used French and British guns; and of 4,400 tanks the U.S. War Department had ordered, only 15 reached France — after the war ended.

Ludendorff kept pressing, but in a series of attacks and counterattacks known as the Second Battle of the Marne, the Germans finally had to abandon their salient threatening Paris. Then, on August 8, 1918, a date that Ludendorff called "the black day of the German Army," British, French, Canadian, and Anzac divisions, behind more than 450 tanks, hit along the Somme near Amiens, catching Ludendorff off guard and panicking his troops. By September 2 the Germans were back to the Hindenburg Line and Ludendorff's resolve had cracked. "The war must be ended," he wrote the kaiser.

American Offensives in High Gear

In mid-September, Pershing massed 550,000 American troops, supported by 110,000 French colonial soldiers and an armada of over 600 American, French, Portuguese, and Italian planes, to quash a bulge protruding from the Hindenburg Line east of Verdun. Here, near St.-Mihiel, the Germans had been dug in since 1914. From their positions they had watched their enemy's massive buildup. Ludendorff had already started a gradual pullback, but Pershing struck before it could be completed.

At dawn on September 12, Pershing's forces attacked. By nightfall of September 13, the attackers had won all major objectives. By September 16 they had cleared the salient and taken 15,000 prisoners.

Meanwhile Marshal Foch had told Pershing to prepare the AEF for an even tougher assignment: the assault on a formidable system of German trenches in the area of the Meuse River and the Argonne Forest. If the Americans could break through there, they could cut the rail lines that supported the German armies in France.

On September 26 the Americans attacked on a 25-mile front. But after several days the advance stalled. The Germans had filled a 15-mile-deep zone with trenches, machine-gun nests, concrete pillboxes, and every kind of trap and obstacle. Six weeks of fighting in the Meuse-Argonne sector cost the Americans 120,000 casualties, but they met their objective: breaching the innermost German line.

While the Allies were battering its defenses, Germany was crumbling from within. In the fall of 1917, a small group of sailors had begun agitating for peace negotiations;

At about 5:00 A.M. on November 11, 1918, German and Allied representatives, meeting in a railway carriage at Compiègne, France, signed an armistice agreement that would take effect six hours later, at the 11th hour of the 11th day of the 11th month of the year.

It was the middle of the night in America. At 3:00 A.M. the Associated Press wires flashed news of the armistice to New York. In the harbor, ships' horns split the night air. Newspaper presses rolled out an extra. Daylight brought nationwide revelry. At the Metropolitan Opera, Enrico Caruso went hoarse singing the anthems of the Allies for a cheering, stamping crowd. Across the country, jubilation reigned. In Washington, President Wilson drove through celebrating throngs to address Congress. That evening, crowds kindled 48 bonfires, one for each of the states, in the Ellipse behind the White House. The symbolism was fitting, for seldom if ever had the states been so unified in a national cause.

His fighting done, Sgt. Alvin C. York poses for a portrait after the war. A religious conscientious objector at the war's start, York, as a private in October 1918, singlehandedly overcame a machine-gun unit, killing 15 Germans and capturing 132.

two of them were executed. Metalworkers went on strike in January 1918. In that month President Wilson announced his Fourteen Points, a peace plan calling on Germany to withdraw from occupied lands and supporting self-determination for the peoples of Europe. The plan was noteworthy for what it did not demand: the partition of Germany.

By October the Germans had accepted Wilson's Fourteen Points, but sought better terms for an armistice. Then the pace of events quickened. Austria-Hungary gave up. German sailors mutinied, refusing to fight. On November 9, as the Meuse-Argonne offensive forged ahead, rebels seized Berlin. The kaiser, having taken refuge with his army in Belgium, had little choice. He abdicated his throne and fled to Holland. With him went the last obstacle to peace.

Yanks of Company M, 6th Infantry, at Remoiville, France, cheer the armistice. Enemies meet (inset) to sign the cease-fire in a railcar in a forest near Compiègne.

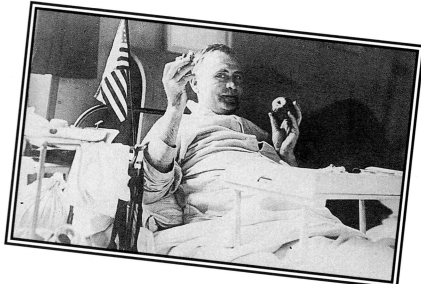

With a concertina, the tricolor, and the Stars and Stripes, four happy Allies in France salute the war's end. Hospitalized near Paris but looking almost cheerful as he displays his snacks, a wounded doughboy (above, right) waits for word of his passage home.

A Yank stands guard near the Rhine River in the sector of Germany occupied by Americans after the armistice. By the fall of 1919, most American troops had left Europe.

Who Won the War?

Of course, the Allies lost less than the Central Powers. But even the victors were badly hurt, and they failed to fashion a durable peace. Medicine advanced, but influenza had the last word in causing human misery.

The war was a disaster for every major belligerent except one: the United States. The map of Europe was changed forever. Four empires had collapsed: Germany, Austria, Russia, and Turkey. A fifth and sixth, Britain and France, emerged from the conflict spiritually and materially exhausted. Though the sheer size of combat forces — 65 million — foiled attempts at precise accounting, as many as 10 million soldiers had perished in battle, and twice as many had been wounded. Four million civilians had lost their lives.

In the face of these almost unbearable losses, it was comforting for some to believe that the Allies had won, at least, a victory for democracy and liberal thinking. Gone were the pampered princes and archdukes of imperial Europe, the Ottoman sultans and Romanovs and Hapsburgs, and in their stead stood the new independent nations of central Europe: Austria, Hungary, Czechoslovakia, Poland, Finland, Estonia, Latvia, and Lithuania, all vaguely democratic, all fiercely nationalistic. Turkey surrendered its Arab lands to the British and French, and colonial peoples the world over saw reason to hope that the new egalitarian spirit sweeping the globe would include them too. For a time it seemed that the Wilsonian principles of national sovereignty and political self-determination would create a just and lasting peace and a new age of international cooperation. But such was not to be.

Many have said that the Allies won the war but lost the peace, and it is true that the peace conference at Versailles created as many problems as it solved. Forced to admit responsibility for the conflict and pay billions in war reparations, Germany's infant democracy was hamstrung from the start, but the terms were not so severe as to prevent a resurgence of German militarism. Worse, because Germany had sued for peace before the Allies invaded, many Germans believed that they had not really lost the war but had been stabbed in the back by Jews, Bolsheviks, and Socialists.

Underestimating the depth of German resentment may have been the costliest mistake of the century. Ten months after the armistice, a corporal named Adolf Hitler attended his first meeting of an anti-Semitic group that would later name itself the National Socialist German Workers' Party. Though no one knew it yet, the winds of tyranny were blowing again in Europe. By the end of the 1920's, totalitarian regimes had subverted parliamentary democracy in Italy and Russia; Poland, Hungary, Turkey, and Yugoslavia had all reverted to one-man rule.

Not all the war's legacies were so ruinous. Spurred by wartime needs, technological advances came quickly and

then just as quickly found peacetime applications. Lessons learned from tanks made better tractors. Lightweight alloys developed for aviation proved a boon to automotive engineers, and in Germany economic isolation gave birth to flourishing chemical and plastics industries. Out of the war came airplanes that flew faster, farther, and higher and captured worldwide fascination. By war's end, the warring nations had built some 200,000 aircraft, and the armistice freed hundreds of trained pilots to fly passengers and mail.

Medical Advances From the Battlefield

New weapons, the abominable conditions of trench warfare, and the millions of wounded added up to an unprecedented medical challenge. High-velocity bullets and artillery shrapnel inflicted massive tissue damage, and wounded soldiers lying in the manure-rich fields of France were at great risk of contracting gas gangrene and tetanus. Poison gas caused nearly 185,000 Allied casualties. In the trenches, waterborne diseases such as cholera and dysentery were always a threat. Crowded, unsanitary conditions permitted the breeding and spread of lice and fleas, carriers of the bacteria that causes typhus.

Doctors, nurses, and medics struggled heroically to save lives. Chlorine in the drinking supply cut disease rates, and immunization not only reduced typhus deaths but laid the basis for better understanding of the body's immune system. For the first time motorized ambulances saw wide use, as did X-rays and the restoration of blood volume by transfusion. French army surgeon Alexis Carrel and British chemist Henry Dakin joined forces and developed a surgical therapy to irrigate and sterilize wounds without harming adjacent tissues. Psychiatry, still in its infancy, gained respect by treating shell shock, a post-battlefield mental illness characterized by hysteria, disorientation, and paralysis. Similarly, the ravages of war hastened advances in physical therapy, plastic surgery, prosthetics, orthopedics, anesthesiology, and the treatment of respiratory trauma.

Still, nothing could have prepared medicine for the influenza that raged across the globe in 1918. The loss of life was staggering. Worldwide, as many as 27 million people perished, half a million in the United States alone. For every American killed in the war, the flu, and the pneumonia that accompanied it, killed 10. Coffins became valuable, and when Washington, D.C., health officials learned that a shipment, bound for Pittsburgh, lay at the railroad station, they arranged to have it go no farther. All found use in the nation's capital.

In the United States the epidemic reached its peak in the last week of October 1918, when 21,000 died — the highest domestic one-week mortality rate on record. Then, unaccountably, it faded. By the spring of the next year, the virus had ceased its rampage. It has never been identified, although other flu viruses, ball-shaped organisms so small that 30 million can fit on the head of a pin, have since been isolated and studied. To this day no one knows why the 1918 virus turned so deadly. Perhaps, as many have suggested, influenza was nature's way of showing humanity who was still boss.

In London, on his way to Versailles, President Woodrow Wilson (above, left) rides with King George V of England. As peace talks began, influenza engulfed the world. A Massachusetts tent camp (above) optimistically offered fresh air to cure flu.

Established in 1918, the Distinguished Service Cross (left) was awarded to U.S. Army officers and enlisted men for extreme heroism in combat.

Chapter 3

THE UNRULY DECADE

Prohibition uncorks a spirit of exuberance.

Flappers, fast cars, and faster airplanes.

Jazz and tabloids. Scandals and fads.

Valentino and the Babe. Then . . . Crash!

Thomas Hart Benton's 1930 mural "City Activities and Dance Hall" portrayed the passions of the 1920's.

Mustered out of the army in 1918 at the end of World War I, these soldiers celebrate their departure from Camp (later Fort) Dix, New Jersey.

AMERICA SIDESTEPS WORLD LEADERSHIP

After the most devastating war humanity had yet seen, Western Europe was ready to believe that a fresh wind was coming across the Atlantic with a promise of renewed hope. But was America ready to lead?

When the guns fell silent over Europe, the victorious Allies reacted with joy and bewilderment. Frontline soldiers stayed in their trenches, scarcely daring to believe an end had come. A hundred miles or so to the west, a multitude of delirious Frenchmen sang "La Marseillaise" against the backdrop of the dazzlingly illuminated Paris Opéra.

In America ecstatic throngs turned out with parades and other celebrations to welcome home the returning doughboys. The fuzzy-cheeked lads who had gone overseas to fight were coming back heroes, and they carried themselves with a newfound sense of worldly self-assurance. "How ya gonna keep 'em down on the farm (after they've

seen Paree)?" asked a popular song lyric. It was a good question. And like those returning heroes, the nation itself appeared to have grown up and to be ready to assume its rightful place in the first rank of world powers.

It was in this upbeat atmosphere that President Woodrow Wilson sailed to France for peace negotiations. Wilson arrived in December of 1918, the first incumbent U.S. president to step on European soil, and his reception was tumultuous. The French cheered his train all the way to Paris, where adoring throngs awaited him. Similar adulation flowed toward him in London and Rome.

The American president brought with him a peace plan based on his famous Fourteen Points, the visionary

Wilson received the Nobel Peace Prize in 1919. He was the third American to win the Peace Prize, after Theodore Roosevelt in 1906 and Elihu Root in 1912.

precepts for international accord he had announced earlier that year. The plan included self-determination for European nationalities, an end to secret diplomacy, and even more ambitiously, a League of Nations to settle future international disputes. It was a sublimely idealistic document.

But no sooner did Wilson sit down in Paris with the delegates of the 32 negotiating states than his plan met with the grim realities of European politics. Italy wanted a piece of the Balkans; Great Britain hoped to remain the foremost naval power; France, twice in 48 years invaded by Germany, intended to cripple its hated neighbor; Ukrainians, Poles, Slavs, Magyars, Jews, and others demanded homelands, sometimes claiming the same piece of earth.

For Germans the Treaty of Versailles was a humbling document. Germany saw its once mighty army dismantled and its Rhineland region declared a demilitarized zone. The treaty exacted reparations, later set at $32 billion, and required Germany and Austria to accept full blame for the war. American delegates were horrified. Herbert Hoover predicted that the harsh terms would "ultimately bring destruction." Wilson himself was inclined to believe the treaty was too punitive, but he signed it in exchange for Allied support of his precious League.

▲ **Wilson arrived in Dover, England, in December 1918 and was met by King George V's uncle, the duke of Connaught, and girls who strewed roses in his path.**

Flawed Peace

On June 28, 1919, after months of hard negotiating, President Wilson signed a peace treaty at the palace of Versailles, near Paris. But the U.S. Senate failed to ratify the treaty, and the United States remained technically at war with Germany until 1921. Many Germans considered the Versailles treaty unfair, and Adolf Hitler was later to take full advantage of their bitterness. Although France's Premier Georges Clemenceau and Britain's Prime Minister David Lloyd George sat at Wilson's side at the signing, both had snubbed the ailing Wilson during the negotiations and had even come to blows with each other. (Clemenceau actually challenged Lloyd George to a duel!) On the day of the signing, the French delegates, who had won most of their objectives, could not conceal their glee, while the Germans behaved like chastened offenders. It was not an auspicious day for world peace.

▶ **Henry Cabot Lodge, powerful Republican senator from Massachusetts, offered to stop opposing "Wilson's treaty" if the president dropped the provision that would send U.S. troops to help defend League of Nations members. Wilson refused, and Lodge continued to prevent the treaty's ratification.**

Back home, when he submitted the Versailles treaty for Senate approval, Wilson faced an even tougher fight. Isolationist Republicans, who wanted no more of Europe's nasty squabbles, objected in particular to U.S. membership in the League of Nations and sponsored an amended treaty.

The president rejected their modifications and took his case to the people, crossing the country aboard the presidential train, *The Mayflower*. It was a punishing ordeal. At 62 years of age, against the advice of doctors, Wilson traveled a grueling 8,000 miles and made more than 30 prepared speeches. Three weeks into the trip, his strength gave out entirely. *The Mayflower*, blinds drawn, sped back to Washington.

A few days later the President suffered a massive stroke. For weeks he could not sit up or even sign his name. It soon became clear that the reins of presidential power had not passed to Wilson's vice president, Thomas Marshall, but to his wife, Edith. The first lady in effect ran the country, with a bit of help from Wilson's doctor and his secretary.

On March 19, 1920, the Senate voted 49–35 for the amended version of the treaty, still 7 votes short of the two-thirds majority needed for ratification. Wilson left office in March 1921 and died three years later, a beaten and embittered man. Yet he understood better than anyone that America could no longer stand apart in splendid isolation. The League limped along, but without the United States, it carried little weight in world affairs.

PROHIBITION SETS OFF A SPREE

Hoping to promote sobriety, morality, and good health, legislators passed a sheaf of laws banning the sale of liquor. The result was nearly 14 years of illicit drinking.

I t was 12:01 in the morning of January 16, 1920, and across America — from the smallest town to the largest city, from Los Angeles to New York and everywhere between — could be heard the sounds of tavern doors closing, of corks going back into bottles, of folks crying in their last legal beers. Only two weeks old, the 1920's had dried up. Prohibition lay hard on the land.

Anti-Saloon Lea-guers and members of the Women's Christian Tem-perance Union (WCTU) greeted the day with joy and optimism. In John Kramer, the new Prohibition commis-sioner, they found their voice. "This law," he proclaimed, "will be obeyed in cities large and small, and where it is not obeyed it will be enforced. . . . The law says that liquor to be used as a beverage must not be manufactured. We shall see that it is not manufactured. Nor sold, nor given away, nor hauled in anything on the surface of the earth, or in the air."

He could not have been more wrong. Never was a law destined to be so flagrantly violated by so many, and at such great profit. Remembered as "a great social and eco-

▲ *Three thirsty ladies at a Milwaukee brewery stand ready to hoist their beer steins the moment Prohibition ends.*

▲ **Prohibition sparked an immediate outcry, especially from men. To these neatly turned-out New Yorkers, the law was both foolish and unfair.**

Amendment XVIII

1. After one year from the ratification of this article the manufacture, sale, or trans-portation of intoxicating liquors within, the importation thereof into, or the exportation thereof from the United States and all territory subject to the juris-diction thereof for beverage purposes is hereby prohibited.

2. The Congress and the several States shall have concurrent power to enforce this article by appropriate legislation.

▲ **Prohibition's driving text was the 18th Amendment to the Constitution, approved by Congress in 1917. Two years later, three-fourths of the states had ratified the amendment, making it the law of the land.**

nomic experiment, noble in motive," Prohibition was not one law but many: the 18th Amendment itself, which prohibited the sale, transport, and manufac-ture of all intoxicants, from beer to whiskey; the National Prohibition Act, or Volstead Act, by which the 18th Amendment was to be enforced; and a bevy of state and municipal regulations that provided for local regulation and penalties. All were ignored equally. Prohibition failed utterly to deter Ameri-cans from manufacturing, selling, and drinking spirits. During the next almost 14 years of legal sobriety, they actually drank more.

Only a few hours after the birth of dry America, the nation received its first taste of things to come when officials seized four stills, two in Detroit and two in Hammond, Indiana. Within the year liquor was pouring over the borders from Canada and Mexico. Fleets of rumrunners assembled off the coasts of New York, New Jersey, California, and Florida, loaded down with liquor from Europe and the Caribbean, where many farsighted American distillers had stockpiled their wares in anticipation of the coming thirst. For every saloon that closed, dozens of speakeasies sprang up in its place. By 1926 officials estimated there were 100,000 speakeasies operating in New York City alone. Breweries, restricted by the Volstead

Act to the manufacture of low-alcohol near beer, simply ignored these legal niceties. In California the acres devoted to growing wine grapes ballooned from 97,000 in 1919 to 680,796 in 1926. Moonshine stills, once limited to backwoods localities, sprang up everywhere: in tenement basements, in the kitchens and bathrooms of private homes, in the darkest reaches of abandoned coal mines.

Drinkers carried and smuggled hooch in every conceivable container, from hip flasks to life preservers. "In time," noted a German tourist in 1927, "I learned that not everything in America was what it seemed to be. I discovered, for instance, that a spare tire could be filled with substances other than air, that one must not look too deeply into certain binoculars, and that teddy bears, which suddenly acquired tremendous popularity among the ladies, very often had hollow metal stomachs."

To the dismay of some, criminalizing liquor had the effect of increasing its appeal to many Americans. What's more, since all drinkers became tacit partners in crime, Prohibition had a democratizing effect. Cultural and class barriers fell with a resounding thud. Once a habit more widespread among laborers, who drank beer, and wealthy Americans, who drank wine and spirits, the use of intoxicating beverages now found a multitude of enthusiastic converts among the traditionally sober middle class.

Enforcing Prohibition proved hopeless. Though many members of Congress were willing to vote "dry" in principle, and thus protect themselves from the wrath of Anti-Saloon Leaguers and other drys, they were less eager about appropriating funds to police the nation's drinking habits. Toward the end of "the noble experiment," Herbert Hoover himself estimated that a police force of a quarter of a million men would be needed to make it work, further demonstrating, as he remarked, "the futility of the whole business." The Prohibition laws, too, were full of holes, voted into the statute books in many cases by men who themselves went right on tippling with the rest of America. Graft was rampant. Federal Prohibition officials and local police, undermanned and underfunded, were hard pressed to withstand the considerable temptations of the liquor trade and the pressures of organized criminals. One Prohibition official called his bureau "a training school for bootleggers."

The hypocrisy was evident to nearly everybody. Far from laying boozing to rest, Prohibition had sparked a national obsession with alcoholic beverages and a widespread contempt for the law. Moreover, it had unintentionally placed control of everything to do with the liquor trade in the hands of criminals. Increased efforts to enforce Prohibition only made matters worse; by the end of the decade, "the era of clear thinking and clean living" had degenerated into a pointless exercise in turning a large segment of the American middle class into lawbreakers. Still, it was not until 1933, after the lowest level of the Great Depression, that Prohibition was finally undone, the first and only amendment ever to earn the dubious distinction of having been repealed.

A painting by New York artist Ben Shahn shows some ingenious ways a gentleman tippler might hide his whiskey.

▲ *Federal agents proudly display a moonshiner's captured backyard still. But for every still raided, hundreds more continued to operate undetected.*

A lady bootlegger could carry a full gallon in each leg of these copper bloomers. More discreet, a book-shaped flask held a generous nip.

SPEAKEASIES AND BOOTLEGGERS

"Mother makes brandy from cherries;
Pop distills whiskey and gin;
Sister sells wine from the grapes on our vine —
Good grief, how the money rolls in!"

No sooner had the 18th Amendment taken effect than many Americans' ideas about good citizenship seemed to evaporate. The production, sale, or transporting for sale of alcoholic beverages was illegal, but breaking the law — bootlegging — was widely winked at, as the popular ditty above attests. Formerly law-abiding families fired up kitchen stills and filled their bathtubs with homemade gin. Not nearly so innocent were the big-time bootleggers who claimed they purveyed real whiskey and were lauded as public benefactors. Yet these same sellers often cut their supplies with industrial alcohol and other toxic substances, then sold the adulterated stuff at immense profit.

The handiest outlet for bootlegged hooch was the speakeasy, the illicit reincarnation of the corner tavern. No doubt the atmosphere of romance, danger, and secrecy that surrounded speakeasies contributed to their popularity. Adding to the allure was the assortment of colorful types who ran the leading speaks. Few other hostesses could project such brazen good cheer as Mary Louise (Texas) Guinan, former cowgirl, vaudevillian, and silent-movie actress who became queen of the New York nightclub scene. Drinking in Miss Guinan's establishments was not cheap — the cover charge alone was between

▲ With "Hello, Sucker!" and a big smile, Texas Guinan (seated, in dark dress) greets a customer at one of her speakeasies.

Clip joint, bathtub gin, cement overshoes, the one-way ride — never has a decade so enriched the American vocabulary with memorable idioms of lawlessness and vice.

Names of bootleg booze promised kicks, if nothing else. White Lightning was corn liquor from Virginia, which also produced Old Stingo and Jackass Brandy (from peaches). The entire South liked Squirrel Whiskey, a moonshine so strong it made men climb trees. The Midwest went for Pumpkin Wine. Chicago's Yack Yack Bourbon, laced with burnt sugar and iodine, was also a favorite. White Mule, Old Horsey, Happy Sally, Soda Pop Moon — the list went on and on. Discriminating tipplers looked for the Real McCoy, smuggled in pure and unadulterated from the Bahamas by legendary rumrunner Bill McCoy.

Any of these potions could get a drinker lit, lubricated, fried, canned,or corked. More would make him stinko or spifflicated, all the way up through ossified, embalmed, and blotto to out like a light. The morning after would bring the jumps, the shakes, or — worse yet — the screaming meemies.

$5 and $25, depending on the night — but for nearly a decade Texas packed them in.

Prohibition enforcement produced its own share of colorful characters. Two less likely agents of the law can hardly be imagined than Izzy Einstein and Moe Smith, tipping the scales at well over 200 pounds apiece. Masters of disguise, they shut down speakeasy after speakeasy, still after still. To nab a moonshine operation in a New York City cemetery, they posed as thirsty gravediggers; at Cornell University, Izzy donned a varsity-letter sweater to ensnare campus bootleggers. So successful were this Tweedledum and Tweedledee of law enforcement that during their five years as Prohibition agents they brought in nearly 20 percent of all Prohibition cases tried in New York City.

Scarface Al Capone was hardly the decade's only crime boss, but he was certainly the most ruthless. "I call myself a businessman," the bull-necked Chicago gangster explained, then added ruefully that many others did not. "When I sell liquor it's bootlegging. When my patrons serve it on silver trays on Lake Shore Drive, it's hospitality." With his private army of 700 gunslingers, Capone seized control of all the Windy City's 10,000 speakeasies, and he edged into gambling, prostitution, and racketeering operations throughout the Midwest. Scores of policemen and politicians were on his payroll. No one knows how much money he hauled in, but conservative estimates place his gross take at $100 million a year. The drys looked upon him as evil incarnate, but to Chicago's many tipplers he was a savior.

Capone's climb to the top left a trail of bullet-riddled corpses. As rival gangs battled for a piece of the action, Cook County suffered nearly 400 mob slayings a year. The vio-

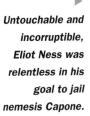

Public Enemy Number One, crime boss Al Capone, kept the good times flowing — at the point of a gun.

Untouchable and incorruptible, Eliot Ness was relentless in his goal to jail nemesis Capone.

lence culminated on February 14, 1929 — St. Valentine's Day — when Capone ordered the death of North Side boss Bugs Moran. Seven North Side gang members were waiting at a garage for a shipment of hijacked liquor. Pretending to be policemen, Capone's men disarmed their victims, lined them up against a wall, and cut them down with machine-gun fire. Moran escaped, but his crime career was over.

As the body count rose, Capone's popularity sank. A vigorous public relations campaign by the Chicago Crime Commission, and the invention of the Public Enemies List, helped speed his downfall. In October 1931 he was arrested for income tax evasion and sentenced to 11 years in prison.

Nobody was more pleased than Eliot Ness, of the U.S. Justice Department's Prohibition Bureau, who had battled for years to put Capone away. The crime czar himself was unrepentant. "All I ever did was supply a demand," he reminisced.

When a thirsty motorist tried to smuggle in booze from Mexico, customs officers from Marfa, Texas, seized all 110 bottles.

Elegantly dressed patrons sip bootleg drinks at a New York speakeasy, as seen by painter Ben Shahn's unsentimental eye.

NORMALCY GOES AWRY

With the end of the war, American voters yearned for a return to earlier times. Handsome, affable Warren Harding offered prosperity at home and disengagement abroad. Then everything started to tumble apart.

The American mood in 1920 was not good. The recent war had strained the economy and plunged it into recession. Unemployment was widespread, and agriculture, the mainstay of the economy, foundered under low farm prices. At the same time, the general cost of living had soared. Industry was buffeted by labor unrest, and threats from anarchists and other radicals (see p.110) troubled the nation. No help was forthcoming from the White House. President Wilson, disabled by a stroke, showed no interest in domestic policy, and his dreams of world leadership left most Americans cold. Clearly the time was ripe for a Republican to assume control. The only question was who.

There seemed to be two good choices: Gen. Leonard Wood, political heir of the late Teddy Roosevelt, and Gov. Frank O. Lowden of Illinois. The two ran neck and neck all the way to the Chicago convention, in June. There, vote after vote resulted in deadlock. Then, on the seventh and

When the Harding oil scandals came to light, cartoonists had a field day at the Grand Old Party's expense.

eighth ballots, fourth-place candidate Warren G. Harding, junior senator from Ohio, began to gain steam. With his craggy good looks and friendly manner, Harding was difficult to dislike; he had diligently campaigned as a compromise candidate in anticipation of a deadlocked convention. On the 10th ballot the nomination was Harding's. Nine months later he sailed into the White House, having trounced Democratic candidate James M. Cox and his running mate, Franklin D. Roosevelt, with the largest popular majority in history up to that time: 60.2 percent.

Harding's overwhelming victory came as a surprise even to himself. Born and raised in rural Ohio, he had attended tiny Ohio Central College and entered the newspa-

Campaigning from his front porch in Ohio, Harding (front row, left) plays host to Broadway star Blanche Ring and singer Al Jolson; Mrs. Harding holds a scroll. An ornate medal (right) served as a memento of Harding's nomination.

After Harding died, his name was linked to several women other than Florence Harding (bottom). One was Carrie Phillips (top), wife of a Marion store owner. Another, unwed mother Nan Britton (middle), claimed her daughter's daddy was the president himself.

On November 2, 1920, women all across the U.S. defied critics and hecklers and marched to the polls to vote in their first presidential election. It was a triumph that had taken many decades to bring about. Opposition to woman suffrage, and to the 19th Amendment that made it the law of the land, had been long-standing and loud. Before Prohibition, liquor interests had warned that temperance-minded women voters would close the saloons. The political bosses feared that do-gooders would initiate government reforms. And many Southerners felt that black women's votes would doom discriminatory Jim Crow laws. Still others found the "most excitable part of the human race" emotionally ill equipped for politics, despite the fact that women in Wyoming Territory had voted as early as 1869 and elsewhere in the West since the 1890's.

Hardly anyone felt the earth tremble when women finally cast their ballots, however. The League of Women Voters had prepared the way with instructional pamphlets, voting demonstrations held in department stores, and drills staged in mock election booths. Turnout was light in many locations. But in places like New York (left), the first state east of the Mississippi to ratify the 19th Amendment, "every woman not suffering from Spanish influenza voted."

per business, purchasing the bankrupt *Marion Star* with two friends, whom he later bought out. Under Harding's leadership the *Star* prospered, and in 1898 he made his first leap into politics. Urged on by an ambitious and well-connected wife, Florence de Wolfe (whom he called Duchess), he ran for the Ohio Senate.

In the climate of intrigue and corruption that permeated Ohio politics at the turn of the century, Harding distinguished himself as a man of quiet virtue, honest and deeply loyal. He was known as a skillful mediator and would come to earn the nickname the Great Handshaker. His only apparent fault was a fondness for what he called "bloviating," a kind of windy speechmaking that struck at least one listener as resembling "an army of pompous phrases marching across the landscape in search of an idea." The general thrust of Harding's politics was harmonious good fellowship, and he rode it to the United States Senate in 1914. Six years later the

President Harding (seated at center) relaxes with (seated from left) Henry Ford, Thomas Edison, Harvey Firestone, and Protestant churchman William Anderson. Said Edison of Harding: "Any man who chews tobacco is all right."

American public, weary of postwar turmoil and nostalgic for a simpler time, lifted Harding and the values of industrious, neighborly Marion to the presidency.

Harding had spent virtually nothing on his campaign, preferring to remain in Marion and greet voters — some 600,000 — from his front porch. He rejected Wilson's vision of America's role in world affairs, and largely ignored the zealous idealism of the reform-minded Progressives, who had been ardent supporters of Teddy Roosevelt in the previous decade. "America's present need is not heroics, but healing," Harding proclaimed, "not nostrums, but normalcy." In his inaugural address, he sounded the same comforting refrain: "Our supreme task is the resumption of our onward normal way."

Shortly after Harding took office, it became increasingly clear that some of the old Ohio friends who came with him to Washington were not highly principled characters. At the notorious Little Green House on H Street, the president met Attorney General Harry Daugherty and other cronies of his "poker cabinet" for late-night sessions of cards, bootleg liquor, and off-color stories.

Harding's administration was unapologetically probusiness, but the complexities of economic legislation dismayed the president himself. "I can't make a damn thing out of this tax problem," he once confessed. "I listen to one side, and they seem right, and then . . . I talk to the other side, and they seem just as right." Fortunately, along with his more dubious appointments, Harding had also named to his Cabinet a few supremely competent men. With Herbert Hoover as commerce secretary and Andrew Mellon as treasury secretary, the Harding administration paved the way for the economic expansion of the later 1920's.

But Harding and the presidency were soon in trouble. "I never find myself done," he complained. "I don't believe there is a human being who can do all the work there is to be done in the president's office." To compound his troubles, Mrs. Harding became gravely ill with a kidney infection. The handsome Harding, who had long suffered digestive and heart ailments, began to look wan and exhausted. In mid-January 1923 he caught a severe case of the flu, which sent him into visible decline.

Skulduggery Too Vast to Ignore

Ill health was only the beginning of Harding's troubles, however. Rumors of financial double-dealing on the part of his Ohio cronies had begun to circulate. The easygoing Harding at first paid no attention; he was a man for whom trust in others came all too naturally. But the evil was real, and it would soon explode in an avalanche of corruption on a scale not seen since the days of Ulysses S. Grant. The first hints emerged early in 1923 from the unlikely quarter of the Veterans Bureau. It seems that bureau director Charles R. Forbes, a member of the so-called Ohio Gang, was peddling government medical supplies on the open market. There was also a matter of kickbacks on hospital construction contracts. Harding, deeply shaken, angrily confronted Forbes, grabbing him by

The first president to address the nation over radio, Harding received this photo to mark the occasion.

A celebrated hunter of Reds, U.S. Attorney General A. Mitchell Palmer (right, with young admirer) aspired to the White House but never made it. Neither did Socialist Eugene V. Debs (below), who launched his 1920 presidential campaign from a jail cell.

FOR PRESIDENT · CONVICT NO. 9653

Radicals Left and Right

Profound social stresses affected the U.S. in the first two decades of the 20th century. Unrestricted immigration up to World War I had opened the gates to a surge of foreigners — many of them from southern and eastern Europe, poor, illiterate, and often Catholic or Jewish. Clinging to their native languages and old ways, they were often targets of scorn and prejudice. Moreover, many immigrants were drawn to labor unions, which in turn were mainly blamed for an epidemic of strikes — some 3,000 in 1919. Americans often found it difficult to distinguish between union activity for better working conditions and conspiracies by foreign-born anarchists, Communists, and Socialists.

Radical leftists were in fact on the rise. Some joined the American Communist Party, formed in 1919 after the revolution in Russia led by Bolshevik Vladimir Lenin. The Bolsheviks advocated the overthrow of existing governments and promised more revolutions would follow. Was any nation now safe?

One evening in June 1919 U.S. Attorney General A. Mitchell Palmer was preparing for bed when a powerful blast rocked his house. On Palmer's front porch lay the corpse of the man who had delivered the bomb, and alongside him was an anarchist pamphlet. Palmer, to that point restrained in his dealings with radicals, now took drastic action.

On November 7, 1919 — the second anniversary of the Russian Revolution — federal agents, under orders from Palmer, set upon alleged radical centers in 18 U.S. cities

Beginning at age 15, firebrand Elizabeth Gurley Flynn was active in the labor movement, later in the Communist Party.

Radicals and convicted murderers Bartolomeo Vanzetti and Nicola Sacco were executed in 1927, despite a lack of solid evidence.

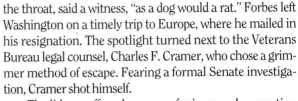

and arrested hundreds of immigrants for deportation. Palmer's men cast a wider net the next year, rounding up some 10,000 leftists. Americans who found Palmer's methods excessive were told that the Red conspiracy must be stopped at any cost.

An array of reactionary groups took up the cry, denouncing and persecuting persons whom they deemed un-American. No group was more savage than the Ku Klux Klan. This white supremacist organization, born after the Civil War, had died out in the early 1870's only to be resurrected in 1915. From a mere 2,000 members in 1920 the ranks of the Klan swelled to over 2 million by mid-decade. Its primary target was still blacks, but the KKK widened its following by attacking immigrants, Catholics, and Jews. Across the U.S. night

riders roved the countryside. By the light of flaming crosses, they flogged, tarred and feathered, and lynched their enemies.

In the early 1920's many blacks rallied behind the charismatic Marcus Garvey, who argued that they could find justice only in their original homeland. His "Back to Africa" message attracted some 2 million followers, few of whom actually made the trip to Africa. After Garvey was jailed for mail fraud in 1925, his movement fell apart.

By the end of the decade, the appeal of radical voices, whether from the left or the right, had declined, partly because of the prolonged boom in industry. Troubling currents of bigotry and labor-management antagonism remained, but the American mainstream would prove deep and wide enough to assimilate all but the most alienated.

Marcus Garvey dressed as "provisional president" of the African nation he yearned to create.

the throat, said a witness, "as a dog would a rat." Forbes left Washington on a timely trip to Europe, where he mailed in his resignation. The spotlight turned next to the Veterans Bureau legal counsel, Charles F. Cramer, who chose a grimmer method of escape. Fearing a formal Senate investigation, Cramer shot himself.

The lid was off, and rumors of crimes and corruption surrounded the Harding administration. One target of suspicion was Jesse Smith, an unofficial aide to Daugherty, who allegedly could fix any problem for a price. Like Cramer, Smith shot himself. "What's a fellow to do," Harding was overheard saying, "when his own friends double-cross him?"

Worse was yet to come. In 1922 two oil executives, Edward L. Doheny and Harry F. Sinclair, had secretly won exclusive drilling rights at naval oil reserve sites at Elk Hills, California, and Teapot Dome, Wyoming. These oil interests had been major backers of Harding's campaign. Furthermore, the rights had been awarded not through competitive bidding, but in exchange for a payoff to Interior Secretary Albert B. Fall. Teapot Dome, like Watergate half a century later, became synonymous with corruption, cover-up, and scandal at the highest levels of government. The beleaguered president sought the counsel of Herbert Hoover. "Mr. Secretary, there's a bad scandal brewing," he lamented. "What do you think I ought to do?" The upright Hoover advised his boss to come clean; but Harding, extolling loyalty above all other virtues, could not implicate his friends. His distress deepened. In the summer of 1923, while vacationing in Alaska, the president fell ill. Returning to California, he checked into San Francisco's Palace Hotel on July 29. Four days later, with his wife at his bedside reading aloud from *The Saturday Evening Post*, Harding suffered a cerebral hemorrhage and died.

Hymns for Harding's Funeral Train

The news of Harding's death elicited a tremendous outpouring of affection. At every stop, the funeral train that returned his body to Washington and thence to Marion met grieving throngs, still unaware of the scandals that would later cloud his reputation. Mourners stood beside the track singing his favorite hymns: "Onward, Christian Soldiers" and "Lead, Kindly Light." At the time of his inauguration, Harding had said, "I cannot hope to be one of the great presidents, but perhaps I may be remembered as one of the best loved." If only for the moment, his wish had come true.

Sober and taciturn, Coolidge stayed calm in any crisis, a quality that inspired the "Keep Cool" slogan used on stickers (bottom of this column) during his 1924 campaign. Big business was positively exuberant about his hands-off economic policies, as a 1920's cartoon (below) illustrates.

KEEPING COOL WITH CAL

In an era of booming stock markets and bathtub gin, the prim New Englander in the White House seemed oddly out of step with the times. But though he said little and appeared to do even less, most Americans just loved Calvin Coolidge.

At a time when Puritanism . . . is at its lowest ebb," wrote columnist Walter Lippmann, "the people are delighted with a Puritan." The sobersided individual in question was Calvin Coolidge, the nation's 30th president, known to almost everyone as Silent Cal. Dour, taciturn, with pale blue eyes and a tight-lipped smile, he appeared, said one wit, to have been "weaned on a pickle." Yet Coolidge possessed a flinty integrity that seemed just right.

A conservative Republican from New England, Coolidge firmly believed that the best government was the one that governed least. This precept had propelled him through local politics to the governorship of Massachusetts. Along the way he acquired a vivacious young wife, Grace Anna Goodhue, who taught at a school for the deaf. Poking fun at his own lack of conversation, he quipped that his bride, "having taught the deaf to hear . . . might perhaps cause the mute to speak."

What pushed Governor Coolidge into national prominence was his forceful handling of the 1919 Boston police strike. When the city's patrolmen walked off the job with demands for higher pay and the right to join a union, Coolidge called in the National Guard. "There is no right to strike against the public safety by anybody, anywhere, any time," he declared. The next year, as delegates to the Republican National Convention cast about for a vice presidential nominee, their glance fell upon Coolidge.

In Washington, while President Warren Harding's fast-dealing cronies raided the public till, Coolidge marched to his own distinctive drummer. At dinner parties his tart Yankee manner seemed quaintly amusing. "Mr. Coolidge," one waggish matron told him, "I've made a rather sizable bet with my

▼ The president gave moral support to these bewigged ladies urging a monument to Thomas Jefferson, but completion of the Jefferson Memorial was 15 years away.

▲ Harking back to his boyhood on a Vermont farm, Coolidge strikes a rustic pose.

With what looks like bemused dignity, Silent Cal plays cowboy at a 1927 Fourth of July gala in South Dakota.

Decked out in full tribal headdress, Coolidge stands with leaders of the Sioux Indians, who made him an honorary tribesman. The president had a natural flair for publicity. For those admirers who sewed, there was a Coolidge thimble.

On a snowless day at the White House, the president and first lady try out new skis, giving a welcome endorsement to the winter sports industry.

friends that I can get you to speak three words this evening." Replied the vice president: "You lose."

The news of Harding's sudden death found Coolidge vacationing at his father's farm in Vermont. It was shortly after midnight. Coolidge senior, a notary public, swore in the new president by the light of a kerosene lamp. Then both men went back to sleep.

As he took office, the scandals of the Harding administration were just bursting into full public view. Moving with deliberate speed, he fired Attorney General Harry Daugherty and ordered a special investigation that sent Harding's secretary of the interior, Albert Fall, to jail for taking bribes. Then he settled down to provide the same minimalist government he had given Massachusetts. His popularity soared. In 1924, campaigning under the slogan "Keep Cool With Coolidge" — and riding a ground swell of business prosperity — he won reelection by a landslide.

Over the next four years Coolidge cut taxes, trimmed costs, and managed to lop $3 billion off the national debt. Above all, he took pains to avoid any unnecessary action. "Many times, if you let a situation alone," he liked to say, "it takes care of itself." In dealing with Congress, he would carefully study new legislation and then find reasons for dismissing it. In all, he vetoed 50 bills; Harding had vetoed 6. When petitioners approached him with their proposals, he employed a well-honed tactic: "If you keep dead still they will run down in three or four minutes."

His do-nothing approach did not amuse everyone. Pundit H. L. Mencken commented on the president's habit of taking two-hour naps: "Nero fiddled but Coolidge only snored." But with the nation prospering and at peace, most people agreed with Supreme Court Justice Oliver Wendell Holmes, Jr.: "While I don't expect anything astonishing from [Coolidge], I don't want anything astonishing."

In the summer of 1927, Coolidge issued a brief statement: "I do not choose to run for president in 1928." He did not elaborate. Dead of a heart attack five years later, he was buried at his birthplace, Plymouth Notch, Vermont, beside his father and son Calvin, who had died at 16 in 1924.

Declining to run for a second term, Coolidge retired to Northampton, Massachusetts, to write and pursue the elusive New England brook trout.

FROM ACES TO AIR TRAVEL

Suddenly pilots were no longer war heroes but merely stuntmen. But by the decade's end, the airplane had spawned a national mail service and a plethora of fledgling airlines.

One of the crazier barnstorming stunts was aerial tennis, which required hidden cables to tie the players to the wing. No feat was thought too daring or too silly if it drew a crowd of paying customers.

AIR MAIL
is Socially Correct

the First Ounce *10* for each additional Ounce

The U.S. officially launched airmail in May 1918 with this Curtiss Jenny stamp, good for up to an ounce. Ten years later (above) the Post Office was promoting airmail as affordably stylish.

After the glory and excitement of World War I, pilots who had honed their skills dogfighting German air aces faced a bumpy landing. Most of them returned to workaday jobs that offered no glamour. Eddie Rickenbacker, America's most famous ace, became a car salesman. But a few diehards tried to parlay their experience into civilian flying careers.

Some became barnstormers, flying from town to town and executing breathtaking routines of aerial acrobatics for admiring crowds. And some were wing walkers who actually swaggered across the aircraft in flight, hung by their fingers from fuselages, and climbed from one plane to another on rope ladders. Inevitably, some crashed. Yet despite the dangers and the terrible pay — World War I ace Dick Depew

said the greatest danger was "the risk of starving to death" — the barnstormers wanted only to fly. After each performance spectators would pay $5 to $15 for a three-minute "joy hop." Some 10 million people took rides.

It was the U.S. Post Office that transformed airplane flight from a carnival curiosity into a serious national endeavor. Starting in 1918, the Post Office began airmail service, first using government planes and pilots, then contracting the work out to private operators. Flying the mail was not for the fainthearted. Hours in cramped, noisy cockpits tortured mind and body, and bad weather brought the added discomfort of bone-chilling wet and cold. With no radios and few navigational instruments, pilots found their way by looking for landmarks. "If a farmer painted his barn a different color, we'd be lost," one recalled. Another flier judged his speed by listening to the air stream past his open cockpit: "If it's whistling pretty loud and shrill, you're going too fast. If it's barely whispering, then you're near a stall." Little wonder that 31 of the first 40 mail pilots on the New York–Chicago run died in crashes. But with salaries ranging from $800 to $1,000 a month, other young men stepped eagerly forward to take the risk.

Charles A. Lindbergh, Jr., who flew the mail from St. Louis to Chicago, fixed his eye on a far higher reward: the glory of making the first nonstop flight from New York to Paris. A U.S. Navy seaplane had made the passage in 1919 with fuel stops at Newfoundland and the Azores. Now, New York hotel owner Raymond Orteig was offering $25,000 to the first pilot to fly direct from the United States to continental Europe. Six men had tried, and all six had crashed to their death. Lindbergh, undaunted, climbed into his single-engine monoplane, *The Spirit of St. Louis,* on May 20, 1927, and took off from Long Island's Roosevelt Field. Thirty-three hours and twenty-nine minutes later he touched down at Le Bourget in Paris. And the world went crazy. "The greatest feat of a solitary man in the records of the human race," one newspaper trumpeted. No longer was he called the Flying Fool. Now he was the romantically evocative Lone Eagle. Congress voted Lindbergh a Medal of Honor. Partygoers danced to a new step called the Lindy Hop.

Twenty-five-year-old Lucky Lindy's triumph sparked an upsurge of enthusiasm for travel by air. Within a year the number of air passengers quadrupled. Companies like Boeing and National Air Transport, both airmail carriers, began flying regular passenger routes. By the end of the decade there were 44 scheduled U.S. airlines and many nonscheduled ones. Transcontinental Air Transport, in a joint deal

Air travelers proudly plastered their suitcases with stickers like these. More than 400 airlines, big and small, vied for mail and passengers in the 1920's.

◄

These eight stewardesses, hired by United Airlines in 1930, were aviation's first. All were trained nurses, and not one was over 25 years old or weighed more than 115 pounds.

Lindbergh poses with The Spirit of St. Louis before taking off on his solo transatlantic flight. His success inspired millions, including songwriters (right).

with the Pennsylvania Railroad, provided cross-country service from Los Angeles to New York. Passengers flew during daylight, then transferred to sleeper cars at night. The trip took 48 hours.

As more people flew, plane travel became increasingly safe and comfortable. Adventurous travelers in the early 1920's would hop mail flights and ride among the letter sacks. Then came wicker chairs in heated cabins, where the passengers munched sandwiches handed out by flight attendants. As often as not the plane they boarded was a Ford Tri-Motor, an immensely popular model that made its debut in 1925 as the nation's first metal-skinned commercial aircraft. Henry Ford, whose Tin Lizzies had put America on wheels, was the builder. His aircraft was dubbed the Tin Goose. Ford Tri-Motors remained in service in some parts of the world for the next 30 years.

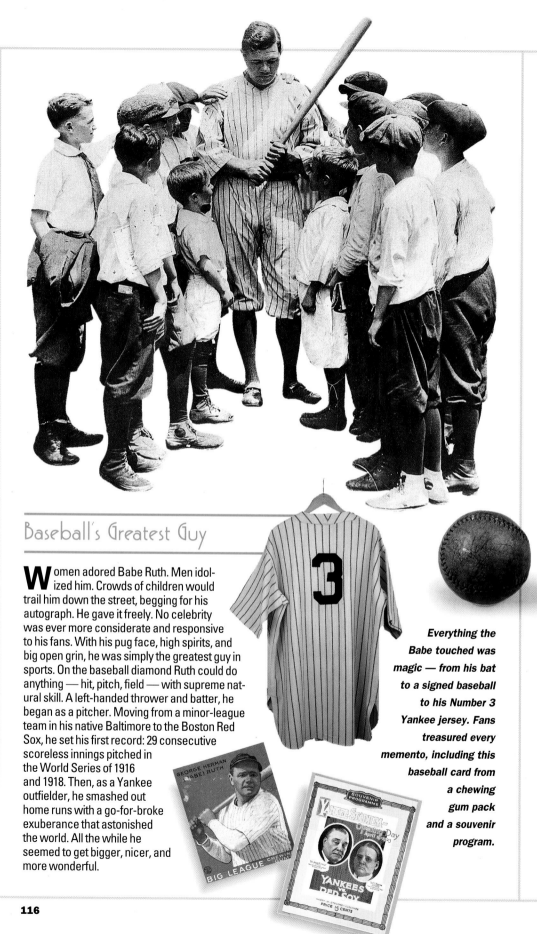

Baseball's Greatest Guy

Women adored Babe Ruth. Men idolized him. Crowds of children would trail him down the street, begging for his autograph. He gave it freely. No celebrity was ever more considerate and responsive to his fans. With his pug face, high spirits, and big open grin, he was simply the greatest guy in sports. On the baseball diamond Ruth could do anything — hit, pitch, field — with supreme natural skill. A left-handed thrower and batter, he began as a pitcher. Moving from a minor-league team in his native Baltimore to the Boston Red Sox, he set his first record: 29 consecutive scoreless innings pitched in the World Series of 1916 and 1918. Then, as a Yankee outfielder, he smashed out home runs with a go-for-broke exuberance that astonished the world. All the while he seemed to get bigger, nicer, and more wonderful.

Everything the Babe touched was magic — from his bat to a signed baseball to his Number 3 Yankee jersey. Fans treasured every memento, including this baseball card from a chewing gum pack and a souvenir program.

THE BABE AND OTHER GIANTS

It was a golden age of American sport, with boxers like Dempsey, football's Red Grange, Tilden in tennis, and, greatest of them all, the Bambino.

When George Herman Ruth (known as Babe or the Bambino) arrived in New York in 1920 to play for the Yankees, baseball was in trouble. The year before, eight players of the Chicago White Sox were accused of taking bribes. "Say it ain't so, Joe," a young fan pleaded with one of them, Shoeless Joe Jackson. But a remorseful Jackson had to nod yes, it was true. The game of baseball, and professional sports in general, seemed permanently tainted.

Then came Ruth. He stepped up to the plate, a big paunchy man with a remarkably dainty grace, and whacked balls out of the park with amazing consistency. He hit 54 home runs his first season as a Yankee. The next year he hit 59. He became the Sultan of Swat, and he restored the luster to America's national game.

What the Babe did for baseball, another extraordinary athlete did for the ancient sport of boxing. Jack Dempsey, the Manassa Mauler, crashed into the national consciousness on July 4, 1919, when he demolished champion Jess Willard in just three rounds. There seemed to be no stopping him. In 1921 he knocked out Frenchman Georges Carpentier before more than 80,000 fans, drawing boxing's first million-dollar gate. He demonstrated his fierce courage in 1923, when he kayoed Luis

At Chicago in 1927, Dempsey crumpled Gene Tunney. But the controversial 17-second "long count" gave Tunney time to recover, then win.

Man o' War raced two years and took all but 1 of his 21 starts. He was the greatest thoroughbred ever.

Tennis aces for the ages, Helen Wills (far left) and Bill Tilden were the first Americans to win at Britain's Wimbledon. Tilden took six U.S. titles, while Wills won every match she played between 1927 and 1932.

Firpo, of Argentina, in the second round, after Firpo had knocked him out of the ring in the first round.

Even when he made his exit in 1927, Dempsey did it with flair. His opponent was Gene Tunney, light-heavyweight champ of the World War I AEF. At Philadelphia in 1926 Tunney had outboxed Dempsey, who had grown flabby from three years of high living. But a year later in Chicago, Dempsey sent Tunney sprawling. By the rules of boxing, Dempsey should then have stepped to a neutral corner. But he was slow in doing so, thus giving Tunney time to regain his feet and win the fight.

In football the nation lavished its applause on Notre Dame coach Knute Rockne, who almost always found a way to win. And it thrilled to the exploits of Red Grange, the

Coach Knute Rockne, here cuddling the Notre Dame mascot, won 105 football games from 1918 to 1931, with only 12 defeats.

Galloping Ghost of Illinois, who in 1924 scored 4 touchdowns and ran 262 yards in the first 12 minutes of a game against Michigan.

If the 1920's provided some of the greatest legends in sports, part of the reason may have been the decade's extraordinarily fine sportswriters. Damon Runyon, Ring Lardner, and Paul Gallico made people care passionately when Gertrude Ederle swam the English Channel or when swimmer Johnny Weissmuller splashed to another Olympic record. They chronicled the two-year career of Man o' War, the chestnut supercolt who won 9 of his 10 starts in 1919 and all 11 in 1920, and was outrun only once, by a horse named Upset. They recorded the years of golfer Bobby Jones, who addressed each shot "with all the certainty of a natural phenomenon" and won 13 national championships. And after Notre Dame beat Army in football in 1924, the words of sportswriter Grantland Rice conferred immortality on four student athletes. Of Notre Dame's backfield, Rice wrote: "Outlined against a blue-gray October sky, the Four Horsemen rode again. In dramatic lore, they are known as Famine, Pestilence, Destruction, and Death. These are only aliases. Their real names are Stuhldreher, Miller, Crowley, and Layden."

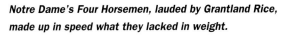

Notre Dame's Four Horsemen, lauded by Grantland Rice, made up in speed what they lacked in weight.

117

JOURNALISM, WICKED AND WISE

Never had America enjoyed such a varied or attention-grabbing diet of reading matter. Tabloid newspapers dished up titillating sagas of sex and crime. At the same time, some lively new magazines offered more uplifting fare.

Columnist Damon Runyon earned acclaim for his colorful stories of low-life guys and dolls.

On The New Yorker's first cover, a dandified Eustace Tilley squints through his monocle at the world.

Drawing by Rea Irvin; © 1925, 1953, The New Yorker Magazine, Inc.

F irst came the illustrated *Daily News*. The premier issue appeared on June 26, 1919, in a tabloid-size format designed for easy reading on crowded New York subways. Since then, sensational headlines of the tabloid press have screamed for the nation's attention: "Brooklyn Vice Barons Lure Innocent Girls to Sin Dens!" "Boys Foil Death Chair!" "Mate Gives Cheating Wife to White Slave Torturers!" By 1924 the *News* had the largest circulation of all the dailies in America, and its competitors were not far behind.

The strongest challenge came from William Randolph Hearst, titan of American journalism, who in 1924 brought out the look-alike *Daily Mirror*. Hearst promised his readers "90 percent entertainment and 10 percent information — and the information without boring you." Close behind came physical culture guru Bernarr MacFadden and his sensation-packed *Daily Graphic*.

Sex and violence were the essentials, with a large dose of celebrity scandal — as the tabloid imitations created on these two pages suggest. (The basic facts are real, and so are the photos; the headlines and text simulate the period's look and style.) The disappearance of Hollywood evangelist Aimee Semple McPherson was splashed across front pages in May 1926. A month later, when McPherson stumbled out of the California desert claiming to have been kidnapped, the tabloids covered her ordeal in horrified, heartrending detail. Then came the kicker: evidence that McPherson may have made up the whole story to disguise a lovers' tryst.

A good murder did wonders to boost circulation, and when fresh bodies were lacking, the editors simply dug up old ones. In 1926 the *Daily Mirror* revived the four-year-old Hall-Mills case, in which the corpses of Episcopal minister Edward W. Hall and a comely parishioner, Mrs. Eleanor Mills, had been discovered together on an abandoned New

Where was Aimee?

Was She Abducted? Or Did She Just Pretend?

HELD AGAINST MY WILL!

HOLLYWOOD – "Sister Aimee" **Semple McPherson,** the famous revivalist preacher whose thousands of ~~devoted~~ followers have anxiously ~~awaited her~~ revelation in the ~~...~~

SHOCKING NEW EVIDENCE IN HALL-MILLS MURDER:

"PIG WOMAN" TESTIFIES!

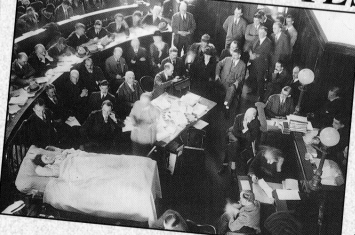

SOMERVILLE, N.J. – Dramatic testimony from bedridden Jane Gibson, known as the "Pig Woman," tightened the case against society matron Frances Stevens Hall, charged with murdering her husband four years ago in a jealous rage. Speaking in whispers, the dying Mrs. Gibson, who suffers from cancer, told how she had seen the accused lurking near the site where the bodies were found on an abandoned tract not far from her own pig farm. She also spotted Mrs. Hall's two brothers, "Crazy Willie"

Jersey farm. The killer had never been found, so the *Mirror* proposed a conspiracy masterminded by Hall's socialite wife. The accused were acquitted, but the story made juicy reading for weeks.

Then came Daddy and Peaches. The split-up of 51-year-old-millionaire Edward (Daddy) Browning and child-bride Frances (Peaches) Heenan after a year and a half of marriage gave the tabs a field day. Peaches told all to MacFadden's *Graphic*, which illustrated her marital saga in concocted photos it called composographs. The one at right shows how, on the couple's wedding night, Daddy had brought along a pet goose and barked like a dog. Daddy's eccentric behavior, Peaches claimed, made married life miserable.

When sensationalism palled, readers could turn to a flock of vigorous new magazines. DeWitt Wallace, a young war veteran, borrowed $5,000 and started *The Reader's Digest* in a basement in New York City's Greenwich Village. Within a decade its circulation reached half a million. Two other newcomers, Britton Haddon and Henry Luce, rewrote the week's news in crisp prose, added photographs, and distributed the results nationwide. Within three years *Time* was turning handsome profits.

Highbrow audiences subscribed to such journals as *The American Mercury*, edited by H. L. Mencken and George Jean Nathan. Immensely influential, the magazine served up criticism, commentary, and Mencken's witty diatribes against the booboisie of small-town America. For irreverence and a lighter touch, there was *The New Yorker*. Editor Harold Ross's adroit concoction of fiction, humor, and thoughtful observation was definitely not, as he liked to say, "for the old lady in Dubuque." But its readers loved it, and *The New Yorker* has remained the very model of urban literary sophistication.

THE READER'S DIGEST

THIRTY-ONE ARTICLES EACH MONTH FROM LEADING MAGAZINES EACH ARTICLE OF ENDURING VALUE AND INTEREST IN CONDENSED AND COMPACT FORM

FEBRUARY 1922

The first issue of The Reader's Digest condensed stories from McClure's Magazine, House Beautiful, *and* Scientific American.

A Daily Graphic EXCLUSIVE

WOOF! WOOF! DOGG-BE GOOF?

HONK! HONK! IT'S THE BONK!

Daddy and Peaches' Wedding Night!

▶ **A man for all genres, Ring Lardner wrote sports, humor, fiction, and a column on the American scene, all of which made him one of the decade's most widely read journalists.**

▼ **The acerbic H. L. Mencken, cofounder of The American Mercury, *lashed out at almost everybody.***

TENNESSEE MONKEY TRIAL:
Was It Adam or the Apes?

Attorneys Clarence Darrow (left) and William Jennings Bryan (right) heatedly debate the right of Tennessee schoolteacher John T. Scopes (inset) to teach evolution.

VERDICT IN SCOPES TRIAL AWAITED
FUTURE OF SCIENCE, EDUCATION, HANGS IN BALANCE

DAYTON, TENN. – Renowned attorneys Clarence Darrow and William Jennings Bryan today made their closing arguments in the trial here of John T. Scopes, the local schoolteacher charged with propounding the Darwinian theory of evolution in his science classes, in defiance of a court order.

The verdict, hoped for tomorrow, is expected to have far-reaching implications for American public school education. It will determine the extent to which local religious groups can dictate school policy.

The theory, developed by naturalist Charles Darwin some 50 years ago, holds that all life on earth, including mankind, has "evolved" over the eons from simpler creatures—implying that man's closest ancestors were apes. This notion is offensive to many fundamentalist Christians, as it contradicts the account of

PLAIN LIVES, SIMPLE PLEASURES

The 1920's were the last time that cars, electric appliances, paid vacations, retail chains, and candy bars could be called newfangled. Some things stayed the way they had always been.

▲ **One hand milking, the other adjusting his radio receiver, this farmer comfortably straddles the old and the new.**

Beyond the glitter of the rich and famous, in the small towns and rural areas, America of the 1920's was in many ways closer to the 19th century than it was to the Jazz Age. Church membership grew right along with the population, and churches remained the best places for newcomers to get acquainted. Doctors made house calls, venturing out at all hours and in every weather to treat a fever or deliver a baby. Many children walked miles to school; the standardized yellow school bus was nearly a decade away. And while more and more people were buying automobiles, the railroad was still the most dependable way to travel to the city. On the farms horses gave way very slowly to tractors.

Band concerts, county fairs, hometown ball games, family picnics, group sings around the parlor spinet — these were still the main entertainments. On Sundays after church everyone would peruse the papers, usually reaching first for the new features in the comics section. Then the family would sit down to a belt-stretching feast, often a roast with all the trimmings. In many places the biggest event of the year was when the circus came to town.

But even as the old ways persisted, America was undergoing profound and lasting changes. For the first time more than half the nation — 51 percent of its citizens — lived in urban areas, according to the 1920 census. Suburbs rolled out beyond the city limits, their growth fueled by improved roads and rising auto sales. Older enclaves, such as Cleveland's Shaker Heights and Detroit's Grosse Pointe, expanded 7-fold to 10-fold. Beverly Hills, in Los Angeles, grew to 25 times its former size.

At the same time, most Americans found they had more money to spend and more time to spend it. By mid-decade 40 percent of the population was earning at least $2,000 a year, enough to place it comfortably in the middle class. A factory worker made a few dollars more than $1,500, on average, and a teacher, not quite $1,300. Doctors and lawyers pulled down over $5,000. Farm incomes stayed low, to be sure, and it never paid to be a migrant laborer. But the majority of Americans felt life was looking up.

While wages grew, the time spent earning them began to shrink. The norm of the 6-day work week contracted to 5½ days as more and more businesses granted a Saturday half-holiday. In 1923 the Gary, Indiana, steelworks changed from a 12-hour day to 8-hour shifts. Ford went on a five-day week in 1926, and International Harvester presented its employees with what seemed like the ultimate in company largess: two weeks of paid vacation.

A quiet revolution was altering the American home. Electrification came first in the cities, more slowly in the smaller towns, where the

Even in cities the milkman continued to make deliveries by horse-drawn wagon. As long as their horses could do the job, many deliverymen stuck with animal power.

© & ® Tribune Media Services
All Rights Reserved

Little Orphan Annie (and Sandy) debuted in 1924 and won the hearts of comic-strip readers. Unlike most cartoons, her adventures followed a week-by-week story.

Ice cards in a window told the iceman how much ice to deliver, in cents or pounds, to refill the home icebox. Though sales of refrigerators soared, millions of households still did it the old-fashioned way.

Piggly Wiggly combined low prices with the trailblazing idea of self-service in its "grocerterias," forerunners of supermarkets. Sprouting across the South, this chain grew from just over 500 stores in 1920 to 2,500 in 1929.

central power plant might have shut down at night. Some rural areas had to wait another decade or two for public electricity. But as power lines began to stretch across the American heartland, and as the price of electricity went down, more and more families began reaping its conveniences. Edison's light bulbs replaced the smoky glow of kerosene lamps, radios blared, telephones jangled, refrigerators took the place of iceboxes. As a 1926 General Electric ad intoned: "Any woman who is doing any household task that a little electric motor can do is working for 3 cents an hour; human life is too precious to be sold at a price of 3 cents an hour."

The increasingly centralized populations — earning more money, spending fewer hours on the job — represented a new breed of consumers. For them, it was no longer necessary to make things at home. Almost everything, from cookies to suits, now came ready-made and conveniently packaged. National chain stores, selling prepackaged national brands, grew by leaps and bounds, spanning the continent. J. C. Penney added an average of 100 stores a year thoughout the 1920's, and The Great Atlantic & Pacific Tea Company averaged 3 new store openings every day during the decade.

It was a great time to launch national brands, and many of the newcomers became household names. For breakfast, Wheaties and Rice Krispies; for lunch, a can of Libby's tomato soup with a sandwich (using commercially baked, not homemade, bread) of Peter Pan peanut butter and Welch's grape jelly. For dessert, Hostess cakes and Eskimo Pies, and for snacking, Baby Ruth, Mounds, and Milky Way candy bars. Sanka to wash it down, and Brillo to help do the dishes.

Not everyone liked the changes, to be sure. "Radios and telephones make people farther apart," an invalided worker told the authors of *Middletown,* a 1929 study of a small Midwestern city. "Instead of going to see a person as folks used to, you just telephone nowadays."

But even in the large cities, some things stayed reassuringly the same. All through the 1920's milk still came in bottles. It would arrive on the doorstep before breakfast, brought by the local milkman, who would take away the empties left out the night before.

Mortimer in a silent cartoon, he became Mickey in the sound cartoon Steamboat Willie *(1928) and rose to be America's most popular animated character.*

THE PHENOMENAL FLAPPER

Sassy, smart, and ready for anything, a new kind of rebel danced into view. In dress, manners, and morals, she kicked up her heels and led the way, much to her parents' everlasting dismay.

To some, she was a daring revolutionary. To H. L. Mencken, caustic critic of American manners and mores, she seemed "a somewhat foolish girl, full of wild surmises and inclined to revolt against the precepts and admonitions of her elders." What no one could deny was her breezy devil-may-care exuberance. The 1920's marked the nation's first youth culture, in which a generation of under-25-year-old Americans cut loose as never before and launched a whole new set of styles, attitudes, and ways of behaving. By far their most visible representative was the flapper.

Whatever she did — whether dancing the Charleston at a college fraternity party or joyriding in a roadster with one of her many beaux — she loved to be seen. To make sure she stood out, she dressed for shock

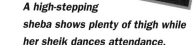

▲ *A high-stepping sheba shows plenty of thigh while her sheik dances attendance.*

value. In her mother's time a woman's costume typically used some 19 yards of cloth and swathed the wearer from chin to toe. No longer. In 1920, in one exultant leap, hemlines rose from ankle to mid-calf. From then on, dresses got smaller, thinner, and lighter so fast they could almost be seen to shrink. Waistlines dropped; busts flattened. Sleeves became shorter or simply disappeared. Cotton stockings gave way to silk or rayon hose, rolled down at the top to allow a glimpse of bare kneecap. The idea was to look carefree and boyish — and ready to play.

Even as the public was reeling from the shock of the disappearing skirt, it was hit by another: bobbed hair. In what amounted to a rite of passage into flapperhood, girls

Helped by two perky young starlets, a Los Angeles man proudly shows off his extra-floppy oxford bags.

All dressed down for New Year's Eve, an exuberant flapper displays her high-voltage Charleston style.

▼ *The latest bathing suits of 1926 seem tame today, but back then, some women shrank at showing so much skin.*

John Held, Jr.

No one captured the cheerful silliness of the flapper era more fully than cartoonist John Held, Jr. In drawings for *The New Yorker, College Humor,* and the covers of *Life* (top), he depicted a stylishly pert young creature with turned-up nose and turned-down hose who brazened her way through life's adventures with a wonderful combination of feckless innocence and worldly sophistication. Held himself had little taste for Jazz Age partying. Born in Utah, he arrived in New York at age 21 with $4 in his pocket. Soon he was earning $2,500 a week, a princely sum. He bought an estate in Connecticut staffed with its own golf pro.

Revelers at a New York City nightclub kick up their heels in a Charleston chorus.

▼ Beads and bows give a coy distinction to this flapper's evening gown.

began visiting men's barbershops to have their long tresses clipped into ultrashort cuts that barely grazed the ears. They rouged their cheeks and plucked their eyebrows. Still another change, if less visible, was just as significant. In a late-decade survey of 1,300 young women with jobs, fewer than 70 confessed that they still wore old-fashioned corsets. Release from constricting whalebone, hooks, laces, and attached garters went right along with other gestures of liberation and letting go.

In fact, flapper styles were a faithful barometer of social change, and as hemlines shortened and undergarments vanished, the country's flaming youth seemed bent on ever more outlandish behavior in the pursuit of pleasure. Much of the frivolity centered around college campuses. A flapper would arrive at a frat party and rush to the ladies' room to "park her girdle" (assuming her mother had insisted she wear one). Then, accompanied by a male escort in baggy pants

Swimwear models strike a daring classical pose as the Three Graces.

and with patent-leather hair, she would cut a rug on the dance floor, puff forbidden cigarettes, sip bootleg liquor (called by such names as hooch and giggle water), and gleefully offend propriety. The evening might continue with a fast ride in an open convertible and, perhaps, some more or less heavy petting. "None of the Victorian mothers . . ." wrote F. Scott Fitzgerald, the flapper's leading chronicler, "had any idea how casually their daughters were accustomed to be kissed."

But a flapper's pleasures were not all so risqué. She loved to dance: clinging fox-trots, romantic tangos, and most of all the Charleston. The Charleston arrived in 1924 in an all-black Broadway show called *Runnin' Wild* and took the country by storm. At first it was considered immoral and was banned in many places, but before you could say "Get hot!" the flapper was swinging her elbows and kicking up her heels in clubs and on campuses across the U.S. Her latest male admirer did his best to keep up, and together the sheik and his sheba were simply the cat's meow.

YES! NO SHORTAGE OF FADS

A giddy quest for the new and different spawned all kinds of odd diversions: mah-jongg, crossword puzzles, flagpole sitting, dance marathons, a self-improvement craze, and much more.

Weary runners in the 1928 Bunion Derby, a 3,000-mile race from Los Angeles to New York, labor down the homestretch. Of 241 entrants only 55 finished.

One day in 1922 the bandleader Frank Silver was taking a stroll through the town of Lynbrook, New York. Feeling hungry, he stepped over to a sidewalk fruit vendor for something to eat. "Got any bananas?" he asked.

"Yes!" came the heavily accented response. "We have no bananas!"

A light bulb flashed in Silver's brain, and he began to think up some lyrics. His piano player, Irving Cohn, supplied a catchy tune. The song became a runaway smash hit. Perhaps that is not surprising, for a streak of nuttiness popped up in America in the 1920's, leading to a succession of wonderfully nonsensical fads and crazes.

They began with a retired French pharmacist named Émile Coué, who in 1921 came out with a seemingly sure-fire prescription for personal happiness. The key was to repeat a simple saying: "Day by day in every way I am getting better and better." The miraculous powers of autosuggestion, Coué declared, would then turn the saying into reality. "We are what we make ourselves and not what circumstances make us," he reasoned.

Drawn in by Coué's positive and encouraging message, some 40,000 clients a year flocked to his clinic in Nancy, France. By the time he visited the United States in 1923, ballyhoo headlines were proclaiming his wonders: "Two Cripples Walk" and "Coué Makes Palsied Man Run." And folks everywhere were learning how to "Coué away" everything from a headache to a heartache.

Hard on Coué's heels came a heated love affair with anything exotic. Late in 1922 a British archeologist, Howard Carter, digging near Luxor, Egypt, stumbled upon the 3,000-year-old tomb of the pharaoh Tutankhamen. Inside was a dazzling trove of royal Egyptian treasure.

◄

Maestro of self-improvement Émile Coué (farthest right in photo) drills disciples in his method for making life better.

Hollywood starlets help
promote the mystique of
mah-jongg by playing the
game in Oriental finery.
A deluxe set (below) cost
up to $500, more than a
Model T Ford.

▼ All nine contestants in the first Miss America Pageant,
held in 1921 at Atlantic City, pose in the very latest
beach attire. After two event-filled days, the title went
to Margaret Gorman, of Washington, D.C.

Suddenly a King Tut craze was sweeping the country. Clothes, jewelry, hairstyles, even furniture, took on a mysterious pharaonic glitter.

Another exotic fad swept in from China in the form of a game called mah-jongg. With its carved bone tiles and their wonderfully inscrutable markings, mah-jongg had caught the fancy of Joseph Babcock, an American oil executive in Soochow. Babcock simplified the rules, added roman numerals to the tiles, and in 1922 launched his version of the game on the American market.

Propelled by a huge advertising campaign, Babcock's mah-jongg took off. By 1923 more than 1,600,000 sets had been sold. Mah-jongg clubs sprang up, where members entrusted their fortunes to the hazard of tiles marked "wind," "dragon," or the mythical "sparrow of a hundred intelligences." For authenticity, players decked themselves out in brocade robes and took refreshment from lacquered trays. As the frenzy grew, Chinese manufacturers ran out of calf shinbones, used to make the tiles, and had to order fresh supplies from Chicago slaughterhouses. Then, as suddenly as it had hit, the mah-jongg mania evaporated. By mid-decade importers of the game were declaring bankruptcy, and cheap sets could be bought for a dime.

One fad that survived to become a permanent institution was the crossword puzzle. The *New York World* had pioneered the form in the previous decade, but it took two fledgling book publishers, Richard Simon and Max Schuster, to spread crosswords across the land. Their very first venture, in 1924, was a collection of puzzles. To promote it they used an eye-catching gimmick: a No. 2 pencil attached to each volume. Everybody wanted this intriguing new book, and within a few months the nation was crossword puzzle crazy. One railroad stocked its cars with dictionaries; ocean voyages became crossword orgies; a minister turned his sermon into a crossword puzzle; college teams dueled in crossword tournaments. One man became so absorbed in a puzzle that he was jailed for refusing to leave a restaurant. He welcomed his 10-day sentence because he could do puzzles in peace and quiet.

Toward the middle of the decade, the fads began to lose their giddy sparkle and took on a more earnest, muscular quality. An ex-sailor, boxer, and stuntman known as Shipwreck Kelly promoted himself by sitting on flagpoles for days on end. One year he spent 145 days on various masts and flagstaffs. Kelly had many imitators. In Baltimore 15-year-old Avon Foreman perched on a sapling in his backyard for 10 days. When Avon descended, the mayor of Baltimore wrote a tribute praising his "grit and stamina."

Endurance became everything. Most grueling of all were the dance marathons, which became popular late in the decade. Couples shuffled through excruciating weeks in the hope of winning the often sizable prize money. Eventually exhaustion took over, and by then it was no longer fun.

◀

Perched high above a movie theater in Union City, New Jersey, Shipwreck Kelly waves hello. His seat atop the flagpole is a small platform equipped with stirrups.

◀

Marathon dancers kept going until they dropped, like this brother-and-sister Chicago couple, who had danced 3,327 consecutive hours.

HOT, BLUE, AND AMERICAN

A typical living room in 1920 featured a piano stacked with sheet music and a windup phonograph with records of operatic and music-hall favorites. Something was missing.

A whole new sound was about to burst onto the scene: jazz!

Chock-full of innuendo and nonsense words, such as boop-a-doop, up-tempo tunes provided fitting background music for those zany times when youth ran wild and made whoopee. The Sheik of Araby (top) may have sung of desert passion to his lady-love, yet even an ordinary swain could woo his girl with a song sheet and a little practice.

From the start jazz meant excitement, energy, pleasure. Jazz was alive — hot! Many heard in it a spirit of joyous revolt. It captured all that the wild young things of the 1920's wanted to be. No one knows the exact origin of the word, and its meanings were many, but above all it was a new musical style — marked by syncopation, improvisation, and blue notes — created by black people in the South.

The primary birthplace of jazz was New Orleans, among the black Creole population, which had roots in both African and European musical traditions. After the Civil War, when the military bands stationed in New Orleans broke up, band instruments were often bought by the families of freedmen, who had long traditions of teaching music to their children. By 1900 there were scores of brass bands in New Orleans, playing for dances, parades, picnics, and funerals. They drew some of their tunes from popular white mainstream sources but developed them with the vivid harmonies and rhythms characteristic of African music. Flowing into this musical mix were other great streams of black music: ragtime and the blues. Some of the bands flourished in Storyville, the notorious red-light district of New Orleans. It was there, in the dozens of honky-tonks, that many of the early jazzmen, such as Kid Ory, Jelly Roll Morton, and Joe (King) Oliver, began to "play hot." This was musicians' slang for a sound replete with "bent" notes, growls, and plenty of vitality.

Louis Armstrong (left) created the Hot Five studio group (above) with his wife, Lil Hardin Armstrong, and with Johnny St. Cyr, Johnny Dodds, and Kid Ory. They rarely got radio play, still their re-styled New Orleans sound reached appreciative ears.

The Incomparable Satchmo

The story of Louis (Satchmo) Armstrong began at the bottom of that hard and colorful world on July 4, 1900. He and his mother lived in the midst of a myriad of honky-tonks, including a music and dance emporium called Funky Butt Hall. "Before the dance," he remembered, "the band would play out front for about a half hour and us little kids would all do little dances. Then we'd look through the cracks in the wall of Funky Butt." When Louis was 12, he shot a pistol in the street celebrating New Year's Eve and was sent for more than a year to the Waifs' Home for Boys. It was in the home's brass band that he learned to play instruments, progressing from tambourine to lead cornet. Armstrong's musical gifts developed quickly, and after he was released, he was befriended by King Oliver, the top jazz cornet in New Orleans. The young Armstrong sold sacks of coal by day and played cornet in the honky-tonks at night while studying the horn with Oliver.

Paul Whiteman (top, right) led his orchestra to great heights of popularity by toning down the jarring elements of what a 1921 *Ladies' Home Journal* called "unspeakable jazz." Pianist Jelly Roll Morton and his band, the Red Hot Peppers (bottom, right), deliver up some spicy down-home jazz. Morton wrote his tunes in musical notation, making him the first jazz composer.

After the United States entered the world war in 1917, the U.S. Navy closed down Storyville. Many of the bands scattered. Oliver went north to Chicago and in 1920 formed the Creole Jazz Band. In 1922 he sent for Armstrong, who by that time was unsurpassed for his technique and his ability to improvise. Little of the music was written down. Lil Hardin, the band's classically trained pianist, who later wed Armstrong, recalled her amazement when Oliver told her the signal for the band to join in after his intro: "When you hear two knocks, just start playing." Oliver and Armstrong would plunge through their breaks at full tilt, never clashing a note. The astonished audiences loved it.

Jazz bands flourished in the nightclubs and speakeasies of Prohibition-era Chicago. The famous Jelly Roll Morton (who claimed to have invented jazz in 1902 by playing ragtime while stamping his foot in 4/4 time) came to Chicago with his Red Hot Peppers in 1926. The brassy sound fit perfectly into the gangster-controlled speakeasies.

Jazz Enters the Mainstream

Black musicians created jazz, but the popularity of the new music quickly attracted white imitators, who learned the black style and were playing the New Orleans sounds before World War I. The first major white group was the Original Dixieland Jazz Band, led by trumpeter Nick LaRocca.

No doubt the top talent among the white jazz soloists was Bix Beiderbecke, from Davenport, Iowa. Enthralled by the recordings of the Original Dixieland Jazz Band and the New Orleans Rhythm Kings, Beiderbecke learned the jazz cornet by playing along with records. He died at 28, but his style continued to be a major influence on jazz musicians.

Beiderbecke played for the most popular dance band of the 1920's, the "symphonic" jazz orchestra of Paul Whiteman. A classical violinist, Whiteman organized his orchestra in 1919 and hit pay dirt overnight in the record business. The orchestra's first recording, in 1920, sold 2 million copies. One record sold 3.5 million copies, which was amazing since there were only about 7 million phonographs in the United States at the time. His success enabled him to hire the best white jazz musicians, including Beiderbecke and both Tommy and Jimmy Dorsey.

While Whiteman played downtown New York, uptown the bands of Fletcher Henderson and Duke Ellington were riding the wave of the Harlem renaissance, presaging the big band era of the 1930's. All-black Broadway shows, such as Eubie Blake and Noble Sissle's *Shuffle Along,* of 1921, kept people begging for more right up to the end of the decade. White Manhattanites came north in droves for Harlem shows, which featured comedians, chorus girls, singers, such as Ethel Waters, and dancers, like Bill (Bojangles) Robinson. In 1927 the elegant and original Ellington began playing at the famous Cotton Club to a mostly white audience. People paid well for the thrill of being in such a colorful and exotic place as Harlem after midnight, and it flourished. And if they listened closely, underneath the gaiety and din they could hear the howl of jazz announcing it was here to stay.

Dubbed the Empress of the Blues, Bessie Smith sang an emotionally charged brand of country blues laced with jazz that made her famous among her mostly black audience.

George Gershwin's genius with symphonic jazz had musicians improvising, music lovers humming, and men and women "pulling and mauling each other" to get into the premiere of Rhapsody in Blue.

127

DREAM FACTORIES

The decade's brightest stars blazed in silent splendor in the fantasy world of the silver screen, bringing passion, laughter, and the spice of scandal to a rapt America. Then they began to talk, a change that spelled disaster for some and even greater acclaim for others.

All the adventure, all the romance, all the excitement you lack in your daily life are in — Pictures." So trumpeted an advertisement in *The Saturday Evening Post*, and it was true. Movies brought people's dreams to life through the stars of the silver screen.

Paid six-figure salaries, backed by awesome publicity machines, stars were the ultimate in national glamour. During the 1920's moviegoers bought 100 million tickets a week, nearly 1 for every U.S. citizen, to see their idols in movie theaters, some as magnificent as palaces.

As the 1920's began, Mary Pickford, dubbed America's Sweetheart, and her husband, the dashing Douglas Fairbanks, already glittered in the Hollywood sky. So did Lillian Gish, famous since the days of D. W. Griffith's *Birth of a Nation* (1915). Other stars rose overnight to join them. One was the sultry Rudolph Valentino (above), whose 1921 film *The Sheik* made him America's most sighed-over actor. Men were baffled; film mogul Adolph Zukor said Valentino's acting consisted of widening his eyes and flaring his nostrils. But so adept was Valentino at setting female hearts aflutter that when he died in 1926, grieving fans rioted at his funeral.

The Great Lover made great box office, but the moviegoing public was aghast when in 1921 a 23-year-old actress named Virginia Rappe died after an alleged sexual assault in the hotel suite of the film comedian Fatty Arbuckle. (Arbuckle was later cleared, but his movie career was finished.) Fearing for their profits, studio heads banded together to hire an industry chaperone. He was Will Hays, a Presbyterian elder and high Republican official. Besides instituting such standards as the seven-foot rule (kisses could last no longer than seven feet of film), the Hays Office decreed that movies must show "compensating values," meaning that the bad guys had to lose in the end.

In practice, films could show five or six reels of sin as long as virtue eventually triumphed. No one used this formula to better effect than the

Hollywood's firmament included "It" girl Clara Bow (draped across chaise at top), Douglas Fairbanks, and Mary Pickford (right).

◄ **In *Safety Last* (1923) comic Harold Lloyd scrambled up a skyscraper to impress his girlfriend.**

◄ **The Gish sisters, Dorothy and Lillian (the younger by 2½ years), were silent film stars both individually and together.**

*Rudolph Valentino secured his place as the
Great Lover of filmdom in* The Sheik.

flamboyant director Cecil B. De Mille. In his 1923 film *The Ten Commandments*, worshippers reveled around the golden calf while Moses sought God on the high mountaintop, thus satisfying everybody. Other directors pushed good taste to its limits, particularly in films about liberated youth, a staple of the 1920's. Joan Crawford doing the Charleston in *Our Dancing Daughters* (1928) caught the very essence of exuberant Jazz Age hedonism.

The decade produced some of the funniest comedy scenes ever filmed. Acrobatic Harold Lloyd played a youthful Everyman who was constantly tripping up, but whose luck always carried the day. Charlie Chaplin won immortality as the soft-hearted little tramp. In movie after movie his gallantries toward the leading lady were thwarted by comic circumstance. Then there was the deadpan Buster Keaton, who battled technology at every turn. In *The General* (1926) Keaton captured a

*Charlie Chaplin's little tramp (right)
displayed a ragged elegance in* The Gold
Rush *(1925), while
rescue dog Rin-Tin-Tin
was voted the
nation's favorite
star in 1926.*

RIN-TIN-TIN

runaway train and won the girl of his dreams almost in spite of himself.

Westerns galloped to new heights with a fresh crop of heroes who rode the range in the name of truth and justice. Such he-men as Tom Mix, Hoot Gibson, and Buck Jones thrilled the hearts of young boys. Adults, meantime, had their passions stirred by romantic dramas such as *Flesh and the Devil* (1927), in which Greta Garbo rocketed to stardom opposite John Gilbert. Or they delighted in the provocative ways of the impish Clara Bow, dubbed the "It" girl in 1926. ("It" was sex appeal leavened with nonchalance.)

Everything changed in 1927, when sound came to the movies. "Wait a minute, you ain't heard nothin' yet," exclaimed Al Jolson in *The Jazz Singer*, and the Hollywood heavens shook. Clara Bow, it turned out, spoke with an accent few found pleasing. John Gilbert's flutelike tenor voice seemed positively unnatural for the romantic hero his fans knew. The careers of Vilma Banky, Pola Negri, and Norma Talmadge went into permanent eclipse. Yet, other stars gained. Despite her foreign accent, Garbo flourished as never before. So did a mouse called Mickey, who tootled his way into American hearts when Walt Disney put a sound track on an animated cartoon called *Steamboat Willie* in 1928.

*Gloria Swanson portrayed
a modern woman in the
silent melodrama* Prodigal
Daughters *(1923).*

▼ *This low-tech
contraption filmed
football action in* Brown
of Harvard *(1926).*

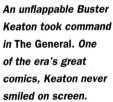

*An unflappable Buster
Keaton took command
in* The General. *One
of the era's great
comics, Keaton never
smiled on screen.*

*Clad in a color
later reserved
for villains,
good guy Hoot
Gibson could
shoot in any
direction.*

RADIO NETWORKS THE NATION

Born in a cacophony of static and squawks, radio matured into a clear-voiced adult that beamed news, comedy, music, sports, and, of course, commercials. Americans were all ears.

▼ **In the first scheduled commercial broadcast, an announcer at KDKA relays the news of Warren G. Harding's election as president.**

The airwaves carried crooner Rudy Vallee to stardom.

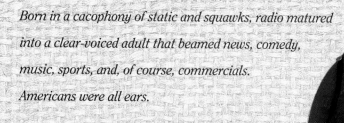

▶ *An early classic, this 1923 Atwater Kent Model II receiver has a horn-of-plenty speaker and four tubes. It was battery-powered.*

wo banjo players plunked away, filling the air time between news reports. It was November 2, 1920, Election Day, and radio station KDKA, of Pittsburgh, Pennsylvania, had turned on its new transmitter to give the election returns. No other signals disturbed the airwaves. Commercial broadcasting, and with it a new age of mass communication, was making its solitary debut.

For 10 months KDKA was alone on the air. Then everywhere other stations sprouted. In Chicago a stockyard applied for a license, in Los Angeles a laundry. In 1922 there were 30 stations; a year later, more than 550, all broadcasting on the same two frequencies. Only low transmitter wattage, and the long distance between stations, kept broadcasters from garbling one another.

As stations proliferated, so did listeners. Thousands of amateur radio buffs built their own primitive receivers, using a fragment of germanium crystal, coiled copper wire, and headphones. Placing the headphones in a soup bowl created a loudspeaker effect, which allowed the whole family to listen in, but reception was far better on a factory-made set. By mid-decade Americans were buying brand name radios, such as Westinghouse and Atwater Kent, at the rate of 1.5 million a year. Sales in 1925 amounted to a staggering $400 million, with some 50 million listeners tuning in.

Many manufacturers also owned stations. KDKA, for example, was founded by Westinghouse, which hoped to lure potential customers into

On the Scene With McNamee

Almost everyone knew the voice of Graham McNamee (right). A young concert baritone and semipro ballplayer, McNamee wandered into New York's WEAF one day and ended up as the decade's most popular announcer. Besides sports, McNamee sometimes broadcast the news: he reported the 1924 Republican convention and Lindbergh's triumphant return from Paris, in 1927. The secret of his success, he said, was to make each listener "feel that he or she is there with you in the press stand, watching the pop bottles thrown into the air; Gloria Swanson arriving in her new ermine coat; McGraw in his dugout . . . giving signals."

purchasing its radios. But another source of revenue soon took command: paid commercials. Not everyone approved of the invasion by hucksters of the new medium. As early as 1922 Commerce Secretary Herbert Hoover, charged with the regulation of broadcasting, worried that radio would "be drowned in advertising chatter." He might just as well have saved his breath.

Before long, advertisers were not only buying air time, they were creating their own radio programs. The Ipana Troubadours serenaded toothpaste; the Cliquot Club Eskimos, soda pop; the A&P Gypsies, groceries. In 1928 the American Tobacco Company's flamboyant president, George Washington Hill, poured his advertising money into a broadcast campaign for Lucky Strike cigarettes, suggesting to women that they smoke to stay svelte. "Reach for a Lucky Instead of a Sweet," the slogan advised. Sales of Luckies jumped nearly 50 percent.

Comics, Crooners, and Competing Networks

For Americans everywhere, radio opened up an ether-borne treasure chest of comedy, drama, information, and wonder. As early as 1921 a listener within receiving range could catch stock market reports, newscasts, weather reports, and the World Series. The next year brought the New York Philharmonic's first broadcast. A pantheon of invisible idols took shape in the nation's living rooms. Graham McNamee, the first announcer to name himself on the air, received 50,000 fan letters in a year. A machine-gun speaking style (217 words a minute) won celebrity for newscaster Floyd Gibbons. There was newfound fame for Broadway transplants like the cowboy-philosopher Will Rogers and the vaudeville comic Ed Wynn. Working in an empty studio disconcerted Wynn, however.

One of the first studio audiences, a group of scrubwomen and others, was assembled to laugh at his jokes.

Some of radio's biggest stars came from nowhere. Women seemed to melt at the nasal greeting, "Heigh-ho, everybody!" of a hitherto obscure New England bandleader named Rudy Vallee, who dubbed himself the Vagabond Lover. Two struggling performers from Chicago renamed their blackface act *Amos 'n' Andy* and, playing all the parts themselves, created a hit for Pepsodent, even though the show's portrayal of blacks would be unacceptable today.

By the decade's end every third household in America boasted a radio, and the industry's revenues were edging up toward $1 billion. The dominant figure was David Sarnoff, who in 1926 had created the National Broadcasting Company (NBC). Sarnoff's radio experience went back to 1912, when, as a 21-year-old Marconi Wireless operator, he picked up distress signals from the S.S. *Titanic* and relayed the news of her sinking to a horrified nation. Now, with NBC, he set an industry pattern by using leased transcontinental telephone circuits to link affiliated local stations.

Within months competition arose from the 27-year-old son of a cigar manufacturer, William S. Paley. Taking over a nearly bankrupt chain of 16 radio stations, Paley launched the Columbia Broadcasting System (CBS). In two years CBS had 70 affiliates to NBC's 75. The ensuing battle for America's ears (and eyes) would last through the century.

In a trick photograph, radio comics Freeman Gosden and Charles Correll confer with their famous on-air characters, Amos and Andy.

Ed Wynn, dolled up for a radio audience that could never see him, wears his trademark vaudeville striped blazer.

CAN I HELP YOU?

ON THE ROAD

Nearly 23 million automobiles had swarmed onto America's roadways by 1929. With them came gas stations, trailer parks, road signs, traffic jams, and the first links in a national highway system.

It did not take a crystal ball to see that the nation was hooked on cars. In 1909 the United States produced 828,000 horse-drawn carriages and 123,900 automobiles; by 1929 the figures were 4,000 carriages and more than 4 million cars. "Why on earth do you need to know what's changing this country?" snapped one Midwesterner. "I can tell you what's happening in just four letters: A-U-T-O!" Every family that could afford a car bought one, and many families that could not. Explained one motorist, who owned a car but no indoor plumbing: "Why, you can't go to town in a bathtub!"

The point was to get moving — to town or any other place that was somewhere else. Farmers sped to market, city folk explored the countryside, vacationing factory workers took their families on week-long auto safaris to national parks and forests. Sunday driving became a national pastime, even for churchgoers. For young lovers, cars offered round-trip tickets to romance, far from the prying eyes of family and neighbors.

As the automobile worked its way into the fabric of American life, scores of new models came onto the market to fit every taste and budget. While only the very rich could summon up the $7,000 it took to buy a sporty Pierce-Arrow, almost any middle-class family could afford a $700 Chevrolet. The Model T Ford, which stayed in production until 1927, cost as little as $290, or only $5 a week on the installment plan. The price went up to $495 for the Model A, which replaced it, but the new Ford offered such state-of-the-art improvements as safety glass windshields, hydraulic shock absorbers, simpler gears, and self-starting ignitions. Who could resist?

A souvenir postcard (top) shows how a parked car could be as much fun as a moving one — particularly compared with the pace of Sunday traffic in St. Louis, Missouri (left).

Motorists enjoy a car-side picnic at Franconia Notch, New Hampshire, a canyon in the White Mountain region.

nificent hodgepodge of roadside eateries appeared: wigwams, pagodas, giant milk bottles, miniature Mount Vernons serving ice cream and hot dogs. Even more important, the ease of auto transport began to change living patterns. Suburbs rolled out from the city limits, with Tudor cottages, Italian villas, and Spanish-style bungalows replacing what were once hayfields and apple orchards.

As Americans took to life on the road, they learned how to travel with all the comforts of home. The "autocamping" craze began when wealthy auto buffs built "house cars" fitted with beds, kitchens, and roof decks. Soon middle-income enthusiasts were adapting old auto chassis for mobile living. At first the "tin canners" would pitch their tents in any nearby field. But enterprising businessmen began constructing roadside tourist cabins. Then in California, in 1926, innkeeper Arthur Heineman opened the first motel, a term he coined because he could not fit the words *Milestone Motor Hotel* on his entrance sign. The age of the automobile had clearly arrived.

The newest look in urban transit was the Checker cab, which made its debut in 1922 when the Checker Motors Corporation of Chicago began manufacturing its own vehicles. Soon Checker franchise drivers were carrying riders in cities across America.

Whatever the vehicle, the decade's motorist set out with a sense of adventure. Some 3 million miles of roadway crisscrossed the nation in 1920, most of it consisting of unpaved rural lanes intended for horses. Road signs, when present, tended to be an unreadable confusion of crude arrows, skulls and crossbones, and other strange icons. Some early routes were marked by daubs of colored paint on tree trunks and fence posts, a system that broke down entirely in the treeless, open spaces of the West.

Improvement came quickly, however. The world's first three-color traffic light went up in Detroit, in 1919. State highway departments began laying down asphalt, and with the Federal Highway Act of 1921, the federal government stepped in as well. New York's Bronx River Parkway, the first limited-access auto route, opened in 1923, and the first cloverleaf interchange, at Woodbridge, New Jersey, opened in 1929. By the decade's end the government was building 10,000 miles of paved highway each year.

The auto wrought other transformations on the landscape. Filling stations sprang up on vacant lots. Giant billboards crowded the highway panorama. A mag-

Workmen place road markers on the 3,389-mile-long Lincoln Highway, the country's first coast-to-coast auto route, begun in 1914 with funds from the fledgling auto industry.

Filling stations doubled as grocery stores, sandwich shops, or, as here in upstate New York, a post office.

1906 ◆ Stanley Steamer
The Stanley twins made their first steam-driven vehicle in 1897, and the last Stanley appeared in 1924, when gasoline-powered cars dominated.

FOR THE LOVE OF CARS

There came panting and chugging up that flat thoroughfare a thing . . . vaguely like a topless surrey, but cumbrous with unwholesome excrescences fore and aft, while underneath were spinning leather belts and something that whirred and howled and seemed to stagger. . . . 'Git a hoss!' the children shrieked, and gruffer voices joined them. 'Git a hoss! Git a hoss! Git a *hoss!* '" Thus, in *The Magnificent Ambersons*, did the American novelist Booth Tarkington describe the coming of the automobile to an Indiana town. Since those days at about the turn of the century, Tarkington's mechanical monster has become part of the American way, and it has changed our daily lives, our cities, our countryside. For all of this — or despite it — America remains a nation of car lovers, perhaps because the car still represents personal freedom in a world that seems increasingly constricting. On these two pages, a few of the cars we have loved sit for portraits.

1909 ◆ Waverly Electric
Despite running cleanly, quietly, and cheaply, electric cars could not go fast enough, nor far enough between recharges, to suit America's taste.

1927 ◆ Ford Model T Runabout
This sporty roadster appeared just before Chevrolet first topped Ford in annual car sales. Henry Ford responded by building the Model A.

1929 ◆ Duesenberg Dual Cowl Phaeton
The rich and famous owned Indiana-built Duesenbergs. Phaeton meant 4 doors, 2 cross seats, and a top that folded back.

1933 ◆ Packard Sport Phaeton Dietrich
Famous designer Ray Dietrich had a hand in custom-styling this majestic touring car.

1948 ◆ Studebaker Starlight
"First by far with a postwar car!" Studebaker crowed about its new look.

1930 ◆ Ford Model A
Sturdily built, and under $500, it sold 1.3 million in 1930, but the Depression cut sales by half in 1931.

1951 ◆ Mercury Station Wagon
"Woodies," with real wood paneling, were popular before and after World War II.

1956 ◆ Lincoln Continental Mark II
At nearly $10,000, it cost too much for most Americans, but almost everyone agreed it was a classy classic.

1956 ◆ Ford Thunderbird Convertible Coupe
Ford made fewer than 16,000 of these T-Birds in 1956. Ageless good looks have made them collectors' pets.

1957 ◆ Volkswagen Beetle
Also known as the Bug, the German gem began winning America with a 1949 price of $1,280.

1957 ◆ Chevrolet Corvette
Introduced in 1953, 'Vette sports cars, with fiberglass bodies, wowed car lovers, especially the elegant 1956 and 1957 models.

1978 ◆ Datsun 280Z
Then known widely as Datsun, the Japanese carmaker Nissan won praise for these Z-cars of 1970–78.

1958 ◆ Cadillac Coupe
Tail fins seemed to have a life of their own on General Motors' top-of-the-line cars, Cadillacs, in the mid-1950's.

1967 ◆ Oldsmobile Toronado
It reprised the 1966 model's front-wheel drive, great handling, and fastback styling.

1992 ◆ Plymouth Voyager AWD
Like their cousins the truck-cars (right), roomy, boxy vans caught on with Americans starting in the 1980's.

1993 ◆ Ford Bronco
Trucklike personal vehicles were hot sellers in the 1990's, reflecting perhaps a nostalgia for rugged simplicity.

WRITERS WHO DAZZLED AND DARED

Some lived in Paris in self-imposed exile. Others stuck closer to their American roots. Literary rebels, they brandished their pens with such exuberance and style that they created a new era in American letters.

Critic Van Wyck Brooks, harking back to the generation that came of age in the 1920's, described it as "the one in which everyone hated, often without visible reason, the town in which he was born." Brooks meant, of course, his fellow writers and intellectuals — rebellious souls for whom all gods were dead, all causes lost, and who found their native soil oppressively confining. Lashing out against everything from Puritan morals to cultural boorishness to the consumer economy, they told the truth as they saw it, whatever the cost. Like true anarchists, they dropped a bomb of prose so brilliant and new on the reading public that they brought America to the forefront of the international literary scene.

Some writers expressed their disenchantment by looking American society squarely in the face and calling it deficient. Sinclair Lewis burst into prominence with his novel *Main Street* (1920), in which he attempted to exorcise his childhood demons by building in words a Midwestern town just like the one where he grew up. In a clear, unromantic, often biting voice, Lewis took aim at the narrow smugness of small-town life — "the village virus," as he termed it. Two years later he attacked the decade's business ethic with *Babbitt*, a novel about a bumptious Midwestern realtor who represented most of what Lewis found objectionable about America.

Astonishingly, both books were runaway best-sellers: popular tastes at the time leaned more often to Western adventure or sugary romance novels. But publishing was

Ernest Hemingway poses with a marlin he caught off Key West in 1929. In approach and subject, his lean writing stressed courage and manly skill.

Tennis-playing dramatist Eugene O'Neill drapes an arm around daughter Oona, the future Mrs. Charlie Chaplin.

The Fabulous Fitzgeralds

No writer cut such a shimmering swath through the 1920's as F. Scott Fitzgerald. With his pretty wife, Zelda, the very model of a Jazz Age flapper, he seemed to personify the era's heedless energy and romance. He set the tone with his first novel, *This Side of Paradise* (1920), a tale of driven, party-going youth in Princeton and New York City. Then he and Zelda set out to live like his characters. They supped in nightclubs, danced on tabletops, splashed about in a fountain in front of New York's Plaza Hotel, rode down Fifth Avenue on the roof of a taxi. Wherever they went, they courted attention.

To pay for these high jinks, Scott wrote dozens of magazine stories and one of the decade's most highly praised novels, *The Great Gatsby* (1925), about a Long Island bootlegger. But as time went on, the fun turned sour. The money ran out, Fitzgerald's drinking began to get out of control, and Zelda, always unstable, suffered a severe nervous breakdown.

Sinclair Lewis

one of the decade's growth industries, with readership expanding and titles accelerating off the presses. American publishers brought out 10,187 new titles in 1929, nearly double the number a decade earlier. There was room for every type of work, no matter how difficult, contrary, or experimental.

Much of what was new and exciting emerged from the bohemian byways of New York City's Greenwich Village. Playwright Eugene O'Neill went there to find himself. Son of a prominent actor, O'Neill by age 24 had dropped out of Princeton, gone to sea as a deckhand, sold sewing machines, prospected for gold, reported for a newspaper, been married and divorced. Washing up in the Village, he rubbed shoulders with thieves, hustlers, radicals, feminists, artists. And he began writing plays: *Anna Christie* (1921), *Desire Under the Elms* (1924), *Strange Interlude* (1928), and some 40 others, injecting a note of stark, brooding realism that utterly transformed the American theater.

New York attracted scores of other young writers eager to stretch their talents. John Dos Passos looked in but quickly left; his experimental *Manhattan Transfer* (1925) poured such contempt upon what he saw that one critic likened the book to "an explosion in a cesspool." But most writers settled in quite happily. Edna St. Vincent Millay, a Greenwich Village resident, thrived on the area's heady ideas and easygoing ways: "My candle burns at both ends;/ It will not last the night;/ But, ah, my foes, and, oh, my friends —/ It gives a lovely light!" Her verses caught on, and she became that rare phenomenon, a serious poet whose books made the best-seller lists.

Edna St. Vincent Millay

To those writers who felt they could remain in America not a moment longer, escape to foreign lands was the only solution. So escape they did: to Paris, London, the Riviera. Free-flowing liquor, cheap living, and more sophistication lured some of the most talented American-born writers of the 20th century. F. Scott Fitzgerald (see box at left) breezed through France. T. S. Eliot settled in England to forge a brilliant new idiom of poetic expression. Poet Ezra Pound moved to Italy, where he savaged modern life ("a botched civilization") in dense, cryptic verse that challenged traditional perceptions.

The brightest beacon was Paris, which enjoyed a boom of small publishing houses, such as Black Sun Press, and provocative literary magazines, such as *transatlantic review*. Newly arrived writers would head for the Café Dôme or the Dingo bar to see and be seen. They might have caught up on the latest books and gossip at Shakespeare and Company, a cozy bookstore run by Sylvia Beach, daughter of a Baltimore clergyman. Most assuredly they made their way to the Left Bank apartment of the formidable Gertrude Stein, a California intellectual and writer who had established herself in Paris before the war and who ran a perpetual salon for the up-and-comers.

Beyond the gossip and aperitifs there was serious work to be done: new styles to be tested, new truths to be told. Urged on by friends, Ernest Hemingway quit his job as a journalist and devoted himself entirely to fiction. The result was his first novel, *The Sun Also Rises* (1926), which told of disillusioned American expatriates (much like the author and his pals) on a trip to Spain. Between the lines ran an undercurrent of discontent and shattered dreams. *A Farewell to Arms* (1929) followed next and then other novels and stories, all delivered in taut, stripped-down prose, which became the hallmark for a new kind of tough-guy American literature. It proclaimed in no uncertain terms that Hemingway, and his fellow American writers both abroad and at home, were a force to be reckoned with.

The Algonquin Round Table

Not all American writers of the 1920's worked in Village garrets or Paris cafés. In Manhattan a group of wits enlivened the dining room of the Algonquin, a midtown hotel whose Round Table became a home away from home for a glittering set of literary luminaries. Their humor relied largely on rapid-fire delivery of the barbed insult. Dorothy Parker, a magazine editor and composer of light verse (e.g., "Men seldom make passes / At girls who wear glasses"), was a master. Nor were the others far behind.

This Al Hirschfeld cartoon of the Round Table shows (clockwise from bottom left) Parker, humorist Robert Benchley, journalist Alexander Woollcott, columnist Heywood Broun, playwright Marc Connelly, columnist Franklin P. Adams, novelist Edna Ferber, and playwrights George S. Kaufman and Robert Sherwood. At the smaller table (left rear) sit Broadway stars Alfred Lunt and Lynn Fontanne with *Vanity Fair* editor Frank Crowninshield hovering paternally nearby.

T. S. Eliot moved to London in 1914 and wrote some of the century's most acclaimed poems in the English language, including "The Waste Land" (1922). He became a British subject in 1927. Here he explains some fine points of literary theory.

SCIENCE CAPTURES THE PUBLIC'S FANCY

From archeology to zoology, from outer space to the depths of the human psyche, a flood of astonishing discoveries shed light on some ancient mysteries while promising a better life for everyone.

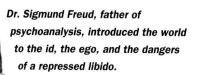

Dr. Sigmund Freud, father of psychoanalysis, introduced the world to the id, the ego, and the dangers of a repressed libido.

A rtificial silk. A cure for tetanus. Anti-knock gasoline. A new hormone isolated. A giant star measured, and the structure of atoms laid bare to mathematical scrutiny. Scarcely a week went by that the newspapers failed to announce some startling achievement in science or technology. Men with slide rules and laboratory coats became celebrities. As one editorialist noted, the words *science teaches us* were enough to settle any argument.

No area held such a grip on the public's attention as the rapidly developing field of psychology. With its batteries of tests and personality charts, psychology seemed capable of solving any human problem, from crime to divorce to early morning blues. Businesses hired psychologists to run their personnel departments. Schools brought in testing agencies to determine students' IQ's (intelligence quotients). Parents debated the values of nature versus nurture and raised their children according to the precepts of Dr. John B. Watson's book *Behaviorism*. Thousands of anguished men and women, turning for help to psychiatry, clocked countless hours attempting to probe their unconscious minds.

Sex became a favorite topic of polite conversation, prompted in part by the writings of Sigmund Freud. When the Viennese doctor traced the cause of certain mental illnesses to sexual repression, an eager public took this finding as an excuse for almost anything. Taboos came crashing down in the name of scientific enlightenment — much to the dismay of churchmen, educators, and many others. So heated was the sexual debate that Robert Benchley, then a drama critic at *Life,* wrote in exasperation: "Sex as a theatrical property is as tiresome as the Old Mortgage. . . . I am sick of rebellious youth and I'm

George Washington Carver, to help black farmers in the South, discovered how to make nearly 300 products from peanuts, including axle grease and shaving lotion.

After the worldwide 1918–19 flu epidemic took half a million American lives, schoolchildren learned lessons like this one in the importance of preventive medicine.

The Wizard Who Folded Space

W hen Albert Einstein visited the United States in 1921, he was already a world celebrity. Two years earlier, astronomical observations had confirmed his general theory of relativity, which said that space is curved. The concept was beyond most news reporters, who mobbed his stateroom to ask him about everything else — from world politics to his thoughts on the New York City skyline to when the universe would end.

The cover of a 1928 Tom Swift novel envisions the birth of color television.

Scottish inventor J. L. Baird (left) displays his TV transmitter and the wooden dummy that was his star, while Vladimir Zworykin (right) shows his new cathode ray tube.

sick of Victorian parents and I don't care if all the little girls in all sections of the United States get ruined. . . . "

Laboratories discovered or produced a chestful of wondrous cures and treatments: the hormone insulin, used to control diabetes; vaccines against tetanus, whooping cough, and tuberculosis; vitamins B_1, which prevents beriberi, and C, the antiscurvy agent. A generation of youngsters dutifully choked down spoonfuls of cod-liver oil, which contains rickets-preventing vitamin D. Researchers isolated the streptococcus bacteria, the cause of the killer disease scarlet fever. In 1928 a British bacteriologist, Alexander Fleming, discovered penicillin, the first antibiotic. That same year Harvard's Philip Drinker devised his respirator, the iron lung, and George Papanicolaou invented the Pap test for detecting cervical and uterine cancer.

The research departments of the nation's mighty business corporations poured out a flood of inventions, swelling the number of patent applications during the 1920's to more than 800,000. Among the new products were hand-held cameras, Kodak film, the Geiger counter, paint sprays, cigarette lighters, antifreeze, electric shavers, aluminum pots and pans, such plastics as vinyl and acetate, magnetic tape, hybrid corn, and the tommy gun.

Some achievements laid the groundwork for future marvels. For more than 40 years, inventors had been searching for ways to transmit moving images over the airwaves. Then in 1926 a Scottish engineer, John Logie Baird, displayed the world's first television picture, a fuzzy image of a ventriloquist's dummy named Bill. Baird's equipment was crude, but a better system was at hand, based on Vladimir K. Zworykin's cathode ray iconoscope, the forerunner of modern TV technology.

Some branches of science pushed beyond the boundaries of earth itself. In Auburn, Massachusetts, physicist Robert H. Goddard sent the first liquid-fueled rocket on a short flight in 1926, opening the way to space travel for future generations. Meanwhile, a 100-inch reflecting telescope, then the world's largest, went into operation at California's Mount Wilson Observatory. New stars came into view, and new galaxies were mapped. Astronomer Sir Arthur Eddington delved into the birth of stars, and America's E. P. Hubble found evidence that the universe was expanding outward. This information, coupled with the startling theories of a shy shaggy-locked physicist named Albert Einstein (who said that matter was energy and that space and time were both relative to how you viewed them), was heady material indeed. But to even the most befuddled observer, it was obvious that science had no limits.

Robert H. Goddard shows off his liquid-fueled rocket. When it was launched in March of 1926, it covered a distance of 184 feet at an average 60 m.p.h.

The Treasure Trove of Tutankhamen

For years archeologists had been frustrated in their search for treasures from the royal tombs of ancient Egyptian pharaohs. Most concluded that grave robbers had long since made off with anything of value. Howard Carter, an Englishman with little formal education, was an exception. Generously financed by the earl of Carnarvon, Carter spent 10 years digging in and around the Valley of the Kings, hoping to find something.

In October of 1922 Carnarvon reluctantly agreed to fund one more season. A month later Carter opened the 3,200-year-old tomb of the boy-pharaoh Tutankhamen. It was nearly intact: "Details of the room within emerged slowly from the mist, strange animals, statues, and gold — everywhere the glint of gold."

The world's press hailed the achievement, and by 1924, when Carter uncovered the polished funerary mask at left, King Tut had become a household name.

THE GREAT PROSPERITY ENGINE

Most Americans, seeing corporate profits skyrocket and personal incomes rise, came to think that business could sustain an expanding prosperity and provide everyone with a steadily increasing share of the wealth.

Behind all the hoopla and razzmatazz of post–World War I America lay a single supremely vital fact: never before had the country seemed so prosperous. After a sharp stumble in 1920–21 (a 24 percent drop in industrial output and an unemployment rate that reached nearly 12 percent), the economy took off. Factories hummed, jobs multiplied, and a seemingly endless gusher of consumer products poured out. In 1923 the nation's total output of goods and services surged ahead by an extraordinary 14 percent. The momentum continued, with a few minor pauses, until 1929. It was the swiftest expansion of national wealth that anyone could remember. When President Coolidge told a group of newspaper editors that "the chief business of the American people is business," most Americans wholeheartedly agreed.

Leading the parade was the auto industry. By 1926 a Model T Ford was rolling off the assembly line every 10 seconds of the working day. General Motors (GM) was catching up fast, with Chrysler not far behind. And that was only half the story, for the brisk pace of auto production spurred business in a score of related industries. Steel for bodies and frames, rubber for tires, plate glass for windshields — all were in greater demand. And the oil companies, once mainly purveyors of kerosene, began pumping out a new leaded gasoline said to quiet engine knock.

At the same time, giant utility companies were taking shape to supply the needs of manufacturers and to light the lamps and run the household gadgets of private consumers. Cheap electric power sparked further demand. So fierce was the appetite for Hoover vacuum cleaners that the company could not keep up. A specialist was brought in to streamline production, and output shot up to 1,000 new Hoovers a day.

Scientific Approaches, Sacred Missions

Specialists from many fields contributed to the boost in productivity. Efficiency experts descended, stopwatches in hand, to conduct time and motion studies in the nation's factories. Engineers refined product designs and assembly line techniques. New principles of scientific management emerged, and to learn about them, would-be executives enrolled in business schools. Something must have sunk in, for corporate profits spurted ahead during the decade by 62 percent. America's businessmen came to see themselves as national heroes, charged with a sacred mission to do good by doing well. "The man who builds a factory builds a temple," Coolidge declared, for that man would thereby create jobs and increase the general welfare.

Man and machine are one in Lewis Hine's 1920 photo of a mechanic adjusting the steam pump in an electric-power house.

In the early 1920's Raymond Hood won out over 300 architects with his soaring Neo-Gothic design for the 33-story Chicago Tribune building.

Skilled workers, like these at the Yale & Towne Manufacturing Company, saw their real wages increase about 50 percent during the decade.

Spurred by copywriters like Bruce Barton (seen here with his wife, Esther) and by the growth of radio and national magazines, advertising expenditures leapt from $400 million in 1917 to $2.6 billion in 1929.

No group spread the gospel of material well-being with more unabashed vigor than advertisers. On roadside billboards, in magazines and newspapers, over the radio, in the morning mail — everywhere Americans looked or listened they were told to buy, and buy some more. Indeed, it was their duty to spend, they were told, and if they had to work a little harder to earn more dollars, all the better. "Looking at the ads makes me think I've GOT to succeed," declared a householder named Andy Consumer in a high-pressured magazine sales pitch that trumpeted the virtues of the advertising industry itself.

The industry had its own highly vocal prophet, Bruce Barton, who claimed his inspiration came from the very highest source. In *The Man Nobody Knows*, a best-seller in 1925 and 1926, Barton declared that the world's first marketing genius was none other than Jesus Christ. "He picked twelve men from the bottom ranks of business and forged them into an organization that conquered the world," the author wrote, and he went on to add that Christ's parables were "the most powerful advertisements of all time. . . ." That the decade's hucksterism tended to aim at such non-Christian traits as greed, snobbery, and fear seemed not to matter. An ad for a popular mouthwash asked, "Often a bridesmaid but never a bride?" then suggested that perhaps the problem was halitosis. The point was to sell.

If the customer lacked the ready cash for a new car or a washing machine, ads encouraged him to buy on the installment plan. Before World War I, most people's use of credit began and ended with a home mortgage. Ten years after the war, credit was the American way to buy cars. Credit also propelled a boom in construction, which began in the decade's early years. Investment in new buildings, by both private and public sectors, nearly doubled,

By 1924, when this photograph was taken, huge generators like this one were powering the electrification of America.

reaching $16 billion in 1927 — a level that would not be equaled until 1941.

Cities took on a new, more jagged profile as skyscrapers transformed the business centers. In Chicago, construction of the Neo-Gothic Tribune Tower, 33 stories high, began in 1923. Other corporate spires soon followed — in Pittsburgh, Omaha, Memphis — culminating, in 1930, in New York's magnificent Art Deco Chrysler Building. The piercing, energetic thrust of these mighty buildings seemed to echo the nation's highest aspirations and to promise that the good times would last forever. When, in 1928, Herbert Hoover declared that "we in America are nearer to the final triumph over poverty than ever before in the history of any land," the president was only repeating what many people throughout the world already believed.

◄

A delegation of visitors inspects the long line of cars rolling off the Ford assembly lines in Kearny, New Jersey.

Proud People That Good Times Forgot

In 1923 this young coal miner in Pennsylvania lived and worked under miserable, unsafe conditions for very little pay.

If they could, farmers — whether using mule or steam or gas power to harvest wheat — tried to make up for falling prices by producing more, which only served to make matters worse. ▼

The prosperity of the 1920's barely touched some Americans. Costly new machinery produced more than debt-ridden farmers could sell profitably; technology permitted factory and mine owners to hire fewer workers.

A Nebraska farmer, gazing out on rolling acres of ripening wheat, saw nothing but trouble. Each year his land yielded its bounty in greater abundance. But prices were dropping, and each year crops brought in less money. During World War I, like so many other farmers across the nation, he had taken out a mortgage in order to extend his holdings and to buy the tractor and other equipment that made his record harvest possible. Now he couldn't meet his mortgage payments, and he had no idea where to find the cash.

The farmer was not alone in his misfortune. While much of the nation was enjoying an affluence it had scarcely dreamed possible, vast numbers of Americans found they had been left behind. In the proud old river towns of New England, antiquated shoe factories and textile mills were closing down. Coal mining, shipbuilding, lumbering, railroads, the merchant marine — the building blocks of the old prewar economy — were also in trouble.

Agriculture had been by far the nation's largest business at the decade's start, providing occupation for one-

third of its citizens. The United States produced more than half the world's cotton, two-thirds of its corn, and huge quantities of other farm goods, including tobacco. But even as the decade's rich harvests filled storehouses to overflowing, demand was falling. Prohibition cut the market for barley nearly in half. Then the government, to shield domestic producers, raised stiff tariffs against foreign manufactured goods. Other countries naturally responded with tariffs of their own. Since sales abroad were an important source of farm revenue, the vise merely tightened. Their markets cut off, thousands of farmers were driven out of business. In 1925 the number of farm bankruptcies totaled 8,000. By the decade's end some 1.5 million farmers had left the countryside to look for work in the cities and towns.

The Struggle for a Decent Living

Nowhere was the squeeze more painful than in the rural South. Crops like cotton and tobacco were raised mostly by tenant farmers and sharecroppers, the latter of whom had to turn the bulk of their harvest over to the landowners. Often malnourished, always in debt, they fled the land in droves. Some found employment in the region's growing mill towns, which were taking over from those of New England as the nation's main textile producers.

But life as a wage earner in the mills was often no better. Revenues were falling in textiles as well; so to cut costs and maintain profits, the mill owners stretched shifts to 12 hours a day, 6 days a week. Weekly paychecks dwindled, by 1928, to as low as $18 for adult males, while women worked at half pay, and children for even less.

Low wages, long hours, and deplorable working conditions set off a ground swell of labor unrest. The machinery of

In the 1920's John L. Lewis, dynamic head of the UMW, survived a series of cruel setbacks for labor.

◄

Although 2 million additional women joined the work force over the decade, they took mainly low-income jobs that men did not want, becoming teachers, nurses, office clerks, and garment workers, like those pictured at left.

Mine owners often sought, and got, court injunctions against bringing food to striking coal miners. This well-stocked truck, near Canton, Ohio, reached hungry strikers.

mass production was rapidly replacing workers, many of whom could not find other full-time employment. In 1920 strife broke out in the coal mines of Pennsylvania and West Virginia. The fiery, bushy-browed John L. Lewis, newly elected president of the United Mine Workers (UMW), set out to organize the work force at Matewan, West Virginia, where a day's labor in the coal mines paid as little as $2. The mine owners brought in "detectives," who began evicting union sympathizers from company housing. Violence spread throughout the state, with pitched battles between gun-toting miners and company guards. Eventually the National Guard restored order. But thousands of miners lost their jobs. And the UMW lost membership and prestige that it would not regain until well into the next decade.

In most of the nation's older industries, labor suffered similar reverses. Court injunctions ended hundreds of strikes; even armed intervention became common. When garment workers in New York City walked off the job and onto the picket lines in 1926, the police arrested 8,000 of them. In 1929 blood flowed in Gastonia, North Carolina, where police fired on picket lines. The strike leaders were charged with conspiracy and murder.

In an era characterized by optimism and increased material well-being, such turmoil hardly seems possible. But while most Americans profited as the economy boomed — from the pre–World War I years to 1928, the number of persons reporting assets of over $1 million rose from 7,000 to 35,000 — others labored just to maintain a decent standard of living.

AND THEN CAME THE CRASH

In a decade of easy credit, frantic speculation, and rising fortunes, millions of Americans grabbed at almost any opportunity to win their pot of gold. It would prove shockingly illusory for most of them.

The Election of 1928

When Herbert Clark Hoover rose to deliver his inaugural address, in March 1929 (above), he had achieved a solid victory over his Democratic opponent, Alfred E. Smith. The differences between the presidential candidates could not have been more striking. Hoover was a dour Quaker and a public servant who shied away from the campaign trail and abhorred publicity. He had risen from humble beginnings in rural Iowa to become a wealthy mining engineer, and then applied his business skills to the organization of food relief in post–World War I Europe.

Al Smith was a cigar-chomping, backslapping politician. His strong accent ("radd-ee-o" and "horspital") betrayed his origins on New York City's Lower East Side and alarmed many voters who saw cities as hotbeds of modern evils. Most damaging to his presidential aspirations was that he was Catholic. Smith worked hard to assure voters that his religious beliefs in no way influenced his official actions, but the rumor mill spun anyway: If you elect Al Smith, Protestant marriages will be annulled; he'll build a tunnel linking the Vatican to Manhattan.

Unfounded tales of drunken binges, fueled by Smith's anti-Prohibition stance, quashed any hope he had of becoming president. Given the times, though, probably no Democrat could have won. As Will Rogers said, "You can't lick this prosperity thing."

n December of 1919 a dapper, diminutive former bank clerk named Charles A. Ponzi opened the Securities and Exchange Company in Boston's financial district. Ponzi promised that by exploiting inequalities in foreign exchange markets, he would double his customers' investments every 90 days.

It sounded too good to be true. But Ponzi paid out as promised; by midsummer of 1920 he was taking in $1 million a week, and had become something of a national hero. But suddenly his bubble burst. The *Boston Post* reported that Ponzi was a convicted forger. What is more, his business had been a total scam: he was simply paying off old customers with the money that flowed in from new ones. Ponzi was sent to jail. And for each customer who got rich, many more went broke.

Once out of jail, Ponzi turned up in Florida in 1925, at the height of a land boom seemingly tailor-made for him: both the swindlers and the "suckers" who resold their properties were making lots of money. (The hapless Ponzi was indicted for fraud in less than a year.) Beginning after World War I and continuing at a dizzying pace, developers had bought large stretches of beachfront and palmetto grove, carving out lots and selling them off at enormous profit. Miami's population swelled to 75,000 by 1925, more than doubling in just five years. Here was a place in the sun for all America, the sales pitch proclaimed, and, not incidentally, a great place to invest in real estate.

Americans heeded the call by the tens of thousands, arriving by auto and by railroad to be feted with banquets, bused to a myriad of investment opportunities, and pried loose of their investment dollars. If a buyer found that his investment lay in a swamp or even under water, no matter: he could unload the deed on someone else for double or quadruple the purchase price. Properties that had sold for a few thousand dollars a decade earlier were now fetching as high as $250,000. A lively and profitable market sprang up in slips of paper, called binders, that represented an option to buy a particular tract.

The boom could not last. By early 1926 Florida had more house lots for sale than there were families in Amer-

The Democrats' donkey lacked the kick to help Smith overcome years of boom under the Republicans.

For the staggering fee of $50,000, an aging William Jennings Bryan on a float at Coral Gables promotes Florida living.

ica. Then in mid-September a hurricane devastated much of south Florida. Four hundred people died, as did the dreams of quick riches in real estate.

Speculation Grips Wall Street

Incredible, but often true, tales of Wall Streeters making fast money in the stock market were luring millions of citizens, wealthy and not, to try their luck. The Great Bull Market saw volume on the New York Stock Exchange soar from 227 million shares in 1920 to an unprecedented 920 million in 1928. The volatility of the market gave everyone the chance to win, or lose, big bucks.

The Radio Corporation of America (RCA) launched in 1919, became a speculator's delight. Its stock traded in 1921 for $2.50 a share; by 1927 a share reached $85, and in the next two years, adjusted for stock splits, it rose to an astonishing $573.75. And it wasn't just RCA. The market seemed destined to move in only one direction: up.

Anyone with a few spare dollars could ride the Wall Street bull. Stories about the trained nurse who made $30,000 in the market and the financier's valet who netted a quarter million traveled fast. And if a potential player lacked cash, he could buy on margin, permitting him to pay a small percent of the stock's purchase price. His broker would put up the rest. Buying on margin entailed some risk, for if the

Con man Charles Ponzi cashed in on America's get-rich-quick fantasies, only to die penniless in 1949.

stock's price dropped, the investor could be forced to sell all his holdings at a loss. But risk was the last thing on anyone's mind. When the market suffered a sharp downturn in 1928, it quickly recovered and kept climbing. There were signs of trouble, such as banks closing and factories running at a loss, but almost everyone ignored them.

The top was reached in early September of 1929. Then prices started dropping, picked up speed, and on October 24 — Black Thursday — began a free-fall. At 1:30 P.M. a consortium of worried bankers sent Richard Whitney, an exchange vice president, to the floor with purchase orders totaling $20 million. Cheers went up from the traders. The market steadied.

But on Tuesday, October 29, panic erupted again. Sell orders poured in, many driven by the forced liquidation of margin accounts. More than 16,400,000 shares traded hands, a record that would stand until 1968. The tape ran late, so nobody knew how much money he was losing.

Soon the damage was all too clear. At the day's end, close to $15 billion in market value had simply vanished; by mid-November the figure had risen to $30 billion, and an estimated 3 million people were out of work, versus 700,000 a month earlier. The bull market was over, and with it had crashed the high-flying hopes of an entire decade.

▲ *Early skepticism about the Florida land boom inspired this biting January 16, 1926, cover of* Judge.

▶ *Chalk-wielding stock clerks had trouble keeping up with the record-setting pace in 1929; brokers traded over a billion shares.*

Chapter 4

The Down- and-Up 1930's

On the farms and in the cities, Americans

and their president fight the Great Depression —

and prevail, only to feel the ominous rumblings

of another European war.

Nature added to Depression woes with dust storms like this one in Cimarron County, Oklahoma, 1936.

Hope, humor, and Hoovervilles

Herbert Hoover's State of the Union address in December 1929 described economic woes as merely "a reduction in the consumption of luxuries and semi-necessities by those who have met with losses, and a number of persons thrown temporarily out of work."

▲ **The stock market crash forced all kinds of people into situations they had never before imagined. To draw attention to his plight, a hard-hit businessman offers to sell his luxury automobile to passing pedestrians at a bargain price.**

America's financial community picked itself up from the 1929 crash with the rueful humor of a man recovering from a wild night on the town. The New York Stock Exchange, determined to dispel gloom about the economy, rang in the new year with a whoop and a holler. A brass band played on the trading floor, confetti flew, and brokers jigged and pirouetted between the trading booths. For a while it seemed to have worked: stock prices actually rallied in the first four months of 1930. But in May the stock market began to wobble, and prices broke again, to continue their dismal trend downward.

The rich shrugged off their losses with a well-studied nonchalance. George F. Baker, Jr., chairman of New York's scandal-ridden First National Bank, boasted that he had dropped $15 million. (He was more close-lipped about how,

An Apple a Day . . .

The sudden appearance of apple sellers on urban street corners in the fall of 1930 came about through a brainstorm that typified the go-getting spirit of American business even in a slump. Apple growers in the Northwest had such a bumper crop in 1930 that they had a hard time finding markets. Then an official of the International Apple Shippers' Association came up with the idea of distributing crates of apples on credit to the unemployed for resale.

The association immediately began sending shipments of apples to cities, where eager hordes of poor men gathered at loading docks to pick them up. The campaign even had a slogan — Buy an apple a day and eat the Depression away! — that captured the euphoric hope of the scheme. One day Wall Street brokers got together and bought the entire stock of the peddlers in their area, auctioned it off, and distributed the profit to the peddlers.

But soon the novelty of the idea wore off. Peddlers had to work longer and longer hours to sell a crate, and resorted to price wars to move the product. The wholesalers began to raise prices, and they sorted fewer of the bruised and spoiled apples from the good ones. Peddlers ended up working all day for a few pennies of profit. To add insult to injury, unemployment statistics were lowered when the impoverished peddlers were classified as employed, and President Hoover tried to portray the peddlers as prosperous entrepreneurs, saying, "Many persons left their jobs for the more profitable one of selling apples."

◀

On May 20, 1931, springtime seemed to hold little promise for these unemployed men, among the hundreds who made their home in this bleak Hooverville on Banksville Road in Pittsburgh.

WRAP YOUR TROUBLES IN DREAMS
(And Dream Your Troubles Away)

Words by
TED KOEHLER
and
BILLY MOLL
Music by
HARRY BARRIS

Introduced by
BING CROSBY
"of Three Rhythm Boys"

MADE IN U.S.A.

▲ Tin Pan Alley songsmiths did their best to lift America's spirits with lighthearted tunes offering cheerful homilies, such as this one, published in March of 1931.

a few years earlier, he had netted $22 million in a single day's trading.) The novelist Theodore Dreiser was set back some $75,000, but around the dinner table he would inflate the sum to $300,000, presumably for dramatic effect. When reports began circulating that several bankrupt moneymen had committed suicide, Eddie Cantor — who himself lost a painful $2 million — added a joke to his Broadway routine, in which a hotel reservations clerk asks a guest: "Do you want the room for sleeping or for jumping?" (In fact, the suicide rate stayed level for 1930.)

High-Level Optimism, Mainstream Misery

A number of astute Wall Streeters had foreseen the crash and left the market in time. Bernard Baruch, adviser in financial matters to Presidents Harding and Coolidge, had shifted his assets into bonds, cash, and gold. Similar tactics had saved Joseph P. Kennedy, who remarked, "Only a fool holds out for the top dollar." In fact, Kennedy was among the many bears who made money by reentering the market to take advantage of bargain stock prices.

But the collapse hurt many Americans badly, and the brunt of the disaster fell on those least able to afford it. In the three years following the crash, 9 million savings accounts were wiped out, and people stopped spending. All sorts of businesses — 86,000 of them — unable to sell their products or services, shut their doors. Millions of people were thrown out of work; no one was sure how many, but the total kept rising.

At first the nation responded by denying that anything was really wrong. Billboards proclaimed: "Forward, America! Nothing Can Stop U.S.!" Patriotic Midwesterners sported buttons that read, "I'm sold on America. I won't talk depression." New York's dapper mayor, Jimmy Walker, thought some upbeat Hollywood movies might lift people out of the dumps and prompt them to spend.

Herbert Clark Hoover's unceasingly optimistic pronouncements on the economy inspired a sardonic humor among the poor. Rural folk who had success hunting jackrabbits said they were dining on "Hoover hogs." Beggars with empty pockets pulled them inside out to fly their "Hoover flags." And groups of the homeless lived in makeshift villages dubbed Hoovervilles.

Communities sprang up wherever there were warm, dry spaces to crawl into. People lived in unused pipes stored in pipe yards, in huge ovens at closed steel plants, and in old trolley cars. Squatters in Detroit burrowed into a sandpile, hollowing out their homes and putting in chimneys. The denizens of a St. Louis Hooverville worshiped at a church

In May 1932, 20,000 World War I veterans met in Washington, D.C., and set up camp. Calling themselves the Bonus Expeditionary Force, they vowed to stay until they were advanced a bonus due them in 1945.

Planned in the 1920's, the Empire State Building was to be the very incarnation of American power and wealth. Instead, when it was opened in May of 1931 — thanks partly to the toil of brave riveters who worked nearly a quarter of a mile up — its 102 stories remained largely empty throughout the Depression. The 80-foot steel dirigible-mooring mast that topped it was never used.

that they had constructed out of orange crates.

In the consumer spending boom of the 1920's, Americans had borrowed heavily. On the eve of the crash, the nation's total nongovernment debt, both personal and corporate, had reached $100 billion. The Wall Street banks and brokerage houses held the bulk of the IOU's; indeed, they were creditors to the world, having lent large sums overseas to support governments in Europe and Latin America, thereby bolstering foreign markets for American goods.

With the collapse on Wall Street, the whole debt structure came tumbling down. The banks, stripped of their funds, had virtually no credit to extend. The overseas loans dried up, and the once-lucrative foreign trade diminished to a trickle. Their confidence badly shaken, businesses started cutting back. The economy sputtered to a halt.

Breadlines were among the most sobering sights of the Depression. The specter of hundreds, even thousands, of ragged and famished men and women lining up every day for a loaf of bread or a bowl of soup was unnerving to Americans used to abundance. In the depths of the crisis, New York counted 82 breadlines providing 85,000 meals a day. The notorious Chicago gangster Al Capone established his own private breadline. When he appeared at baseball games, he got standing ovations for his generosity. To President Hoover, however, the breadlines did not signal a catastrophe. As the president saw it, "Nobody is actually starving. The hoboes, for example, are better fed than they have ever been. One hobo in New York got 10 meals in one day."

Hoover's Late Efforts Fall Short

Even so, the one individual who seemed capable of solving the whole complicated mess was the man in the White House. President Hoover was probably the savviest person in Washington on economic matters, having served with distinction as secretary of commerce for his two predecessors. During World War I and its aftermath, he had headed a relief agency that sent millions of dollars in food and clothing to the devastated populations of a battle-scarred Eu-

▶

Despite the fine location, sandwiched between a hotel and a restaurant, this barber seems to lack customers, who may have opted to spend 10 cents on a meal next door instead of a shave.

rope. Surely he could and would do the same for America.

In his sober, methodical way, Hoover began to take the actions he felt the nation needed. In December of 1930, in an effort to create jobs, he launched a $100-million program of dam building, road construction, and other public works. He signed a relief bill for farmers, extending loans to purchase cattle feed. Hoping to stimulate trade, he gave foreign nations a one-year moratorium on repaying debts to the United States. Early in 1932 he created the Reconstruction Finance Corporation, with a potential funding of $2 billion, to prop up the nation's faltering banks, insurance compa-

On July 28, 1932, Hoover sent in the army, commanded by Gen. Douglas MacArthur (shown above left with aide Maj. Dwight D. Eisenhower), to remove the remaining veterans.

nies, and other institutions and to prevent further job losses.

It was too little and too late. As the breadlines lengthened and the jobless lists multiplied, Hoover stood firm against direct federal relief for Americans. A government dole, he believed, would bankrupt the treasury and sap the nation's moral strength. And he was convinced that the crisis would eventually correct itself. "Prosperity," he declared, "is just around the corner." But as time went on, that corner continued to recede into a cloudy future.

Violence, born of desperation, flared sporadically. In 1930, 1,100 men waiting in a breadline could not bear the sight of truckloads of food being delivered to a hotel; so they surrounded the trucks and emptied them. A man waiting in line to sign up for relief funds was stunned to see another man dive headfirst down a stairway. "He was gonna get on relief even if he had to go to the hospital to do it," the first applicant said. People who had been well-to-do before the crash were driven to despair by the prospect of subsistence living. A Chicagoan recalled a friend whose $25,000 salary was cut to $5,000: "He walked right over to the Board of Trade Building, to the top, and jumped." Others found it within themselves to cope with the drastic reversals the Depression dealt them. A banker who had lost everything went to work as a caddie at his old golf club.

In some cases being poor eroded long-standing racial barriers. A black man remembered life by the railroad tracks: "Twenty-five or thirty would be out on the side of the rail, white and colored." Black and white, the hoboes slept, ate, and looked for work together. "It didn't make any difference who you were, 'cause everybody was poor."

Readers and Writers Confront the Depression

In their time of economic trouble, Americans looked to their writers for solace, advice, and hope. Not surprisingly, escapist literature fared well in the 1930's. One of the biggest successes was James Hilton's *Lost Horizon,* which set millions of readers to dreaming of life in mythical, carefree Shangri-La. The most popular fiction book of 1931 and 1932 was *The Good Earth,* Pearl Buck's family saga set in faraway China. In the following year the adventure yarn *Anthony Adverse* transported its readers to Napoleon's world and made author Hervey Allen rich when it sold 300,000 copies in just six months.

Historical novels with heroic themes showing readers that the nation had undergone trials in the past and had triumphed were also successful. But the one that most captured the popular imagination was Margaret Mitchell's epic, *Gone With the Wind,* which topped the best-seller list for fiction in 1936 and 1937. Its spunky heroine, Scarlett O'Hara, saw her genteel society destroyed, lost her fortune, starved, and emerged tougher from the ordeal, proclaiming at the end of the book that "tomorrow is another day."

Books offering down-to-earth advice also climbed the best-seller lists. The best of the genre was Dale Carnegie's *How to Win Friends and Influence People* (1936), which told readers how, by following a few simple rules, they could become popular and respected.

Some of America's greatest writers did their finest work during the Depression. William Faulkner published four major

Pearl S. Buck

Dale Carnegie

books in the 1930's, including *Light in August* and *Absalom, Absalom!* In such books, wrote critic Malcolm Cowley, this "poet in prose, a creator of myths" wove "a legend of the South." Another Southern writer, Thomas Wolfe, published his first novel, *Look Homeward, Angel,* in 1929. The sequel, *Of Time and the River,* came out in 1935. Three years later Wolfe was dead, just before his 38th birthday. His essentially hopeful outlook is expressed in the opening lines of *Look Homeward, Angel* with a meditation on "that dark miracle of chance which makes new magic in a dusty world."

Not every writer shared Wolfe's optimism. John Dos Passos published a massive trilogy, *U.S.A.,* peopled with cynical crooks and goodhearted suckers. The trilogy ends with a vagrant musing on his disenchantment with the American dream.

Near the end of the decade, John Steinbeck focused on a small segment of the rural population and captured the turmoil and tragedy of the Depression. His great novel, *The Grapes of Wrath,* depicts the ordeal of the Dust Bowl farmers and their harrowing exodus to California. In the sufferings of the Joad family, readers found echoes of their own misfortunes, and the book became a best-seller. If Steinbeck exhorted readers to face the failures of America's economic system, he also portrayed the strength and endurance of the American people. Ma Joad says it best: "We ain't gonna die out. People is goin' on — changin' a little maybe, but goin' right on."

William Faulkner

John Steinbeck

151

BLACK CLOUDS OVER THE FARMS

Far across the Great Plains, the worst drought in U.S. Weather Bureau history burned crops, turned the soil to dust, and sent thousands of destitute farm families trekking to California.

They came with terrifying suddenness — churning black clouds that looked, from afar, like mountains moving across the prairie. When they hit, the sky went dark, and an avalanche of fine dust piled up everywhere, burying livestock, drifting over houses, filling mouths and lungs with choking particles. To a farm economy already reeling from the Depression, the storms aimed a devastating blow. And they added a haunting phrase to the American lexicon: Dust Bowl.

After a year of mostly good rains and harvests in 1931, precipitation dropped alarmingly in the years following. Some 300,000 square miles of Great Plains territory, stripped of its protective buffalo grass by decades of plowing and grazing, turned dry, then drier, and then to dust. The stricken area included much of Colorado, New Mexico, Nebraska, Kansas, Oklahoma, and Texas.

Then, in November 1933, a black cloud rose up in the Dakotas, swept east, and darkened the sky over Chicago. The next day its shadow fell upon Albany and parts of New England as the airborne particles headed out to sea. In April 1935 the dust of the Great Plains settled over the Capitol itself, adding urgency to the proceedings inside. (The senators were hearing testimony on a bill to control soil erosion.) It was an ecological disaster that provided important lessons to a later, more environmentally aware era.

Gritty Humor, Grim Devastation

Midwestern farmers managed to wring a bit of humor from the situation and told dust jokes. According to one, a truck driver spotted a 10-gallon hat resting atop a dust drift, picked it up, and uncovered the head of a cowboy. "Can I give you a lift?" the startled driver asked. "Nope, I'll make it on my own," the cowboy replied. "I'm on a horse."

But toughness and a sense of humor could not prevent the tremendous damage these "black blizzards" inflicted on the Great Plains. A single immense dust storm, on May 11, 1934, blew away 300 million tons of topsoil, roughly the amount of earth dredged from the Panama Canal. It tossed the equivalent of 3,000 hundred-acre farms into the air.

The dust clouds struck with deadly speed. Farmers caught in their fields, or just a few steps from shelter, could be engulfed by dust and die of suffocation. Repeated exposure to the fine powder caused pneumonia and other respiratory ailments. To protect themselves, some people slept with wet cloths on their faces. Farmers and ranchers strung guide wires so they could find their way from house to barn in order to feed the livestock when a storm blew in. In the hardest-hit regions, agriculture ceased and cattle died from eating dust-covered grass.

The devastation in the Dust Bowl touched off an enormous migration of farm families, lasting for years. Altogether perhaps as many as 350,000 people loaded their belongings onto rickety vehicles and headed west in search of a promised land. Most traveled to California's San Joaquin Valley, where large orchards and cattle ranches offered seasonal work. But there were never enough jobs for the thousands who arrived monthly during the worst times.

Many of the migrants crowded into ramshackle settlements built of tent canvas and packing crates. Some found places at one of more than a dozen camps run by the Farm Security Administration (FSA), which offered washrooms and recreational facilities. A lucky few scraped together the $3 a month required to buy a tiny plot on which they could build their own house. All faced the scorn of Californians, who resented the influx of impoverished newcomers. They became known as Okies, the derogatory term applied to all migrants whether or not they came from Oklahoma.

The migrants just hunkered down and took it. After the privations of the Dust Bowl, they felt lucky to have food in their bellies and occasional work at $3 a day. With their eyes on the future and hope in their hearts, inch by inch they struggled to get ahead. "Jest like the cat eatin' grindstone," one man said, "a little bit at a time."

Dust Bowl Troubadour

The decade's most lyric spokesman for the downtrodden was folksinger Woody Guthrie (above), who hopped a freight train at age 15 to play his guitar in hobo encampments. When the dust storms hit, the Oklahoma-born Guthrie moved on to California, where he became a union organizer. His favorite audiences were the poor, the dispossessed, and children.

Guthrie poured the rueful humor and wounded pride of the Dust Bowl experience into songs that stand as American classics: "Hard Traveling," "So Long (It's Been Good to Know Yuh)," and many others. After the Depression he continued to champion the underdog. His "This Land Is Your Land" was a theme song of the 1960's civil rights movement.

Whipped along by 50-m.p.h. winds, a giant "black blizzard" — all dust, no rain — boils across the Colorado prairie. ▶

In California a migrant family shows off its new bungalow, built with FSA help. It might have lacked plumbing and electricity, but it was home.

Staying put in Indiana, this farm couple took a federal loan to tide them through the dry years.

FDR PLEDGES A NEW DEAL

Rejecting advice that he wage a safe, stay-at-home campaign, Roosevelt toured the country talking about a wide range of issues. He was vague about solutions, but there was no question that he meant to take action.

This cast-metal electric clock, a popular premium from the 1930's, leaves little doubt as to who was the pilot of America's ship of state.

▼ **Written for the 1929 movie, Chasing Rainbows, "Happy Days Are Here Again" was FDR's unofficial victory song in 1932.**

In June 1932 Democrats convened in Chicago to nominate a candidate for president. Since nearly everyone assumed that any Democrat could defeat Herbert Hoover, there was a fierce contest for the nomination. Not until the fourth ballot did the governor of New York, Franklin D. Roosevelt, emerge the winner. He then broke all precedent by flying to Chicago to accept the honor in person and to address the troubled country: "I pledge you, I pledge myself, to a new deal for the American people." That card player's phrase, new deal, would become the name for President Roosevelt's programs.

Years before, the young Roosevelt had been his opponent's effusive admirer, saying of Hoover, "I wish we could make him president of the United States. There couldn't be a better one." Yet Hoover appeared dour and bitter during the campaign, while Roosevelt exuded confidence and energy. His promises were not so different from Hoover's, but he seemed less hesitant about using government intervention to solve the economic crisis. To the tune of "Happy Days Are Here Again," he toured the country, shaking hands, chatting with local officials, making speeches from the rear of his train. To no one's surprise, FDR won the popular vote by 7 million, carried 42 states, and received 472 out of 531 electoral votes.

On the night of Election Day, as his son James helped Roosevelt into bed, the president-elect spoke the fears he had hidden in the campaign. "I'm just afraid that I may not have the strength to

Holding on to son Franklin Jr.'s arm, a confident, jubilant candidate Roosevelt gives a cheerful wave to supporters at a campaign stop in 1932.

► **Because of the assassination attempt on FDR, this specially prepared New Yorker cover never saw print.**

do this job. After you leave me tonight, Jimmy, I am going to pray. I am going to pray that God will help me, that He will give me the strength and the guidance to do this job and to do it right. I hope you will pray for me, too, Jimmy."

Bullets in the Night

In early February, with his inauguration still a month away, Roosevelt went on a 12-day fishing trip in the Bahamas. Upon his return he addressed a large crowd gathered in Miami's Bay Front Park. As FDR was leaving, shots rang out. Several people were hit, including Chicago's Mayor Anton J. Cermak, who was standing near the president-elect.

Later, at the hospital, the mortally wounded Cermak told Roosevelt, "I'm mighty glad it was me instead of you. I wish you'd be careful. The country needs you." The dying

▶ *With his arm around vice presidential candidate John Nance Garner, FDR leaves Topeka, Kansas, for the beginning of what would be thousands of miles of rail campaigning.*

mayor's sentiments were echoed by millions of Americans, many of whom had learned of the assassination attempt immediately after it happened, because of the ever-widening reach of radio. The gunman, Giuseppe Zangara, was an Italian immigrant and unemployed bricklayer who harbored a hatred of "all officials and everybody who is rich." He was speedily tried and executed.

Many felt that the assassin's target had been not only FDR but America's hope for the future. It was widely noted that the president-elect had stayed calm in the face of mortal danger. From this baptism by fire both Roosevelt and the country's faith in him emerged newly strengthened.

"The Only Thing We Have to Fear"

On March 4, 1933, Roosevelt rode in the open presidential car to his inauguration. Seated beside Herbert Hoover, who barely spoke throughout the ride, FDR saw a somber crowd, under tight security because of the assassination attempt. Then, in the blustery March wind, he assured his listeners that "the only thing we have to fear is fear itself." He closed the address by asserting: "The people of the United States have not failed. . . . They want direct, vigorous action."

Some months earlier, a friend had assured Roosevelt that he would be remembered as the greatest American president if he succeeded and as the worst if he failed. Confiding his understanding of the seriousness of the crisis, FDR answered, "If I fail, I shall be the last one." Now that he was in the White House, Roosevelt could no longer simply talk about America's problems and his proposed solutions. The time had come to act — to take the direct, vigorous measures he had promised. The nation held its breath.

Grit and Grace

Franklin Delano Roosevelt's political career began in 1910, when the 28-year-old patrician from Hyde Park, New York, narrowly won a seat in the state senate. In 1913 he accepted a job offer from President Wilson to be the assistant secretary of the navy, and in 1920 he ran as vice president on the Democratic ticket. The ticket was defeated by Warren Harding and Calvin Coolidge; yet Roosevelt was soon planning future campaigns. Even as a young man, Franklin had said that he thought he had a real chance to be president, following in the footsteps of his distant cousin Teddy. Now FDR was clearly destined for higher office.

Then disaster struck. In the summer of 1921, while vacationing with his wife, Eleanor, and their children at his summer home on Campobello Island, off the coast of Maine, Franklin fell ill. Doctors diagnosed his symptoms — paralysis of the lower extremities — as polio. There was a possibility that he would remain crippled for the rest of his life.

Anyone else might have abandoned all political plans. Not Roosevelt. For the next seven years he kept up a strenuous regimen of daily exercise. In heavy steel braces and on crutches, he struggled again and again to reach the foot of Hyde Park's 200-yard driveway. He swam in the 88-degree waters of a spa in Warm Springs, Georgia. He kept hoping he would graduate from crutches

to a cane and eventually walk unencumbered. His hopes were futile. By the time he ran for governor of New York in 1928, Roosevelt knew that he was permanently handicapped.

To accept the disability was by no means to admit defeat. The illness had given him a new perspective on life: "If you've spent two years in bed trying to wiggle your big toe, everything else seems easy." Once in office as New York's governor, Roosevelt took charge. As the Depression deepened, he was one of the few governors in the country who created state relief programs. Beginning in 1930, he instituted a series of emergency measures in New York State that amounted to a dress rehearsal for the New Deal.

One incident, witnessed by only a few, epitomized the special combination of grit and grace that was FDR. At the Democratic convention of 1936, Roosevelt was making his way to the podium to deliver his acceptance speech, supported on one side by his son James and on the other by a cane. His hip joints gave way, one of his steel braces snapped, and he fell. With practiced speed, his Secret Service men raised him while others moved in to shield him from onlookers. The pages of the speech were picked up and put in order. "Clean me up," he requested. Minutes later the curtain parted and FDR was at the podium, standing tall, relaxed, and smiling.

FDR about age 10

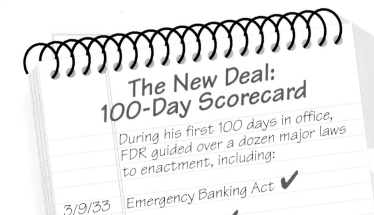

The New Deal: 100-Day Scorecard

During his first 100 days in office, FDR guided over a dozen major laws to enactment, including:

3/9/33	Emergency Banking Act	✔
3/20/33	Economy Act	✔
3/31/33	CCC established	✔
4/19/33	End of gold standard	✔
5/12/33	Federal Emergency Relief Act	✔
5/12/33	Emergency Farm Mortgage Act	✔
5/18/33	TVA established	✔
5/27/33	Truth in Securities Act	✔
6/13/33	Home Owners' Loan Act	✔
6/16/33	National Industrial Recovery Act	✔
6/16/33	Farm Credit Act	✔

ONE HUNDRED DAYS OF CHANGE

"At the end of February," wrote the columnist Walter Lippmann, "we were a congeries of disorderly panic-stricken mobs and factions. In the hundred days from March to June we became again an organized nation confident of our power . . . to control our own destiny."

Franklin D. Roosevelt, who had pledged action the day before in his inaugural address, proclaimed on March 5, 1933, a national bank holiday. The week before, millions of panicky citizens had withdrawn their assets in cash. The nation's banking system was on the verge of collapse; Roosevelt was determined to save it. The Treasury buzzed as new appointees put their heads together with old officials to create a program that would work. The new president's top priority was to calm fears — the public's fear of losing their hard-earned savings and the bankers' fear of being put out of business.

Within four days Congress, summoned by Roosevelt to an emergency session, had passed a new banking act. On Sunday evening, March 12, FDR broadcast the first of his famous fireside chats, to announce the reopening of the banks: "I can assure you that it is safer to keep your money in a reopened bank than under the mattress. . . . Let us unite in banishing fear. It is your problem no less than it is mine. Together we cannot fail."

FDR's blend of serenity and confidence touched off an enthusiastic response. All over America long lines of people queued up to redeposit their money in the banks. As the humorist Will Rogers put it, "The whole country is with him, just so he does something."

This was only the beginning. FDR had much more up his sleeve. Major programs were coming to restore purchasing power by correcting the worst imbalances in the economy, to enact reforms that would prevent another stock market crash, and finally, to launch a vast public works program creating new jobs.

To help formulate these programs, FDR had brought with him to Washington a group of college professors, called by his secretary Louis Howe, somewhat sarcastically, the Brain Trust. FDR had chosen some Brain Trusters for key Cabinet posts; others remained unofficial advisers. They in turn attracted more New Dealers, as they came to be known,

Louis Howe (far right), FDR's trusted adviser, chairs a White House meeting with Brain Trust professors (from left) Adolf Berle, Jr., Rexford Tugwell, and Raymond Moley.

and overnight Washington was revitalized. Seldom has such a high concentration of idealists, colorful personalities, hard-working intellectuals, and monumental egos assembled at the seat of power.

Coming from a wide variety of backgrounds, the Brain Trusters represented many conflicting points of view and approaches. FDR saw himself as a man of action, not a philosopher. He was brilliant at getting the best from this very diverse group. He explained his presidential role as similar to that of a quarterback: "If the play makes ten yards, the succeeding play will be different from what it would have been if they had been thrown for a loss." The president would not know until the next play was completed what would be his call on the play after next. To a young man who asked him what his philosophy was, Roosevelt responded, "Philosophy? I am a Christian and a Democrat — that's all."

▼ In 1933 NRA supporters mounted a huge parade in New York City: 250,000 marchers and 2 million spectators.

Fireside Chats

Many presidents have wished to conduct the real business of government behind closed doors. Not FDR. Instead, he tried to give people the feeling that they were participating in the decision-making process. More than once, both friends and enemies complained

about FDR's indirection and even deviousness, but no one could ever accuse him of not taking his program to the people.

This he did via the fireside chats, broadcasts he made often, starting the week he took office. "My friends," FDR began, and then he seemed to open his heart to the millions who backed him.

The reaction was overwhelmingly positive. A Brooklyn man wrote, "I felt that he walked into my home, sat down, and in plain and forceful language explained to me how he was tackling the job I and my fellow citizens gave him." Republicans could complain and call FDR a mealy-mouthed demagogue. But to many people eager to believe his soothing voice, FDR was a savior.

FDR kept up a dizzying pace. In all, 15 major bills were introduced and passed during those euphoric first 100 days, ranging from refinancing farm and home mortgages to guaranteeing bank deposits. The National Industrial Recovery Act set up the National Recovery Administration (NRA) and created the Public Works Administration (PWA), designed to provide jobs through a $3.3-billion program of construction projects. Other bold strokes included the establishment of the Civilian Conservation Corps (CCC) and the Tennessee Valley Authority (TVA), providing for a vast system of dams and hydroelectric plants to produce power for rural folk in the South who had never had it before. To critics it seemed an ill-sorted package; some called it creeping socialism. But its positive impact was profound.

A New Role for Government

The NRA, with its Blue Eagle thunderbird emblem bearing the words "We Do Our Part," seemed the most revolutionary of all the New Deal measures. It sought to check the downward spiral of output and prices and established government regulation of wages, hours, and working conditions. Some 2 million employers were persuaded, coerced, or stampeded into signing an NRA agreement, or else they could not display the high-flying Blue Eagle. NRA parades were staged in cities and towns across the country to encourage more converts. For millions, the NRA represented the best hope of the New Deal. For many conservatives, it became a hated symbol of government regulation. For everyone, the national political scene had been transformed.

Ladies raise their mugs in a toast after Congress passed a bill legalizing 3.2-percent beer and wine in March 1933.

157

GETTING AMERICANS BACK TO WORK

New Deal employment programs inspired confidence in government and support for FDR.

"It's the first time in my recollection," a workman remarked, "that a president ever got up

and said, 'I'm interested in and aim to do something for the workingman.' "

From 1935 to 1943, when it disbanded, the WPA put a total of 8.5 million people to work on 1.4 million separate projects.

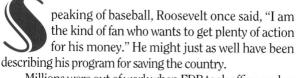

Harry L. Hopkins (left) and Harold L. Ickes share a rare companionable moment in 1938. Shrewd, intelligent, and rivalrous, both men held top government positions throughout FDR's long presidency.

Speaking of baseball, Roosevelt once said, "I am the kind of fan who wants to get plenty of action for his money." He might just as well have been describing his program for saving the country.

Millions were out of work when FDR took office, and so many had hit rock bottom that emergency relief programs were a top priority in the early days of the New Deal. FDR's choice to head up a Federal Emergency Relief Administration (FERA) was the veteran social worker Harry L. Hopkins, whose philosophy was outspokenly radical: "I believe people are poor because we don't know how to distribute the wealth properly." The cornerstone of FERA's action was work relief. Criticism was at first muted. As one politician put it, no one was going to shoot Santa Claus just before Christmas. ("The hell they won't," Hopkins retorted. "Santa Claus really needs a bulletproof vest.")

The New Deal proposed much more than a bit of leaf raking and ditch digging to put suppers on the table. With the Public Works Administration, Roosevelt had launched federal construction projects on a scale hitherto unimaginable. Ground for new highways, subways, bridges, schools, hospitals, and other public works was broken everywhere under the auspices of the Department of the Interior and its head, Harold L. Ickes, a reformer who had served as a campaign worker for Theodore Roosevelt a generation earlier.

Soon FDR saw the need to create another giant agency, which would complement the PWA with short-term projects: the Works Progress Administration (WPA). At the head of this new enterprise Roosevelt placed Harry Hopkins. Ickes and Hopkins became bitter rivals. Ickes favored grants to states and cities to pay for projects. Hopkins called for spending on labor itself: "We're for labor — first, last, and all the time. WPA is labor — don't forget that." Hopkins's philosophy and programs led to charges that the government was throwing money out the window on boondoggles, or useless make-work projects. The critics were not only Republicans. The administration itself was divided, with Ickes leading the opposition to Hopkins and the WPA. He wrote in his private diary at the time: "I am for substantial, worthwhile and socially desirable public works, while Hopkins is for what has come to be known as boondoggling."

Controversial Projects, Lasting Legacies

Despite the controversy, the WPA's achievements were considerable. Included under the WPA umbrella was a vast federal arts program. Thousands of murals and sculptures were commissioned. To this day WPA art can be seen on the walls of many post offices, courthouses, and other federal buildings. In addition, WPA money brought symphony orchestras and theater to people who had never in their lives seen anything of the sort. A federal writers' program for unemployed writers led to the creation of a state guidebook series so excellent that several of the guides have remained in print ever since. To charges that taxpayers' money was being misspent, supporters could reply with a quote from George Washington's address to Congress in 1790: ". . . there is nothing which can better deserve your patronage than the promotion of science and literature."

The WPA put thousands of painters, sculptors, and designers to work across America. Artist James M. Newell created this study for a post office mural in Dolgeville, New York.

The Federal Theatre Project brought 1,000 shows to cities and small towns and entertained some 25 million people, many of whom had never before seen a live production. These actors perform The Swing Mikado.

Saga of the Soil Soldiers

The New Deal had barely got off the ground when a second wave of Bonus Army veterans marched on Washington. Instead of calling out federal troops as Hoover had done the summer before, FDR quelled the protesters with kindness. They were given an army camp, and Eleanor Roosevelt visited with the men while her husband conferred with their leaders. In no time the marchers were enrolled in FDR's new brainchild, the Civilian Conservation Corps (CCC), also known as the C's, Soil Soldiers, or Roosevelt's Tree Army.

Enrollment in the CCC was open to unemployed youths, ages 18 to 25, as well as to needy vets. Enrollees wore olive-drab uniforms, lived in barracks under near-military discipline, and received $30 a month, most of which was held back to be sent to the folks at home. For six months to a year, the men worked on such projects as forest conservation, flood and erosion control, land drainage and reclamation. Soon the Soil Soldiers were building roads and fire towers, planting millions

Above: A Soil Soldier plants a pine seedling in Montana. Below: A CCC camp at Schroon River, New York.

of trees, combating forest-destroying insects and blights, and maintaining trails and campsites in parks throughout the nation. (Camp David, Maryland, a presidential hideaway ever since FDR used it for meetings with British Prime Minister Winston Churchill during World War II, was built by the CCC.)

Within months after its launching in the spring of 1933, the CCC had already become the biggest government labor force in U.S. history. By the time the last Soil Soldiers folded their tents early in World War II, over 2.5 million men had served in the CCC.

A few union leaders criticized the CCC as "forced labor," but overall it was one of the New Deal's most highly regarded programs. No one accused the Soil Soldiers of goldbricking or boondoggling. "If a boy wants to go and get a job after he's been in the C's," one Tree Army veteran boasted, "he'll know how to work." Another said, more simply: "It made a man of me, all right."

THE SPLENDID SILVER SCREEN

Mickey Mouse and Shirley Temple, Groucho Marx and Greta Garbo, Busby Berkeley and Fred Astaire —

Hollywood kept America chuckling, gasping, and applauding all through the bad times.

"When the spirit of the people is lower than at any other time, during this Depression," President Roosevelt said, "it is a splendid thing that for just fifteen cents an American can go to a movie . . . and forget his troubles." It was 1936. Most people had money only for necessities, and for the movies.

By the end of the decade, Americans were buying 80 million movie tickets every week at prices as low as 10 to 15 cents each. That ticket bought a lot, too: a newsreel, a cartoon, a short subject, previews of coming attractions, and a double feature.

Of course, little had to do with reality, but that was the point. Production code censors banned words like *hell* and *damn,* along with brutal murders and the horizontal position in love scenes. In the movies people died without bleeding and bred without mating. And some of the most popular characters were not even people.

Hollywood called Walt Disney's studio the Mouse Factory, and the mouse was Mickey. In the dark days of 1933, Disney had set the country singing "Who's Afraid of the Big Bad Wolf?" from *The Three Little Pigs,* but cartoons about mice appealed even more. Among Mickey's early devotees were Italian dictator Mussolini and Queen Mary of England. Only Adolf Hitler was immune, and German propaganda declared the animated rodent "the most miserable ideal ever revealed . . . mice are dirty."

Across town from the Mouse Factory, the world's best-paid moppet ($100,000 a picture in 1938, more than Gable or Garbo) single-handedly kept 20th Century-Fox afloat. Shirley Temple sang, danced, giggled, and melted stony hearts in *Dimples, Curly Top,* and *Little Miss Marker* while

Elegance in motion, Ginger Rogers and Fred Astaire danced through 10 hit movies and spun a new ideal of American glamour.

Busby Berkeley's Footlight Parade (background, this page) and Born to Dance with Eleanor Powell (background, next page) formed fantasy backdrops to Hollywood's golden age of musicals.

▲

The pluckiest heroine of 1939 was Dorothy, played by Judy Garland, in The Wizard of Oz. She closed her eyes, clicked her ruby slippers, and whirled off to stardom.

Winsome Shirley Temple started acting at age three and made 27 films by the decade's end.

▶

Veteran Hollywood comic Stan Laurel hits his partner, Oliver Hardy, with a well-placed sight gag.

her mother stood by during filming shouting, "Sparkle, Shirley! Sparkle!"

Just as upbeat were the kaleidoscopic productions of choreographer Busby Berkeley, with dozens of long-legged beauties. Also, Fred Astaire and Ginger Rogers twirled with magical grace. Astaire's first screen test read: "Can't act. Slightly bald. Can dance a little." But the grand success of *The Gay Divorcée* in 1934 saved RKO Pictures Corporation, and the studio insured Astaire's legs for $1 million. His debonair charm played off Rogers's glamorous sex appeal, and both could dance the spots off a leopard.

A raft of brilliant comedies perked up weary audiences. Comedy ranged from Mae West's sensuous innuendo ("When women go wrong, men go right after them") to the inspired mayhem of the Marx Brothers in *Duck Soup, Animal Crackers,* and *A Night at the Opera*. There were working-girl comedies, like *She Married Her Boss*, family comedies, such as the Andy Hardy series, and screwball comedies, like Howard Hawks's *Bringing Up Baby*. All had happy endings.

The biggest movie year of all, 1939, saw two all-time masterpieces. One was *The Wizard of Oz*. The other, *Gone With the Wind,* should have been a disaster. The producer, David O. Selznick, auditioned 1,400 actresses for the role of Confederate belle Scarlett O'Hara including such notables as Joan Crawford and Tallulah Bankhead, then chose virtually unknown Vivien Leigh, who was British. Production gobbled up three directors, a stable of screenwriters, and a colossal $4,250,000. Nobody knew if audiences would sit through a film lasting nearly four hours, more than twice the usual length. Nor could anyone predict the reaction when Clark Gable, as dashing Rhett Butler, delivered his censorship-defying line, "Frankly, my dear, I don't give a damn!" Some 300,000 people turned out for the Atlanta premiere, and everybody loved it. Like Scarlett herself, the audience seemed to feel that no adversity was painful enough to break one's spirit.

Swedish-born Greta Garbo starred in Queen Christina, **about Sweden's 17th-century monarch.**

Walt Disney's 1937 Snow White and the Seven Dwarfs (above) **was the first full-length animated film ever. In Bringing Up Baby** (right), **Cary Grant and Katharine Hepburn played nursemaids to a pet leopard.**

Clark Gable and Vivien Leigh burned up the screen in Gone With the Wind, **the decade's most talked-about film.**

LAND OF LISTENERS

ON THE AIR

Imagine, in the depths of the Depression, the magic of live radio shows starring Fred Allen, Bing Crosby, Lily Pons, Orson Welles, Kate Smith, Edgar Bergen, Duke Ellington, Gracie Allen, Arturo Toscanini, and many more.

Their pocketbooks may have been hurting, but Americans had never enjoyed a more richly varied fare of entertainment than they did in the 1930's. It was the golden age of radio. By the end of the decade, 85 percent of the population owned a radio and thrilled to the news, sports, and entertainment that came "free" to their living rooms. The industry had become the fourth largest in the nation and the most pervasive medium of communications ever.

Daytime listeners found companionship and vicarious romance in the serials — later known as soap operas because of their sponsors — that dominated early afternoon hours five days a week. One of the longest lasting, *The Romance of Helen Trent,* for 27 years posed the same question: "Can a woman over 35 find romance?" Youngsters hurried home from school to tune in to their favorite adventure shows, such as *Buck Rogers in the 25th Century, Jack Armstrong, the All-American Boy,* and *Tom Mix and the Ralston Straightshooters.* Audiences not only listened, they bought sponsors' products and mailed off the proof-of-purchase to collect the freebies offered to boost sales: a Green Hornet ring or a Captain Midnight code-o-graph. After just one announcement, 42,000 fans sent in a cigar band to get a picture of Kate Smith.

Westerns, like *The Lone Ranger,* and mysteries, like *The Shadow,* were among the not-to-be-missed evening radio dramas; and listeners of all ages sat transfixed waiting for the masked rider's stirring shout of "Hi-yo, Silver!" and the phantom avenger's spine-tingling question, "Who knows what evil lurks in the hearts of men?"

The phenomenal success of *Amos 'n' Andy* had demonstrated to network executives, and to advertisers, that tickling the national funny bone could be as profitable for them as it was pleasing to the public. In just three years after its debut in 1928, the show had become an institution, with some 42 million listeners — including Herbert Hoover, J. Edgar Hoover, and Henry Ford — tuning in for a ritual 15-minute dose of belly laughs from 7:00 to 7:15 P.M. every weekday. The show's white creators, Freeman Gosden and Charles Correll, might be drummed off the air today for portraying offensive racial stereotypes, but in the 1930's they were national icons.

The show's success inspired a proliferation of comedies starring former vaudevillians. Raspy-voiced George Burns smoked a cigar and played the straight man to scatter-brained Gracie Allen as she searched for an imaginary lost brother. Jack Benny parlayed his reputation as the stingiest man in the world into an enormously successful radio career, to the accompaniment of "Love in Bloom" squeaked

The Shadow, which made its radio debut in 1930 and ran for 24 years, inspired many fan clubs and this pulp magazine.

On CBS, "Doctor" George Burns says to Gracie Allen: "This won't hurt because there's no sense. There's no feeling."

Jack Benny (left) and Fred Allen spent years hilariously feigning a fierce on-the-air feud.

Edgar Bergen and his dummy Charlie McCarthy appeared on NBC's Chase and Sanborn Hour on Sunday evenings.

out on his violin. And Fred Allen held forth with acerbic wit, fueling an on-the-air running battle of insults with Jack Benny. Only Franklin Roosevelt's fireside chats commanded a larger audience than the radio face-off between the pair on March 14, 1937. Ventriloquist Edgar Bergen and his devilishly feisty dummy Charlie McCarthy, the Magnificent Splinter, exchanged caustic banter with each other and a parade of celebrity guest performers.

Almost as popular as the comedy shows were musical programs featuring an incredible variety of styles and stars. Bing Crosby, Kate Smith, Lawrence Tibbett, and Lily Pons all sang. Bandleaders Paul Whiteman and Guy Lombardo conducted their pop orchestras. Weekly broadcasts of grand opera emanated from the Metropolitan Opera House in New York, and such eminent symphonic conductors as Arturo Toscanini wielded their batons.

A new kind of torrid, fast-paced dance music entered the mainstream thanks to radio and big bands. Based on the driving rhythms and superheated riffs developed by black jazz musicians in the 1920's, it added a rollicking dance beat and tight musical arrangements to produce swing. Clarinetist Benny Goodman created a sensation in August 1935 when he introduced it midway through an on-radio engagement at the Palomar Ballroom, in Hollywood. The young crowd went wild. Swing became a craze, spawning a whole new vocabulary — jitterbug, jukebox, disc jockey, and dozens of other words and phrases — and a whole new set of energetic dance steps, like the big apple and the lindy. One alarmed psychologist felt compelled to warn against swing's "dangerously hypnotic influence . . . cunningly devised to a faster tempo than 72 bars to the minute —

Surrender, Earthlings!

The Mercury Theatre had been on the air only a few months and had no sponsor. Orson Welles, the show's talented 23-year-old producer, was hardly a household name. But the show he planned for the evening of October 30, 1938, would change that forever. Welles announced that it was an adaptation of a book, *The War of the Worlds,* by H. G. Wells. But many people were listening to Edgar Bergen and Charlie McCarthy and tuned in late. All they heard was dance music interrupted by "news flashes" reporting the invasion of armed Martians. The fantasy became reality to Americans made jumpy by daily broadcasts of the crisis in Europe. Orson Welles's prank set off a panic. People called the police, packed their bags, or simply huddled at home, terror-stricken. Welles issued an apology, WCBS announced repeatedly that it had been a hoax, and by the next day nearly all that remained was a recognition of the stunning power of radio.

faster than the human pulse." By 1940 hundreds of dance orchestras — including the big bands of Duke Ellington, Fletcher Henderson, Count Basie, Artie Shaw, Tommy and Jimmy Dorsey, Glenn Miller, and Harry James — were swinging for fans in live concerts and on network broadcasts across the land.

▼ *Benny Goodman's virtuoso clarinet and crowd-pleasing renditions of familiar tunes earned him the title "King of Swing."*

Glenn Miller kept his fans coming back for more with hits such as "Little Brown Jug," "In the Mood," and his signature song "Moonlight Serenade."

Bandleader Kay Kyser combined music and quiz show formats on his Kollege of Musical Knowledge.

◄ *Duke Ellington's extraordinary musical abilities first attracted widespread acclaim in Harlem's Cotton Club from 1927 to 1932.*

163

CHAMPIONS IN BODY AND SPIRIT

Big changes were in the air, and many of the era's most gifted athletes faced challenges that had nothing to do with how well they played their game.

Every decade has its harbingers of things to come, but in sports the 1930's had more than their share of portentous events and significant beginnings. Increasingly, professional athletes caught the scent of more money to be made. The odious "color line" was still in place, but in a few sports black athletes got the chance to show how very good they could be. The Cincinnati Reds erected lights at their park and played the first night baseball game, against the Philadelphia Phillies, on May 24, 1935. College basketball took off as a spectator sport.

Mildred Ella (Babe) Didrikson, perhaps the greatest woman athlete ever, outperformed most men in baseball, basketball, billiards, diving, swimming, and tennis. She electrified women's track and field (right). Then, still in her early twenties, she turned to golf. She was the dominant woman player for 20 years, courageously winning the 1954 U.S. Women's Open just a year after surgery for the cancer that killed her 2 years later. Along the way, she married a genial giant of a wrestler named George Zaharias.

Meanwhile, the other phenomenal Babe, from whom Didrikson's fans had borrowed her nickname,

◀ *Sportswriters called Jesse Owens the Ebony Antelope, and at the 1936 Olympics he showed the crowds what that meant.*

At the 1932 Olympics in Los Angeles (souvenir playing cards, left), Babe Didrikson set world records in the 80-meter hurdles and (shown here) the javelin throw.

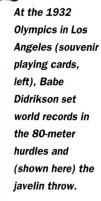

was pushing his employers to pay him what he thought he was worth. When the Yankee owners grudgingly gave Ruth a 1931 salary of $80,000, more than President Hoover made, the Babe tried to defuse accusations of ungentlemanly avarice by pointing out, "I had a better year than the president." True. When Hoover threw out the first ball in the 1931 World Series, fans booed the man most blamed for the Depression.

In other sports, too, there were hints of the big money to come for athletes. Playing more than 80 head-to-head tennis matches on a 1938 tour, Fred Perry and Ellsworth Vines earned $34,000 each, a princely sum at the time.

Madison Square Garden in New York was the cradle of a national obsession with college basketball. There, to the surprise of almost everybody, college doubleheaders drew large, lusty crowds. Those events set the stage for the first National Collegiate Athletic Association (NCAA) postseason tournament, in 1939, which then, as now, matched up the best teams in the country. Eventually, basketball brought some colleges whopping TV revenues.

Whether the best teams of the 1930's could have been even better is a question that will always haunt American sports, for black athletes were kept off most squads. In 1933

The New York Renaissance, a black team, was equal to any team in all-white pro basketball.

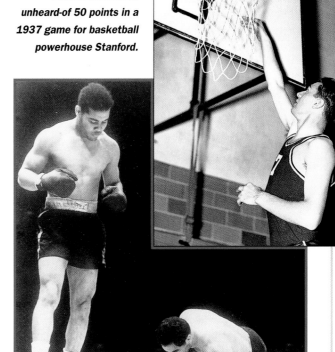

Using his revolutionary one-handed shot, Hank Luisetti scored an unheard-of 50 points in a 1937 game for basketball powerhouse Stanford.

After playing 2,130 straight games (still a record), Yankee Lou (Iron Horse) Gehrig announces his retirement, July 4, 1939. Two years later he was dead of a degenerative nerve disease.

Olympic gold medals in 1928, 1932, and 1936 propelled Norwegian skater Sonja Henie to Hollywood stardom.

Avenging an earlier defeat, Joe Louis leaves a down-and-out Max Schmeling on the mat after only 2 minutes and 4 seconds of the first round in their second fight, in 1938.

Fans loved the David-and-Goliath script when upstart Don Budge (left) beat old pros Fred Perry (middle) and Ellsworth Vines (right) in 1939.

the New York Renaissance, an all-black professional basketball team, took seven of eight games from the best white team of the era, the Original Celtics of New York City. The 1933–34 Rens played 134 games and won 127.

Boxing was open to black athletes, and a poker-faced Alabama native named Joe Louis made the most of it. The Brown Bomber turned professional in 1934 at the age of 20, and in 1937 he won the world heavyweight championship by knocking out James J. Braddock in eight rounds.

The year before, Max Schmeling had knocked out Louis in the 12th round. After that bout Schmeling sneered: "He fought like an amateur. This is no man who could ever be champion." But in 1938 Louis devastated the German heavyweight and humiliated Nazi Germany, which had made Schmeling a symbol of Aryan superiority.

A similar scenario had unfolded at the 1936 Olympics in Berlin, where Nazi sympathizers disparaged the black superathlete Jesse Owens. He burst their balloon of racist hot air by taking four gold medals.

ON STAGE: ROMP AND REALISM

Dorothy Stickney and Howard Lindsay starred in Life With Father, which set a Broadway record of 3,224 performances.

Luther Adler plays the boxer, and Art Smith, his manager, in Odets's Golden Boy (1937), about a prizefighter who wants to be a concert violinist.

When the sun went down, New York City's Times Square theater district lit up the Depression-era sky, offering high-stepping musicals, sharp-edged comedy, and deep social relevance.

Satire," quipped playwright George S. Kaufman, "is what closes Saturday night." But for the worldly-wise audiences of the 1930's, satire played just fine. *Of Thee I Sing*, with the book by Kaufman and Morrie Ryskind and songs by George and Ira Gershwin, was an uproarious musical parody of American politics, which opened in December 1931. A year later it was still running strong.

Even the dizziest, most upbeat comic turns did not hesitate to touch on the issues of the day. Irving Berlin's *As Thousands Cheer* (1933) lampooned everything from the New Deal to Paris sensation Josephine Baker. *Pins and Needles* (1937), a musical review performed by members of the International Ladies' Garment Workers' Union (ILGWU), stuck it to the bosses. Increasingly, Broadway musicals reached toward the higher arts for inspiration. George Abbott took the plot for *The Boys From Syracuse* (1938) straight out of Shakespeare. Richard Rodgers and Lorenz Hart's *On Your Toes* (1936) featured dance sequences choreographed by ballet master George Balanchine. George Gershwin's *Porgy and Bess* (1935), a poignant story of poor blacks in the South, was a musical synthesis of folk, jazz, and operatic forms.

The straight dramatic theater addressed volatile topics head-on. John Wexley's *They Shall Not Die* (1934) protested the rape charges against the Scottsboro boys, nine black teenagers accused of assaulting two

Broadway spoofed the classics in this musical based on Shakespeare's Comedy of Errors.

white women on an Alabama freight train. Maxwell Anderson's verse play *Winterset* (1935), based on the Sacco and Vanzetti case, took a hard look at the American justice system. The Southern sharecroppers portrayed in the stage version of Erskine Caldwell's

A tap-dancing bevy of scantily clad chorines enlivens Cole Porter's Anything Goes, one of his best-remembered and most frequently staged musical confections.

Tobacco Road (1933) were so true to life that one reviewer swore he detected the "smell of hot dust . . . and dried food leavings" wafting through the proscenium arch.

Some of the decade's most innovative stagings occurred beyond the glitter of Broadway. The government-sponsored Federal Theatre Project, set up to provide jobs in the dramatic arts, spawned such avant-garde talents as Orson Welles, the 21-year-old prodigy who rocked the theater world with his voodoo *Macbeth* (1936), set in Haiti. The Group Theatre, a privately funded repertory company, experimented with audience participation. For Clifford Odets's *Waiting for Lefty* (1935), it transformed a Greenwich Village theater into a meeting hall and the audience into taxi union members locked in a dispute with their bosses. Each performance closed with ringing chants of "Strike! Strike! Strike!"

The cast of **Tobacco Road** *brought the rural South to Broadway in controversial scenes that dealt frankly with issues of poverty, ignorance, and degradation.*

But even in an age of confrontation, it was still possible to find old-fashioned escape. Noël Coward's *Private Lives* (1930) doled out belly laughs instead of diatribes. Clarence Day's *Life With Father* (1939) returned to simpler turn-of-the-century times. Cole Porter musicals, such as *Anything Goes* (1934), served up farcical escapist fare. It enchanted audiences with the madcap antics of a playboy in pursuit of an heiress, an evangelist turned nightclub singer, and a gangster on the lam. The stellar cast, led by Ethel Merman, belted out such Porter gems as "You're the Top," "I Get a Kick Out of You," and the peerless title song. For a couple of hours it was possible to forget there was a Great Depression.

In the musical **On Your Toes,** *George Balanchine's violent, erotic production number "Slaughter on Tenth Avenue," starring Ray Bolger, set a new standard of choreography for the Broadway stage.*

Todd Duncan and Anne Brown *played the title roles in the tragic story of* **Porgy and Bess,** *hailed as "an American Folk Opera."*

VICIOUS CRIMINALS, VIOLENT ENDS

During the Depression a slew of killers and kidnappers provoked widespread fear — no one was safe if the Lindbergh baby wasn't — but even some law-abiding citizens admired bank robbers.

Clyde Barrow (left) and Bonnie Parker (below, right) once shot their way out of a hideout near Joplin, Missouri, leaving behind the negatives of the pictures reproduced here.

▲ Murders, bank robberies, and jailbreaks made John Dillinger Public Enemy Number One, with both state and federal governments offering rewards.

As if the Depression were not misery enough, many Americans felt that their nation had become a hotbed of heinous criminal acts. Early in the decade came the repugnant kidnapping and death of little Charles Lindbergh, Jr. (see box, next page), and there seemed to be no stopping the epidemic of kidnappings, bank robberies, and gruesome murders all over the country. For anybody who read the newspapers or listened to the radio, it was hard to avoid thinking that desperate criminals lurked everywhere. That perception was not entirely unwarranted. Measured by murders per size of population, the United States led the world in homicide.

A horrified public wondered where this criminal element had come from and what had caused the surge of lawlessness. Some said it was the repeal of Prohibition in December 1933 that was forcing bootleggers to find income to replace their profits from booze. Others blamed the offenders' battered-down families, who were trying to grub their way through the Depression on used-up farmland or

in big-city slums. Still others said that the Depression had spawned a hatred of anyone who seemed to have it better. Bankers were obvious targets, according to this theory, but it came to include anyone who had a job — gas station attendants, grocers, postal workers, and especially, law enforcement officers.

Some even viewed their gangsters as folk heroes. John Dillinger, the most notorious of the bank thieves, was to many a modern-day Robin Hood: "He robbed those who became rich by robbing the poor. I am for Johnnie," said one citizen of Dillinger's native Indiana. Dillinger's flair for the dramatic made some people forget that he had killed at least 10 people. His gang once posed as a movie company on location in front of a Sioux Falls bank. While thousands milled around hoping to catch a glimpse of a real star, real criminals, posing as movie actors, robbed the bank and made a swift getaway. After a nationwide manhunt, Melvin Purvis and other federal agents, tipped off by the madam of a brothel, shot down Public Enemy Number One in July 1934 outside a North Side Chicago movie theater.

Most of the big-name criminals from those years died as violently and as publicly as John Dillinger had. In May the infamous Bonnie and Clyde had driven into an ambush set up by a former Texas Ranger captain outside Arcadia, Louisiana. Going 85 miles an hour, the car careened out of control as their bodies absorbed more than 50 bullets. Bonnie Parker, a 23-year-old tough-talking, cigar-smoking, quick-shooting former waitress from Kansas City, and her 24-year-old Texas-born lover, Clyde Barrow, had

sped through the Southwest knocking off small-town banks, grocery stores, and gas stations. The lawless pair made a lark of their crimes, snapping souvenir photos of themselves and murdering passersby and law officers indiscriminately. After a nationally publicized manhunt, they were finally ambushed. Some 12 firearms, including 3 submachine guns were found in their car.

Charles (Pretty Boy) Floyd succeeded John Dillinger as Public Enemy Number One. He robbed so many banks in Oklahoma that the insurance rates doubled in just one year. He relied on the machine gun as his weapon of choice; for a while he even had one mounted on his car. His nickname, which he thoroughly detested, was said to have been supplied by an admiring Kansas City bordello madam. Floyd met his demise in October 1934 when he was chased down

◄ Police in Pueblo, Colorado, took this mug shot of Pretty Boy Floyd when they arrested him for vagrancy in 1929.

▶ Ma Barker — thief, kidnapper, and murderer — enjoys a peaceful moment with lover Arthur Dunlop. Insets: The sons she raised in her image, Dock (left) and Freddie (right).

by a 100-man posse outside of East Liverpool, Ohio.

Baby Face Nelson, who wanted to be known as Big George and who had always resented the fact that he never got as much media attention as his onetime partner, John Dillinger, became the next Public Enemy Number One. When federal agents finally cornered him, outside Barrington, Illinois, Nelson killed two of them, staggered back to the G-men's car with 17 slugs in his body, and made a getaway with his wife and another gangster. That evening, they tossed his dead, naked body into a ditch near Niles, Illinois, where it was found the next day.

For matrimonial devotion, however, George Barker is unsurpassed in gangster lore. The 55-year-old Ma Barker left her plodding husband, George, so that she could wheel and deal to get her remaining three sons out of prison. (One had already committed suicide.) Once out, sons Freddie and Dock moved in with Ma and her new lover and took to robbing banks and kidnapping wealthy men. They were fabulously successful at both ventures: one bank job netted $250,000, and the ransom for a Minneapolis banker came in at $200,000. In January 1935 Ma and her son Freddie, now living near Oklawaha, Florida, were killed in a six-hour machine-gun battle with federal agents. Her spurned husband had their bodies — and those of his other sons — returned to Welch, Oklahoma, and buried each of them within sight of his gas station there.

The Crime of the Century

Kidnappings increased at a frightening rate as the Depression deepened; in Chicago alone police logged some 200 in 1930 and 1931. But the abduction of the 20-month-old son of Anne and Charles Lindbergh (right) in March 1932 shocked the nation and aroused Congress to make kidnapping a federal offense. The press swooped down in droves, and the carnival atmosphere added to the Lindberghs' suffering. After the baby was taken from his home in New Jersey, investigators found a ransom note with Germanic misspellings. Two weeks later a retired Bronx teacher claimed to have contacted the kidnapper and agreed to pass along the $50,000 in demanded ransom. Lindbergh paid, but the baby was not returned. Police questioned suspects all over the country, to no avail. Every so often a ransom bill turned up, but no one could trace the source. In May truckers found the baby dead in the woods near the Lindbergh estate. More than two years passed before police arrested Bruno Richard Hauptmann (left), a Bronx carpenter with a record of petty crime in Germany. Hauptmann claimed he was innocent; when some of the ransom money was found in his garage, he said a friend had left it there. Hauptmann was tried in Flemington, New Jersey, a small town overrun by souvenir hawkers, curiosity seekers, and the press. The macabre circus ended when the jury of eight men and four women found him guilty. Hauptmann, still swearing his innocence, went to the electric chair on April 3, 1936, even though a confession would have saved him.

► *J. Edgar Hoover's campaign to make the FBI America's premier crime-fighting force included these 1935 publicity shots. A G-man tests a submachine gun in the bureau's soundproof underground shooting range, and scientific sleuths inspect evidence in the FBI crime laboratory.*

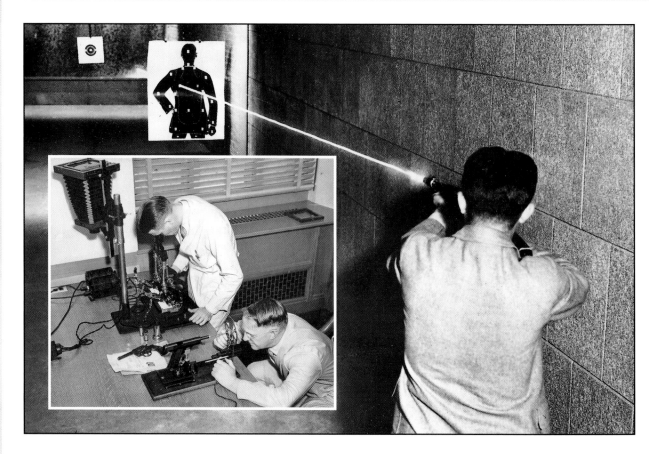

Prohibition's end coincided with a crime wave that led to the strengthening and expansion of the FBI. Here Director J. Edgar Hoover examines his network of field agents.

DIRECTOR OF LAW AND ORDER

By raising personnel standards, instituting rigorous training programs, and insisting on the best scientific equipment, J. Edgar Hoover promoted his FBI as the nation's best weapon against crime.

The dramatic crime wave sweeping the country demanded "action, and action now," as President Roosevelt had pledged in his inaugural address. But there was no such thing as a national police force, and the Department of Justice, largely manned by party hacks, was often referred to as the Department of Easy Virtue.

Within the Justice Department there was the little-known Bureau of Investigation, headed by J. Edgar Hoover, who had been appointed in 1924 at the age of 29. Shortly after taking office, Hoover fired a third of the staff and then raised the hiring standards for new employees. He brought the management style of a military martinet to the bureau and transformed it into a formidable crime-

fighting force. By 1930 he had a file of 3 million fingerprints and had established a crime laboratory to evaluate evidence. But the bureau's jurisdiction was still limited to glamourless investigative donkeywork, such as tracking down perpetrators of federal bank frauds or violators of the 1910 Mann Act, the white slave traffic law that prohibited transporting women across state or national boundaries for immoral purposes. Agents were not even authorized to make arrests or to carry firearms.

Then, in response to the Lindbergh case (see p. 169), Congress passed a law making kidnapping across state lines a federal crime. In addition, robberies of national banks, assaults on federal officers, and many other crimes involving interstate felonies became federal offenses. Federal agents finally got permission to carry guns and make arrests. Hoover, once admiringly described by a reporter as a "sledgehammer in search of an anvil," had created a department ready for its new responsibilities.

Moving fast, Hoover's bureau compiled a list of 6,000 gangsters and suspicious persons, and it elevated a few to a new and highly publicized Public Enemies List. The bureau's agents were in on the capture or killing of the era's most notorious criminals: John Dillinger, Pretty Boy Floyd, Baby Face Nelson, Ma Barker and one of her boys, and more. By early 1935 Hoover and his agents — now known as G-men; the G for *government* — were very much admired. By the end of that year the bureau had been renamed the Federal Bureau of Investigation (FBI), and its members had become folk heroes.

How a Legend Grew and Grew

Hollywood is what made the difference. Its mythmakers zoomed in on gangster cases, and on the FBI, and turned them into popular entertainment. The first movie, *G-Men,* starred James Cagney, and it was a box office knockout. Quickly absorbing this lesson in the value of publicity, Hoover involved himself in the launching of a new comic strip, a radio show, and pulp magazines like *G-Men* and *The Feds.* All pushed the bureau as the model of clean-cut virtue and scientific efficiency, and Hoover as a model director. FBI communications with the media emphasized that the director was in personal charge of every important investigation. To publicize his starring role, Hoover began showing up at the capture of high-profile criminals and talking to the press afterward. On one such occasion he crowed:

Melvin Purvis led the team of agents that killed John Dillinger. After a falling-out with Hoover, he left the FBI and did promotional work, like this how-to-fight-crime manual for Post Toasties.

▼ **The Boys Clubs of America presented "Public Hero Number One" their Distinguished Service Medal in 1936.**

"The man who said he'd never be captured quit like the yellow rat he is and the rest of gangland is at heart." And in 1935 Hoover started the National Police Academy, a training school for local police officers from across the country, creating yet another powerful constituency for the director and the bureau.

As success piled upon success, the FBI gained more muscle. In 1936 FDR gave Hoover a mandate to seek out subversives deemed to be threatening national security. By 1940 nearly 1,000 special agents staffed the bureau, compared with just over 300 at the decade's start.

As the bureau grew dramatically in size and prestige, more and more people saw the director as a man who could do no wrong. Tracking down a bank robber and his wife in New York City, Hoover shooed away city police while he and a squad of 25 G-men poured gunfire, then tear gas, into the fugitive's apartment. He defended his actions by saying, "The taxpayers got what they paid for, the apprehension of criminals." A passionate defender of morality and discipline, he scorned "the maunderings of fanatics and tuffet heads, who . . . allow the new youth to do anything it pleases."

By 1940 some magazines and newspapers were expressing concern that Hoover was trampling on civil liberties. But the success of "Public Hero Number One" could not be denied. Kidnapping had virtually disappeared, bank robberies were down, recoveries in interstate thefts had doubled, and the FBI conviction rate stood at an impressive 80 percent.

Thousands of Junior G-Men (Melvin Purvis's club for kids) aspired to become the topflight, clean-cut professionally trained crime buster this photo publicized.

This baby was among the children of the Flint, Michigan, autoworkers who staged a parade on January 10, 1937.

TOUGH BOSSES, TOUGH WORKERS

After years of unrest marked by more than 20,000 strikes, bloodshed, and seemingly endless setbacks, the labor movement rebounded with the help of public support.

Organized labor suffered a near fatal blow during the Depression. High unemployment decimated membership ranks and permitted employers to fire workers with impunity. Unions, organized by craft and skill in the American Federation of Labor (AFL), had begun to lose the confidence of many of their rank-and-file members.

A number of laborers actually worked at gunpoint. Richard B. Mellon, chairman of the Pittsburgh Coal Company, explained to Congress in 1928 why he kept machine guns in the coal pits: "You cannot run the mines without them." Congress apparently agreed. Many employers spent huge sums hiring spies and goons to weed out union troublemakers. Organized protests were routinely squelched by local authorities. A Youngstown, Ohio, district attorney stated publicly: "Give me 200 good, tough armed men and I'll clean up them sons of bitches on the picket line."

But labor persevered. Conditions were so bad, there was little choice. An unskilled autoworker described his

In May 1937, police attack protesters near the Republic Steel plant in South Chicago. Two weeks later (below) some 8,000 CIO members with their families protest police brutality in Monroe, Michigan.

plight: "You might call yourself a man if you was on the street, but as soon as you went through the door and punched your card, you was nothing more or less than a robot. Do this, go there, do that. You'd do it." A wife described her working husband: "You should see him come home at night, him and the rest of the men. . . . So tired like they was dead. . . . And then at night in bed, he shakes, his whole body, he shakes." Another wife glumly added: ". . . they're not men anymore, if you know what I mean."

New Weapon: The Sit-down Strike

Championing the workers' cause was a six-foot three-inch mountain of a man of Welsh descent, John L. Lewis. Lewis drove a Cadillac and wore custom-made underwear, but he used his booming voice and biblical oratory to fight uncompromisingly for the United Mine Workers (UMW). He saw to it that he was always photographed scowling; to be seen smiling might indicate softness.

Toughness paid off. Lewis won for the UMW "all the things deputy sheriffs usually shot people for demanding," a magazine wrote. In late 1935 Lewis, along with such progressive union leaders as David Dubinsky and Sidney Hillman, proposed a plan to unite all skilled and unskilled workers on an industry-wide basis. Their plan frightened conservative AFL leaders, who referred to the insurgents as "pinkos" and kicked them and what would become a new union, the Congress of Industrial Organizations (CIO), out of the AFL.

The CIO's big test came at the end of 1936. Newly organized autoworkers in a Flint, Michigan, General Motors plant simply stopped working and sat down. It was the first sit-down strike in the United States, and its leaders included Walter P. Reuther, who would remain a force in the labor movement until his death in 1970, and his brother Victor, who later outlined the conditions that faced the Flint strikers: "Flint's mayor, chief of police, clergy, newspapers, and even its judges were under the thumb of General Motors." The strike spread: 60 plants in 14 states were affected.

The strikers in Flint hung on for 44 days. Wives, family members, and friends cooked for them in a makeshift kitchen outside the plant and hoisted the food up through the windows. When GM attempted to halt food delivery and turned off the heat inside, Lewis and Labor Secretary Frances Perkins convinced Governor Frank Murphy to intervene for a peaceful settlement. "Morale was very high . . . "

▼ *After a bitter and debilitating power struggle, which lasted for nearly 20 years, the AFL and the CIO would merge in 1955.*

recalled a striker. "It started out kinda ugly because the guys was afraid they put their foot in it and all they was gonna do is lose their jobs. But as time went on, they begin to realize they could win this darn thing, 'cause we had a lot of outside people comin' in showin' their sympathy." Victory came when GM agreed to recognize and bargain with the United Automobile Workers (UAW) in all 60 plants.

New Target: The Steel Industry

Lewis's next target was United States Steel, which had recorded gross earnings of over $35 million in 1934. The average steelworker earned $369 per year, and most steelworkers were part-time. Safety conditions were deplorable: in a single year more than 200 workers were killed, more than 1,000 permanently disabled, and more than 21,000 temporarily laid up. Lewis believed that if he won over U.S. Steel, other steel companies would follow. "If the crouching lion can be routed, it is a safe bet that the hyenas in the adjacent bush may be scattered along the plain." Surprisingly the chairman of U.S. Steel agreed, without a fight, to sign a contract with the CIO.

Other steel companies were not so easily won over. On Memorial Day, 1937, in Chicago some 1,500 workers, with their wives and children, gathered for a demonstration outside the Republic Steel plant. A doctor described it as "simply a family picnic sort of thing: little kids, people dressed up in their Sunday shirts." But the laughter soon turned to screams as 150 cops attacked the crowd with tear gas, nightsticks, and guns. Within 15 minutes, 10 demonstrators lay dead and more than 100 were wounded.

Labor lost that round, but public opinion was turning against management-sponsored violence and toward the rights of the workingman. Over the decade, union membership, helped by favorable New Deal legislation, increased from fewer than 3.5 million to nearly 9 million, and politicians at all levels had to acknowledge the power of organized labor.

◀

Jailed in Russian Poland for union activity, David Dubinsky escaped to America in 1911. As head of the International Ladies' Garment Workers' Union (1932–66), he helped launch the CIO but left it and rejoined the AFL in 1940.

LANDSLIDE FOR THE NEW DEAL

The forces arrayed against President Roosevelt in 1936 ran the gamut from financiers to Communists, but he still won 60 percent of the popular vote.

FDR and Eleanor stump together in Kansas City (top); often in 1936 they campaigned separately. The opposition, meanwhile, struck back hard, as in the cartoon above, which appeared on the cover of a satiric anti-New Deal pamphlet.

The presidential election of 1936 was bitterly fought, and its lopsided result marked a smashing personal triumph for the Democratic incumbent. From the beginning President Roosevelt knew the campaign would hinge on how people felt about him: "There is only one issue in this campaign," he told an adviser. "It's myself, and the people must be either for me or against me."

The people against FDR were easy enough to spot. The millionaire John Pierpont Morgan, Jr. absolutely prohibited FDR's name from being mentioned in his house. When FDR visited Harvard, his (and Morgan's) alma mater, the president was booed by students and alumni who believed he had turned his back on his social class.

On the far right, Father Charles E. Coughlin, a Roman Catholic priest who had launched his own political party, railed against communists, Jews, capitalists, and "Franklin Double-Crossing Roosevelt" on national radio. Coughlin's

Financier J. P. Morgan epitomized the upper-class enmity toward Roosevelt and his programs.

Social Security

When in June 1934 President Roosevelt set up a committee, chaired by Secretary of Labor Frances Perkins, to study economic security, he told her that "there's no reason why everybody in the United States should not be covered . . . from the cradle to the grave." Perkins didn't think politicians would pass something so comprehensive, even though most European countries had done so a generation earlier. The Social Security Act authorized welfare payments and set up insurance for the aged, unemployed, and disabled. It was meant to supplement personal savings and private pension plans and covered about half the work force. Businessmen fought hard against a bill they felt would destroy initiative and discourage thrift. The left condemned it as too conservative and charged FDR with selling out to big business. In August 1935 the bill passed — and passed overwhelmingly. Few congressmen wanted to go on record as being against the interests of older people. The law signaled acknowledgment by the federal government that it had a responsibility for the everyday well-being of senior citizens. FDR had insisted that the program be funded by equal worker and employer contributions because he thought that future administrations would thus have a harder time taking away benefits. The initial payroll deduction was 1 percent of a worker's wages up to $3,000 per year.

A monthly check to you—

FOR THE REST OF YOUR LIFE · · BEGINNING WHEN YOU ARE 65

GET YOUR SOCIAL SECURITY ACCOUNT NUMBER *promptly*

APPLICATIONS ARE BEING DISTRIBUTED AT ALL WORK PLACES

WHO IS ELIGIBLE · · EVERYBODY WORKING FOR SALARY OR WAGES (WITH ONLY A FEW EXCEPTIONS, SUCH AS AGRICULTURE, DOMESTIC SERVICE, AND GOVERNMENT WORK). APPLICATIONS FOR SOCIAL SECURITY ACCOUNTS ARE AVAILABLE THROUGH EMPLOYERS. IF YOU DO NOT GET ONE FROM YOUR EMPLOYER, ASK FOR ONE AT THE POST OFFICE.

HOW TO RETURN APPLICATION

1. HAND IT BACK TO YOUR EMPLOYER, or
2. HAND IT TO ANY LABOR ORGANIZATION OF WHICH YOU ARE A MEMBER, or
3. HAND IT TO YOUR LETTER CARRIER, or
4. DELIVER IT TO LOCAL POST OFFICE or
5. MAIL IT IN A SEALED ENVELOPE ADDRESSED POSTMASTER LOCAL DO IT NOW. NO POSTAGE NEEDED.

—Social Security Board

INFORMATION MAY BE OBTAINED AT ANY POST OFFICE

has just taken his seat in the dental chair for what is certain to be a long and painful ordeal."

But polls suggested that the contest was close, and some businessmen who were pushing anyone but Roosevelt tried to scare workers about Social Security by putting slips in their paychecks: "You're sentenced to a weekly pay reduction for all your working life. You'll have to serve the sentence unless you help reverse it November 3rd." Roosevelt fired back. "Never before in all our history have these forces been so united against one candidate as they stand today," he said. "They are unanimous in their hate for me — and I welcome their hatred."

The real measure of public opinion came in the gigantic crowds that flocked to FDR as he campaigned. That popular outpouring was reflected on Election Day. FDR won every state except Maine and Vermont and more than 60 percent of the vote. He had put together a new coalition of voters: the urban working class, organized labor, farmers, and Southerners. For the first time in more than 40 years, the largest bloc of voters in the country considered themselves Democrats, not Republicans.

▼ *At home in the Sunflower State, Governor Landon poses with his family: left to right, John, Margaret Anne (standing), Nancy (later Senator Kassebaum), and wife, Theo.*

LANDON AND KNOX

supporters joined with followers of Dr. Francis E. Townsend, who advocated a $200-a-month payment to senior citizens, and with those of Huey Long, the dynamic senator from Louisiana who had been assassinated a year earlier, to back a third-party candidate, William Lemke, dedicated, in Father Coughlin's words, to "taking a Communist from the chair once occupied by Washington." On the left, Norman Thomas, the Socialist candidate, told voters that only he could lead a revolution. Further left, Earl Browder ran on the Communist ticket.

While many raised their voices to criticize Roosevelt, few could get excited about his Republican opponent, Alfred M. (Alf) Landon. A two-term governor of Kansas, Landon was a moderate and decent man, but his rhetorical skills fell somewhat short of inspirational. His campaign slogan was "Life, Liberty, and Landon," but he was described on the campaign trail as having "the unhappy look of a man who

CLIPPING A PRESIDENT'S WINGS

With the New Deal flying high and his popularity soaring, FDR may have thought he was invincible. Then the Supreme Court nullified a key program, and the president responded with an audacious scheme to reshape the Court more to his liking.

Outraged Democrats balked at FDR's "innocent" Court-packing proposal.

▼ **Franklin D. Roosevelt, talking to reporters from his hand-controlled Ford, is brimming with confidence after some six years as president.**

For a while in 1935 it seemed as though the mighty Blue Eagle of Franklin D. Roosevelt's National Recovery Administration (NRA), the New Deal agency set up to regulate business and labor, would be brought down by a sick kosher chicken.

It all started with four brothers who ran a kosher poultry business in Brooklyn. After the NRA was passed, the Schechter brothers signed its Live Poultry Code, agreeing to pay a minimum wage, limit the number of hours for workers, and maintain a certain quality of chicken. In no time the brothers were indicted and convicted on 17 violations of the code, including selling a sick chicken for human consumption. Protesting their innocence, the Schechters carried their fight all the way to the Supreme Court.

A little after noon on a warm spring Monday, May 27, 1935, the white-whiskered 73-year-old Chief Justice Charles Evans Hughes read the high court's unanimous decision striking down the NRA as an unconstitutional infringement on the power of Congress by the president. "This is the end of this business of centralization, and I want you to go back and tell the president that we're not going to let this government centralize everything. It's come to an end," Justice Louis Brandeis told a Roosevelt aide.

President Roosevelt was livid. The Supreme Court had undercut a major program. Furthermore, upcoming decisions threatened the whole New Deal, including Social Security and the Wagner labor law. He asked Attorney General Homer Cummings to prepare some alternative courses of action but waited until he was reelected in 1936 to do anything.

At his second inauguration he indicated that the New Deal was far from over: "I see one-third of a nation ill housed, ill clad, ill nourished," he said in his inaugural address. "The test of our progress . . . is whether we provide

▶ **Two of the triumphant Schechter brothers hoist their lawyer, Joseph Heller, to celebrate their defeat of the NRA in the Supreme Court.**

enough for those who have so little." Most people thought he meant to launch another attack on economic royalists. But Roosevelt had a different target in mind.

Just two weeks later FDR held his annual dinner for the federal judiciary at the White House. It was a pleasant evening, without a hint that he had big plans for changing the Court. Two days later Roosevelt presented his plan to key members of Congress: for every Supreme Court justice who failed to retire after 70, the president wanted to appoint a new justice, up to a total of six. With the addition of six new liberal justices, the conservative anti–New Deal majority on the Court would be smashed. FDR presented this as an "efficiency" measure to help the aged justices with their heavy work load. But it was immediately obvious that the measure was actually aimed at packing the Court in his favor. After winning the greatest landslide in U.S. history, FDR figured he was unstoppable. But he soon learned otherwise.

His New Deal coalition began to crumble. Vice President John Nance Garner came out against the plan; 79-year-old Senator Carter Glass of Virginia resented the implication that a man was washed up at 70. Chief Justice Hughes took the extraordinary step of writing a letter to Congress stating that more justices would actually increase their work load: "There would be more judges to hear, more judges to confer, more judges to discuss, more judges to be convinced and to decide."

FDR continued pushing the plan even as it lost popular support. But as Hugh Johnson, former head of the NRA, noted: "The old Roosevelt magic has lost its kick. . . . The diverse elements in his Falstaffian army can no longer be

Her Song Is Heard

They came from all walks of life: young and old, black and white, rich and poor. On that Easter Sunday, April 9, 1939, they gathered 75,000 strong around the steps of the Lincoln Memorial to hear the African-American contralto Marian Anderson. For many in the crowd, her concert represented a triumph for racial tolerance. Earlier that year, she had been denied the use of Constitution Hall, a building owned by the Daughters of the American Revolution (DAR), for a performance. Suspecting bigotry, some members of the DAR, most notably Eleanor Roosevelt, resigned. Then Anderson's backers had a brilliant idea: let her sing at the Lincoln Memorial. And there, from the moment she began to sing "My country! 'tis of thee!" Marian Anderson became a symbol of racial justice.

kept together and led by a melodious whinny and a winning smile." It wasn't that the president had lost popularity; he hadn't. But Congress and the public resented what appeared to be a power-grabbing scheme by the president.

Ironically, the justices themselves reversed course and upheld other key elements of the New Deal, such as Social Security, the Wagner Act, and a state minimum wage law. Later the president liked to say that he had lost the battle but won the war since he got what he wanted from the Court. But never again would Congress support him without question. And his next years were marked by a recession and high unemployment, which topped 19 percent in 1938.

The national debate shifted, focusing increasingly on tensions in Europe and Asia and on what, if anything, America should do. Roosevelt surprised much of the nation when he decided to try for an unprecedented third term in 1940. The threat of war and Roosevelt's desire to be succeeded by a liberal Democrat (the major contenders for the nomination were conservative) influenced his decision. His Republican opponent, Wendell Willkie, a utility executive with no political experience, attacked the New Deal. He charged that interfering with business had not returned the nation to prosperity. Toward the end of the campaign, Willkie even labeled FDR a warmonger. But the president assured the country: "Your boys are not going to be sent into any foreign wars." Although the New Deal had been floundering, FDR was still personally popular, and perhaps the country wanted someone they knew in office for the troubled times ahead. When the ballots were counted, Roosevelt had won convincingly, 27 million votes to Willkie's 22 million.

Wendell Willkie, here campaigning in Jersey City, attacked FDR's bid for a third term with slogans like "No man is good three times" and "No crown for Franklin."

GOING PLACES AS NEVER BEFORE

In spite of the Depression — some said because of it — adventurous Americans, rich and poor, expanded their travel horizons in ways that were almost always faster, sometimes cheaper, and often riskier.

Airship Tragedy

Charles Lindbergh had become an emblem of optimism and adventure in the late 1920's. If he could hop in an airplane and fly from New York to Paris all by himself, then there was nothing Americans couldn't do. The Depression dealt this optimistic outlook a body blow, but a few gallant, and well-heeled, aerial pioneers continued to push the limits of how far we could go and how fast — and became instant heroes.

America hailed Wiley Post, a one-eyed ex-oilman and para-chute jumper, when he and his navigator circled the globe in the record time of 8 days, 15 hours, and 51 minutes in 1931. Two years later, equipped with a radio navigational device and an autopilot to help him fly the plane, Post became the first person to fly around the world alone. And this time he did it in less than eight days. A shocked nation mourned in 1935 when he and his friend Will Rogers died in a plane crash in Alaska. The quest for records cost a number of aviators their lives. Amelia Earhart, or Lady Lindy as she was known to her adoring public, became the first woman to fly solo across the Atlantic, in 1932; but she disappeared

For wealthy travelers in the 1930's, nothing rivaled the luxurious airships built by Germany's Zeppelin Company. The *Hindenburg*, flagship of the new "average traveler's" fleet, could reach about 80 m.p.h. and had 25 passenger cabins, complete with hot and cold running water. Leaving Frankfurt on May 3, 1937, it had 36 passengers and 61 crew members. Due at Lakehurst, New Jersey, at 6 A.M. on May 6, the *Hindenburg* was delayed by head winds and was just passing over Times Square at 3:07 P.M. By 7 P.M. a ground crew of more than 200 and a large crowd eagerly awaited the arrival. Passengers first knew something was wrong when they saw people on the ground freeze and then run from the ship. Only 32 seconds elapsed from the first flame appearing in the stern to the bow hitting the earth. Miraculously, 62 people survived. But the horrifying photos, films, and radio broadcasts helped to doom passenger airships.

When completed in 1931, the George Washington Bridge, here being built, joined New Jersey and New York City. The economical 1939 Crosley (left) promised 60 miles per gallon.

Hoboes rode the rails for free in the 1930's. The postcard below touts a precursor of today's high-speed roads.

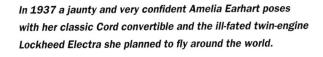

In 1937 a jaunty and very confident Amelia Earhart poses with her classic Cord convertible and the ill-fated twin-engine Lockheed Electra she planned to fly around the world.

five years later in the Pacific while attempting to circle the world at the Equator. A search by the navy — involving 4,000 men in 10 ships and 65 airplanes over 16 days — found nothing.

These kinds of tragedies led some to call for curbing risky flights; such grandstanding was senseless and discouraging to would-be passengers on the young domestic airlines. Discouraging, too, was the tiny, cramped space for passengers in most airliners. But in 1932 Trans World Airlines (TWA) engaged the Douglas Aircraft Company to design a plane more suitable for passengers than for cargo. The result was the Douglas Commercial-1 (DC-1). Its innovative wing flaps made landing slower, safer, and much smoother. Its design was further refined in the quicker, more comfortable DC-2. But it was the DC-3, completed in 1935, a plane big enough to accommodate sleeping berths for passengers, that became the most widely used plane of all time.

Of course, not many Americans were ready to

Britain granted a subsidy to Cunard–White Star to complete the construction of the luxury liner Queen Mary, here escorted by biplanes in 1936.

try plane travel. Nor could many afford cruises on luxurious ocean liners, like France's *Normandie* and Britain's *Queen Mary,* which came into service in 1936 with exotic wood interiors, hand-woven carpets, and sterling silver fixtures. Even as the rich and famous patronized these "floating palaces," most folks had to rely on trains and cars.

The cheapest way to travel was to steal a ride on a freight train: you didn't have to pay a thing, as long as the railroad bulls (police) didn't catch you. Almost anyone, of course, would have preferred to ride in an automobile. Though car production fell 75 percent from 1929 to 1932, car registrations dropped just 10 percent.

Manufacturers either adapted to lower demand or went bust. Particularly hard hit were makers of luxury cars, such as the Deusenberg, Stutz Bearcat, Pierce-Arrow, and air-cooled Franklin, none of which survived the Depression. By 1939 General Motors, Chrysler, and Ford made 90 percent of the cars in America.

President Roosevelt's New Deal was in full swing, and by the end of the decade, Public Works Administration (PWA) funds helped finance America's first express tollway: a 160-mile run from Harrisburg to Pittsburgh, the first leg of what would become a turnpike stretching across Pennsylvania. This road was built so straight in places that it proved hazardous: some motorists suffered from highway hypnosis. Nevertheless, with a few improvements it became the prototype for future superhighways.

THE WORLD OF TOMORROW

The New York World's Fair glowed with visions of plenty, beauty, and social harmony, all brought within Americans' grasp by the wondrous alchemy of science and technology.

The 1939 New York World's Fair, wrote a journalist, "was such an upbeat antidote to the Depression — the implied promise of better times was palpable." Set atop a marshy landfill in Flushing, Queens, the fair offered a look at a happier future. It was, as *Life* magazine put it, "a boast by America about America for Americans." Millions of visitors came to "The World of Tomorrow" to peek into a TV studio, walk through a hydroelectric dam, watch machine-made lightning, and hear the voice of Albert Einstein in a vivid sound-and-light show.

Sixty nations and more than 100 corporations participated in this monument to democracy and technology. Grover Whalen, the fair's president, dismissed mounting tensions in Europe and assured potential investors there would be no war: "Why, the king of Egypt told me positively that there'll be no war. . . . A wave of enthusiasm for our New York World's Fair is sweeping Europe. That's what Europe is thinking about, not war."

Visitors came away believing in a not-too-distant future of 14-lane highways, air-conditioned high-rises towering over slum-free cities, a TV in every home, and a cancer cure. Many wore an "I Have Seen the Future" button after eyeballing General Motors's Futurama, Norman Bel Geddes's stunning conception of the landscape in 1960.

▲ *In 1939 New York's bold planner Robert Moses proposed a bridge connecting Manhattan's southern tip and Brooklyn. The project never got off the ground.*

Industrial designers like Norman Bel Geddes (top) and Raymond Loewy (right) streamlined the look of the future. Above: Geddes applied the concept of aerodynamic streamlining to his models of buses and cars. Loewy came up with this design for a Pennsylvania Railroad train.

PENNSY

Even household objects took on the new sleek look. Walter Dorwin Teague designed this 1933 table radio; the clock's Art Deco style was enormously popular in the 1930's.

Frank Lloyd Wright (below), a genius who called his work organic architecture, was nearly 70 when he designed this innovative weekend retreat, called Fallingwater, for Pittsburgh department store owner Edgar Kaufmann in 1936.

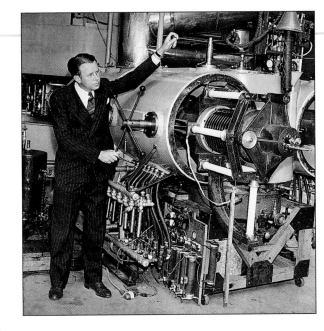

► Ernest O. Lawrence won the 1939 Nobel Prize for physics for inventing and developing the cyclotron, known as the atom smasher.

Not far away, in midtown Manhattan, a project that would change the New York City landscape was nearing completion. Begun in 1931, Rockefeller Center was a complex of skyscrapers and shops, offices and services — a city within a city. Mayor Fiorello La Guardia's ambitious planner, Robert Moses, meanwhile, supervised the construction of a dozen new bridges and tunnels and several major highways, so that a motorist could drive nearly all around the congested city without stopping for a traffic light.

On the West Coast, engineer Joseph B. Strauss coordinated the construction of the remarkable Golden Gate Bridge in San Francisco, opened in 1937. Meanwhile, in the stifling heat of the Nevada desert, thousands of men had worked to pour 6 million tons of concrete into Hoover Dam, the largest masonry structure built up to that time: 660 feet thick at its base, and nearly two-thirds as high as the Empire State Building. At opening ceremonies President Roosevelt christened it Boulder Dam; not until the late 1940's did Congress restore its original name. Dam building was a

favorite New Deal project. The TVA harnessed the Tennessee River with a vast complex of dams and powerhouses. In the Northwest a series of giant projects, topped by the enormous Grand Coulee Dam, tamed the Columbia River.

Not only were dams and highways technological marvels, they also embodied the new sense of visual design that was sweeping America. The apostle of the futuristic look was a voluble industrial designer named Raymond Loewy, who preached the gospel of streamlining. Loewy smoothed the lines of the chunky Coldspot refrigerator for Sears, Roebuck, and sales quadrupled. He pioneered the shape of Studebaker cars, of Greyhound buses, of Pennsylvania Railroad trains, of ballpoint pens and ocean liners.

Only a few of those who came to the World's Fair could see technology's full implications, however. One man who saw into the future was Albert Einstein. In the summer of 1939, after the World's Fair opened, he sent a letter to President Roosevelt urging the development of atomic energy, a pursuit that would soon give human beings a fearsome new force to reckon with.

► This poster features the symbols of the New York World's Fair: the over-600-foot-tall needlelike Trylon and the almost-200-foot globe, the Perisphere.

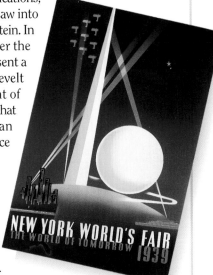

Buffalo ◑ 1901

The Lackawanna Railroad promoted its scenic route, along the Delaware River through the "gap" between New Jersey and Pennsylvania, to the Pan-American Exposition, whose aim was to further the prosperity of the Western Hemisphere.

St. Louis ◑ 1904

Officially named the Louisiana Purchase Exposition in honor of President Thomas Jefferson's 1803 acquisition of 827,987 square miles of North America from France, the St. Louis world's fair spread over 1,240 acres. Its theme was education.

Every Year ◑ The 4th of July

Everyone has a favorite way to celebrate America's birthday. These boys re-create the famous *Spirit of '76* by American painter Archibald Willard. Others go to a baseball game, have their annual extended family picnic, watch fireworks, and just enjoy being American.

San Francisco ◑ 1915

The Panama-Pacific International Exposition paid tribute to Balboa's reaching the Pacific in 1513, the Panama Canal's opening (1914), and San Francisco's recovery from the 1906 quake.

GREAT CELEBRATIONS OF THE CENTURY

When the 100th birthday of Miss Liberty rolled around in 1986, New Yorkers gave her a party to remember. The festivities included a parade of tall ships and the wondrous fireworks at left. For the hundreds of thousands of well-wishers that crowded New York City's shorelines, the hoopla rivaled the city's Bicentennial blowout just 10 years before. (See "The Bicentennial," pp. 368–69). In good times and bad, Americans have given themselves some memorable wingdings. Though tragedy clouded the first of the century's great fairs, when President McKinley was shot at the Buffalo exposition, America bounced back three years later with a spectacle that convinced one wide-eyed New Yorker that St. Louis was no longer a backward prairie town. "The cascades and fountains were leaping in the still lagoon," 21-year-old Harper Silliman wrote his bride-to-be back in Massachusetts, and "I could almost imagine myself to be present at some great festival in Athens two or three thousand years ago." Such transcendent fantasies, whether of a glorious past or a fabulous future, are the common thread of the grand fairs and extravagant expositions remembered on these two pages.

San Francisco World's Fair ◗ 1939

Visitors to the Golden Gate International Exposition could stroll the 1,000-foot-long Court of the Seven Seas (above), one of several avenues radiating from the 400-foot-tall Tower of the Sun in the background. This "Pageant of the Pacific" dedicated itself to world peace and brotherhood.

Chicago World's Fair ◗ 1933

The Windy City gave itself a 100th-birthday bash, celebrating "A Century of Progress" since the city's founding in 1833. In the depths of the Depression, the fair's upbeat themes drew 38.6 million people.

New York World's Fair ◗ 1964

"Peace Through Understanding" (souvenir button, left) was its theme and its symbol, the Unisphere (below, seen through illuminated fountains).

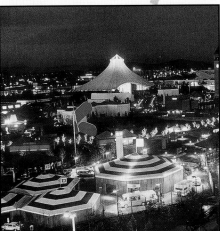

Seattle World's Fair ◗ 1962

The Century 21 Exposition presented the good life that advances in science and technology could bring in the 21st century, as envisioned by exhibitors from 48 countries.

New York's World Fair ◗ 1939

The Perisphere, a huge white globe, and the Trylon, a tapering 728-foot-tall column, took center stage in "The World of Tomorrow," a Utopian vision of marvels to come. But what came first was the horror of world war.

Spokane ◗ 1974

Reflecting the environmental and social concerns of the time, Expo '74, dominated by an American Indian tepee pavilion, rose on a 100-acre park that had been an industrial site. The fair addressed problems created by progress.

A GREEDY GANG OF DICTATORS

Ironfisted strongmen emerged from the chaos following World War I, each intent on

grabbing absolute power, restoring national pride and prosperity, and humbling all enemies.

The dictators who emerged following World War I came in all sizes, shapes, and philosophies, but each one sought total control of his country.

After V. I. Lenin died in Russia in 1924, Joseph Stalin won a vicious power struggle and assumed leadership of the ruling Communist Party. He purged the government of potential rivals, including Lenin's heir apparent, Leon Trotsky, and launched the first of his five-year plans to industrialize the economy. Seeking to improve farm productivity, Stalin ordered all landowning peasants to give up their land or face exile, forced labor, or execution. By 1933 he had collectivized more than 80 percent of Soviet farms, but millions of kulaks, peasants who opposed collectivization,

were murdered or died of man-made famine. Stalin then set his secret police on his enemies within the party and the army; he killed or exiled roughly half the officer corps, some 35,000 men. He then turned on the secret police who had carried out his murderous schemes and replaced them with henchmen he deemed even more loyal. All this was done, Stalin explained, to ensure the U.S.S.R.'s security and to advance communism.

The threat of communism promoted the standing of dictators in other countries. The stridently anti-Communist Benito Mussolini postured and blustered as Il Duce (The Leader) for more than a decade, promising "peace, work, and calm . . . with love if possible, with force if necessary." Then in 1935, hoping to resurrect the imperial splendors of ancient Rome, he set his sights overseas — on Ethiopia.

Ethiopia's army carried muskets, swords, and spears; its barefooted cavalrymen wore lion skins. In October of 1935, 250,000 Italian troops swarmed across the border against an Ethiopian army a tenth that size. Ethiopia's Emperor Haile Selassie asked the League of Nations for help. He got none. Less than a year later, a defeated emperor

A month before this photo was taken in August 1936, Francisco Franco vowed to lead a fascist revolt against his government.

▲

Joseph Stalin's smile at the party congress in 1934 masks plans for a brutal purge.

Ever the pompous posturer, Benito Mussolini (left, center) struts before supporters in 1939. Ethiopia's Haile Selassie (below) had no hope of beating the Italian air force (bottom) but his forces put up a brave fight for seven months.

warned the League: "It is us today. It will be you tomorrow."

Halfway around the world, another League display of impotence cost 2 million Chinese lives. In September 1931 Japan had invaded Manchuria and conquered it within four months. The League condemned the aggression, but did nothing else. Six years later Japan took advantage of an ongoing civil war between Communists and Nationalists and invaded northern China, with massive destruction, looting, and killing in city after city. The worst was Nanking, where 20,000 girls and women were mutilated, raped, or killed and 20,000 young men were used for bayonet practice, gunned down, or doused with gas and set afire.

Adolf Hitler, meanwhile, planned a German empire. Defeated, angry over the humiliating losses in the Treaty of Versailles, mired in economic chaos, and torn by violent politics, Germany was ripe for Hitler's spellbinding oratory, which hypnotized millions with promises of glory, power, and vengeance. A decorated World War I corporal who was unemployed in the lean years after the war, Hitler spoke for the "little people" of Germany and had support in the army and big business. His National Socialist Party got one-third of the votes, and he was appointed chancellor. Then, during the same hundred days that opened FDR's first term, Hitler abolished the German republic, banned rival political parties, outlawed trade unions, and eliminated free speech. Gangs of Nazi Brownshirts beat up Jews, Communists, and intellectuals.

◀

In October 1938, Japanese soldiers celebrate in Hankow — named the capital of China after the fall of Nanking — captured after an 89-day siege.

The government burned books and declared modern art degenerate. In 1936 Hitler sent troops into the Rhineland, German territory that had been demilitarized by the Treaty of Versailles. He expected Britain and France to resist, but they did nothing, freeing him for further aggression.

In Spain the fall of the monarchy in 1930 gave rise to a weak republic, which struggled against extremists of both the right and the left. Street violence, political assassination, and rumors of revolution peaked in July 1936, when most of the Spanish Army, under Gen. Francisco Franco, rebelled.

Franco and the Fascists Win Spain

From the start it was ugly. Franco called his Fascist cause a holy war to defend the church, the exiled monarchy, and Spain itself. The Loyalists (loyal to the republic) claimed that freedom, democracy, and humanity would stand or fall with them. Atrocities multiplied: a Madrid cathedral gutted by a mob, priests lynched, thousands of civilians killed by German bombs in the town of Guernica. Germany and Italy aided Franco, sending large shipments of arms and then troops. The republic's support came from the Soviet Union and from the international leftist communities, including some 3,000 Americans who manned the Abraham Lincoln Brigade in Loyalist trenches.

Finally, early in 1939, Franco took Barcelona and Madrid. Italian and German troops went home as heroes; Loyalists slipped over the French border in defeat. Ernest Hemingway, a Loyalist sympathizer in Spain while a reporter, immortalized the preview to World War II in *For Whom the Bell Tolls*. George Orwell, wounded fighting against Franco, returned to find his country "sleeping the deep, deep sleep of England, from which I fear . . . we shall never wake till we are jerked out of it by the roar of bombs."

▶

Hitler, his chief aide Hermann Goering, and Propaganda Minister Joseph Goebbels acknowledge cheers in Berlin a few days after the annexation of Austria, on March 12, 1938.

EUROPE BOWS TO A BULLY

"Britain and France had to choose between war and dishonor. They chose dishonor. They will have war." That view of the 1938 Munich accord, attributed to Winston Churchill, proved terribly right.

For years Winston Churchill had warned that dictators were pushing the world into war, and he urged England to rearm. When the Nazis militarized the Rhineland in 1936, Churchill cried out against it both in Parliament and in a syndicated newspaper column. The Reich, he wrote, "is arming more strenuously, more scientifically and upon a larger scale, than any nation has ever armed before." Outraged subscribers protested the "nationalistic" articles by Britain's "number one warmonger."

In early 1938 Churchill predicted that Hitler would move next into Austria, but on March 2 Prime Minister Neville Chamberlain assured Parliament that Austria was

All newlyweds received a copy of Mein Kampf (above), in which Hitler predicted Germany's rise to "lord of the universe." At Bad Godesberg on September 22, 1938 (top), Neville Chamberlain seemed unalarmed by Hitler's shocking demands.

◀

German cavalry entering Düsseldorf signaled Hitler's remilitarization of the Rhineland in March 1936. The expected opposition from France never came.

safe. Ten days later German troops goose-stepped across the border, uniting the two countries. Churchill urged an alliance of nations to stop Hitler's aggressions. While Parliament debated Churchill's proposal, Hitler paraded in Vienna before cheering crowds, proclaimed the end of the "Shame of Versailles," and declared that 6 million Austrians were now citizens of his Greater Reich.

Next, he turned to the Sudetenland, where a largely German population chafed under Czech rule. All summer Hitler ranted about the "oppression" of the Sudeten Germans; in August, Germany mobilized. Chamberlain flew to Munich to reason with the fuehrer. He bargained for hours with Hitler, Mussolini, and French Premier Édouard Daladier — but no Czechs — then agreed that a third of Czechoslovakia would be ceded to Germany. Chamberlain returned to England, confident that he had secured "Peace with honor . . . peace for our time." Churchill was undeceived. "We have sustained a total and unmitigated defeat!" he thundered. "This is only the beginning of the reckoning!"

Meanwhile, in Germany, Jews were forbidden to worship, hold most jobs, or own property. On November 7, 1938, a teenage Polish Jew killed a member of Germany's Paris embassy to avenge Nazi treatment of Jews. An enraged Hitler ordered retaliation, and a wave of sanctioned vandalism struck German Jews. So many shops and synagogues were destroyed that the night of November 9–10 was called Kristallnacht ("Crystal Night") for the shards of glass that littered the streets. The Nazis further humiliated the Jews by fining them to pay for the cleanup.

In March 1939 Hitler annexed more of Czechoslovakia and created a puppet state of the rest. Britain and France pledged "total and unqualified support" for Poland. In May Hitler and Mussolini signed the Pact of Steel, agreeing to come to each other's defense in case of war. Hitler called the

Nothing pleased the fuehrer more than a show of loyalty from Germany's young men, seen marching below at a propaganda rally. As Hitler's power became more absolute, the headline on the recruiting poster at left, "Youth Serves the Fuehrer," became more like an order.

This woman in Cheb (inset), a Sudeten border town, weeps openly as she and other residents salute the advancing Wehrmacht.

plight of Germans living in western Poland, intolerable. Only fear of the Soviet Union kept him from attacking.

Then on August 23 Germany and the U.S.S.R. stunned the world by announcing a joint treaty of nonaggression. It openly assured mutual neutrality in case of war and secretly divided up Poland. Hitler was free to attack.

Where did America stand during all this deal making?

For a long time President Roosevelt was publicly neutral. During the Czech crisis, he wrote Hitler that the U.S. had "no political involvements in Europe" and that the Munich agreement had produced a "universal sense of relief." But by 1939 he was reminding a reluctant Congress that "we, too, have a stake in world affairs."

Even after Germany invaded Poland on September 1, 1939, many Americans saw going to war as the worst of evils. Some were isolationists who formed the America First Committee, which sought to keep the country neutral. Committee members included Charles A. Lindbergh, North Dakota Senator Gerald P. Nye, and Gen. Robert A. Wood. Many other Americans were pacifists, and others discounted the dangers of German, Italian, and Japanese militarism and racism. As the debate intensified, however, it became increasingly clear that American involvement was all but inevitable.

Chapter 5

WORLD WAR II
HOME FRONT & BATTLEFIELD

The bleak days just before and after Pearl

Harbor slowly give way to a dawning realization that

the United States and its Allies can and will win

on land, on the sea, and in the air.

A marine sprints through a hail of Japanese machine-gun fire on Okinawa, the last great battle in the Pacific.

BLITZKRIEG, SITZKRIEG, AND FALL

A victory parade through Paris sends Wehrmacht regiments strutting past the city's majestic Arc de Triomphe. While German troops occupied northern France, the south became an independent pro-Nazi state with its capital at Vichy. What was left of the French Army fled to Africa, bringing tears to the eyes of patriots at home (above, right).

With swift and overwhelming fury, Hitler's armies swarmed into Poland, Scandinavia, and France. Then they turned on the U.S.S.R., badly underestimating the ferocity of "General Winter."

After months of diplomatic negotiation designed to prevent it, the worst finally happened. On September 1, 1939, moving with the speed and precision of an irate cobra, the armed might of Adolf Hitler's Nazi Germany thrust across the border deep into neighboring Poland. England and France jumped in on Poland's side. World War II had begun. It would claim 50 million lives, destroy industry and commerce from the Urals to the Irish Sea, and leave much of Asia devastated.

The conflict ushered in a new dimension in military terror: blitzkrieg, or "lightning war." Hitler's Wehrmacht struck with massive force, moving into Poland 1.5 million strong. Panzer divisions with some 1,700 tanks led the way, racing ahead to cut supply lines, sever communications, and isolate defensive positions. Overhead swept an armada of 2,000 Luftwaffe aircraft: Heinkel bombers, Messerschmitt fighters, and Junkers dive bombers, the fearsome Stukas. By the end of September, Poland had been wiped from the map. Germany annexed its western half, while in the east the Russians took over, as previously agreed in a secret deal between Hitler and Soviet Premier Joseph Stalin.

After smothering Poland, Hitler paused to take

stock. Western Europe experienced several months of eerie calm — the so-called sitzkrieg, or "sitting war." Then, in the spring of 1940, Hitler struck again, hitting Denmark and Norway. His next targets were France and the Low Countries. As the German armies penetrated deep into France in mid-May, panzer commander Gen. Erwin Rommel brimmed with elation. "It was not just a beautiful dream," he recalled. "It was reality."

Britain sent 10 divisions to head off the German advance, but by May 26 Hitler's panzers had sped across Belgium and reached the English Channel near Dunkirk. The British Expeditionary Force found itself cut off, along with almost half the French First Army and the entire Belgian Army. The Belgians would soon surrender. Only a massive rescue operation led by the Royal Navy prevented a total disaster. The Germans barely stopped to take notice. On June 14 they entered Paris. A week later an exultant Hitler laid down his terms to the French at Compiègne, in the same railroad car that was used for the German surrender in 1918.

The news for the Allies grew steadily worse. On June 10 Benito Mussolini, Fascist premier of Italy, had joined the war on Hitler's side and ordered an attack on France by way of the Alps. President Franklin D. Roosevelt voiced the world's scorn: "The hand that held the dagger has struck it into the back of its neighbor." Romania, Bulgaria, Yugoslavia, and Greece fell quickly to the Germans. But in the summer of 1941 Hitler made a fatal miscalculation.

Despite his secret agreement with Stalin, Hitler had long cast an envious eye on the vast fertile expanses of the

◄ At Dunkirk a volunteer rescue fleet of more than 800 vessels, from steamships to sailing yachts, snatched 380,000 trapped and bombarded Allied troops from certain capture or death.

▼ Rallying its forces, and clad in heavy winter uniforms like the one in the poster below, the Red Army moved up to defend Moscow. Soviet horse cavalry (bottom), part of a force 200,000 strong, could operate in almost any weather and helped turn the tide.

U.S.S.R. Against the advice of every general on his staff, Hitler decided to invade. "We have only to kick in the front door," he declared, "and the whole rotten edifice will come tumbling down."

So on June 22, 1941, Hitler sent the largest invasion force the world had yet seen, 162 divisions with a total of 3 million men, to conquer the largest country on earth. In the first months the Germans thrust northward along the Baltic coast to the outskirts of Leningrad. They captured Kiev to the south and pushed past Odessa to the Crimea. They struck east toward Moscow. Their successes were all but incredible. Hundreds of thousands of Soviet troops were captured or killed, and vast agricultural and mineral resources were brought under German control.

Then autumn arrived. Roads turned to mud in the October rains, slowing the panzer formations to a walking pace. A mid-November freeze solidified the roads, allowing a successful dash to Moscow. But by early December, when the Germans reached the city's suburbs, the nights had turned bitter cold. "General Winter" was in command.

Temperatures sank as low as 40 degrees below zero. The deep chill bit through the Wehrmacht's uniforms and up through the hobnails of boots. Thousands of frostbitten feet turned gangrenous and had to be amputated. Gun oil congealed, and machine guns jammed. Tank and truck batteries went dead. At the same time, Stalin's troops, reinforced by fresh divisions from Siberia, began to counterattack. "We have seriously underestimated the Russians, the extent of the country, and the treachery of the climate," a German commander observed. By Christmas the Germans had begun to fall back.

"THEIR FINEST HOUR"

As German bombers rained fire on Britain, and RAF fighter pilots rose to meet them, a dauntless leader emerged who made survival heroic, victory attainable, for his beleaguered people.

On a London rooftop an aircraft spotter scans the sky. St. Paul's Cathedral, in background, withstood heavy bombing.

With France gone, Britain stood alone, the only free nation blocking Hitler's dominance over Western Europe. Now, with his armies poised at the English Channel, Hitler offered an astonishing proposal: recognize his conquests on the Continent, and he would leave England alone. If not, he would invade.

When England, predictably, refused to deal, Hitler drew up plans for Operation Sea Lion, a massive cross-channel assault by 250,000 combat troops. He first had to gain air superiority over the landing sites, a job left to Field Marshal Hermann Goering's Luftwaffe.

In July of 1940 German attack planes began testing the British defenses, bombing and strafing coastal towns and Channel shipping. Small flights of Royal Air Force (RAF) fighter planes — Hurricanes and Spitfires, many piloted by RAF volunteers in their early twenties — mounted the skies to engage the German aircraft in swift, spiraling dogfights. Though outnumbered, the British often won.

Next Goering prepared a massive raid on RAF ground installations: airstrips, hangars, communications posts, radar warning towers, airplane factories. More than 2,000 German fighters and bombers stood ready at airfields in occupied France, Belgium, and Holland, awaiting his take-off signal. Against them, the British defenders could loft only 700 first-line fighters, plus a number of older craft.

The first squadrons attacked in bright sunshine on August 13 — Eagle Day, in the German code designation —

launching an aerial siege of brutal intensity, which came to be known as the Battle of Britain. Week after week, month upon month, multiple waves of Luftwaffe bombers, accompanied by their Messerschmitt fighter escorts, swept overhead to lay down patterns of fiery destruction.

The RAF pilots scrambled to intercept them. Sometimes they flew as many as six or seven missions a day and returned so tired they would drop to sleep the moment their wheels touched the runway. On one extraordinary day, August 15, the Germans launched nearly 1,800 sorties (missions by single planes), and the British nearly 1,000. The RAF lost 34 fighters, but it sent 75 German planes spinning down in flames, a two-to-one ratio that British pilots would maintain overall in the months ahead.

A few days afterward Britain's new prime minister, the gruff, indomitable Winston Churchill, arose in the House of Commons to pay them tribute. "Never in the field of human conflict," he rumbled, his bulldog jaw thrust defiantly forward, "was so much owed by so many to so few."

Inevitably, the air war escalated. On August 24, German pilots strayed off course and accidentally dropped bombs on London. An angry Churchill responded by ordering raids on Berlin. After four such hits, Hitler, stamping in fury, vowed: "We will raze their cities to the ground."

So began the Blitz, a sustained attack on Britain's great cities.

CHURCHILL THE MAGNIFICENT

Soldier, war correspondent, master politician, orator, author, national leader, world statesman — in more than half a dozen roles, Winston Churchill made a mark on history. But his finest hours came in the dark war years, stepping jauntily through the smoking rubble of London, his hand raised in his V-for-victory salute. "I have nothing to offer but blood, toil, tears, and sweat," he said on becoming prime minister at the age of 66, in May 1940. A month later, in the House of Commons, he proclaimed: "We shall not flag or fail ... we shall defend our island ... we shall never surrender." He was lovingly caricatured as a toy bulldog (above) with the words "Hitler terror" written on his steel helmet.

Ground crews worked like demons to keep Britain's outnumbered airplanes aloft. Above: Stirling bomber. Above, right: Spitfires prepare for takeoff.

own roofs to brave nightly raids. Others would gather their bedding and march to the relative safety of a shelter or the Underground, the city's deep-dug subway system. When Buckingham Palace took a hit on September 11, Londoners were gratified to learn that the royal family, too, was resolved to stick it out.

Over the months, as the Luftwaffe shifted its bomb-sights to England's civilians, the RAF was given breathing space to rebuild its shattered airfields and to equip its depleted squadrons with new planes and pilots. Eventually Hitler, realizing he would never achieve air superiority over England, had Operation Sea Lion quietly put to rest.

The London Blitz continued well into 1941, with a final holocaust on the night of May 10–11, which took 1,212 lives. The raids then ceased entirely. They had spanned eight months, turned 250,000 Londoners out of house and home, and taken the lives of 40,553 men, women, and children. But London, and all England with it, had endured.

Nearly a year before the first German attack, Churchill had stood before Commons to proclaim his country's determination. "Let us . . . so bear ourselves," he said, "that if the British Empire and its Commonwealth last for a thousand years, men will still say: " 'This was their finest hour.' "

And so it was.

▼ As a precaution against the Germans' possible use of gas, these English children wear masks for an air raid drill.

London was hit again, on September 7, by a force of 320 bombers and 600 fighter escorts, and for the next 57 nights running. Liverpool, Manchester, Bristol, and Birmingham also felt the fury of Nazi raids. The bombs took such a toll on Coventry, struck November 14, that when Churchill visited to survey the wreckage, he broke down and wept.

But London suffered worst. The Luftwaffe was dropping high explosives and incendiary bombs, and floating 2½-ton land mines down by parachute. The resulting fires consumed whole blocks. The glow from the burning dock-yards in the city's East End, which were hit repeatedly, could be seen from 30 miles away. "It was like a lake in Hell," said a survivor. Streetcar wheels welded themselves to the melting tracks. "Send all the pumps you've got," one firefighter called, "the whole bloody world's on fire."

Thousands of Londoners fled to the countryside. But millions more remained behind to operate the machinery of government and industry. Some of them stayed under their

▶

Londoners share tea, chat, and play darts in an underground shelter as German bombers pay a visit to the city above.

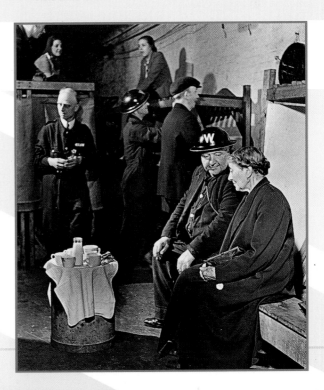

"ARSENAL OF DEMOCRACY"

At Roosevelt's urging, a reluctant America began to arm. FDR met Churchill, Lend-Lease delivered vital war aid to the hard-pressed Allies, and able-bodied young men reported to their local draft boards.

To Americans of 1940 the war overseas seemed a world away. Although sympathetic with the embattled democracies, most people balked at the idea of being directly involved. It took all of President Franklin D. Roosevelt's considerable political skills to prod the country into an all-but-fighting stance as "the great arsenal of democracy."

A vocal isolationist minority resisted the change. Many isolationists were bitter over what they saw as futile American sacrifices in the war of 1914–18. "The People Say NO War!" proclaimed posters of the isolationist America First Committee. Senator Burton K. Wheeler, with bitter anti-New Deal sarcasm, denounced a proposal to aid Britain as "a plan to plow under every fourth American boy." And some citizens were actively pro-German. Members of the German-American Bund adopted the Nazi salute and held military exercises in support of Hitler's Reich.

Ranged against the antiwar crusaders were those who advocated intervention on the side of the democracies. The Committee to Defend America by Aiding the Allies was organized by the newspaperman William Allen White. Leading supporters included *Time-Life* publisher Henry Luce and the playwright Robert Sherwood, who pointed out that even two broad oceans could no longer guarantee safety from dictators' warplanes, ships, and submarines.

"I Like Your President," Said Churchill

Most Americans, even isolationists, saw the Allies as good guys and the Axis as bad guys. Edward R. Murrow's riveting radio broadcasts from blitz-torn London during the Battle of Britain contributed to America's admiration for the plucky English. Meanwhile, the United States took practical steps to help. In an ingenious swap designed to silence antiwar critics, Roosevelt gave the British 50 "obsolete" destroyers in exchange for long-term leases on eight British naval and air bases in the Caribbean and North Atlantic.

Much more was needed. By December 1940 Britain had nearly run out of funds to buy urgently needed war supplies. In a press conference Roosevelt revealed what was on his mind: "Suppose my neighbor's home catches fire, and I have a length of garden hose. . . . I don't say to him . . . 'Neighbor, my garden hose cost me $15; you have to pay me $15 for it!' . . . I don't want $15 — I want my garden hose back after the fire is over." After two months of debate, Congress gave in to this folksy argument and to British Prime Minister Winston Churchill's appeal, "Give us the tools and we will finish the job." The act that became known as Lend-Lease allowed Britain — and, later, 37 other nations — to borrow or lease any equipment the president deemed vital to the defense of the United States.

In August 1941 Roosevelt and Churchill, who had been corresponding since the beginning of the war, decided to meet. With German subs prowling the

Headed for duty at Fort McClellan, Alabama, in October 1940, a soldier kisses his girl good-bye as his train leaves the Delaware, Lackawanna, and Western terminal in Hoboken, New Jersey.

▶

Bound for Britain laden to the gunwales with Lend-Lease war matériel, and on constant watch for U-boats, a convoy of Liberty ships churns through the heavy seas of a North Atlantic storm. The United States gave $50 billion in aid by the war's end.

Atlantic, they took extreme precautions. Churchill sailed secretly for Canadian waters on a camouflaged Royal Navy battleship. Roosevelt went on the presidential yacht for what was billed as a fishing trip, then quietly boarded a U.S. Navy cruiser heading north. The two leaders met off Newfoundland on August 9, 1941. "I like your president," Churchill told the American ambassador on his return to England. And Roosevelt cabled Churchill: "It is fun to be in the same decade with you." The joint declaration they had agreed on, the Atlantic Charter, expressed their countries' aims in a war that the United States had not yet officially joined. Renouncing territorial ambitions, they called for freedom of the seas, self-determination of nations, freedom from want and from fear, and the establishment of a "permanent system of general security."

America prepared for its own defense. In September 1939 the country's standing army had consisted of some 188,000 men, all volunteers, and was ranked 17th in the world. One year later, in the fall of 1940, Congress approved the first peacetime draft in U.S. history. In step with the armed forces, industry, too, was gearing up for war. Field Marshal Hermann Goering, the chief of the Luftwaffe, had ridiculed American mass production as good only for manufacturing refrigerators and razor blades. He was quickly proved wrong. U.S. plants, exceeding goals once thought impossible, were soon turning out an average of 60,000 warplanes and almost 1,000 cargo ships a year.

At sea the United States was drawing perilously close to open warfare. To protect aid shipments, U.S. warships began escorting supply convoys across the Atlantic. Even so, attacks by German U-boats took an increasing toll. On October 17, 1941, shortly after Roosevelt ordered the navy to shoot Axis warships on sight, a German torpedo struck the destroyer *Kearney*. Two weeks later another torpedo hit the *Reuben James*, sinking it and taking the lives of 115 crewmen. The war was coming home to American families.

▼ *Protesting the Lend-Lease bill — and the risk of war it seems to pose for America — angry mothers pray before the Capitol in Washington, DC.*

▲ *A leather-lunged drill sergeant introduces some recruits to the sweet discipline of military life in an infantry regiment at Fort Dix, New Jersey. More than a million men were drafted before the nation officially went to war, and thousands of them passed through Fort Dix on their way to posts elsewhere in the United States and abroad.*

THREAT FROM BELOW

Both sides used submarines with deadly effect and consummate courage, but it was the German U-boat campaign that almost changed the course of World War II. Part of Hitler's grand strategy called for U-boats to blockade the British Isles and starve Britain into submission.

Groups of U-boats, known as wolf packs, prowled the Atlantic and the Caribbean for convoys. Their hunting grounds were the sea-lanes by which the United States supplied beleaguered Britain and the Sovet Union. By mid-1942 the U-boats were sinking Allied ships at the rate of one every four hours.

The turning point came in May 1943, with improved sub-detection devices and more warships and airplanes to shield the convoys. The next month just six ships fell victim to U-boat torpedoes. The Battle of the North Atlantic took a grim toll in lives and ships. Altogether the Allies lost 2,778 ships, 2,603 of them merchantmen. The Germans lost some 780 of the 1,162 U-boats they put to sea.

"A DATE WHICH WILL LIVE IN INFAMY"

On Sunday, December 7, 1941, at 7:49 in the morning, Japanese attack planes swooped down without warning and dropped their bombs on the U.S. naval base at Pearl Harbor, on the Hawaiian island of Oahu. A stunned and horrified America suddenly found itself at war.

Commander Mitsuo Fuchida, leading 183 carrier-based fighters and bombers of the Japanese Navy, scanned the target area with binoculars. Below, at the huge Pearl Harbor naval base, lay 8 battleships, 9 cruisers, 29 destroyers, and 39 lesser craft — the bulk of the United States Pacific Fleet.

Fuchida ordered his radioman to send out the signal to strike: *"To, To, To."* Then he dropped a wing and rolled in for the attack. Moments later he broadcast a second message: *"Tora, Tora, Tora"* ("surprise achieved").

Though the raid on Pearl Harbor was planned in utmost secrecy, anti-Western feeling among the Japanese was well known. For more than a decade Japan had aggressively expanded its power in the Pacific. Then, in September 1940, in an act of defiance addressed to the entire free world, Japan signed an alliance with Germany and Italy. America was horrified. President Franklin D. Roosevelt froze Japanese assets and placed an embargo on oil and steel shipments to Japan. Diplomats from both countries met in Washington in late 1941 to defuse the crisis.

But even as the diplomats parleyed, the Japanese strike force — 6 carriers and 14 escort vessels — was steaming toward Pearl Harbor. U.S. naval intelligence, which had broken the Japanese code, knew that the fleet had gone to sea, but since the Japanese sailed under radio silence, their whereabouts remained a mystery. On December 6, 1941, President Roosevelt appealed directly to Emperor Hirohito for peace. That same day, the strike force approached its launch point.

On Sunday morning, December 7, a sailor named Dick Fiske was just coming off watch on the battleship *West Virginia*, which was moored at Ford Island, in Pearl Harbor. "We saw the dive bombers coming in," Fiske said, "and we

Above, left: Days before the Pearl Harbor attack, U.S. Secretary of State Cordell Hull (center) talked peace with diplomats from Tokyo.

Addressing a joint session of Congress — and, through radio, the entire nation — President Roosevelt calls for a declaration of war against Japan. Three days later, on December 11, 1941, Germany and Italy declared war on the United States.

thought they were army planes. Just another exercise. A friend of mine said, 'Let's go over to the port side and watch them dropping torpedoes on us.' " The next thing Fiske remembered "was a hellacious loud noise, and a wall of water that looked like a 50-foot wave came across the deck and washed us both to the other side of the ship."

Doris Miller, heavyweight boxing champ of the *West Virginia*, was a mess attendant and was not trained in gunnery. But he sprinted to a machine gun. "It wasn't hard," he said. "I just pulled the trigger and she worked fine." Miller became the first black man to win the Navy Cross, that service's second-highest decoration for gallantry.

Marine private James Cory, aboard the battleship *Arizona*, was opening the window of his battle station to get a clear view. "The bombs struck forward — forward of us," he said. "The bridge shielded us from flames coming aft. . . . But still, around the edges in these open windows came the heat and the sensation of the blast. We cringed there." A 1,760-pound bomb had pierced the bow and ignited the ship's huge forward magazine. A sailor on the nearby *Nevada* saw the *Arizona* "jump at least 15 or 20 feet upward in the water and sort of break in two." More than 1,000 American sailors and marines perished in the fireball.

Private Cory and a buddy jumped overboard and swam for their lives. "There were bomb splashes nearby," he said. "There was strafing in the water. You could feel the impact of the bullets. There was a tremendous amount of confusion and noise and all this sort of thing. Our own oil was bubbling up and congealing. . . . It was catching fire slowly and incinerating toward us." The two men struggled ashore. They were then "lifted up into the air and flung down" as a bomb detonated somewhere near them. Both men survived.

Caught at their berths on Pearl Harbor's Battleship Row, three of the U.S. Navy's most powerful vessels burn unchecked. Damage to the West Virginia *(left) and* Tennessee *(center) was repaired. But the* Arizona *still lies on the bottom, under a white marble memorial to her dead.*

By 8:12 A.M. seven battleships lay heavily damaged or sunk, some resting on the harbor bottom with their twisted wreckage breaking the water. The second wave, of 170 Japanese attackers, arriving just before 9 A.M., kept pounding the battleships and scored major hits on other, smaller ships. The Japanese also destroyed 188 aircraft, most of them on the ground. They killed 2,403 Americans and wounded 1,178.

Returning to their carriers, the Japanese pilots urged their commander, Vice Admiral Chuichi Nagumo, to send a new wave against the American fleet's docking and fueling facilities. Nagumo refused. The operation had already succeeded beyond anyone's hopes. He took his fleet to the safety of the Central Pacific.

In fact, the Pearl Harbor attack was a major strategic blunder. Most of the ships sunk or damaged there were repaired, some within a few weeks. The U.S. Pacific Fleet's three aircraft carriers, major targets, were not present and thus escaped damage. They would soon inflict terrible vengeance on the Japanese Navy. Even more significant, Pearl Harbor united the American people in a crusading zeal that sustained them throughout the war.

Calling upon Congress to declare war, President Roosevelt began solemnly: "Yesterday, December 7, 1941, a date which will live in infamy. . . ." Then he rallied the nation with these words: "With confidence in our armed forces, with the unbounding determination of our people, we will gain the inevitable triumph. So help us God."

Millions of Americans wore enameled lapel pins proclaiming that they would "Remember Pearl Harbor."

AMERICANS ON
THE ALERT

The attack on Pearl Harbor shattered America's sense of security. That Christmas season of 1941 saw a flurry of home-front preparations aimed at defending the country against rumored invasions from any or all directions.

A blind World War I veteran organized farmers in a small Oregon town into a guerrilla band that dug foxholes and practiced the evacuation of dairy herds. Elementary schools taught children to spot enemy warplanes by their silhouettes. Wisconsin Legionnaires urged the formation of an army of experienced deer hunters: 25,000 sharpshooters ready for an assault via the polar route.

On the East Coast, private pilots in light aircraft flew for the Civil Air Patrol, spotting and harassing German submarines and even sinking two with pint-size bombs. By January 1942 5 million men and women had signed up with the Office of Civilian Defense. During air raid drills volunteer wardens with white helmets and bright armbands saw to it that blackout shades were pulled down and lights doused. Some 115,000 wardens were on call in New York City alone. One of their duties was to make sure that the lights of Broadway were dimmed at night so that Allied ships would not stand out against the glow of the city and make easy targets for German U-boats prowling offshore.

Only once did an enemy plane bomb the U.S. mainland. In September 1942 a Japanese officer, Nobuo Fujita, released incendiary devices over the Oregon woods. He had hoped to start a conflagration, but the flames just sputtered out.

JAPAN THRUSTS OUTWARD

In the wake of its Pearl Harbor strike, and of similarly devastating air attacks that same day on U.S. forces in the Philippines and British forces at Singapore, Japan moved with practiced precision to carve out a vast realm in the Pacific.

By December 1941 the Japanese were masters of an empire on the western rim of the Pacific. They controlled Manchuria, Korea, much of Indochina, eastern China and its ports, Taiwan (then called Formosa), and a few smaller islands.

It was not enough. Japan's leaders hated the Western presence in their part of the world and craved to replace it with their own imperial system. In their Greater East Asia Co-Prosperity Sphere, the banner of the Rising Sun would fly over an area that spanned some 5,000 miles, from the Kurile Islands in the north through vast stretches of the South Pacific. It would include Burma, the Dutch East Indies, the Philippines, the British colonies of Hong Kong and Malaya, plus Thailand and New Guinea.

Between the Japanese and the fulfillment of their dream lay what seemed to be a disorganized and dispirited foe. Australia and New Zealand needed time to reach full fighting strength. In the East Indies and the Philippines, valiant Dutch and Filipino units were plainly outmatched; so for the time being were British imperial forces in Burma and India. As for the Americans, the U.S. Navy was apparently in bad shape after Pearl Harbor; and Japanese strategists doubted the will of Ameri-

◄

Near victory in the Philippines, Japanese soldiers raise flags and swords on Bataan. Assured of the glory of their conquests, Japan's forces fought courageously and often pitilessly.

While U.S. and Filipino troops above ground awaited the inevitable Japanese landings, support personnel crowded Corregidor's tunnels.

can boys to fight a long and bloody war thousands of miles from home.

The Japanese underestimated the Allies' fighting spirit. In New York City alone, hours after the Pearl Harbor attack, hundreds of young men waited all night outside army and navy recruiting stations, hoping to be among the first in their neighborhood to enlist.

But it would take months to train and equip the new recruits and to deploy them in combat. In the interim the Japanese taught the armed forces of the United States a terrible lesson. Just 10 hours after striking Pearl Harbor, the Japanese sent a bomber force to attack Clark Field, in the Philippines, the principal U.S. air base in the Far East. The American pilots had just returned from morning patrols and were relaxing in the mess hall. Suddenly enemy bombers began unloading on the B-17 Flying Fortresses parked in neat rows on the runway aprons. In a matter of hours more than a third of the American air power in the region was demolished.

The same day, December 8, on the far side of the International Date Line, the Japanese attacked Guam and Wake Island and destroyed the U.S. air base at Midway. Hong Kong fell on Christmas Day. Japanese infantry columns advanced through Thailand, which surrendered without a fight, and down the Malay Peninsula toward Singapore. The British enclave of Singapore had been hit by Japanese bombers the same morning as Pearl Harbor. The city fell to Japanese troops on February 15, 1942. Next came the Dutch East Indies and the Solomon Islands.

Meanwhile, a Japanese expeditionary force had landed in the Philippines and swept southward. By January 7, 1942, a combined force of U.S. and Filipino defenders, under Gen. Douglas MacArthur, had withdrawn onto the rugged Bataan Peninsula. Then began a campaign that horrified and

transfixed the American people — and hardened their resolve to beat the Japanese into submission.

The defenders were sick, starving, short of munitions, and just about out of luck. Unrelenting attacks by the Japanese pressed them into a shrinking perimeter of land. Still, they held on. Early in March, when MacArthur left for Australia on President Roosevelt's orders, he announced with supreme confidence, "I shall return."

His return would take years. On April 9 the exhausted defenders of Bataan were forced to surrender. Then began the infamous Death March, on which the surviving Filipinos and Americans, now prisoners, were brutally herded through choking dust and sweltering heat to Camp O'Donnell, some 60 miles to the north. Along the way their captors systematically killed anyone too weak or too sick to keep up. "If you fell," said an American survivor, "you were dead. They bayoneted you right away."

Acts of brutality became routine. Once, a group of prisoners, parched with thirst, was ordered at gunpoint to wade a stream, but forbidden to drink from it. One man, in desperation, tried to dip his hands into the water. "He was 12 feet from me," a soldier related. "They shot him. Some guards on the bridge just popped him off."

The Filipinos fared worse than the Americans. During the march, according to some estimates, they died at some 10 times the rate of their American comrades. And those who withstood the march were subjected to equally rough treatment when they reached Camp O'Donnell. Of nearly 70,000 Americans and Filipinos captured at Bataan, some 23,000 perished before the war's end.

Some U.S. forces retreated from Bataan to the nearby island of Corregidor, at the entrance to Manila Bay. There, in a network of tunnels, they hung on for another month. When they finally surrendered — on May 6, 1942, five months less one day after Pearl Harbor — the entire Western Pacific belonged to Japan.

With a total length of 38 inches and a 29-inch single-edge blade, this Japanese Army katana was a sword meant for killing, not for ceremony. Officers carried their katanas into action.

TRADITION OF EMPERORS

When Shomu (top) reigned in the 8th century, Japanese emperors had vast power and the status of gods. As time passed, they lost their earthly power, but continued to be seen as divine. Real power lay with the feudal lords and, by the 20th century, with

the army and navy. Military leaders like Hideki Tojo backed Japanese aggression in the 1930's. Tojo and his cadre knew they had to appear subservient to the emperor to win popular support. Thus, at a military review in 1940 (above), Tojo bowed humbly to Emperor Hirohito. At the war's end, most Japanese still revered Hirohito. A new constitution made the will of the people paramount while retaining the emperor and his line as a national symbol. Tojo was hanged as a war criminal in 1948.

OUTFLANKING THE DESERT FOX

For Gen. Erwin Rommel, Germany's master tactician, North Africa was the best of times and the worst of times. His stunning victory at Tobruk elevated him to field marshal, but when he was forced to retreat from Kasserine, he was relieved of his command.

GI's and Tommies lower themselves into an assault craft headed for Algeria's shore. Operation Torch, Involving more than 500 ships, was the largest amphibious invasion thus far.

For most of the 107,000 U.S. and British soldiers who clambered down the landing nets of troopships in early November 1942, North Africa was a land known only from books and movies, if at all. But long before the next six months were over, these men would have the names of Bizerte, Kasserine Pass, Maknassy, and dozens of other sun-scorched places between Casablanca and Cairo etched in their memories. On such battlegrounds GI's and Tommies would fight the best troops Germany and Italy could throw at them.

Operation Torch, the code name for the combined U.S.-British landings, struck at Oran, Algiers, and Casablanca. Its overall commander, Lt. Gen. Dwight D. Eisenhower, directed the invasion from his headquarters within the Rock of Gibraltar, on the other side of the Mediterranean.

Before Torch, Seesaw Battles

For more than two years before Operation Torch, Italian forces, aided by their German allies, had been trying to dislodge the British from East and North Africa. The prize was control of the entire Mediterranean area, including the Suez Canal. In June 1940 Italy's dictator, Benito Mussolini, launched the first of thousands of air attacks against the British-held island of Malta. In September he invaded Egypt. By February of the following year, British troops, under the command of Lt. Gen. Sir Archibald Wavell, had routed the Italians in Libya and Egypt. The hard-fighting British, it seemed, could be stopped only by their afternoon tea; so Hitler sent one of his best commanders to rescue his floundering allies.

The general was Erwin Rommel. Rommel took charge of the Afrika Korps, his main attack force, on February 12, 1941. For the next 15 months, the fighting seesawed. Rommel launched his first offensive on March 24 but failed to take Tobruk, a strategic garrison on the coast of Libya. By year's end the British, now led by Gen. Sir Claude Auchinleck, pushed Rommel back halfway across Libya.

On May 26, 1942, Axis forces counterattacked, with Rommel commanding some 760 tanks, 240 of which were virtually useless. On June 21 he seized Tobruk in a lightning one-day assault, and Hitler promoted him to field marshal. Next, Rommel pursued the retreating British Eighth Army eastward but was stopped at the coastal village of El Alamein, a scant 150 miles northwest of Cairo, Egypt's capital. The Axis seemed certain to take Cairo, but the newly appointed British commander in the Middle East, Gen. Sir Harold Alexander, and commander of the Eighth Army, Lt. Gen. Bernard L. Montgomery, had other ideas. Patiently Alexander built up the army at El Alamein with fresh troops and supplies. On October 23 nearly 900 of his big guns began a barrage on enemy positions. Two days later the revitalized Eighth Army had knocked out 90 percent of the tanks Rommel had deployed at El Alamein, and on November 4 a badly battered panzer army, with Montgomery in pursuit, began to draw back toward Tunisia.

For the British, El Alamein was a desperately needed success. Winston Churchill later wrote: "It may almost be said that before Alamein we never had a victory. After Alamein, we never had a defeat." To celebrate this turning point, Churchill asked that church bells be sounded all over Britain. (The bells had been silenced since 1940 and were to have been rung as a signal that England had been invaded.)

Four days after the Germans began their retreat, Eisenhower's Operation Torch invaded North Africa. Now Rommel faced two big armies, one to the west and one to the east. Meanwhile, Hitler had fortified German forces holding on to northern Tunisia, and in late February 1943 they joined Rommel in a thrust toward the Kasserine Pass. Allied

◄

Shielding himself from the scorching Egyptian sun with a parasol, British Prime Minister Winston Churchill tours the desert near El Alamein in August 1942.

reinforcements poured in, and Eisenhower ordered artillery units to make a 735-mile dash from Oran to the Kasserine. Rommel retreated. On March 6 Montgomery's Eighth Army dealt him a brutal defeat, and three days later Rommel flew to Berlin to advise Hitler to give up North Africa. He was relieved of his command. In the spring of 1943 an estimated 275,000 German and Italian troops trudged into waiting Allied prisoner-of-war camps.

DUEL IN THE DESERT

The battle for North Africa pitted two masters of warfare against each other: Lt. Gen. Bernard Law Montgomery and Field Marshal Erwin Rommel.

Bernard Montgomery

Montgomery was so meticulous that his painstaking tactics often exasperated impatient superiors. His cautiousness, however, was born not of fear of the enemy but of love for his fellow soldiers. He had witnessed the horrors of World War I, and it made him forever determined to protect the lives of his men, who affectionately nicknamed him Monty.

If Montgomery relied on method, Rommel relied on

Erwin Rommel

instinct, boasting, "I sniff through the country like a fox." The Desert Fox, as he was called, took personal command of each battle, often eluding setbacks with swift improvisation. So great was his ability that even Winston Churchill declared, "We have a very daring and skillful opponent against us . . . a great general."

▲ *The North African campaign stretched from the coast of Morocco to the shores of the Nile, some 3,000 miles away.*

→ Invasion Force Movements
▲ Operation Torch Landings
✳ Major Battle

Carefully concealed behind a makeshift shelter, a German soldier uses a periscope to spot the next target. The Afrika Korps, which was shifted from Europe to Africa with little preparation, underestimated the hostile climate.

▼ *Trapped in his immobilized tank, a panzer crewman has little choice but to surrender to British infantrymen at El Alamein, where the Germans finally met their match.*

THE END BEGINS FOR HITLER

By 1942 Adolf Hitler had set his sights on the Russian city of Stalingrad, which he considered the ultimate test of his country's iron will. Meanwhile, Allied bombers began hammering at a strategic target of their own: Germany.

Introduced in May 1942, this air medal went to members of the U.S. forces who distinguished themselves in flight, both combat and noncombat.

The rosewood-paneled dining car of Adolf Hitler was the pride of the German railway system. On the evening of November 7, 1942, the train carrying that car stopped at a small station outside Munich. Inside, at a table adorned with polished silverware and fresh flowers, sat the fuehrer himself. Unexpectedly, a train of cattle cars pulled alongside and stopped. Hitler peered through his window. Staring back at him through the slatted sides of the cars were what appeared to be human scarecrows, held together by tattered uniforms and blood-stained bandages. They were wounded German soldiers returning from the Battle of Stalingrad, the Russian city that Hitler had ordered taken against the advice of most of his staff. For an instant Hitler looked into the eyes of those who had been part of the 300,000-strong force he had sent to conquer Stalingrad. Then he turned away abruptly from the window, ordered the shades to be drawn, and went on with his dinner.

If Hitler had chosen to take a clear-eyed look at his nation's fortunes, he might have seen the high tide of Germany's invincibility beginning to ebb. The unsuccessful siege of Stalingrad, then in its third bloody month, hinted strongly that the mighty German ground armies that had swept victoriously from one end of Europe to the other were not unstoppable after all. Moreover, as Allied air strength grew, the formidable Luftwaffe was losing the clear-cut advantage it had held at the war's outset.

To Hitler the news from Stalingrad must have seemed unbelievable. How could the ill-equipped defenders of that drab city on the west bank of the Volga continue to hold out after an artillery pounding so brutal that it turned most of the city into rubble? The answer was that Germany had failed to recognize the incredible resourcefulness and steely resolve of the enemy. "Before you die, kill a German," the Soviet high command ordered its soldiers, "with your teeth if necessary!"

At one point in the five-month-long fight for control of the city, the Germans occupied nine-tenths of Stalingrad, but it was a nightmare to hold such gains. "It is hard, often impossible, to distinguish between night and day, for vast clouds of smoke blot out the light," one German soldier wrote. "A street is no longer measured in meters," an officer noted, "but in corpses."

▼ **At Stalingrad the Red Army's cavalry played a key role in thwarting Hitler's Sixth Army. Siberian ponies not only maneuvered through rough terrain, they outlasted panzers rendered immobile in subzero temperatures.**

The staggering death toll at Stalingrad began with heavy casualties on the very first day of battle, when a raid by 600 German bombers left 40,000 dead.

▼ "Forward! Toward Victory!" proclaims a Soviet poster. In the winter of 1942–43 the Soviets thwarted further gains by the Nazis, who, by then, had seized almost as much of the U.S.S.R. as the Mongol hordes did in the 13th century.

On November 19 Soviet forces, strengthened by fresh soldiers, tanks, and artillery, began their counterattack. They cut off and surrounded the German forces. Soldiers battled in blizzards so heavy that casualties, once fallen, could be turned into silent snow mounds in a matter of minutes. On January 31, 1943 after 100,000 of his men were killed in the course of three weeks, the German commander gave up. Fighting ceased on February 2. To the Germans' devastating losses were added thousands of deaths by starvation and exposure to disease in Soviet prison camps. In all, only about 6,000 Axis soldiers of the original attack force of 300,000 are known to have survived to see

nicknamed the Flying Fortress, Americans had brought a powerful offensive weapon into the war. In the first all-American mission, on August 17, 1942, a dozen B-17's won laurels flying through flak and hitting the rail yards at Rouen, in occupied Normandy; all returned safely. But no Allied bombers, British or American, were invulnerable to the swarms of German fighter planes that attacked as the squadrons crossed the English Channel and the North Sea. At one point the chances of a crew member's completing 25 missions were about one in three.

the end of World War II.

About the same time the Germans were giving up at Stalingrad, U.S. heavy bombers made their first highly successful daytime air strike of the war into Germany proper, targeting the naval base at Wilhelmshaven. It was only the beginning of a systematic effort to tear open Germany by means of air power. By March 1944 combined forces of 1,000 Allied bombers would roar daily into Germany. With their B-17 bomber,

Help arrived in December 1943 in the form of U.S. P-51 Mustangs, whose 2,300-mile range enabled them to escort bombers all the way into and out of Germany. Even before the arrival of these Mustangs, however, Allied planes were inflicting terrible damage inside the Third Reich.

In early 1944 Germany was losing more than 2,000 planes per month. By June, when Allied troops were poised for the D-Day landings on the beaches of northern France, their supreme commander, Gen. Dwight D. Eisenhower, offered words of comfort: "If you see fighter aircraft over you, they will be ours."

THE TIDE TURNS IN THE PACIFIC

In the uncertain months after Pearl Harbor, Japan

seemed all but unstoppable. But then came four key

events that changed the course of the war: a raid on Tokyo

and the Battles of Midway, Guadalcanal, and the Coral Sea.

At Midway the agile and accurate Douglas Dauntless dive bomber was the navy's most effective offensive weapon.

On a fine spring morning in 1942, Tokyo residents had every reason to feel good about themselves and their country. Since their nation's surprise attack on Pearl Harbor, the war had been going Japan's way, with mainland and island conquests throughout the Pacific, and U.S. resistance in the Philippines crumbling fast. Tokyo itself sat safe from harm — or so its citizens believed that Saturday morning, April 18. Meanwhile 16 heavily fueled U.S. Army Air Forces B-25 bombers fought their way aloft from the aircraft carrier *Hornet* amid gale-force winds and waves.

Their leader was Lt. Col. James H. Doolittle, a feisty doctor of science who had set a number of aviation speed records, and their main target was Tokyo, some 800 risk-filled miles away. So confident were the Japanese that their land was invulnerable that some of them waved cheerfully upward as the U.S. planes flew over

Each important U.S. Navy ship had an official insignia, such as this one belonging to the Yorktown.

Lt. Col. James H. Doolittle's B-25, headed for Tokyo, lifts off the U.S.S. Hornet. After the raid President Roosevelt told reporters that the planes came from "our secret base at Shangri-la" in order to maintain security. Doolittle, left, won the Medal of Honor for his heroism.

Tokyo and other cities. After releasing their bombs, the planes headed west: 13 of the original 16 reached China and 1 the U.S.S.R. Two other crews were captured in Japanese territory, and three of the fliers were executed.

Even though Doolittle's bombers did little damage, the incursion was a stinging blow to Japan's pride. Smarting from the insult, the Japanese Navy sent a large attack force toward Port Moresby, in New Guinea, thus posing a serious threat to Australia. But timely code-breaking had already alerted the Americans that the Japanese ships were on their way. A three-part naval force with two big carriers, the *Yorktown* and the *Lexington*, headed out to surprise the Japanese.

The Battle of the Coral Sea was about to begin. At first, neither naval force could pinpoint the location of the other's main fleet. Then, on May 7, 1942, American warplanes hit the carrier *Shoho*, sending her to the ocean floor. The next day one U.S. dive bomber pilot, Lt. John James Powers, who

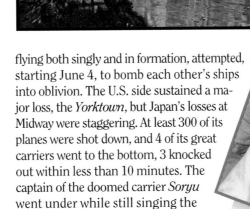

Under towering coconut trees, four marines stroll through their headquarters on Guadalcanal. In addition to the enemy and torrential rains, GI's had to contend with leeches, rats, bats, and crocodiles.

had earlier made a vow to sink an enemy carrier, dived on the carrier *Shokaku*. The bomb he dropped from 300 feet put the ship out of action, but the force of explosions from the stricken vessel sent Powers and his plane crashing into the sea, killing him. His astonishing bravery was honored with a posthumous award of the Medal of Honor.

The U.S. fleet did not come through unscathed. One enemy bomb ripped through four decks of the *Yorktown*. The *Lexington* took two torpedoes and several bombs, but was still afloat. Then, two hours after the Japanese broke off action, she exploded when a generator caught fire. Almost 3,000 crew members arranged their shoes in neat rows on the flight deck, then dropped over the side to waiting rescue ships. Thus ended the first sea engagement ever fought in which ships of the opposing fleets never caught sight of each other. Airmen carried all the attacks.

Only a month after the Battle of the Coral Sea came the most decisive sea confrontation of the war, when the balance of power in the Pacific began tilting unmistakably toward the United States. This was the Battle of Midway. It took place some 1,500 miles off Hawaii when Japan's navy joined in air battles with a less powerful U.S. fleet, which was then about 400 miles away. Airmen,

flying both singly and in formation, attempted, starting June 4, to bomb each other's ships into oblivion. The U.S. side sustained a major loss, the *Yorktown*, but Japan's losses at Midway were staggering. At least 300 of its planes were shot down, and 4 of its great carriers went to the bottom, 3 knocked out within less than 10 minutes. The captain of the doomed carrier *Soryu* went under while still singing the Japanese national anthem.

The Battles of the Coral Sea and of Midway showed the Japanese that U.S. forces were more than a match both on the sea and in the air. But Americans had yet to prove themselves on land. That chance came in the bloody battle for the island of Guadalcanal. Few memories of combat in World War II are more searing than those of the marines who invaded Guadalcanal or of the Japanese who defended it. Guadalcanal was the first of many such invasions in the Pacific by U.S. forces, with devastating losses suffered by Americans and Japanese alike.

At dawn on August 7, 1942, members of the 1st Marine Division waded ashore on the island, which had assumed strategic importance because of the airfield the Japanese were building there. Over the next six months, in rotting jungles filled with disease, intense heat, and Japanese ready to die for their emperor, U.S. troops engaged in some of the most savage fighting of the entire war. Approximately 1,600 Americans and nearly 24,000 Japanese died on the island, but on February 8, 1943, Maj. Gen. Alexander M. Patch could finally report that "the Tokyo Express no longer has a terminal on Guadalcanal."

TOKYO ROSE

Hello, you fighting orphans of the Pacific. How's tricks?" Thus began a radio show hosted by Iva Ikuko Toguri D'Aquino, one of the numerous female radio announcers collectively dubbed Tokyo Rose by the GI's. A nisei (second-generation Japanese-American), she acquired her English growing up in the United States. Though her teasing broadcasts were designed to make servicemen so homesick that they would lose the will to fight, her propaganda, with its blend of corniness and nostalgia, actually raised morale by giving GI's both entertainment and a target for sarcastic humor. In 1949 D'Aquino, then 33, was convicted of treason in a trial held in the United States. She spent six years in a federal prison in West Virginia and was granted a pardon by President Gerald Ford in 1977.

p. 192

p. 226

p. 190

p. 240

p. 222

ARCTIC OCEAN

Germans attack Allied convoys bound for U.S.S.R. 1941–45

★ Reykjavik
ICELAND

• Murmansk

• Archangel

Battle of the Atlantic Sept 1939–mid-1943

FINLAND

NORWAY

Oslo ★

SWEDEN

Helsinki ★

Russo-Finnish Wars Nov. 1939–Mar. 1940 June 1941–Sept. 1944

Leningrad German siege Sept. 1941–Jan. 1944

Stockholm ★

Baltic Sea

★ Tallinn
ESTONIA

★ Riga
LATVIA

Moscow ★

North Sea

Dublin ★
IRELAND

GREAT BRITAIN

Battle of Britain/Blitz July 1940–May 1941 London ★

Allies evacuate Dunkirk May–June 1940

Channel Islands

DENMARK

Copenhagen ★

Wilhelmshaven

Hague ★
NETH.

Arnhem Sept. 1944

BELG.

Brussels ★

Hamburg ★

Peenemünde

DANZIG

LITHUANIA

Vilnius ★

EAST PRUSSIA

Dnieper R.

Kursk July 1943

Bergen-Belsen

Hanover ★ Berlin

Treblinka ■

UKRAINE

Kharkov Feb.–Mar. 1943

RUHR

Cologne ★ GERMANY

Warsaw Jewish ghetto uprising, Aug.–Oct. 1944

Kiev ★

Buchenwald

Dresden

ATLANTIC OCEAN

NORMANDY D-Day Jun. 6,1944

Rouen ★

Paris ★

Battle of the Bulge Dec. 1944–Jan. 1945

RHINELAND

LUX.

Allies cross the Rhine at Remagen Mar. 7, 1945

Stuttgart ★

SUDETENLAND

Prague ★

POLAND

Auschwitz-Birkenau ■

Sept. 1941, Aug.–Dec. 1943

CZECHOSLOVAKIA
SLOVAKIA

Dachau

FRANCE

Bern ★
SWITZ.

Vienna ★

AUSTRIA

Budapest ★
HUNGARY

Odessa ★

Vichy capital of unoccupied France

VICHY

Marseilles ★

Allies land Aug. 15, 1944

Corsica

ITALY

ROMANIA

Ploiesti

Belgrade ★

YUGOSLAVIA

Bucharest ★

CRIMEA

Sevastopol ★

Black Sea

PORT.

Lisbon ★ Madrid ★

SPAIN

Sardinia

Rome Allies liberate June 4, 1944 ★

Anzio Allies land Jan. 22, 1944

Monte Cassino Jan.–May 1944

Salerno Allies land Sept. 9, 1943

Sofia ★
BULGARIA

Tirana ★
ALB.

Istanbul •

TURKEY

SPANISH MOROCCO

MOROCCO

ALGERIA

TUNISIA

Palermo •

Sicily

July 9–10, 1943

Malta Axis bombing raids Dec. 1941–July 1942

GREECE

Athens ★

Crete

Cyprus

Mediterranean Sea

PALESTINE TRANS-JORDAN

FOR NORTH AFRICAN CAMPAIGN, SEE P. 201.

LIBYA

EGYPT

El Alamein July 1942; Oct.–Nov. 1942

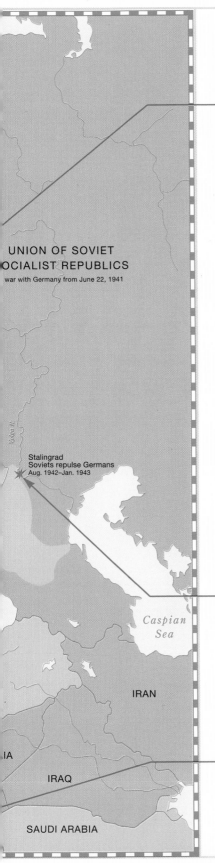

UNION OF SOVIET
OCIALIST REPUBLICS
war with Germany from June 22, 1941

Stalingrad
Soviets repulse Germans
Aug. 1942–Jan. 1943

Caspian
Sea

IRAN

IA

IRAQ

SAUDI ARABIA

p. 191

THE WAR IN EUROPE

The map tells the story: Without going to war, Germany expanded west, south, and east. When it loosed its armies, the Allies staggered, then swept to victory.

Key

■ Germany up to Sept. 1, 1939

■ Axis powers and Axis-aligned nations, Sept. 1939–42

■ Areas conquered by Axis, Sept. 1939–42

■ Neutral nations

■ Allied nations and Allied-aligned nations, Sept. 1939–42

⊛ Capitals

✳ Battles

⬕ Allied invasions

⬙ Important Allied bombings

⬙ Important Axis bombings

■ Concentration/extermination camps

⇢ Convoy routes

p. 202

p. 201

Long before German armies smashed into Poland on September 1, 1939, Hitler, by fair means or foul, had been acquiring territory, building his military strength, and forging alliances in Europe. The German expansion of the 1930's began in January 1935, when the people of the Saar, a region bordering France and Germany, voted to return to German rule after more than 15 years of administration by the League of Nations. Emboldened, Hitler the next year flagrantly ignored the Treaty of Versailles and remilitarized the Rhineland (see map), which included the Saar. Exactly two years later, taking advantage of Austrian economic and sociopolitical disorder, he brought Austria under German rule in the notorious *Anschluss* (union). A little more than six months later, Hitler began absorbing Czechoslovakia piece by piece into his Third Reich. Jumping north, Hitler then gobbled up the Baltic seaport territory of Memel in Lithuania. In less than five years, Germany had enlarged itself by thousands of square miles; and it counted among its European partners Italy, Bulgaria, Romania, and Hungary.

Bursting the Axis Bubble at Last

Threats, deceit, and Machiavellian alliances had served Hitler well. For almost three years after he attacked Poland, it seemed that armed aggression would serve him even better. By the fall of 1942, as the map shows, Germany and its Axis friends ruled an empire that stretched from the gates of Moscow to the shores of the Atlantic, from the deserts of Africa to the Arctic Ocean. But then came the British victory at El Alamein in North Africa and the heroic Soviet stand at Stalingrad. Momentum swung to the Allies. Amphibious invasions struck Axis-held Europe from the south and west; the Soviets rolled in from the east. Allied bombers rained destruction on the heart of Germany. East and west, Germany itself was breached, and the Allied armies poured in. Increasingly desperate, the Nazis accelerated mass slayings at concentration camps. Then Hitler killed himself in his Berlin bunker. On May 8, 1945, the war in Europe was over, five years eight months and seven days after it began.

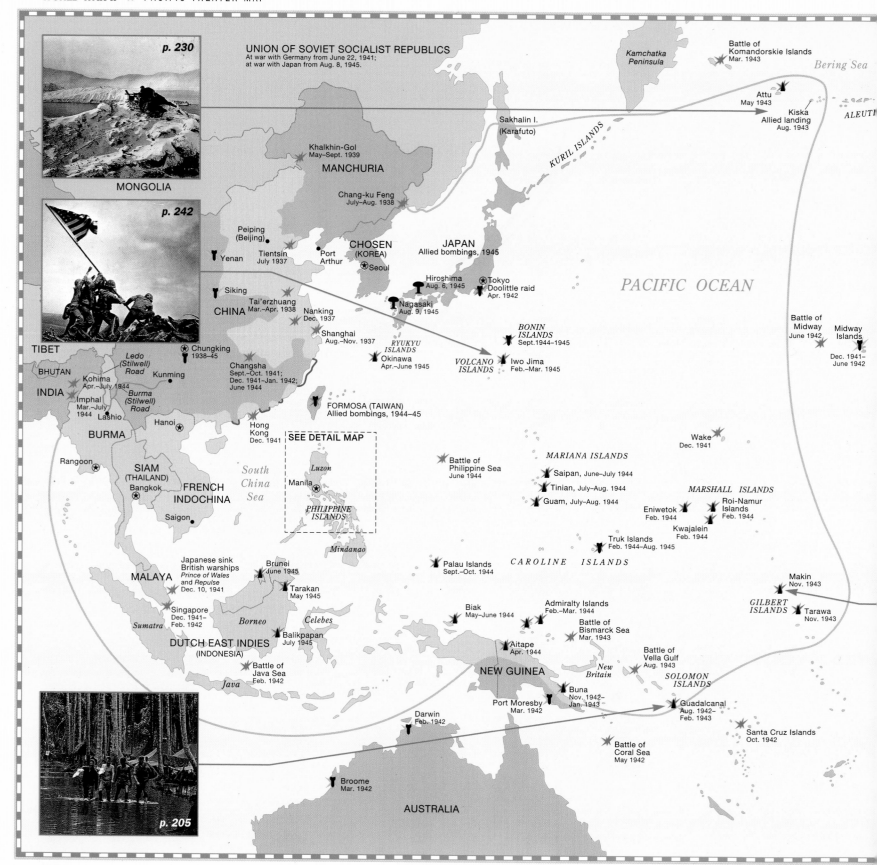

p. 230

MONGOLIA

p. 242

UNION OF SOVIET SOCIALIST REPUBLICS
At war with Germany from June 22, 1941;
at war with Japan from Aug. 8, 1945.

*Kamchatka
Peninsula*

Battle of
Komandorskie Islands
Mar. 1943

Bering Sea

Attu
May 1943

Kiska
Allied landing
Aug. 1943

ALEUTI

Sakhalin I.
(Karafuto)

KURIL ISLANDS

MANCHURIA

Khalkhin-Gol
May–Sept. 1939

Chang-ku Feng
July–Aug. 1938

CHOSEN
(KOREA)

JAPAN
Allied bombings, 1945

Peiping
(Beijing)

Yenan   Tientsin
July 1937

Port
Arthur

Seoul

Hiroshima
Aug. 6, 1945

Tokyo
Doolittle raid
Apr. 1942

PACIFIC OCEAN

TIBET

Siking

CHINA   Tai'erzhuang
Mar.–Apr. 1938

Nanking
Dec. 1937

Nagasaki
Aug. 9, 1945

*RYUKYU
ISLANDS*

Battle of
Midway
June 1942

Midway
Islands

BHUTAN

Chungking
1938–45

Ledo
(Stilwell)
Road

Kohima
Apr.–July 1944

Kunming

Shanghai
Aug.–Nov. 1937

Okinawa
Apr.–June 1945

*BONIN
ISLANDS*
Sept.1944–1945

Iwo Jima
Feb.–Mar. 1945

Dec. 1941–
June 1942

INDIA   Imphal
Mar.–July
1944   Lashio

Burma
(Stilwell)
Road

Changsha
Sept.–Oct. 1941;
Dec. 1941–Jan. 1942;
June 1944

*VOLCANO
ISLANDS*

Hanoi

BURMA

Rangoon

Hong
Kong
Dec. 1941

FORMOSA (TAIWAN)
Allied bombings, 1944–45

SEE DETAIL MAP

Wake
Dec. 1941

SIAM
(THAILAND)

Bangkok

*South
China
Sea*

Luzon

Manila

Battle of
Philippine Sea
June 1944

MARIANA ISLANDS

Saipan, June–July 1944

FRENCH
INDOCHINA

*PHILIPPINE
ISLANDS*

Tinian, July–Aug. 1944

MARSHALL ISLANDS

Saigon

Guam, July–Aug. 1944

Eniwetok
Feb. 1944

Roi-Namur
Islands
Feb. 1944

Mindanao

Truk Islands
Feb. 1944–Aug. 1945

Kwajalein
Feb. 1944

Makin
Nov. 1943

MALAYA

Japanese sink
British warships
Prince of Wales
and *Repulse*
Dec. 10, 1941

Brunei
June 1945

Tarakan
May 1945

Palau Islands
Sept.–Oct. 1944

CAROLINE   ISLANDS

*GILBERT
ISLANDS*

Tarawa
Nov. 1943

Singapore
Dec. 1941–
Feb. 1942

Sumatra

Borneo

Celebes

Biak
May–June 1944

Admiralty Islands
Feb.–Mar. 1944

Battle of
Bismarck Sea
Mar. 1943

DUTCH EAST INDIES
(INDONESIA)

Balikpapan
July 1945

Aitape
Apr. 1944

Battle of
Vella Gulf
Aug. 1943

Battle of
Java Sea
Feb. 1942

Java

NEW GUINEA

*New
Britain*

*SOLOMON
ISLANDS*

Darwin
Feb. 1942

Port Moresby
Mar. 1942

Buna
Nov. 1942–
Jan. 1943

Guadalcanal
Aug. 1942–
Feb. 1943

Battle of
Coral Sea
May 1942

Santa Cruz Islands
Oct. 1942

Broome
Mar. 1942

AUSTRALIA

p. 205

THE WAR IN THE PACIFIC

p. 197

p. 197

HAWAIIAN ISLANDS
(U.S.)

Pearl Harbor
Dec. 7, 1941

Key

Japanese empire as of 1933

Occupied by Japan
before Dec. 7, 1941

Occupied by Japan
after Dec. 7, 1941

Neutral versus Japan for all or part of war

Allied-held throughout war

— Limit of Japanese advance

— Japanese naval blockade

⊛ Capitals

✳ Battles

✴ Allied invasions

✴ Allied air and naval strikes

▼ Japanese invasions

▼ Japanese air strike outside occupied area

☗ Atomic bomb

— Roads

p. 224

p. 224

THE WAR IN THE PHILIPPINES

Aparri
Dec. 1941

Vigan
Dec. 1941

Luzon

Lingayen Gulf
Dec. 1941,
Jan. 1945

*PHILIPPINE
ISLANDS*

Camp O'Donnell
Clark Field

Manila

Bataan and
Corregidor
Jan. 1941–
May 1942,
Feb. 1945

Lamon Bay
Dec. 1941

Mindoro

Legaspi
Dec. 1941

Samar

Battle for
Leyte Gulf
Oct. 1944

Panay

Leyte

Cebu

Leyte
Oct. 1944

Palawan

Negros

Bohol

Japan held sway over approximately 25 percent of the earth's surface before America and its allies rallied and began to push the tenacious Japanese back toward their home islands, the Land of the Rising Sun.

L ike its Axis partner Germany on the other side of the globe, Japan had already won large chunks of territory before it attacked any Western power in World War II. As the Germans were claiming regions that they considered rightfully theirs in Europe (see map, pp. 206–07), Japan was doing the same on the Asian mainland (map at left). At the same time, in a curious twist of history, Japan, which had been on the Allied side in World War I, was busy building military bases on some of the Pacific island groups, such as Truk and Palau, that Germany had lost to Japan as a result of that earlier war.

Japan, the Land of the Rising Sun, aspired to nothing less than domination of Eastern Asia and the Western Pacific. To achieve this grand design, Japan knew it would have to take on the United States sooner or later. Secretly it chose the place and time: the U.S. naval base at Pearl Harbor in the Hawaiian Islands, December 7, 1941. For the Japanese the success of its first strike was critical. As the smoke cleared over Pearl Harbor — and for many months thereafter — it looked as if Japan's daring move had succeeded brilliantly. Victory followed victory for Japan, until by mid-1942 fully a quarter of the world fell under its rule.

But the Japanese had missed something very important at Pearl Harbor: America's aircraft carriers, which were at sea on December 7. At the Battle of Midway those carriers tipped the scales America's way. From Midway on, and with Pearl Harbor's facilities back in business, Japan's defeat was inevitable, though the terrible toll in human lives would keep mounting for more than three years as the Americans fought their way across the Pacific.

For Americans, the Philippines came to stand for both the agony of defeat and the thrill of victory. The loss of Bataan and Corregidor in 1942 was a heavy blow. Two and a half years later, when Gen. Douglas MacArthur announced, "I have returned" as he walked ashore on the island of Leyte, Americans felt that the world was beginning to right itself.

THE MUD-RAIN-AND-FROST GUYS

Tough, sassy, grudgingly good-humored, they saw the war from the level of a foxhole. And while they griped about the food, the officers, and the absence of women, they fought with a dogged courage that changed the world.

Kilroy was here!

Some wags said the initials *GI* stood for "galvanized iron" (as in garbage cans). The more accepted translations were "general issue" or "government issue," referring to the uniforms and the mountains of gear the armed services gave out to recruits. But *GI* came to mean the U.S. Army enlisted man.

"They were the underdogs. They were the mud-rain-frost-and-wind boys. They had no comforts, and they even learned to live without the necessities. And in the end they were the guys without whom the Battle of Africa could not have been won." That was how correspondent Ernie Pyle described the American infantrymen in 1943. Even the enemy came to respect them. German Field Marshal Erwin Rommel praised "the speed with which the Americans adapted themselves to modern warfare," aided by "their tremendous practical and material sense and by their lack of all understanding for tradition and useless theories."

Home, humor, and the love of a sweetheart were never far from a GI's mind. He decorated his tent or barracks with pictures of his wife or girlfriend, or with pinups of Betty Grable, Rita Hayworth, and lesser-known beauties, like Hollywood hopeful Chili Williams, whom *Life* magazine first presented in a two-piece polka-dot bathing suit. GI's painted whimsical names, slogans, and cartoon characters on their tanks, airplanes, ships, trucks, and even guns and bombs. The favorite characters were not all glamorous. Author-soldier William Saroyan's creation "The Sweetheart of Company D" was a part-dachshund mutt called Shorty.

SNAFU, Kilroy, and Joe and Willie

The overseas GI was endlessly resourceful. He turned tin cans into pots or skillets and supplemented his woefully unappetizing (if virtually unspoilable) diet of C and K rations with fresh vegetables, eggs, and wine bought or bartered from locals he met as he slogged through the mud according to some grand strategic plan of which he had little knowledge. An oil drum with holes punched in the bottom made a serviceable field shower. One marine unit in the South Pacific rigged up a wind-powered washing machine using an old airplane propeller. The

Ernie Pyle, shown here on Okinawa just days before a Japanese bullet killed him, wrote unforgettable columns that made the folks back home feel the hardship and danger of GI life.

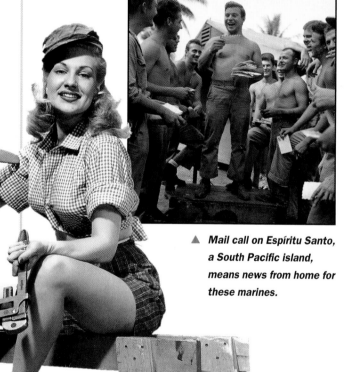

Leggy starlet Chili Williams, one of the GIs' most popular pinups, radiates enthusiasm for tools of war.

▲ *Mail call on Espíritu Santo, a South Pacific island, means news from home for these marines.*

◄ *A soldier's mess-hall diet often came out of cans: powdered eggs, dried milk, baked beans.*

ONE MAN'S VIEW OF THE WAR

▲ **Bill Mauldin's characters Willie and Joe were grubby, unshaven, and bleary-eyed, but Mauldin himself was just a kid. A writer who met him at Anzio in 1944 wrote, "When he is tired, he looks all of sixteen."**

Already a published cartoonist at 18, when his Arizona National Guard unit was federalized in 1940, William Henry (Bill) Mauldin went on to create some of the enduring images of World War II. Wounded at Salerno in 1943, Mauldin stayed close to the action in Italy and France, depicting the combat infantryman's exhaustion, misery, grim humor, and irreverence toward military authority. His drawings became a popular feature in the service paper *Stars and Stripes,* but they offended some serious-minded civilians and military brass, who didn't think our guys should look like bums or ridicule their officers. Furthermore, said Lt. Gen. George S. Patton, Jr., Sergeant Mauldin's cartoons were obviously bad for morale. Hundreds of thousands of his fans, including General Eisenhower, did not agree. After the war Mauldin became a nationally syndicated political cartoonist.

◄ **Mauldin's own favorite cartoon shows a cavalry sergeant putting his broken-down "iron pony" out of its misery.**

"Th' hell this ain't th' most important hole in th' world. I'm in it."

GI spiced his language with terms like SNAFU (Situation Normal, All Fouled Up) and Mae West (the flier's life vest, whose girth reminded him of the voluptuous entertainer). Perhaps his most famous creation was the elusive Kilroy, who always seemed to arrive at any particular place before anybody else, leaving the message "Kilroy was here" scrawled on walls from Paris to Polynesia.

GI's raced to mail call, and the lucky ones pored over letters from home, which had been addressed to an anonymously numbered APO (Army Post Office). When they wrote back, their letters had to pass through the unit's censor, who was charged with removing any information that might reveal the troops' whereabouts. For reading material a GI had special armed forces editions of books and magazines. He devoured the army weekly, *Yank,* and the daily newspaper *Stars and Stripes*, published by and for enlisted

▲ **The U.S. Army weekly, Yank, appeared worldwide from April 1942 through 1945.**

The pungent canned meat called Spam went everywhere the Army went, as George Baker's Sad Sack discovers.

WAR WORDS

Hundreds of expressions sprang up to accommodate the facts of wartime life. Much of this lingo covered things that no one had ever dreamed of before, but it was all wonderfully descriptive.

bazooka - an antitank rocket launcher; named after a novelty musical instrument it somewhat resembles.

blackout - the extinguishing or hiding of lights in case of an air raid. Also, momentary loss of consciousness in an accelerating plane.

blitz - a heavy air raid; from the German word for "lightning."

buzz - to fly over low in an airplane. Buzzing bathing beaches was a favorite stunt.

dogface - a U.S. Army infantryman.

Dear John letter - When your wife or sweetheart sent you one, you knew it was all over between you.

flak - antiaircraft fire; from German *Fliegerabwehrkanone*, an antiaircraft gun.

flattop - an aircraft carrier.

GI - a serviceman. "G.I. Joe" was a comic strip that first appeared in *Yank* in 1942.

gung ho - dedicated and enthusiastic; from the Chinese slogan meaning "Work together!" Gen. Evans Carlson picked it up while assigned to observe Mao Tse-tung's army in 1937–38, and he later introduced it to his 2nd Marine Raider Battalion.

gooney bird - a C-47 transport plane.

▼ *Comedian Bob Hope performs at a World War II military hospital in the South Pacific. He also entertained the troops in two later wars, Korea and Vietnam.*

▲ *Somewhere in France, Berlin-born anti-Nazi film star Marlene Dietrich belts out a ballad for GI's. Her theme song, "Lili Marlene," expressed a whole world of wartime loneliness.*

men. For *Yank*, cartoonist George Baker created an ever-unlucky private, Sad Sack. And Pulitzer Prize–winning Bill Mauldin captured the GI spirit in a pair of sardonic dogfaces named Willie and Joe (see box, previous page).

For readers at home, a trusted authority on the heart and mind of GI Joe was Ernie Pyle, whose syndicated column reached 14 million people. Slight, middle-aged, and balding, Pyle traveled with the infantry in North Africa, Europe, and the Pacific, always trying to make his readers see what the GI's saw and feel what they felt. He succeeded so well that he won a Pulitzer Prize. When he was killed by Japanese machine-gun fire on an island near Okinawa, the men he had celebrated erected a marker on his grave: "At This Spot the 77th Infantry Division Lost a Buddy, Ernie Pyle, 18 April, 1945."

In War, Winds of Social Change

First Lady Eleanor Roosevelt visited almost as many battle areas as the ubiquitous Kilroy, and more than 300,000 other women served as volunteers in the army, navy, marines, and coast guard. They did just about everything short of fighting, from nursing to truck driving. Though not all GI's welcomed them into the all-male military world, some who at first jeered at them later praised their work. Wacs (Women's Army Corps members) and army nurses went coolly about their duties close to battle lines. Women pilots ferried planes from factories to air bases, tested new aircraft, and trained male fliers. Their ferry service had no official military status, and its survivors had to wait more than 30 years before Congress voted them veterans' benefits. Even so, their skill and courage, and the strong performance of thousands of other women in uniform, challenged prevailing stereotypes and pointed the way to opportunities for women in the decades ahead.

Black servicemen, too, set social change in motion during World War II. Heavyweight boxing champion Joe Louis won admiring headlines by enlisting in the army. In combat uniform with rifle and bayonet, he became one of the first black Americans to be featured on a patriotic poster. Black officers and enlisted men served in segregated units, usually noncombat ones, and they were barred from many off-duty recreational facilities. Black truck drivers in the Army Transportation Corps' Red Ball Express rushed more than 5,000 tons of supplies a day to the fast-moving U.S. First and Third Armies in France in the late summer of 1944. And black engineers worked under fire from Germany to Burma.

Late in the war, as manpower became short, black volunteers were accepted to fill the ranks of depleted combat units. For a time they fought side by side with white soldiers in traditionally white regiments, though in all-black

The Women's Auxiliary Ferrying Squadron (WAFS) flew planes from factory to airfield, sometimes shuttling them as far as England; here WAFS chief Nancy Love takes the controls of an army trainer. Unlike army Wacs and navy Waves (right), the women in WAFS were technically civilians.

platoons. The barriers began to rise again at the war's end, when the black soldiers were ordered back to their former units. Many protested that they wanted to return home as members of victorious combat regiments. Some of their white buddies agreed: "If they were good enough to fight with us, they're good enough to come home with us." Finally, in 1948, the armed forces became fully integrated.

Common Bonds

Entertainers, such as Bob Hope and Marlene Dietrich, followed punishing schedules, endured no-frills military travel, risked disease, and dodged danger to bring GI's live shows. The USO (United Service Organizations) became a kind of super impresario, sending scores of performers hither and yon to entertain GI's stationed across America and around the globe. From 1941 to 1947, USO Camp Shows presented an amazing 428,521 performances. The sizes of the audiences ranged from tens of thousands to a mere 25 or so at the more lonely outposts.

Between American servicemen and their Allied comrades-in-arms there was much respect and a lot of good-natured rivalry. With waves of GI's arriving in England, the British were soon wryly describing the Yanks as "overpaid, oversexed, and over here." The Americans replied that the Brits were "underpaid, undersexed, and under Eisenhower." The Americans were amazed by stories of Scottish commandos proudly wearing their regimental kilts on daring raids into France. And like their American counterparts, the Tommies loved poking fun at their officers and at military life in general. ENSA (Entertainments National Services Association), the British equivalent of the USO, was affectionately mocked as showing "Every Night Something Awful."

◄

Late in the war a GI hands out caramels to a cluster of children in the bomb-blasted railroad station in Caserta, Italy.

Kilroy was here!

Are you a girl with a Star-Spangled heart?

JOIN THE WAC
THOUSANDS OF ARMY JOBS NEED FILLING!
Women's Army United States

Have you got what it takes to fill an important job like this?

Enlist in the **WAVES**
INQUIRE TODAY AT ANY NAVY RECRUITING STATION OR OFFICE OF NAVAL OFFICER PROCUREMENT

jerrican - a five-gallon can for gasoline or water, originally of German Army make, adopted by the Allies in 1942.

Joe Blow - any soldier.

jungle juice - home-brewed booze concocted by servicemen in the Pacific.

K ration - a day's combat ration in three cardboard boxes, consisting of food, cigarettes, gum, water purification and salt tablets, and matches.

liberate - to loot, commandeer, appropriate.

milk run - an easy or routine air force mission.

Sad Sack - hero of a comic strip appearing in *Yank*.

snow job - deliberately confusing, flattering speech.

socked in - prevented by weather from taking off in an airplane.

SOP - short for "standard operating procedure," meaning "the way we do things here."

task force - a grouping of units for a given tactical operation.

COURAGE UNDER TYRANTS' HEELS

As the Axis cracked down hard, both at home in Germany and Japan and in the conquered lands, small groups behind the front lines strove valiantly to resist the new order. Meanwhile, Allied bombers wreaked another form of terror.

"Give me five years," Adolf Hitler promised the German people during his rise to power, "and you will not recognize Germany." Such boastful rhetoric played a vital role in the fuehrer's master plan. "Hitler promised everybody something," explains one historian, "and a lot of people almost everything." He knew that there was only one way to achieve his imperial dream of a "thousand-year Reich," and that was to make all Germans share it.

The declaration of war troubled most Germans, but each new victory in Europe and the U.S.S.R. boosted their sense of national pride. Military success also brought Germans something more tangible. After two decades of economic privation following World War I, relief came in the form of long-scarce goods. Daily necessities as well as luxuries, such as Norwegian furs, French perfume, and Dutch dairy products, began to flow in from countries conquered by the Germans.

By late 1942, however, as thousands of wounded soldiers returned from the eastern front, Germany's short-lived halcyon days were over. Hoping to hasten Hitler's demise by breaking the spirit of his people, the Allies adopted a strategy of around-the-clock attacks, which some U.S. journalists dubbed terror bombing and which reached their height of fury in raids like the one on Dresden in February 1945. U.S. and British air squadrons dropped so many incendiary bombs on the splendid old city that it burned for a week. "Never would I have thought," mourned one eyewitness, "that death could come to so many people in so many different ways."

A poster by U.S. artist Ben Shahn decried Nazi atrocities in Czechoslovakia.

This is Nazi brutality

THE PLOT THAT FAILED

Few Germans would voice their opposition to Adolf Hitler for fear of retribution, but some were willing to risk their lives to bring down the Third Reich. One group came close to succeeding. In June 1944, when Germany's ultimate defeat seemed assured, a number of prominent Germans, including both high-ranking army officers and influential civilians, began making plans to take over the government. Hoping to stop further bloodshed and to salvage some vestige of their country's honor, the plotters intended to outlaw the Nazi Party and the Gestapo, halt the extermination programs, negotiate peace with the Allies, and withdraw from all occupied territories. But they knew that first they would have to kill Adolf Hitler.

The man who volunteered for that mission was Col. Claus Schenk, count von Stauffenberg, a staff officer with direct access to the fuehrer. A war hero and intellectual who represented the

Stauffenberg

German aristocratic tradition, Stauffenberg had for years detested the Nazi regime. "I feel I must do something now," he confided to his wife, "to save Germany."

On July 20, 1944, at a meeting in Hitler's supreme command headquarters, in East Prussia, Stauffenberg placed a briefcase containing a time bomb near the fuehrer's feet, then excused himself to make a phone call. Another officer not involved in the plot accidentally kicked the briefcase, then moved it a few feet away. When the bomb exploded, Hitler escaped with only slight injuries. The Gestapo swung into action. Over the remaining months of the war, about 5,000 anti-Nazi Germans, including Stauffenberg, were executed for their complicity in the plot, or merely for their association with the plotters.

◄

Flanked by storm troopers, who used strong-arm tactics to intimidate foes of nazism, Hitler leads his retinue of jackbooted Nazi officers past rows of swastikas at a rally in northern Germany.

To keep Germans loyal, the Nazi Party employed every tool imaginable, from propaganda to terror. Hitler's dreaded secret police, the Gestapo, was ruthless in ferreting out and crushing even the slightest hint of opposition. People were urged to spy on family members for any sign of disloyalty. Listening to a foreign radio station was an act of treason, punishable by death.

Nazi Crackdown, Anti-Nazi Intrigue

The notorious chief of Hitler's "evil guardian angels," as the SS (short for Schutzstaffel, the Nazi police unit) was once described, was Heinrich Himmler, who in the early days boasted that his corps was so elite that even a filled tooth was enough to disqualify a candidate. Under Himmler's leadership, SS men became masters in the art of interrogation by torture. One concentration camp guard was fond of greeting new arrivals with the chilling welcome: "This is hell, and I am the devil." As the war widened, the SD (short for Sicherheitsdienst, the Nazi security service) and the Gestapo (secret police) extended their control to the occupied countries of Europe. Under Hitler's Night and Fog decree, enemies of the Reich were to be disposed of by being made to disappear into "night and fog," that is, without a trace.

Even in the face of such tactics, resistance flared. In 1941 a Munich student, Hans Scholl, founded the underground White Rose movement to mobilize fellow Germans against Nazi tyranny. Scholl and two other members (one was his sister Sophie) were arrested and guillotined in 1943. Other groups plotted to assassinate Hitler himself; none were successful. After surviving the explosion of a bomb that was placed near him in a briefcase on July 20, 1944 (see box at left), Hitler crowed that he was immortal.

But Hitler's megalomania could not stop the Allied bombing raids that were tearing apart his country and its people. In July and August 1943, for example, the Allies launched a massive assault on Hamburg, Germany's largest port and second-largest city. Virtually nonstop for nine days U.S. and British bombers unleashed their fury on Hamburg. Both the city and its population were devastated: 10 square miles lay in ruins and an estimated 50,000 civilians lost their lives. Across the country, people feared that what happened to Hamburg could happen to them — and in many cases it did. By the end of the war, most of Germany's large towns and cities were so ravaged by bombs that, true to Hitler's promise, they were unrecognizable.

WARRIORS OF THE SPIRIT

Most who warred against nazism on its own territory were unarmed civilians. Some took direct action, such as hiding people wanted by the Gestapo. Others, like Protestant theologian Dietrich Bonhoeffer, led double lives. While ostensibly working for Germany's intelligence service, Bonhoeffer was at the same time transmitting messages to the British from anti-Nazi resistance leaders. The Nazis eventually caught and executed him.

Others served by keeping a record. The most celebrated of these witnesses was Anne Frank (below), a German-Jewish teenager who died in a concentration camp. The Frank family had fled Germany for Amsterdam in 1933 to get away from nazism. When the Nazis marched into Holland, the family hid for two years in the attic of a friend's unused warehouse. In August 1944 the Gestapo learned of the family's hideout, and the Franks were taken to concentration camps. All died except for Anne's father, Otto. After the war Otto returned to Amsterdam and there, on the warehouse floor, he discovered a diary that Anne had kept up to the time of her arrest. *The Diary of a Young Girl* remains the most vivid, warmly human document of the entire war.

One who resisted simply by living to tell the tale was Elie Wiesel (above). A gifted child of Jewish parents in Romania, young Elie had already written a book-length Bible commentary when, at age 15, he was taken to Auschwitz. Survival in a death camp was a matter of luck. Elie's parents and sister perished. Convinced that Providence had chosen him to bear witness to the Holocaust, the term he applied to the wholesale murder of Jews by the Nazis, Wiesel wrote his first book, *Night*, which appeared in English in 1960. A citizen of the United States since 1957, he was awarded the Nobel Peace Prize in 1986.

Bonhoeffer, Wiesel, and Anne Frank were exceptional, but they were not alone. There were many warriors of the spirit. Most belonged to that unsung multitude who braved the Nazi terror and perished without leaving a trace.

BRAVE RESISTANCE ACROSS EUROPE

TOOLS OF A TRICKY TRADE

Routine searches and draconian punishments made the arts of disguise and concealment vital to resistance operatives; this inspired the invention of such ingenious low-tech espionage gadgetry as a real poison-pen (left) and a book hollowed out to conceal a handgun (below). Resisters hid items such as coded messages in the heels of their boots, and built radio receivers in a myriad of deceptive shapes.

Under the heel of German occupation, most people in the vanquished countries of Europe were simply glad to stay alive. The governments of France and Denmark, hoping to make the best of a bad situation, urged compliance with the enemy. Leaders of other defeated countries — Belgium, Luxembourg, the Netherlands, Norway, Poland, Czechoslovakia, Greece, Yugoslavia — fled to London, where they set up governments in exile. In BBC broadcasts they urged compatriots to sit tight and await liberation by the Allies.

Inevitably, small acts of resistance began to occur. Brave individuals hid persons sought by the Nazis. Young Danes wore red, white, and blue in solidarity with the British. Clandestine pamphlets and newspapers appeared. Factory workers staged job slowdowns when the product was intended for the Germans. Others, working with Allied intelligence services, ferreted out military secrets and radioed them to London and Moscow. Ham operators in Holland and Czechoslovakia were conspicuously active, and many paid with their lives. Sabotage became a key resistance tactic. In 1943 Norwegian underground fighters destroyed a heavy-water plant, effectively halting Germany's A-bomb program.

As the resistance increased, Germany's occupation troops began to crack down. On June 4, 1942, Czechoslovakia's notorious

A propaganda photo extols the courage of Yugoslav women partisans under the command of resistance leader Josip Broz (Tito). They are shown undergoing training before assignment to combat.

Nazi governor, Reinhard (Hangman) Heydrich, died of injuries sustained during an attempt on his life by British-trained agents. In a frenzy of reprisals the Germans killed more than 1,000 Czechs and later slaughtered 3,000 inmates of a local concentration camp.

In many occupied lands citizens banded together to wage guerrilla war. Soon after Hitler's battalions marched into the U.S.S.R., Soviet resistance fighters began attacking German supply lines, blowing up trains and bridges, and harassing rear-guard area military posts. By 1944 the Soviet partisans numbered as many as 300,000 men and women, controlled 200,000 square miles of territory, and effectively tied down 25 German field divisions. In both Greece and Yugoslavia, rival partisan factions armed variously by Moscow or London battled the German occupiers, and sometimes each other. In Italy anti-Fascist guerrillas resisted sweeps by German divisions. When fallen dictator Benito

▲ Two Greek freedom fighters wear pickup uniforms but carry no-nonsense carbines supplied by the Allies.

A marksman with the French Resistance, shod in homemade straw boots, guards a road in Brittany.

Mussolini was captured and executed, in 1945, Italian partisans carried out the deed.

Some resistance efforts backfired, with dire consequences. In 1944, as Soviet troops approached Warsaw, the local Polish underground revolted against their German occupiers. When the smoke cleared, 85 percent of Warsaw was smoldering rubble and 250,000 Poles lay dead. Soon after, the Soviets moved in and set up a Communist government.

But for every failure, resistance fighters scored a dozen victories. One of the most notable was achieved by the French, who in 1942 relayed Germany's coastal defense plans to London, thus helping Eisenhower plan the Normandy invasion two years later.

A Yugoslav partisan captain and his executive officer scan the horizon from a snowy pass in the Balkans.

SAVED BY THE DUTCH

Underground fighters saved many downed Allied airmen. Typical is the story of a B-17 hit by flak over Leipzig in June 1944. Limping homeward on two engines, the crew had to bail out over Holland. A Dutch underground unit lodged the men in a small room made of hay bales. They spent six months there, joking about their predicament: "Gosh, wish Errol Flynn was here. Wonder what he'd do to get us out of this fix." Finally the Germans learned where they were hiding, and the airmen had to shoot their way out. In reprisal the Germans executed 117 local civilians, but the fugitive airmen remained at large to greet arriving Canadians in April 1945.

TERROR AND TRAGEDY IN ASIA

When news of the victory at Pearl Harbor reached the Japanese people, the prospect of plunging into a global war drew mixed reactions. "I never thought I should live to see . . . such a thrilling day, such an auspicious day," one citizen declared. "The good ship Japan has just been sunk," another lamented, fearing what lay beyond the glow of early triumph. In the short term Japan would extend its rule to more than 1 million square miles of territory and more than 150 million people, but as a result of the war, at least 2.5 million Japanese would be counted dead or missing and more than 10 million would lose their homes.

As the Japanese took over Southeast Asia, they Nipponized vanquished countries. They replaced the Roman calendar with the Japanese one. Western languages, one order decreed, "have ceased to exist." When a native happened to meet up with a Japanese, the native either bowed or received a slap in the face.

Secret Police and Phony Co-Prosperity

Japan did not accept Western ideas about humane treatment of prisoners or civilians. Japan's secret police, the Kempei Tai, were notorious for pulling out their victims' fingernails during interrogations. Shortly after Japanese soldiers conquered Singapore, in February 1942, they massacred more than 5,000 Chinese residents, some of whom were doomed simply because they had tattoos, which were believed to symbolize membership in a secret criminal group.

Presenting themselves as liberators who had lifted the yoke of European oppression, Japanese conquerors tried to minimize resistance from their subjects by emphasizing their common Asian heritage and by touting the benefits of a new and supposedly self-sufficient economic community, the Greater East Asia Co-Prosperity Sphere. Among themselves, impoverished Southeast Asians mocked Japan's charade, referring to it as the Co-Poverty Sphere.

In a scene staged by the photographer, Japanese soldiers frolic with Filipino schoolgirls. Despite such token togetherness, the Philippines smoldered under Japanese rule.

Since Japan had been at war with China for more than four years before Pearl Harbor, the Japanese people had grown accustomed to hardship and sacrifice, but their fortitude faced even harsher tests after 1941. "To live at all," recalled Foreign Minister Mamoru Shigemitsu, "the people reverted to a primitive existence." Rice imports fell to almost nothing as the Americans took command of the seas, and hardy, fast-growing pumpkin replaced rice as the national staple. Buddhist monks were conscripted to work in factories. Faced with shortages of both manpower and clothing, many women forsook centuries-old traditions. They traded their kimonos for baggy trousers and did what had to be done to keep family and society together.

No amount of sacrifice and courage, however, could triumph over the lethal rain of bombs that fell on Japan beginning in 1944, and that would culminate a year later in the atomic devastation of Hiroshima and Nagasaki. As one Japanese civilian said after a raid on Tokyo: "We finally began to realize . . . that the government had lied when it said we were invulnerable. We then started to doubt that we were also invincible."

THE FIGHTING FILIPINOS

WE WILL ALWAYS FIGHT FOR FREEDOM!

A U.S. poster rallied support for the Filipino resistance movement, which was secretly led by U.S. advisers.

AMERICAN INDUSTRY GOES TO WAR

While America's fighting men stood ready to make the ultimate sacrifice, home-front citizens

kept them well armed and fully equipped by making some sacrifices of their own.

When France fell to the Nazis in June 1940, America's defense industry was contributing only about 2 percent to the nation's total industrial production. Four years later defense accounted for 45 percent of national output.

In round-the-clock shifts, workers built new plants and retooled old ones to turn out everything from cargo ships to carbines by the thousands. As American industry hummed into high gear, it needed hundreds of thousands of new workers, and women answered the call. Before the war some 12 million women constituted about a fourth of the labor force. By the fall of 1943, coaxed by slogans such as Do the Job He Left Behind, over 30 percent more women — close to 16 million in all — were at work outside their homes.

The popular song "Rosie the Riveter" celebrated the women who took over factory jobs, especially traditionally male tasks, such as riveting and welding. Norman Rockwell painted Rosie as a muscular Amazon for the cover of *The Saturday Evening Post* magazine. The inspiration for the Rosie legend may have been one Rosie Bonavita, who, with the help of another woman, pounded 3,345 rivets into the wing of a fighter plane in a record six hours.

New factories sprouted in cornfields and cow pastures. Near Detroit, at a creek named Willow Run, Henry Ford built a 70-acre aircraft plant, which was called the "most enormous room in the history of man." Aviation pioneer Charles Lindbergh referred to it as "a sort of Grand Canyon of a mechanized world."

Factories alone could not work miracles, however. In the past airplanes and ships had been put together one at a time. Now plant managers had to figure out by trial and error how to assemble them on a mass-production basis. J. D. Kindelberger, North American Aviation president, commented: "You cannot expect blacksmiths to learn how to make watches overnight." Nevertheless, U.S. industry rose to the occasion. By 1944 bombers were coming off Henry Ford's assembly line at the rate of one every 63 minutes.

A dynamic dam builder of the 1930's brought mass production to America's wartime shipyards. He was Henry J. Kaiser, the contractor for the Hoover, Bonneville, and mammoth Grand Coulee dams. Kaiser became one of World War II's civilian heroes by adapting prefabrication

Rosie the Riveter's air of unshakable confidence proclaimed that American women could do anything if only they set their minds (and muscles) to it.

Spurred on by posters like the one touting the Woman Ordnance Worker (WOW) (upper left), workers assembled planes, such as the B-17F (circle inset), at record speeds and completed an entire Liberty ship (left) in only 10 days.

"THE GIRL HE LEFT BEHIND IS STILL BEHIND HIM" She's a WOW

▲ Americans nationwide answered the call to fight shortages with scrap drives like this one, led by Boy Scouts. It collected over 80 tons of rubber.

HERE'S OUR ANSWER PRESIDENT ROOSEVELT

YOUR SCRAP
...brought it down

KEEP SCRAPPING
Rubber · Metal · Rags

GIVE TO A COLLECTOR,
SALVAGE DEPOT OR SELL TO A DEALER

▼ Champions of the Allied armored forces, these M-4 Sherman tanks receive finishing touches from Ford mechanics, 1942.

and assembly-line techniques to building ships. His methods dramatically shortened shipbuilding schedules and created jobs that could be quickly learned by unskilled workers.

On the home front Americans soon learned that fighting a war meant doing without. The War Production Board (WPB) took control of all steel, copper, aluminum, rubber, silk, and nylon after Pearl Harbor and quickly stopped the manufacture of 300 kinds of items it deemed nonessential, a list that included refrigerators, beer cans, toothpaste tubes, and wire clothes hangers.

Americans launched what seemed to be a perpetual scavenger hunt for reusable rubber and metal. Boy and Girl Scout troops scoured attics, basements, and garages for old automobile and bicycle tires, overshoes, aluminum pans, rubber mats, and hot-water bottles. Hollywood and

THE CASE OF THE PHONY FISHERMEN

Shortly past midnight on June 13, 1942, John C. Cullen, a rookie coastguardsman, was patrolling the beach at Amagansett, Long Island — 105 miles east of New York City — when he spotted four men emerging from the fog. "We're fishermen from Southampton and ran aground here," announced one of the men, identifying himself as George Davis. Cullen told them to come back to the Coast Guard station with him. "I don't want to kill you," responded Davis, who then offered Cullen a bribe to forget what he had seen. Outnumbered and fearing for his life, Cullen accepted the money ($260) and walked away in the fog.

As soon as the strangers were out of sight, Cullen raced back to the station to report the incident and turn the money over to his superior. A search the next day uncovered a duffel bag containing four German Navy uniforms and four waterproof boxes filled with TNT, timing devices, and incendiary bombs.

Davis, whose real name was Georg Dasch, was actually the leader of a team trained by German intelligence. All had lived in the United States years earlier. Along with four others, who landed near Jacksonville, Florida, a few nights later, Dasch and his comrades were to plant bombs at a number of targets from New York to the Midwest.

Once the four men arrived in New York City, however, their top-secret operation fell apart. They went on a spree — drinking, gambling, and womanizing. When some of the men started blabbing about their exploits, Dasch and another member of the group, Ernest Burger, turned themselves in. Within two weeks all eight would-be saboteurs were in custody. Death sentences for Dasch and Burger were commuted to 30 years and life, respectively, but they were released and deported to Germany in 1948. The other six men were put to death in the electric chair to discourage future sabotage missions.

Broadway pitched in with gusto, as when the actress Merle Oberon lent her beauty to orchestrating an aluminum drive at the Stork Club, a stylish New York night spot.

At the start of the war President Franklin D. Roosevelt had called upon the United States to achieve such an overwhelming superiority in weapons that the Axis could never catch up. His country did not disappoint him. When Roosevelt and Stalin met in Tehran, late in 1943, the Soviet dictator proposed an admiring toast: "To American production, without which this war would have been lost!"

MAKE DO OR DO WITHOUT

When you ride ALONE you ride with Hitler!

Join a Car-Sharing Club TODAY!

Whether it meant cutting down on cigarettes, driving less, eating less meat, turning the front lawn into a cabbage patch, or resisting the blandishments of black marketeers, folks at home strove to do all they could for the war effort.

Very quickly after Pearl Harbor, home-front consumers learned a new refrain: "Use it up, wear it out, make it do, or do without." If tempers frayed because of the long workdays and limited goods, complainers were stopped short with an impatient, "Hey! Don't you know there's a war going on?"

Many companies were quick to discover that a patriotic image was good for business. "Lucky Strike Green Has Gone to War," proclaimed the American Tobacco Company to explain the switch from green to white packages; supposedly, green dye contained precious metals that were vital to the war effort. Whatever the package color, home-front smokers frequently waited in block-long lines to purchase their favorite brands, since most cigarettes went to the GI's.

By the summer of 1942 gasoline was scarce, and many filling stations closed. In December the Office of Price Administration (OPA) dealt out A, B, and C windshield stickers. An A sticker entitled the car's driver to coupons for four (later three) gallons of gas per week, which authorities suggested should be used for grocery shopping, going to church, and other such unfrivolous activities. The B and C stickers — for drivers who used their cars to commute to defense-related jobs, for example — permitted larger purchases.

The gas shortage touched almost everyone's life. Pleasure driving all but stopped. Retail stores eliminated home deliveries; milkmen rediscovered horses and wagons. Home-front workers made car pooling an American institu-

DO YOUR BIT! SKATE TO WORK SAVE GAS

A poster lashed out at solo driving (above, left), while in a promo stunt for the 1942 Broadway musical **Roller Vanities** *these girls show off an alternative.*

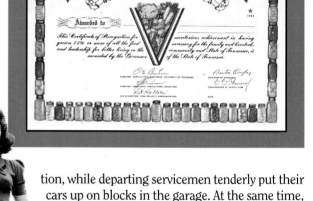

Every purchase seemed to require a sticker or a stamp, and you got special ration tokens in change. But in Tennessee growing your own dinner could have won you a citation (below).

tion, while departing servicemen tenderly put their cars up on blocks in the garage. At the same time, express buses suspended service, plane tickets were unavailable for ordinary civilian travel, and the government took over steamships.

Inevitably "Mr. Black," as black marketeers came to be collectively known, appeared on the scene. Some black-market crooks forged gas coupons; others stole real ones from OPA offices. Mr. Black also found ways to procure and sell T coupons, meant to give truck drivers all the gas they needed to keep essential goods moving. To help cut down cheating, OPA inspectors checked the stickers and license plates of cars parked at movie houses and sporting events, looking for people who drove too often for mere pleasure.

Travel restrictions were an inconvenience, but food shortages cut closer to the bone. Coffee was added to the list of rationed goods, and so was sugar. Sugar imports from the Philippines had been cut off, and ships that normally transported sugar from Cuba and Puerto Rico, and coffee from South America, were appropriated for defense. Ration boards set an allotment of half a pound of sugar per week for each man, woman, and child, which was not much in the days before prepackaged mixes, when many housewives made puddings and pies from scratch and put up their own jams and jellies.

Less Butter, More Vegetables

By July 1943 the Allies began to win the battle against U-boats, and more cargo space became available for nonmilitary shipments. Coffee rationing ended, and the weekly civilian allotment of sugar rose to three-quarters of a pound per person. Meanwhile, by February 1943 the military's need to send food overseas had brought rationing to canned meat and canned fish. In March other canned foods were added, followed by fresh meats, butter, and cheese.

In principle the rules of food rationing were simple. For each month the ration board gave every person, regardless of age, two books: one with blue coupons for canned goods, and the other with red coupons for meat, butter, and cheese. At first the monthly allotment of blue coupons provided about 2 pounds of canned fruits and vegetables, while the red coupons covered 28 ounces of meat plus 4 ounces of cheese. Depending on national supplies, these allotments went up or down. And sometimes unanticipated shortages in one region or another made it impossible to find the foods for which a shopper had coupons.

Americans found a number of ways to stretch their coupons. One called for ingenuity in the kitchen (see box at right). But the best and most patriotic coupon-stretcher was the victory garden. Americans followed the advice of Secretary of Agriculture Claude R. Wickard with feverish enthusiasm and spaded up everything from a few square feet of land to acres. Flower beds became cabbage patches, and grass surrendered to lettuce. What wasn't eaten fresh went into mason jars as homemakers returned in droves to the old-fashioned art of putting up their harvest. So successful was the program that by 1943 victory gardeners were gathering more than one million tons of vegetables each season, about 40 percent of the nation's needs.

EATING TO WIN THE WAR

Although it isn't / Our usual habit
This year we're eating / The Easter Rabbit.

So went a poem in a 1943 issue of *Gourmet* magazine, when World War II made sugar, dairy products, meat, and coffee scarce or unavailable. With rationing in effect from early 1942 through 1946, preparing meals became an experiment in creativity. American women stretched everything to the limit and substituted foods they could get for ones they couldn't. Pork, fish, chicken, or even horsemeat replaced beef. Casseroles and stews were made from whatever icebox leftovers the family would tolerate. And meatless meals meant families sitting down to supper and facing Cottage Cheese Loaf as the "meat dish." For dessert they might have had a sugarless Yankee Doodle Prune Pie with a low-shortening Victory Pie Crust. Not enough java to serve with it? Then chicory was added to the brew, or coffee drinkers took President Roosevelt's wry advice and rebrewed their grounds. Even the White House went on an austerity plan: reduced portions for the help. Homemakers cut down on baking, and restaurants put less sugar in their sugar bowls to help "build final and complete victory." Most Americans regarded the lack of sugar — and of almost everything else they most loved — with a resigned acceptance that was usually more wistful than grumbling. The popular columnist Walter Winchell summed it up best:

Roses are red, violets are blue.
Sugar is sweet. Remember?

Learning early to conserve, a young patriot shows his ration book, which holds the monthly allotment of food stamps he needs to buy canned goods.

One of 20 million Americans to grow a victory garden, this parking lot owner in downtown New Orleans spaded up enough asphalt to grow 30 pounds of tomatoes, 100 ears of corn, and 75 fine heads of cabbage.

Hard Fighting in the Soft Underbelly

Striking directly into Europe, Allied troops battled their way up the Italian peninsula — to the noisy delight of most Italians. Unfamiliar place-names dominated the morning headlines: Salerno, Anzio, Monte Cassino.

Lashed by a summer gale, the armada of 3,000 ships rolled and pitched in heavy seas off Malta. Crammed in troop carriers, some 160,000 U.S., Canadian, and British soldiers fought varying degrees of seasickness and prebattle jitters. Their destination: the island of Sicily. Above the invasion fleet an airborne force of some 4,000 men — glider troops and paratroopers — droned ahead to open the assault behind the beaches. It was July 9, 1943, and Operation Husky had begun.

Next morning, the troops stormed ashore. Lt. Gen. George S. Patton, Jr., sporting his ivory-handled revolvers, led the U.S. Seventh Army onto Sicily's south coast. The British Eighth Army, commanded by Gen. Bernard L. Montgomery, landed to the east. The island's defenders, 350,000 Germans and Italians, under Field Marshal Albert (Smiling Albert) Kesselring, fell back to regroup.

Operation Husky was the first Allied thrust into Western Europe, and it aimed at the "soft underbelly" of Axis power, as Winston Churchill put it. And despite a few major blunders — Allied antiaircraft fire downed a number of Allied planes, for example — the campaign was a success. Italian units, never eager to march for Hitler's generals, surrendered in droves. The island's civilians greeted the Allies as liberators, embracing them and plying them with wine

Seventh Army troops roll into Palermo, capital of Sicily (top), while jubilant residents wave flags and shout welcoming slogans: "Long live America!" and "Down with Mussolini!" Later, in newly liberated Rome (circle inset), a Yank private wins a grandmotherly kiss.

and fruit. The harsher experiences of war were never far away, however. As the Allies pushed Kesselring's remaining 60,000 Germans into a corner in the northeast, heavy fighting took many casualties. General Patton, visiting a field hospital, noticed a private who, though unwounded, was occupying a bed. "It's my nerves," confessed the soldier, who suffered from shell shock. Patton flew into a rage and called the man a coward; then he slapped him with a glove. The story reached the newspapers, and the resulting furor brought Patton a scolding from higher-ups.

In mid-August Kesselring withdrew his surviving forces across the Strait of Messina to the Italian mainland. Enemy resistance appeared to be dissolving. Benito Mussolini, Italy's Fascist head of state, had been replaced, and the new government was conducting secret armistice negotiations. All that was needed to take Italy out of the war, it seemed, was to land a few troops on the mainland.

Fierce German Counterattacks

But no one had reckoned with the strength of German determination. Hitler poured in men and weapons. Montgomery's Eighth Army landed first, on September 3, at Reggio di Calabria, on the Italian toe. Then, six days later and 200 miles up the Italian boot, Lt. Gen. Mark W. Clark's U.S. Fifth Army splashed ashore at Salerno, a day's march south of Naples. All hell broke loose.

Kesselring sent a panzer division, backed by heavy artillery, against the Salerno beachhead. In desperate fighting, in which clerks, cooks, and musicians served as riflemen, the GI's stopped the Germans less than two miles from the beach. It took another three weeks of bloody fighting to dislodge the enemy from the surrounding hills. Recalling an

Warned of a pending attack by Allied bombers, two Benedictine monks at Monte Cassino pack treasured books and parchments, including an 11th-century Latin grammar, for emergency shipment to the Vatican. After the monastery had been obliterated, German soldiers set up gun nests in the ruins, slowing the Allied advance.

assault on a hilltop observation post, Sgt. Ross Carter, of the 504th Parachute Infantry Regiment, said: "I'd never known real terror until that moment."

Eventually the Germans abandoned Naples and retreated north to a fortified line. Here stubborn German resistance, combined with freezing rain and blizzards, brought the Allies to a standstill. In response, Clark decided to try an end run. He landed a 50,000-man Anglo-American force, under U. S. Maj. Gen. John P. Lucas, at the small port of Anzio, 33 miles south of Rome.

The Germans, moving in quickly with eight divisions, turned Anzio into a death trap. Two giant 280-millimeter railroad guns, nicknamed Anzio Express and Anzio Annie, hurled 550-pound projectiles into the Allied positions. Panzer-led assaults hammered the hapless beachhead.

British forces, meanwhile, stepped up their attacks on the main line of German defenders. Their focal point was the town of Cassino, overlooked by a 1,400-year-old monastery atop 1,703-foot Monte Cassino. On February 15, Allied bombers destroyed the monastery. The town came next, obliterated on March 15 by 1,000 tons of bombs and some 195,000 artillery shells. British, French, and Polish ground troops waged a brutal and costly campaign to take Cassino. By the end of May, the town and monastery were in Allied hands, and Clark's force had broken out of Anzio .

As the Germans fell back, Clark ordered a dash for Rome. On June 4, 1944, almost nine months after they landed in Salerno, the grimy, exhausted soldiers of the Fifth Army entered the Eternal City. It was the first of the three Axis capitals to fall to the Allies. In a radio address to the nation, President Roosevelt announced Rome's liberation: "One down and two to go."

IRON PONIES OF THE WAR

One day in 1941 a flying wedge of 18 odd-looking boxlike vehicles charged onto a German airfield in North Africa with their specially fitted Vickers machine guns blazing. Within minutes they destroyed or damaged 37 planes, then bounced off into the desert before Rommel's people had time to figure out what had hit them. Manned by British soldiers, the American jeep had just made its combat debut. First developed in 1940, this olive-drab box on wheels weighed a quarter-ton, had four-wheel drive, got 20 miles to the gallon, and could go just about anyplace. The word *jeep* came both from the designation GP

(general purpose) and from the name of a cartoon character, Popeye's pal Eugene the Jeep. On mountainsides, through jungles, and across trackless wastes the world over, jeeps became the iron ponies of the Allied effort. Well-nigh indestructible and easy to fix when they did break down, they towed antiaircraft guns, served as ambulances and mobile command posts, and sometimes dashed out ahead of the tanks. Also, their radiators were occasionally tapped to get hot water for shaving. More than 600,000 were built by 1945. A tamer postwar version was developed, and jeeps have been with us ever since.

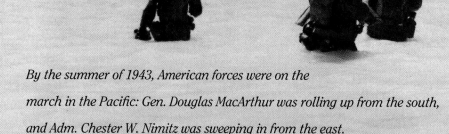

ISLAND BY ISLAND TOWARD TOKYO

Adm. Chester W. Nimitz

▶

American infantrymen wade ashore at Makin, an atoll near Tarawa, following an intense bombardment by navy guns.

By the summer of 1943, American forces were on the march in the Pacific: Gen. Douglas MacArthur was rolling up from the south, and Adm. Chester W. Nimitz was sweeping in from the east.

For Japanese garrisons in the far-flung outposts of the South Pacific, the reports were not good. In early March 1943, Allied bombers swooped down on a Japanese troop convoy in the Bismarck Sea, northeast of New Guinea, and all but demolished it. The pilots used a new, lethally effective technique called skip bombing, and it sent 12 of the convoy's 16 vessels plunging to the bottom. Some 3,000 Japanese soldiers and seamen lost their lives.

Allied airmen soon delivered a second sharp blow. Adm. Isoroku Yamamoto, Japan's top naval commander, was making a morale-boosting inspection tour of island bases east of New Guinea. On April 18 a squadron of U.S. P-38 fighter planes flying from newly liberated Guadalcanal pounced on Yamamoto's plane over the island of Bougainville. Japan's most brilliant military leader, the strategist of Pearl Harbor, spun earthward to a fiery death.

In every sector Allied forces were swinging over to the offensive. On the ground in New Guinea, U.S. and Australian troops, under Gen. Douglas MacArthur, pushed through malaria-riddled jungles to clean out Japanese strongholds. On MacArthur's right flank Adm. William Halsey, nicknamed Bull, led a series of amphibious assaults on the 700-mile-long Solomon Islands .

Meanwhile, in the vast reaches of the Central Pacific, the Pacific Fleet, under Adm. Chester W. Nimitz, struck Japanese bases on widely scattered mid-ocean islets and coral reefs. The first target was Tarawa, a heavily fortified atoll in the Gilbert Islands. On November 20, after intensive naval bombardment, a division of marines hit the beach.

The navy's guns had pounded Tarawa's defenses with 3,000 tons of high explosives — enough, presumably, to obliterate all resistance. Not so: the Japanese, dug into the coral in steel-lined bunkers, withstood the shelling. As

With majestic aplomb, General MacArthur leads his aides to the beach at Leyte in the Philippines, shortly after U.S. Sixth Army assault troops had cleared the way. "I have returned," the general declared, keeping a promise he had made back in 1942. It took four months of bitter fighting to complete the island's capture.

the marines rushed ashore, they faced withering fire from Japanese shore batteries and automatic weapons.

Individual acts of heroism propelled them forward. Lt. William D. (Hawk) Hawkins, a 29-year-old Texan, single-handedly assaulted a cluster of machine-gun nests, running from one to the next to toss hand grenades through the firing slits. Wounded, he kept going — "I came here to kill . . . not to be evacuated," he shouted — until an explosive shell claimed his life.

Adm. Isoroku Yamamoto

Gradually the firing sputtered out. "The Americans," one Japanese commander had predicted, "could not take Tarawa with a million men in a hundred years." Four days were all they needed. But four days of hell! The marines lost 1,115 dead and 2,234 wounded. Of 5,000 Japanese defenders, only 17 men survived.

Adm. William Halsey

The U.S. fleet moved on through the Pacific, landing troops on the Admiralty Islands, the Marshalls, the Carolines. New tactics and equipment — including amtracs (amphibious tractors) to get ashore and flame throwers to wipe out enemy bunkers — helped reduce casualties. Even so, the advances came at a terrible cost in lives.

American strategy called for taking a trio of islands in the Marianas: Saipan, Tinian, and Guam. The U.S. fleet, 535 vessels strong, approached in mid-June 1944 and quickly scored a remarkable victory. The Japanese moved up a carrier force, much smaller in size, and a four-day battle ensued in which U.S. Navy pilots sank three Japanese carriers and shot down hundreds of enemy planes, a rout the Americans dubbed The Great Marianas Turkey Shoot.

Capturing the islands was another matter. The Japanese defenders on Saipan, ordered to die for their emperor, hurled themselves against the Americans in repeated banzai attacks. Both sides took heavy losses. The Japanese, running out of ammunition, charged with bayonets tied to sticks. The corpses piled so high that U.S. machine gunners had to keep moving their weapons just to clear their firing lanes. The Americans suffered 16,525 casualties, while the Japanese lost some 29,000, many of them in the largest suicide attack of the war.

▶
Mission accomplished, the U.S.S. Langley leads a task force of Pacific Fleet carriers and battleships back to base after pounding enemy positions in the Phillippines.

While U.S. pilots blasted the enemy from the sky, submarine skippers struck from below, like this one peering through his periscope (bottom, right). Crews boasted of their kills with homemade battle flags (below). A cartoonlike fish figure identified the submarine, while each Japanese flag represented a merchantman or warship either maimed or destroyed by the sub.

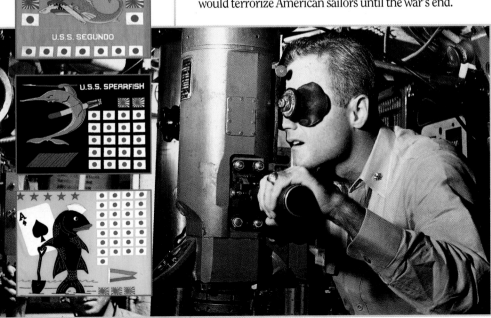

The Allies' two lines of assault — MacArthur moving up from New Guinea and Nimitz's armada of ships sweeping in from the east — began to converge. In late October 1944, 132,000 of MacArthur's men stormed a beach at Leyte in the Philippines. A few hours later the general himself waded in. Already Japan's last great carriers and battleships were steaming toward Leyte for a final do-or-die confrontation with the U.S. Third and Seventh fleets.

The Battle for Leyte Gulf lasted three days, spread over hundreds of miles of ocean, and saw no fewer than 282 warships engage in combat. It was the largest armed struggle in naval history. When the smoke cleared, the Japanese Navy lay crippled beyond repair. But in its death throes it launched a horrifying new weapon: the kamikaze attack. A Japanese pilot crashed his plane onto the U.S. escort carrier *St. Lo,* killing himself and irreparably damaging the ship. Attacks by kamikazes ("divine wind," in Japanese legend) would terrorize American sailors until the war's end.

TIGHTENING THE NOOSE

At an airfield in England, General Eisenhower tells D-Day airborne troops, "Nothing less than full victory!" Dropped north of St.-Lô, they faced snipers, mine-tipped sticks, and flooded landing zones.

In retrospect, Hitler's fate was sealed when the Western Allies stormed and held the Normandy beaches and Red armies smashed into Poland. But the Germans had other ideas.

"You are about to embark upon a great crusade!" With these forceful, inspiring words Gen. Dwight D. Eisenhower launched Operation Overlord against the Atlantic wall of German-occupied Europe. Beginning in the small hours of June 6, 1944, two days after the capture of Rome, Operation Overlord eventually sent almost a million Allied troops across the English Channel and onto the invasion landing sites of France. It was a massive logistical undertaking put together piece by piece in deepest secrecy over the previous 13 months.

Up to the last possible moment, the Allies tried to confuse the Germans with a blizzard of feints and fake plans, all designed to conceal their true objective: the broad beaches of Normandy, in northwest France. As zero hour approached, Allied warships began a thunderous bombardment, 2,000 planes dumped bombs on German seacoast defenses, and three divisions of paratroopers leapt from the dark skies to hold off German reinforcements and gain control of the roads behind Utah Beach for the American advance through the marshes there.

Nevertheless, at Omaha Beach the U.S. 1st Infantry Division met heavy artillery and machine-gun fire. Soon hundreds of dead bodies drifted in the surf while many drowned in tanks that sank before they could reach the shore. Those who made it to the beach were still in grave danger. If vehicles stopped, they became sitting ducks for the murderous German fire.

Meanwhile, some 1,500 miles to the east in northern Europe, the Soviets were headed for a climactic showdown. Since their victory at Stalingrad early in 1943, they had barely survived a German counteroffensive. Then, on July 5, 1943, Soviet and German tanks clashed at Kursk, in southwestern Russia, igniting the greatest tank battle in history and shattering the myth that German tank units, the panzers, were invincible. In June 1944, about two weeks after D-Day, Soviet Field Marshal Georgi Zhukov launched 166 divisions, more than a million men, in a major westward offensive into Poland.

Out of Normandy and Across France

In Normandy the Americans, too, were learning hard lessons about tank warfare. While trying to capture the rail hub of St.-Lô, the Americans found the countryside crisscrossed with hedgerows — tall banks of dirt topped with thornbushes and trees, which concealed German machine guns, tanks, and mortars. In climbing over the hedgerows, U.S. tanks exposed their thinly armored undersides to enemy fire. Many of these vehicles were lost before an American farm boy, Sgt. Curtis G. Culin, Jr., welded a set of steel plates to the front of his tank. Equipped with such "horns," these rhino tanks, as they were nicknamed by grateful fellow tankers, enabled U.S. armor to cut right through hedgerows and outflank German tanks.

Overhead, massive Allied air power had all but driven the outnumbered Luftwaffe from the skies. Wave after wave of planes bombed and strafed the German defenses with devastating results. A bitter joke circulated through the German ranks: "If you see a white plane, it's an American. If you see a black plane, it's the RAF. If you see no plane at all, it's the Luftwaffe."

With St.-Lô secured, U.S. armor poured through a gap at Avranches and headed south and west, gaining as much as 40 miles in a single day. An officer who personified aggressive tank warfare, Lt. Gen. George S. Patton, Jr., now led the Third Army after the successful completion of the Sicilian campaign. Just past midnight on August 7, 1944, Hitler ordered four panzer divisions to unite for a counterattack. But the Allies, having broken the German codes, knew what was coming. Canadian and British forces, striking from the north, joined Patton's forces, moving up from the south, and trapped many of the Germans in a pocket near Falaise, where planes and artillery inflicted heavy casualties. By August 19 the battle for Normandy was over. German

Tourists for a moment, soldiers of the U.S. 4th Infantry Division gawk at the Eiffel Tower after the liberation of Paris, August 1944.

A Frenchwoman of Belfort, near the German border, gives this GI a big wide-armed welcome to her newly liberated town.

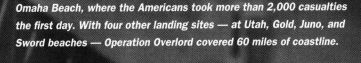

Nowhere on D-Day did the Allies meet worse going than at cliff-ringed Omaha Beach, where the Americans took more than 2,000 casualties the first day. With four other landing sites — at Utah, Gold, Juno, and Sword beaches — Operation Overlord covered 60 miles of coastline.

LETTER FROM A WOUNDED SOLDIER

When Charles dictated this letter for a Red Cross nurse to send to his mother, a month had passed since he received his combat wounds (for which the United States confers the Purple Heart, above). One eye gone and the other virtually sightless, he wanted to reassure his family about his injuries. Later, sight came back in his right eye as he had faith it would, although his doctors at first had been pessimistic. In the half century after shrapnel felled the infantry second lieutenant as his unit advanced into Germany near Aachen, Charles fulfilled his prewar dream of becoming a professional writer. Married to his wife, Betty, since 1947, he has a son, a daughter, and two granddaughters. He considers himself a lucky man.

My dearest Mother,

I have been informed that now since a certain period of time has elapsed since my injury it will be O.K. to tell you about it. I'll begin with my head and work down. . . . As you probably guessed, my eyes have been my chief worry lately. I lost my left eye and my right eye was sympathetically affected but the doc has been working hard on it and he says it is going to be O.K. So far though I can't see too well with it. They are making me a very handsome artificial eye for the left side. The eyes are made of the same material they make false teeth of, so, I go to the dentist to have it fitted which seems quite funny. Speaking of the dentist, remember . . . all those damn fillings I got and how I fought . . . to keep them from pulling teeth. Well, I'll be damned if a piece of shrapnel didn't come along and knock out all my front teeth and some of the back ones. It also broke my jaw. . . . This hasn't bothered me much except for the fact that I have to be on a liquid diet all the time and you know my appetite. The rest are getting peanut butter, hash, potatoes and all those things while my mouth waters, but the time is almost up now and they'll be able to take the wiring out of my jaw.

Charles in 1943 . . .

Then I got two shrapnel wounds in my chest which went rather deep and penetrated my lungs, but they patched them up and tapped my lungs for excess fluid so that now I can breathe O.K. . . . But at first it was my most serious wound. Then I got a big wound in the back of my left shoulder which broke the shoulder and most of my ribs on the left side. These are all healing up. . . . The main thing lately has been my eye but as I said I am getting an artificial one for the left side and the right one will be O.K. The army doctors are doing a wonderful job over here. Some of them are the best in the world in their particular specialty, so, don't worry. I know that you will feel much better now that you know what is wrong with me. . . . My mind is O.K., it is not shell shocked and I don't have the jitters. I'll look a little different but I'll still be the same old guy. There is no more news as to how long I'll be here or where I'll go next but I'll let you know as soon as I find out.

. . . and 50 years later

Give my love to all the family and I'm really looking forward to seeing you and father. . . . Won't we have a lot to talk about. All my love to you both,

Your devoted son,
Charles

◀ *These U.S. paratroops were to thrust north toward British forces dropped near Arnhem in the Netherlands. But the linkup failed, and the Germans held Arnhem and its bridge.*

losses in the pocket fight alone were 10,000 killed, 50,000 captured, and 500 tanks destroyed.

As the enemy withdrew across France toward the Rhine, thousands of Frenchmen rose up against the Germans occupying Paris. Enraged, Hitler ordered the city destroyed. Ignoring him, the local commander offered to surrender. Eisenhower, a sound politician as well as a good general, supported the right of the Free French leadership to accept the German capitulation.

No Easy Road Into Germany

The invasion of Germany was next on the Allied agenda. On September 17 the Allies on the northern flank tried to break through into the Reich in a daring but ill-fated assault by way of the "back door" from the Netherlands. Paratroopers planned to seize key bridges over the Lower Rhine, but a counterattack kept Allied units from reaching the Red Devils of the British 1st Airborne Division, isolated at Arnhem. Trapped without hope of victory or escape, many of the British were forced to surrender.

The Allies began a more methodical advance along the entire front, and then Hitler took a desperate gamble. On December 16, 1944, he sent three German armies roaring out of the hilly Forest of Ardennes in a fierce counterattack into Luxembourg and Belgium. His goal: to seize the port of Antwerp and cut off the British Army from its supply bases, thus forcing it back to England in another Dunkirk.

Opposing the Germans were only six American divisions, some assigned to this hitherto quiet sector for rest and training. The Germans quickly overwhelmed them and opened a huge bulge in the Allied lines, 65 miles deep and from 10 to 25 miles wide. Trapped in the key town of Bastogne were American paratroopers of the 101st Airborne Division. The Germans called for surrender. "Nuts!" replied their commander, Brig. Gen. Anthony McAuliffe.

Along a chaotic front the Battle of the Bulge soon involved 1 million men. Patton swiftly wheeled his troops around and headed them toward Bastogne. By the end of December, the bulge was collapsing. Bastogne was liberated on December 26—not a moment too soon for its defenders, who were down to their last rounds of ammunition. As the Allies resumed their advance to the Rhine and the massive Red Army continued its offensive across Poland, Germany was caught in an ever-tightening vise.

Texts country boy Audie Murphy enlisted in the army at the age of 17. He fought in North Africa and Europe, winning more decorations than any other U.S. soldier: 24 medals from his own country, 3 from France, and 1 from Belgium. After the war he starred in war movies and westerns.

In the eerie quiet of a fresh snowfall, U.S. soldiers guard their forest position north of the Meuse River in Belgium, early January 1945. Three weeks earlier German armies had launched the desperate counterattack now known as the Battle of the Bulge, which threw the entire Allied advance into a confused, if temporary, turmoil.

Guarding an ice-rimmed passage in the Aleutian Islands, U.S. marines hunker down in the snow with their machine gun.

◀

Chugging across the wide Irrawaddy River on a makeshift barge in December 1944, a British unit joins the southward push that eventually broke the Japanese stranglehold on Burma.

BRUTAL BYWAYS: BURMA AND THE ALEUTIANS

From the steaming forest of a former British spice colony to Alaska's dank, frigid out islands, the war against

Japan spanned a 22,000-mile front and touched some of the world's most remote and punishing climates.

Some of the most vicious, and heroic, fighting of World War II erupted on the far reaches of Japanese expansion. One short, bitter action occurred on American territory in the northern Pacific: the Aleutian Islands, off Alaska. Another bloody campaign — involving American, British, Chinese, Indian, and many other Allied nationalities — ground on for years in Southeast Asia, with Burma as its epicenter.

During the Battle of Midway, in June 1942, the Japanese had put troops on Attu and Kiska, two small, deso-

late islands of the Aleutian chain. In the grand military strategy of the war, this had little significance, but it allowed the Japanese to boast that they occupied American soil. Determined to reclaim its territory, the United States sent 11,000 troops to Attu on May 11, 1943. Waiting for them were more than 2,300 Japanese soldiers, battle-ready despite heavy bombardment by American planes. In fact, many of the bombs had missed their targets because of the dense, ever-present fog that shrouded the region. After 18 days of bitter fighting in tundra mud, the Japanese commander,

Distinctive shoulder patches worn by U.S. troops include the blue-and-green shield of a behind-the-lines Burma unit (left) and the lotus-blossom triangle (right) of the army engineers who built the Ledo-Burma Road.

realizing that reinforcements would not arrive in time, ordered his remaining 1,000 men to make a desperate attack. When 100 were killed, the rest, determined to die on the battlefield, blew themselves up with hand grenades. Just 28 of the Japanese defenders survived to be taken prisoner. But the victory was costly for the Americans as well: some 600 U.S. soldiers lost their lives.

On August 15, 1943, the Allies invaded nearby Kiska with a combined force of over 34,000 Americans and Canadians. Once again fog aided the enemy. Weeks earlier the Japanese, obscured by a white wall of mist, had evacuated their entire garrison of nearly 6,000 men, leaving three dogs behind. When the Allies landed, visibility was so poor that some soldiers mistook each other for the enemy. Twenty-five GI's were killed and 31 wounded by friendly fire.

Toughing It Out in Burma

When the Japanese occupied Burma in May 1942, they acquired rich oil fields and mineral deposits and also cut the Burma Road, a main overland supply route into China. Without Allied aid sent over this lifeline, Generalissimo Chiang Kai-shek's Nationalist Chinese Army stood little chance against the determined Japanese troops. Adding to Chiang's worries were corruption in his ranks and distrust of the Chinese forces loyal to the Communist leader Mao Tse-tung. For nearly three years Allied planes, often shepherded by Flying Tiger fighters (see box below), flew oil and munitions over the "hump" (the Himalayas) to enable Chiang to keep fighting.

Bound for China over the "hump" of the Himalayas, a U.S. C-46 Commando hauls four tons of cargo to help Chinese troops halt the Japanese invaders.

Early in 1945 U.S. convoys again rolled into China from India and the south, using the Ledo and Burma roads and this 21-curve stretch on the last leg to Chungking.

Meanwhile, aiming to wrest India from British control, the Japanese expanded from Burma into the Indian state of Assam. The Chindits — a mélange of British, Burmese, and Gurkhas — under Brig. Orde C. Wingate, and Merrill's Marauders, an American force led by Brig. Gen. Frank D. Merrill, responded by blowing up railroads and bridges and engaging the Japanese in savage jungle battles.

In its climate and terrain, Burma was unmatched for pure torment. It mingled sodden swamps, jagged mountains, and parched plains, where temperatures frequently soared well over 100°F. To make matters worse, soldiers had to contend with monsoons, ever-present leeches, and swarms of stinging insects. Tropical diseases claimed many lives, and festering wounds brought down equal numbers. One GI summed up Burma as "the worst experience I have ever been through."

Only a major offensive could dislodge the tenacious Japanese from Burma, and that job fell to the brilliant British commander Lt. Gen. Sir William Slim. Displaying a mastery of both conventional and guerrilla warfare, Slim maneuvered his Anglo-Indian troops to isolate large chunks of the Japanese Army. Near Rangoon, on April 27, 1945, Japanese armed with explosives mounted on poles led suicide attacks on British tanks. But the tide had already turned. In January 1945 the Burma Road, with extensions to Ledo, India, and Chungking, China, had reopened. It was one of the great engineering feats of any war and ensured that hundreds of thousands of Japanese troops would be kept busy in China, thereby sharply reducing the Japanese manpower available to stem U.S. advances in the Pacific.

TIGERS WITH SHARKS' TEETH

Aviators known as American Volunteer Group (the Flying Tigers) began helping China against Japan in 1941. Each earned about $600 a month from the Nationalist Chinese government, plus $500 per Japanese plane downed. Organized by Claire Chennault (inset), a retired U.S. Army pilot serving as adviser to the Chinese, the Tigers got their name from the sharks' teeth they painted on the noses of their Curtiss P-40B Tomahawk fighter planes. Chennault's superbly drilled fliers inflicted heavy losses on the Japanese while suffering only light casualties. In July 1942 Chennault was recalled to active duty with the U.S. Army Air Forces and continued to distinguish himself in the air war over China and Burma. He was a major general when he retired in 1945.

Boom and Upheaval at Home

The turmoil of war overseas reverberated through America, changing it in ways that were often unexpected, sometimes funny, occasionally shattering. Jobs beckoned, romance blossomed, neighborhoods shuddered, and teenagers felt their oats.

◄

Soldiers or civilians, Americans were on the move in the spring of 1942, crowding gates like this one for the New York train at Union Station, Washington, D.C.

For Americans, going to war meant uncertainty, upheaval, and fear for loved ones in the service. But World War II also brought something that had been sorely missed for a decade or more: jobs. Month by month, war shook the United States out of the Depression. If there was no work near home, people who had never left their hometowns picked up their lives and moved. Families patched up old jalopies and set out for the factories of Detroit or the shipyards and aircraft plants on the Gulf and Pacific coasts.

An estimated 15.3 million Americans relocated. The South boomed. The population of Mobile, Alabama, jumped more than 60 percent; that of Norfolk, Virginia, almost 45 percent. Nearly 2 million people moved to California. And more than 7 million left rural areas, as farmhands became soldiers and defense workers. To compensate for the lost manpower, farmers upped their use of machines and fertilizers and grew some 30 percent more food in 1945 than in 1940, thus keeping America fed and helping to feed its hungry Allies as well.

Wherever the jobs were, housing was at a premium. Converted garages, attics, even chicken coops, rented for top dollar. Newcomers took whatever space they could afford, whether in trailers, tents, or shantytowns. Some workers lived in their cars. Others rented "hot beds," which cost 25 cents for eight hours: when the day shift left in the morning to go to work, the night shift crawled into the vacated beds for some sleep.

As the armed services drained millions of men from the labor force, women filled civilian jobs. This often meant that neither parent could provide adequate child care, and children became "eight-hour orphans," left to fend for themselves in new and sometimes dangerous neighborhoods. In some places the waves of arriving residents strained social-service facilities, crowded schools, overbur-

VICTORY SUITS VS. ZOOT SUITS

The armed forces' demand for textiles led to shortages of wool and rayon, causing fashion changes at home. When their tweed and worsted suits wore thin, men mixed unmatched coats and pants. The so-called Victory Suit was matched, but it saved fabric by being single-breasted and without vest, lapels, or cuffs. The War Production Board banned ruffles, pleats, and patch pockets (right) and restricted the yardage in clothes. The result was a tailored look in women's fashions (upper right).

Women in factories gamely wore slacks and covered their hair with bandannas or woven-mesh snoods. Denied silk and nylon hosiery, women painted their legs with makeup and drew lines on the backs of their calves to simulate seams. Despite austerity and high taxes, sales of jewelry and furs increased, thanks to defense jobs putting cash in workers' pockets.

Bucking the fabric-saving trend were men (far left) sporting zoot suits: long coats called drapes with three to six inches of padding at the shoulders, and baggy "peg leg" trousers fitted snugly at the ankles. A broad-brimmed hat completed the effect, proclaiming its wearer to be a jive-talking hepcat. Zoot-suiters' women friends also favored long jackets, which the women wore with short skirts.

dened hospitals, and all but swamped law-enforcement agencies.

With long work hours, poor living conditions, and blacks and whites struggling for identity in changing communities, racial tensions crackled. One hot afternoon in June 1943 blacks and whites scuffled in a Detroit park. Rumors of gang killings swept the city. Mobs, armed with stones and clubs, rioted. Violence continued for more than 30 hours before federal troops restored peace; by then, the rioting had killed 34 people and injured more than 700. Two months later, a racial clash in the Harlem area of New York City left six dead and 543 injured.

Civil Rights, "Dear Johns," and Teens

In response to these and other race riots, more than 200 commissions on interracial understanding sprang up, and the government spurred enforcement of antidiscrimination rulings. Some blacks began to get better jobs, though segregation persisted. Nonetheless, gains that blacks made during the war laid the groundwork for desegregation and equal-opportunity legislation afterward.

Meanwhile, amid the uniforms, the bands, the marching, the sailings, and the furloughs, romances bloomed and the marriage rate jumped, as it normally does during war.

As a lot of parents grumbled, wartime teenagers went wild for boyish Frank Sinatra, who started crooning solo in 1943.

Some hasty marriages succeeded, but a lot ended as abruptly as they began. Even stable marriages faced severe strains with husbands gone for months or years, and home-front families adapting to new ways of coping and living. For GI's, mail call might bring a dreaded "Dear John" letter, breaking off an engagement and telling the soldier good-bye.

Filling jobs left by servicemen and defense workers in fields such as transportation, retailing, and construction, millions of teenagers found they had more money and greater freedom than they had ever dreamed of having. With their new independence came an exuberance that many adults found appalling. For example, some 30,000 young fans — mostly teenage girls — showed up outside the Paramount Theatre in New York in October 1944 to hear silken-voiced Frank Sinatra. Though fewer than 4,000 got inside, their swooning screams at times drowned out his singing. Outside, 700 riot police tried to keep order. Often dismissed as "just bobbysoxers" because of the anklets (bobby socks) girls wore with loafers or saddle shoes, these wartime adolescents were, for better or worse, the vanguard of the teen revolution of later decades.

Two U.S. Navy lieutenants use a dress sword to cut their wedding cake. Now grandparents, this couple made their wartime marriage work.

Mr. and Mrs. Gustav J. Nickel
announce the marriage of their daughter
Virginia Elizabeth
Lieutenant (jg) W.A.V.E.S.
to
Richard Charles Nehring
Lieutenant (jg) United States Naval Reserve
on Tuesday, the second of January
Nineteen hundred and forty-five
Winnetka, Illinois

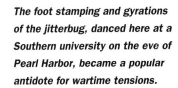

The foot stamping and gyrations of the jitterbug, danced here at a Southern university on the eve of Pearl Harbor, became a popular antidote for wartime tensions.

233

Servicemen applaud a show at New York's Stage Door Canteen.

"FOR THE BOYS"

Nothing was too good for U.S. servicemen on leave. Young ladies feted them, starlets lionized them, and songwriters and bandleaders kept them dancing to the latest popular tunes.

Almost anywhere they went in America, and often overseas as well, GI's found a home away from home. And what homes many of them were! In California, Bette Davis and John Garfield launched the Hollywood Canteen, where some of the brightest names in movies volunteered to entertain and mingle with the GI's. Across the country, in New York, the American Theater Wing's Stage Door Canteen gave lonesome servicemen a place to dine or dance, or just sip coffee and chew the fat with pretty Broadway chorus girls, all without paying a cent. Out across the land thousands of churches and civic groups sponsored dances, set out picnics, and arranged ball games "for the boys."

More than 1 million Americans donated their time to help run 3,035 USO centers. Churches, museums, yacht clubs, barns, railroad cars, and even log cabins housed USO facilities, where coffee and doughnuts were plentiful, jukeboxes blared, and invitations to home-cooked dinners were almost impossible to avoid.

USO hostesses were usually in their late teens or twenties, the same age as the GI's. And while they were carefully screened and closely chaperoned, and dating was strictly forbidden, romance blossomed. Many girls married the soldiers or sailors they met at USO canteens.

Willie Gillis, Norman Rockwell's jug-eared GI, scarfs down all the goodies he can eat, and is rendered speechless by the attention.

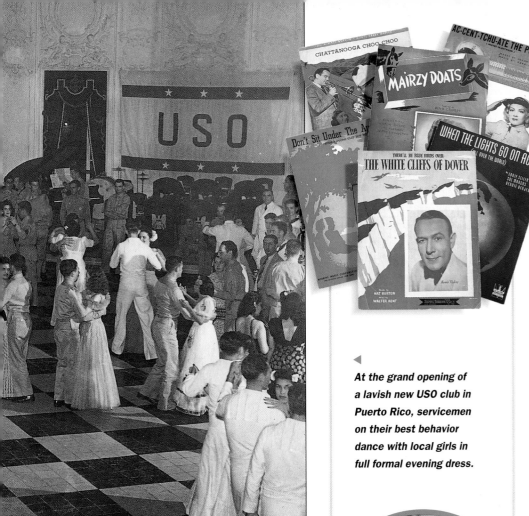

At the grand opening of a lavish new USO club in Puerto Rico, servicemen on their best behavior dance with local girls in full formal evening dress.

Wartime songs ranged from sprightly and cute ("Mairzy Doats") to achingly poignant ("When the Lights Go On Again All Over the World").

kept the GI's dancing — and all America with them. The big bands of Harry James, Artie Shaw, Tommy Dorsey, Benny Goodman, and dozens of others packed ballrooms and nightclubs. People jitterbugged and lindy-hopped to numbers like Glenn Miller's "Chattanooga Choo Choo," which sold 1 million records and was one of the period's biggest hits. (An appreciative RCA gave Miller a disc of the song sprayed with gold paint, making it the industry's first "gold" recording and launching a promotional gimmick that persists today.) Sentimental ballads, like "The Nearness of You" and "The White Cliffs of Dover," sent couples into slow, clinging fox-trots.

Among the era's most evocative tunes was Irving Berlin's "White Christmas," sung by Bing Crosby in the 1942 film *Holiday Inn*; it expressed a longing for home and family that touched the heart of wartime America. Other Hit Parade numbers rang a note of high patriotism, like Kate Smith's soaring rendition of "God Bless America." But the music that best summed up the national mood came from the concert hall. It was the opening four notes of Beethoven's Fifth Symphony, which echoed the *dot, dot, dot, dash* rhythm of the letter *V* in Morse code. *V* stood for *Victory*, and it was tapped on car horns and flashed in lights throughout the free world.

Kate Smith autographs a calling card addressed to Hitler at a U.S. Navy submarine base in New London, Connecticut. The buxom singer toured far and wide to entertain the troops.

Points of embarkation — like San Francisco, San Diego, New York City, and Honolulu — were places to have a fling before shipping out to the war zones, and the port cities went all out to give GI's a great time. As one amazed soldier put it, "Even if you got money, they don't let you spend it." In New York soldiers and sailors were treated to free or half-price tickets to Broadway shows, including *Oklahoma!*, which opened in 1943. The composer Irving Berlin's smash musical *This Is the Army* opened with a cast of 300 soldiers. The showman Billy Rose put on a star-studded extravaganza at Madison Square Garden and raised $10 million to fund USO activities.

Radios and jukeboxes

Bing Crosby reprised his 1942 hit song "White Christmas" in a 1954 movie of the same name.

Berlin's hit show, a spoof on life in boot camp, beat a rousing patriotic drum.

ALL KINDS OF PATRIOTS

Taxpayers, auctioneers, Hollywood stars, sports heroes, writers and photographers, radio newscasters, even advertisers — all America did its bit to help win the war and bring the boys home.

▼ **This dramatic mural in New York City's Grand Central Station glorified the American fighting man and the American way of life while exhorting civilians to purchase war bonds.**

There were dozens of ways to be patriotic, and Beardsley Ruml found one of them. Treasurer of Macy's department store and an expert on installment plans, Ruml, who was also chairman of the New York Federal Reserve, sold the government on a wonderful new method of meeting the war's staggering costs: a pay-as-you-go income tax. Employers withheld a minimum of 20 percent in taxes from each employee's paycheck beginning in 1943, thus providing Uncle Sam with a steady, year-round income.

The government also raised money by selling some $135 billion worth of war bonds, which offered investors an irresistible mixture of patriotism and profit. A bond that cost $18.75 would be worth $25 in 10 years time; one for $37.50 would return $50. Children could buy war stamps for as little as a dime and paste them into a special book that would buy a war bond when filled.

War bond rallies became major events, attracting thousands of buyers and earning hundreds of thousands of dollars in direct bond purchases and auction sales. At a rally

"THAT GOVERNMENT · BY THE PEOPLE SHALL NOT PERISH FROM THE EARTH"

THAT WE MAY DEFEND THE LAND WE LOVE

THAT THESE MAY FACE A FUTURE UNAFRAID

THAT WE MAY BUILD FOR A BETTER WORLD

BUY DEFENSE BONDS AND STAMPS NOW!

A junior Uncle Sam helps drum up war stamp sales on a New York City street.

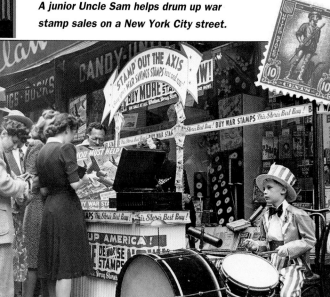

Joe DiMaggio & son

◄ *Mickey Mouse, Donald Duck, Pluto, the Seven Dwarfs, and other Disney characters decorate this certificate given to buyers of war bonds.*

held in Gimbel's basement in Manhattan, a $75 violin donated by comedian Jack Benny brought in a cool $1 million.

Hollywood went to war in the only way it really knew how: with lots of publicity. After an air raid drill one studio bigwig gushed, "Oh, it was a big success. The magazine photographers were there and got swell pictures." But Hollywood also turned its many creative talents to helping the war effort. In dozens of films dramatizing the heroism of American servicemen and their allies, movie audiences could experience the excitement of battle, the thrill of comradeship, and the promise of ultimate victory (see "Making War in the Movies," next page).

Many Hollywood stars traded make-believe battle for the real thing. Gene Autry, Jackie Coogan, Douglas Fairbanks, Jr., Henry Fonda, Burgess Meredith, Robert Montgomery, and James Stewart (later to win the Distinguished Flying Cross) all volunteered for service. Clark Gable, though over the age limit at 41, enlisted nonetheless.

BASEBALL HEROES GO TO WAR

Forty-eight hours after Pearl Harbor, Bob Feller enlisted in the navy. Barely 23 years old, he was the fastest, perhaps the best, pitcher in all baseball, but he believed his duty was to his country.

About 4,000 major and minor leaguers followed Feller. Like him, Joe DiMaggio, Ted Williams, and other top players lost valuable years but returned to reach new heights. Some, like Washington shortstop Cecil Travis, who hit .359 in 1941 but suffered frozen feet in the Battle of the Bulge, never had another good season. For most, however, military service simply meant playing ball in a different uniform: just having the athletes around was good for GIs' morale. Morale was also why President Roosevelt allowed professional baseball to continue at home. It was, he said in January 1942, a "recreational asset." The fans agreed, turning out in droves to watch teams of players too old or too young for the military.

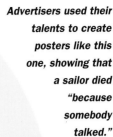
Bob Feller

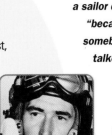
Ted Williams

► *Advertisers used their talents to create posters like this one, showing that a sailor died "because somebody talked."*

...because somebody talked!

The news media also pitched in, sending more than 500 photographers and correspondents to cover the war. Families gathered around the radio for reports from Edward R. Murrow ("This . . . is London.") and William L. Shirer and for commentary by Gabriel Heatter ("Ah, there's good [bad] news tonight . . .") and H. V. Kaltenborn, with his famous rolling *r*'s.

The War Advertising Council produced posters with public-service messages, such as "Loose Lips Sink Ships," a warning that spies might overhear casual talk about troop movements. And no one objected when military censors inked out words from servicemen's letters if it meant bringing the boys home safe, sound, and victorious.

Colleges went on playing football during the war, and Army vs. Navy was a national event. Below, Army's 1944 backfield (left to right): Tom Lombardo, Dean Sensanbaugher, and the famous duo, big Doc Blanchard and speedy Glenn Davis.

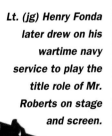

Lt. (jg) Henry Fonda later drew on his wartime navy service to play the title role of Mr. Roberts on stage and screen.

▲ *Maj. James Stewart receives the Air Medal after his 10th combat mission. By war's end he was a full colonel.*

► *Lt. Clark Gable, U.S. Army Air Corps, sights his target on a practice range, 1943.*

MAKING W★A★R IN THE MOVIES

When D. W. Griffith's Civil War epic, *The Birth of a Nation,* premiered in 1915, Americans saw their first great war movie. Ever since, war movies have held a special place in the hearts of Americans. Far more than mere entertainment, war movies have informed, inspired, and sometimes infuriated their viewers. As a genre, they have dramatized some of the most significant and heartwrenching events of the 20th century. And they have mirrored changing public attitudes toward the wars America has fought in the 100 years in which it has risen from relative isolation to being the most powerful nation on earth. In America's rise, perhaps the greatest event of all was World War II, and so it is here that we take a nostalgic look at a few of the movies that helped define our feelings not only about that war but about ourselves and all wars.

WORLD WAR 1

All Quiet on the Western Front ★ 1930
This version of Erich Maria Remarque's searing novel relates the horrors of war in the trenches from the viewpoint of young German students who joined the kaiser's army.

Sergeant York ★ 1941
The eve of America's entry into World War II was a perfect time for Gary Cooper to play a hillbilly who becomes a hero by single-handedly capturing more than 100 Germans soldiers in 1918.

THE SPANISH CIVIL WAR

For Whom the Bell Tolls ★ 1943
For moviegoers of 1943 the Spanish Civil War prefigured the Allied war on fascism. Ernest Hemingway's classic novel became a film starring Gary Cooper and Ingrid Bergman.

THE MEXICAN REVOLUTION

They Came to Cordura ★ 1959
Five soldiers and one woman trek to a remote outpost in the Mexico of 1916 during the U.S. expedition against revolutionary general Pancho Villa's forces, which nearly resulted in war. The movie played to U.S. audiences worried about the Communist threat next door in Cuba.

WORLD WAR II

The Great Dictator ★ 1940
Charlie Chaplin as The Great Dictator, Adenoid Hynkel (left), and Jack Oakie as Napoloni (right) hilariously lampoon the all-too-real rise of dictators Hitler and Mussolini.

Casablanca ★ 1942
Cynical loner Humphrey Bogart meets old flame Ingrid Bergman in a nest of spies and double agents in Axis-leaning French North Africa. He quickly decides to join the fight for freedom.

Bataan ★ 1943
Starring Robert Taylor, this saga of U.S. defeat in the Philippines appeared only a year after the actual events and reinforced the public mood of grim determination.

Guadalcanal Diary ★ 1943
Audiences who had seen newsreel coverage of U.S. victories in the Solomon Islands only months earlier could now see Hollywood's dramatic re-creation of the events.

PT 109 ★ 1963
This rendering of John F. Kennedy's deeds as a PT boat commander in the Pacific was released the year of the presidential assassination.

Patton ★ 1970
Filmed at the height of the Vietnam War, this blockbuster about Gen. George S. Patton, Jr., showed hawk and dove alike that in a popular war a tough-minded military man could attain the status of hero.

The Sullivans ★ 1944
Many moviegoers wept when they saw this heartrending tale of five brothers who die bravely in action while serving in the U.S. Navy.

THE KOREAN WAR

Pork Chop Hill ★ 1959
Starring Gregory Peck, this starkly realistic drama takes moviegoers back to the final bloody moments of the Korean War.

M*A*S*H ★ 1970
Audiences needing relief from daily Vietnam body counts found humor in this story of an army medical unit trying to stay sane in Korea.

Song Of Russia ★ 1944
Robert Taylor plays a U.S. symphony conductor touring the U.S.S.R., in a film designed to arouse pro-Soviet sentiments.

13 Rue Madeleine ★ 1946
James Cagney heads a group of agents in occupied France in this thriller, presented in the style of *The March of Time* documentaries.

THE VIETNAM WAR

The Green Berets ★ 1968
John Wayne's blood-and-thunder epic of Special Forces operations in Vietnam met with mixed reactions from a public torn by debates about the war.

Apocalypse Now ★ 1979
A powerful statement that the hell of war is rooted in the human heart, this nightmarish film played to a public still grappling with the lessons of Vietnam.

Born on the Fourth of July ★ 1989
Tom Cruise stars in this grim dramatization of paralyzed Vietnam veteran Ron Kovic's real-life story.

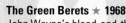

Stalag 17 ★ 1953
William Holden thrills audiences as a sergeant suspected of being a spy in this grimly humorous saga of life in a German prisoner-of-war camp.

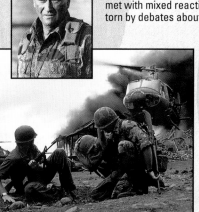

VICTORY IN EUROPE

By the spring of 1945, Allied forces were racing through Germany on their way to Berlin. With Hitler's suicide in an underground bunker, the thousand-year Reich came crumbling down.

▲ Armored tanks of the U.S. First Army roll across the Rhine River at Remagen, thus passing the last barrier to final victory. Some 650 pounds of explosives, set by the town's German defenders, had failed to destroy the bridge.

Dodging machine-gun bullets, Sgt. Alex Drabik, of the U.S. First Army, sprinted across the Ludendorff Bridge, at Remagen, a town straddling the Rhine River. It was the afternoon of March 7, 1945, and for nearly a week the Germans had been blowing up Rhine crossings, hoping to stem the Allied advance. But at Remagen the dynamite charge had failed. Quickly Drabik's company carved out a bridgehead. Gen. Dwight D. Eisenhower had dreaded the logistical problems of bringing his armies across the Rhine. Now the river had been spanned.

Other units soon followed. Gen. George S. Patton's Third Army charged across the river some 80 miles to the south. The British, under Field Marshal Bernard L. Montgomery, swept over to the north. In a pincers movement, the Allies trapped over 300,000 enemy troops in the Ruhr, Germany's industrial core. Allied planes flew more than 42,000 sorties, smashing Luftwaffe bases and wiping out Germany's air power. On April 11 the U.S. Ninth Army reached the Elbe River, only 53 miles west of Berlin.

There the Americans stopped, on Eisenhower's orders. A month earlier, the three Allied leaders — Winston Churchill, Joseph Stalin, and an ailing Franklin D. Roosevelt — had met at Yalta, in the Crimea, where they agreed that Soviet troops should enter Berlin first. Indeed, the Soviets had marched through Poland, swept past the Oder River, and were poised for a final assault on the Nazi capital.

Death Camps and Nazis at Bay

As the Allies closed in, Adolf Hitler retreated to the Führerbunker, a 19-room underground command center beneath the Reich Chancellery garden, in Berlin. He ordered movements for troops that had ceased to exist, and with members of his inner circle he studied astrological charts, searching for signs of a saving miracle. He ranted against his generals and the German people. Factories, railroads, reservoirs, and food supplies should be destroyed, he commanded; if he was to perish, so must Germany.

Meanwhile, the British and Americans were discovering a horror that made it difficult to show Germany any mercy: the death camps. On April 14 British soldiers entered

◀ *An exuberant camaraderie marked the meeting of GI's and their Red Army allies at Germany's Elbe River.*

The grief of an entire nation at FDR's death from a cerebral hemorrhage on April 12, 1945, at Warm Springs, Georgia, seems to flow with the tears of this Marine Corps accordionist. With full military honors the president's body was put aboard a train to Washington, and his name appeared on the Pentagon's regular casualty list, along with the name of every serviceman who died that day.

▲ *The Allied triumvirate — Churchill, Roosevelt, and Stalin — huddle at Yalta, a Soviet resort, to shape the map of the postwar world.*

Germany's top-secret security weapon, the Enigma Machine, put all messages typed on it into a supposedly unbreakable code. But early in the war British cryptologists decoded Enigma, an intelligence coup that helped speed the Allied victory.

the Bergen-Belsen concentration camp and gazed in appalled disbelief at "a precinct littered with corpses, people dying of starvation." In the next few weeks Americans encountered similar spectacles at Buchenwald. At Dachau the scenes were so awful that enraged GI's executed some of the SS guards on the spot. Eventually it was determined that Hitler had killed 6 million Jews along with 5 million Slavs, Gypsies, and other presumed undesirables.

On April 13 Joseph Goebbels, Hitler's minister of propaganda, had telephoned the Führerbunker in a state of wild excitement. Their astrological studies had convinced Hitler and his advisers that the second half of April would bring a dramatic turning point. "My Fuehrer," Goebbels exclaimed, "I congratulate you. Roosevelt is dead!" For once the Nazi propaganda master was telling the truth.

The day before, Vice President Harry S. Truman had taken the presidential oath of office in the White House Cabinet Room. He confirmed that the war would continue until Germany and Japan surrendered unconditionally.

In Italy, British and U.S. armies broke through the last German defense line into the Po Valley, capturing Bologna as well as other cities. In Germany, Patton's Third Army rolled east toward the Czech border. Other units moved south into Bavaria and Austria.

▶

Jubilant New Yorkers swarm into Wall Street to celebrate the end of fighting in Europe.

On April 25 a U.S. patrol on the Elbe converged with a Soviet unit in a historic meeting that cut the Reich in two.

Soviet tanks and infantry moved into Berlin, destroying German resistance in savage hand-to-hand street fighting. Their opponents were mostly teenage boys and bewildered old men. But more than 5,000 Nazi defenders battled a fire raging through the parliament building. In the nearby Führerbunker, with the sounds of battle echoing all around, Hitler shot himself in the mouth with a pistol. His companion, Eva Braun, took cyanide. Their bodies were placed in a shell hole and burned.

Exactly one week later, on May 7, in a modest schoolhouse in Rheims that served as Ike's headquarters, the Germans signed a document of unconditional surrender. The news was announced May 8, the official V-E Day, and a grateful world went wild with celebration.

VICTORY OVER JAPAN

More than 1,000 miles, and months of potentially devastating combat, lay between the farthest Allied advances and Japan's home islands. Then came Hiroshima, and a flash of fire that ended the war in a matter of days and changed the world forever.

President Harry S. Truman stared at a cable an aide had just handed him: DIAGNOSIS NOT YET COMPLETE BUT RESULTS SEEM SATISFACTORY. The cryptic wording concealed a fact of shattering significance. That morning, July 16, 1945, at a test site in the New Mexican desert, American scientists had exploded the world's first atom bomb. Truman relayed the news to a few top assistants. No one else was allowed to know. American sailors and GI's continued their bloody island-by-island progress across the Pacific. The Japanese fought on with courage and savage desperation, spurred by a national pride that allowed no room for surrender. The number of dead and wounded continued to mount relentlessly on both sides.

Five months earlier,

on February 19, two entire marine divisions plus reserves had stormed ashore on tiny Iwo Jima, a desolate pile of volcanic rock and ash equipped with three airfields. It took them almost a month of hand-to-hand combat to clear out the defenders, who had dug themselves into a honeycomb of caves and tunnels in the rock. Over 6,800 marines lost their lives; it was the worst casualty rate in the corps's 168-year history. Of the island's 23,000 Japanese defenders, almost all were annihilated. And at Okinawa, the next major Allied target, the toll was even more alarming. More than 100,000 Japanese died, including large numbers of civilians.

It seems unbelievable that the Japanese could keep going. Army Air Forces Maj. Gen. Curtis E. LeMay was systematically bombing every military and industrial target on the home islands. Huge formations of B-29 Superfortresses, flying out of bases in the Marianas, hit factories, railroads, oil dumps. Japan became so starved for oil that its giant battleship *Yamato,* sailing to help defend Okinawa, could not return for lack of fuel.

Just as terrible was the toll on Japan's civilians. In one raid, on March 9, 300 B-29's showered Tokyo with incendiary bombs, igniting a fire storm so intense that otherwise unharmed people dropped dead from suffocation. More than

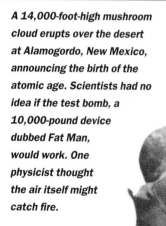

A 14,000-foot-high mushroom cloud erupts over the desert at Alamogordo, New Mexico, announcing the birth of the atomic age. Scientists had no idea if the test bomb, a 10,000-pound device dubbed Fat Man, would work. One physicist thought the air itself might catch fire.

In a formal ceremony aboard the U.S.S. Missouri, *Foreign Minister Mamoru Shigemitsu signs the documents that ended history's most destructive war while Gen. Douglas MacArthur (at microphone) stands in full, imperious command.*

Mass euphoria swept the world with the news of Japan's surrender, as this sailor, embracing a nurse in New York City's Times Square, enthusiastically demonstrates.

80,000 residents were killed. As the spring wore on, LeMay was sending 500 planes on fire raids every other day.

But the end would come sooner than anyone knew. Ever since April 1943, nuclear scientists at Los Alamos, New Mexico, had been secretly working to develop the ultimate victory weapon. Brig. Gen. Leslie R. Groves, the army administrator in charge of the project, called the scientists "the largest collection of crackpots ever seen." But the "crackpots" included some of the world's greatest minds, such as physicists J. Robert Oppenheimer and Enrico Fermi. And with the benefit of two years time and $2 billion in government money, the bomb was now ready for testing.

The trial took place on a desolate stretch of sand called Alamogordo, 200 miles south of Los Alamos. A fireball with a core heat three times greater than the sun's roared up from the desert floor, casting a glow so intense it could have been seen from Mars. The vibrations rattled windows more than 200 miles away. The only journalist present, William Lawrence of *The New York Times*, wrote: "One felt as though one were present at the moment of creation when God said, 'Let there be light.'"

President Truman, at a summit conference in the Berlin suburb of Potsdam, passed the news to Winston Churchill and Joseph Stalin. The three Allied leaders issued a stern ultimatum to Tokyo: surrender or suffer "complete and utter destruction." The Japanese made no reply.

So early on August 6, 1945, Col. Paul W. Tibbets, Jr., lifted off the island of Tinian in *Enola Gay*, a B-29 bomber he had named for his mother. He headed for Hiroshima, a Japanese seaport of 240,000 inhabitants. In the plane's belly rode a 9,000-pound atomic device nicknamed Little Boy. At 8:17 A.M. Little Boy dropped toward its target, Hiroshima's Aioi Bridge. Moments later a fireball incinerated everybody and everything within 2,000 yards of the bridge. Outside that radius the wounded lay writhing and screaming. Entire trains were flung off their tracks like toys. The remains of factories sailed skyward in a whirlwind of air.

Three days later a second atom bomb fell upon Nagasaki. Japan was finished. A sorrowing Emperor Hirohito told his war council, "I cannot bear to see my innocent people suffer any longer," and announced his decision to surrender.

The official ceremony, on Sunday, September 2, 1945, had the formal pomp of a scene from grand opera. Eleven tight-lipped Japanese emissaries climbed aboard the battleship *Missouri*, anchored in Tokyo Bay, and signed the instruments of surrender while thousands of U.S. servicemen looked on. Then the Japanese departed as silently as they had arrived. World War II was history.

For millions of Americans, this image of five marines raising the Stars and Stripes atop Iwo Jima's Mount Suribachi meant that the indomitable courage of the nation's fighting men would bring ultimate victory.

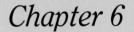

Chapter 6

POSTWAR CHALLENGE AND CHANGE

Emerging from the war stronger than ever,

a nation ready for fun gets a rude shock as the

Soviet sphere becomes our dedicated adversary

in every aspect of world affairs.

A pair of baby boomers and their parents face the future: a new house on a new lot in a postwar subdivision.

A PEACE TO BE BUILT

Clement Attlee (Britain), Harry S. Truman (U.S.), and Joseph Stalin (U.S.S.R.) pose for posterity at Potsdam, Germany.

"Today we are faced with the pre-eminent fact," wrote FDR, "that, if civilization is to survive, we must cultivate the science of human relationships — the ability of all peoples, of all kinds, to live together and work together in the same world, at peace."

In July 1945 Harry S. Truman, president of the United States for just three months, wrote to his mother and sister: "I am getting ready to go see Stalin and Churchill. I have to take my tuxedo, tails . . . high hat, low hat, hard hat. . . . I have a briefcase filled with information on past conferences and suggestions on what I'm to do and say. Wish I didn't have to go. . . ." Truman was preparing to leave for Potsdam, a suburb of Berlin, for his first major international conference and his first meeting with Winston Churchill and Joseph Stalin. Following up on the tenuous postwar alliance forged at Yalta, the Big Three were convening to decide how to shape the peace. Before the conference began, Truman wrote in his diary: "I hope for some sort of peace — but I fear that machines are ahead of morals by some centuries and when morals catch up there'll be no reason for any of it." That very afternoon he received word of the successful atom bomb test in New Mexico.

The leaders had to decide how to administer a defeated Germany, already portioned into four zones of military occupation (France having the fourth zone). At Potsdam, Germany was divided into Eastern and Western zones, and everyone agreed to its demilitarization. Other borders had to be established in Europe. East Prussia was divided between Russia and Poland. Poland was moved 200 miles west, into what had been Germany. In fact, the Big Three altered the entire map of Eastern Europe. No timetable was set for democratic elections in Eastern European countries; so Soviet occupation meant they would fall within the Soviet sphere of influence. (The Soviets would soon force totalitarian regimes on Bulgaria, Hungary, Poland, Romania, and, in 1948, Czechoslovakia.)

The Big Three took one other important action. They issued an ultimatum, the Potsdam Proclamation, demanding Japan's unconditional surrender. Not only had Truman secured Stalin's agreement to enter the war against Japan, but he decided while at Potsdam to use the atom bomb if Japan failed to respond to the Potsdam Proclamation, which only hinted at the bomb's existence and power.

Building a lasting peace meant first putting Europe back together again. The cityscape on these pages is viewed from the cathedral in Cologne, Germany, which, miraculously, suffered little damage. Below, Berliners return home in July 1945 after evacuating their besieged city.

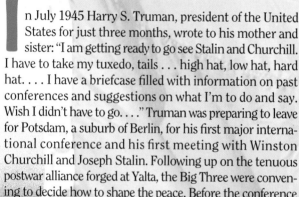

Adm. Karl Doenitz, who was to receive 10 years in prison, addresses the war crimes court in Nuremberg in October 1946. Seated in front of him, from left to right, are Hermann Goering (death), Rudolf Hess (life in prison), Joachim von Ribbentrop (death), Wilhelm Keitel (death), Ernst Kaltenbrunner (death), and Alfred Rosenberg (death).

But Potsdam left many questions unanswered. And the Big Three itself changed in mid conference: Winston Churchill lost his bid for reelection, and Clement Attlee of the Labor Party replaced him as Britain's representative at Potsdam. Truman thought Churchill had talked too much at the conference, and he had no use for Attlee at all. Truman was well aware that Stalin was a brutal dictator, but he liked him anyway, although he was surprised Stalin was such a "little bit of a squirt" (five feet five inches). He came away from the meeting with the mistaken impression that he could work with him in the future. Stalin later told Nikita Khrushchev that he found Truman worthless.

Forums to Punish War and Promote Peace

The Potsdam conferees agreed that surviving Nazi leaders should be prosecuted for "crimes against humanity." The Nuremberg trials began in November 1945 and lasted for nearly a year. Of the 22 Nazis tried by the international tribunal, 12 received death sentences, 3 life imprisonment, 4 shorter prison terms, and 3 were acquitted. Trials against accused Japanese war criminals, begun in May 1946, ended with prison terms for 16 and death sentences for 7.

The best hope for the resolution of future disputes lay in the United Nations. At a conference in San Francisco less than two weeks after Truman assumed the presidency, delegates from 50 nations, including Harold Stassen for the United States, had agreed on a charter for the body. The preamble expressed lofty goals: " . . . to save succeeding generations from the scourge of war . . . to reaffirm faith in fundamental human rights . . . to establish conditions under which justice and respect for . . . international law can be maintained, and to promote social progress and better standards of life." The U.S. Senate approved the charter, although it had reservations about the limits the charter would place on America's self-determination.

The new organization appeared to have advantages over the League of Nations: All the major nations that had emerged victorious from the war belonged. The Security Council, especially its five permanent members (the United States, the Soviet Union, Britain, France, and China), had vital decision-making powers; although smaller nations had argued against granting the five nations veto rights, the balance of power between the Security Council and the larger General Assembly at least reflected the real relationships among members. And the U.N. was more committed than the League to addressing social and economic issues.

The war had left a drastically changed world. Western Europe lay in ruins. World War I veteran Truman remarked after seeing Berlin: "I never saw such destruction." Churchill, whose own country was bankrupt, called Europe "a rubble heap, a charnel house, a breeding ground of pestilence and hate." Old nations had been swallowed up, new ones created. Eastern Europe was falling increasingly under the influence of the Soviet Union. Japan's empire had crumbled, along with the European colonial empires in the Far East. And across the world, the Russians and the Americans eyed one another warily.

Senator Arthur Vandenberg adds his signature to the U.N. charter at the San Francisco Opera House on June 26, 1945.

On May 12, 1945, these GI's at Fort Dix, New Jersey, learned that they were about to become civilians. The army's demobilization system gave credits for each of the following: months of service, months overseas, battle stars, combat decorations, and each child under 18.

COMING HOME

"The guys who came out of World War II were idealistic," recalled wounded veteran Harold Russell. "They sincerely believed that this time they were coming home to build a new world."

▲ Sam Macchia, wounded in both legs in Normandy, greets his mother and father back home in New York.

When discharged, veterans received an emblem for honorable service, the Golden Eagle lapel pin (above, left, twice actual size), popularly known as the "ruptured duck."

When the news of Japan's surrender swept across the United States in August 1945, over 12 million Americans were in uniform, 7 million of them overseas. Harry S. Truman, the spunky Missourian who never ran from a tough decision, needed to determine how quickly he should demobilize those troops.

Intense pressure to act quickly came from many fronts. Railroad presidents pressed for the speedy return of former employees so that other veterans could be transported home and new consumer goods shipped to market. The United Mine Workers lobbied to have their 30,000 boys sent home right away. Servicemen's wives and sweethearts bombarded Washington with calls and letters. One bewildered senator received 200 pairs of baby bootees in the mail, all carrying the identical message: "I miss my daddy!" As the demobilization got under way, GI's stationed in major foreign cities, such as Manila, Paris, Frankfurt, and London, demonstrated noisily that it was going far too slowly.

Within a year of V-J Day, however, only a little over 3 million Americans remained in uniform. The next year that number dwindled to 1.5 million. Truman would later conclude that he had proceeded too hastily, leaving the military disabled and the forces abroad in a skeletal state: "The program we were following was no longer demobilization — it was disintegration of our armed forces." Veterans, of course, were overjoyed to be home.

No vet would ever forget what it meant to come out of the terrifying, destructive war alive and feel the warm embrace of loved ones. But, for many, the return to civilian life would prove difficult. The sudden influx of millions of

On January 24, 1946, jobless veterans leave Philadelphia for Harrisburg to ask the governor for unemployment benefits.

GI's into the ranks of those seeking work strained an economy that was shifting from wartime to peacetime production. Ten days after V-J Day, 1.8 million workers received pink slips; six months later 2.7 million were out of a job. Labor union leaders, angered that wages and salaries remained flat as corporate profits mounted, staged loud and frequent strikes. Price controls were lifted and costs soared. Scarce goods — such as beer, clothes, beef, lumber, and nails — became hot items on a growing black market.

For veterans trying to readjust to civilian life, the search for a place to live became a nightmarish ordeal. In Tuckahoe, New York, a school superintendent set up house in a classroom every day after hours until the school board made him move. One Englewood, Colorado, veteran dragged a sofa into city hall and had his wife nurse their baby there. Many families made condemned buildings, attics, sheds, even chicken coops, their homes.

Returning servicemen received a much-needed boost from Congress, which passed legislation, quickly dubbed the 52-20 Club, allowing for the disbursement of $20 weekly for 52 weeks to unemployed veterans. Although the legislation remained in effect for four years, and over that time 52-20 beneficiaries collected $3.7 billion, fewer than 1 in 100 of those eligible for the funds tapped them each year.

The capstone of postwar aid, the GI Bill of Rights, had been passed in 1944. The $14.5 billion it provided (until being phased out in 1956) enabled more than half of the veterans of World War II to attend college or technical school. Classrooms bulged with new students, schools expanded their facilities, and in 1949 and 1950 more than twice the number of degrees were conferred than had been granted 10 years earlier. A long-running boom in education had begun.

AMERICA'S BABY DOCTOR

Almost from the moment it was published in 1945, *The Common Sense Book of Baby and Child Care* became the child-rearing bible for hundreds of thousands of parents. Dr. Benjamin Spock, a New York pediatrician with a background in psychology, wrote his guide for a receptive audience: young marrieds wanted to put the war behind them and start a family. The book sold some 750,000 copies in its first year and has become a perennial best-seller. *Baby and Child Care* changed the nation's ideas about raising children. Whereas a popular behaviorist in the first half of the century, John B. Watson, had advised parents not to hug and kiss children, or "let them sit on your lap," Dr. Spock insisted that love, reason, and parental example were essential elements in the healthy development of the child. He encouraged parents to use their common sense and assured them that "there's a happy medium between adapting to the baby's individual needs and maintaining a sensible control over him." He felt strongly that a mother's place was in the home, particularly during the first three years of a child's life. He opposed excessive rigidity, leading some detractors to accuse him of fostering permissiveness. Through his gentle counsel, this "father" to 76.4-million baby boomers, born between 1946 and 1964, reshaped America's concept of child care.

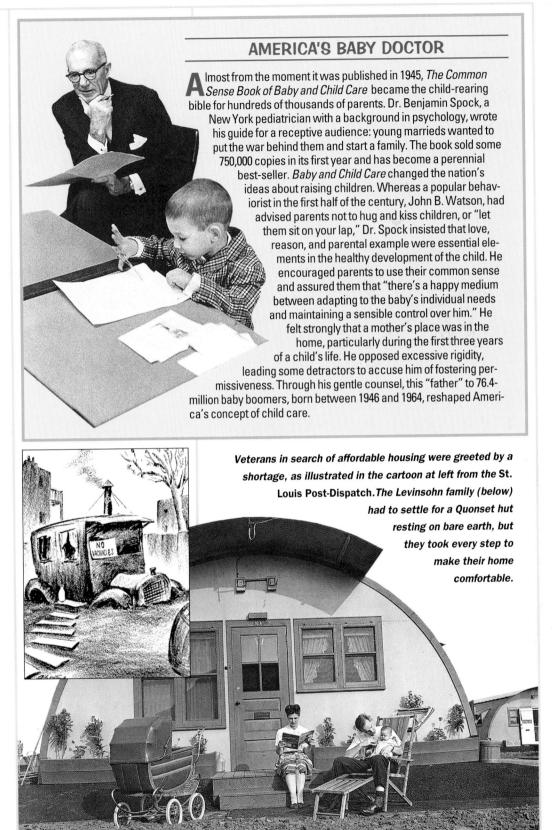

Veterans in search of affordable housing were greeted by a shortage, as illustrated in the cartoon at left from the St. Louis Post-Dispatch. The Levinsohn family (below) had to settle for a Quonset hut resting on bare earth, but they took every step to make their home comfortable.

FASHION STATEMENTS, TRENDY LOOKS

The postwar fashion era reflected an odd mix of seemingly contradictory attitudes: a devil-may-care,

let's-try-anything sentiment and a yearning to return to a normal way of life and simply follow the leader.

World War II had been over for just 18 months when an obscure dress designer named Christian Dior sent a file of models down a Paris runway wearing what seemed like a thousand excess yards of fabric. Waists were tiny, hips and bosoms rounded, skirts flared to within 12 inches of the ground; with its voluptuous curves and ample skirts, the New Look harked back some 50 years to the Victorian period. "God help the buyers who bought before they saw this," gasped one American store rep. Women who had been forced to make do with skimpy this and skimpier that — because clothing regulation L-85 of the War Production Board limited the amount of fabric manufacturers could use — reveled in the folds, tucks, and swishing sounds that came along with skirts big enough to topple over a set of tenpins. Within a year, stores were selling knockoffs of the $450 originals for $20 or less. The New Look had its dissenters, of course, such as the 300,000 members of the Little Below the Knee Club.

A Touch of Zaniness in America's Fashions

Daily life during the postwar years was shaped by a longing for conformity. Very few men, women, or children wished to be left out or left behind. For the average middle-class American, the urge to keep up with the Joneses turned into a way of life. Extravagantly endowed with new opportunities and obligations and deeply awed by the certainty that technological advances would soon transform ordinary life almost beyond recognition, Americans were at once giddy and anxious. "Let's try something new!" was the prevailing impulse. "Let's do it together" was its ever-cautious companion.

▶ Even though the sack dress enjoyed wide popularity at the end of the decade, its nightgown variety never caught on. Outlandish dark glasses, such as the ones shown at the upper left, were all the rage, particularly when worn with a bikini.

Bermuda shorts, named for their island of origin, won ▲ over college students and young adults of both sexes.

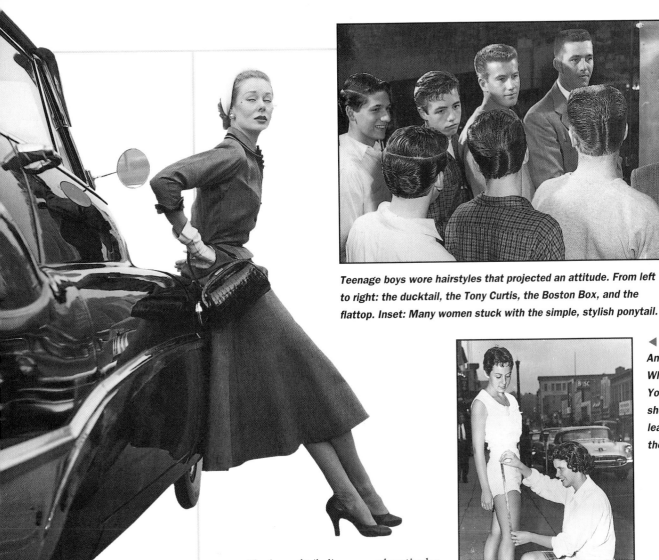

Teenage boys wore hairstyles that projected an attitude. From left to right: the ducktail, the Tony Curtis, the Boston Box, and the flattop. Inset: Many women stuck with the simple, stylish ponytail.

◄ An ordinance for White Plains, New York, provided that shorts must reach at least halfway down the thigh.

► This teenager spent some time perfecting her outfit: rolled-up jeans, a man's flannel shirt, scuffed and dirty saddle shoes, and bobby sox.

▲ Designer Christian Dior dominated the world of high fashion throughout the decade. This model sports his look from head to toe.

◄ For the woman who aspired to reach the top of the fashion ladder, a complete outfit demanded the very latest in accessories, from sophisticated millinery styles to tasteful jewelry and hand wear.

The lure of tribalism proved particularly strong among teenagers. Now that the lean war years had ended, parents indulged their children, leaving more money at their disposal than any earlier generation had enjoyed. Poodle skirts, sweater sets, motorcycle jackets, white bucks or saddle shoes were some of the pricier spoils of parental indulgence. And the kids purchased their fair share of flash-in-the-pan items as well. Extra earnings from babysitting and lawn-mowing jobs went to buy ankle bracelets, golf-ball-size cuff links, garrison belts, and crinoline petticoats. But the most conspicuous display of youthful mass lunacy, a succession of *de rigueur* hairstyles, cost the wearer very little: for the girls, poodle cuts, beehives, pageboys, and pixies; for the boys, crew cuts, flattops, Apaches, pompadours, and the infamous ducktail, which foreshadowed the next decade's hair rebellions.

Even middle-class adults succumbed to trendy fashion statements. Women donned tube dresses, short shorts, pop-it necklaces, and a new line of at-home wear, featuring lounging pants and velveteen pajamas. The designer of the bikini — named for postwar nuclear bomb tests at Bikini atoll in the Pacific — touted the swimwear's "explosive potential." A few bold men ventured beyond the staid male fashions of the time and put aside gray flannel suits to sport pink dress shirts, string ties, and Bermuda shorts — even at the office.

In an odd bit of symmetry, the postwar era closed as it had begun, with an out-of-left-field style. The inelegant sack dress appeared just as veterans of Dior's New Look were wondering where their tiny waists had gone. Amid howls of protest, the shapeless chemise flared for a season, then mercifully sputtered out.

251

"AN IRON CURTAIN HAS DESCENDED"

▶

Gen. George C. Marshall, army chief of staff during World War II, later served as secretary of state (1947–49) and secretary of defense (1950–51). He won the Nobel Peace Prize in 1953 for the European Recovery Program, which put a stricken Europe back on its feet.

Amid fears of Soviet expansion in Europe, the Truman administration decided that the containment of communism would be the linchpin of American foreign policy.

Europe lay destitute in the spring of 1947. Severe shortages of food and fuel, rampant disease, and faltering economies had left the Continent in shambles. Conditions were particularly perilous in Greece, where a civil war raged between Communists and defenders of the crown. The devastation made Europe vulnerable to lurking dangers: would the Soviet Union attempt to bring more countries into its sphere of influence? Speaking at Westminster College in Fulton, Missouri, on March 5, 1946, Winston Churchill (above) warned of Soviet expansion, declaring: "From Stettin in the Baltic to Trieste in the Adriatic an iron curtain has descended across the Continent." The shattered European nations required a massive infusion of outside aid.

Truman Gets Tough on Communism

Almost one year after Churchill delivered his iron curtain speech, Britain announced it could no longer afford to give aid to Greece and Turkey. President Truman decided to act. He presented a plan to key members of Congress, and in the discussion that ensued, Senator Arthur Vandenberg remarked: "Mr. President, if that's what you want, there's only one way to get it. That is to make a personal appearance before Congress and scare the hell out of the country."

On March 12, 1947, Truman did just that, asking for $400 million in economic and military assistance for Greece and Turkey. "I believe that it must be the policy of the United States," he said, "to support free peoples who are resisting attempted subjugation by armed minorities or by outside pressures." That policy of containment came to be called the Truman Doctrine. A month later the dawning era got its name from a speech delivered by financier Bernard Baruch: "Let us not be deceived — today we are in the midst of a cold war." Veteran American diplomat and Russian scholar George Kennan published a forceful argument that communism could be contained with strength. The battle lines of the Cold War were drawn.

In late spring of 1947, the lengthening Soviet shadow loomed ominously over Eastern Europe. The French Communist Party was flexing its muscles, and Italian voters seemed poised to choose a Communist majority. Against this backdrop, Secretary of State George C. Marshall outlined a bold plan to aid European recovery. In a commencement address at Harvard University on June 5, 1947, he offered economic assistance to all of Europe, including the Soviet Union (which rejected the overture). As, in early

CARVING OUT A NEW NATION

Although keeping the Soviets in check dominated America's foreign policy in the postwar era, another issue demanded prompt attention: how to compensate the Jewish survivors of the Holocaust. Since the late 19th century, Jewish Zionist leaders had been pressing for a homeland for their people in Palestine, site of the ancient kingdom of Israel. Beginning in the 1920's, great numbers of Jews emigrated to the largely Arab region; as the Nazis rose to power, Jewish refugees poured in. When World War II ended, Britain, which had controlled Palestine since 1918, referred the question of the Jewish state to the United Nations. In November 1947 the U.N. voted to divide Palestine into two states, Arab and Jewish, responsibility for which would be turned over to the U.N. within six months. Jews around the world celebrated the decision, and Arabs condemned it as a declaration of war. President Truman, along with most Americans, supported

the Zionist cause. Secretary of State George C. Marshall argued for a U.N. trusteeship until the differences between Palestinians and Jews could be resolved; he called attention to the growing value of Middle East oil reserves and asserted that partition could lead to war, possibly involving the Soviets. Great Britain thought partition unworkable. Dr. Chaim Weizmann, who would become Israel's first president, wrote Truman a letter urging: "The choice for our people, Mr. President, is between statehood and extermination. History and providence have placed this issue in your hands and I am confident that you will yet decide in the spirit of moral law." Just 11 minutes after Israel was proclaimed a state on May 14, 1948, the United States became the first country to grant it formal recognition. The next day five Arab states invaded Israel. For the first time in more than 2,000 years, the Jews had an independent homeland, but at the price of unending turmoil in the Middle East.

1948, Congress debated the European Recovery Program (later known as the Marshall Plan), Czechoslovakia fell to a Communist-led coup; in April Congress approved initial outlays of money for the plan. The impact of the Marshall Plan on a Europe still devastated by war was dramatic. Needy citizens received food and clothing; new trains hauled goods along freshly laid tracks; dikes were erected in the Netherlands; mines hummed to life, and factories geared up. "Ordinary thanks are inadequate," wrote the editor of a British newspaper. "Here is one of the most brilliant successes in the history of international relations." A London paper called the Marshall Plan "the most . . . generous thing that any country has ever done for others." As distrust toward the Soviets mounted, the plan forged new bonds of friendship between the United States and Western Europe.

Tensions flared dangerously in June 1948, when the U.S.S.R. attempted to force the United States, Great Britain, and France to abandon West Berlin, which lay 110 miles inside East Germany. The Soviets blocked all land routes connecting the city to West Germany. Within a week, bread and meat supplies diminished to one month's worth. Gen. Lucius D. Clay, U.S. commander in Berlin, warned: "If we mean . . . to hold Europe against communism, we must not budge . . . the future of democracy requires us to stay." Some military officers proposed ramming through the railroad blockade with an armored locomotive, but General Clay called Gen. Curtis E. LeMay, U.S. Air Force chief in Europe, and asked: "Curt, can you transport coal by air?" The Berlin Airlift was born.

The airlift depended on clockwork precision: as soon as a plane touched down, crews worked feverishly to unload it and send it back aloft within 30 minutes. For 321 days, medicine, food, coal, and other vital goods were flown into Berlin, to the outrage of the Soviets.

By the fall of 1948, some 5,000 tons of supplies were arriving daily. The Berlin crisis proved the need for an alliance that would protect Western Europe against Soviet aggression. On April 4, 1949, 10 European countries, the United States, and Canada signed the North Atlantic Treaty, which provided that an attack on any member nation would be regarded as an attack on all of them; NATO (North Atlantic Treaty Organization) was set up to coordinate military assistance. Finally, in May 1949, the Soviets lifted the blockade in Berlin, handing the West its first real Cold War victory.

Young airlift spotters watch a four-engine C-54, carrying 10 tons of supplies, as it nears West Berlin from Frankfurt. "The sound of the engines is like music to our ears," wrote one victim of the Soviet blockade.

FIERY HARRY PULLS AN UPSET

At one campaign stop after another, a shout would rise up from the crowd — "Give 'em hell, Harry!" Truman later remarked, "I never gave anybody hell, I just told the truth and they thought it was hell."

It was probably the worst night of Harry Truman's long political career. For nearly four hours in the sweltering July heat, the president sat in a cramped and stuffy room while the delegates to the National Democratic Convention reluctantly nominated him their candidate in the 1948 election. The Democrats would have preferred to choose almost anyone else, but they were stuck with Harry. The mood of the nation that year was gloomy. The euphoria over America's victory in World War II had been eroded by a wave of troubles: strikes crippled major industries, inflation raged, and shortages in housing and consumer goods dampened the hopes of war veterans looking forward to raising families. Many laid the blame for the nation's troubles squarely on the president's shoulders. "To err is Truman," people said, and they meant it. When Truman took the podium to accept the nomination, it was nearly 2:00 in the morning. Most of the radio and television audience (this was the first

▲ **At a campaign stop in Bridgeport, Pennsylvania, Harry draws an appreciative crowd. His campaign literature included a 16-page comic book (inset) featuring him as the hero, a ploy that critics deemed unbecoming to the office.**

◀

A Chicago Tribune *cartoon* comments on the Southern Democrats' split from the party because of its liberal civil rights plank.

year of national TV coverage) had gone to bed and did not hear Truman's feisty promise of victory. Few of them would have questioned former Congresswoman Clare Boothe Luce's assessment that Truman was "a gone goose."

When his party fragmented, Truman seemed to face even greater odds. Southerners outraged by the Democratic civil rights platform bolted away and formed the States' Rights Party (Dixiecrats) behind Gov. Strom Thurmond of South Carolina; left-leaning Democrats created the Progressive Party and picked former Vice President and Secretary of Commerce Henry A. Wallace to be their candidate.

The Republican choice, Gov. Thomas E. Dewey of New York, serenely contemplated the wreckage of the Democratic Party. Although humorless and stiff — Alice Roosevelt Longworth once joked that Dewey looked like "the little man on top of the wedding cake" — Dewey had earned a reputation as a tough crime-busting district attorney. He had lost to FDR in 1944, but most of the nation felt that his day had come. Opinion polls showed Dewey way ahead of Truman, and one newspaper advised the Democrats to "im-

Thomas E. Dewey takes California Gov. Earl Warren on a tour of his farm shortly before asking Warren to join the ticket.

▶

Strom Thurmond decried integration of the armed forces as "un-American"; Henry Wallace promised to eliminate segregation and end the Cold War. Thurmond won 39 electoral votes, and Wallace, not a single state.

Dixiecrat Strom Thurmond

Progressive Henry A. Wallace

mediately concede the election to Dewey and save the wear and tear of campaigning."

But wear and tear was exactly what Harry Truman had in mind. In June he had taken a 12-day train trip across the country. At stops along the way, he stood on the rear platform of the train and lambasted the "do-nothing" Congress. The farm states were solidly Republican, but this Democratic president from Missouri had a rapport with farmers: he understood their problems and spoke their language. Big-city reporters may have snickered, but Truman detected a faint political rumbling that the pollsters had missed.

Truman also knew that Americans tend to root for the underdog who fights back. Early in September a pollster announced that Dewey's lead of 44 percent of the vote, to Truman's 31 percent, would prove insurmountable. Truman ignored the report and continued on his whistle-stop campaign. He told the crowds that he favored price controls to stop inflation, an expansion of Social Security, an increase in the minimum wage, and more money for housing, roads, and schools. He hammered away at Dewey, the 80th Congress, and the financial powers on Wall Street. He delivered his message in a salty style that caused some listeners to cringe and many others to support him: If you vote Republican, he warned one group, "you're a bigger bunch of suckers than I think you are!"

On the evening of Election Day, Dewey confidently awaited the returns in a Manhattan hotel. Despite early reports of a Truman lead in the East, Dewey's campaign manager announced victory at 4:30 P.M. Meanwhile, Truman rested up in the resort town of Excelsior Springs, Missouri. After a Turkish bath, he went to his room and had a ham-and-cheese sandwich and a glass of buttermilk. He listened to some early returns and went to sleep around 9:00 P.M.

Awaking at midnight, he switched on the radio and learned that he was 1.2 million votes ahead. When he awoke again at 4:00 A.M., he was ahead by 2 million votes. Truman left for Kansas City, saying, "It looks like I've been elected."

Truman's upset stunned the press and particularly the pollsters, who had failed to forecast a last-minute shift by undecided voters to the Truman camp. The president's driving, down-to-the-wire campaign had paid off. A coalition of various interests, including labor, the Farm Belt, and urban voters, had gathered behind him. A surge among black voters helped make up for votes that had gone to the Dixiecrats. But Truman suspected all along that he would emerge victorious. In the middle of the campaign, when all the experts were counting him out, he had remained confident. "Everybody's against me," Harry said, "but the people."

On a brief stop in St. Louis during his triumphant post-election return to the capital, a beaming Truman displays a newspaper headline that mistakenly announced his defeat.

RISING FEARS OF COMMUNIST SUBVERSION

"Party labels don't mean anything anymore," said Hollywood's George Murphy. "You can draw a line right down the middle. On one side are the Americans; on the other are the Communists and Socialists."

◀
Uncle Sam sifts the Truman administration for Communists in a Buffalo Courier Express cartoon.

▼ **In March 1949 anti-Communist hysteria led protesters to picket outside a meeting of the Cultural and Scientific Conference for World Peace in New York. Composer Dimitri Shostakovich headed the Soviet delegation.**

"When we have these fits of hysteria," President Truman observed, "we are like a person who has a fit of nerves in public — when he recovers, he is very much ashamed." The hysteria — a rising suspicion that the nation was riddled with Red agents, Communist spies trying to subvert the government and destroy the American way of life — was all too apparent.

It began with the end of World War II, and it grew in volume as the Cold War intensified. In September 1945 an officer at the Soviet Embassy in Canada defected, carrying with him evidence of widespread Soviet espionage in North America. That same year, the scholarly journal *Amerasia,* which covered foreign policy issues in the Far East and which had been critical of Chiang Kai-shek and the Chinese Nationalists, ran a story that had been lifted from a secret State Department briefing paper. How had the editor, an avowed Communist sympathizer, obtained this document? Clearly someone in government had given it to him. Belonging to the Communist Party was not a crime. Thousands had joined up in the Depression years, and during the war the U.S.S.R. had been a major ally. But the fear that the Kremlin's agents had penetrated the corridors of American government sent an ominous chill across the land.

Under pressure from Congress and the Justice Department, Truman introduced some anti-Communist measures of his own. In 1947 he established a Federal Employee Loyalty program by executive order. Over the course of four years, more than 3 million Americans were screened and cleared; several thousand resigned, but only 212 were dismissed for misconduct or as security risks.

To those eager to find it, Communist influence was everywhere. Had Soviet agents penetrated the boardrooms of American capitalism? A booklet put out by a conservative think tank contained the following advice on "how to spot a Communist in your own business": familiarize yourself with the Communist Party line as printed in left-wing publications and watch how workers respond to anti-Communist labor leaders. What about education? Fearful that left-wing professors might fill students' heads with Marxist propaganda, state legislatures and college administrations began to demand that educators sign loyalty oaths. Some 11,000 professors in the University of California system alone were required to take the pledge. Failure to do so could end in a

As president of the Screen Actors Guild, Ronald Reagan told Congress that while he knew of members who followed "tactics we associate with Communists," he knew no guild member who belonged to the party.

person's firing, as over 120 recalcitrant professors at UCLA found out.

The anti-Communist fervor invaded libraries too, which emptied their shelves of everything suspect, from Communist organs, such as the *Daily Worker,* to mainstream publications, such as *National Geographic.* Even books on Robin Hood came into question. Didn't the bandit of Sherwood Forest steal from the rich and give to the poor? In the turbulent sea of suspicion, voices of moderation were all but lost.

Congress Seizes the Initiative

The noisiest, most persistent investigative body was the House Committee on Un-American Activities (HUAC), which had been set up in Congress in 1938 to investigate foreign subversion. Turning its sights from Nazis to Communists, HUAC aimed at a target sure to gain maximum attention: Hollywood.

As part of the war effort, several studios had made pro-Soviet films. Then a series of labor strikes hit the film industry — instigated, some studio heads suggested, by Communists. So in 1947 the committee held two weeks of hearings to expose the contamination. Scores of industry witnesses — from producers Walt Disney and Jack Warner to actors Robert Taylor, Gary Cooper, George Murphy, and Ronald Reagan — took the stand. Some decried Communist infiltration of the Screen Writers Guild and other unions. So-called unfriendly witnesses faced the obligatory question: "Are you now or have you ever been a member of the Communist Party?" Refusing to respond on the grounds that the question violated their First Amendment rights, 10 of those who were subpoenaed, including writers Ring Lardner, Jr., and Dalton Trumbo, headed off to jail on charges of contempt. But the Hollywood Ten were not the only casualties. Perhaps as many as 500 writers, directors, and actors were suspended from work when their names ended up on studio blacklists established to satisfy HUAC.

The next year, 1948, the committee turned its attention to the State Department. In the sweltering heat of a Washington August, a tall, handsomely tailored former State Department official named Alger Hiss strode into a congressional caucus room to refute allegations that he

Stars who came to Washington to protest Red hunts in Hollywood included (from the bottom row, left to right) Richard Conte, Lauren Bacall, Humphrey Bogart; Paul Henreid, June Havoc, Geraldine Brooks; Marsha Hunt, Evelyn Keyes; Jane Wyatt, Danny Kaye; Mrs. Sterling Hayden, Gene Kelly; and, behind Kelly, Sterling Hayden.

had been a Communist. With his upper-class bearing, good looks, and record of high achievement in a number of key government posts, Hiss seemed the embodiment of the public-spirited American. Now, in his early forties, he headed the prestigious Carnegie Endowment for International Peace. That such a man could betray his country seemed unimaginable. Yet this was the charge leveled against him.

His accuser, Whittaker Chambers, projected quite a different image. Dumpy and disheveled — "a fat, sad-looking man in a baggy blue suit," according to one reporter — Chambers had joined the Communist Party in the 1920's. In 1938 he underwent a change of heart and, renouncing communism, became an ardent patriot. He later joined the staff of *Time* magazine, where he rose to the rank of a senior editor. Now, under subpoena, he began to identify associates in his old Communist cell. Hiss was the most prominent.

Hiss met the allegations with cool disdain. Did he know Chambers? At first he answered no, then at a second hearing conceded he had known Chambers, but under a different name. Had he let Chambers stay in his Washington house? Yes. In fact, he had also

given him a used car. A freshman congressman from California, Richard M. Nixon, doggedly pursued this line of questioning; and as Hiss and Chambers continued to offer conflicting versions of the same events, Hiss's story began to unravel. It became clear that Hiss had been more deeply involved with Chambers than he was willing to let on.

The Plot Thickens

After Chambers repeated his charges against Hiss on radio's *Meet the Press,* Hiss sued him for libel. Chambers next produced an assortment of papers that he said Hiss had passed on to him and that he had hidden away after emerging from the Communist underground 11 years earlier. Some were notes in Hiss's handwriting; others were summaries of State Department documents, which experts attested had been typed on Hiss's old Woodstock typewriter. Chambers gave investigators as further evidence several rolls of microfilm, which he dramatically removed from a hollowed-out pumpkin on his Maryland farm. This proof led to Hiss's indictment. Because the statute of limitations on espionage had expired, Hiss was charged with two counts of perjury for having lied about his relationship with Chambers and about having transmitted confidential material to him.

The proceedings shifted from the caucus room to the federal courts, where distinguished public servants, including Supreme Court Justice Felix Frankfurter, testified to Hiss's good character, while Chambers was assailed as a self-confessed traitor. The jury failed to reach a verdict, and a second trial was set. This time the prosecutor hammered away at the documentary evidence, the "pumpkin papers." Hiss was found guilty and sentenced to five years in prison. His conviction was the most compelling evidence so far that Communist infiltration of the government had posed a threat to national security. Hiss staunchly maintained his innocence and repeatedly sought to have his conviction overturned on appeal.

Several weeks after the first Hiss trial had ended, on August 5, 1949, the State Department released a white paper conceding that China had been lost to Mao Tse-tung and the Communists. "We picked a bad horse," muttered Harry Truman. Over the previous four years, America had provided $2 billion in support to the Nationalist forces of Chiang Kai-shek, but Chiang's government was corrupt, inefficient, and militarily inept. When the Communists won, forcing the Nationalists to retreat to Taiwan, Chiang's American supporters hinted darkly at a pro-Communist conspiracy within the U.S. government. Had America betrayed its wartime ally Chiang Kai-shek? Henry Luce, the conservative publisher of *Life* and *Time,* along with other members of the so-called China Lobby, apparently thought so. They

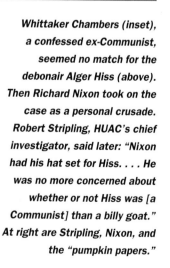

Whittaker Chambers (inset), a confessed ex-Communist, seemed no match for the debonair Alger Hiss (above). Then Richard Nixon took on the case as a personal crusade. Robert Stripling, HUAC's chief investigator, said later: "Nixon had his hat set for Hiss. . . . He was no more concerned about whether or not Hiss was [a Communist] than a billy goat." At right are Stripling, Nixon, and the "pumpkin papers."

Chiang Kai-shek and his Wellesley-educated wife meet with Gen. Joseph Stilwell in Burma in 1942. After the war $2 billion in American aid did not save China for Chiang.

Since the end of World War II, the rising fear of communism had been tempered by the knowledge that America had the atom bomb and the U.S.S.R. presumably could not develop one for years. But in September 1949, startling news reached the Truman White House. An American B-29 had detected the unmistakable radioactive fingerprint of an atomic blast somewhere over the wasteland of Soviet Siberia. The four-year American monopoly on atomic weapons vanished in a flash. How had the Soviets so quickly mastered the construction of the world's most destructive weapon? Few Americans understood the complexities of an atomic chain reaction, but it seemed plausible that Communist spies must have relayed the bomb's secret. Less than five months later, that suspicion was confirmed by the confession of British spy Klaus Fuchs (see pages 272–273). Never before had Americans felt so vulnerable. The stage was set for the dramatic charges of Sen. Joseph R. McCarthy.

accused the State Department of having Soviet leanings and of making a shambles of American foreign policy. One Republican congressman even charged Truman's secretary of state, Dean Acheson, with being on the Kremlin payroll. Hard-liners began referring to Acheson as the Red Dean. In December 1949, Republicans in both houses of Congress passed a resolution urging Dean Acheson's firing; President Truman ripped it in two. But for years the hunt continued for the traitors who had "lost" China.

Assistant secretary of state under Roosevelt (1941–45), Truman's "top brain man," Dean G. Acheson, served him as undersecretary (1945–47) then as secretary of state (1949–53).

Just a year after the Communists had proclaimed the People's Republic of China in October 1949, thousands of Chinese carrying likenesses of Mao Tse-tung parade to celebrate National Day. The decades-long struggle between the Communists and Nationalists for control of China effectively ended when Mao drove Chiang Kai-shek from the mainland.

EMBRACING SUBURBIA

While some social critics found the new suburban communities drably conformist, residents disagreed: "Levittown was like a godsend. . . . We all got along because we all started with a clean slate, we were all in the same situation."

Developments like Levittown, New York (right, about 1950), made possible the American dream of marriage, homeownership, and parenthood (inset, above right) for thousands of young people who longed for wholesome stability.

B y the end of 1945, American GI's were streaming home at the rate of 1.25 million each month, only to find there was no place to live. Many vets and their families had to double up in crowded apartments or occupy unused military barracks. Others moved in with in-laws.

It was two years before William J. Levitt came up with the idea that went a long way toward solving the crisis: why not apply the assembly-line production techniques of the auto industry to housing? In Nassau County, New York, Levitt purchased 6,000 acres of potato fields, and within a few months, a whole prefabricated community stood where none had been before. A hundred houses appeared at a time: plain, boxy structures, all looking very much alike. Not glamorous, but the price was right: the smallest house cost under $8,000, and the government would help finance it with low-cost loans provided under the GI Bill. Couples camped out for days for the chance to buy. By 1951, 82,000 residents lived in Levittown's 17,447 homes.

A Home of One's Own, at Last

The postwar suburbs were hardly posh, but neither could they be called slums. Individual houses might have been small and lacking in architectural grace notes, but what did it matter? They still were houses, and they filled an aching need. Men and women who had suffered the deprivations of the 1930's, and years of wartime separation, yearned for the opportunity to blossom: a patch of grass, a large and healthy family, the comfort and security of their very own home. Here was their chance. Thanks to a robust economy, the GI Bill, and federally subsidized mortgages, the American dream was back on line.

So began the postwar move to the suburbs. Of the 13 million homes constructed in the 1950's, 11 million sprang up on the fringes of city limits. One and a half million

New Yorkers fled the boroughs for surrounding areas, and the population of Orange County, south of Los Angeles, tripled.

Part of that surge was attributable to a rapidly increasing birth rate. Brides and grooms were younger than at any other time during the century; the average age of marriage for men dropped to 22 and for women to just 20. The divorce rate stabilized, and the birth rate exploded. By 1957 it had reached an all-time high of 4.3 million, or one baby every seven seconds. Some 30 million new Americans came into the world between 1950 and 1959, creating a boom that would echo across the land for decades.

Every migration leaves a vacancy, and the rush to the suburbs forever changed urban America. Once the center of life for young professionals, cities increasingly became places in which to work and shop. A mass commuter culture evolved as office workers poured into downtown business districts each morning, and eagerly headed home at 5 P.M. Before long, many stores joined the urban exodus, and industrial parks sprouted along the expressways.

"YOUNG MEN IN GRAY FLANNEL SUITS"

The new suburbia was not without its critics. As early as 1950, David Riesman, a sociologist at Harvard University, shook national complacencies with a best-selling book, *The Lonely Crowd,* which examined suburban conformity. Then Columbia professor C. Wright Mills presented a detailed and often scathing portrait of middle-class life and values in *White Collar* (1951) and *The Power Elite* (1956). In *The Organization Man*, William H. Whyte wrote that Americans had become obsessed with "togetherness," "team work," and "group think," sacrificing individuality to get ahead in huge corporate conglomerates.

Criticism of suburbia was not confined to academia. Fiction writers joined the chorus, notably Sloan Wilson with his partly autobiographical novel, *The Man in the Gray Flannel Suit* (1955), which was made into a movie starring Gregory Peck (inset, center) in 1956. It is the story of a young couple, Tom and Betsy Rath, who struggle against the pressures of middle-class conformity. Tom is a war veteran commuting to an ad agency job he doesn't much like, and which pays him not enough money. Their house is too small for their three children; the furniture is old and worn. What should have been an upwardly mobile couple enjoying the fruits of honest labor is shown instead to be a sorely discontented pair, deep in debt and scurrying to keep up with their neighbors, who, it turns out, are equally unhappy. The book's title comes from Tom's sudden realization that "all I could see was a lot of bright young men in gray flannel suits rushing around New York in a frantic parade to nowhere." Then Tom looks down and discovers, to his horror, that he, too, is wearing gray flannel. In the end, Tom and Betsy confront their problems and work them out; both their marriage and their principles remain intact. But the issues Wilson portrayed struck a resonant chord with millions struggling to attain the American dream.

High employment and rising wages swelled the ranks of the middle class, whose enormous buying power soon boosted the economy. Enticed by Madison Avenue pitchmen to buy ever-larger slices of the good life, Americans took material consumption to new heights. A nation with 6 percent of the world's population drove 75 percent of its automobiles, consumed nearly half its energy, and produced almost half of its manufactured products.

And yet, despite so many outward signs of prosperity, anxieties lurked at the core of suburban life. Many suburbanites were living beyond their means. Homeownership, the pride of the decade, floated largely on bank loans: the equity stake was often a mere $1,000. Most cars were bought on credit, and personal indebtedness ballooned as suburban dwellers struggled to "keep up with the Joneses." Real wages did rise by 30 percent during the decade, to be sure. But worries about the threat of Soviet nuclear attack became the stuff of nightmares. Perhaps the frenetic pace with which suburbanites gobbled up material goods stemmed, in part, from life's very precariousness, the fear that everything — houses, cars, swimming pools — could vanish in a second. The face of suburbia wore a smile, but a nervous one.

◄

Eager homeowners arrive in droves at Lakewood, a community of new tract housing outside Los Angeles, which the builders pronounced ready for occupancy in 1953.

261

THE GOLDEN AGE OF TELEVISION

"Make no mistake about it," predicted Wayne Coy of the Federal Communications Commission in 1948,

"television is here to stay. It is a new force unloosed in the land."

Within six months of its debut in 1951, *I Love Lucy* had bumped Milton Berle from the top spot in the ratings and was rewarded with an $8-million contract from CBS. When Lucille Ball became pregnant, she and her husband, Desi Arnaz, worked this happy condition into the script. They shot an episode celebrating the future arrival of Little Ricky, and CBS aired it Monday, January 19, 1953 — the very day Lucille Ball actually gave birth. Seventy percent of all TV households in America tuned in, far more than watched the televised broadcast of President Dwight Eisenhower's inauguration the next day.

Lucy's success was just one example of the explosive growth of television. In 1945 TV was an exotic toy. Three years later Milton Berle had an audience pushing 5 million. Berle, a popular nightclub comic noted for borrowing jokes, became the first big television star. Starting with a mixture of wacky costumes, old vaudeville routines, and a parade of wisecracking burlesque buddies, Uncle Miltie hosted *The Texaco Star Theater* and made Tuesday nights *his.*

Berle's closest rival was gossip columnist Ed Sullivan, who hosted a Sunday night variety show called *The Toast of the Town.* Sullivan — who, said comedian Fred Allen, "will be around as long as somebody else has talent" — debuted in 1948 and remained on the air for 23 years. TV won new audiences for show biz veterans Jimmy Durante and Red Skelton and also for Groucho Marx, whose *You Bet Your Life* quiz program became a launching pad for his own outrageous one-liners. Sid Caesar and Imogene Coca brought viewers 90 minutes of sheer hilarity in *Your Show of Shows.*

Sitcoms, born on radio, learned to spread their wings on TV. *The Goldbergs* made the transition. Burns and Allen continued trading gags (George: "What do you think of TV?" Gracie: "Wonderful! I hardly ever watch radio anymore."). Jackie Gleason played Brooklyn bus driver Ralph Kramden

Television reached 17 million living rooms by 1951, delighting viewers with the high jinks of "Uncle Miltie" Berle (above), with Kukla, Fran and Ollie (on screen), and with lots more.

◄ **Lucy and Desi head for California on episode 110 of** I Love Lucy, **with their friends the Mertzes (Vivian Vance and William Frawley) riding in the back seat.**

▼ **Ed Sullivan gave dozens of top stars their first big break when he booked them on his show.**

▼ **As a duck falls from above, showing that a lucky contestant has said the secret word on** You Bet Your Life, **Groucho Marx delivers an impromptu wisecrack.**

in *The Honeymooners,* about a working-class family dreaming of, and scheming up, ways to make it in America.

Any similarity between the typical on-screen family and life as Americans lived it was purely coincidental. The wives on *Father Knows Best* and *Leave It to Beaver* cooked and cleaned in dressy dresses and heels, pearls and earrings. *The Adventures of Ozzie and Harriet,* featuring the real-life Nelson family, familiar to radio listeners, at first had to take place on Saturdays, lest viewers think Ricky and David were missing school.

Detective shows tried at least to give the appearance of realism. *Dragnet* — starring Jack Webb as Joe Friday, the laconic Los Angeles police sergeant asking persistently for "the facts, ma'am, just the facts" — enjoyed a highly successful run from 1952 to 1959.

As broadcast hours increased and more homes tuned in, television found a new role to play: electronic babysitter. Soon after *Howdy Doody* began in 1947, the tube's potential for influencing kids grew by gleeful leaps and bounds. Next came *Kukla, Fran, and Ollie,* which charmed adults as well as youngsters. *Ding Dong School,* a show for toddlers starring soft-voiced Miss Frances, and *The Mickey Mouse Club* both enjoyed enormous success. *Captain Kangaroo* debuted in 1953 and stayed on the air for three decades.

Bus driver Jackie Gleason of The Honeymooners *warns TV wife Audrey Meadows — "One of these days, Alice . . . Bang, zoom!" — as Art Carney and Joyce Randolph look askance.*

Your Show of Shows *was one of the funniest variety programs ever, thanks to gag writers Mel Brooks, Woody Allen, and Mel Tolkin and to the comic aplomb of co-host Sid Caesar (with cigar).*

◀

The Lone Ranger (Clayton Moore) and his companion, Tonto (Jay Silverheels), get ready to ride. They galloped on screen in 1949 and stayed until 1957 in one of TV's most popular horse operas for kids.

▼ *Flesh-and-blood image of the Man of Steel, George Reeves played Superman — intrepid defender of "truth, justice and the American way" — on TV from 1952 to 1957.*

In Paddy Chayefsky's Marty, perhaps the most celebrated of all 1950's live television dramas, Nancy Marchand, as Claire, brings a sweet touch of romance to the drab life of a lonely Bronx butcher, played by Rod Steiger.

Jack Webb (left), director and star of Dragnet, just wants the facts. Ben Alexander plays his partner, Officer Frank Smith.

Westerns, too, were kids' favorites, beginning with *Hopalong Cassidy* (1949), starring William Boyd, and followed quickly by *The Roy Rogers Show, The Gene Autry Show,* and *The Lone Ranger.* By 1958, viewers could choose from more than 20 regularly scheduled westerns each week, many of them targeting an adult audience. James Arness spent 20 years playing the stalwart Marshal Matt Dillon in *Gunsmoke.* James Garner's *Maverick* was an affable poker-playing antihero just one step shy of a con man.

If such series seldom rose to real drama, viewers had only to spin their dials. In 1947 the *Kraft Television Theatre* broadcast TV's first live production, and soon TV was offering more than 10 live dramas every week. Prestigious showcases, such as *Playhouse 90* and *Studio One,* featured written-for-TV plays, like J. P. Miller's *Days of Wine and Roses,* Rod Serling's *Requiem for a Heavyweight,* and Reginald Rose's *Twelve Angry Men.* Rod Steiger, Sidney Poitier, Paul Newman, Joanne Woodwood, Anne Bancroft, and Eva Marie Saint all launched their careers on television.

Meanwhile, TV news departments emerged as powers within the networks. Coverage of political conventions and congressional hearings attracted huge audiences, loyal to particular anchormen, like NBC's Chet Huntley and David Brinkley, who first worked together at the 1956 national political conventions. But no one was more admired than Edward R. Murrow, whose sad eyes and smoldering cigarette became national icons of journalistic integrity. As host of CBS's *See It Now,* Murrow examined controversial issues, such as illiteracy, racism, Senator Joseph R. McCarthy's demagoguery, and the cancer-causing potential of cigarettes.

From the beginning, television had its critics. Intellectuals mocked it as "the idiot box" or "the boob tube," and

With clean-cut friends like these — the original cast of Walt Disney's Mickey Mouse Club — what grade-schooler could resist becoming a Mousketeer and wearing a pair of rodent ears? Premiering in 1955, the show delighted a generation of children with its clever mix of cartoons, songs, and skits.

▼ One of America's great investigative journalists, Edward R. Murrow, pioneered the TV documentary with See It Now on CBS, and brought the camera into newsmakers' living rooms with Person to Person.

▼ On the quiz show Twenty-One, emcee Jack Barry presides while Charles Van Doren (left) and Herb Stempel (who blew the whistle on Van Doren) ponder a question from isolation booths, which were supposed to ensure honesty.

even defenders worried when, by the end of the decade, the average family spent some five hours a day in front of the screen. Murrow himself called it "the real opiate of the people" and wondered if even the best TV news coverage could ever "sort out the charlatan from the statesman."

The mania for quiz shows in the late 1950's certainly provided fertile ground for chicanery. Charles Van Doren was no statesman, but he was an earnest young Columbia instructor who came

across as brilliant and likable, and he became a TV star. Van Doren, seeming to strain for answers, won thousands of dollars on *Twenty-One*. Three years later he admitted to a House subcommittee that it had all been a hoax: the producer had given him the answers. Columbia fired Van Doren and so did NBC, which had taken him on as a commentator at $50,000 a year. Even so, popular sympathy ran with Van Doren, and a poll suggested that most people, given the chance, would have done just the same thing.

The Today Show on NBC — with affable host Dave Garroway and his more-or-less-silent partner, J. Fred Muggs — set the style for chatty morning news programs.

RELIGION RESURGENT

Polls regularly showed that 95 percent of Americans considered themselves religious. And some came to believe, as a writer for The Christian Century *did, that it was "un-American to be unreligious."*

Editor of the *Cleveland Press* Louis B. Seltzer wrote a piece for his paper one day in 1952 that alluded to the need for religion in a material world: "We abound with all of the things that make us comfortable. We are, on the average, rich beyond the dreams of the kings of old. . . . Yet . . . something is not there that should be." The response was immediate. Letters and phone calls poured into Seltzer's office; 41 newspapers picked up the editorial for their own pages. He had touched a chord.

The 1950's found a prosperous America experiencing a profound religious resurgence. People flocked to the nation's churches in growing numbers: by 1955 half the adult population, 49 million congregants, regularly attended services. Expenditures on church construction rose from $409 million to nearly $1 billion.

Increasingly prayer accompanied the events of daily life: on railways, where dining car menus came with a suggested grace; during radio programs, which scheduled breaks to allow time for private meditation; and before athletic contests. When New Yorkers found themselves at a loss for words in their moment of need, they turned to Dial-A-Prayer, a one-minute telephone service set up by the minister of a local church. Drivers along America's byways could find spiritual solace at roadside and drive-in churches and by turning to their own dashboards, which, peopled by images of holy figures, became moving altars.

Piety Wins in Washington and in the Media

Among a growing number of Americans, belief in God became intertwined with patriotism. As one minister put it: "An atheistic American is a contradiction in terms." In 1954 Congress added the words "under God" to the Pledge of Allegiance. Two years later, the phrase "In God We Trust," made the nation's official motto not long before, was engraved on all U.S. currency. When the Supreme Court ruled "released time" constitutional, allowing students to leave public schools early one day a week for religious instruction, Justice William O. Douglas's opinion read: "We are a religious people whose institutions presuppose a Supreme Being." President Dwight D. Eisenhower stated his view of the place of God in government: "The Almighty takes a definite and direct interest day by day in the progress of this nation." And, in those Cold War times, many believers saw their faith as a bulwark against communism. FBI Director J. Edgar Hoover urged Americans: "Since Communists are anti-God, encourage your children to be active in the church."

With polls indicating 9 out of 10 Americans believed in God, Hollywood produced religious blockbuster movies — *The Ten Commandments, Quo Vadis, The Robe* — and smaller films treating spiritual themes. "He was everybody's kind of guy. . . . He was God's kind of guy," ran the ad for *A Man Called Peter,* about a U.S. Senate chaplain.

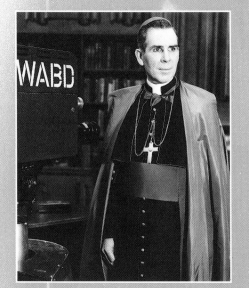

The dynamic, yet straightforward and humorous, style of Bishop Fulton J. Sheen (above) appealed to his television viewers. The Reverend Billy Graham (right) was at his best in spacious arenas, where he urged thousands to come forward for Christ.

A NEW POPE

On October 28, 1958, white smoke rose from a chimney above the Sistine Chapel in the Vatican to signal the election of a new pope. Angelo Giuseppe Roncalli, the aging cardinal and patriarch of Venice, seemed to be a "caretaker" choice by the College of Cardinals. Taking the name Pope John XXIII (shown above in his first official photograph), he moved swiftly to demonstrate that his reign would differ from that of his predecessor, Pope Pius XII. Within months, his evident compassion, humility, and sense of humor won over millions around the world. Then, in 1959, he stunned the church hierarchy by calling for an ecumenical council, the first in nearly 100 years. Finally convened in 1962, the council, called Vatican II, initiated numerous changes in Roman Catholic religious life and liturgy, among them that church officials could substitute the vernacular for Latin in the Mass, and that discrimination of any kind, and anti-Semitism in particular, was to be condemned. Pope John XXIII, who died in June 1963, won praise from church officials and the people alike for his reforms.

▲ *Rev. Norman Vincent Peale and his wife pose with his best-seller, which taught "a simple yet scientific system of practical techniques of successful living that works."*

◀

Wilson Prock, pastor of a Bronx, New York, church, greets one of the 200 worshippers to arrive for the first of a series of services held at the Whitestone Bridge Drive-In.

A few clergymen, aware of the power of the media, reached out to audiences in print and through radio and television. The best-selling book *Peace of Mind* (1946) by the Radio Rabbi, Joshua Loth Liebman, inspired Bishop Fulton J. Sheen to write *Peace of Soul* (1948) and evangelist Billy Graham, *Peace With God* (1952). A 1952 edition of the Bible, the Revised Standard Version, sold 26.5 million copies in its first year. After the Bible, Rev. Norman Vincent Peale's *The Power of Positive Thinking* (1952), which remained on best-seller lists for 186 weeks, ranks as one of the best-selling works of spiritual literature in history. The pastor of New York's Marble Collegiate Church, Peale combined popular psychology with religion, advising readers to "cast out those old, dead, unhealthy thoughts" and trust in God. In 1953 his radio program reached 1.5 million listeners; his television show would ultimately attract 5 million viewers.

Fulton Sheen, the Roman Catholic auxiliary bishop of New York, went on the radio with *The Catholic Hour* in 1930, but he reached the pinnacle of his teaching ministry when his *Life Is Worth Living* ran on national TV weekly in the years 1952 to 1957. At its height the program was watched by 10 million people; in 1953 Sheen topped the popular Milton Berle program in the Nielsen ratings.

But the clergyman who acquired the greatest mastery over the media was Rev. Billy Graham. Through his best-selling books, his radio show (*Hour of Decision*), numerous TV appearances, and worldwide Crusades for Christ, Graham preached old-time religion, calling on sinners to repent and be saved. When accused of being more adman than preacher, Graham countered: "I am selling the greatest product in the world; why shouldn't it be promoted as well as soap?" Though critics found him overzealous, many Americans affirmed the urgency of Graham's message.

Popular TV shows reflected the nation's religious resurgence. Here, the Anderson family of Father Knows Best pauses to say grace before eating a humble turkeyless Thanksgiving dinner.

HOLDING THE LINE IN KOREA

In the aftermath of the North Korean invasion of South Korea, political leaders and the American public

supported President Harry Truman, who said, "If we are tough enough now, there won't be any next time."

It came like a bolt out of nowhere: at 4:00 in the morning of June 25, 1950, some 90,000 soldiers from North Korea stormed across the border into South Korea. The very next day, with most of South Korea's forces in headlong retreat, American fighter planes swept in from their bases in Japan. The U.S. Seventh Fleet steamed toward the area. And shortly thereafter the first American ground troops were sent in. "We've got to stop those sons of bitches no matter what," Truman declared.

The United Nations Security Council (minus a boycotting U.S.S.R.) voted unanimously to send in troops. For the first time in history, a world organization was mobilizing to stop aggression. Some 16 nations sent troops, but for all practical purposes, it was a United States and South Korean show. The United States contributed over 50 percent of the ground troops, more than 80 percent of the navy, and more than 90 percent of the air force.

Brilliance, Miscalculation, Stalemate

At the end of World War II, U.S. troops had occupied the Korean peninsula south of the 38th parallel, while the U.S.S.R. took over in the north. The arrangement was meant to be temporary, but as in so many other theaters throughout the Cold War world, the lines hardened and froze. The result was two Koreas: a Soviet-sponsored Democratic People's Republic of Korea in the north and the American-backed Republic of Korea in the south. No one knew what role the Soviets had played in the attack, but government leaders assumed that Russia had orchestrated it and believed that America had to stop the Communist aggressors.

Supplied with Soviet-made tanks and weapons, the North Korean Army pushed U.N. forces, using World War II – vintage equipment, down the length of Korea until by early August the defenders held a mere toehold of ground on the southeast coast. There, along a 75-mile perimeter enclosing a pocket around the port of Pusan, they dug in.

The man who broke the stalemate was Gen. Douglas MacArthur. Then age 70, and supreme U.S. commander in the Far East, MacArthur devised a plan of astonishing boldness: an amphibious assault at the west-coast port of In-

TRUMAN SACKS MACARTHUR

As the Chinese offensive in Korea continued, Gen. Douglas MacArthur began calling in public for an expansion of the war into China. Truman refused and asked MacArthur to clear any future statements with the White House. By March of 1951, U.S. troops had pushed the Chinese back to the 38th parallel. MacArthur proposed cutting them off at the Yalu River by seeding its banks with radioactive waste. Truman said no. Then on April 5, Minority Leader Joe Martin read a letter on the House floor that was written by MacArthur and condemned the limited war strategy. It asserted, "There is no substitute for victory." Truman resolved to fire his general because, as he said, "I could no longer tolerate his insubordination." Amid fears that the news might leak, the announcement was rushed out at 1:00 A.M. on April 11. Truman said that he did not want MacArthur "to be allowed to quit on me." Reaction was swift. Senator William Jenner claimed that the country lay "in the hands of a secret coterie" controlled by Soviet agents. Senator Richard Nixon charged Truman with giving "the Communists and their stooges . . . what they always wanted — MacArthur's scalp." In Worcester, Massachusetts, Truman was hanged in effigy. On April 19 MacArthur stood before Congress. "I address you with neither rancor nor bitterness in the fading twilight of life, with but one purpose in mind: to serve my country." A record audience watched his masterful performance on television. "I now close my military career and just fade away — an old soldier who tried to do his duty as God gave him the light to see that duty. Good-bye." The public acclaim that followed the speech was unprecedented. But as Truman had anticipated, the adulation did not translate into support for MacArthur's strategy. Eventually, MacArthur did fade away. Civilian control of the military was reaffirmed.

chon, some 250 miles behind enemy lines. "I can almost hear the ticking of the second hand of destiny," the general declared. "We must act now or we will die."

So on September 15, after an air strike and naval bombardment, U.S. marines scrambled up 12-foot sea walls and sent the North Koreans reeling. It was the most brilliant stroke of MacArthur's long career. The troops holding Pusan linked up with the marines, and the U.N. forces sped inland, liberating Seoul. Then the forces turned north, reached the 38th parallel, and swept into North Korea.

It was a fateful step. What had begun as a U.N. police action to defend the south had now expanded into an offensive drive for all Korea. Truman approved the action, but with deep reservations: should the fighting spill over into China, directly across the Yalu River to the north, it might

On December 24, 1950, U.N. forces blew up the North Korean port of Hungnam before withdrawing to reinforce the Eighth Army in South Korea. The port was demolished to prevent the Communists from using it following the defeat of the U.S. forces at Chongjin Reservoir a few weeks earlier.

precipitate World War III. MacArthur remained cocky. The Chinese were far too weak to pose a real danger, he assured Truman. The GI's would be home by Thanksgiving.

It was not to be. As the U.N. armies neared the Yalu, they began trading gunshots with Chinese units. Then on November 27 some 360,000 Chinese troops attacked in force, swarming U.N. positions in the east and the west and swallowing up entire regiments. The defenders reeled back, recovered, and withdrew again as wave after wave of Chinese reinforcements poured across the Yalu. "The whole mountainside turned out to be Chinese," recalled one general.

American jet fighters, such as these Republic F-84's, gave U.N. forces dominance of the skies during the Korean War.

The U.N. forces retreated through the mountains of North Korea in the arctic cold of an early winter. Eventually the Chinese advance was halted near the 38th parallel, along a rim of low-lying peaks later dubbed Heartbreak Ridge and Pork Chop Hill. Again, the war had reached a stalemate. Again, MacArthur proposed a solution: all-out war against China. But MacArthur's lobbying showed little respect for civilian control of the military. Truman had no alternative but to fire him.

The war sputtered on another two years while delegates from both sides met to negotiate an armistice. Finally, on July 27, 1953, they signed an accord at Panmunjom, in the no-man's-land between the two front lines. By then, almost 34,000 Americans had been killed in action, and some 103,000 more had been wounded. Casualties among North and South Koreans, military and civilian, numbered in the millions. And for all the slaughter, the boundary between North and South Korea had shifted by no more than a few dozen miles.

Men from the U.S. 7th Infantry Division eat turkey for Thanksgiving dinner near the Yalu River on November 23, 1950. Just a few days later, the Chinese entered the war, forcing the U.N. troops to retreat.

Candidate Eisenhower ignored pundits' gibes, like "the extremely General Eisenhower," and led an affable campaign designed to appeal to the middle road of the American electorate.

REPUBLICAN NATIONAL

AMERICA SAYS "I LIKE IKE!"

Democratic candidate Adlai Stevenson may have been urbane and eloquent, but General Eisenhower's stature as a war hero, and the nation's shift to the right politically, guaranteed victory for the Republican Party in 1952.

don't think he has any politics," wrote the county clerk in Abilene, Kansas, when a high official of the Republican Party inquired into Gen. Dwight D. Eisenhower's party affiliation. The assessment might have damaged any other potential presidential candidate; but in 1952, Eisenhower's reputation as nonpartisan, a man above politics, was a key to his enormous popularity. The Democrats had been in office for 20 years. Rumors of corruption within the Truman administration were rife, and investigations into Communists in government, ongoing. The Korean conflict dragged on, and many Americans hoped that this war hero, supreme commander of the Allied forces during World War II, would end the stalemate. In 1948 both political parties had courted Eisenhower. Four years later Ike (having turned out to be a Republican) would be nominated to run for president on the first ballot at the 1952 Republican Convention.

In March of that year, President Truman, whose popularity rating hovered around 26 percent, had announced he would not run again. He asked Illinois governor Adlai Stevenson to seek the nomination in his stead. Stevenson, a moderate who had held public office under Roosevelt and Truman, was stunned. "The President wants me to save the world from Dwight Eisenhower," he told a friend. Not until delegates launched a genuine draft at the convention did he consent to be the Democratic candidate. The race was on, but Eisenhower stumbled out of the starting gate.

Ike's early performance seemed flat and lackluster. He made banal pronouncements — "The great problem of America today is to take that straight road down the middle"

◄ *Candidates Richard Nixon and Dwight Eisenhower, alongside their wives, Patricia and Mamie, raise their arms in victory after being nominated at the 1952 Republican Convention.*

— prompting reporters to joke, "He's crossing the 38th platitude again." Six weeks into the campaign, a major newspaper declared: "Ike is running like a dry creek."

Meanwhile, Stevenson, who was not well known to much of the electorate, dazzled listeners with his elevated speaking style and sharp wit. One journalist remarked that "his gifts are more imposing than those of any president . . . in this century." But Stevenson's assets would also prove to be liabilities. Some considered him haughty and patronizing. The press branded him an "egghead," and others hinted that his intellectual pretensions smacked of socialism. Stevenson responded with characteristic aplomb: "Eggheads of the world unite — you have nothing to lose but your yolks." But the attacks hurt his bid nonetheless.

Before long the Eisenhower campaign picked up steam. Ike recorded a series of pithy TV ads in which he addressed the concerns of ordinary citizens. He began to criticize Stevenson for making light of serious problems. As he became accustomed to the grueling schedule of appearances, he spoke with greater confidence. And he hammered away at the issues, termed K_1C_2, for Korea, corruption, and communism.

But on September 18 scandal rocked the Eisenhower campaign. The *New York Post* headlined a story "Secret Nixon Fund" and reported that Ike's running mate, Richard M. Nixon, maintained a secret slush fund. The fund, earmarked for Nixon's fight against communism, did exist, but it was no secret. Nevertheless, some Republicans suggested that Nixon withdraw, and Eisenhower himself called for a careful examination of the matter. Nixon decided to take his case directly to the American people via television.

As an audience of some 55 million watched, Nixon reviewed the fund and denied any misuse of its contents. In so doing, he laid out his own finances for public inspection. He was not a rich man, Nixon said. He owned a 1950 Oldsmobile and owed

▶ *This shot of Adlai Stevenson's worn-out shoes by an alert photographer might have helped mitigate his elitist image. But the Republicans managed to turn even Stevenson's down-at-the-heel footwear to their own advantage.*

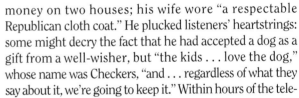

▼ *Countering slush fund charges, Richard Nixon spoke to TV viewers about his daughters, Julie and Tricia, and their puppy, Checkers. Nixon broke down in tears after the broadcast because he felt his appeal to voters had failed.*

money on two houses; his wife wore "a respectable Republican cloth coat." He plucked listeners' heartstrings: some might decry the fact that he had accepted a dog as a gift from a well-wisher, but "the kids . . . love the dog," whose name was Checkers, "and . . . regardless of what they say about it, we're going to keep it." Within hours of the telecast, supportive telegrams deluged Republican headquarters. By casting himself as the common man, Nixon had saved his candidacy and given the whole campaign a boost.

On October 24, Eisenhower made a dramatic announcement that likely clinched the election for him. During a speech in Detroit, he vowed that as president, he would "forgo the diversions of politics and concentrate on the job of ending the Korean War." He would take "a personal trip to Korea." Thereafter, all the polls indicated that Eisenhower would win the election handily.

Ike won the popular vote by a margin of more than 6,500,000. While some Americans lamented the end of an era under the Democrats, most looked forward to what they felt would be the firm leadership of General, now President, Eisenhower.

LOYALTY ON TRIAL

For a while in the early 1950's, America was caught up in the idea that all problems could be solved by ferreting out and destroying Communists.

On February 3, 1950, the British government announced that physicist Klaus Fuchs, who had worked on the atom bomb project at Los Alamos, had confessed that he had passed atomic secrets to the Soviets. The revelation confirmed America's worst fears. Indiana Senator Homer Capehart railed: "How much more are we going to have to take? Fuchs and Acheson and Hiss and hydrogen bombs threatening outside and New Dealism eat-

Separated by a screen, Ethel and Julius Rosenberg are transported in a police van to their jail cells after being found guilty of espionage and conspiracy.

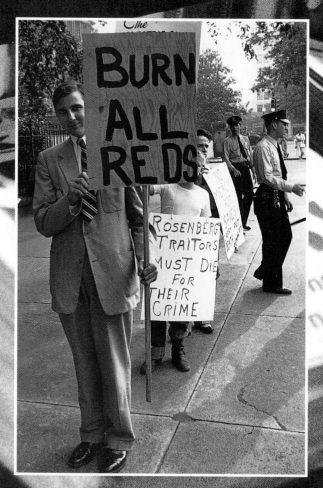

Pickets outside the White House march in support of the death penalty for the treasonous Rosenbergs.

Klaus Fuchs, who passed atomic secrets to the Soviets for eight years, served nine years in prison before being deported to East Germany.

ing away at the vitals of the nation. In the name of Heaven, is this the best that America can do?"

Less than a week after the Fuchs confession, Senator Joseph R. McCarthy rose to provide an answer. At the McLure Hotel in Wheeling, West Virginia, he said America was in trouble. Foreign policy failures, such as allowing China to fall to the Communists, could be traced to Communist infiltration of the U.S. government and particularly of the State Department. "I have in my hand a list of 205," he declared, waving a paper, "a list of names known to the Secretary of State as being members of the Communist Party and who nevertheless are still working and shaping policy in the State Department."

A gasp rose from the audience, and within days, the charges echoed across the front pages of the nation's newspapers. The effect was just what McCarthy wanted. In four years as the Republican senator from Wisconsin, he had done little to capture wide attention. But with elections coming up, he looked for a way to further his career.

In speech after speech, McCarthy lashed out. He

Sophie Rosenberg, Julius's mother, leads a demonstration to stop the scheduled execution, less than a week away.

inveighed against "parlor pinks and parlor punks," against "egg-sucking phony liberals" and the "Communists and queers who sold China into atheistic slavery." Truman and Acheson became "Pied Pipers of the Politburo." McCarthy's diatribes were denounced by many, including Edward R. Murrow on TV, but the public at large supported him.

Some news reports seemed to lend credence to what McCarthy was saying. Four months after Klaus Fuchs's con-

fession, one of his accomplices, Philadelphia chemist Harry Gold, was arrested. Gold in turn implicated another Los Alamos employee, army machinist David Greenglass. From there the trail led to Greenglass's wife, Ruth, and sister Ethel Rosenberg and her husband, Julius. All were arrested, and all confessed, except for Ethel and Julius Rosenberg. The Rosenberg case dragged slowly through the courts, with each appeal upholding the original conviction and its terrible consequence: the death sentence. At any point the Rosenbergs could have saved themselves by pleading guilty and asking for clemency. They did not. "Always remember that we were innocent," they wrote in a letter to their sons, "and could not wrong our conscience." Amid great protest, they were put to death in the electric chair at Sing Sing, the state prison in Ossining, New York, on June 19, 1953.

Even after the Republicans swept into office in 1952, McCarthy, intoxicated by his newfound power, stepped up his attacks. At the end of 1953, the senator turned his attention to the U.S. Army. In his widening hunt for subversives, he challenged the routine promotion of a captain, Irving Peress, who held left-leaning beliefs. The army mounted a counterattack. It seemed that McCarthy's top aide, 27-year-old Roy Cohn, had made repeated attempts to arrange a commission for his friend Pvt. G. David Schine and had warned he would "wreck the Army" if it was not granted. In March 1954 the army charged McCarthy and Cohn with using the threat of investigation as a form of blackmail.

For 36 days, 20 million Americans watched the Army-McCarthy hearings unfold on television. At one table sat Army Secretary Robert Stevens and the army's special counsel, the courtly Massachusetts lawyer Joseph Welch. At the other was McCarthy, disheveled and combative, and Cohn. No match for Welch's deft questioning, McCarthy resorted to smear and innuendo. He accused a junior member of Welch's own law firm of being a Communist. Welch listened in growing fury, and then he responded: "Until this moment, Senator, I think I never really gauged your cruelty or recklessness. . . ." "Point of order! Point of order!" McCarthy cried. But Welch continued: "Let us not assassinate this lad further, Senator. You have done enough. Have you no sense of decency, sir, at long last? Have you left no sense of decency?" The entire room broke into applause.

And so, then, did most Americans. The U.S. Senate formally condemned McCarthy in December 1954, after which he finished out two more years as senator and slid into rapid decline. He died in 1957, but the fears and ideas he exploited survived him.

▲ Joseph R. McCarthy (left) and his top counsel, Roy M. Cohn, discuss strategy in 1953. That year the two men considered investigating the CIA before they set their sights on Communist infiltration of the U.S. Army.

▲ In April 1954 army counsel Joseph N. Welch, seated next to Army Secretary Robert Stevens, presents a memo denying that the army tried to impede McCarthy's inquiry.

William Glackens ●
Beach Umbrellas at Blue Point, 1915
A member of the so-called Ashcan School of New Realists, Glackens found inspiration in the colorful bustle of real people in and around eastern cities.

Mary Cassatt ●
After the Bath, 1901
Pennsylvania-born Cassatt focused on women's daily lives. An Impressionist, she lived in France from 1874 until her death in 1926 at 82.

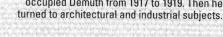

Charles Demuth ● *The Circus,* 1917
Studies of nightclub and vaudeville entertainers, like this watercolor-and-pencil work on paper, occupied Demuth from 1917 to 1919. Then he turned to architectural and industrial subjects.

Georgia O'Keeffe ● *Red Canna, c.* 1924
Lyrical evocations of the inner structure of flowers followed O'Keeffe's minimalist drawings and cityscapes and preceded the desert motifs of her New Mexico work.

George Luks ●
The Polka Dot Dress, 1927
A member of The Eight, the nucleus of the Ashcan School, Luks rejected New York's upper crust and turned his gaze on the city's common people.

Grant Wood ●
Daughters of Revolution, 1932
Resisting European modernism, Wood and fellow painter Thomas Hart Benton chose a realistic style that became known as Regionalism. His prim "daughters" stand before Emanuel Leutze's *Washington Crossing the Delaware.*

AMERICAN PAINTING MAKES ITS MARK

To the typical American art lover at the turn of the century, impressionism was modern art, and the postimpressionists Cezanne, Gauguin, and Van Gogh were just reaching respectability. Then in 1913 the Armory Show opened in New York City. It exhibited the freshest in American art, including some of the painters represented on these two pages (Glackens, Luks, and Stuart Davis, then 18 years old), and work considered avant-garde in Europe — cubism and fauvism, for example. By the late 1940's, America, in particular New York City, could claim to be the center of the Western art world, thanks in part to an influx of artists from war-torn Europe. Abstract expressionism, led by Pollock and de Kooning (see next page), as well as by Mark Rothko and others, dominated Western art for several years, until such styles as pop art (see pp. 344–45), minimal art, and a rebirth of realism arose to fascinate artists and connoisseurs alike.

Jacob Lawrence ⬤ *Migration Series,* 1940–41
On 60 masonite panels measuring 12 in. by 18 in., Lawrence memorialized the century's ongoing exodus of blacks from the rural South to northern cities.

Jackson Pollock ⬤
No. 3, 1949: Tiger, 1949
Using the technique later dubbed action painting by a critic, Pollock spread this canvas on the floor, stood over it, and dripped oil, enamels, string, and cigarette shreds on it. For him it broke the tyranny of traditional art.

Andrew Wyeth ⬤
Roasted Chestnuts, 1956
Perhaps America's favorite painter at the end of the 20th century, Wyeth created richly detailed images heavy with a sense of solitude. Much of his work reflects his love for Pennsylvania's Brandywine Valley, his lifelong home.

Willem de Kooning ⬤ *Composition,* 1955
After exhibiting his controversial series of wildly incongruous female figures, de Kooning then created a number of abstractions like this one.

Stuart Davis ⬤
General Studies, 1962
Cubism, jazz, and the city's pulse infuse Davis's work, whose abstract forms, bold colors, random scrawls, and visual echoes of familiar objects are major elements of American modernism.

Edward Hopper ⬤
People in the Sun, 1960
Nearing 80 when he painted this haunting scene of people facing a late afternoon sun, Hopper uses light and shadow to heighten the isolation and trancelike self-absorption of the individuals in the group.

Frank Stella ⬤
Sacramento Mall Proposal #4, 1978
In his teens Stella forsook representational painting for abstract expressionism. Then, taking a further step to concentrate on stripes and rectangles, he became known as a leader of "minimal art."

Janet Fish ⬤
Gold Tea Set, 1986
Realism and conventional subjects continued to captivate many late-20th-century artists like Janet Fish, whose still lifes sparkle with light and color.

LEARNING TO LIVE WITH SUPERBOMBS

Comparing the atom bomb to the hydrogen bomb, Winston Churchill wrote: "The atomic bomb, with all its terrors, did not carry us outside the scope of human control . . . in thought or action in peace or war."

At the highest levels of government, debate raged over development of the so-called superbomb. Many scientists, led by J. Robert Oppenheimer, director of the Manhattan Project, objected to the undertaking on moral grounds. Hiroshima was bad enough; the prospect of working on stronger weapons, capable of eradicating whole populations, raised fundamental questions about the role of science. A few scientists hypothesized that the detonation of the hydrogen bomb might start a chain reaction and incinerate the globe itself. Others, notably Hungarian-born physicist Edward Teller, disagreed. Fusion weapons were possible, asserted Teller, and they were inevitable. And woe betide the nation that sat on its hands and let the Soviets build one first.

The question of the H-bomb was settled in early 1950, when British physicist Klaus Fuchs confessed to passing nuclear secrets on to the Soviets over an eight-year period. What else did the Kremlin know? Truman elected to err on the side of caution, and on January 31, 1950, he announced that development of the hydrogen bomb would proceed under Teller's direction. Less than two weeks later, Albert Einstein appeared on television to warn that "radioactive

The photo above, of the first thermonuclear detonation, was taken 2 minutes after zero hour, at about 12,000 feet some 50 miles away. Physicist Edward Teller (inset, left) championed the bomb's development. J. Robert Oppenheimer (inset, top), who headed the Manhattan Project, opposed it.

276

As fear of nuclear war increased, gimmicks for surviving an attack multiplied. A Los Angeles couple (far left) Christmas shops in fallout gear. A prefabricated family shelter (left), produced by the Walter Kidde Nuclear Laboratories, sold under the brand name Kidde Kocoon.

A group of pacifists demonstrates their opposition to nuclear war by refusing to take shelter during an air raid drill in New York City.

poisoning of the atmosphere, and hence annihilation of any life on earth, has been brought within the range of technical possibilities...."

Thus the early 1950's became the age of nuclear anxiety, marked by a frantic civil defense craze. In manuals such as *You Can Survive an Atomic Attack*, federal civil defense officials advised Americans to stockpile food and water, purchase Geiger counters, plan escape routes, and build backyard shelters. Schools instituted nuclear-attack drills. Not everybody believed such measures would save them, but most Americans adopted a positive outlook as they made preparations for the possibility of a nuclear strike. A Los Angeles mother of three told reporters that her backyard shelter would "make a wonderful place for the children to play in." In a publicity stunt, newlyweds Maria and Melvin Minnison spent a two-week honeymoon in an 8- by 14-foot steel-and-concrete box buried 12 feet under their backyard and emerged smiling.

Both Sides Get the Hydrogen Bomb

In the fall of 1952, Teller's H-bomb was detonated: a fireball 5 miles wide lit the Western Pacific sky, sending a mushroom cloud roiling 25 miles into the air. The heat at ground zero was estimated at five times the temperature of the sun's interior. The closest observers — some 50 miles away — watched dumbstruck as Elugelab, a mile-wide atoll in the Marshall Islands, disappeared.

A blast of such magnitude was impossible to hide. Newspapers reported that the bomb could have flattened San Francisco, Spokane, St. Louis, or Washington, D.C., and vaporized a large part of New York City. A congressional subcommittee estimated that in a thermonuclear con-

frontation, 20 million Americans would perish on the first day.

The development of the H-bomb — matched by Russia a mere nine months later — brought a fundamental change to military strategic planning; both sides had the bomb and the rocket technology to deliver it. The result was a nuclear stalemate lasting four decades. The H-bomb also seemed to deflate public interest in surviving, let alone winning, a nuclear confrontation. Evidence accumulated that fallout could prove lethal hundreds of miles downwind from ground zero, and that strontium 90, a by-product of nuclear testing, had made its way into the food chain, appearing in the milk people bought at the corner grocery. Against such awesome power, backyard shelters seemed insignificant; quickly they filled with bicycles, flowerpots, and old snow tires. Where once Americans had faced the prospect of nuclear confrontation with gritty optimism, a new fatalism emerged. When asked what he would do should war come, a New York City bank teller replied that he would "run under the bomb and get it over with quickly." Concerns about the growing Soviet arsenal of intercontinental ballistic missiles (ICBM's) further eroded American confidence in the future.

America's atomic fears surfaced in books and movies, notably Nevil Shute's novel *On the Beach*. Published in 1957 and made into a movie two years later, Shute's tale of the last survivors of a nuclear holocaust, awaiting certain death as a radioactive cloud approaches them, put a human face on the grim abstraction of atomic annihilation.

THE COURT CANCELS "SEPARATE BUT EQUAL"

The Supreme Court's unanimous 1954 decision on public school segregation ruled separate educational facilities "inherently unequal" and set in motion a civil rights revolution that changed the nation forever.

Each morning, eight-year-old Linda Brown crossed a railroad yard in Topeka, Kansas, to catch a bus that took her to school 25 blocks away. Just four blocks from her home stood another elementary school. Why, Linda wondered, was the nearby school only for whites?

In 1951 that question was getting harder for parents to answer. President Harry Truman had integrated the military and was pushing for civil rights laws. In baseball, the first black to play in the major leagues, Jackie Robinson, had been named Rookie of the Year in 1947. The black middle class had begun to gain momentum. And, still, the fundamental right of all children to equality in education was being denied due to the segregation of public schools.

Oliver Brown, Linda's father, decided to act. When he took Linda to the local school and the principal refused her admission, he sued. *Brown* v. *Board of Education* became one of five lawsuits used by the National Association for the Advancement of Colored People (NAACP) to battle segregated schooling across the nation.

An Appeal for Justice

NAACP lawyer Thurgood Marshall thought he had a good case to challenge the segregation laws. At the heart of the issue was the argument that "separate but equal" facilities — hospitals, public transportation, schools — fulfilled the Constitution's promise to uphold the rights of all citizens. In practice, black schools were poorly funded and black teachers were underpaid. "We conclude that in the field of public education . . . 'separate but equal' has no place," wrote Chief Justice Earl Warren in 1954 in an opinion signed by all nine justices. In 1955 the Court unanimously directed the states to desegregate public schools "with all deliberate speed."

The South called for "massive resistance." In Virginia, officials closed public schools, some for up to two years. In Congress, 82 representatives and 19 senators signed a Southern Manifesto that accused the Supreme Court of

◄ *On December 21, 1956, Rosa Parks at last rode legally in the front of a Montgomery bus (far left). Some nine months later, 15-year-old Elizabeth Eckford (left) was jeered as national guardsmen turned her away from Central High School, Little Rock.*

► *Before he became the nation's first black Supreme Court justice, in 1967, Thurgood Marshall won 29 of 32 cases he brought before that body. Here he arrives to argue against Orval Faubus's use of the National Guard in Little Rock.*

abusing its powers. Six years after the Brown decision, four Southern states had not integrated a single public school.

Attempts to desegregate schools and other facilities were often followed by violence. But, under the charismatic leadership of Dr. Martin Luther King, Jr., pastor of a Montgomery, Alabama church, blacks met violence with non-violence: they turned the other cheek. In December 1955 a seamstress named Rosa Parks refused to surrender her seat on a crowded bus to a white man, and she was arrested. Montgomery blacks decided to boycott the bus company and asked the 27-year-old King to organize the campaign.

In a matter of days, 90 percent of black bus riders were walking, carpooling, or bicycling to their destinations. During the 381-day boycott, King's house was bombed and he was jailed twice: for conspiring to organize an illegal boycott and for a minor traffic violation. In November 1956 the Supreme Court ruled against the bus company.

Resistance to the growing civil rights movement did not end there. In 1957 a Senate filibuster, kept alive for 24 hours and 18 minutes by Strom Thurmond of South Carolina, nearly derailed a federal initiative, the Civil Rights Act of 1957. But it passed, in large part because of the efforts of the Senate Democratic majority leader, Lyndon B. Johnson.

Intervention by the President

President Eisenhower, who tried to avoid involvement in the civil rights fray, was compelled to act in 1957 when Orval Faubus, governor of Arkansas, pitted state law against federal law. The crisis began that September when Faubus ordered the Arkansas National Guard to surround Little Rock Central High School in order to stop nine blacks from enrolling. On September 3 the black students braved a white mob, only to be turned away at the school doors. When 15-year-old Elizabeth Eckford walked alone through the crowd, the scenes of whites screaming curses at her flashed across the country — indeed, around the world.

Under court order, Faubus sent the Guard home on Friday, September 20, leaving 150 city policemen to protect the black students the next week. On Monday over 1,000 whites attacked blacks and sympathetic whites outside the school. Police made no move to protect them; one officer simply removed his badge and walked away. The next day, Eisenhower took control of the Arkansas National Guard and brought in 1,100 paratroopers. Central High was integrated, but troops had to remain there for the entire school year. The struggle for civil rights was far from won.

◀ *In the racially tense Montgomery of 1956, Reverend King, his wife, and daughter Yolanda share a family moment.*

Earl Warren (inset) was in his first year as chief justice when the Court issued the historic school desegregation decision. On May 17, 1957, more than 15,000 people, including Dr. Martin Luther King, Jr., and Roy Wilkins, gathered in Washington to mark the third anniversary of the decision.

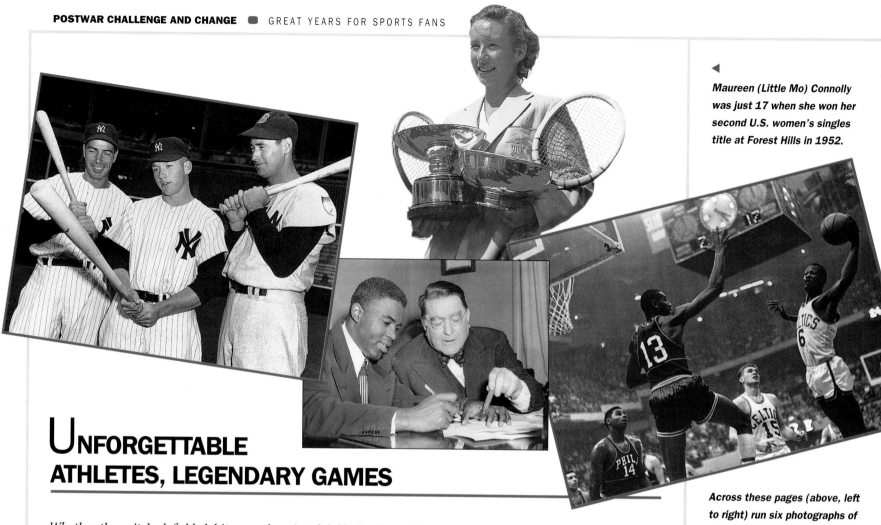

◄

Maureen (Little Mo) Connolly was just 17 when she won her second U.S. women's singles title at Forest Hills in 1952.

UNFORGETTABLE ATHLETES, LEGENDARY GAMES

Whether they pitched, fielded, hit, passed, sprinted, lobbed, rebounded, jabbed, or putted their way into the record books, America's sports figures captivated fans and gave television viewers hours of entertainment.

As the battlefields of World War II grew silent, America welcomed home baseball heroes like Ted Williams, the Splendid Splinter of the Boston Red Sox; Joe DiMaggio, New York's Yankee Clipper; and Stan the Man Musial, the pride of the St. Louis Cardinals. They returned to a game about to undergo major changes.

Branch Rickey, the Brooklyn Dodgers president, would soon break the color barrier in the majors, and he had just the man to do it: multitalented Jackie Robinson, a 195-pound, 6-foot, 28-year-old graduate of UCLA, who had a fierce competitive spirit. Rickey knew that racial slurs, spikings, beanballs, taunts from fans and players, even his own, and blacks-only hotels lay in wait for Robinson. Before offering him a contract, as Jackie told *Reader's Digest* years later, Rickey tested him: "Let's say I'm a hotel clerk. You come in with the rest of your team. I look up from the register and snarl, 'We don't let niggers sleep here.' What do you do

then?" Several questions later, Rickey explained, "I want you to be the first Negro player in the major leagues. I've been trying to give you some idea of the kind of punishment you'll have to absorb. Can you take it?"

He could. Throughout the 1947 season, Robinson was the model of decorum. He won Rookie of the Year honors, and his success on the field opened major league baseball to other black athletes. Roy Campanella, a three-time Most Valuable Player, and Don Newcombe became teammates. Across town, the New York Giants introduced center fielder Willie Mays, the Say-Hey Kid, in 1951.

That same year, the Dodgers and Giants played what many fans consider the most exciting baseball game of all time. From a 13½-game deficit, the Giants had steadily gained on the Dodgers. The regular season ended with the teams in a dead heat, forcing a three-game play-off. They split the first two games. In the ninth inning of the third

Across these pages (above, left to right) run six photographs of sports greats. A 19-year-old Mickey Mantle is flanked by two established stars, Joe DiMaggio and Ted Williams. Branch Rickey uses his cigar to point to the dotted line in Jackie Robinson's 1950 contract. Wilt the Stilt Chamberlain (above) goes up to block Bill Russell's shot at Boston Garden in 1959. Ben Hogan, winner of eight Grand Slam tournaments, tees off in Miami. Rocky Marciano lands a right to Jersey Joe Walcott for the heavyweight title in 1952; he was never defeated. A 25-year-old medical student, Roger Bannister, breaks the four-minute mile on May 6, 1954.

game, the Dodgers led 4–2. With two men on base and one out, Bobby Thomson, the Giant third baseman, came to the plate. Reliever Ralph Branca threw a strike.Then he unwound another pitch that streaked in high and inside. Thomson swung and hit "the home run heard around the world." Pandemonium broke loose in the stadium; Thomson felt as though he were "living one of those middle-of-the-night dreams" of glory. Before the decade ended, both the Giants and the Dodgers would leave New York for the West Coast.

But New York City's other baseball franchise, the Yankees, stayed put and played the game as if they owned it in the 1950's. With superb pitching, the power hitting of sluggers like Mickey Mantle, and Casey Stengel's inspired managing, between 1949 and 1960 the Yankees won 10 pennants and 7 World Series, 5 of them in a row.

Thrilling Stories in Every Sport

Champions emerged in a wide variety of sports. California's Bob Mathias captured the grueling Olympic decathlon in 1948 and 1952. The next year Maureen Connolly stroked and smashed her way to win the grand slam of tennis — the championships of Australia, France, Britain, and the United States — the first woman in history to do so. In 1957 and 1958, Althea Gibson, one of the first black tennis stars, won both the British and American national championships. In boxing, Joe Louis finally retired and Rocky Marciano took control of the heavyweight crown. Sugar Ray Robinson, called pound for pound the best fighter of all time, fought his way to the middleweight title five times.

Professional football mesmerized the entire country on a mild December day in 1958, when 50 million viewers tuned in to the National Football League championship game between the New York Giants and the Baltimore Colts, a contest many call the best football game ever played. The Colts tied the score seven seconds before the clock ran out, sending the game into sudden-death overtime. The Giants could do nothing on their first possession and punted. The Colts, with the incomparable Johnny Unitas at the helm, marched 80 yards up the gridiron in 13 plays, finally winning 23–17 when fullback Alan Ameche plunged over the goal line from the Giant one-yard line.

The story in professional basketball was the Boston Celtics, led by playmaker Bob Cousy and 6-foot 10-inch defensive standout and center Bill Russell. In 1959 the Celtics won their first of eight straight National Basketball Association championships.

Professional golf provided the drama of one of sport's greatest individual comebacks, that of the diminutive Bantam Ben Hogan. For 17 agonizing months after a near fatal automobile accident in 1949, Hogan wondered whether he could ever compete again in the sport he so dearly loved. But he won the U.S. Open in 1950 and the Open and the Masters in 1951. Seven years later Arnold Palmer's charge to victory in the televised 1958 Masters would attract a whole new generation to the sport.

Hall of Fame pitcher Dizzy Dean tries his hand at play-by-play for the Dumont network in September 1950. Telecasts hooked new fans and soon became a major source of income for the owners.

BRIDEY, DAVY, HOWDY, AND A LOT MORE

Emerging from two decades of depression and war, and riding the crest of a booming economy, Americans spent much of their leisure time lurching from one fad to another. Perhaps the most amazing aspect of all the craziness was its unrelenting variety.

The phone-booth-stuffing craze originated in South Africa and, in 1959, enjoyed a few months' popularity in the United States, primarily on the West Coast.

The Bomb had created an age of anxiety. Many people seemed to work, or play, harder as a way of coping with the thought that their world might vanish in an instant. Perhaps the perilous times made the idea of reincarnation especially attractive, for the story of a Colorado housewife who claimed to have experienced a previous life in 19th-century Ireland touched a chord. The best-selling book *The Search for Bridey Murphy* was serialized in over 35 magazines and newspapers. Hostesses threw "come-as-you-were" parties and served "reincarnation cocktails."

The 1950's were also a time of unprecedented general prosperity. Not only would Americans have a chicken in every pot but a car in every garage, a washing machine in every basement, a television set in every rec room, and, thanks to fluoride, a perfect set of teeth in every child's mouth.

The first toy that every kid had to own — the by-product of a marine engineer's research — practically leapt off the shelf when a Philadelphia store displayed it early in 1947. The Slinky, a springy coil of wire that, among other feats, "walked" downstairs, sold like hotcakes for several years before settling down to become a classic.

The Slinky was just the beginning of America's feverish accumulation of goods. By 1948, when some 100,000 American homes boasted TV sets, children were greeting one another with a bouncy "It's *Howdy Doody* time." Kids collected souvenirs of the show's characters: Howdy Doody hats, pajamas, bathing suits, watches, and Clarabell horns; and they dressed up as Princess Summerfallwinterspring. The country turned into one big circus, thanks to Buffalo Bob Smith, the show's host, and to shrewd marketing.

Television brought the children of America a series of heroes with product tie-ins. Few kids had heard of

At the height of the Davy Crockett hysteria in 1955, the opportunity to get a real coonskin cap caused near riots by youthful Crockett fanatics. ▶

Davy Crockett before Walt Disney broadcast a three-part series on the Indian fighter beginning in December 1954. Disney offered an idealized version of Davy: he was clean shaven, cuss free, and smartly outfitted in spotless fringed leather and a coonskin cap with a tail. Coonskin caps became all the rage, and, by the spring of 1955, when suppliers had run out of coonskins, kids donned caps made of rabbit, muskrat, and who-knew-what, even in 80-degree weather. Four million 45 records of Davy's theme song were sold, and an estimated $100 million worth of Davy T-shirts, lunch boxes, sheets, towels, and buckskins. It couldn't last and it didn't. Davy the man had lived for 50 years; Davy the fad barely made it to 11 months.

Among college students, a strange new rite of spring developed in 1952, the panty raid. The phenomenon began when male undergraduates at the University of

WILL TRADE ANYTHING FOR A DAVY CROCKETT CAP

◄

This 15-inch marionette was one of a series of puppets, based on Howdy Doody show characters, produced in the early 1950's.

▼ *Most people were happy to master one Hula-Hoop, but experts, young and old, delighted in seeing how many they could spin at once.*

Michigan swept across campus and descended on a women's dorm demanding tokens of esteem from residents. The coeds responded by tossing their undergarments from windows and balconies, and the rite was soon adopted on campuses across the country. Adults everywhere shook their heads in dismay. Inevitably some raids resulted in minor injuries and property damage, and university officials were compelled to crack down on them.

While certain postwar fads incited generational distress, a handful seemed to reinforce notions of family togetherness. Scrabble and canasta, both of which had been around for years, were rediscovered in the 1950's and became wildly popular overnight.

Near the end of the decade, a passion for knockoffs of the bamboo hoops used in Australian gym classes seized the nation with a grip mightier even than that of Davy Crockett himself. In 1958 everyone who was not bedridden seemed engaged in the struggle to keep a brightly colored, lightweight plastic hoop orbiting somewhere above his or her hips. By Halloween, when the fad petered out, 100 million had been sold. At $1.98 apiece, the Hula-Hoop may well have been one of the least expensive muscle toners ever on the market.

NOVEL EVENTS

Two first novels published in the 1950's saw pockets of moral decay beneath the surface of American life. The books had several things in common. Both sought to expose hypocrisy and did so using strong, blunt language that shocked or titillated readers. Both were banned in some schools and libraries, and they were instant best-sellers, particularly among students. J. D. Salinger's *The Catcher in the Rye* (1951) chronicled two days in the life of 16-year-old Holden Caulfield, an articulate youth given to musings about phoniness and corruption who runs away from his prep school to New York City. *Peyton Place* (1956), by Grace Metalious, tells a sordid tale of lust, rape, incest, and adultery set in a picture-perfect New England town. *Peyton Place* sold 60,000 copies in its first 10 days, and the 1957 movie caused a new surge in paperback sales. Salinger won critical acclaim, but he became a recluse and published nothing after the mid-1960's. Although Metalious's future as a novelist looked promising, she subsequently published two unsuccessful novels. She died in 1964 at the age of 39.

▼ *In the spirit of togetherness that became an American ideal in the 1950's, this family of five bounces its way through a fun-filled afternoon on pogo sticks.*

ROCK AND ROLL COMES TO STAY

Favored with unprecedented buying power, teenagers contributed to the spectacular success of rock and roll, a music largely written and performed by members of their own generation.

The year was 1956. The New York *Herald Tribune* called him "an unspeakably untalented and vulgar entertainer." Popular television emcee Ed Sullivan declared him "unfit for a family audience." But just weeks after he had condemned Elvis Presley, Sullivan bowed to public demand and booked him for three guest spots on his show, at $50,000 a performance. By Elvis's third appearance, Sullivan instructed his camera crew to shoot the rock and roller from the waist up, cutting off from view the gyrating hips that made Elvis a sensation at 21.

A poor truck driver from Memphis, Elvis was discovered when he dropped into Sun Records to cut a disc for his mother's birthday. The head of the studio, Sam Phillips, had been on the lookout for "a white boy who could sing colored" and signed Elvis up. RCA liked what they heard, bought his contract, and launched a publicity campaign that included national TV appearances.

Presley brought rock and roll into the mainstream, but he didn't invent it. Rock's origins go back to the early 1950's, when black gospel, blues, and jazz were melded into what was called rhythm and blues. Because of its association with blacks, this music was largely relegated to small, indepen-

On radio stations in Cleveland and New York City, disc jockey Alan Freed spun the records and promoted the rock music teenagers wanted to hear.

"If I stand still while I'm singing, I'm dead, man," said Elvis Presley. "I might as well go back to driving a truck." His onstage gyrations thrilled teenagers, horrified their parents, and helped propel Elvis to the heights of musical royalty as the King of Rock and Roll.

Rock and roll's greatest poet, Chuck Berry, is as much renowned for his athletic "duck walk" as for his personal sound on the electric guitar, displayed in classic songs such as "Johnny B. Goode."

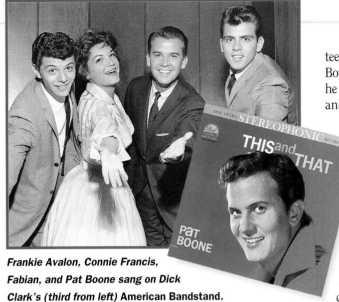

Frankie Avalon, Connie Francis,
Fabian, and Pat Boone sang on Dick
Clark's (third from left) **American Bandstand.**

▼ *Texas country boy Buddy*
Holly and his backup group,
the Crickets, made numerous
rock and roll hits before
Holly's untimely death at the
age of 22 in an airplane
crash, which also took the
lives of Ritchie Valens ("La
Bamba") and The Big Bopper
("Chantilly Lace").

dent recording companies and black radio stations. But, attracted by the sexually charged imagery and driving beat of rhythm and blues, young white music fans began to listen as well. Cleveland disc jockey Alan Freed tapped into the burgeoning market and, in 1951, launched *Moondog Rock and Roll Party*. In doing so, Freed became the first to employ the term *rock and roll* to define a genre of music. In March 1952 he organized what is generally regarded as the first-ever rock and roll concert, featuring black performers and drawing an audience that was two-thirds white.

In 1953 a white country singer named Bill Haley recorded the rock song "Crazy, Man, Crazy," which became a minor hit. Haley and his group, the Comets, developed a hybrid of rock and roll, combining rhythm and blues, country and western, and swing. Filmgoers were electrified by his "Rock Around the Clock," in the movie *The Blackboard Jungle*, for some viewers their first taste of rock and roll.

Gradually black rock and roll stars became recognized nationwide. Chuck Berry — who recorded "Maybellene" in 1955, followed by dozens of hits, including "Rock and Roll Music" and "Sweet Little 16" — was arguably the most influential, but Little Richard ("Good Golly, Miss Molly") and Fats Domino ("Blueberry Hill") had great runs, and Bo Diddley made hits as well. White artists such as Buddy Holly ("That'll Be the Day," "Peggy Sue") and Jerry Lee Lewis ("Whole Lot of Shakin' Goin' On") took inspiration from black performers.

Attempts to bring rock to a wider audience continued, most notably on a new TV program out of Philadelphia hosted by the 27-year-old impresario Dick Clark. In 1957 the show went national as *American Bandstand*. Every afternoon, for an audience that ultimately reached 40 million, rock stars lip-synched their songs while teens danced the new steps, among them the Hand Jive, the Bop, the Stroll, and the Slop. Clark engaged every hit maker he could for the program, from girl groups, such as Ronnie and the Ronnettes and the Shirelles, to street-corner singing groups, such as The Platters and Dion, to clean-cut pop singers, such as Annette Funicello and Bobby Darin. The cleanest cut of all the young performers was Pat Boone, who frequently rerecorded songs by other artists, many of them black ("Tutti-Frutti," "Ain't That a Shame").

Even the likes of Pat Boone could do little to silence rock and roll's critics, one of whom cautioned that the music "inflames and excites youth like jungle tom-toms readying warriors for battle." Still, record sales tripled, and by 1958 teenagers were buying 70 percent of all the albums issued. The decade's end saw adult resistance to rock soften. "Just as hot jazz of the twenties (then anathema to our grandparents) did not destroy our parents, and swing (anathema to our parents) did not destroy us," wrote Arnold Shaw in the May 1959 *Harper's*, "it is quite unlikely that rock 'n' roll will destroy our children."

Flamboyant Little Richard, seen here in a 1957 movie,
claimed credit for being the architect of rock and roll.

BIG MOVIES, BELOVED STARS

After a record-setting year in 1946, movie revenues began a precipitous decline. Hollywood responded with new technologies, a spate of science fiction and horror flicks, big-screen blockbusters, and some outstanding performances by old and new stars.

◄

In Alfred Hitchcock's 1959 thriller North by Northwest, *Cary Grant is pursued by a murderous crop duster and winds up climbing down Mount Rushmore.*

Postwar Hollywood seemed the creation of a malicious screenwriter who harbored a grudge against the movies. While most of the country was ready to savor prosperity, movieland languished in the doldrums. In 1947, 90 million Americans went to the movies each week; by 1950 it was half that, with 3,000 theaters closing by the summer of 1951. Television was the reason, and Hollywood fought back: CinemaScope, VistaVision, and Todd-AO expanded the screen to gargantuan proportions, each claiming a better image. Cinerama surrounded the audience, using broad, curved screens, three projectors, and stereophonic sound. In 1952 audiences peered through red-and-green Polaroid glasses at their first 3-D production, *Bwana Devil.* That film was quickly followed by other grade B movies in which everything from spears to rockets seemed to leap from the screen. But Cinerama was limited to the few theaters that could afford the expensive equipment. And it didn't take long for people to joke that 3-D stood for "Dead, Dead, Dead."

The good news in the movie business was the advent of the drive-in. Some 2,000 opened between 1947 and 1950. Teenagers swarmed to these "passion pits," which also drew families seeking informality and a good bargain. From the comfort of their automobiles, moviegoers cringed as biological aberrations lurched and slithered across the screen

Playing a second-rate club singer, Marilyn Monroe sings "That Old Black Magic" in the 1956 adaptation of William Inge's play Bus Stop.

◄

James Dean was an icon of disaffected youth. This shot is from Giant *(1955), which costarred Rock Hudson and Elizabeth Taylor, and was completed only a week before his death.*

in horror pictures, many of them inspired by the nuclear arms race: *The Fly, The Creature From the Black Lagoon, Them, The Thing, The Blob* (versus Steve McQueen). Some science fiction fantasies, such as *Destination Moon*, thrilled audiences with special effects; others, like *The Day the Earth Stood Still* and *The Invasion of the Body Snatchers* won critical praise and developed cult followings.

The studios unleashed a parade of big-budget extravaganzas as well. Henry Fonda, Audrey Hepburn, and an army of extras reenacted Napoleon's retreat from Russia in *War and Peace*. David Niven globe-trotted in *Around the World in 80 Days*. Charlton Heston, as Moses, led his people out of Egypt in *The Ten Commandments,* a Cecil B. DeMille production. Critics may have panned the epics, but audiences flocked to them.

A cluster of young movie actors, including Kirk Douglas, Gregory Peck, William Holden, Paul Newman, and Richard Widmark, joined Spencer Tracy, Humphrey Bogart, John Wayne, and other established stars in the Hollywood firmament. And a new breed of leading man, restless and tormented, came to the screen. Montgomery Clift made his acclaimed debut in *The Search* (1948). Marlon Brando reprised his Broadway role in *A Streetcar Named Desire* (1951), then turned in an Academy Award–winning performance in *On the Waterfront* (1954). James Dean established the archetype of the troubled teen in *East of Eden* and *Rebel Without a Cause,* both released in 1955, the year he died, at 24, in a car accident.

This scene between Burt Lancaster and Deborah Kerr broke Hollywood taboos. From Here to Eternity (1953) *won the Academy Award as did the film's supporting actors, Frank Sinatra and Donna Reed.*

While female stars of the 1930's and 1940's, such as Joan Crawford, Katharine Hepburn, and Myrna Loy, continued to make box office magic, younger actresses rose to stardom: 13-year-old Elizabeth Taylor in *National Velvet* (1945); Grace Kelly in *High Noon* (1952); Natalie Wood in *Rebel Without a Cause* (1955); Doris Day, an audience favorite, in *The Man Who Knew Too Much* (1956) and *Pillow Talk* (1959); Kim Novak in *Picnic* (1956); Audrey Hepburn in *Roman Holiday* (1953), for which she received an Academy Award; and the inimitable Marilyn Monroe in *The Asphalt Jungle* (1950), *Gentlemen Prefer Blondes (*1953), *How to Marry a Millionaire* (1953), and *Some Like It Hot* (1959). But, for sheer Hollywood, nothing could beat the fancy stepping of Gene Kelly, Debbie Reynolds, Donald O'Connor, and Cyd Charisse in *Singin' in the Rain* (1952).

Movies were not all glamour and glitter, however. The studios also made well-crafted films dealing with serious issues. Elia Kazan exposed anti-Semitism in the film version of Laura Z. Hobson's *Gentleman's Agreement* (1947). John Ford's western *The Searchers* (1956) examined bigotry, too. And a number of movies, among them *The Caine Mutiny* (1954) and *Bridge on the River Kwai* (1957), took a hard look at military ethics.

◀ *Robert Mitchum starred as a psychopathic preacher in* The Night of the Hunter (1955), *the only film directed by Charles Laughton.*

▼ *Clad in black leather and jeans, a brooding Marlon Brando plays Johnny, leader of a gang of motorcycle hoods, in Stanley Kramer's 1954 production* The Wild One.

NEW MAGIC ON OLD BROADWAY

The stage was bursting with talent of every kind. Composers, lyricists, and choreographers recreated American musical theater, and gifted playwrights woke up Broadway with brilliant dramas.

The New Haven tryout looked like a disaster. "No Girls, No Gags, No Chance!" grumbled one New York critic. So much for quick judgments. At opening night on Broadway, as the soaring cadences of "Oh, What a Beautiful Mornin' " swept over the audience, everyone knew that *Oklahoma!* was something extraordinary. Richard Rodgers and Oscar Hammerstein II, two old pros now working together for the first time, had achieved an almost operatic fusion of song and story. Dances by newcomer Agnes de Mille flowed into the action with amazing grace. The result was pure, jubilant enchantment. *Oklahoma!*, which opened in 1943, was still lifting the nation's spirits more than 2,200 performances later.

The golden age of American musical theater had arrived. Rodgers and Hammerstein made magic again in 1945 with the musical drama *Carousel.* Then came *South Pacific,* with a dozen hit tunes and a provocative May-September pairing of Mary Martin and Metropolitan Opera star Ezio Pinza. Rodgers and Hammerstein went on to create *The King and I,* among other works, and in 1959 *The Sound of Music,* their final show together, opened.

Other Broadway veterans picked up the new operettalike style. Irving Berlin wrote his most brilliant score for *Annie Get Your Gun* (1946), thus allowing Ethel Merman to blast her way to superstardom. Cole Porter, brushing up on his Shakespeare, chimed in with *Kiss Me, Kate* (1948). Some remarkable new talents caught fire. Alan Jay Lerner and Frederick Loewe unrolled their first Broadway hit in the Scottish mists of *Brigadoon* (1947), then soared into box office heaven with *My Fair Lady* (1956). Who could resist the courtly Rex Harrison, as speech professor Professor Henry Higgins, teaching Julie Andrews's cockney Eliza Doolittle to say "The Rain in Spain Falls Mainly in the Plain"? *My Fair Lady* charmed Broadway audiences through an aston-

Composer Richard Rodgers (above) and librettist Oscar Hammerstein (top) teamed up on nine Broadway musicals, including South Pacific *in 1949. Based on a book by James Michener, it starred Mary Martin as navy nurse Nellie Forbush, shown here romping through "Honey Bun" at a talent show.*

Demanding "Shall We Dance?" a puckish Yul Brynner, as ruler of old Siam, attempts a waltz with Gertrude Lawrence in The King and I *(1951). It was his first Broadway show and her last.*

ishing run of 2,717 performances. And composer Leonard Bernstein joined 27-year-old Stephen Sondheim to create the riveting music and lyrics for *West Side Story* (1957).

Serious drama flourished, too. A long-silent Eugene O'Neill — not a word since winning a Nobel Prize in 1936 — returned to the stage in 1946 with *The Iceman Cometh.* Set among the patrons of a seedy bar, the play heralded the last, strongest phase in the career of America's greatest playwright. Eleven years later, the posthumous production of O'Neill's *Long Day's Journey Into Night,* based on his own tormented family, would win a Pulitzer Prize.

Fresh dramatic voices gained attention. Arthur Miller made his Broadway debut in 1947 with *All My Sons,* then followed it in 1949 with *Death of a Salesman,* a work so powerful that the first-night audience refused to leave the theater. Everyone seemed to know Willy Loman, a huckster down on his luck, and his fall from grace hit hard. Miller's harrowing look at the dark side of the American dream won a Pulitzer Prize. His next play, *The Crucible*

▲ **In a balletic rumble in West Side Story, *two street hoods fight over a woman. Jerome Robbins's choreography won high praise from critics.***

▼ **Brutal and passionate, a 23-year-old Marlon Brando torments Jessica Tandy in A Streetcar Named Desire, *an emotion-packed drama by Tennessee Williams (inset).***

(1953), focused with the same gritty realism on the notorious witch trials of colonial Salem. No one missed the grim parallels with Senator Joe McCarthy's anti-Communist crusade (see pp. 272–273).

Another major new talent dealt in bittersweet flights of fantasy and pathos. Tennessee Williams burst into the limelight in 1945 with *The Glass Menagerie,* about a widowed mother thinking back to the "gentleman callers" of her Southern girlhood and about her crippled, withdrawn daughter. The narrator, Tom Wingfield, sets the tone: "Yes, I have tricks in my pocket, I have things up my sleeve. . . . I give you truth in the pleasant disguise of illusion."

Illusion dominated Williams's next triumph, *A Streetcar Named Desire* (1947). Marlon Brando, young and unknown, played the brutish Stanley Kowalski, who assaults and crushes the forlorn pretense of gentility indulged in by his sister-in-law, Blanche DuBois. Blanche's passionate credo might belong to all the defeated dreamers of Williams's plays: "I don't want realism. I want magic. Yes, yes, magic!" *Streetcar* won Tennessee Williams his first Pulitzer Prize; a second came in 1955 for *Cat on a Hot Tin Roof.*

The list of distinguished American dramatists was growing substantially. Carson McCullers won praise for the 1950 stage adaptation of her novel *The Member of the Wedding.* William Inge hit Broadway with *Come Back, Little Sheba* and earned a Pulitzer Prize for *Picnic.* And Archibald MacLeish, taking inspiration from the biblical Job, penned the 1958 verse drama *J.B.,* also winning a Pulitzer.

▲ **At a moment of crisis in Death of a Salesman, *Lee J. Cobb, as despairing Willy Loman, confronts his wife (Mildred Dunnock) while sons Biff and Happy (Arthur Kennedy and Cameron Mitchell) look helplessly on.***

Sputnik Beeps a Challenge

As America answered the Soviet success with its own satellite, Wernher von Braun promised that space travel would "free man from . . . the chains of gravity," opening to him "the gates of heaven."

After the Soviets launched the world's first artificial satellite (model at left), Premier Nikita Khrushchev crowed that in the near future the U.S.S.R. would be "turning out long-range missiles like sausages."

On Friday, October 4, 1957, at the Baikonur Cosmodrome in Kazakhstan, U.S.S.R., a rocket engine gave off a shattering roar. "And then suddenly came a bright light," reported an eyewitness. "Flames burst from the launch pedestal . . . and slowly and confidently the white body of the rocket moved upwards."

Driven into the sky by 264,000 pounds of thrust and trailing a fiery plume, the rocket penetrated the blackness. Within minutes, it had streaked to more than 500 miles above the earth's surface and was speeding around the planet at an average velocity of 17,896 miles an hour. Suddenly an aluminum sphere, just short of 2 feet in diameter and weighing slightly more than 184 pounds, separated from the rocket's third and last stage. Four antennas whipped out from its surface. Two radios clicked on, emitting a steady beep . . . beep . . . beep. The sphere, dubbed *Sputnik* (Russian for "traveling companion"), began to circle the earth. The shiny Soviet "moon" had become our planet's first artificial satellite.

That evening in the United States, the event became real for millions of Americans as the chirping of *Sputnik* interrupted their favorite radio and television programs. The first reaction was shock, and then anger and fear set in. Senator Stuart Symington sounded an alarm. "The recently announced launching of an earth satellite by the Soviets," he warned, "is but more proof of growing Communist superiority in the all-important missile field." If the Soviets could send a satellite whirling around the world, could they not use the same technology to deliver a nuclear bomb to a

U.S. city? Concern increased when, just a month later, the Russians launched a much larger satellite, *Sputnik II*, carrying an 11-pound dog, Laika. Senator William Fulbright expressed his conviction that far more than the launch of satellites was at stake. "The real challenge we face," he said, "involves the very roots of our society. It involves our educational system, the source of our knowledge and cultural values."

Some observers, including President Eisenhower, downplayed the significance of Russia's achievement. "One small ball in the air," the president scoffed, "something that does not raise my apprehensions, not one iota." The chief of naval operations belittled *Sputnik* as "a hunk of iron almost anybody could launch."

But an anxious American public sought answers to two simple questions: How did the Russians get ahead of us? How can we catch up?

Dr. Wernher von Braun, the former technical director of wartime Germany's rocket program, and now chief of development at the U.S. Army Ballistic Missile Agency at Huntsville, Alabama, provided some answers. He assured Americans that the problem had to do with timing, not lack of talent: "We could have done what they did if we

▲
Uncle Sam tries to recover his balance as Sputnik I *whizzes overhead in* The Detroit Free Press *cartoonist Frank Williams's depiction of the impact of the Russian satellite on American scientific pride.*

▼ *By sending a living mammal, the dog, Laika, into orbit, the Soviets gave a clear indication that they were getting close to manned space flight.*

Flying saucer sightings, which began in the late 1940's, fueled interest in UFO's (unidentified flying objects). This comic book purports to give documented proof supporting claims of extraterrestrial visitations on Earth.

FLYING SAUCER ENCOUNTERS

O n June 24, 1947, Kenneth Arnold, a businessman and trained pilot, spotted "saucerlike things ... flying like geese in a diagonal chainlike line" as they approached Mount Rainier. By the end of the year, hundreds of sightings had been reported, marking the dawn of an era of "flying saucers." The U.S. Air Force, responsible for investigating each event, concluded that most of the phenomena were either man-made or of natural origin. But there were some that the air force could not explain. At various times during the summer of 1951, science professors at Texas Tech observed lights in the sky over Lubbock. A local teenager even managed to photograph some of them. In July 1952 an air traffic controller in Washington, D.C., saw mysterious blips on his radar screen coming from the sky over the White House and near Andrews Air Force Base, a report confirmed by at least one commercial pilot.

Books, movies, comic books, tabloids, and TV shows featured tales of alien encounters. An "abductee" named Buck Nelson, who claimed to have traveled to Mars, the Moon, and Venus, sold $5 packets of hair taken from a 385-pound Venusian dog. In the California desert, George Adamski met a blond long-haired creature from Venus called Orthon, who made him "feel like a child in the presence of one with great vision and much love. ...." Howard Menger told *Tonight Show* viewers he had been born on Saturn and later cut a record called "The Song From Saturn."

Believers gave various explanations as to why aliens would wish to visit Earth: the explosions of the atom and hydrogen bombs, Communists in league with extraterrestrials, and after 1957 the threatened invasion of the aliens' territory by space satellites. Many charged that the air force was covering up data that proved UFO's existed. With no hard, irrefutable physical evidence, the debate over the existence of UFO's continued as the 1950's drew to a close.

James Van Allen looks on (inset, below) as Wernher von Braun explains the workings of the Jupiter-C rocket, which got the U.S. space program on track with Explorer *(right).*

started in 1946 to integrate the space flight and missile programs." Sensing the country's impatience, President Eisenhower authorized the launching of a U.S. satellite as soon as possible. Two efforts went full speed ahead, one by the navy's Vanguard team and the other by Von Braun and the army's Jupiter-C team.

On the morning of December 6, 1957, Americans flicked on their TV sets to watch the Vanguard missile launch the nation's first satellite, at Cape Canaveral, Florida. Kurt Stehling, the propulsion engineer, described what happened next: "It seemed as if all the gates of hell had opened up. Brilliant stiletto flames shot out from the side of the rocket near the engine. The vehicle agonizingly hesitated a moment, quivered again, and in front of our unbelieving shocked eyes, began to topple."

But the U.S. space program didn't collapse. Von Braun's Jupiter-C rocket lofted the little *Explorer* satellite into orbit on January 31, 1958. Although it weighed in at just over 30 pounds, *Explorer* delivered a hefty dividend. As it soared to a height of more than 1,500 miles, physicist James Van Allen monitored the number of electrically charged particles encountered in outer space. Abruptly the signals stopped. The instrument had become overloaded as it passed through areas of space thick with charged atoms. No one had guessed that such bands, which came to be known as Van Allen belts in honor of their discoverer, existed.

By July, Congress had set up the National Aeronautics and Space Administration (NASA) to plan and execute space exploration, and within a year, NASA named seven men America's first astronauts. Congress also passed the National Defense Education Act to enrich the nation's pool of quality scientists and teachers and to make the United States, if not first in space, best in space. The beep, beep of *Sputnik I* had turned out to be a wake-up call.

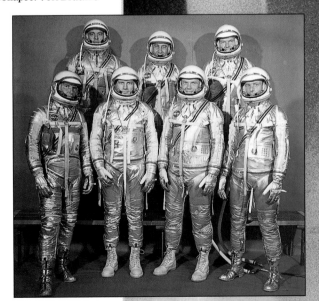

In 1959 NASA named its first astronauts (clockwise from back row, left): Alan Shepard, Virgil Grissom, Gordon Cooper, Scott Carpenter, John Glenn, Donald Slayton, and Walter Schirra.

LIVING ON THE BRINK OF WAR

According to John Foster Dulles, the defense policy under Eisenhower gave America "a bigger bang for a buck."

The key strategy of brinkmanship meant the United States would risk war if an adversary refused to back down.

When this photo of Ho Chi Minh was taken in May 1954, he had defeated the French at Dien Bien Phu, ending an eight-year war that had cost 400,000 lives.

President Eisenhower welcomes President Ngo Dinh Diem of Vietnam for a state visit in May of 1957. The United States had helped install him and backed him for the next eight years.

After the defeat of Japan in World War II, the French were ready to reclaim their holdings in Southeast Asia. But they were not prepared for the redoubtable Ho Chi Minh, leader of the nationalists in French Indochina. Ho appealed to the United States for military support and aid, which were granted in 1945. But after China and the Soviet Union recognized Ho's government, American support for him became impossible.

Instead, Presidents Truman and Eisenhower both provided military aid to the French forces fighting the Vietnamese rebels and found they had backed a loser when Ho won a decisive victory at Dien Bien Phu in 1954. That same year the Geneva Accords were signed. Laos and Cambodia were given their independence, and Vietnam was divided in half, with the Communists taking power in the north and Prime Minister Ngo Dinh Diem's non-Communist government controlling the south. Elections were scheduled for 1956 to decide who would govern a united Vietnam, but they were never held. Diem, fearing a Communist victory at the polls, canceled the election and staged his own rigged balloting in its place. He laid claim to 98 percent of the vote.

In Saigon, his capital, Diem faced a chaotic situation, with various religious, political, and criminal factions plotting against him. He unleashed a repressive crackdown on his enemies, while local Communist sympathizers, known as Vietcong, launched a terrorist campaign to oust him. President Eisenhower refused to commit U.S. troops on a large scale, but he did send a number of military advisers to aid the Saigon government. Most Americans had never heard of Vietnam, but Washington policymakers saw it as a crucial piece in a geopolitical puzzle. Eisenhower's support was based on the domino theory, which he first described in a 1954 news conference. "You have a row of dominoes set up, you knock over the first one, and what will happen to the last one is the certainty that it will go over very quickly. So you have the beginning of a disintegration that would have the most profound consequences."

As Eisenhower wrestled with the tangled situation in Vietnam, another crisis flared up in Asia. In September 1954 Chinese Communist troops began to shell offshore islands held by Chiang Kai-shek's forces. Fearful that this provocation could escalate into full-scale war, Eisenhower, through diplomatic channels, made it clear to Mao Tse-tung that the United States stood ready to use nuclear weapons if necessary. The shelling stopped, and an uneasy peace settled over the troubled rim of the Far East.

Eisenhower's primary concern, of course, was the worldwide spread of communism. By the late 1950's the reins of power in the most powerful Communist country had passed to the hands of stout, pudgy-faced Nikita Khrushchev. Khrushchev was a tough, shrewd former coal miner who seemed to offer a refreshing change from the arctic chill of the Stalin era. In the summer of 1955, Khrushchev, then the head of the Communist Party, and President Eisenhower met for the first time when the first summit conference since World War II convened in Geneva. Khrushchev set the tone as he announced, "Things are different now," but it was Eisenhower who made a startling proposal. Saying "I have had enough of war," he offered to have the United States and the U.S.S.R. trade a "complete blueprint of our military

Secretary of State John Foster Dulles had to maintain a delicate balancing act in foreign policy, as shown in this 1954 cartoon from The Washington Star.

▼ Nikita Khrushchev, here addressing the National Press Club in 1959, was the first leader of the Soviet Union to visit America.

The 1956 uprising in Hungary, led by civilians and some factions within the army (left, an armed girl on patrol; above, insurgents aboard an army tank), was doomed once the Soviet Union invaded with force.

ALASKA AND HAWAII MAKE FIFTY STRONG

America's 27th flag was first raised at 12:01 A.M. on July 4, 1960, at Fort McHenry National Monument in Baltimore, Maryland.

The Cold War dominated American foreign policy, but it had an effect on one area of domestic politics that few had anticipated.

Hawaii had become an American territory in 1900; Alaska, in 1912. By the early 1950's both had been petitioning for statehood for many years without success. Since 1912, when Arizona and New Mexico became the 47th and 48th states, respectively, no new state had been admitted to the Union.

Arguments against statehood for Hawaii and Alaska ran that the two territories lay outside the contiguous 48 states and at a great distance from them. Alaska's population was small, and its economy weak; Hawaii's racially mixed population raised unfounded fears among some Americans that Hawaiians would not be loyal to the United States. Partisan politics also figured in the slow move to statehood: Hawaii was traditionally Republican; Alaska, Democratic.

But by the late 1950's, most of these objections had become moot. With the advent of the commercial jetliner, the problem of distance became considerably less relevant. The partisan politics issue could be settled by linking the admission of the two territories: Republicans in Congress would vote in favor of Alaskan statehood if fellow Democrats could be counted upon to vote for Hawaii. Alaska's economy was on the upswing, boosted by the construction of an extensive Distant Early Warning System along the Bering and Arctic

The post office issued each of these seven-cent airmail stamps within moments of the proclamation of statehood for Alaska and Hawaii.

coasts. And a Senate review of Hawaii's qualifications for statehood, conducted in the early 1950's, had concluded: "If the ultimate test of loyalty and patriotism is willingness to fight and die for one's country, then Hawaii has nobly met this test." Furthermore, World War II had made clear the geographical importance of Hawaii and Alaska, and Cold War defense considerations mandated a strong military presence in both areas.

After winning congressional approval in June 1958, Alaska became the 49th state on January 3, 1959. President Eisenhower signed the proclamation and unveiled a new flag — to become official on July 4 — featuring the traditional 13 stripes and 7 staggered rows of 7 stars in each row. (Ike confessed he preferred another design, one with 9 rows of stars, alternating 5 and 6 stars to a row.) On August 21, 1959, Hawaii was admitted as the 50th state. The new flag, reconfigured to accommodate Hawaii's star, now displayed 9 staggered rows alternating 6 and 5 stars each, and it became official the following July 4.

Alaska joined the Union as the largest state. At 591,000 square miles, it is twice as big as Texas and nearly one-fifth the size of the entire United States. With the smallest population of any state, Alaska was entitled to one representative. All of its first congressmen were Democrats.

Hawaii, with some 6,400 square miles, ranks 47th in size. Hawaiians surprised some political pundits by electing a Democrat and a Republican to the Senate and a Democrat to the House of Representatives (Daniel K. Inouye, a World War II combat hero).

establishments, from one end of our countries to the other, as a prelude to disarmament." To police the agreement, he suggested that both the Soviet Union and the United States open their skies to aerial photography.

The Russians did not accept the "open skies" proposal, but the conference ended on a note of goodwill between the superpowers. Not every American official, however, shared the optimistic spirit of Geneva. Just a few months after the summit conference, the hard-line Secretary of State, John Foster Dulles, gave an interview to *Life* magazine describing his strategy of creative confrontation with the Soviets. "You have to take chances for peace, just as you have to take chances in war," Dulles said. "The ability to get to the verge without getting into the war is the necessary art . . . if you are scared to go to the brink, you are lost." But in an era when war meant worldwide nuclear destruction, the concept of brinkmanship was a chilling one. Ignoring Dulles's bellicose stance, Khrushchev stunned the Soviet Union and the world by declaring that war between Communist and capitalist nations need not be inevitable; it was possible for the two sides to enjoy "peaceful coexistence."

Khrushchev had welcomed a warming of relations between the United States and Russia, but his speech had other, unintended results. His denunciation of Stalin caused hopes to soar in the Eastern European countries under Soviet domination; but when a more liberal regime gained power in Hungary, Khrushchev crushed it. The Western world, whose sympathies Khrushchev had so adroitly secured, was repelled by photographs of Red Army tanks rolling through the streets of Budapest. Thousands of Hungarian citizens were killed during three days of street fighting in November 1956. Eisenhower and Secretary of State Dulles had backed off from giving the Hungarians U.S. military support once the Soviets invaded.

A Series of Crises in the Middle East

On October 29, 1956, Israel invaded the Sinai Peninsula in an effort to expand its security zone. Two days later, France and Great Britain bombed military targets in Egypt and sent in troops to regain control of the Suez Canal, which Egyptian leader Gamal Abdel Nasser had nationalized. President Eisenhower, who had not been contacted before the incidents, demanded that the forces be pulled out. Recognizing a rare opportunity to divide the North Atlantic Treaty Organization (NATO) allies, Khrushchev threatened to launch missiles against Britain and France if their troops were not withdrawn. Yielding to pressure from Eisenhower and the U.N., the British, French, and Israelis pulled out, but the diplomatic turmoil lasted for weeks, offering the world a nerve-racking demonstration of brinkmanship.

The next summer the Middle East flared into crisis again. Iraq's King Faisal II was assassinated by military officers who objected to their country's ties to the West. Neighboring Jordan and Lebanon feared similar coups. In a show of force, Eisenhower sent the Sixth Fleet to the Mediterranean. The marines landed in Lebanon, where they remained for a few months without major incident.

Communism Strikes Closer to Home

In Cuba, just 90 miles from Florida, a young nationalist named Fidel Castro formed a band of guerrillas and ousted the corrupt dictator Fulgencio Batista in January 1959. Many Americans viewed Castro's takeover with favor and elevated him to the status of folk hero. The U.S. government initially supported Castro, but relations deteriorated rapidly as he stepped up his anti-American rhetoric and moved increasingly to the left.

The closing months of Eisenhower's presidency were haunted by a confrontation with the Soviets. Since 1956 the CIA had been flying reconnaissance missions over the Soviet Union. U-2 planes, capable of flying at altitudes over 220,000 feet, had gathered invaluable intelligence. But on May 1, 1960, the Soviets shot down a U-2 and captured its pilot, Francis Gary Powers. The incident, coming just weeks before a planned summit in Paris, ruined hopes for a productive meeting. A. J. Liebling described the administration's posturing in *The New Yorker:* "After denying we did it, admitting we did it, denying Ike knew we did it, admitting Ike knew we did it, saying we had a right to do it and denying we were still doing it, we dropped the subject." Khrushchev denounced American "banditry" and relished his propaganda triumph.

In his farewell address, Ike wearily confessed to feelings of disappointment. He had kept us out of war, the president said, but a lasting peace was not in sight. He issued a warning: " . . . we must guard against the acquisition of unwarranted influence . . . by the military-industrial complex. The potential for the disastrous rise of misplaced power exists and will persist."

Francis Gary Powers's ID card told the Soviets who he was after they shot down his U-2 plane (below): a U.S. agent for the Defense Department. A Soviet trial (inset) found him guilty of spying and he was sentenced to 10 years in prison.

EPOCHAL FIRSTS IN SCIENCE AND MEDICINE

Who could have guessed in 1946 that the descendants of an electronic behemoth called ENIAC would change the world or that the dreaded poliomyelitis would be banished by a simple inoculation?

◄ *J. Presper Eckert, in the foreground, and John W. Mauchly, behind Eckert, work at ENIAC, the first fully electronic digital computer.*

▲ *By 1959, transistors had made a big impact on the consumer market, most notably inside small, powerful radios that could be carried almost anywhere.*

On February 14, 1946, the War Department unveiled a top secret machine called ENIAC, an acronym for Electronic Numerical Integrator and Computer. Developed to calculate the trajectories of artillery shells, it consisted of 18,000 vacuum tubes and several miles of wiring, weighed 30 tons, and took up 3,000 cubic feet of space. J. Presper Eckert, one of the inventors, predicted, "The old era is going, the new one of electronic speed is on the way. . . ." But the computer would have to be brought down to a manageable size.

The insignificant-looking transistor proved to be the first step in the shrinking process. Bell Laboratories announced its invention in 1948, and by 1954 nearly all hearing aids used the tiny transistor in place of vacuum tubes. Within a few years IBM had built a transistorized computer that was far smaller, and consumed 95 percent less power, than ENIAC. The U.S. government became intensely interested in the promotion of microelectronics after the Soviets launched Sputnik in October 1957. By 1959 Jean Hoerni of Fairchild Semiconductor had devised a transistor that fit on a wafer of silicon crystal, which led to a critical invention for the nascent computer industry: the integrated circuit. The stage was set for the age of computers.

While the electronics industry advanced apace, a series of stunning discoveries was transforming the world of medicine. Every summer, year after year, as the polio season dragged on, newspapers would print weekly tallies of new cases. In 1952 alone the crippling and sometimes fatal disease had struck almost 58,000 Americans, most of them children. Scientists knew that poliomyelitis, also called infantile paralysis, was caused by a virus that attacked the nervous system. What they didn't know was how to prevent or cure it.

In 1954 a vaccine developed by Dr. Jonas Salk at the University of Pittsburgh was tested in a study involving more than 1,830,000 American children. The experiment was rigorously scientific: 440,000 children got the vaccine,

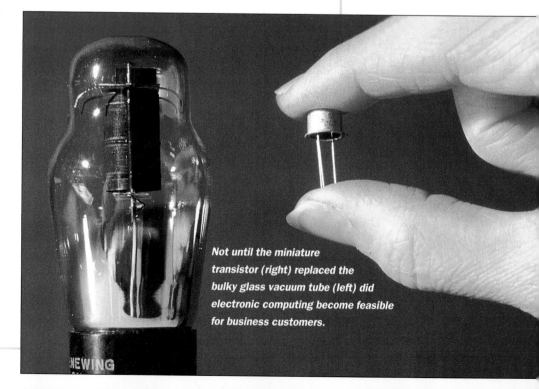

Not until the miniature transistor (right) replaced the bulky glass vacuum tube (left) did electronic computing become feasible for business customers.

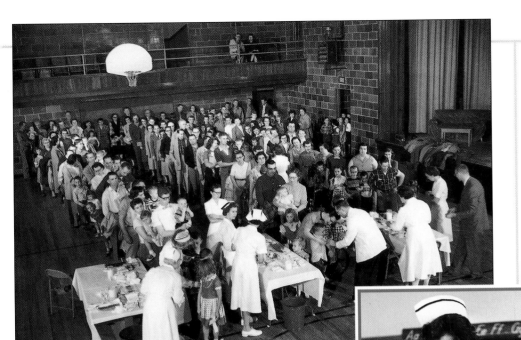

210,000 were injected with a saltwater solution, and a control group of 1,180,000 got neither injection and was simply observed. One participant in the study recounted his experience: "Our teachers marched us into the gym. . . . We didn't know what was going on and most of us were frightened. All we saw were doctors sitting in metal folding chairs and nurses beside them. And then we got our shots . . . [and] a little clip-on badge . . . with two words inscribed on it: 'Polio Pioneer.'" Scientists at the University of Michigan evaluated the test results and concluded, on April 12, 1955,

▲ Dr. Jonas Salk (above) administers polio vaccine to a young Pittsburgh resident. Mass inoculations were sometimes given at high school gymnasiums, such as the one at top in Protection, Kansas.

◄

In 1953 James D. Watson (left) and Francis H. C. Crick illustrate the double-helix structure of DNA with their model. Watson was 25; Crick, 12 years older.

that the vaccine worked. Three years later tests began on an oral form of the vaccine developed by Dr. Albert Sabin.

Important changes were also taking place in the operating room. On May 6, 1953, doctors employed a device during surgery that for the first time took over the work of the heart and lungs. The heart-lung machine, invented by a team headed by Dr. John H. Gibbon, Jr., at Jefferson Medical College in Philadelphia, worked flawlessly.

Studies in Human Traits and Behavior

On April 25, 1953, a team of scientists published the results of its research into the cellular agent responsible for the transfer of genetic traits. They had created a model for deoxyribonucleic acid (DNA), the molecular codifier in the chromosomes, at Cavendish Laboratory in Cambridge, England. The researchers, Francis H. C. Crick and Maurice H. F. Wilkins, both British, and an American, James D. Watson, were awarded the Nobel Prize for physiology or medicine in 1962.

While Crick and his colleagues investigated fundamental components of the cell, another biologist looked into a basic aspect of human behavior: sexuality. Whether Dr. Alfred Kinsey's books on the sex lives of American men (1948) and women (1953) qualified as science or, as many Americans thought, guides to depravity was a hotly debated topic of the times. In *Sexual Behavior in the Human Female*, Kinsey described his work as showing simply that no individuals or couples are identical in their sexual behavior. Louis B. Heller, a congressman from Brooklyn, New York, questioned the value of Kinsey's studies and demanded that the books, which he condemned as obscene, be barred from the mails. Clyde Kluckhohn, a Harvard University professor, thought otherwise: "This book makes an enormous contribution . . . to our knowledge of sexual behavior . . . it is science, serious science." Though Kinsey originally intended his work to be read by physicians and

Dr. Alfred Kinsey

other professionals, hundreds of thousands of ordinary people bought the books, making them bestsellers and opening the way for the frank discussion of human sexuality.

▶ *Flamboyant tail fins, enormously popular and certainly the most eye-catching feature of postwar car styling, served no functional purpose.*

▼ *America's love affair with the road led to a demand for convenient travelers' accommodations. In the 1950's motels more than doubled in number. The sign below marks a Houston motel complex.*

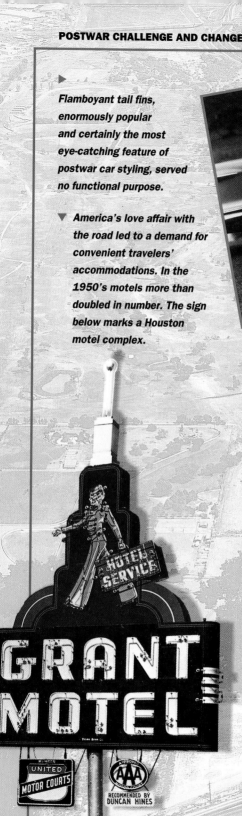

For '59...only Plymouth wagons g...

FOR THE MOTORIST, MORE OF EVERYTHING

Towering fins and acres of gleaming chrome; the throaty purr of a 300-horsepower, high-compression V-8; the elegant lines and nimble cornering of a ragtop sports car — the automobile was the winged chariot of postwar prosperity, a one-way ride to the good life.

The United States emerged from World War II in a deep state of vehicular withdrawal. Gas rationing had curtailed travel, and the conversion of the auto industry to war production had cut the manufacturing of cars from 3.8 million in 1941 to just 84,000 in 1945.

But the good news was that Americans at war's end had money to spend — $100 billion in wartime savings — and when automotive production resumed, they went on a big-ticket buying spree. Spurred by urban flight, rapid population growth, advertising, and easy credit, the annual sales of passenger cars grew to 7.9 million in 1955, the apogee of the postwar boom. By the end of the decade, 77 percent of all American households owned at least one car.

General Motors led the pack, accounting for about half of all passenger car sales, with Ford and Chrysler trailing. By 1955 one-sixth of the gross national product was directly linked to the manufacture, sale, and maintenance of automobiles.

The new cars were longer, wider, and more powerful than ever before. They bristled with technical innovations, such as power steering and brakes, automatic transmis-sions, high-compression engines, padded dashboards, and fiberglass construction. Radios and air-conditioning be-came standard features on many luxury cars. In spite of 5 million annual road accidents, safety did not seem to be an issue with buyers. Tail fins reached ludicrous dimensions, and designers piled on the chrome and air scoops. One industry official remarked that "a square foot of chrome sells 10 times more cars than the best safety door latch." Some models, such as the '53 Corvette and the '57 Chevy, set industry standards for design and engineering. Others did not fare so well.

Named after one of Henry Ford's sons and unveiled with great fanfare in September 1957, the 1958 Edsel was a hodgepodge of bewildering technology, bizarre looks, undistinguished performance, and pointless detail. It lasted a mere two years.

The Edsel was the victim of its own hype, but it also represented, in the words of *Time*, "the classic case of the wrong car for the wrong market at the wrong time." By 1957 the economy had slid into recession, and America's love affair with the gas-guzzling behemoth, which averaged

o many luxury features...and low price,

▲ Aimed squarely at the young family, an advertisement in the November 17, 1958, issue of Life magazine features the latest-model Plymouth station wagon. By the end of the decade, the major car companies directed the largest part of their advertising budget to spots on television.

just 12 miles per gallon, had soured. Reluctantly, domestic manufacturers turned to smaller models. In the meantime, imports had arrived. By the end of the decade, many American families were choosing a lighter, more economical import as a second car. The Volkswagen, a surprisingly efficient import from Germany, established a loyal following, despite general moaning over its peculiar appearance. One thing the VW had going for it was price: $1,300, well below the average American car price of $1,900.

In spite of record auto sales, America's roads were in bad shape, making long-distance travel by car no journey for the frail or timid. Congress stepped in and, under the Interstate Highway Act of 1956, provided for the construction of 41,000 miles of divided expressways. By far the largest public works project ever attempted, the interstate system linked coast to coast and city to city. Americans by the thousands responded by loading up the family station wagon and heading for the open road.

New facilities sprang up catering specially to the motorist. In place of the clusters of tiny cabins and roadside camps that had accommodated travelers in the past came

sleeker, more comfortable motels, with swimming pools and roomside parking. Banks, restaurants, and dozens of other businesses instituted drive-through service. In San Bernardino, California, milk-shake-machine salesman Ray Kroc shook up the culinary world when he walked into a thriving hamburger joint owned by two brothers, Maurice and Richard McDonald. Impressed with their assembly-line cooking method, he persuaded them to let him franchise their product; in 1955 Kroc opened his first McDonald's, in Des Plaines, Illinois, and the rest is history.

The expansion of the American automobile culture had wide-ranging effects. It changed the way Americans worked and played, closed the gap between city and country, and tamed, once and for all, the far reaches of the nation. Many debated the wisdom of these changes, but one thing is certain: by decade's end, the automobile had joined the flag and apple pie as quintessential symbols of American life.

In January 1949 the first Volkswagen arrived for sale in the U.S. (top). Nobody foresaw the car's impact on the American auto industry, especially after only two were sold that year. The McDonald brothers opened their first restaurant in 1940. They sold out to Ray Kroc, who built a McDonald's across the street (above, in 1955) and, subsequently, drove the brothers out of business.

THE TIGHT HUG OF TOGETHERNESS

Alternately hailed as golden sanctuaries of family life, and scorned as the ultimate in 20th-century blandness,

the American suburbs of the 1950's have generated both rhapsodic nostalgia and widespread derision.

In a show of hospitality, the civic groups of Fullerton, California, posted the display at left. They hoped to attract clean-cut American families, such as the one portrayed in television's *Leave It to Beaver* (above).

▼ A perfect TV hostess demonstrates Admiral Corporation's Telebar, a 21-inch screen plus the means for entertaining.

The TV sitcom *Leave It to Beaver* each week portrayed a suburban never-never land populated almost entirely by nurturing moms, wise and loving dads, and healthy, well-adjusted children. If this bucolic idyll did not exactly mirror reality, it accurately reflected most Americans' hopes for what life *should* be.

Survey after survey in the 1950's revealed that 75 percent of American adults considered themselves middle-class. Most of them had either just moved to suburbia or wanted to. Residents of the new suburbs tended to be white and between the ages of 25 and 35, with roughly equivalent incomes. They wore similar clothes, drove similar cars, and filled their kitchens with the same array of laborsaving gadgets. The houses on a given street were identical or slight variations on a theme. But in almost every way, suburban life far surpassed the dreams of young couples who had grown up during the hard times of previous eras. To most, conformity did not seem a problem; it was a relief.

McCall's said that adults could find their "deepest satisfaction" by marrying at an early age and rearing large families. Fewer than 1 in 10 Americans polled answered yes to the question of whether "an unmarried person could be happy." A book called *Modern Woman: The Lost Sex* traced every problem, including alcoholism, juvenile delinquency, and war, to neurotic career women. Instead, the media

glorified something called togetherness, which seemed to consist of weekend barbecues, drives in the family station wagon, and hours of fellowship in front of the TV set.

At the heart of suburban culture was a profound change in the ways families organized their daily lives. The growing size of young families, and the close quarters of tract developments, established the idea of "the neighborhood" as an extended, ever-shifting support group. Families were transient: Atlas Van Lines estimated that the average corporate manager relocated 14 times in his career. As a result, suburban mothers relied on one another to help with domestic chores and babysitting. Suburbanites were almost relentlessly social; from PTA to weekly bridge groups to cocktail parties, there was always a reason to gather.

Trouble in Paradise

Although more husbands were helping out with chores and child rearing, by far the biggest change for men was the rise of huge corporations. During the decade, over 3,000 smaller companies were swallowed up by 500 larger ones. By 1959, 200 corporations controlled 50 percent of the nation's business assets. Junior executives disappeared daily into these impersonal behemoths to become nameless, interchangeable cogs in the wheels of progress. If, as *Parents* magazine reported, the 1950's father no longer played the role of a woodshed disciplinarian, most likely he was either still at work or else just too tired.

The "keeper of the suburban dream," said *Time*, was the housewife. Closed out of the well-paying jobs they had held in wartime, and excluded from most professions, women turned their energies to the home, becoming the domestic engines of middle-class life. Throughout the 1950's, only about one-third of the college undergraduate population was female, and even those women who earned degrees hesitated to seek outside careers. At a Smith College commencement, Adlai Stevenson reminded young women of their duty "to restore valid, meaningful purpose to life in the home" and to keep their husbands "truly purposeful."

While most women found happiness as suburban homemakers, some felt bored and isolated, a troublesome response to what, after all, had been billed as paradise. Other cracks began to appear in the smooth countenance of suburban life. Juvenile delinquency was on the rise; even good kids seemed drawn to rebels like James Dean or Jerry Lee Lewis. Alcohol consumption was increasing. As the decade closed, *The New York Times* reported a general restlessness among women, who "felt stifled in their homes." Perhaps that feeling — combined with the economic pressures of the suburban lifestyle — explains why 40 percent of all women over 16 decided to enter the labor force.

SUBTERRANEAN VOICES: THE BEAT GENERATION

While most of the country eagerly pursued the American Dream, a small group of nonconformists was busy running as fast as it could in the opposite direction. These latter-day bohemians saw no particular virtue in politics or current events; most did not bother to read the newspaper, and few owned TV sets. They

Novelist Jack Kerouac

shunned work and scorned middle-class life, preferring to inhabit, as one of them insisted, a netherworld "of dingy backstairs 'pads,' Times Square cafeterias, be-bop joints, night-long wanderings, meetings on street corners ... and the streets themselves."

They were the Beat Generation, so-called by Jack Kerouac, one of their early spokesmen, who probably heard jazz musicians using the term "beat" to mean exhausted or down-and-out. Poet Allen Ginsberg referred to his fellow Beats as "subterraneans."

Out of the Beats' opposition to convention emerged a gritty, experimental new literature. Beat authors liked to shock. They peppered their writings with references to drugs and sex, used obscene language, and borrowed slang from black culture: "hip," "cat," "dig," "square," "bread." Inspired by the fast-paced bebop riffs of saxophonist Charlie Parker, trumpeter Dizzy

Young Beats filled clubs to hear a new sound called bebop, played by innovative jazzmen, like Charlie (Bird) Parker, seen here in 1946.

Gillespie, and pianist Thelonius Monk, they cultivated a hard-hitting, improvisational writing style. "I saw the best minds of my generation destroyed by madness, starving/ hysterical naked,/ dragging themselves through the negro streets at dawn looking for an angry fix ..." began Allen Ginsberg's poem "Howl," which he recited at a San Francisco gallery on October 7, 1955. Jack Kerouac tapped out "spontaneous prose" on a 120-foot roll of Teletype paper to create *On the Road*, a rambling narrative about "the raggledy madness and riot of our actual lives ... the senseless nightmare road." (As Truman Capote later remarked, "That's not writing, it's just ... typing.") Gregory Corso blurted nonsense phrases, such as "Fried shoes. Like it means nothing."

The 1957 publication of *On the Road* brought the Beats major public recognition: the book sold 500,000 copies. The press dubbed them beatniks and mocked their unkempt hair, their sandals and beards, their dark verse and their seedy hangouts. But at least one TV program portrayed a beatnik: *The Many Loves of Dobie Gillis* debuted in 1959 with the scruffy character Maynard G. Krebs, who never uttered a syllable unless he prefaced it with the word *like*.

Publisher Barney Rosset confers with writers (from far right) Allen Ginsberg, Gregory Corso, and Peter Orlovsky at a Greenwich Village party.

Chapter 7

The Clamorous 1960's

A dizzying decade of highs and lows sees triumph and tragedy in civil rights, JFK slain, flower power, Super Bowl I, the ordeal of Vietnam, and men on the moon.

An uncertain Alabama sky silhouettes the voting rights march from Selma to Montgomery in March 1965.

JFK PROCLAIMS A NEW FRONTIER

Kennedy took to the White House the dreams of a new generation, born in the 20th century, and left to posterity a legacy of high hopes and expectations.

Afresh snowfall blanketed Washington, D.C., on the bitterly cold day of January 20, 1961. President Dwight D. Eisenhower, one of the oldest persons to hold the office, stood bundled against the chill air while his successor, John F. Kennedy, took the oath. At age 43, Kennedy was the youngest man ever elected to the presi-

dency and the first born in the 20th century. Tanned and coatless, he addressed the crowd gathered before the Capitol: "We observe today not a victory of party but a celebration of freedom . . . signifying renewal as well as change."

During the campaign Kennedy had promised to pioneer a New Frontier, conquering "uncharted areas of science and space, unsolved problems of peace and war, unconquered pockets of ignorance and prejudice, and unanswered questions of poverty and surplus." Now, in the same ringing tones, he sent a warning to America's Cold War enemies: "We shall pay any price, bear any burden . . . to assure the survival and success of liberty." And he summoned all

John F. Kennedy is sworn in as the 35th president by Chief Justice Earl Warren. Looking on are Jacqueline Bouvier Kennedy; exiting President Dwight D. Eisenhower; Kennedy's vice president, Lyndon B. Johnson; and Eisenhower's vice president, Richard M. Nixon.

When President-elect John F. Kennedy invited Robert Frost to read a poem ("The Gift Outright") for the 1961 inauguration, many felt JFK had magnanimously honored an old poet. To those who admired Frost's work, however, the poet's acceptance was more of an honor for the new president — and Kennedy himself may have agreed.

Frost's poems spoke in a familiar American voice, that of a canny but wondering, God-fearing but skeptical New Englander, if not precisely a nature lover, then a man on intimate terms with nature's kindnesses and cruelties. A student at Dartmouth and Harvard, resident of England for three years before World War I, Frost was not the rustic he appeared to be, though he did own a succession of New England farms. Among his famous lines are "Two roads diverged in a wood, and I — / I took the one less traveled by . . . ." from "The Road Not Taken." He died two years after JFK's inauguration, at the age of 88.

Americans to the cause: "Ask not what your country can do for you — ask what you can do for your country." The audience came to its feet in a standing ovation.

Jack Kennedy had always been close to politics. His mother's father, John F. (Honey Fitz) Fitzgerald, had been mayor of Boston and his paternal grandfather, a Massachusetts legislator. Kennedy's father, the self-made millionaire Joseph P. Kennedy, Sr., served as Franklin Roosevelt's chairman of the Securities and Exchange Commission; in 1937 he was named ambassador to Great Britain.

Born in 1917, the second son in a large Irish Catholic family, Jack was not the obvious choice to inherit the Kennedy legacy. A sickly child, he also had a weak back that would bother him all his life. Nevertheless his cleverness and boundless energy, verging on recklessness, won him many friends. While enrolled at Harvard College, he wrote the best-seller *Why England Slept,* about Britain's unpreparedness for war, which he based on interviews in 1939 with European officials. After graduating in 1940, the 23-year-old Kennedy tried and quit business school, then enlisted as a seaman in the navy prior to Pearl Harbor. Eventually commissioned an officer, he captained *PT-109,* a torpedo boat, in the South Pacific. When, on August 2, 1943, a Japanese destroyer cut his craft in two, Kennedy, towing an injured shipmate, swam with nine other crew members to a nearby island; four days later all were rescued. He was awarded the Purple Heart and the Navy and Marine Corps Medal, and his actions, related in John Hersey's *PT-109,* helped vault him into politics. Recuperating in the United States, he learned that his older brother, Joseph junior, the family's political heir apparent, had been killed on a bombing mission over Europe. Joe senior now shifted his political ambitions to Jack.

In 1946 Kennedy ran for Congress in a Boston district and won handily, thanks to his father's financial backing and the energetic electioneering of the Kennedy clan. Then, in 1952, after three uneventful terms in the House of Representatives, he sought a seat in the U.S. Senate. He ran against the Republican

Joseph P. Kennedy, Sr., with Joe junior and Jack, departs in 1938 for Great Britain, where he served as U.S. ambassador.

Tens of millions of viewers tuned in to watch each of the four televised presidential debates pitting Nixon against Kennedy.

incumbent, Henry Cabot Lodge, Jr., and won by some 70,000 votes while the Republican Eisenhower was winning the presidency in a landslide. Kennedy served on the Senate Labor Committee, the Government Operations Committee (headed by Sen. Joseph R. McCarthy), and on the McClellan rackets committee investigating corruption in the labor unions. In 1955, bedridden after back surgery, he wrote *Profiles in Courage*, a collection of essays on American statesmen who, in times of crisis, put the interests of their country above personal gain. The book won the Pulitzer Prize in 1957. Only 40 years old, Jack had become a national figure. He narrowly lost the vice presidential spot on the 1956 Democratic ticket, but four years later he won his party's nomination for president of the United States.

Kennedy and his opponent, 47-year-old Vice President Richard M. Nixon, stood reasonably close on the issues in 1960, a year when the country enjoyed wide prosperity and faced no international crises. Both candidates took a hard line on communism, stressing the importance of America's economic and military superiority over the Soviet Union; Kennedy charged, however, that under Eisenhower and Nixon the United States had begun to lag behind its great adversary. Both candidates called for civil rights legislation, but Nixon made few overtures toward black voters, while Kennedy actively courted their vote and promised that, as president, he would be their strong advocate.

Narrow Victory, Ambitious Start

The two candidates were tireless, forceful campaigners, effective in their many stump speeches. But the election, close throughout, hinged on a few tense hours in the final weeks, when JFK and Nixon clashed in debates, the first presidential debates ever broadcast live on television and radio. The radio audience judged the debates a draw. But millions of TV viewers came away with a different impression: they saw a calm, confident Kennedy, whom pundits had labeled inexperienced, appear the equal of his seasoned opponent. Nixon, on the other hand, who had refused to wear makeup for the first debate, looked haggard, his face darkened by a five o'clock shadow. But as Election Day neared, many voters wavered: Kennedy's Catholicism left them uneasy. In the end, he won — barely. His margin over Nixon was fewer than 120,000 votes: 49.7 percent of the popular vote to Nixon's 49.5.

Once in office, President Kennedy established his own style of leadership. He assembled a Cabinet drawn from the

Kennedy's attorney general and closest confidant was his brother, Robert.

elite ranks of the academic and business worlds. He named Dean Rusk of the Rockefeller Foundation as secretary of state; Robert S. McNamara of the Ford Motor Company as secretary of defense; McGeorge Bundy of Harvard University as national security adviser; and as attorney general, his brother and campaign manager, Robert. "I don't see what's wrong with giving him a little experience before he goes out to practice law," said Kennedy on the appointment of the 35-year-old Bobby.

This team, skilled as it was, met with mixed results. Congress rejected a number of their domestic initiatives but supported other innovative programs: the Peace Corps sent thousands of volunteers to Third World countries (see box below); the Alliance for Progress sought to ease poverty in Latin America; and in the space race with the Soviets, Kennedy committed the United States to put the first man on the moon (see pp. 320–321).

Kennedy became the first president to hold regular live press conferences on TV. On these occasions he could be witty (upon being informed of a Republican resolution calling him a failure: "I assume it was passed unanimously"), self-mocking (to students working in Washington: "Sometimes I wish I just had a summer job here."); or pointed (how did he view his treatment in the press?: "Well, I'm reading more and enjoying it less"). Few people, even those who disliked his ideas or policies, could help admiring his wit and grace.

The Peace Corps

In early 1960 Congress studied the idea of sending young Americans to developing nations to improve living standards. During a campaign speech in San Francisco that November, John Kennedy proposed a peace corps: "There is not enough money in all America to relieve the misery of the underdeveloped world in a giant and endless soup kitchen. But there is enough know-how and knowledgeable people to help those nations help themselves."

The corps would promote mutual understanding and world peace. The United States also hoped the presence of Americans in the Third World would counter Communist influence there.

On March 1, 1961, shortly after Kennedy took office, he signed the Peace Corps into existence by executive order. His brother-in-law Sargent Shriver was made director. But not everyone shared Kennedy's enthusiasm for the enterprise. Detractors renamed the corps Kennedy's Kiddie Korps; Eisenhower labeled it "a juvenile experiment."

Then, in September 1961, the first volunteers, who averaged 26 years of age, left for their host countries. Eighty men and women arrived in Ghana and Tanganika, now Tanzania, 17 in St. Lucia, and 62 in Colombia. Hundreds of other volunteers were enrolled in eight-week training programs, in which they studied such subjects as Swahili and snakebite treatment.

Peace Corps volunteers Tom Livingston and Georgianna Shine taught in Ghanaian schools. John Arango was sent to Cutaru, Colombia, where he helped reconstruct river wharves, convert a local jail into a health clinic, drain a swamp, and build housing. In 1966 Peace Corps enrollment peaked at 15,550 volunteers serving 50 countries around the globe.

Kennedy's socialite wife, Jacqueline Bouvier, added to the presidential glamour. Her elegantly coiffed hair and stylish outfits, from pillbox hats to A-line dresses, set the fashion for many American women. On a June 1961 presidential trip to Paris, it was Jackie, fluent in the French language and at home in that country's culture, who starred. Clad in a stunning succession of couturier suits, dresses, and ball gowns, her hair done twice daily by France's leading stylist, she was simply *ravissante!*" "I am the man who accompanied Jacqueline Kennedy to Paris," her husband remarked. As for the Kennedy children, photographers found them irresistible: Caroline toddling into the middle of a press conference in her mother's high heels and John-John hiding under daddy's desk.

Some Called It Camelot

Kennedy tastes gave rise to other trends. The clan's mania for sports stimulated a fitness craze. Jack's penchant for James Bond novels made them bestsellers. His partiality for rocking chairs boosted their sales. And when Jackie hosted a TV special, in which she gave a tour of the recently restored White House, over 48 million viewers tuned in.

The Kennedys revived the tradition of White House musicales. Cellist Pablo Casals, violinist Isaac Stern, and others performed for the likes of Robert Frost and André Malraux. One Kennedy guest list included 49 Nobel Prize winners, prompting the president to observe that the event marked "the most extraordinary collection of talent . . . at the White House" since "Thomas Jefferson dined alone." In later years the Kennedy White House was dubbed Camelot.

But the fairy tale was not as perfect as it seemed. America faced troubled relations with some of its neighbors in the Western Hemisphere and also with its Cold War adversaries. The conflict in Vietnam was brewing. And there was talk of Jack's philandering ways. Still, for one brief shining moment — the "thousand days" of Kennedy's presidency — vitality, culture, and wit reigned in the White House.

▲ *A photographer catches John-John playing hide-and-seek under his father's Victorian desk.*

▶

First Lady Jacqueline Kennedy, with children, Caroline and John, Jr., sits for a formal portrait.

▶

Spanish-born maestro Pablo Casals, age 86, takes a bow before the distinguished guests gathered in the East Room of the White House for his cello recital in 1961.

The newly erected Berlin Wall divides a family: A West Berlin couple scale a makeshift ramp to speak with the woman's mother, trapped on the Eastern side. Inset: Improvised gavel before him, Soviet Premier Nikita Khrushchev appears bemused by the response his table pounding theatrics have aroused in the General Assembly of the United Nations.

Hot Spots in the Cold War

Nikita Khrushchev appeared more moderate than other Soviet leaders, but tensions around the globe just worsened. Everywhere Communists took a hard line: Eastern Europe, China, North Korea, Africa.

As the United Nations delegates looked on in astonishment, Soviet Premier Nikita Khrushchev took off his shoe and pounded it vigorously on the table. The gesture was the climax to weeks of theatrics by Khrushchev, from finger shaking to heckling and name-calling. The premier was protesting one delegate's charge that Eastern Europe had been "swallowed up by the Soviet Union," but few doubted that Khrushchev's real aim was to disrupt the proceedings whenever they failed to go his way.

By 1960 Communist right-wingers in the Politburo were pressuring the Soviet leader to reassert Soviet authority in global affairs. Khrushchev heeded the hard-liners in his policy toward Africa, where nations fighting for their independence from Western colonial powers seemed fertile ground for the spread of Soviet influence. The following January Khrushchev announced his "unlimited support" of Third World nations "fighting for their liberation."

But Khrushchev chose Berlin, in Soviet-controlled East Germany, as his flash point. In August of 1961 the Russians erected a concrete and barbed-wire barrier down the middle of the city, cutting the Western sector off from the Eastern zone and obstructing a major escape route for East Germans fleeing the repressive Communist regime. Democratic nations expressed outrage at so blatant an infringement of human rights. President Kennedy visited the wall on the West Berlin side in 1963 and in a moving demonstration of American support for the freedom seekers declared, *"Ich bin ein Berliner"* ("I am a Berliner"). But since he could tear down the wall only by declaring war, it stood as a symbol of the West's helplessness. Kennedy's assassination in the fall of that year (see pages 312–313) cast the nation into weeks of mourning and soul-searching. America's adversaries kept up the pressure everywhere.

Outside the U.S.S.R., the Communist threat presented itself in another ominous form: a mushroom cloud billowing above Lop Nor in the desolate wastes of Sinkiang, China. It was 1964, and Red China had the atom bomb.

▲ The Soviets parade solid-fuel missiles through Red Square on November 7, 1963, during celebrations marking the 47th anniversary of the Bolshevik Revolution. A few months before, the United States, Great Britain, and the Soviet Union had signed the first nuclear test ban treaty.

Two years later dictator Mao Tse-tung incited a movement that would reignite the Communist revolutionary flame in China. Under the banner of the Cultural Revolution, Mao sent forth radicals, among them millions of young people called the Red Guards, to ruthlessly purge China of bourgeois tradition and "corrupt" Western influences. Weddings, funerals, modern art were outlawed; even cosmetics and holding hands were banned. The young fanatics ransacked libraries, burned books, and shut down universities, driving professors into the countryside to perform manual labor and undergo "political reeducation." Most of the middle class was exiled or exterminated. Leaders of the Communist Party's moderate faction were paraded in dunce

◀ *A leader of the paramilitary group the Red Guards rallies supporters in the port of Shanghai in February 1967. Mao Tse-tung's protégés laid siege to many of China's major cities in an effort to set up communes in place of local governments.*

▼ *Bloodied but defiant Czech students wave their nation's flag from atop a Soviet tank in August 1968. Over 500,000 troops invaded Prague, the Czechoslovakian capital, that summer to enforce Leonid Brezhnev's directive reversing the Prague Spring reforms.*

caps before student courts and forced to renounce their deviation from the teachings of Mao. In the grim years of "purification," nearly 500,000 Chinese lost their lives.

But the greatest humiliation to the United States in this Cold War decade came not from China but from China's close ally, North Korea. In 1968 the North Koreans seized the intelligence ship the U.S.S. *Pueblo* as it cruised in international waters off their coast. For almost a year the North Koreans held Capt. Lloyd Bucher and his crew, brutally torturing the men to exact confessions of spying. Some U.S. senators called for military retaliation. Instead, the United States made futile appeals to the Soviet Union and the United Nations to intervene. But not until the U.S. government submitted an official admission of intrusion into North Korean waters and issued an apology were the captives released.

By this time Khrushchev had been unceremoniously removed and replaced by Stalinist hard-liner Leonid Brezhnev. Under the new leader, the Soviets cracked down on nations in the Eastern European bloc that had begun to test the limits imposed by their Soviet masters. Czechoslovakia, led by Alexander Dubcek, was enjoying an unheard-of measure of liberty in political and artistic activity. The new freedoms culminated in the Prague Spring of 1968, a brief interlude when the press went uncensored and students rallied openly for more reforms. In August, Soviet tanks rumbled into Czechoslovakia and silenced the voices of change.

The Six-Day War

In the 1960's hostilities between Israel and the neighboring Arab nations in the Middle East escalated. Commandos from Syria and Jordan mounted an unrelenting barrage of border raids on the Jewish state. Israel retaliated forcefully and, by early 1967, had won decisive victories in battles against the Arab aggressors. Egyptian president Gamal Abdel Nasser ordered United Nations troops to leave the Arab-Israeli border and sent Egyptian troops into the Sinai in preparation for all-out war.

Then, on June 5, 1967, Israel struck without warning. The Israelis wiped out or severely damaged four enemy airfields and annihilated the Egyptian army. They occupied the Sinai Peninsula and annexed the Gaza Strip (Egypt), East Jerusalem and the West Bank (Jordan), and the Golan Heights (Syria).

The Six-Day War dealt a crippling blow to the Arab states. Their ally, the Soviet Union, also suffered a serious embarrassment; but, thanks to Soviet Premier Aleksey Kosygin's first-time use of the hotline to the United States, a superpower confrontation was averted.

▲ *Jubilant Cuban campesinos (farmers) make their way on horseback to a July 26th celebration marking the day in 1953 when Fidel Castro and his followers initiated their revolt. Inset: Nikita Khrushchev and Castro make a show of their mutual support during a 1961 rally in Moscow's Red Square.*

CONFRONTING CARIBBEAN TURMOIL

When Cuban rebel Fidel Castro overthrew Fulgencio Batista in a "freedom coup," many Americans thought they had gained a friend in Latin America. Little did they know Castro would soon align Cuba with their greatest foe.

By 1960 the the situation in Cuba had become deeply troubling: Premier Fidel Castro had seized American-owned oil refineries and businesses, nationalized the country's major industries, and cozied up to the Soviet Union. Soviet loans, arms, and advisers arrived in a steady stream. The same Castro who had once firmly proclaimed, "Power does not interest me" now headed a Communist police state — right on America's doorstep.

Something had to be done. Pres. Dwight D. Eisenhower ordered CIA Director Allen Dulles to secretly train thousands of anti-Castro refugees living in Florida for an assault on Cuba. By March 1961, Dulles was urging the new president, John F. Kennedy, to set loose the clandestine force on the island nation, with the assurance that once the commandos landed, the Cuban people would rise up to throw off Castro's yoke. An uneasy Kennedy gave the go-ahead, but to

At the height of tensions between Cuba and the United States — the 1962 missile crisis — Castro staged a display of Soviet weaponry in his capital, Havana.

maintain the illusion that it was a Cuban-sponsored operation, he ordered: "There will not be . . . any intervention in Cuba by the United States. . . . The basic issue . . . is between the Cubans themselves."

The Bay of Pigs invasion was a fiasco from the start. On April 15, eight B-26 bombers manned by Cuban exiles fired on Castro's airfields, knocking out some planes but leaving key aircraft unharmed and, worse, tipping Castro off to the coming invasion. The dictator swiftly rounded up thousands of suspected dissidents, dashing any hope of a civil uprising. On the night of April 17, 1,400 troops landed on the island. The CIA had led them to expect a smooth landing on a deserted beach; instead, their boats ran aground on coral reefs within sight of a public park. Within 24 hours of the landing, Castro had sent 20,000 Cuban regulars to the area to block the drive inland. The next day four B-26's left Nicaragua for an attack on Castro's forces, but failing to take into account the difference in time zone, the pilots arrived at their targets an hour before their escorts. Castro's jets swatted them down like flies. By nightfall on the third day of the invasion, Castro had won.

"The Other Fellow Just Blinked"

The Soviet buildup in Cuba continued. On October 16, 1962, alarming news reached Kennedy: aerial photographs revealed that the Soviets were installing ballistic missiles on the western side of the island. The missiles could be fitted with nuclear warheads. Wider ranging missiles, spotted two days later, could reach targets as far west as Montana. Were the Soviets, through Castro, planning a secret attack? Thirteen days of crisis ensued. Kennedy called together his closest aides to decide on a course of action — the Soviet missiles had to be destroyed or removed, and promptly — but the president warned: "[Khrushchev] can't permit us to take out their missiles, kill a lot of Russians, and do nothing." Defense Secretary Robert McNamara advocated the use of a naval blockade to force Khrushchev's hand while enabling him to withdraw the missiles quietly.

On October 22 Kennedy apprised the nation of its danger: "The purpose of these bases," he said in a televised address, "can be none other than to provide a nuclear strike capability against the Western Hemisphere." All-out nuclear war suddenly seemed possible. The United States girded itself. The entire fleet of B-52's was sent aloft, the largest ground force since World War II was assembled, and scores

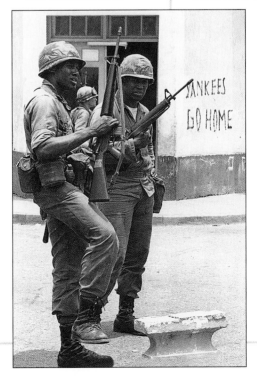

▼ *Determined to prevent "another Cuba," President Johnson sent 20,000 U.S. troops to the Dominican Republic during an outbreak of civil unrest in 1965.*

of warships and air squadrons swept the Caribbean. "I guess this is the week I earn my salary," Kennedy remarked. For four days while the nuclear clock ticked, Khrushchev remained silent. But at sea, Soviet freighters, confronted by the U.S. Navy, stopped dead in the water. "We're eyeball to eyeball," said Secretary of State Dean Rusk, "and I think the other fellow just blinked." Then, late on October 26, a letter arrived from the Soviet leader: the weapons would be removed if the United States pledged not to invade Cuba.

Hours later a second letter demanded the United States remove its own missiles from Turkey, which were within striking distance of the Soviet Union. Kennedy answered the first missive, agreeing to its condition, and ignored the second, and on October 28 Khrushchev promised to remove the missiles from Cuba. This time, Kennedy had won.

Throughout the 1960's, Castro called repeatedly for revolutions in other parts of the Western Hemisphere. Che Guevara, Castro's top lieutenant, roamed Latin America in an effort to ignite civil uprisings without success; in 1967 he and his small guerrilla band were captured by government troops in the Bolivian jungle and Che was killed. The United States refused to abandon its naval base at Guantánamo Bay, on the southeastern shore of the island, and relations with Cuba subsided into a hostile tolerance.

NOVEMBER 22, 1963

It would be a date Americans could never forget: where they were, what they were doing, when the news reached them that President Kennedy had been shot. A nation mourned.

Just after noon on a sun-splashed Friday, President John F. Kennedy's motorcade made its way past cheering crowds along its 11-mile route through downtown Dallas, Texas. So balmy was the fall weather that Kennedy rode in an open limousine, without benefit of the usual protective bubble. Smiling and waving, the president sat in the back seat next to his wife, Jackie, who looked luminous in a pink suit and pillbox hat. Texas Gov. John B. Connally, Jr., and his wife greeted well-wishers from the fold-down jump seats in front.

The presidential caravan glided down Main Street and turned right then left onto a less populated side street. Suddenly, the sharp crack of gunshots shattered the air. Pandemonium set in. Governor Connally collapsed in his wife's lap. "My God, they are trying to kill us all!" he cried, critically wounded in the chest. Jackie reached out to help Secret Service agent Clint Hill clamber over the rear of the limousine as it sped toward the hospital. Police ran toward a nearby grassy knoll, thinking the shots had come from that direction. A bullet had pierced Kennedy's throat and another hit him in the head. Within minutes, a team of doctors at Parkland Hospital was working frantically to keep him alive; miraculously the president showed vital signs. To no avail. At 1 P.M. Central Standard Time on November 22, 1963, a half hour after the bullets had reached their mark, Kennedy, age 46, was pronounced dead.

Soon after the shooting, police had entered the Texas School Book Depository, a building less than 90 yards from the point where Kennedy and Connally had been hit. Eyewitnesses had spotted an armed man in a sixth-floor

On the day he turned three, John junior bade his father farewell at St. Matthew's Cathedral.

One of the last glimpses of John F. Kennedy shows the president, first lady, and Gov. John B. Connally settling into their open limousine for the ride through Dallas.

window of the building. A search turned up a bolt-action rifle fitted with a telescopic sight. One worker was missing: 24-year-old Lee Harvey Oswald, a clerk who filled book orders. Oswald was an ex-marine and a qualified sharpshooter. He had lived in the Soviet Union and championed pro-Castro causes. Within little more than an hour after JFK was shot, police arrested Oswald inside the Texas Theater. He had taken cover there after killing veteran police officer J. D. Tippit, who had stopped him for questioning.

A President Is Buried; Oswald Shot

John Kennedy's lifeless body was transferred to *Air Force One* for the flight back to the capital. Vice President Lyndon Johnson took the oath of office in the plane's cramped quarters before it left the tarmac. Then he turned and gently instructed the pilot, "Let's be airborne."

The plane landed, and the casket was transferred to Bethesda Naval Hospital and then to the White House. The Kennedy family gathered for a private ceremony in the East Room of the White House, where, almost 100 years before, the murdered Lincoln had lain. On Sunday afternoon, a horse-drawn caisson bore the flag-draped casket to the

◄

Citizens line Memorial Bridge to pay their last respects as the caisson bearing Kennedy's casket, followed by a three-mile-long funeral cortege, crosses the Potomac River.

towering Capitol rotunda. An honor guard representing all the armed services kept watch around the catafalque. The Navy Band sounded a heartrending dirge, a measured "Hail to the Chief." Then Senate Majority Leader Mike Mansfield delivered a eulogy, denouncing "the bigotry, the hatred, prejudice, and the arrogance which converged in that moment of horror" to bring the president down. Some 250,000 people waited in line for six or more hours to file past Kennedy's bier as tens of millions more watched the ceremony unfold on television.

Even as Senator Mansfield spoke, Oswald lay dying of gunshot wounds sustained while in police custody. His killer was nightclub owner Jack Rubenstein, known as Jack Ruby, who claimed to be a fierce Kennedy admirer. When Ruby saw "a smirk on [Oswald's] face," he told his brother Earl, he decided to shoot. (Shortly after Lyndon Johnson took office, he named a special commission, under Chief Justice Earl Warren, to look into the Kennedy assassination. The 888-page Warren Report, issued after the commission had spent nearly a year collecting 26 volumes of testimony by 552 witnesses, concluded that Oswald had acted alone in killing Kennedy.)

On Monday morning, the funeral cortege departed from the Capitol Rotunda and proceeded up Pennsylvania Avenue. In a gesture symbolic of the fallen chieftain, a riderless charger with boots reversed in the stirrups accompanied the caisson. Bagpipes wailed, muffled drums resounded. Delegates from 92 nations joined the retinue at the White House and, led on foot by Mrs. Kennedy together with the slain president's brothers, Attorney General Robert Kennedy and Senator Edward Kennedy, continued on to St. Matthew's Cathedral. Richard Cardinal Cushing celebrated the mass and prayed, "May the angels, dear Jack, lead you into Paradise." The procession resumed, passing the Lincoln Memorial toward Arlington National Cemetery. At the grave site, atop a hill overlooking the Potomac River, there were final prayers, the sound of taps, the crash of a rifle volley. The widow accepted the folded flag. She lit the eternal flame and departed. All was silent.

Less than 48 hours after the Dallas police arrested Lee Harvey Oswald (above), he was fatally shot by Jack Ruby. Numerous conspiracy theories have since arisen linking Oswald to an array of groups from the Soviet KGB to organized crime.

Vice President Lyndon Johnson, flanked by his wife and a grief-stricken Jacqueline Kennedy, takes the oath of office before Judge Sarah T. Hughes.

LYNDON TAKES THE REINS

Propelled into the presidency, Johnson struck the theme of continuity: he would advance "the forward thrust of America" initiated by Kennedy. But LBJ set an even greater national goal: to erase poverty altogether and establish the Great Society.

Lyndon Baines Johnson was a six-foot-three-inch-tall tower of contradictions. Sophisticated and vulgar, shrewd and naive — "gentle and solicitous as a nurse" and "as ruthless and deceptive as a riverboat gambler" — he used the full range of his complex character to get things done. Johnson's Texas-style presidency came as a jolt to a nation newly accustomed to the polished demeanor of its assassinated leader. But LBJ's unpredictable behavior rarely hampered his extraordinary effectiveness on behalf of his country.

During a tour of Appalachia, Johnson talks to a destitute coal miner and father of eight in Inez, Kentucky.

A volunteer with the Job Corps shows an Arkansas youth how to operate a lathe.

The son of a hardscrabble Texas rancher and state legislator, young Johnson took on odd jobs as a shoeshine boy and a cotton picker to supplement his family's meager finances. He worked his way through college, taking a year off to teach Mexican-American children. Speaking later of this formative experience, he said: "Somehow you never forget what poverty and hatred can do when you see its scars on the hopeful face of a young child."

Johnson came to Washington in 1931 at age 23 as the assistant to a congressman. Convinced that government should improve the lot of every American, he supported the New Deal policies of President Franklin Roosevelt. "You get yours, he gets his, and we all share" was how one admirer summed up Johnson's personal creed. He returned to Texas to marry Claudia Taylor, known as Lady Bird, and built a political base from his position as head of the state's National Youth Administration. Beginning in 1937, LBJ served for over a decade in the House and then won a seat in the Senate in a runoff tainted by accusations of

With characteristic flourish, LBJ flings the last of 126 pens used to sign the $1.1- billion Appalachian aid bill into law.

fraud; his 87-vote margin earned him the ironic nickname Landslide Lyndon. In 1953 his Senate colleagues made him minority leader, and two years later, when the Democrats gained control of the upper chamber, he became majority leader. Johnson lost the Democratic nomination for president in 1960 to John Kennedy, who then selected Johnson as his running mate.

"An End to Poverty and Racial Injustice"

Catapulted by tragedy into the presidency, Johnson charged into command. He single-handedly broke the congressional logjam that had stymied Kennedy. Using every ploy in his repertoire — cajoling, pleading, bullying — he got Congress to act on stalled legislation. Civil rights were his special concern, and LBJ worked around the clock to persuade legislators to pass a bill, initiated under Kennedy, which had languished in committee for months. "Do you know what it is to be black?" he challenged fence sitters. The trailblazing Civil Rights Act, enacted in July 1964, barred discrimination against minorities in employment and in places of public accommodation, protected voting rights, and made further advances in school desegregation.

In the election of 1964, Johnson thrashed conservative Republican Barry Goldwater, whose hawkish views contrasted sharply with Johnson's more prudent approach to military matters. And whereas Goldwater sought to dismantle domestic programs, Johnson presented a utopian vision of the United States: "The Great Society rests on abundance and liberty for all. It demands an end to poverty and racial

▶ Even after having announced his decision not to seek reelection in 1968, Johnson labored around the clock to carry out his duties as chief executive. Here he "relaxes" in the pool with grandson Lyn and dog Yuki while tending to some presidential homework.

▼ At the 250-acre LBJ Ranch, familiarly known as the Western White House, Johnson entertained dignitaries, met with advisers, and, above all, enjoyed the role of a working Texas cowpoke. Here he ropes and wrangles an obstinate calf.

injustice. . . ." President Johnson surged ahead with his domestic policies, which were rubber-stamped by the heavily Democratic legislature. Congress enacted bills that provided funding to schools serving needy schoolchildren and created the first federal scholarships for college students. LBJ championed measures to accelerate research into life-threatening diseases, and he established Medicare for the elderly.

Under Johnson, new agencies took shape: the departments of Housing and Urban Development and of Transportation, the National Foundation on the Arts and the Humanities, and the Administration on Aging. Nearly a billion dollars earmarked for the Office of Economic Opportunity in its first year alone went to administer the Job Corps, designed to assist the chronically unemployed; Head Start, preschool instruction for disadvantaged children; Volunteers in Service to America (VISTA), a domestic Peace Corps; and half-a-dozen other antipoverty programs.

Johnson presided, all told, over the passage of the most significant legislation since the days of FDR, and over the greatest splurge in domestic spending in the nation's history. Federal expenditures on health, education, and for the welfare and Social Security programs more than doubled in the years 1965 to 1970.

Lyndon Johnson took pride in never retreating: once he had embarked on an undertaking, he saw it through to the very end. He fervently advanced his notion of the Great Society, succeeding to a degree as perhaps no other president could have. But, clear-sighted in his domestic policy, Johnson would lose his way in the twisted labyrinth of the Vietnam War.

" I HAVE A DREAM . . . "

By the reflecting pool of the Lincoln Memorial, on August 28, 1963, civil rights supporters assemble to hear Martin Luther King, Jr. (right) deliver his "I have a dream" address. In 1964, at 35, Dr. King became the youngest recipient of the Nobel Peace Prize.

Martin Luther King, Jr., called upon civil rights workers to "stir the social conscience of . . . the nation." And they did — through sit-ins, Freedom Rides, registration at all-white schools, and marches.

In February 1960 four black college students seated themselves at the whites-only lunch counter of a Greensboro, North Carolina, Woolworth store. They ignored the hostile looks cast their way and waited all day for service they knew would never arrive. The next day 20 more students joined the 4 at the Woolworth's counter. Within two weeks, sit-ins were being staged in 15 other cities. In Nashville, Tennessee, protests came to a head when a bomb blast destroyed the home of a lawyer who defended sit-in participants. After an estimated 6,000 protesters marched on City Hall, Nashville mayor Ben West ordered the luncheonettes opened to all. By summer's end, blacks and whites ate side by side in restaurants across the South.

In using nonviolent means to bring about change, the students had followed the teachings of Rev. Martin Luther King, Jr., leader of the civil rights movement and head of the Southern Christian Leadership Conference. "Segregation is on its deathbed," King pronounced upon their success.

Segregation was indeed in the throes of death, but it did not go quietly. The next major challenge facing civil

rights workers was to desegregate interstate bus terminals. James Farmer, director of the Congress of Racial Equality, organized the Freedom Rides: a group of volunteers would travel on buses between Washington, D.C., and New Orleans and on the way deliberately disregard signs designating segregated seating and whites-only bus terminal facilities. "We were counting on the bigots . . . to do our work for us," explained Farmer. "We figured that the government would have to respond." The Freedom Riders departed on May 4, 1961. As the journey progressed, antagonism toward them escalated. At first they were taunted, then threatened. In the Deep South violence broke out. An incendiary bomb was tossed into a bus in Anniston, Alabama. A gang of thugs attacked riders in Birmingham. And in Montgomery a mob numbering in the thousands fell on the riders as their bus pulled into the station. The initial Freedom Rides ended in Jackson, Mississippi, but they galvanized other campaigns. By the end of the year, integration came to interstate travel.

Soon another barrier fell, the one barring blacks from entering traditionally white Southern universities. In 1962, James Meredith was blocked from enrolling at the University of Mississippi by Gov. Ross Barnett. After days of confrontation, U.S. marshals were summoned to escort Meredith to the campus. That night full-scale rioting broke out, resulting in two deaths. Only when President Kennedy ordered army troops to the scene did fighting cease. The next year two black students peacefully integrated the University of Alabama

▲ **Little Rock, Arkansas, students do schoolwork during a lunch counter sit-in. Inset: A poster pictures the widow of NAACP activist Medgar Evers, who was killed by a sniper in the doorway of his home in 1963.**

▼ **Flanked by federal officials, James Meredith enters the University of Mississippi campus.**

despite Gov. George Wallace's threat to stand in the doorway himself to keep them out.

The fight against segregation intensified. In the spring of 1963, Reverend King initiated continual demonstrations in Birmingham, Alabama, which he dubbed "the most segregated city in the U.S." The infamous Birmingham police chief, T. Eugene (Bull) Connor, ordered the arrests of hundreds of protesters, including young children and King himself. When, in early May, thousands of demonstrators thronged downtown Birmingham, Connor met them with attack dogs and fire hoses. As the media captured every nasty turn of the confrontation, the King forces gained leverage. Local officials and businessmen finally backed down and agreed to desegregate some public facilities and to hire blacks. A committee was set up to help resolve future problems.

In the Shadow of Lincoln

In August 1963 some 200,000 civil rights advocates, black and white, marched on the nation's capital. "Civil Rights — Now!" "Integrated Schools — Now!" "Decent Housing — Now!" their placards read. Following behind King, A. Philip Randolph, Roy Wilkins, and Whitney Young in the first rank, marchers strode down Constitution Avenue and spilled onto the Mall in front of the Lincoln Memorial. King spoke movingly of his hopes for the future: "I have a dream that one day on the red hills of Georgia the sons of former

▼ **Demonstrators in Birmingham, Alabama, huddle in a doorway against the fierce blast of a fire hose. The water's force tore the clothes off some protesters' backs.**

Black Muslim leader Malcolm X

▼ On March 21, 1965, three thousand voting rights marchers cross the Edmund Pettus Bridge toward the Jefferson Davis Highway, leading from Selma to Montgomery. Inset: A young supporter at a California rally.

slaves and the sons of former slaveowners will be able to sit down together at the table of brotherhood . . . that my four little children will one day live in a nation where they will not be judged by the color of their skin, but by the content of their character." The audience answered in chorus to his freedom call. Orderly to the end, they filed into the night.

The Voter Registration Drive

Black voters had long been discriminated against in Southern states, where literacy tests and poll taxes discouraged most of them from registering and racist intimidation kept others away from the polls. During Freedom Summer in 1964, organizers initiated an all-out effort to register black voters in Mississippi. Fifteen volunteers were killed. But it was the murders in June of two white Northern volunteers, Andrew Goodman and Michael Schwerner, and a black Mississippi resident, James Chaney, that shocked the nation most. The three disappeared shortly after their car was stopped for speeding. Their lifeless bodies were found weeks later.

The very week of the murders, a 75-day filibuster in the U.S. Senate was broken, and on July 2 the Civil Rights Act of 1964, the most comprehensive such legislation in U.S. history (see p. 315), was signed into law by President Lyndon Johnson. The federal government now stood four-square behind the fight to end racial discrimination. "Stronger than all the armies is an idea whose time has come," said conservative Illinois Senator Everett Dirksen.

By early 1965 Reverend King decided the time was ripe to dramatize the push for black voter registration and to muster support for a voting rights bill. He chose Selma, Alabama, as the demonstration site, hoping that the strong-arm tactics of Sheriff James G. Clark would bring attention to the cause: "Bull Connor gave us the civil rights bill," explained a King aide, "and Jim Clark is going to give us the voting rights bill." The Selma protesters were viciously attacked and several were killed. On March 15, President Johnson went before Congress to urge passage of a voting rights bill, saying that Selma exhibited "the effort of American Negroes to secure for themselves the full blessings of American life." "We shall overcome," he declared, invoking the battle cry of the civil rights movement. On March 21 some 3,000 protesters left Selma for a 54-mile march to the Alabama capital. Four days later they entered Montgomery, where 25,000 people joined them in a victory rally. That August, Congress passed the Voting Rights Act of 1965.

Days after the Voting Rights Act was signed into law, violence erupted again, this time in Watts, a black neighborhood in Los Angeles. Watts exploded in racial rioting after a black motorist resisted arrest and was shoved into a squad

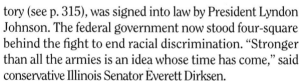

Summer after hot summer, as Dr. King's dream remained unfulfilled, racially motivated violence erupted in America's cities: New York in 1964, Watts in 1965, Chicago, Cleveland, and San Francisco in 1966, Newark and Detroit (left) in 1967. The flames were fanned by militants such as Stokely Carmichael (inset), who, after James Earl Ray shot King in April 1968, told followers, "Get your gun."

After three volunteers for the Freedom Summer black voter registration drive were killed, a new group of recruits signed up for the cause. Above, a student talks to a potential voter.

car; onlookers charged police brutality. Within hours area residents took to the streets; as many as 80,000 rioters went on a spree, torching buildings and looting stores. Some 14,000 national guardsmen helped the Los Angeles police restore order. The violence had exacted a heavy price: 34 persons were killed, 891 injured, and 3,758 arrested.

As racial tensions shifted northward, many inner city blacks rejected the nonviolent strategies of Dr. King for more radical alternatives. The separatist message of the Nation of Islam attracted new adherents: Black Muslims exhorted blacks to found their own schools, businesses, and, ultimately, their own nation. Their most charismatic spokesman, Malcolm X, left the Nation of Islam in 1964 to form his own sect. Then, on February 21, 1965, Malcolm was gunned down, and a more extreme group came to the fore. They were the Black Panthers, headed by Huey P. Newton and Bobby Seale, who armed themselves and provided black communities with "protection" from the police.

On April 4, 1968, the last hope of nonviolence as a tactic seemed all but lost when Dr. King himself was assassinated in Memphis. King, evidently foreseeing his own death, had told his followers: "I just want to do God's will. And He's allowed me to go to the mountain. And I've looked over, and I've seen the Promised Land. I may not get there with you. But I want you to know tonight that we as a people will get to the Promised Land." Through peaceful means King had wrought revolutionary change.

Black Pride: Claiming an Afro-American Heritage

SING of our Race! SING out our Destiny / to your sons, to your warrior sons — in the ghettos, / on the tenant farms, / in the swelling cities by the Western Sea." So the American poet Rolland Snellings (who later adopted the Muslim name Askia Muhammad Touré) celebrated the reaffirmation of black society and culture that took place in the 1960's.

Prominent black leaders sought to establish the unique identity of their communities, apart from the context of white America. Alternatives to the word *Negro* were proposed: *black, Afro-American* — or just *African.* Malcolm X encouraged blacks to follow his example and drop their surnames, which he termed "slave names given by the slavemaster to our fathers during slavery time." And blacks reexamined their heritage and strove for a more vital connection to their African past.

Instead of straightening their hair to conform to white standards of beauty, blacks began to style their hair in Afros or braids and adorn it in African fashion. Many wore African jewelry, headwear, and garments, from *bubas* (scoop-necked dresses) and *djellabas* (flowing robes) to *dashiki* shirts and *gele* turbans. "Black is beautiful" became a theme of the times.

The new sense of pride influenced worship practices. Some blacks turned to African faiths, such as the religion of the Nigerian Yoruba, who recognize over 400 gods and spirits. And in 1966 a black American created *Kwanzaa* (Swahili for "first"), a Christmastime festival during which participants recite African tales, prepare traditional meals, and reflect on guiding principles by which to live.

"ONE GIANT LEAP FOR MANKIND"

"Before the first men tasted time, we thought of you. You were a wonder to us,

unattainable. . . . Now our hands have touched you in your depth of night."

— *American poet Archibald MacLeish, on the Moon landing*

On April 12, 1961, Soviet cosmonaut Yuri Gagarin circled the Earth once and landed safely 450 miles southeast of Moscow, the first human being to orbit the planet. Gagarin's astonishing flight, following as it did on the heels of several Soviet space triumphs, dealt a hard blow to American pride. A month later Project Mercury astronaut Alan Shepard, Jr., rocketed into space for a 300-mile, 15-minute suborbital loop. It was a significant feat for America's space program, but it was a poor second to the Russian's 24,600-mile flight.

Sensing the nation's mounting anxieties about the Soviet challenge in space,

Cosmonaut Yuri Gagarin strapped into Vostok I

Top: Astronaut Edward H. White II, tethered to the Gemini 4 capsule, takes his historic 22-minute walk in zero gravity as the craft orbits Earth on its June 3–7, 1965, flight.

A souvenir "medal," complete with space-suited figurine, commemorated the first Moon landing.

FIRST
MICHAEL COLLINS
EDWIN E. ALDRIN
NEIL A. ARMSTRONG
ON THE MOON JULY 21st 1969

President John Kennedy made a bold promise. He vowed to land a man on the Moon "before this decade is out. . . . No single space project in this period will be more impressive to mankind. . . ." Vice President Lyndon Johnson put his full support behind the president's goal and would continue to do so throughout his own presidency.

Naysayers labeled the Apollo mission to the Moon extravagant, even unattainable. It would cost $24 billion, use the labor of nearly half a million workers, and tie up much of America's scientific brainpower for several years. But Apollo's advocates argued that "whoever controls space may well control the Earth," and the public raised few objections. Led by the National Aeronautics and Space Administration center (NASA) in Houston, the massive program of research, development, and training sped forward.

In February 1962 John H. Glenn, Jr., orbited the Earth three times. Three more Mercury flights followed, and the program was termed a success. "We are through the gates," exulted one Mercury team member.

The next step for the United States was the two-man space shots of the Gemini program. This time an on-board computer calculated many of the spacecraft's functions, from complex maneuvers to reentries. In June 1965 Edward White became the first American to walk in space while James McDivitt took pictures from inside the capsule. White wore a 21-layered "Moon suit." It shielded him from radiation, temperatures ranging from minus 150° to 250° F, and micrometeorites traveling hundreds of times faster than a bullet. A gold-coated "umbilical" cord anchored White to his craft as he moved by the propulsion of a jet gun. The astronaut, exhilarated by his encounter with the infinitude of space, called his return to the module "the saddest moment of my life."

Meanwhile, a Soviet cosmonaut had walked in space three months before White, and the Russians claimed the first woman in space and the first unmanned soft landing on the Moon. But in the mid-1960's Soviet technology reached its limit, and the Russians began to recycle old craft. Still, they kept up a convincing propaganda campaign and, to all outward appearances, remained neck and neck with the United States in the space race.

Barely under way, the Apollo program suffered a terrible setback: in January 1967 astronauts Virgil (Gus) Grissom, Ed White, and Roger Chaffee died in a

Despite an instrument failure, John Glenn (shown prior to suiting up for takeoff) successfully completed his mission.

flash fire that incinerated the interior of their module during a training exercise on the ground. The module design underwent substantial alterations, and in December 1968 *Apollo 8* orbited the Moon 10 times. In May 1969 *Apollo 10* flew to within nine miles of the lunar surface.

The true test came on July 16, 1969. Years of work and billions of dollars had led up to this one flight, *Apollo 11*. The rocket blasted off. Four days later, Michael Collins orbited the Moon in the command ship *Columbia* as Neil Armstrong and Edwin (Buzz) Aldrin, Jr., dropped toward the lunar landscape in the landing vehicle *Eagle*. Pilot Armstrong, realizing the module's automatic navigation was steering them toward rough terrain, seized the controls and touched the craft down safely in the smooth Sea of Tranquillity. "The *Eagle* has landed," he reported back to NASA.

Armstrong emerged from the craft as a television cam-

Buzz Aldrin makes his imprint on the Moon while Neil Armstrong, reflected in Aldrin's visor, takes pictures. Bottom right: Quarantined to be checked for "space bugs," the Apollo 11 astronauts are greeted by President Richard Nixon.

era, mounted on the base of the lunar lander, beamed stunning images back to Earth. When his foot touched the ground, he said, "That's one small step for a man, one giant leap for mankind." In their bulky space suits, Aldrin and Armstrong frolicked like bears, moving strangely in gravity a sixth that of the Earth. They collected Moon rocks, set up experiments for later research, and shed equipment to lighten the return trip. They spoke to President Richard Nixon and then lifted off to hook up with *Columbia*. The astronauts splashed down safely on July 24. Americans were euphoric: less than a decade after humanity's first fleeting moments beyond the safe blanket of the Earth's atmosphere, President Kennedy's promise had been fulfilled.

HORNET + 3

RICH YIELDS FROM SCIENCE

In many fields of knowledge — from astronomy to space technology, aeronautics to marine biology, computers to medicine — scientists made dazzling finds.

Telstar *was the world's first practical communications satellite.*

The 264-pound Tiros I enabled scientists to monitor cloud formations and track cyclones.

Signals from Europe are bounced off Telstar *and* Early Bird *and reach the ear of "Big Horn," a 340-ton antenna in Andover, Maine.*

Almost five years to the day before *Apollo 11* delivered Armstrong and Aldrin to the Moon, Americans got their first close-up look at the lunar landscape. *Ranger 7*, an unmanned rocket, took 4,316 stunning photographs as it approached, and finally crash landed on, the Moon's Sea of Clouds. Another space wanderer, *Mariner 4*, gave a revealing look at Mars in 1965. *Mariner* pictures showed a terrain devoid of higher forms of life, the Martians of science fiction tales. The question of whether simple life could survive the planet's harsh environment remained open.

As spacecraft probed the void, a new generation of astrophysicists explored the cosmos by training their telescopes on distant astral phenomena. In 1963 astronomers at the Palomar Observatory outside San Diego discovered quasars, luminous energy sources at the centers of galaxies billions of light years from Earth. Quasars seemed to provide a tantalizing clue to the origin and destiny of our own universe. In 1967 Jocelyn Bell, a student studying under Antony Hewish at Cambridge University, made another crucial observation: she detected signals coming from pulsars, densely compacted stars (every cubic inch weighs about 10 billion tons) that scientists theorized were formed in the aftermath of the collapse of supernovas.

In the 1960's NASA entered a partnership with industry to come up with practical

▶

These women of Project Tektite II leave their underwater dormitory to conduct experiments in the ocean surrounding St. John, Virgin Islands.

uses for space technology. NASA launched the first weather satellite, *Tiros I*, in 1960. With each 100-minute orbit of the Earth, *Tiros* recorded shifting climate patterns in thousands of overlapping snapshots. The satellite *Telstar* transmitted television broadcasts across the Atlantic Ocean beginning in 1962, the first link in future worldwide communications. And the *Early Bird* satellite, introduced in 1965, greatly expanded the transatlantic telephone network .

Back on Earth, aviation experts devised aircraft that dispatched passengers to their destinations at record speeds. American Airlines inaugurated jet service between New York and California in 1959, cutting transcontinental flight time from eight hours to less than five. The Soviets sent aloft the world's first supersonic transport (SST), the Tupolev TU-144, in 1968. British and French com-

Before it began its test run, the X-15 plane was carried aloft under the wing of a B-52 bomber.

Other vaccines first administered in the 1960's prevented the childhood diseases of measles, rubella (German measles), and spinal meningitis. In the field of obstetrics, doctors used amniocentesis, a procedure whereby amniotic fluid is drawn from the mother's uterus for genetic analysis, to diagnose inherited disorders before a child's birth. And surgeons found an invaluable tool in the laser, which could be used to perform delicate eye operations and to destroy cancerous growths.

The 1960's also saw the federal government's role expand in public health. Congress passed legislation to enforce safety on the nation's highways. The surgeon general's report of 1964, which linked smoking and lung cancer, made an enormous impact over time, convincing tens of thousands of Americans to kick the habit.

From the computer silicon chip, patented in 1961, to the industrial robot, introduced in 1962, science and technology pervaded daily life. The relentless march of progress left some casualties in its path. Power generators produced toxic waste hazards. Residue from pesticides threatened animal life and the food supply. Oil tanker accidents and offshore drilling leaks contaminated beaches. Ordinary citizens were beginning to realize that modern technology had drawbacks as well as benefits. The road to a better tomorrow, it seemed, had some hazardous curves that would have to be negotiated with great care.

panies teamed up to develop their own SST, the Concorde, which made its maiden voyage in 1969 and, within seven years, was shuttling jet-setters and business clients across the Atlantic in under four hours. Among experimental aircraft, America's X-15, equipped with a liquid-fueled rocket engine, achieved mind-boggling speeds of 5,000 miles per hour, seven to eight times the speed of sound.

While aeronautical engineers broke the sound barrier, marine biologists plumbed the depths of the underwater world. President Kennedy's proclamation spurred them on: "Knowledge of the oceans is more than a matter of curiosity. Our very survival may hinge upon it." Fittingly, astronaut Scott Carpenter joined the crew of *Sealab II* to help test man's endurance in water pressures at 200 feet below sea level. The *Tektite I* aquanauts lived for two months in a high-tech laboratory, studying marine life under the Caribbean Sea.

Medical Miracles and Health Warnings

In medicine, too, goals that had once seemed fanciful rapidly became realities. South African doctor Christiaan Barnard performed the first successful heart transplant in 1967. The recipient survived a mere 18 days, but a second transplant patient lived for more than 19 months. By decade's end, 148 patients, including an eight-day-old baby, had received healthy hearts. Victims of coronary artery disease found new hope in the coronary artery bypass operation, a procedure that, by the 1990's, had become more common than an appendectomy.

The crippling disease polio has been almost eradicated in the United States, due in large part to the development of an oral vaccine approved in 1961.

▼ Dr. Christiaan N. Barnard performed the first heart transplant, at Groote Schuur Hospital in Cape Town, South Africa.

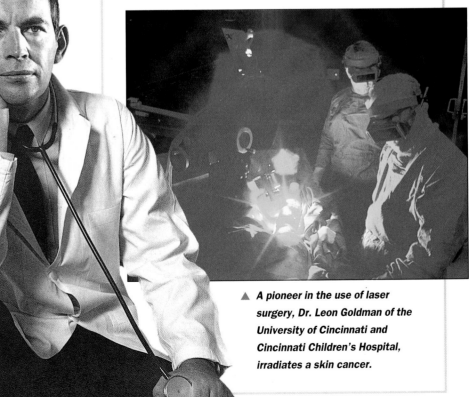

▲ A pioneer in the use of laser surgery, Dr. Leon Goldman of the University of Cincinnati and Cincinnati Children's Hospital, irradiates a skin cancer.

LOOK, KIDS! CRAZY FUN AND GAMES

Before protests, alternative lifestyles, and general rebellion became popular pursuits, some teens spent their after-

school hours doing little more than surfing, skateboarding, cruising, and dancing till dawn.

If youth culture took hold in the 1950's, in the early 1960's it took over. Teenagers looked at the workaday routine of their parents and, finding the older generation wanting, embarked on their own quest for pleasure.

One sign of the times was the surfing craze, with its worship of the deep suntan, the muscled male, the overexposed female ("Itsy Bitsy Teenie Weenie Yellow Polkadot Bikini" was a top song in 1960), and, most important, the cool attitude. Surfing bliss meant to "hang ten" (toes, that is) and "shoot the curl" (beneath the crest of a breaking wave) in Malibu, California; Waikiki, Hawaii; Queenscliffe, Australia — wherever the perfect wave rolled in. Teen idols Frankie Avalon and Annette Funicello starred in movies, including *Beach Party, Bikini Beach,* and *How to Stuff a Wild Bikini,* that glamorized the carefree lifestyle of the beach bum. And music groups such as the Surfaris, the Pyramids, and the Beach Boys — four clean-cut youths with a catchy

California sound — spread the gospel to the rest of the nation in dozens of recordings. "Everybody's going surfing, surfin' U.S.A.," sang the Beach Boys, and land-locked youth donned baggies (loose shorts), Pendleton shirts, and tennies (tennis shoes) and hopped onto asphalt surfers (skateboards) in a simulation of ocean surfing.

When the sun went down, the partying began. Set up a phonograph, get out the record collection, dim the lights, and any teenager could turn the family rec room into a dance floor. Everyone wanted to try out a sexy new step, the twist, popularized in 1960 by singer Chubby Checker on Dick Clark's television show *American Bandstand*. Twisters

▼ **Souped-up automobiles, such as this custom-painted 1933-vintage Ford, were the envy of every hot-rodder.**

▼ **Poster boy Edd "Kookie" Byrnes of the TV program *77 Sunset Strip* sculpts his hairstyle to perfection.**

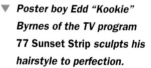

The Beach Boys don Pendleton shirts in the photo shoot for the cover of their first album, Surfin' Safari.

The Barbie Phenomenon

Behind the invention of the first Barbie® doll is the story of a real little girl. Barbara Handler loved dressing paper dolls in cutout clothes. Her dolls weren't the baby-faced innocents usually associated with child's play; instead, they resembled adults and had wardrobes to match.

Barbara's parents, Ruth and Elliot, started the toy company Mattel in 1945. In 1950 Ruth had an inspiration: to create a three-dimensional version of Barbara's paper doll and market it to girls her daughter's age.

Barbie hit the toy stores in March 1959. She was made of vinyl plastic with holes in her feet so she could be propped up on a stand. She came wearing a zebra-striped one-piece bathing suit, over her curvaceous 5¼" x 3" x 4¾" frame, and sported hoop earrings, shoes, and hep cat sunglasses. Her wardrobe boasted 22 outfits, from pedal pushers to a wedding gown.

Little girls adored Barbie and, by 1963, were sending her 500 letters a week. Mattel, Inc. became one of the largest toy manufacturers in the country.

◀

"Grab your board and go sidewalk surfin' with me," sang surf music duo Jan and Dean. In 1965 manufacturers sold $30 million worth of skateboards to avid practitioners of the sport.

▼ *Goldie Hawn, the dizzy blonde comedienne of* Laugh-In *fame, lounges in little more than body paint, a fad made popular in discotheques beginning in the mid-1960's.*

didn't make contact; instead, they gyrated in place as if drying their backs with a towel while rubbing out a cigarette with their feet.

Some "oldsters" expressed horror at the new development. "What has happened to our concept of beauty and decency and morality?" demanded former President Dwight D. Eisenhower. *Time* magazine advanced the theory that twisters might be reenacting "some ancient tribal puberty rite." But the dance quickly caught on with the jet set, and in trendy clubs from New York City's Peppermint Lounge to Whisky à Go-Go on Sunset Strip in Hollywood, hipsters could be seen twisting the night away. Before long, it seemed the entire over-30 crowd had joined the dance mania, co-opting the twist altogether. It was time for teens to take up some new steps. "Anyone who still believes the Twist is in," wrote reporter Gloria Steinem in 1965, "proba-

bly also thinks that a girl is called a 'chick.'" Spin-off dances proliferated: the swim, monkey, pony, the shag, the dog, mashed potato, frug, wobble, watusi, and a dance whose only rule was to follow the beat, the jerk.

The beach and the dance floor were popular spots for meeting and pairing up, but adolescent life still centered around the automobile. The surfer's dream car was the modest woody, an old wood-paneled station wagon. "Revheads" (surfing lingo for people who preferred automobiles to surfboards) lavished attention on their "muscle cars" — Pontiac 409's, Barracudas, Stingrays, Dodge Chargers, Mustangs — the last of the great fuel-guzzlers. They also customized earlier cars, "chopped and channeled" them, "Frenched" the headlights, or "headers," and installed Hollywood mufflers, or "glasspacks," in the exhaust system to give their 400-horsepower engines a throaty roar. Singing groups intoned paeans to the automobile in tunes from "Little Deuce Coupe" to "Hey Little Cobra." In a hit song by Jan and Dean, "The Little Old Lady From Pasadena" drag races through town to a chorus of voices urging, "Go granny, Go granny, Go granny, Go!" In teen paradise the road and the surf beckoned, the sun always shone, and the party never ended.

▶

Dancers contort themselves in the twist. Singer Chubby Checker instructed twisters to take a prizefighter's stance, swivel hips, twist feet, and move the body side to side.

AN EXPLOSION OF NEW SOUNDS

Rock music erupted in the soulful syncopations of the Motor City groups, in the potent voice of folk, and in the harmonies and discordances of the British bands.

With $700 in his pocket and a fervent desire to escape the Detroit ghetto, a young black songwriter named Berry Gordy, Jr., established his own production company, Motown Records. Motown signed on dozens of black artists drawn from the rich pool of talent found in Detroit at the time: The Four Tops, The Temptations, The Marvelettes, Smokey Robinson and The Miracles, Little Stevie Wonder — the list goes on. The Motown look and sound were perfected by The Supremes, three slinky female vocalists, including Diana Ross, whose smooth voices matched their choreographed moves.

Meanwhile, a white entrepreneur, Phil Spector, was at work developing his own unique music — a "Wall of Sound" — by throwing everything from Moog synthesizers to glockenspiels behind his singers. The recording technique would earn Spector a string of gold records and the nickname The First Tycoon of Teen before he hit age 25.

The title song of this 1964 Supremes album topped the Billboard charts for two weeks.

Far from the glitter of Spector and Motown, in the smoke-filled coffeehouses of San Francisco and New York's Greenwich Village, new currents stirred in the countercultural world of folk. The movement started with three clean-cut college boys, the Kingston Trio, whose rendition of the traditional song "Tom Dooley" became a smash. But to many, the pure sound of the solo voice accompanied by acoustic guitar, as performed by Joan Baez, came to epitomize folk and the directness of its message. Baez performed old American songs as well as new tunes, many of them composed by a scruffy young man from Hibbing, Minnesota, named Robert Zimmerman, or Bob Dylan, as he called himself.

▶ **Jimi Hendrix, who died of a drug overdose at 27, wailed out masterful guitar licks.**

▼ **Bob Dylan outraged folk-music purists when he "went electric" in 1964.**

▲ **Listeners loved the velvety tones of Smokey Robinson's Miracles.**

▶ **Beatles Paul McCartney, Ringo Starr, George Harrison, and John Lennon**

▲ Belter Janis Joplin rocked the 1967 Monterey Pop Festival.

▲ Jim Morrison and The Doors evolved a hallucinatory rock style.

▼ Supercharged vocalist James Brown came to be known as the Godfather of Soul.

▼ Aretha Franklin earned the title First Lady of Soul.

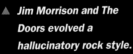

Dylan's lyrics bespoke a growing social consciousness among many of America's youth: "Mothers and fathers throughout the land. . . . Your sons and your daughters are beyond your command." His "The Times They Are A-Changin' " and "Blowin' in the Wind" became anthems for participants in the 1960's protest movement.

Another 1960's rock revolution originated on the other side of the Atlantic, in Great Britain. Growing up in Liverpool, the foursome who would become the Beatles listened to gospel-based styles and the progenitors of rock and roll: singers such as Chuck Berry, Elvis Presley, Buddy Holly, and Little Richard. Then the group, known first as the Quarrymen, began to write their own distinctive music. Upbeat, tuneful recordings such as "Love Me Do" and "Please, Please Me" were early hits in

The versatile group, The Mamas and the Papas, bridged the genres of rock and folk music.

England. With their American tour in 1964, the Beatles, already an international phenomenon, launched a full-scale "British invasion" of the United States. On the heels of the winsome mop tops came the Dave Clark Five, the raw intensity of Britain's Rolling Stones, whose sexually charged performance on the *Ed Sullivan Show* caused the host to apologize for booking them, and then dozens of other English groups, including the Animals, Zombies, Yardbirds, and the Who.

A new generation of American artists met the British challenge. Out of a fertile mix of protest, the folk scene, and the hippie movement arose a slew of fresh groups. They wore rock's antiestablishment uniform of long hair and weird clothing and adopted colorful names, such as The Mamas and the Papas, The Lovin' Spoonful, The Mothers of Invention , The Grateful Dead, and Jefferson Airplane.

Many of the groups used music as a weapon to assault conventional values or to shock. The Doors spun haunting, poetic images in "Light My Fire." Country Joe and the Fish mocked the wages of the Vietnam War with "Feel Like I'm Fixin' to Die Rag." Guitarist Jimi Hendrix twisted "The Star-Spangled Banner" into an electrified scream of protest. Simon and Garfunkel softened the message in "Sounds of Silence": "The words of the prophets are written on the subway walls." Many of the rock artists would burn out, and some died of drug overdoses, but not before they had forever changed popular music.

SUPER YEARS FOR SPORTS

Television, sponsors, team owners, and the athletes themselves discovered to their delight that America's appetite for sports seemed to just grow and grow.

More teams, greater TV revenues, shiny new stadiums — all these fed the sports boom of the 1960's. Major league baseball expanded from 16 teams to 24, professional football from 12 franchises to 26, professional basketball from 11 clubs to 25. TV revenues, boosted by competition among the networks, ballooned. In 1965, for instance, the National Football League (NFL) signed with CBS for $28 million; two weeks later the rival American Football League (AFL) made a deal with NBC for $36 million. Multiuse stadiums, suitable for more than one sport, sprang up in a dozen cities. The glitziest was the roofed, air-conditioned $32-million Houston Astrodome.

Such splendid trappings called for stellar performances, and the decade's athletes responded. In baseball the 1961 season saw New York Yankee Roger Maris, in the last

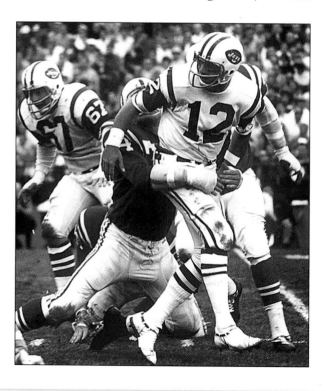

Wilma Rudolph won the Olympic 100- and 200-meter races and the 400-meter relay in Rome.

◄ Cocky Joe Namath (No. 12) "guaranteed" his Jets would beat Baltimore in the 1969 Super Bowl, and they did.

▲ Green Bay coach Vince Lombardi is credited with saying: "Winning isn't everything . . . it's the only thing."

game of the regular season, best the record 60 home runs Babe Ruth had belted in 1927. Maris had a 162-game schedule, compared to Ruth's 154 games, but baseball allowed both marks. The next year Los Angeles Dodger Maury Wills surpassed another immortal's record, stealing 104 bases to eclipse Ty Cobb's 1915 total of 96. Los Angeles Dodgers pitcher Sandy Koufax was a sensation in 1965. Worried before the season that arthritis in his left elbow would end his career, Koufax never missed a start, struck out a record 382 batters, and pitched a no-hitter. St. Louis Cardinals pitcher Bob Gibson compiled a record earned-run average of 1.12 during the 1968 season, the same year Detroit Tigers pitcher Denny McLain won 31 games, a total that some argue will never be matched. Perhaps the decade's biggest baseball surprise was the 1969 New York Mets, a team of no-names that became the first expansion team to capture a pennant; they then won the World Series.

Pro football had fullback Jim Brown of the Cleveland Browns and quarterback Johnny Unitas of the Baltimore Colts. No one man could stop Brown. Said one opposing player after a game: "I made almost as much yardage as he did — riding on his back." Unitas, the coolest of quarterbacks, was famous for engineering come-from-behind wins. Once, after he overcame an earlier 20-point deficit in the last minutes of a game, a rival marveled: "Unitas led his team down the field three times, like a man walking a dog."

Super Bowl I, in 1967, pitted the Green Bay Packers, winners of four NFL titles in the previous six years, against the Kansas City Chiefs of the upstart AFL. The Packers thrashed the Chiefs, 35–10. The result seemed to prove the superiority of the NFL, but two years later quarterback Joe Namath of the New York Jets, dubbed "Broadway Joe" for his showmanship on and off the field, gave the AFL its first Super Bowl win.

College football flourished as well. Attendance topped 20 million in 1960 for the first time, then grew by 1 million annually.

Pro basketball's greatest scorer of the decade was the seven-foot center Wilt Chamberlain, who in 1962 made 100 points in one game, breaking his own record of 78 points. The greatest team, the Boston Celtics, won its eighth consecutive National Basketball Association (NBA) championship in 1966. Undeniably the Celtics had gifted individual players, but they meshed so well that the team was greater than the sum of its parts.

Soon to enter the pros was seven-foot college phenom Lew Alcindor, who, in 1969, led UCLA to its third straight NCAA championship. As Kareem Abdul-Jabbar, he became a major force in pro basketball for almost 20 years.

Led by coach Red Auerbach (above), playmaker John Havlicek (above, left), and superstar center Bill Russell, the Boston Celtics were a well-oiled machine.

Arnold Palmer and Jack Nicklaus, as likable as fierce competitors can be, staged epic battles on the golf links. Arnie won the U.S. Open in 1960, the British Open twice, the Masters four times. The long-driving Nicklaus, then 22, became Palmer's chief rival in 1962, beating him in a play-off to win the U.S. Open. In tennis, Billie Jean King, in 1967, captured the women's singles, doubles, and mixed-doubles titles, both in the U.S. and Britain. And Arthur Ashe, in 1968, won the first U.S. Open. Like many athletes of the 1960's, Ashe quickly learned about product endorsements. "The idea," he confided, "is to have a Coke in one hand, a Wilson racquet in the other . . . when they take my picture."

Americans made their mark on the decade's three Olympics. Among the gold medalists in Rome in 1960 were Wilma Rudolph (photo, preceding page) and Rafer Johnson, the latter in the grueling decathlon. In 1964, in Tokyo, swimmer Don Schollander took four golds. The Mexico City games of 1968 produced another American decathlon winner, Bill Toomey; and discus-thrower Al Oerter became the Olympics' first four-time winner of this event. Reflecting the turmoil of the times, two black American track medalists, Tommie Smith and John Carlos, raised clenched fists on the victory stand in a black power salute to protest racial discrimination at home.

"Float Like a Butterfly, Sting Like a Bee"

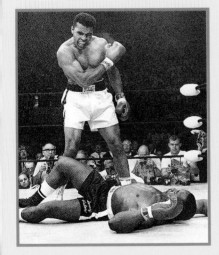

Not a few sportswriters and boxing fans have called Muhammad Ali the greatest heavyweight fighter of all time. Ali agreed, describing himself as "the greatest" and "a man/ With iron fists and a beautiful tan./ He talks a lot and he boasts indeed/ Of a powerful punch and blinding speed."

That kind of unabashed self-promo-

tion got Ali a lot of press coverage and made him enemies as well as friends. From the time, as 18-year-old Cassius Clay, he won the light-heavyweight title at the 1960 Summer Olympics in Rome, there were people who saw him as a loudmouth (Gaseous Cassius) and wanted him humbled. But it would be years before any boxer would humble Ali. After he turned pro in 1960, he won 19 straight bouts, often predicting in what round he would finish off his opponent. He earned the chance to meet the heavyweight champion, the menacing ex-convict Sonny Liston. Before their fight in Miami Beach on February 25, 1964, just 3 of 46 ringside boxing writers picked Clay to win. Clay himself predicted that he would "float like a butterfly, sting like a bee," and knock out Liston in the eighth round. "Round eight to prove I'm great," Clay had announced at the prefight weigh-in. For once Ali had sold himself short. A hurting, bleeding Liston could not

continue after the sixth round. Cassius Clay, at 22, was heavyweight champion of the world.

That same year, Clay made a momentous decision. Changing his name to Muhammad Ali, he became a follower of the Nation of Islam. He went on fighting superbly (defeating Liston again in a rematch, shown at left), but his chosen religion was leading him toward a confrontation that would cast a shadow over his name for many years. On April 28, 1967, in the middle of the Vietnam War, the champion refused to be drafted into the U.S. Army. Though he repeatedly explained (right) that his religion did not allow him to serve, a court convicted him of refusing induction, boxing authorities stripped him of his title, and he was effectively barred from boxing.

Three and a half years later the U.S. Supreme Court reversed Ali's conviction. It took him three more years, but he regained the heavyweight title. If Ali's judg-

ment was often questioned, his courage in the ring was not. In 1975, in the Philippines, he fought Joe Frazier in one of the most brutal bouts in history. Ali, with characteristic rhyming flair, had billed the bout as the "Thrilla in Manilla." He won, but after it was over, reporters asked him to describe the fight. Slowly and gravely Ali responded, "It was next to death."

ALL-AMERICAN FOOD & DRINK

Banana Split
This favorite dessert, with a three-scoop minimum and a reputation as a belly buster, made its appearance around 1920.

Milk
After pasteurization became commonplace around the turn of the century, Americans drank increasing amounts of milk.

Bacon and Eggs
Early risers nationwide hunker down to this rib-sticking breakfast. Pass the jelly and dig in!

Processed Cheese
Gourmets may scoff, but it's an institution in cheese steaks and grilled sandwiches.

Jell-O
Around 1900 a New York cook mixed powdered gelatin, fruit flavors, and sugar and dubbed the "dessert with a wiggle" Jell-O.

Kool-Aid
First available only through mail order in 1914, this number-one-selling powdered soft drink has wet whistles for decades — from thirsty youngsters to parched soldiers in Operation Desert Shield.

When an ice cream vendor at the 1904 St. Louis Purchase Exhibition ran out of serving dishes, a neighboring vendor reportedly gave him a paper-thin pastry rolled into a cone, and the rest is history. An all-time favorite, popcorn, was supposedly brought by a Wampanoag brave to the first Thanksgiving. Peanut butter was originally created by a Missouri doctor as a health food.

Whether stumbled upon by accident or born of entrepreneurial genius, some foods are known the world over as uniquely American. But for every favorite native dish, there is one with a distinctly foreign origin. Pizza, bagels, and chow mein all arrived with immigrants, underwent Americanization, and are now as familiar as southern-fried chicken and corn on the cob. With the influx of newer immigrants from the Pacific Rim and former Soviet-bloc nations, Americans will open their minds and palates and continue to add new tastes to America's cooking pot.

Dagwood Sandwich
Cartoon character Dagwood Bumstead first slapped together his famous snack on April 16, 1936.

Peanut Butter
More than half of America's peanut crop goes to producing the sticky stuff.

Home Canning
Every rural American homemaker knew the secrets of preserving the garden's bounty — using a process developed by a French confectioner to save Napoleon Bonaparte's armies from starvation.

Apple Pie
Eaten plain, deep-dish, or à la mode, it has long been a national favorite.

Turkey
Two truly native Americans, turkey and cranberries, continue to take center stage at Thanksgiving dinners.

Coca-Cola
Concocted in 1886 by an Atlanta pharmacist as a headache tonic, the carbonated, sugared soda won 20th-century popularity as "the pause that refreshes."

A Cavalcade of Confections
The Hershey Bar made its debut in 1894, followed by Cracker Jack (1896), Whitman's Sampler and Life Savers (1912), and M&M's (1941).

Potato Chips
This crispy snack was once called Saratoga Chips, after the resort where it was invented.

Ice Cream
Americans adore it, consuming some 24 quarts of ice cream per person a year.

Frozen Foods
Scientist Clarence Birdseye learned to quick-freeze caribou steaks in Labrador in 1914, thus starting a new food industry.

The Best Spinach You've Ever Tasted
OR DOUBLE YOUR MONEY BACK!

SnowCrop

TV Dinner
The first — this one features chicken parmigiana —appeared in the early 1950's.

Popcorn
Once called "rice corn" or "parching corn," it reigns as the undisputed king of movie-time snacks.

Hot Dogs
Germans brought them over; Nathan's in Coney Island made them famous.

Breakfast Cereal
Born of a health movement begun in the late 19th century, and spearheaded by men like Dr. John H. Kellogg and C. W. Post, cereals like these have endured over the decades.

Post grape-nuts
Natural Wheat & Barley Cereal

WHOLE GRAIN WHEATIES
The Breakfast of Champions

Kellogg's CORN FLAKES
The Original and Best.

French Fries
Called chips in England, and *pommes frites* in France, these sizzly spuds are an American staple.

McDonald's

READER'S DIGEST
LIVE LONGER COOKBOOK
500 DELICIOUS RECIPES FOR HEALTHY LIVING

A Cup of Coffee
A mortar and pestle for grinding coffee came over on the *Mayflower*. Ever since, Americans have been coffee lovers.

Hamburger
Roadside stands helped to popularize this ground-meat sandwich. Give it the works!

Healthy Eating
The news that healthy eating means better living has Americans practicing in their kitchens what the nutrition experts preach.

Whole Grain total
MULTIVITAMIN SUPPLEMENT CEREAL WITH IRON & ZINC
INCLUDES BETA-CAROTENE AS 20% OF VITAMIN A
100% daily allowance of 12 vitamins & minerals

How to Draw

This impish-looking mod sports an op-art miniskirt and matching cap.

Mod, mini, maxi, and more

A spirit of rebellion took hold of the fashion world as a crop of young, imaginative designers disassembled and reinvented the art of dressing.

Fashion started off conservatively enough. Young, demure Jacqueline Kennedy — who as First Lady reportedly spent $50,000 on clothes in 16 months — became the role model for style-conscious women. No rebel, she took her cues from the Parisian couturiers who had long led the fashion world. Her bouffant hairdos, pillbox hats, and sleeveless shifts sent thousands of women scurrying to shops and hairstylists in search of the Jackie look.

Meanwhile, strange things were afoot in London — in the boutiques along Carnaby Street, a little byway off the main shopping artery, and on the King's Road. A new generation of designers, most of them from working-class backgrounds and still in their twenties, was busily rewriting the book on taste.

Mod style turned the world of high fashion on its ear. For the boys, as exemplified by the rock group the Beatles, mod meant high pointy-toed boots, mop hair, lapelless jackets, and stovepipe pants; mod girls wore high-rise hairdos, tiny leather skirts, and fishnet stockings. The queen of mod designs, Mary Quant, set the tone for the decade. "Good taste is death. Vulgarity is life," she proclaimed. What was the point of fashion? Quant summed it up: "Sex." In women's clothing, constraints of every kind were discarded. Bras and slips were out, and girdles disappeared, never to return. Ready-to-wear was in, along with synthetic materials, flashy colors and prints, and rising hemlines (Quant and French designer André Courrèges share credit for popularizing the miniskirt).

The first American designers to enlist in the clothing revolution were a group of young turks operating on the fringe of Seventh Avenue, center of the New York fashion scene: Rudi Gernreich,

A doe-eyed, 91-pound slip of a girl named Twiggy became the modeling sensation of the decade. Born Leslie Hornby in a working-class London suburb, Twiggy turned herself into an industry.

Deanna Littell, Betsey Johnson, and others. The creative force behind the Paraphernalia boutique, Paul Young, heralded the American fashion movement: "Personally, I've always thought anybody who takes fashion seriously is ridiculous. . . . nothing about wearing [clothes] should be taken seriously." Trendy shops offered op-art dresses that oscillated with patterns and swirls; pop-art designs, which

▲ *Diana Vreeland, editor in chief of* Vogue *magazine in the 1960's, readies model Marisa Berenson for a photo shoot.*

▶

The wearer of the bouffant applied liberal amounts of hair spray to keep her elegantly styled coif in place.

borrowed their motifs from the world of popular culture, such as consumer packaging; and outfits made of metal, vinyl, and other industrial and man-made materials. Paraphernalia designer Johnson explained, "It was: 'Hey, your dress looks like my shower curtain!' The newer it was, the weirder — the better."

Men also experienced a fashion emancipation. They began to "do" their hair in expensive cuts, permanents, and blow-dried styles. The traditional tailored shirt underwent

radical change as designers worked in new silhouettes, a bolder palette — shocking pinks, cobalt blues — and wild prints. Jackets came in strange shapes and a wide variety of materials, from velvet to suede. In 1966 designer Pierre Cardin introduced close-fitting, standing-collared Nehru shirts and jackets. The same year, Cardin caused a sensation at his Paris showing when his "cosmonaut" male models walked the runway in helmets and zipped sleeveless jackets over matching turtlenecks. (Cardin had labeled neckties a "very bourgeois idea.") A spokesman for the venerable menswear store Brooks Brothers objected to the idea that the turtleneck might be donned as formal evening wear: "We will not go along with this evening business." But even Brooks Brothers couldn't stem the tide, and soon men's clothes were as outrageous as women's.

Rules remained to be broken. Elisa Stone's fashion workshop hit the cover of *Harper's Bazaar* in August 1967 with a dress composed of transparent theatrical lighting gel. "I loved the idea that my clothes were not going to last," she said. "I thought of them as toys." Giorgio Sant' Angelo created an outfit from corrugated cardboard. Spain's Paco Rabanne used contemporary chain mail. Betsey Johnson's wearable "happening" was a dress made of blotting paper planted with seeds: when watered, it sprouted blossoms. Diana Dew wired her designs with lights and supplied a portable battery pack. Paper and plastic dresses, skirts for men, the neo-Egyptian look, space-age garb — the fashion world had gone completely bonkers.

By the end of the decade, the flea market and the second-hand clothing store had usurped the place of the boutique. Anything could be deemed fashionable as long as it made the wearer feel good. And high fashion, as Coco Chanel once knew it, lapsed into a series of fads that fizzled as fast as they flamed.

▶

Skirts reached near oblivion with the micro; then hemlines fell briefly to midcalf and later dropped to the ground.

◀ *Peggy Moffitt, model and muse for the "farthest out" of American designers, Rudi Gernreich, strikes a theatrical pose.*

LITTLE SCREEN, BIG SCREEN

Keir Dullea starred in the film 2001: A Space Odyssey *as part of a team of astronauts bound for Jupiter.*

Television won viewers with comedies and action-packed dramas. Hollywood fought back

with everything from mature themes to HAL, Julie Andrews, and wide-screen spectacles.

In *The Dick Van Dyke Show, My Three Sons*, and *Hazel*, the 1960's brought television viewers the standard situation comedy set in a loving home. But there was also a new crop of TV sitcoms characterized by far-fetched conceits and wild flights of fancy.

An array of wacky characters crowded the airwaves: *The Beverly Hillbillies*, with its family of unlikely hick millionaires living in a posh California neighborhood; *Green Acres*, about sophisticated city folk transplanted to the sticks; *The Addams Family*, a clan of ghouls who can't understand why they don't fit in; and *The Munsters*, headed by a Frankenstein look-alike and his vampire wife. Witches, genies, and extraterrestrials populated *Bewitched*, *I Dream of Jeannie*, and *My Favorite Martian*. And *Gilligan's Island* stranded on a deserted island a skipper, professor, millionaire couple, movie star, farm girl, and first mate, Gilligan, and

◄

The Clampetts (Buddy Ebsen, Max Baer, Jr., Donna Douglas, and Irene Ryan) struck oil on their Ozarks property and headed west in The Beverly Hillbillies.

never bothered to explain how such a motley group had assembled for a pleasure cruise in the first place. Other shows, like *My Mother the Car, Mr. Ed*, about a talking horse, and *The Flying Nun*, scraped the depths of comedy for entertainment.

TV heroes also took a variety of forms. The physicians on *Dr. Kildare* and *Ben Casey* solved new medical crises each week; on *The Man From U.N.C.L.E.*, spies Napoleon Solo and Ilya Kuryakin fought James Bond style against the evil THRUSH; the crack *Mission Impossible* team never encountered a mission that was. Other programs parodied pop heroes. Maxwell Smart of *Get Smart* bungled his espionage assignments on a weekly basis but always apologized — "Sorry about that, Chief." On *Batman*, the Caped Crusader and Robin protected Gotham City from a cluster of colorful criminals. "SPLATT!" "POW!" "CRUNCH!" flashed on the TV screen as the Dynamic Duo took out the Riddler, King Tut, the Penguin, and other cartoon villains.

The establishment came in for some hard knocks on *The Smothers Brothers* and for more lighthearted jabs on *Laugh-In* (one guest was presidential hopeful Richard Nixon, who asked the audience to "Sock it to me!"). But *Bonanza*, with its homespun philosophy and frontier wisdom, was strictly old-fashioned fare.

As television's small screen came to dominate entertainment, Hollywood mounted wide-screen spectacles — *El Cid* (1961), *Cleopatra* (1963), *The Bible . . . in the Beginning* (1966) — and brought audiences "adult" fare, such as *Butterfield 8* (1960), starring Elizabeth Taylor as a party girl, and *The Apartment* (1960), with Jack Lemmon as a junior executive who lends his apartment to his superiors for trysts.

At the same time, a younger generation of filmmakers was creating an eye-opening alternative to typical Hollywood fare, borrowing technical innovations and themes from such European directors as François Truffaut (*Jules and Jim*), Michelangelo Antonioni (*Blow-Up*), and Jean-Luc Godard (*Breathless*). American Stanley Kubrick directed *Lolita* (1962), based on the Vladimir Nabokov novel about a middle-aged man's obsession with a 12-year-old seductress; *Dr. Strangelove* (1964), a send-up of nuclear war; and *2001: A Space Odyssey*, in which a leading character is HAL, a spaceship computer that develops a mind of its own.

Two Julie Andrews vehicles served as welcome antidotes to other cinematic visions of the 1960's: Mary Poppins *and* The Sound of Music *(right). The latter broke box office records.*

HAL was only one of a vivid assortment of antiheroes who came to the screen: Dustin Hoffman played a success-bound young man who rejects the career track in *The Graduate* (1967); Paul Newman was *Cool Hand Luke* (1967), a convict on a chain gang; Peter Fonda and Dennis Hopper portrayed spaced-out bikers searching for America in *Easy Rider*. Few of the new films stirred up as much controversy as Arthur Penn's *Bonnie and Clyde* (1967), in which a pair of petty Depression-era bank robbers, given glamorous appeal by actors Faye Dunaway and Warren Beatty, embark on a crime spree. Such movies challenged the viewer's outlook in exciting, often disturbing ways.

▲ Adam West played Batman in the comic-book-for-TV classic, which premiered in January 1966. Adults and kids alike enjoyed the program's campy stylishness and its device of casting stars as "guest villains."

◀ Star Trek, with William Shatner (Captain Kirk), DeForest Kelly (Bones), and Leonard Nimoy (Spock), lasted a scant three seasons, but the program made "trekkies" of legions of fans.

Hollywood's memorable treatment of the hippie counterculture, Easy Rider *(1969), made antiheroes and martyrs out of the asocial drifters played by Dennis Hopper (who also directed), Peter Fonda, and Jack Nicholson.*

ACTING OUT, ACTING UP

Executing a sharp left turn, theater roared in with avant-garde riddles, audience participation, and rowdy free-for-alls. Some folks were not amused.

As the 1960's began, Neil Simon put a final polish on his first Broadway comedy, *Come Blow Your Horn,* and a stylish new president took a brief shining moment of inspiration from the tuneful fantasy *Camelot.* A decade later the curtain rose on *Che!,* a 1969 Off-Off-Broadway production advocating violent revolution and featuring live pornography on the public stage. On opening night the entire cast was hauled to the police station on charges of obscenity and public indecency.

The years between saw a progressive drift toward the offbeat, the experimental, the provocative, and the just plain weird. First in the cellars and lofts of Greenwich Village in New York City, then other locales, and finally on Broadway itself, the countercultural turmoil of the times swept through the proscenium arch and exploded onstage.

Much of the excitement arrived from abroad. English playwright Harold Pinter made his American debut in 1961 with *The Caretaker,* a work of ambiguous dialogue and menacing silences. He followed with *The Dumb Waiter, The Birthday Party,* and *The Homecoming,* each sending an eerie existential mood across the footlights. Eugène Ionesco's comic *Rhinoceros* had nothing to do with animals; instead, it was the dark absurdity of human existence that obsessed the author. After his works of the 1950's, *Waiting for Godot* and *Endgame,* in which life's meaninglessness is discussed at length by the characters, Samuel Beckett went on to create *Krapp's Last Tape* and *Happy Days.* One import, *Marat-Sade,* was set inside an insane asylum; as directed by Britain's Peter Brook, it shattered theatrical decorum with two hours of angry, uninhibited mayhem.

At the same time, America spawned a bumper crop of outspoken new talents. Edward Albee's *Who's Afraid of Virginia Woolf?,* an acid-etched portrait of family strife, opened to rave notices in 1962 and helped save an otherwise disastrous Broadway season; a new Albee play or adaptation appeared almost every year thereafter. Bitter send-ups, like

▲ **The cast of Hair, the tribal-love-rock musical that won Broadway's heart, celebrates the joys of youthful rebellion.**

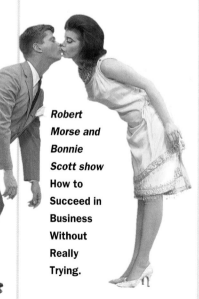

Robert Morse and Bonnie Scott show How to Succeed in Business Without Really Trying.

Carried aloft by his Living Theater troupe, Julian Beck puts a radical spin on Sophocles' classical tragedy Antigone.

Lenny and His Magic Baton

The sedate world of classical music erupted with new vitality. Gleaming concert halls opened in New York, Houston, and other cities. Composers like John Cage and Elliot Carter shattered musical conventions. But no one projected the spirit of the times with more energy and sheer genius than Leonard Bernstein, music director of the New York Philharmonic.

Years earlier, a dashing 25-year-old Bernstein made headlines by filling in for an ailing conductor at Carnegie Hall. The spotlight never left him. He wrote symphonies, operas, and ballets, gave piano recitals, wrote books, lectured at universities, and hosted television shows. People hummed his tunes from *On the Town, Wonderful Town, West Side Story,* and other Broadway shows. When he took over the Philharmonic in 1958, his podium style, full of animated leaps and arm flourishes, fascinated concertgoers. So, to be sure, did his politics: radical chic, as writer Tom Wolfe dubbed them. But his passion for music came through loud and clear, and the public adored him. "It's a great love affair, what's going on out there," he once said, and he was right.

MacBird, a blank-verse parody that heaped ridicule on President Lyndon Johnson, fed a growing appetite for political satire. Black voices began making themselves heard following Lorraine Hansberry's 1959 success with *A Raisin in the Sun.* Poet LeRoi Jones won an Obie award for *The Dutchman.* Actor James Earl Jones gained national acclaim for his portrayal of black heavyweight boxing champion Jack Johnson in *The Great White Hope,* which opened in Washington, D.C., before moving to Broadway.

The most daring productions mixed radical politics with a heady dose of sexual revolution. Spontaneity became the cry as alternative venues, such as Café La Mama in Greenwich Village, pushed the limits of theatrical expression. The actors in Julian Beck's Living Theater took part in sit-ins and antibomb rallies, then romped onstage to shed clothes, shout ritual slogans, protest drug laws, and generally outrage the Establishment. At the Performance Group's *Dionysus in '69,* ticket holders sat on the floor or perched on wooden scaffolding while the cast cavorted about in the nude — a dramatic technique critic John Simon dismissed as "group therapy for actors."

▶ *In* The Caretaker *by Harold Pinter, Alan Bates and Robert Shaw give shelter to a tramp, played by Donald Pleasance. Everyone suffered in the end.*

▼ *The nightclub routines of comedian Lenny Bruce sizzled with angry wit and four-letter rhetoric. Commentator Walter Winchell called him the "man from outer taste."*

Nightclub comedy grew steadily darker. Early in the decade, a gifted pair of Chicago improvisers, Mike Nichols and Elaine May, delighted viewers with ad-lib routines based on audience suggestions. Then came the bitter racial monologues of Dick Gregory, which gave a new sting to "black humor." A TV gag writer named Woody Allen, launching out on his own, dredged up laughs from the murky tides of urban neurosis. Nothing was sacred to Lenny Bruce, who mocked religion, motherhood, the law, and the flag. Arrested repeatedly for obscenity and drug use, he died of an overdose in 1966.

One bright spot continued to illuminate conventional Broadway theater: musical comedy. Perky acting and an inspired story line reaped a 1961 Tony award for Frank Loesser's *How to Succeed in Business Without Really Trying.* Zero Mostel made a hilarious hit of *A Funny Thing Happened on the Way to the Forum.* Carol Channing started belting out the upbeat songs of *Hello, Dolly!,* which opened in 1964 and ran for 2,844 performances. Next came Barbra Streisand as *Funny Girl,* followed by the *Man of La Mancha* galloping in pursuit of "The Impossible Dream." Even when the counterculture invaded, as in *Hair,* the promise of a brighter future, an "age of Aquarius" free from the torments of war and racial strife, shone through. Meanwhile, boy continued to meet girl in *The Fantasticks,* a bit of lyrical whimsy that opened in 1960 at a tiny 152-seat theater in Greenwich Village. It played through the decade and every decade since — America's longest-running show ever.

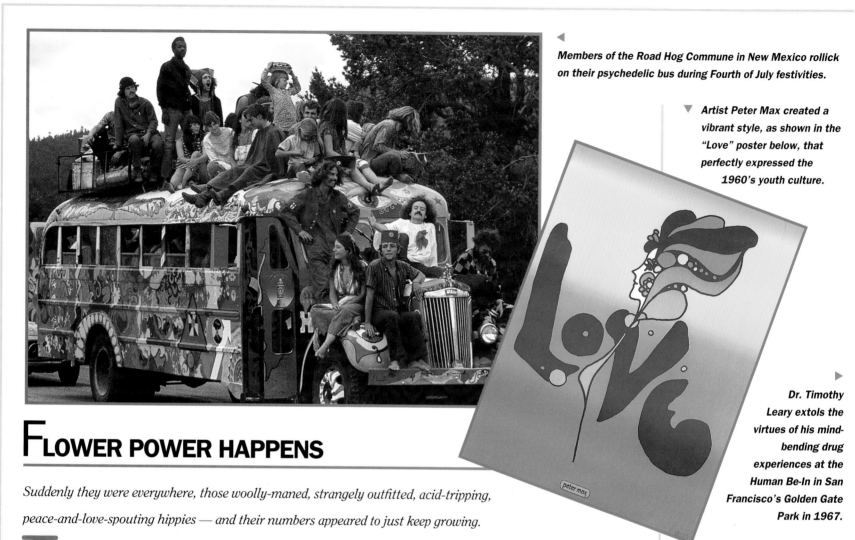

Members of the Road Hog Commune in New Mexico rollick on their psychedelic bus during Fourth of July festivities.

Artist Peter Max created a vibrant style, as shown in the "Love" poster below, that perfectly expressed the 1960's youth culture.

Dr. Timothy Leary extols the virtues of his mind-bending drug experiences at the Human Be-In in San Francisco's Golden Gate Park in 1967.

FLOWER POWER HAPPENS

Suddenly they were everywhere, those woolly-maned, strangely outfitted, acid-tripping,

peace-and-love-spouting hippies — and their numbers appeared to just keep growing.

The gradual creeping of men's hair over the forehead and ears and down the shoulders was perhaps the first sign that the Age of Aquarius had arrived. It started during the presidency of tousled John Kennedy, and before long, mustaches, beards, and long sideburns flourished everywhere. *Life* magazine spotted the culprits: "The Beatles did it!"

The Establishment tried to reverse the shaggy trend. The headmaster of a highly prestigious prep school warned educators: "A sloppy head is indicative of a sloppy mind." A Kentucky father bought his mop-topped son a dog license. In Connecticut a businessman rented a billboard: "Students of Norwalk: Beautify America, Get a Haircut." But what was the use? Even former President Lyndon Johnson grew his hair long once he retired.

By that time, city streets and college campuses were swarming with a new breed of alienated youth called hippies. But hippies were a gentle lot. They pieced together bizarre outfits from clothing items found in secondhand stores, attic trunks, and funky shops: bowler hats, fringed jackets, western boots, bell-bottoms, tie-dyed shirts, Victorian shawls, and army fatigues. And they donned headbands, love beads, peace symbols, and flowers, lots of flowers, tucked behind ears, woven into the hair, crowning their heads.

To some, the blissful, or spaced-out, look typical of the hippie seemed drug induced, and often it was. The future high priest of the drug world, psychologist Timothy Leary, taught at Harvard University in the early 1960's. Then he began to experiment with, and promote the use of the hallucinogen LSD (lysergic acid diethylamide), and Harvard dismissed him. Leary felt LSD had led to his spiritual awakening, and he sought converts.

Buddhist monk Suzuki-roshi taught meditation and founded San Francisco's Soto Zen Center.

Flower child and clothes designer Eileen Levy gathers a hatful of blossoms.

Dr. Leary's Harvard colleague Gunther Weil cavorts in the Berkshire Mountains, MA.

Hippies adhered to Leary's creed: "Turn On, Tune In, Drop Out," or in other words, take drugs, raise your consciousness, and drop out of school, work, society. They drifted, joined communes, and scraped up just enough money and food to survive. They said, "make love, not war," staged "be-ins," "love-ins," and "happenings," and hung out in city parks and on mystical retreats strumming beat-up guitars and intoning yogic chants.

Public reaction to the hippies varied. The old guard tended to agree with *Li'l Abner* cartoonist, Al Capp, who called them a "herd of semi-domesticated animals . . . uttering their mating cries and scratching their pelts." A kinder observer, Bishop James Pike, likened the flower children to the early Christians.

The hippie scene culminated in 1967 with the "Summer of Love" in San Francisco. During the previous decade, the Haight-Ashbury district of the city had become a countercultural mecca for the Beat Generation. Then, in the 1960's, the Haight attracted a huge influx of flower children. The streets teemed with rootless, jobless young people in search of a peaceful, free-form existence. Poets recited their works on street corners. Self-appointed prophets spoke to all who would listen. A charitable farm commune called The Diggers doled out free food and clothing.

As word of the Haight phenomenon spread, the media and tourists descended on the district. Buses ran the "Hippie Hop," taking gawking passengers on "a safari through Psychedelphia, the only foreign tour within the continental limits of the United States." The summer wore on. Strange organizations sprang up, such as the True Light Beavers, who built shrines out of garbage. Souvenir stores and head shops selling drug paraphernalia multiplied.

The situation degenerated further. Squalor set in and crime became rampant. The food supply dwindled, and growing numbers of sick, tired, hungry flower children began an exodus. A feeling of doom befell Haight-Ashbury as "weather prophets" predicted that the Great California Earthquake was coming. The higher hippie ideals of love, peace, and the rejection of materialism had been undermined. It seemed they could survive the real world for only a brief moment.

The Grateful Dead (below) became a musical voice of the peace-and-love generation. The band's house was a major attraction on bus tours of Haight-Ashbury

In the summer of 1969, some 400,000 rock-music fans flocked to a dairy farm in upstate New York for the Woodstock Festival, turning tiny Bethel into the third largest city in the state. The first day the sun shone, then the sky opened up; but the audience stuck it out together through the mud and grime.

VIETNAM BECOMES AMERICA'S BATTLE

Out of the small nation of South Vietnam, prized as a

bulwark against communism in Southeast Asia, grew

a war that would rack the souls of Americans.

In the early 1960's few Americans questioned their nation's involvement in Vietnam. Ho Chi Minh, the formidable Communist leader of North Vietnam, had to be contained. From his capital city of Hanoi, Ho was supporting guerrilla actions in South Vietnam in an effort to reunite the two countries under his Communist rule. Reflecting the United States' view that anything was better than the spread of communism in the region, Vice President Johnson lauded Ngo Dinh Diem, the South Vietnamese president, as "the Winston Churchill of south Asia."

The New York Times warned that the struggle in Vietnam was one "this country cannot shirk." Chairman of the U.S. Joint Chiefs of Staff, Gen. Lyman L. Lemnitzer, predicted that if South Vietnam were to fall, "We would lose Asia all the way to Singapore."

By 1959 the terrorist activities of the Vietcong, a Hanoi-backed guerrilla force composed of Communists, peasants, and opponents of Diem, had escalated into open warfare in some sectors of the South. The United States threw its support behind the South Vietnamese government in Saigon, sending it billions of dollars in aid, military advisers — by 1961 there were 700, by 1962, 3,000, and by the end of 1963, 16,000 — and providing nonmilitary expertise. In 1961 President Kennedy committed the first U.S. troops there,

◄

Vice President Johnson and his South Vietnamese counterpart, Nguyen Ngoc Tho, wave each other's national flag during Johnson's May 1961 visit to the Asian country.

The first U.S. helicopters used in Vietnam were CH-21's, here shown landing to pick up South Vietnamese troops in 1962. Inset: Johnson meets with his top military advisers in mid-1964 at the LBJ Ranch to discuss the deepening commitment of the United States to the conflict in Vietnam.

400 men from the Special Forces group, or Green Berets. But Diem, aware of his pivotal role in U.S. Cold War policy, became "a puppet who pulled his own strings." He and his brothers, including head of the secret police Nhu, along with Nhu's beautiful and imperious wife, ran South Vietnam as a private fiefdom. They jailed opponents, censored the press, discriminated against the Buddhist majority, and handed out patronage appointments to loyal, often incompetent followers.

In 1963, just as Diem had gained the upper hand, Buddhist monks began to stage dramatic protests that included acts of self-immolation. Diem grew increasingly reclusive, and Nhu expanded his influence. Kennedy concluded that America could no longer afford to prop up Diem's doomed administration. With the support of the U.S. government, a junta overthrew the South Vietnamese president that November; he was executed by his captors.

Just a few weeks later, Kennedy himself fell to an assassin's bullet, and Lyndon Johnson became president. At first Johnson took a cautious position on Vietnam. "We don't want to . . . get tied down in a land war in Asia," he assured a crowd during a 1964 presidential campaign stop. But the situation in South Vietnam rapidly deteriorated: the junta that had toppled Diem itself collapsed and was succeeded by a series of short-lived military governments. The Vietcong exploited the disarray in Saigon and extended their control to encompass almost half of South Vietnam.

Then, on August 2, 1964, North Vietnamese patrol boats fired on the U.S. destroyer *Maddox* as it plied the Gulf of Tonkin to conduct surveillance. Two days later sonar technicians aboard the *C. Turner Joy*, which had joined the *Maddox*, reported signals indicating that the ships were again under attack, and a battle with nearby North Vietnamese boats ensued. The alleged second assault by the North Vietnamese induced Johnson to order an immediate retaliatory strike on North Vietnamese torpedo boat bases and oil depots.

On August 4 he took to the airwaves: "Aggression by terror against the peaceful villages of South Vietnam has now been joined by open aggression on the seas against the United States," he declared, and asked Congress to grant

▲ U.S. marines of the 9th Expeditionary Brigade land on Red Beach Two at Da Nang in northern South Vietnam.

▼ Along one thread in the web of ancient trade pathways called the Ho Chi Minh Trail, North Vietnamese trucks transport military supplies south.

him extraordinary powers to take "all necessary measures" in repelling armed attacks against United States forces and to "prevent any further aggression." With only two nay votes, Congress passed the Tonkin Gulf Resolution. The resolution, Johnson exulted, was like "grandma's nightshirt — it covered everything." The military made plans to accelerate the bombing of North Vietnam.

Meanwhile, the guerrilla war heated up. In November the Vietcong struck at an air base in Bien-hoa. The following February they hit a military advisers' camp at Pleiku and, in a matter of minutes, killed 8 soldiers and wounded another 126. "The worst thing we could do would be to let this [Pleiku] thing go by," Johnson told the National Security Council. Bombing raids of North Vietnam, dubbed Operation Rolling Thunder, commenced in March. At the same time, 3,500 marines, the first such U.S. force in Asia since the Korean War, waded ashore at Da Nang to protect the air base there. Soon tens of thousands of U.S. troops, together with South Vietnamese units, would begin a series of joint operations against the Vietcong.

By the spring of 1965, the Joint Chiefs had become convinced that drastic steps had to be taken if the United States was to win the war. They called for U.S. combat

forces, currently numbering 80,000, to be doubled. Johnson summoned his advisers for a conference. Only one, Under Secretary of State George W. Ball, opposed the plan for military escalation. Ball foresaw a possibly disastrous end to the war, in which "the mightiest power on earth is unable to defeat a handful of guerrillas." But Johnson yielded to those who sought to expand the U.S. military role.

Hawks, Doves, and the Tet Offensive

Over the next few years, U.S. aircraft would rain down 800 tons of explosives a day on North Vietnam's bridges, ammunition dumps, and oil refineries. By December 1967, 485,000 American soldiers were fighting in Vietnam and some 1.5 million tons of bombs had been dropped on the North, more than the total tonnage used on the enemy during all of World War II. Beginning with the first major battle, in the Ia Drang Valley in 1965, U.S. forces would win every major engagement of the war, causing heavy casualties among the North Vietnamese and Vietcong. But the Communists displayed remarkable resilience. Ho Chi Minh continually replenished the flow of arms and soldiers south by way of the Ho Chi Minh Trail, a network of pathways twisting through the jungles of Laos and Cambodia. By 1967 some 20,000 North Vietnamese regulars made their way to South Vietnam monthly.

As the United States sank deeper into the Vietnam

conflict, the debate at home grew acrimonious. Senator J. William Fulbright of Arkansas charged that the nation's warmaking was "not living up to [America's] capacity and promise as a civilized example for the world." Johnson shot back, labeling Fulbright and other dissenters "nervous Nellies." Within the Johnson administration, the consensus was breaking down. Defense Secretary Robert McNamara had come to consider the war "dangerous, costly, and unsatisfactory." He would announce his resignation in November 1967 and leave office at the end of the following February.

Moreover, public antagonism toward the war mounted. Americans splintered into "hawks," who favored escalation of the conflict, and "doves," who pressed for a negotiated settlement. The opposition to the war was fed by reports and, more graphically, by images of devastation and carnage in newspapers and on television. College campuses across the nation erupted into antiwar demonstrations (see pp. 347–48). Yet, an opinion poll conducted in December 1967 showed that most Americans wanted to "intensify military pressure within limits and see the war through." And Gen. William C. Westmoreland, the commander of the U.S. forces in Vietnam, offered the public a confident assessment of the future: "We have reached an important point when the end begins to come into view."

In fact, the United States and South Vietnamese forces did have the enemy on the run. Then something happened

▲ *Scenes from a war: The incandescent glow of machine-gun fire streaks the air during a "mad minute" in the Iron Triangle. Insets, left to right: Their village under attack by U.S. marines, a Vietnamese mother and her children flee across a river. Wounded medic Thomas Cole comes to the aid of a fallen comrade. Vietnamese troops take Communists captive in the Mekong Delta, a Vietcong stronghold.*

U.S. marines hurl grenades from Mutter's Ridge during close combat near the demilitarized zone bordering North Vietnam. ▶

that forever changed public perception of the war. On January 31, 1968, during the Vietnamese New Year, called Tet, the Communists seized the initiative. Some 70,000 Vietcong and North Vietnamese regulars lunged at dozens of South Vietnamese cities, up to then spared the onslaught of combat. Just before 3 A.M. in Saigon, a suicide squad blew its way into the U.S. embassy compound, killing some guards. Four hours later U.S. troops secured the area.

From a military standpoint, the Tet offensive could have been counted a failure. American and South Vietnamese forces swiftly restored order in most cities. But Tet galvanized the war's critics. "The terrible quality of the war in Vietnam came home to people," explained Johnson aide Harry McPherson. "It appeared that these guys . . . were never going to quit." On March 31 a distraught Johnson appeared on television to announce he had ordered a partial halt to the bombing of North Vietnam and would offer to initiate peace talks with Hanoi. He would not seek reelection. But the war was far from over. It would take its toll on thousands more brave fighting men before coming to a painful close.

◀ *Lyndon Johnson breaks down after listening to a recording taped by his son-in-law Capt. Charles Robb, describing the horrors he experienced during his tour of duty in Vietnam.*

▼ *Amid a forest laid waste by the Battle of Hill 881 North, Vernon Wike, age 19, tries vainly to save a marine's life.*

▲ *A wounded 12-year-old and her neighbor leave their homes behind as they cross a littered battle site toward a waiting evacuation helicopter.*

South Vietnamese soldiers look on as an area on the outskirts of Saigon goes up in a flames following the Vietcong attack known as the Tet Offensive.

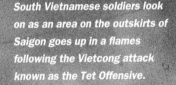

SÀI-GÒN

FERMENT IN THE ARTS

The decade generated writers who delved into the lives of radicals, the ghetto experience, and the minds of criminals, and pop artists who created playful homages to junk food, Brillo boxes, and movie stars.

Though media theorist Marshall McLuhan predicted its demise, the printed word survived, even thrived, during the 1960's. Absurdity and black humor were the hallmarks of a new literature. Joseph Heller's *Catch-22,* whose very title has come to connote a no-win situation, mocked World War II and all war: The antihero Captain Yossarian wants to plead insanity to get out of the military, then learns that, by doing so, he would prove his sanity. Kurt Vonnegut turned science fiction into satire in *Cat's Cradle* and *Slaughterhouse-Five* with a vision of the future world that rivals George Orwell's *1984.* Thomas Pynchon parodied black humor in his first novel, *V.,* a stew of science, politics, pop culture, and philosophy.

The Jewish literary hero, battling angst and his own conscience, gained his voice in the novels of Saul Bellow (*Herzog*) and Philip Roth, whose *Portnoy's Complaint* is a hilarious extended monologue delivered from the psychiatrist's couch. And black writers delineated their experience in autobiographical works, among them James Baldwin's *The Fire Next Time,* about the author's Harlem youth and his encounters with the Black Muslims; *Soul on Ice,* a collection of essays written by Eldridge Cleaver from his jail cell; and *The Autobiography of Malcolm X,* a collaborative effort of Malcolm X and Alex Haley, author of the 1976 bestseller about his African ancestry, *Roots.*

A trio of writers pioneered the "new journalism," a hybrid of reportage and fiction, which bristled with energy. Truman Capote

Writer Norman Mailer

◀

Pop-art guru Andy Warhol and two stars of his cult films, Edie Sedgwick and Chuck Klein, emerge from the underground. Above, one of Warhol's many tributes to the Campbell's soup can.

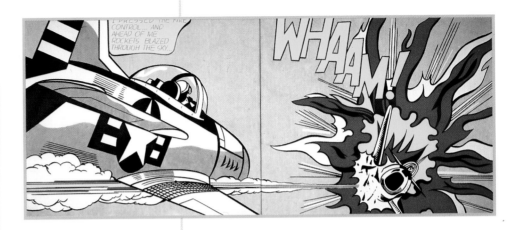

wrote his "nonfiction novel," *In Cold Blood,* in 1966, recounting the horrific tale of two real-life murderers; Norman Mailer vividly described the 1967 antiwar march on the Pentagon in *The Armies of the Night;* and Tom Wolfe chronicled the antics of a band of hippie nomads in *The Electric Kool-Aid Acid Test.*

While several writers took an active role in the events of the day, a group of artists strove to regard their subjects from a remove — the "sublime neutrality" of essayist Susan Sontag. They rejected the action painting of 1950's abstract expressionism and mined popular culture — television, advertising, the consumer market — for new topics. The result was pop art: Andy Warhol's kaleidoscopic images of Coca-Cola bottles, Roy Lichtenstein's magnified comic

Author Susan Sontag

books, and multimedia works such as Robert Rauschenberg's "Monogram," Jim Dine's "5 Toothbrushes on Black Ground," Claes Oldenburg's "Two Cheeseburgers with Everything," and Jasper Johns's "Painted Bronze (Beer Cans)." As James Rosenquist explained: "People looking at my pictures could identify the elements *bam bam bam bam.*"

Pop art enticed the art-buying public, and the market boomed. Original sculptures and paintings commanded record prices, and mass merchandisers joined established

▲ *Taking his inspiration from the pages of action-packed comic books, Roy Lichtenstein painted "Whaam!", now in the Tate Gallery, London.*

▼ *Claes Oldenburg crafted oversized soft sculptures of everyday items, such as restaurant food. Here he props up his giant ice-cream cone, part of a "triptych of edibles."*

auction houses and galleries as sellers of fine art. (Woolworth's offered a work by Spaniard Salvador Dalí for $74,000.) Money flowed into the building and expansion of museums. In 1968 alone, 20 museums opened in the United States, with another 49 under construction.

Art had become big business, and its human subjects and creators, a kind of commodity. Andy Warhol's workshop, The Factory, churned out personalities as well as silk screens. Among writers, Truman Capote and Norman Mailer were known almost as well for their public identities as for their literary output. Capote's black-and-white ball, staged at the Plaza Hotel in New York for 500 of his closest friends, was proclaimed the social event of 1966.

Andy Warhol, the darling of the "beautiful people," defined the pervasive yet fleeting quality of pop fame: "In the future, everybody will be famous for 15 minutes." The fame of Warhol and most of his contemporaries proved somewhat longer lasting.

The vocabulary of pop art was first used in the 1950's to describe artworks such as Jasper Johns's "Three Flags."

This 14-year-old was among tens of thousands of anti-Vietnam demonstrators in New York's Central Park on April 15, 1967.

Free Speech Movement leader Mario Savio speaks with the press at Berkeley in 1964.

▼ Folksinger Joan Baez turned out to sing her support for dozens of causes at hundreds of protests throughout the 1960's and 1970's.

CHALLENGING THE ESTABLISHMENT

The renewed struggle for black civil rights seemed to have a ripple effect. Whether students or pacifists, women or migrant workers, many Americans were ready for a fight against established authority and the status quo.

The employers are going to love this generation. . . . They are going to be easy to handle. There aren't going to be any riots." The speaker was Clark Kerr, president of the University of California system, and the year was 1959. Over the next 10 years, this "easy to handle" generation would assault his university, cost him his job, and shake the nation with waves of protest.

The 1960's were barely a month old when black college students sat down for service at a segregated lunch counter in Greensboro, North Carolina (see p. 316). Nobody could have guessed it at the time, but the lunch counter sit-ins set the tone for the decade. Established authority was in for

some hard knocks, and not surprisingly, young people would do most of the knocking.

It seemed to many adults that students were frequently just looking for an excuse to act up. At the Berkeley campus in September 1964, the university forbade students to make speeches, set up tables, and hand out leaflets on Bancroft Strip, a stretch of sidewalk on college property that was locally famous as a forum for political activity. Students spanning a political spectrum from far left to far right formed what they called the United Front to challenge the university's action. They staged a sit-in at the main administration building, Sproul Hall. Then, led by 22-year-old Mario Savio, protesters renamed themselves the Free Speech Movement and went on agitating.

From the outset Clark Kerr tried hard to calm the turmoil, but he couldn't. Folksinger Joan Baez showed her support for the protesters and delivered stirring renditions of the new anthems of youth and change: songs like "Blowin' in the Wind" and "We Shall Overcome." At one point, as students prepared to take over Sproul Hall again, Baez told them, "When you go in, go with love in your hearts." But there was little love in the hearts of Berkeley police, who roughly dragged the students out.

By the mid-1960's, dozens of colleges, including Yale, Notre Dame, and the University of Kansas, had been hit by demonstrations. Students demanded action on everything from curfew hours and cafeteria food to open admissions policies and revisions in academic programs. Anti–Vietnam War demonstrations, and protests over attendant issues, such as defense-related university research and the presence of military recruiters on campus, escalated along with the war and spilled over into the streets of the nation's capital.

Yippie cofounder Abbie Hoffman

In April 1965, 20,000 students gathered in Washington, D.C., to demand an end to U.S. involvement in Vietnam. In October 1967 a total of 75,000 joined the march on the Pentagon that inspired Norman Mailer's Pulitzer Prize-winning *Armies of the Night*.

Then, in August 1968, the year that saw the assassinations of Martin Luther King, Jr., and Robert Kennedy, and the confirmation that the Vietnam War was far from won, millions of television viewers witnessed what *Life* magazine called "the most widely observed riot in history," at the Democratic National Convention in Chicago (see p. 350). At the center of the clash with Mayor Richard Daley's police force were the "yippies," short for Youth International Party members, a bizarre blend of hippie drug culture and student activism. A year after the riot, the trial of the Chicago Eight, eight leaders charged with instigating the outbreak of disorder at the convention, began. The accused included yippie cofounders Abbie Hoffman and Jerry Rubin, as well as Tom Hayden, a founder of the Students for a Democratic Society (SDS). Hayden had called for "a revolutionary change in the American structure," claiming that what he sought was a truly "participato-

SDS leader Tom Hayden

▼ *At San Francisco State College, President S. I. Hayakawa called in 600 police to keep it open in 1968, then faced a more violent strike the next year. In New York City (inset) antiwar protesters burn their draft cards at a 1965 rally.*

◄
*When Kathy Switzer, a
Syracuse University
student, challenged the
Boston Marathon's men-
only tradition in 1967, an
official tried to oust her
from the race, but fellow
runners came to her aid.*

▼ *Betty Friedan was a
42-year-old suburban
housewife when she
attacked the idea of the
happy homemaker in
The Feminine Mystique.*

► *On "Anti-Bra Day" in San
Francisco, a secretary
displays the brassiere she
has doffed and intends to
destroy in the name of
women's liberation.
Organizers of this rally
called on women to send in
their bras for destruction,
and many women around
the world did just that.*

woman to serve in the House of Representatives: "In the political world, I have been far oftener discriminated against
because I am a woman than because I am a black."

Feminism, of course, was not new. Throughout America's history women had fought for improved legal status and
better conditions for working women. As the 1960's opened,
there were few signs that women's roles would become a
heated issue. President John F. Kennedy formed the
Commission on the Status of Women in 1961, and the
Equal Pay Act of 1963 guaranteed women equal pay when
they worked in the same jobs as men. A 1962 Gallup poll
found that three out of five women were at least "fairly
satisfied" with their lives.

Then, the next year, came Betty Friedan's book *The
Feminine Mystique.* Friedan, a mother of three, wrote of
"the problem that has no name," the frustration felt by
housewives. So strong was the response to the book —
3 million people bought it — that, in 1966,
Friedan and others founded the National Organization for Women (NOW), the preeminent
force for women's rights for years to come.

ry democracy." During the trial, defendants read comic
books and threw kisses to jurors in a show of contempt for
the proceedings. When Judge Julius Hoffman denied one
defendant, Black Panther Bobby Seale, access to his lawyer,
Seale screamed, "Fascist, racist pig!" Hoffman ordered Seale
gagged and chained to his chair for the rest of the trial.
Meanwhile, on the Chicago streets outside, the Weather-
men — a radical cadre dedicated to violent revolution — instigated a "Days of Rage" rampage, smashing shops and cars
and battling police.

Protests were at their height at the end of the decade;
by one count, 1969 saw 448 universities disrupted or shut
down by strikes. There were hundreds of sit-ins at Harvard
alone, where in April state police fought students who called
for abolition of the university's ROTC unit. On Moratorium
Day in October, a million people nationwide marched for an
end to the war. A month later 250,000 came to Washington
to demand the withdrawal of U.S. troops.

Feminists, Friedan, and Women's Rights

Just two weeks after the tumultuous Democratic National
Convention of 1968, at the annual Miss America contest in
Atlantic City, feminists crowned a sheep and tossed steno
pads, false eyelashes, and brassieres into "freedom trash
cans." By then feminists were beginning to describe insensi-
tive men as "male chauvinist pigs." Like the civil rights activists, student protesters, and antiwar marchers of the
1960's, a lot of women were fed up. They felt they were suffering injustices due to their gender and no longer intended
to keep quiet about it. Said Shirley Chisholm, the first black

A female reporter helped women attain one important legislative breakthrough, the inclusion of women in the 1964 Civil Rights Act. TV journalist May Craig was interviewing Representative Howard W. Smith of Virginia on *Meet the Press* when the civil rights bill was in congressional committee. Would he, she asked, consider revising the bill to include women? Yes, Smith replied, he might do just that.

In fact, Smith hoped to defeat the civil rights bill by adding women to the list of minorities it covered. When Smith proposed the inclusion of women in the bill before the House, laughter broke out on the floor. The Civil Rights Act of 1964 did pass, and Title VII prohibited discrimination in employment on the basis of sex. The Equal Employment Opportunity Commission was set up to enforce the law, but it would be another eight years of legal maneuvering before the Equal Employment Opportunity Act was passed and the EEOC had any real power.

Cesar Chavez and the California Grape Boycott

Senator Robert Kennedy called him "one of the heroes of our time." To vineyard owners in California's San Joaquin Valley, he was a maverick labor agitator bent on ruining their grape crop. For some 5 million fellow Mexican-Americans, 42-year-old Cesar Chavez appeared to be a savior: a sad-eyed, soft-spoken champion who promised to restore their ethnic pride and win them a fair share of the American dream.

It would take much doing. For decades Mexican-Americans had faced discrimination in jobs, wages, education, and housing. Many crowded into urban slums; others — migrant farm workers — followed the harvest to pick cotton, apricots, lettuce, and other produce. The pay, which averaged a bit over $2,000 a year in the California vineyards, was barely enough to buy food and clothing.

It was here that Chavez launched his crusade. Son of a migrant farm family, he began organizing the workers. In 1965 a strike broke out at Delano, about 120 miles north of Los Angeles, in the heart of the grape country, and Chavez assumed leadership. He spoke in churches and led a 300-mile march to Sacramento, where a crowd of 10,000 rallied before the state capitol.

Cesar Chavez

Then a seeming miracle occurred. Schenley Industries, a major wine maker, signed a labor contract. For more than three decades, labor organizers had been trying to build an effective farm union; at last it was really happening.

Growers of table grapes held out, however. So Chavez's United Farm Workers (UFW) continued to fight. The strike, *la huelga*, became *la causa*, dedicated to advancing the rights of all migrant farm workers and of all Mexican-Americans. As always, Chavez shunned violence, relying instead on the force of his moral conviction. He called for a boycott of California table grapes, and to drive the point home, he embarked on a 25-day hunger strike. Grapes rotted in warehouses as stores across the country refused to carry them. As *New York* magazine reported, many Americans "would rather eat a cyanide pellet than a California grape these days."

Gradually the growers gave in. By 1970 most had signed contracts with Chavez's union. And Chavez moved on to the next target: lettuce.

Life in a migrant workers' camp meant abject squalor for this Mexican mother and her daughter. Many camps lacked running water and sanitation; older children worked full-time in the fields.

THE TUMULTUOUS RACE OF 1968

It was the year of our discontent: campuses seethed with protest, cities burned, the war dragged on, and American voters despaired. To whom could they turn?

When peace candidate Eugene J. McCarthy declared his intention to enter the Democratic race for the presidency, he was warned never to run against a sitting president. But McCarthy yearned for an end to the Vietnam War, and ignoring the pundits, he forged ahead with his campaign. In March 1968 he tallied 42 percent of the vote in the New Hampshire primary. Several days later New York Senator Robert F. Kennedy proclaimed his candidacy. And on March 31, President Johnson stunned the nation by announcing he would not seek reelection. The Democratic nomination was up for grabs. Vice President Hubert H. Humphrey threw his hat into the ring, and later George S. McGovern did the same.

After a strong showing in the Indiana primary, Kennedy surged into the lead and stayed there. Then, on June 6, Kennedy was shot and killed at a victory celebration after he had won the California primary. His assailant, Arab nationalist Sirhan Sirhan, bitterly opposed the candidate's support of Israel. Violence now haunted the campaign. At the Republican National Convention in Miami Beach, security measures were tight. When a riot broke out, 70 policemen armed with shotguns were called in, and reportedly, 4 rioters were killed. Next came the Democratic National Convention in Chicago.

Chicago was Mayor Richard Daley's town, and he ruled it with an iron fist. As radical groups gathered to disrupt the convention — among them the yippies and the National Mobilization to End the War in Vietnam — Daley prepared to face down the insurgents. He posted 12,000 police officers on street corners and atop buildings all around the city. Army troops and national guardsmen were put on alert. What followed was a police riot. Officers and guardsmen teargassed and beat up protesters, innocent bystanders, reporters, anyone who got in the way. Inside the hall Humphrey was closing in on the nomination, but his presidential bid would be badly damaged by the fractured condition of the Democratic Party and the chaos that nearly engulfed the convention proceedings.

From the conventions emerged two relatively moderate candidates, Nixon and Humphrey. But a wild card candidate remained in the race: George C. Wallace, who ran on the American Independent ticket. Wallace had become the governor of Alabama in 1962 and was chiefly known for his strident opposition to civil rights. After a strong showing in several Republican presidential primaries, he entered the 1968 contest as the candidate of the far right. Wallace was a law-and-order man who promised to restore states' rights (a euphemism for the right of state governments to maintain segregation) and win the Vietnam War. He launched broadside attacks on those he considered his enemies: "left-wing theoreticians, briefcase-totin'

In Chicago, national guardsmen went head-to-head with demonstrators directly under the candidates' hotel windows.

Robert Kennedy, pictured with a local assemblyman and bodyguards, campaigned vigorously to win the vital California primary. He was gunned down in the kitchen of a Los Angeles hotel after delivering his victory address.

American Independent George Wallace, who ran with retired Gen. Curtis E. LeMay, attracted large crowds.

bureaucrats, ivory-tower guideline writers, bearded anarchists, smart-aleck editorial writers and pointy-headed professors."

Meanwhile, Hubert Humphrey and his running mate, Senator Edmund S. Muskie, slowly closed in on the Republican lead in the polls. Hampered at first by his association with the unpopular Johnson administration and by his own role as booster for the president's Vietnam War policy, Humphrey asserted his independence as the campaign progressed. On a telecast in September, he announced: "As president, I would stop the bombing of the North as an acceptable risk for peace because I believe it could lead to

success in the negotiations and thereby shorten the war." The statement won great favor among antiwar Democrats and gave his campaign a much-needed lift.

Richard Nixon's campaign was well staffed, amply funded, and united in its purpose. The candidate read the nation's shift toward conservatism. He assured voters that as president he would "restore order and respect for law in this country." Nixon attacked "the vocal minority" — campus protesters and other rabble-rousers whom Middle America found threatening — and he played to voters he termed "the Silent Majority": family-loving, churchgoing, patriotic, and productive citizens.

Nixon filled out the ticket by choosing little-known Spiro T. Agnew, hoping that the Maryland governor would bring in the Southern vote. Agnew's verbal blunders caused Nixon considerable embarrassment — he called veteran cold-warrior Humphrey "squishy soft on communism" and declined to visit a ghetto area because "if you've seen one city slum, you've seen them all" — but Agnew gradually smoothed out his act.

The election was a squeaker. George Wallace siphoned off 13.5 percent of the popular vote. Nixon and Humphrey split the rest, with Nixon edging out the Democrat by less than a percentage point. In his victory speech, Nixon proclaimed that it was the objective of the new administration "to bring America together."

▲ Hubert Humphrey, shown with his running mate, Edmund Muskie, was nominated on the first ballot.

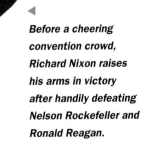

◄ Before a cheering convention crowd, Richard Nixon raises his arms in victory after handily defeating Nelson Rockefeller and Ronald Reagan.

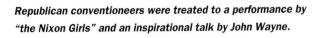

Republican conventioneers were treated to a performance by "the Nixon Girls" and an inspirational talk by John Wayne.

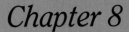
Chapter 8

THE SEESAW 1970's

Watergate stuns, OPEC squeezes, minorities get militant, and the Me Generation finds time to disco and watch Archie Bunker, M*A*S*H, Jaws, Star Wars, and two Godfathers.

Fireworks explode over three famous symbols of democracy on America's 200th birthday, July 4, 1976.

Nixon's HARD ROAD TO PEACE

President Nixon entered the White House with one overriding mandate: to get America out of Vietnam. It took

years and cost another 20,000 U.S. lives, but he scored some notable Cold War breakthroughs along the way.

The greatest honor history can bestow is the title of peacemaker. This honor now beckons America." With these solemn phrases, Richard Nixon, upon his inauguration, declared his ambitions as president. Almost immediately he began withdrawing U.S. combat troops from South Vietnam. But while talking peace was easy, achieving it was another matter entirely.

More than 1 million Americans so far had fought in the jungles of Southeast Asia; some 30,000 had already given their lives. It was the longest armed conflict in the nation's history. In June of 1969, Nixon announced a troop reduction of 25,000 men, the first step in a policy of "Vietnamization," whereby the burden of fighting would gradually shift to the armies of South Vietnam. The United States would supply arms, advisers, and an air shield of bombers and fighter planes; native Vietnamese soldiers would slog through the rice paddies and fire the bullets. The troop withdrawals would continue throughout Nixon's first term. By the end of 1970 total U.S. military strength in Vietnam was down to 334,600 men, from approximately 540,000 when Nixon took office.

Yet every move Nixon made seemed to pull America deeper into the war. Even as his national security adviser, Henry Kissinger, was meeting in Paris with representatives from North Vietnam, attempting to hammer out a cease-fire, the president was secretly stepping up the pressure on

At a press conference on May 9, 1970, Nixon describes the Cambodian incursions. Five days earlier, on the final day of the Kent State confrontation, a student demonstrator tosses back a tear gas canister at an Ohio national guardsman.

Tankers of the U.S. 25th Infantry Division roll into Cambodia. The attack, aimed at Vietcong bases, began on April 30, 1970, and was over by late summer.

the enemy. Clandestine flights of B-52 bombers began roaring over Cambodia to drop their payloads. The strategically vital Ho Chi Minh Trail, the main Communist supply route through Cambodia and Laos, had grown from a jungle footpath into a vast network, hidden by foliage, protected by antiaircraft batteries, and dotted with Vietcong rest-and-resupply camps, arms depots, and field hospitals. Unless these sites were wiped out, Nixon reasoned, South Vietnam could never be defended. Thus the B-52's.

Then, on April 30, 1970, Nixon dropped a bombshell on the American public. Appearing on national television, the president announced he was sending American ground troops into Cambodia. Even as he spoke, a joint U.S. and South Vietnamese assault force, 20,000 strong, was sweeping across the border. The Vietcong sanctuaries had to be cleared, Nixon explained, before America could quit Vietnam. Furthermore, Hanoi's delegates in Paris were digging in their heels at the negotiating table, and American credibility was at stake. "When the chips are down," the president declared, "the world's most powerful nation" cannot afford to act "like a pitiful, helpless giant."

The nation was stunned. Shorten the war by escalating it? "This is madness," exclaimed Senator Edward Kennedy, and many of his congressional colleagues agreed. The Senate repealed the six-year-old Gulf of Tonkin Resolution, which had given legislative sanction to the country's involvement in Southeast Asia.

Home from the battlefront, Green Berets get a joyous family welcome at Fort Bragg, North Carolina.

Even as students protested, New York construction workers marched in favor of Nixon's war policy.

Just days after Nixon's announcement, a second shock sent the nation reeling. At Kent State University in Ohio, a group of student activists had met to protest the Cambodian invasion. The meeting was peaceful, but that evening several hundred other students, fueled by cold beer and warm spring weather, started throwing bottles and smashing windows in downtown Kent. The next night campus demonstrators attacked the ROTC building, burning it to the ground. The authorities called in the National Guard. The final confrontation occurred on May 4, shortly after noon. The guardsmen moved to break up an antiwar rally on the university commons. A melee erupted, with students hurling rocks and insults, and guardsmen responding with tear gas. A salvo of rifle shots rang out. When the smoke cleared, four students lay dead. Ten others were left seriously wounded. In a way that seemed unimaginable, the Vietnam War had come home to America.

Nationwide Protest, No End in Sight

In the wake of Kent State, student strikes shut down more than 400 other colleges and universities across the land. Two more students were killed at all-black Jackson State University in Mississippi. More than 100,000 student demonstrators gathered in Washington to stand vigil before the White House and other government buildings. Nixon, who had earlier branded antiwar activists "bums," was left shaken by the events; he made a 5 A.M. visit to the Lincoln Memorial to reason with protesters there. Still, opposition to the war continued to build.

The president was determined to wind down the conflict at his own pace, leaving a pro-Western government

▲ *Savoring a Cold War triumph, the president and First Lady Pat Nixon tour the Great Wall of China in February 1972. Then, in Moscow, Nixon celebrates détente with Soviet party boss Leonid Brezhnev (left) and Premier Alexei Kosygin.*

▶ *A B-52 Stratofortress, principal arm of America's strategic air might, drops its 54,000-pound payload over enemy territory.*

in control of South Vietnam. "I will not be the first president of the United States to lose a war," he declared. Yet each day victory seemed more elusive. The Cambodian offensive had failed to end the flow of Vietcong troops and supplies. In February 1971 a South Vietnamese assault into Laos backed by U.S. air strikes ended in headlong retreat. And each night on television, the American public found new reasons to dislike the war. In March a military court convicted Lt. William L. Calley of war crimes, reminding viewers that Calley's platoon had massacred more than 100 South Vietnamese villagers at My Lai in 1968. Three months later

The New York Times began publishing the Pentagon Papers, secret Defense Department documents that further eroded the public's confidence in the way the war was being conducted. As *Time* magazine put it: "Vietnam is the wound in American life that will not heal."

Diplomatic Breakthroughs

Even as Nixon's Vietnam policies were dividing the nation, his genius as a statesman was reshaping world politics. One July day in 1971, while vacationing at his home in San Clemente, California, the president delivered yet another TV blockbuster. An invitation had arrived from the People's Republic of China, America's archenemy in Asia, and the president was delighted to accept. Again, the nation was stunned. Richard Nixon, who had battled left-wingers all his political life, traipsing off to shake hands with Party Chairman Mao Tse-tung? Astute observers might have detected the early signs: an end to State Department travel restrictions, the U.S. table tennis team playing exhibition matches in Peking. But the thaw in relations, engineered by Nixon and Kissinger, caught most of the world by surprise.

A few months later Nixon did it again. This time the invitation came from the Soviet Union, and soon Nixon was in Moscow tossing back vodka with Soviet leader Leonid Brezhnev. A new spirit of détente emerged, accompanied by much fanfare and some genuine achievement: cultural exchanges, trade agreements, and a $1-billion sale of American wheat to Russia. Delegates at the Strategic Arms Limitation Talks (SALT), already in progress, drew up their first agreements. With any luck, the lurking terror of nuclear mass destruction might soon be banished from earth.

But nothing would make Vietnam go away. On March 30, 1972, Communist forces launched a massive offensive. Three waves of North Vietnamese troops and guerrillas, armed with Soviet tanks and artillery, stormed into South Vietnam. A drive out of Cambodia reached to within 60 miles of Saigon before being turned back. Nixon responded with an equally massive escalation of U.S. armed might: heavy bombing of North Vietnam, mining of Haiphong Harbor, and a U.S. naval blockade. North Vietnam lost 100,000 men and most of its tanks. Still, the stalemate persisted.

In July, the peace negotiations between Henry Kissinger and Le Duc Tho of North Vietnam resumed after a temporary suspension. Into autumn, Kissinger jetted between Paris, Washington, and Saigon to hammer out an accord. Then, in October, the talks broke down again, and Nixon, in an effort to force Tho back to the negotiating table, ordered a final outpouring of aerial destruction. Starting the week before Christmas, for 12 days straight, U.S. B-52's and other aircraft droned over Hanoi and Haiphong to drop

The Election of 1972

If politics is the national soap opera, the plot twists of the Nixon years deserve a special Emmy award. By his second year in office, the president's popularity had tumbled to 50 percent, and support for his conduct of the Vietnam War, to 34. Police barricaded the White House gates with transit buses as antiwar protesters took to the streets of the capital. Then in 1972 Nixon was reelected by one of the largest victory margins on record.

Others' misfortunes had a part in Nixon's triumph. Well before the election, his most dangerous opponent,

Senator Edward Kennedy, drove off a bridge late one night in Chappaquiddick, Massachusetts, causing the death of a young woman passenger; that temporarily ended Teddy's presidential aspirations. A rifle shot by a would-be assassin crippled Alabama Gov. George Wallace, thus removing a formidable contender from the political far right. Senator Edmund Muskie started strong for the Democrats, then bombed in the New Hampshire primary when false rumors about his wife reduced him to tears of outrage. That left South Dakota's Senator George McGovern (shown above with wife, Eleanor) as the Democratic Party candidate.

Nixon ran a smoothly disciplined campaign and managed to project a skilled, statesmanly image to voters. McGovern came across as a naive prairie populist who promised a quick end to the Vietnam War and who attracted a new breed of political idealist. His campaign was doomed from the start by inexperienced management and the radical image of many of his followers. Republican detractors liked to call him the candidate of "acid, amnesty, and abortion."

The results for McGovern were devastating. Nixon won just under 61 percent of the popular vote and lost only Massachusetts and the District of Columbia. Yet, in defeat, McGovern kept his sense of proportion, telling journalists: "For years I wanted to run for president in the worst possible way — and I'm sure I did."

more than 36,000 tons of explosives in one of the most savage air attacks in history. The Paris talks reopened, and on January 27, 1973, the negotiators signed a cease-fire.

At last the war seemed over. The last of the U.S. ground troops began arriving home. Hanoi released some 600 American POW's. Secretary of Defense Melvin Laird ended the draft. The U.S.-backed government of Gen. Nguyen Van Thieu remained in power in Saigon. "We have finally achieved peace with honor," Nixon announced.

Many Americans thought otherwise. No one could guess how long the Thieu regime would survive. Many thousands of North Vietnamese troops remained in South Vietnam, controlling wide areas of the countryside, poised to resume the battle. Said one returning U.S. veteran: "It isn't peace. And there is no honor."

In the jungles of Southeast Asia, the gunfire never entirely stopped. A civil war was ravaging Cambodia, genocidal in its intensity. In April 1975 rebel forces of the Communist Khmer Rouge took over most of the country, including the capital of Phnom Penh. Meanwhile, fighting broke out again in South Vietnam, with the Communist armies closing steadily southward. Though Nixon had promised Thieu that if the North were to attack, the United States would support him, Congress had prohibited further military involvement in Vietnam. On April 25 Thieu fled the country.

Four days later, as enemy tanks roared into Saigon, U.S. helicopters lifted 1,373 Americans from the roof of the Saigon embassy to the safety of nearby warships. During 18 years of intervention in Vietnam, the United States had spent $150 billion of its wealth and burned away the lives of more than 57,000 of its young men.

The ordeal would haunt America for years.

▲ **Negotiators Henry Kissinger (right) and Le Duc Tho shake hands as they near the signing of the Paris peace accord.**

▼ **In the wake of South Vietnam's surrender, a North Vietnamese tank crashes the gates of the Presidential Palace in Saigon.**

An ADMINISTRATION ON TRIAL

It began as a back-page news item: five men caught breaking into Democratic Party headquarters in Washington. Two years later it ended with a slew of indictments and a president's resignation.

In Washington in the early 1970's, the Watergate complex on the Potomac River was the place to be. Half a dozen members of Congress lived there, several agency heads, and Attorney General John N. Mitchell. It was also where the Democratic National Committee maintained its headquarters. In the wee hours of June 17, 1972, five men broke into the committee offices to bug its phones and rifle its files. A night watchman detected them and called the police. Hardly anyone took notice. "A third-rate burglary attempt" is how White House Press Secretary Ron Ziegler described it. But the Watergate break-in just would not go away.

The five men were no ordinary burglars. James W. McCord, a former agent of the CIA, was security coordinator for the Committee to Reelect the President (later called CREEP); the other four were anti-Castro Cubans who thought their assignment was to look for a connection between the Cuban premier and the Democrats. The break-in had been planned, police learned, by a pistol-packing former FBI

White House Chief of Staff H. R. Haldeman gets ready to testify before the Senate Watergate committee. Later convicted of perjury and conspiracy, he spent 18 months in federal prison.

A Capital Collection of Convicted Cover-uppers

John D. Ehrlichman
Domestic adviser. Convicted of conspiracy, obstruction of justice, perjury:18 months in prison.

John N. Mitchell
Former attorney general and director of CREEP. Convicted in Watergate cover-up: 19 months in prison.

Jeb Stuart Magruder
Deputy campaign director of CREEP. Pleaded guilty in cover-up: seven months in federal prison.

G. Gordon Liddy
CREEP finance counselor. Masterminded Watergate burglary and other illegal acts: 52 months in prison.

E. Howard Hunt
White House consultant. Pleaded guilty to burglary, wiretapping, conspiracy: 33 months in prison.

Charles Colson
Special counsel to the president. Pleaded guilty to obstruction of justice: seven months in prison.

John W. Dean III
Presidential counsel. Implicated Nixon in cover-up. Served four months in prison for obstructing justice.

The soul of integrity, Special Prosecutor Archibald Cox lost his post when he tried to make Nixon hand over the White House tapes. But the tapes became public anyway when the Supreme Court voted 8 to 0 that they be released.

"I'm a plain old country lawyer," Senator Sam Ervin would say in his North Carolina drawl as he craftily pried the truth from reluctant witnesses. In six months of testimony, Ervin's Select Committee on Campaign Practices blew apart the Watergate cover-up.

agent named G. Gordon Liddy, who now worked for CREEP and was assisted by former CIA operative E. Howard Hunt. Could it be that Republican strategists, gearing up for the 1972 election campaign, had broken the law just to snoop on the Democrats?

With Richard Nixon's landslide victory, Watergate faded momentarily from view. But not for long. Liddy, Hunt, and the five burglars were brought to trial. Most of the defendants revealed little about the burglary. But, at sentencing, Judge John J. Sirica read a letter by McCord indicating that pressure had been exerted on the defendants to keep silent, and that some had committed perjury, and it implicated others in the break-in. Meanwhile, two reporters for *The Washington Post*, Carl Bernstein and Bob Woodward, conducted their own investigation. Citing a source known only as Deep Throat, they found out that the burglary had been financed by money from CREEP. John Mitchell, they also reported, maintained a slush fund for sabotaging the Democrats.

Just how far did the circle of involvement reach? Televised hearings began in May 1973 in the Senate, with the deceptively folksy Sam Ervin presiding. They revealed a White House steeped in wiretapping, forgery, and other shady dealings. Viewers learned about the Plumbers, charged with plugging press leaks, and Nixon's "enemies list" of real and imagined foes.

Even more shocking, the hearings showed that Nixon himself may have ordered a cover-up of the break-in. Aides had been instructed to stonewall. Presidential counsel John W. Dean testified that he had been told to "deep-six" a briefcase full of evidence. It seemed apparent that the White House was engaged in a conspiracy to obstruct justice, a criminal offense. But little of this could be corroborated. Then, on July 16, Alexander Butterfield, a Nixon aide, disclosed that since 1971 the president had taped all conversations in the Oval Office. Now almost every charge could be checked.

Even before the hearings had opened, presidential aides John D. Ehrlichman and H. R. (Bob) Haldeman resigned. Then came the Saturday Night Massacre. Nixon, under heavy public pressure, had authorized a Justice Department investigation. But when the special prosecutor, Harvard law professor Archibald Cox, probed too close to Nixon himself, the president ordered him fired. The new attorney general, Elliot Richardson, resigned in protest, as did his deputy, William Ruckelshaus.

At issue were the tapes of White House conversations. Nixon refused to turn them over, citing "national security" and "executive privilege"; instead, he would provide the committee synopses of their contents. Nixon's offer was rejected. Investigators suspected that somewhere in that avalanche of words lay clear evidence of executive complicity: a "smoking gun" proving beyond doubt that Nixon had attempted to block the Watergate investigation. But when the courts finally forced Nixon to give up some of the tapes, a key 18½-minute segment had been erased.

By now Nixon's innocence was in grave doubt. In May 1974 the House Judiciary Committee began impeachment proceedings. The hearings continued through July. Then on August 5 the smoking gun was found: a tape of Nixon ordering the cover-up. The Judiciary Committee voted to recommend impeachment, and on August 9 Richard Nixon became the first American president in history to resign from office.

That same afternoon Gerald R. Ford took over as president. Earlier, Ford had replaced Vice President Spiro Agnew, who had resigned amid charges of taking bribes and cheating on his income tax. Ford was loyal, hardworking, and as plain as a Michigan corn patch. He seemed just the man to heal a scandal-riven nation. "Our long national nightmare is over," he announced, and all America was ready to believe him.

On August 9, 1974, President Richard M. Nixon, surrounded by his family, bids a tearful good-bye to White House aides and Cabinet members.

MINDING OUR PLANET

Faced with the effects of oil spills, smog, strip-mining, pesticide use, and other assaults on nature, Americans decided the time had come to clean up the mess.

April 22, 1970. Seattle high school students spent the day gathering trash. Young people in Atlanta heaped thousands of no-return soft drink bottles into huge mounds. New York City barred automobiles from Fifth Avenue, opening the way to an exhaust-free stroll for 100,000 citizens. In the nation's capital, another sizable crowd gathered for rock music and oratory at the Washington Monument. More than 14,000 schools, colleges, and community groups across the land held workshops, teach-ins, "trash-ins," and other events. For this was Earth Day, when an estimated 20 million Americans turned out for a coast-to-coast ecological Woodstock in favor of clean air, pure water, and wholesale environmental improvement. It was the largest, most upbeat public demonstration since the end of World War II.

Concern over the environment had been growing for nearly a decade. The alarm had been sounded back in 1962 by a crusading book, *Silent Spring*, in which government biologist Rachel Carson warned that unrestricted use of chemical pesticides was destroying much of the nation's wildlife. The newspapers took up the cry, and over their morning coffee, Americans learned that Illinois's drinking water was tainted with nitrates from farmers' fertilizers, that fish suffocated by sewage were piling up on Lake Erie's shores, that bass and salmon had been wiped out downstream from power plants, that Antarctic penguins carried traces of DDT.

The bulletins grew steadily more worrisome. The world was in danger of losing to extinction the black-footed ferret, readers learned, and also the bighorn sheep, the California condor, the whooping crane, even the bald eagle, the very symbol of a proud America. The United States was gobbling up land and resources as if they were snack food: millions of acres ravaged by strip-mining, broad swaths of national forest laid bare by the clear-cutting of timber, a million acres paved over each year. Even more alarming, the world's population had nearly doubled since the century's start, to more than 3 billion souls. By the year 2000 it would double again. In the crush of bodies, how could the planet survive?

▲ **Biologist Rachel Carson alerted the world to the high risks of using chemical pesticides and herbicides.**

▼ **Hikers return to unblemished nature via a backcountry trail in the Cascade Mountains.**

▼ **In Yosemite National Park in California, young environmentalists examine local fauna under the expert eye of a park ranger.**

A nationwide environmental movement began to gain momentum. Old-line conservation groups, like the Sierra Club and the Audubon Society, took on a new militancy and swelled with a deluge of new members. In 1968 protests by nature lovers blocked construction of two U.S. government dams that would have flooded sections of the Grand Canyon. Assaults upon nature continued. In January of 1969 an oil rig in the Santa Barbara Channel blew its top, turning miles of pristine California beachfront into a gooey graveyard for pelicans, porpoises, and fish. An oil slick on the Cuyahoga River in Cleveland, Ohio, caught fire and burned two railroad bridges. But each disaster only sharpened public awareness that things had to change and that no amount of industrial wealth or material progress was worth the price of a permanently damaged world.

By the early 1970's, fully 70 percent of America thought the environment was the nation's most pressing domestic problem. No wonder, then, that Earth Day had enjoyed such sweeping success. Even utility companies, regarded by many as ecological archvillains, joined in with supportive banners, and ad agencies whipped up slogans to express their clients' environmental concerns. Congress took the day off so its members could participate. Earth Day, announced *The New York Times,* was just like Mother's Day: "No man in public office could be against it."

During the course of the decade, Congress drew up a far-reaching program of environmental legislation. Several amendments to the Clean Air Act of 1963 were passed in 1970, giving the government the authority to set air standards. Within months, another bill set up the Environmental Protection Agency. Then came the Clean Water Act, the Endangered Species Act, statutes to limit factory pollution, to protect seacoasts, and to remove the scars left by strip mining. More than 100 million acres of virgin land were set aside for national parks, wildlife refuges, and wilderness areas. When scientific evidence showed that propellants emitted by aerosol spray cans were depleting the earth's ozone layer, with probable dire consequences to the climate, Congress enacted a law to phase out the devices. Some 35 environmental laws took effect during the decade, addressing every aspect of conservation and cleanup, from saving redwoods and protecting songbirds to regulating auto emissions and the disposal of toxic chemicals. And despite several sharp setbacks — the accidental escape of radioactive gas from a nuclear power plant at Three Mile Island in Pennsylvania (see box p. 363), leaks in a toxic dump that forced the evacuation of more than 1,000 families from New York's Love Canal — by the decade's end, large sections of the battered environment seemed to be on the road to recovery.

▲ **An Earth Day activist joins the procession sporting a leafy tiara and a bag stitched to resemble the globe.**

▼ **Tree lovers celebrate Earth Day by planting a large sapling in a city square.**

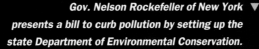
Gov. Nelson Rockefeller of New York ▼ presents a bill to curb pollution by setting up the state Department of Environmental Conservation.

Oil Shock, Stagflation

First OPEC cut off oil exports to the United States, then the gasoline pumps went dry. "Things Will Get Worse Before They Get Worse," predicted one newspaper in 1973. For a moment, things actually seemed to improve. Then double-digit inflation struck.

Christmas of 1973 promised to be the chilliest in years. Food costs were skyrocketing; jobs getting tight. On top of that, the nation faced an acute shortage in one of its most basic commodities: oil. In October the Arab-dominated Organization of Petroleum Exporting Countries (OPEC), a major supplier, stopped all shipments to the United States. Home owners, fearing shortfalls in heating oil, turned down thermostats and stocked up on sweaters. Motorists waited long hours at gas stations, where the lines of cars sometimes stretched for blocks. In New York angry drivers took out their frustration in fistfights. The price tag at the pump delivered another strong punch. Gas in Miami ran as high as $1 a gallon; months earlier it had been 35 cents. Americans, who had long regarded cheap energy and rising prosperity as birthrights, faced a colder, grimmer reality.

The cause of the OPEC embargo lay in the tangled legacy of Middle East political strife: the United States had sent an emergency arms shipment to Israel, then at war with its Arab neighbors, and the Arabs struck back in the best way they knew. A few years earlier the embargo would not have hurt: the United States was producing enough oil to supply its own needs. But by 1973 needs exceeded domestic supply. New factories had sprouted everywhere, and nearly a million new cars were powering onto the highways each year; the United States was consuming 30 percent of the world's available energy. Fully one-third of the nation's oil was imported from foreign sources. As President Nixon's former commerce secretary, Peter Peterson, warned, "Popeye is running out of spinach."

Americans rallied to save energy. Motorists cut their speed to 55 miles an hour, following a new limit set first by individual states and then by federal decree. Gas stations closed on Sundays, and some states introduced rationing. Commuters took to carpooling and

As fuel supplies slowed to a trickle, homemade signs like this one began appearing at gas stations across America. Even fuel-efficient Volkswagens were sometimes left stranded.

To help save fuel, many Americans bicycled, including, it seems, the mayor of Topeka, Kansas.

The 55-mile-per-hour speed limit saved lives as well as gasoline. Set in January 1974, it cut highway fatalities by 1,000 a month.

mass transit. To conserve electricity, the nation went on year-round daylight saving time. In Milwaukee, the Public Safety Committee decided to conduct business by candlelight. President Nixon, citing his doctor's word that it was "really more healthy," urged citizens to lower their thermostats to 68° F. Factories shortened their hours; some colleges canceled midwinter sessions. Airline traffic was cut by 10 percent. Everyone pitched in. "I walk to school every day," reported an eight-year-old Miami boy. "I don't watch much television. And I try not to take a bath."

Other Sources — But No Real Relief

A search began for alternative energy sources and for ways to make appliances, engines, and turbines run more efficiently. Planners rolled out schemes for using coal oil, shale oil, wind power, solar power, and gasohol (90 percent gasoline, 10 percent alcohol). But nothing seemed as good as good old petroleum.

Then as swiftly as it had struck, the oil shortage abated. In March 1974, OPEC lifted its embargo, though its prices remained high. At the same time, construction crews began laying the $8-billion trans-Alaska pipeline across the permafrost, building an 800-mile link between the bonanza oil fields of Prudhoe Bay and the ice-free port of Valdez. Soon Alaskan oil would flow to a thirsty lower 48 at a rate of 1.2 million barrels a day. Americans began shedding their long johns, pushing up their thermostats, and cruising the freeways with the same happy abandon as they always had.

The energy pinch had exacted a painful long-term toll, however. Out on the highways, newer cars tended to be

In the quest for new energy sources, no area seemed as promising as the mighty atom. Nuclear plants had been generating power since 1957, and experts predicted that they might soon supply up to 50 percent of the nation's energy needs. To concerns about nuclear waste and, worse yet, a possible accident, the experts said not to worry: only once in a million years would a major disaster occur. Then came March 28, 1979. Some 800,000 gallons of radioactive water leaked from Unit Two of the reactor at Three Mile Island, Pennsylvania, threatening a meltdown of the reactor core. Some 100,000 citizens fled their homes, and Unit Two was closed down permanently. Since then, not a single nuclear power construction permit has been approved.

Raised on stanchions above the permafrost, the Alaska pipeline opened in 1977 and delivered enough crude oil to displace some $500 of petroleum imports every second.

small, cheap, fuel-efficient imports from Germany and Japan. Meanwhile, domestic automakers, hit by plunging sales, cut production and laid off workers. The cuts spread quickly to other industries — rubber, steel, glass, machine tools — and by 1975 the nation had fallen into the worst economic slump since the Great Depression. The stock market tumbled, interest rates climbed, unemployment soared, and the economy shifted into reverse. At the same time, prices continued to go up. To the bewilderment of economists, the nation was suffering from an unlikely combination of spiraling inflation and stagnant growth — stagflation, as the ailment came to be called.

Inflation became the economic norm of the 1970's. Along with bloated energy prices, the lingering costs of the Vietnam War and other factors combined to keep the inflation rate high. Nixon attacked it early in the decade with a 90-day freeze on wage and price increases. In a dramatic bid to boost production and promote exports, he devalued the currency. For the first time in memory, the U.S. dollar was no longer pegged to a fixed price of gold. But the effects were temporary. Under Nixon's successors, Gerald Ford and Jimmy Carter, the economy stumbled while inflation galloped ahead. By 1979 the rise in prices reached a manic 13.3 percent. Then the worst happened. A harsh winter, followed by an unexpected slump in Middle East oil production and a stiff price hike by OPEC, plunged America into yet another oil crisis. Gas lines, plant closings, rationing schemes — to everyone's horror, it was *déjà vu*.

ALL FOR ME, BODY AND SOUL

Tired of gas lines, turned off by politics, Americans focused on the best topic of all: themselves. They sought fulfillment in everything from hot tubs and singles' bars to macrobiotic diets, encounter groups, pop psychology, and a widening spectrum of religious cults.

In the summer of 1976, *New York* magazine, always quick to spot new trends, ran an inspired article by social critic Tom Wolfe. A cosmic shift had occurred in the way Americans looked at life, Wolfe suggested, in which the public crusades of recent years were being replaced by more personal goals.

To some people this meant adopting the creed of self-improvement. They threw their energies into study groups, exercise schedules, and bizarre new forms of psychotherapy. Others headed for the seductive joys of sexual revolution. Many turned to religion. Whatever their choice, the key word was *self*. The 1970's, Wolfe concluded, were the Me Decade.

If any single spot marked the era's birthplace, it was Big Sur, California, where well-heeled self-seekers gathered at the Esalen Institute for what Wolfe called "lube jobs for the personality." Lodged above the Pacific Ocean in a setting of Eden-like splendor, they shed clothes, plunged into hot tubs, and bared their inner selves in brutally intense encounter sessions. Dozens of similar groups spread across the land as part of the so-called Human Potential Movement, all striving to achieve an ideal of perfect selfhood. Arica, bioenergetics, Gestalt therapy, primal scream, Synanon, Zen meditation — the list of programs and disciplines went on and on.

New techniques of psychotherapy helped propel the movement. *Games People Play*, a self-help guide by psychiatrist Eric Berne, launched a fashion for transactional analysis (TA), which emphasized encounter groups and interpersonal relations.

An exhilarating "lift toss" helps a disciple at the Esalen Institute get in touch with her psyche during a sensitivity training session.

The book sold more than 5 million copies and spent years on best-seller lists until finally edged out by another TA volume, Thomas Harris's upbeat *I'm OK — You're OK*. Equally popular, est (Erhard Seminars Training) drew thousands of participants to weekend encounter sessions. By helping people "get in touch with themselves," former used-car salesman Werner Erhard was soon grossing $10 million a year.

Werner Erhard, est creator

Hand in hand with psychic self-expression, the era's fitness devotees sweated and groaned in search of bodily perfection. Health spas, tennis clubs, exercise centers, and diet clinics boomed. Thousands of otherwise ordinary Americans began eating brown rice, seaweed, and tofu and

Soaking away all inhibition, eight West Coast sybarites luxuriate in the effervescent comfort of a hot-tub party. The 105-degree water was considered to be therapeutic.

Some 40 million Americans took up running, both to stay fit and to experience a promised aerobic euphoria known as runner's high. Here, a massed field of 11,553 swarms into Brooklyn at the start of the 1979 New York City Marathon.

growing alfalfa sprouts on windowsills. Sales of running shoes took off like startled rabbits. At the same time, when the sun went down, thousands more flocked to disco singles' bars in quest of a "relationship." Self-help volumes like *The Joy of Sex: A Gourmet Guide to Love Making* appeared on night tables. A soft-porn aesthetic seeped into Hollywood, where movies like *Last Tango in Paris*, starring a nude Marlon Brando, soon became acceptable.

Often the search for self led into exotic byways of religious experience. The 15-year-old Hindu guru Maharaj Ji, head of the Divine Light Mission, boasted 60,000 disciples, two large estates, and a string of fancy cars. (His mass rally at the Houston Astrodome in 1973 was less successful; an expected UFO failed to show.) Another Hindu leader, Maharishi Mahesh Yogi, preached a yogic discipline he called transcendental meditation (TM) and drew 350,000 followers, including Stevie Wonder and the Beach Boys. Major corporations such as General Foods and AT&T endorsed TM, and *Time* pronounced it "the turn-on of the 70's — a drugless high even the narc squad might enjoy." Meanwhile, young Americans flocked to the Unification Church of Sun Myung Moon, a religious leader from South Korea; or they shaved their heads and danced in the streets with the Hare Krishna sect. And in one of the decade's grimmer footnotes, more than 900 members of the People's Temple followed their deranged messiah, Californian Jim Jones, to the jungles of Guyana and an apocalyptic mass suicide by gunshot and a poisoned Kool-Aid brew.

Back home, a far gentler and happier kind of spiritual commitment was on the rise. By 1977 an astonishing 70 million people defined themselves as born-again Christians. The decade's charismatic Protestantism rivaled the religious awakenings of the 19th century, with mass baptisms, torrid confessionals, and joyous revival meetings. The list of notables who took Jesus Christ as their personal savior included singers Pat Boone and Johnny Cash, former Black Panther Eldridge Cleaver, Watergate felons Charles Colson and Jeb Stuart Magruder, and President Jimmy Carter. The president's sister, Ruth, herself an evangelist, caught the public's eye by converting porno publisher Larry Flint, founder of *Hustler* magazine. And while Pentecostal fervor brought sinners to Christ, it also led some businessmen to nice profits. For example, the Virginia-based Christian Broadcast Network, with 4 stations and 130 affiliates, was pulling in $60 million a year by the decade's end.

Celebrants at a March for Jesus in New York City lift index fingers in a gesture that meant "one way to salvation." Thousands of young people "turned on to Jesus" as an escape from drugs and sex.

Drumming and chanting, youthful devotees of Krishna, the Hindu god, add a new noise to the streets of New York.

Platform shoes, worn by many
women and even some men,
marched onstage in
1970, then
quickly left.

Film star Diane Keaton launched
the Annie Hall look — man's
shirt, baggy pants, floppy hat —
with her laid-back attire in
Woody Allen's 1977 movie.

Hot pants seized the world's
attention in the early 1970's;
these, with matching jacket,
are made of snakeskin.

Hot pants, platforms, and polyester

Never had fashions changed so rapidly or reached such eccentric and bewildering

extremes. Everyone seemed determined to express themselves in what they wore.

There are no rules," announced the fashion magazine *Vogue* in 1970, and the parade was on: hot pants, leisure suits, lycra stretch pants, fake fur, ultrasuede and Naugahyde, floppy bow ties, outsize lapels, elephant bell-bottoms, peasant blouses, Mao Tse-tung caps, slogan-printed T-shirts, ripped jeans, designer jeans, Frye boots, clogs, sandals, platform shoes, plaid shirts, and cowboy hats — all adding up to an exuberant chaos of sartorial self-expression. Some people detected a certain tackiness: "The decade that taste forgot," as one observer put it. Others gloried in the sheer outrageousness of it all. But whatever one's sensibility, the decade offered something for everyone.

The rebellion started in the late 1960's, when fashion designers in Paris and New York, hoping to wean clients away from miniskirts, announced the calf-length midi. The response was all but universal outrage. "If the midi becomes the style, I'll commit suicide or murder," declared one Chicago woman. Groups like GAMS (Girls Against More

Rock star David Bowie helped spawn a gender-bending glitter look with costumes inspired by Japan's Kabuki theater.

Skirt) and SMACK (Society of Men who Appreciate Cute Knees) sprang up to protest what seemed like a descent into terminal dowdiness. In 1971 the midis enjoyed a brief flurry, but for every woman who bought one, thousands more kept their checkbooks in their purses.

As the designers retreated to their cutting rooms, women turned to the shock value of a mode originated by European streetwalkers: hot pants. Skintight, brief as an impulse, they came in satin, velvet, denim, leather, vinyl, and mink, and they could be dyed in one or more Day-Glo colors. Jane Fonda squeezed into them in the movie *Klute*, Liberace played his piano in them, California brides took their vows in white lace versions of them.

The favored footwear for hot pants was the platform shoe. Popularized by rock stars like Elton John — who touched up his platforms with glitter and sequins — the shoes sent wearers clomping and teetering precariously on soles up to seven inches thick. One custom-made pair featured hollow, transparent plastic heels with live goldfish swimming inside.

This was the golden age of polyester, a synthetic fiber that many people hoped would wear out, but didn't. Almost anything could be constructed from it: drip-dry shirts, double-knit blazers, stretch blue jeans, gaucho pants, and the glittery fantasy costumes that people wore to discos. It was also the fabric of choice for that ultimate 1970's statement, the leisure suit. Golfers in Miami and Palm Springs had worn these garments for years, but now they were everywhere, multiplying across the land in every shade of sickly pastel. So offensive did leisure suits become to certain viewers that many of the nation's more elegant restaurants posted signs forbidding them.

Some of the decade's styles took inspiration from earlier times or more exotic places. When Robert Redford and Mia Farrow appeared in *The Great Gatsby,* a Hollywood costume drama based on F. Scott Fitzgerald's novel of the 1920's, fans decked themselves out in pleated skirts, rope necklaces, white suits, and baggy flannels. The Slavic Peasant Look, featuring high boots, large earrings, and flowered print skirts, was briefly popular. President Nixon's visit to Peking, China, spawned a short-lived fascination for Mao jackets and workers' caps.

A Retreat to the 1950's — or Nothing

The decade's biggest nostalgia trip led directly back to the Nifty Fifties. What helped kick it off was a rock-and-roll Broadway musical, *Grease,* which was about the era's hot-rod youth culture and which ran for eight years after it opened in 1972. Then came the TV show *Happy Days,* starring Henry Winkler as Arthur Fonzarelli. A tough-guy 1950's biker with a tender heart, The Fonz won over the nation. There were Fonzie posters, Fonzie knee socks, Fonzie pillowcases. Not every young male plastered his hair into a ducktail, nor did every girl wear saddle shoes, but the black leather jacket became a standard wardrobe item.

One form of rebellion was to affect no style at all, which led, of course, to its own distinctive look. In the spring of 1970, a Danish yoga instructor, capitalizing on the excitement over Earth Day (see pp. 360–361), introduced Earth Shoes, which allowed the wearer to walk as if barefoot, "the way nature intended." The trudge back to nature could also be taken in Birkenstock sandals or Vibram-soled hiking boots, in an ensemble that often included faded jeans, a plaid flannel shirt, and a down vest. The most extreme natural look was to wear no clothes at all, and a momentary fad for "streaking" erupted. A self-proclaimed Streaker of the House ran naked through the Hawaii legislature, and another young man treated the nation's TV viewers to his body in the buff by streaking into the 1974 Academy Awards.

Toward the middle of the decade, a newfound soberness began to infect the fashion world. Men took to wearing

The leisure suit, a 1970's classic, proliferated through mid decade and included this double-knit, flare-legged model from the Montgomery Ward catalog.

Pet Rocks and Lava Lamps

No novelty appeared too outlandish to avoid attracting at least 15 minutes of fleeting fame. Consider the Pet Rock. Little more than a beach stone nested in a fancy box, it came with a manual explaining that it required neither feeding nor paper training. Who would pay $5 for such silliness? At least 5 million people in the autumn of 1975. And how about the Mood Ring, which shifted color according to the wearer's state of mind? In point of fact, the color change occurred when liquid crystals in the ring's clear plastic "stone" responded to changes in skin temperature. That did not discourage as many as 20 million customers from shelling out anywhere from $2.98 (at trinket shops) to $250 (the 14-karat-gold model) for the fun of owning one. Joe Namath, Muhammad Ali, and Sophia Loren all succumbed.

Another decade totem was the Lava Lamp, a cone-shaped fixture that, when plugged in, seethed with molten, multihued excitement. It fit just perfectly on a Parson's table in the archetypal 1970's setting: acrylic shag carpet, exposed brick wall, perhaps a water bed, and a hanging jungle of ferns, spider plants, and begonias, all strung up by a cat's cradle of knotted macramé cords.

MOOD RING

BLACK
Anxious · Excited

AMBER
Nervous · Tense

AMBER-GREEN
Troubled ·Uneasy

GREEN
Sensitive

BLUE-GREEN
Relaxed · Calm

DARK BLUE
Happy · Love

ADJUSTABLE

three-piece business suits, and a "dress-for-success" ethic put women into tailored jackets and conservative-length skirts. Not everyone went along, to be sure. For every Dorothy Hamill hairdo — an austere wedge-shaped cut named for the Olympic figure skater — there was a blow-dried Farrah Fawcett extravaganza, worn by someone hoping to emulate the sex appeal of the *Charlie's Angels* TV star. But the trend was there. In the end, the fashion moguls returned with a vengeance. Every jacket, every polo shirt, every pair of jeans, seemed to be stamped with a designer logo. It became clear that the no-style revolt was over.

HAPPY 200TH, AMERICA!

BUNKER HILL, BOSTON
In British uniforms, Revolutionary War buffs attack the rebels' hilltop positions in a replay of the famous battle.

July 4, 1976, fell on a Sunday. That weekend, right up to the moments when the celebrating reached a crescendo, the skeptics among us were saying that the birthday party would be all glitz and no soul, a tasteless mixture of jingoism and commercialism. But when the party was over, even most of the naysayers had to admit that something rare and wonderful had happened. As they had at the end of two world wars or when Neil Armstrong and Buzz Aldrin stepped out onto the surface of the moon, Americans all over the vast country smiled the same smile, cheered the same cheer. In the end it was not the parades, the fireworks, the speeches, the costumes, the reenactments of glorious events, or even the magnificent tall ships (shown here off Newport, Rhode Island, on their way to New York) that most moved us. It was the feeling that, despite our differences, we were all Americans, and that being an American was something to be very happy and proud about.

BALTIMORE
Grade schoolers show their true colors by creating the Grand Old Flag in chalk.

DALLAS
A fifth-generation Texan decks her hair with American flags, under a wide Bicentennial bonnet.

SEATTLE
For this enthusiastic well-wisher, it was not enough to make a cake for the nation's birthday; he found a way to wear it, too.

CROSS-COUNTRY WAGON TRAIN
Creaking through South Carolina on a Bicentennial journey, these latter-day covered wagons evoked the days of westward expansion.

WASHINGTON, D.C.
A wildly patriotic float joins a Bicentennial parade in the nation's capital. Even in the city of big bureaucracies, it was hard to be blasé about America's 200th birthday party.

PHILADELPHIA
The city where the Second Continental Congress adopted the Declaration of Independence on July 4, 1776, hosted a yearlong party. "Texas Day" (above), was one of 50 celebrations honoring the states.

VERMONT
Standing very tall, Uncle Sam on stilts leads the Bread and Puppet Theater's Independence Day parade in Plainfield, Vermont.

PHILADELPHIA
Red, white, and blue fireworks explode over Independence Hall, or Old State House, where John Hancock signed the Declaration exactly 200 years before.

MR. NICE GUY AND THE PEANUT FARMER

Gerald R. Ford, with wife Betty at his side, takes the oath on August 9, 1974, to become America's 38th president; Chief Justice Warren Burger swears him in. Ford was the only person to serve as both vice president and president without being elected to either office.

With prices rising at more than 11.5 percent a year, Ford launched a campaign to Whip Inflation Now. But unemployment was high, too, reaching 7.1 percent in 1974. Any cure for one evil could worsen the other.

It seemed astonishing: after 25 years in government, Jerry Ford could truthfully say, "I don't have a single enemy." But a series of presidential pratfalls caused voters to turn to a political unknown, a born-again peanut farmer from Georgia who liked to carry his own suitcases.

Three days after assuming office, President Gerald R. Ford told Congress: "I do not want a honeymoon with you. I want a good marriage." It was typical of the new chief executive's down-to-earth, shirt-sleeve style: no romance, just the familiar give-and-take of government as usual. In 25 years in Washington, first as an eager young congressman from Michigan, then as House minority leader, he had earned a reputation as the Eagle Scout of Republican politics: hardworking, plain speaking, scrupulously honest. True, at times he was a bit slow on the uptake, a man who, so the joke went, could not climb stairs and chew gum simultaneously. But Ford had been a star football player at the University of Michigan, a superior student at Yale Law School, and he was clearly no dummy.

One of his early acts as president was to grant an unconditional pardon to Richard Nixon, then under threat of indictment in the Watergate scandal. Ford was hoping to prevent the ghoulish spectacle of a former president being subjected to a court trial and perhaps a prison term. Instead what he got was a firestorm of public abuse. Accusations flew that Ford had struck a deal with Nixon to assure his selection as vice president after Agnew had resigned. The stock market plunged, and Ford's popularity rating dropped from 71 percent to 50 percent.

He never did regain the public's confidence. The worst problem facing his administration was the economy, hit by

Twice in 17 days, President Ford escaped assassination by mentally distraught women: here at Sacramento, California, on September 5, 1975, then again, in San Francisco. Both assailants got life in prison.

soaring unemployment and double-digit inflation. To stem rising prices, Ford tried persuasion. Avoid wasting money, he advised consumers. "Clean up your plate before you leave the table. . . . Guard your health." For good measure, he announced a volunteer program, Whip Inflation Now, and ordered some 12 million WIN buttons for general distribution. To Americans scrambling to make ends meet, it seemed hardly a serious effort.

Surprisingly, inflation did abate slightly, and the economy began to recover. But the president's tightfisted approach to government spending ignited another national brouhaha. Swollen municipal budgets in New York City were threatening to plunge the nation's largest metropolis into bankruptcy, but Ford refused to bail it out with a government loan. "FORD TO CITY: DROP DEAD" is how the New York *Daily News* phrased it. Other large municipalities, fearing they also might need federal help, protested. Eventually the president was persuaded to release the needed funds.

Despite Ford's fiscal restraint, everyone agreed his intentions were good. When a young woman stepped out of a crowd in California and tried to gun him down, the nation was shocked and astonished. How could anyone want to kill such a nice guy? (The would-be assassin, Lynette "Squeaky" Fromme, turned out to be a follower of mass killer Charles Manson.) Shortly after that, another severely addled woman, onetime FBI informant Sara Jane Moore, squeezed off several shots at him.

But Ford had a knack for embarrassing moments. His falls, on a ski slope and getting off a plane, made entertaining news. He also sliced golf balls into the spectator gallery and bumped his head entering the presidential limousine. Having reached the Oval Office through a political quirk, Ford became known as the "accidental" president.

Missteps and Moralizing

In 1976 Ford stood for election in his own right. After a tough primary battle — in which he edged out the charismatic governor from California, Ronald Reagan — he found himself facing a virtual political unknown. "My name is Jimmy Carter, and I'm running for president" is the way Ford's opponent felt obliged to start his stump speeches, just to make sure everybody recognized him.

James Earl Carter, Jr., was a true Washington outsider, a red-dirt peanut farmer and naval engineer from Plains, Georgia, whose experience in politics reached no further than a single term as state governor. He wore blue jeans to work, carried his own luggage, and presented himself as a fiscal conservative with a liberal social agenda. Some people resented his fondness for public moralizing; a born-again Baptist, he taught Sunday Bible classes. But no doubt about it, he brought a new approach to government. "I'll never tell a lie," he vowed. "I'll never make a misleading statement."

Even so, it was a close race. Shortly before the election, Carter gave an ill-advised interview with *Playboy* magazine, in which he shocked the nation by announcing he had "committed adultery in my heart many times." Perhaps he wanted to show that he was no prude, but the remark seemed wildly inept. Ford also bumbled. In a TV debate with Carter, he seemed to deny that the Soviet Union controlled Communist East Europe, a gaffe that became known as Ford's "Polish joke." At election time, Americans scarcely knew whom to pick. Carter just barely held on to his early popular lead and squeaked to victory with 50.1 percent of the vote.

▶

Jimmy Carter's folksy appeal — infectious grin, hearty handshake, and farm-boy background — helped convince voters that he would bring a grass-roots integrity to federal government.

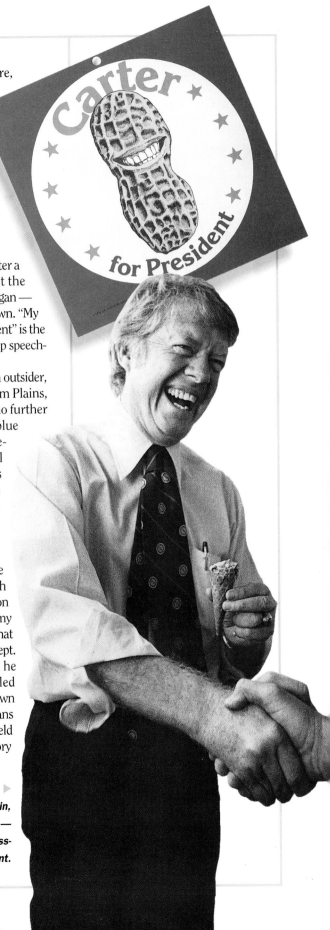

Three national leaders — Israeli Prime Minister Menachem Begin, Jimmy Carter, and Egyptian President Anwar el-Sadat — stand proudly at attention during a White House ceremony to mark the signing of the Camp David peace accord.

CAMP DAVID HOPE, HOSTAGE HORROR

Deeply earnest, with an engineer's mind for absorbing facts and figures, President Carter strove mightily to do good. But despite some important reforms, and a historic peace accord, Carter's presidency ended in frustration.

Some presidents — John Kennedy, for example — liked to read spy stories. Harry Truman preferred history books. For Jimmy Carter, bedside reading was the neo-Calvinist theologian Reinhold Niebuhr, who taught that a politician's highest duty is "to bring justice to a sinful world." No one can say that Carter did not aim high or give his utmost.

Carter moved to Washington resolved to cut costs, relieve poverty, promote civil rights, banish corruption, protect the environment, pursue détente with China and the Soviet Union, and generally encourage good behavior in domestic and world affairs. Right after his inauguration on Capitol Hill, he and First Lady Rosalynn waved aside the government limousine and walked up Pennsylvania Avenue to the White House, demonstrating their sense of the com-

mon touch. Once inside, he trimmed the White House staff, sold the presidential yacht, and ordered subordinates to drive their own cars. More substantial measures soon followed, including civil service reforms and a strict new code of government ethics. The president also moved to deregulate the airline, railroad, and trucking industries and to ease federal control of banks.

Washington is a hazardous city for newcomers, however, and Carter soon ran into trouble. By vetoing a fistful of expensive Western water projects, he ruffled the feathers of important congressmen. Then, launching an oil conservation program designed to relieve the decade's persistent energy worries, Carter declared "the moral equivalent of war." Critics shortened the phrase to MEOW, thereby transforming a lion's roar into a kitten's whine. Other lapses in political etiquette eroded his support even further. His budget director, Atlanta banker Bert Lance, was charged with sloppy financial dealings and forced to resign. A longtime aide from Georgia, Hamilton Jordan, was reportedly seen sniffing illegal substances at a trendy discotheque.

A Triumph of Statesmanship

One area in which the president from Plains came to show surprisingly strong leadership was foreign affairs. Taking his usual high-minded approach, he launched a global campaign for human rights, vowing that "fairness, not force" would guide American policy. This approach struck some people as hopelessly naive, but Carter persisted. He signed an agreement giving control of the Panama Canal to the Panamanians by the year 2000, raising howls of protest from conservatives. No one could fault the president's next initiative, however.

The story began in Jerusalem, the world's holiest city and the setting for some of its most savage hatreds. Here, to everyone's utter astonishment, a strange diplomatic courtship was taking place between those ancient enemies Israel and Egypt. The two nations had been at war for 30 years, with major eruptions in 1948, 1956, 1967, and in the Yom Kippur War of 1973. No peace treaty had ever been signed. Then, almost on impulse, Egyptian President Anwar el-Sadat decided to fly to Jerusalem and meet with Israel's hard-line prime minister, Menachem Begin.

As the two men attempted to talk peace, the old enmities resurfaced. So in stepped Jimmy Carter. Determined to

Iranian militants in the U.S. Embassy show off 1 of the 53 American hostages, most of them embassy staffers, who would spend the next 444 days in Iranian captivity. Freedom came January 20, 1981, just as Carter was leaving the White House.

Shah Mohammad Reza Pahlavi won medical asylum in America, then died in Egypt nine months later.

"Tie a yellow ribbon round the old oak tree," sang Tony Orlando and Dawn. And to honor the hostages, Americans did just that.

Month after month Iranian students paraded through the streets of Tehran denouncing the United States. A death's-head tops this Uncle Sam effigy, and the flags bear slogans reading "Down With U.S. Imperialism" in both English and Farsi.

restore harmony, Carter invited Begin and Sadat to Camp David, the presidential retreat in the Maryland hills. Here, in early September of 1978, they forged the framework for a peace agreement. It was not easy. "The atmosphere is really relaxed," said an Israeli aide, "but when it comes to ideas and positions, that's another story." At one point Sadat, enraged over some point of policy, fled to his cabin and started packing; Carter talked him into staying. After 13 days of intense negotiation, an agreement was reached.

It was Carter's greatest triumph. Then came 1979.

A Disaster in the Middle East

In February the president's brother, Billy — whose worst sin so far had been a genial, good-ole-boy oafishness — was found to be lobbying for Libya, a terrorist state. Then between March and June, the OPEC oil cartel raised the price of petroleum by 65 percent, bringing on the nation's second gas crisis of the decade. The economy stumbled to a

halt. The mighty Chrysler Corporation, the nation's 10th largest business, ran out of money and needed $1.5 billion in government loan guarantees to stay afloat.

The bottom was hit November 4. Some 8,000 miles to the east, in dusty, petroleum-rich Iran, a vengeful mob stormed the American Embassy compound in Tehran and took everyone prisoner. A fundamentalist Islamic revolution, led by the stern Ayatollah Khomeini, had recently overthrown the pro-American shah, who escaped into exile. Carter, knowing the shah to be mortally ill with cancer, allowed him into the United States to seek medical treatment. The Iranians, crying out for the shah's blood, sought a way to retaliate. The result: 66 Americans held hostage in the Tehran embassy.

Thirteen black hostages were set free early on to impress Third World nations. The other 53 remained captives for more than a year. They were blindfolded, beaten, paraded before TV cameras, threatened with immediate execution. An attempt to free them ended in disaster with several helicopters crashing in the desert south of Tehran. All the while Iranian mobs continued to demonstrate, shouting, "Death to America! Death to the Great Satan!" and burning straw effigies of Carter and Uncle Sam. Never, it seemed, had America's star sunk so low. How would it ever rise again?

373

ROCK MEETS DISCO

After the Beatles split up, listeners wondered where rock music would go. Every which way, as it turned out, from soft to hard, funk to punk, glitter to disco.

Their fans were horrified. In the very first year of the 1970's, the Beatles, rock music's reigning superstars, announced they were parting company. John Lennon underwent primal scream therapy, recorded some major hits, including "Imagine," and settled into countercultural married life with Yoko Ono. George Harrison, deep into Hindu philosophy, released the mystical *All Things Must Pass* and other LP's. Ringo made numerous recordings and pursued an acting career. But only Paul McCartney, with his new group, Wings, remained consistently on the charts; by 1979 he was the richest musician in the world. Even so, an era had clearly ended.

It seemed inconceivable that anyone could take their place. But no sooner had the Fab Four's shadow lifted than talented performers sprouted up by the hundreds. The mellow lilt of soft rock drifted in early. James Taylor and Joni Mitchell crooned confessional lyrics in muted tones, as though asking listeners for absolution. Carole King's moody 1971 *Tapestry* sold more than 14 million copies, making it the best-selling LP album up to that time. At the opposite extreme, hard rock bands like the Allman Brothers and Led Zeppelin radiated demoniac waves of cranked-up volume. And the brash, hard-edged voice of black funk groups, such as Sly and the Family Stone and George Clinton and Funkadelic, boomed out across the land.

Many musicians attempted to recapture the Beatles' chameleon charm, mixing soft and hard and borrowing from a range of musical idioms. Flaxen-haired Peter Frampton poured out a cleaned-up rock that some critics termed bland but that teenage girls adored. The mainstream sound of Fleetwood Mac propelled the group to megahit stardom, and its 1977 album *Rumours* won a Grammy award. Others, guessing rightly that rock is the art of performance, donned costumes and struck poses that would have

Disco's hottest tickets included, clockwise on this page from left: Donna Summer, shown on the cover of her hit album Bad Girls; *the Bee Gees, crooning in concert; the Village People, in macho guise as cowboy, Indian, soldier, biker, cop, and construction worker; and John Travolta, in his signature white suit, making a slick disco move on the set of* Saturday Night Fever.

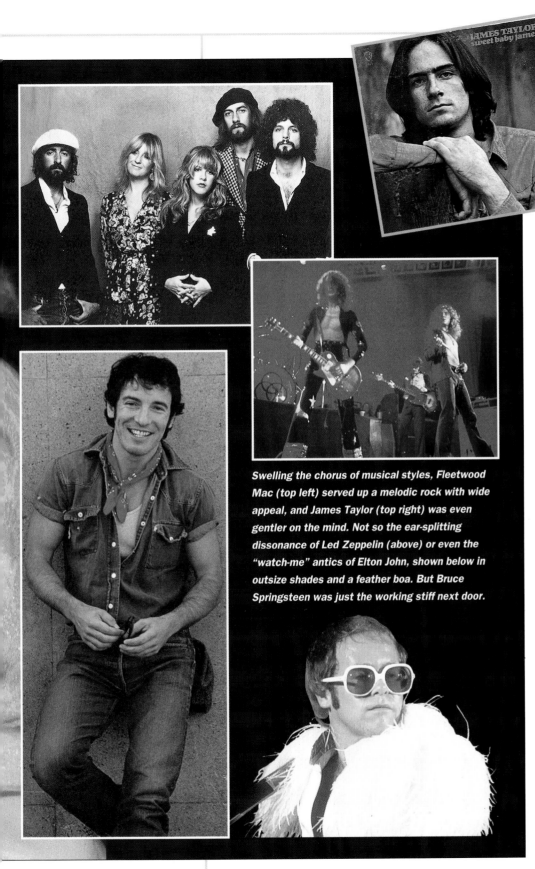

shocked Oscar Wilde. For the purveyors of glitter rock — Elton John, David Bowie, and Alice Cooper among them — outrageousness was all.

And some just presented their own natural selves. When Bruce Springsteen's *Born to Run* LP exploded off the charts in 1975, it seemed to usher in a virile, blue-collar reality: fanfare for the common man.

Dance! Dance! Dance!

Then disco entered the mainstream, offering a fast express to fantasyland. Gays, blacks, and Hispanics in underground after-hours clubs were already gyrating to a pounding, metronomic dance beat that — combined with simple, repetitive lyrics — eventually set the entire country in motion. "Dance! Dance! Dance! — Yowsah! Yowsah! Yowsah!" urged the black disco group Chic, and just about everyone jumped in. "The Hustle," by Van McCoy and the Soul City Symphony, sold 10 million copies in 1975. The next year "Love to Love You, Baby" established Donna Summer as the Queen of Disco. (During the song's 17-minute run, she moaned the title 28 times: "Ooooh, Aaaah . . . Love to Love You, Bay-Bee . . .") Then *Saturday Night Fever,* starring John Travolta as a flashy club dancer, added Hollywood's seal of approval. The sound track LP, featuring the Bee Gees, who revived their careers by mastering the disco sound, sold 25 million copies.

A campy sexual irony was part of the fun. Grace Jones, in a wedding dress and holding a whip, belted out "I Need a Man" on *The Merv Griffin Show.* A game Rod Stewart asked the public "Do Ya Think I'm Sexy?" and came up with a career best-seller. And The Village People, six hulking males, offered straight audiences such gay anthems as "Macho Man," "In the Navy," and "Y.M.C.A." The lyrics offended some listeners, but most of America just kept dancing.

Before the rage subsided, some 20,000 glittering discotheques were amplifying the noise. The most famous electronic temple was New York's celebrity-studded Studio 54, whose owners (before they went to jail for income tax evasion) insisted on "good-looking waiters and abusive doormen." Jackie Onassis, Truman Capote, Bianca Jagger, and even President Carter's mother, Lillian, made the scene. As hour upon hour the dance floor pulsated, DJ's blended their "mixes," adapting songs and volume to the mood of the crowd. When the music peaked and the dancers screamed, as one Los Angeles DJ put it, "They're mine."

Toward the decade's end, a new kind of rock called punk began elbowing its way into the music arena. Groups like the Ramones and the Sex Pistols preached a defiant message of raucous hostility. The fresh, innocent sound of the Beatles was rapidly fading into memory.

Swelling the chorus of musical styles, Fleetwood Mac (top left) served up a melodic rock with wide appeal, and James Taylor (top right) was even gentler on the mind. Not so the ear-splitting dissonance of Led Zeppelin (above) or even the "watch-me" antics of Elton John, shown below in outsize shades and a feather boa. But Bruce Springsteen was just the working stiff next door.

BLOCKBUSTERS HIT MOVIELAND

A crew of bright young directors brought new sparkle to the silver screen, rolling out lavish studio extravaganzas that reaped millions at the box office.

Some came from film school; others started out in television. Martin Scorsese, whose *Mean Streets* gave a tough new edge to the genre of the "gangster picture," had studied to be a priest. Whatever their background, the decade's *wunderkind* directors set out to redefine American film and to make a few bucks along the way. They succeeded beyond anyone's wildest expectations.

Francis Ford Coppola had been working in Hollywood nearly a decade when, at age 31, he won an Academy Award in 1970 for the script to *Patton*. Still, Paramount was taking a long shot when it chose him to film *The Godfather* (1972), from a best-selling novel chronicling the rise of the Corleone crime family. ("He knew the grit," an insider explained.) Against studio objections, Coppola cast Marlon Brando as the family patriarch Don Corleone; insisted on Al Pacino, a little-

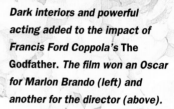

Dark interiors and powerful acting added to the impact of Francis Ford Coppola's The Godfather. The film won an Oscar for Marlon Brando (left) and another for the director (above).

The real stars of George Lucas's Star Wars were two robots, C-3PO and R2D2, who some thought upstaged the human leads, Carrie Fisher, Mark Hamill, and Harrison Ford.

known stage actor, as Corleone's youngest son; and demanded total period authenticity.

The Godfather grossed $43 million and earned Coppola another Oscar. He followed up with *The Godfather, Part II* (1974), a look at Don Corleone's youth. The picture earned him three more Oscars, for best screenplay, picture, and directing. His masterstroke was casting Robert de Niro, until then best known for his tough-guy lead in *Mean Streets,* as the young Don Corleone. (De Niro went on to play a psychopathic killer in Scorsese's 1976 *Taxi Driver,* making him a specialist in nastiness.) Nor was Coppola finished. In 1979 he released the decade's most ambitious film, *Apocalypse Now,* a Vietnam War saga that cost more than $30 million and took years to make.

The next newcomer to hit it big was Steven Spielberg, who got his start by walking onto the Universal lot. Spielberg was assigned low-budget chase movies at first, then, in 1975, at age 28, he was asked to direct *Jaws,* about a killer shark with an appetite for swimmers. To fill the title role, the producers devised a mechanical sea monster, which, unhappily, still had a few kinks when filming began. The studio was frantic. Spielberg rescued the film with inspired cinematic zoom-ins and zoom-outs for blood-chilling effects. No more snickers, just screams. *Jaws* became one of the top grossers ever.

Then Spielberg hit pay dirt again. *Close Encounters of the Third Kind* (1977) took a man and a woman to remote Wyoming for a rendezvous with UFO's and extraterrestrials. The movie was riddled with plot holes and awash in false premises. No matter. Spielberg performed his sleight of hand with the camera, and — presto — people in droves left the theaters feeling wonderful.

George Lucas went straight from USC's film school to Warner Brothers. In 1973, still in his mid-20's, he made the low-budget, highly acclaimed *American Graffiti*. His next move was a 180° swerve into science fiction. *Star Wars* took the best elements of Hollywood's past — the western's stark locales, World War II's aerial dogfights, *The Wizard of Oz*'s Tin Man camaraderie — and transformed them into desert planets, laser-beam spacecraft, and talking robots. Critics likened the result to a cinematic comic strip, but audiences loved it. The movie's gross went ballistic: nearly $300 million by the decade's end.

No movieland event had more critics shaking their heads than the remarkable success story of Sylvester Stallone, creator of *Rocky* and its socko sequels. In 1975 the 29-year-old Stallone — broke, his wife pregnant — penned a screenplay about a down-on-his-luck boxer

Sylvester Stallone poses as the dogged prizefighter Rocky Balboa in the first of many Rocky movies.

Steven Spielberg's Close Encounters of the Third Kind featured dazzling special effects created by electronics wizard Douglas Trumbull.

Director Spielberg enjoys a friendly moment with the star of Jaws.

who miraculously gets to fight the world heavyweight champion. Offered $360,000 for the script, Stallone refused the money unless he could play the lead. People hemmed, people hawed, but he got his way. The Italian Stallion trotted into the ring, and there he stayed year after year.

Hollywood still made all manner of films, of course. Director Bob Fosse had a musical hit with *Cabaret* and followed up with *All That Jazz*. Stars like Jack Nicholson *(Five Easy Pieces, One Flew Over the Cuckoo's Nest, Chinatown)* and Robert Redford *(The Sting, Three Days of the Condor, All the President's Men)* attracted ticket buyers and demanded upward-spiraling multimillion-dollar fees. Sex continued to sell: Jane Fonda played a prostitute stalked by a psychotic murderer in *Klute* and won an Oscar; ex-footballer Burt Reynolds, cavorting bare-chested, became the decade's hottest cinematic stud as well as *Cosmopolitan* magazine's first-ever nude male centerfold.

Other movies bucked the trend and still did magnificently. Robert Altman's *Nashville* challenged audiences with its offbeat casting and controversial plot. And who would have thought that Woody Allen, not everyone's idea of a suave leading man, would win over viewers in his sly urban romance *Annie Hall*? Or that Dustin Hoffman and Meryl Streep, caught in the midst of a bitter child-custody feud, would turn *Kramer vs. Kramer* into a three-hankie must?

Roots: A Megahit

For eight consecutive nights at the end of January 1977, America sat mesmerized. Businessmen canceled meetings, movie houses remained half empty, and even Congress went home early. No one wanted to miss a single episode of *Roots*, a brutal and riveting 12-hour epic of slavery in America, based on Alex Haley's best-selling family history and starring newcomer LeVar Burton (above). Viewers had seen other multipart dramas, to be sure, usually on public television; but *Roots* was the first true megahit. Some 130 million Americans watched at least part of it, giving ABC its highest one-week rating ever. And a new TV staple, the miniseries, came into being.

At home with All in the Family: *Carroll O'Connor and Jean Stapleton as Archie and Edith, with Rob Reiner and Sally Struthers*

ARCHIE, MARY, HAWKEYE, AND FRIENDS

Accustomed to a diet of silly comedies, conventional drama, and wacky variety shows, TV viewers were about to get the shock of their lives.

The year 1971 marked a watershed in American television. Three old soldiers marched off camera: poker-faced Ed Sullivan, clowning Red Skelton, and syncopating music-maker Lawrence Welk. In swaggered Archie Bunker, the blue-collar hero of *All in the Family*, carrying a satchel of blustery quirks and stubborn ethnic prejudices that made people's hair stand on end. "Archie Bunker ain't no bigot," TV's new everyman told a black neighbor, "it ain't your fault you're colored." Viewers did a quick double take and burst out laughing. Enter the real-life sitcom, which served up brash humor along with social relevance. Television would never be the same again.

All in the Family brought a gritty, tell-it-like-it-is immediacy to the tube. Archie, played by Carroll O'Connor, shared his Queens, New York, home with "dingbat" wife Edith (Jean Stapleton), good-natured daughter Gloria (Sally Struthers), and long-haired son-in-law Mike (Rob Reiner), whom he referred to as meathead. The show dealt regularly with hitherto taboo subjects, such as racism, rape, impotence, and menopause. Mike got a vasectomy. Gloria made friends with a transvestite. ("She's a nice fella," Archie grudgingly admitted.)

Audiences could not get enough. *All in the Family* continued for 12 years, one of the longest runs in television. Several of its characters moved on to shows of their own, establishing *Maude* and *The Jeffersons* as decade hits.

Another sitcom with a social conscience, *The Mary Tyler Moore Show*, struck a particularly resonant chord with career women. *MTM* depicted the weekly comic travails of Mary Richards, an aspiring TV executive (played by Mary Tyler Moore) who works as associate producer for a Minneapolis news program. Mary was over 30, still single, and spunky as all get-out. When her boss, Lou Grant (Ed Asner), asked personal questions during a job interview, she at first protested; then, like many other job seekers in the 1970's, she swallowed her pride. Lou: "What religion are you?" Mary: "Mr. Grant, you're not allowed to ask that. . . . It's against the law." Lou, persisting: "Are you married?" Mary, in a tiny voice: "Presbyterian."

Over seven seasons, *The Mary Tyler Moore Show* won 27 Emmys, including 3 for best comedy, 5 for writing, and 14 for acting. And it spun off three successful series: *Rhoda, Phyllis,* and *Lou Grant.*

For a country deeply divided by the Vietnam conflict, *M*A*S*H,* a black comedy about a Mobile Army Surgical Hospital unit in the Korean War, tugged hard on raw emotions. Amid the bloodshed and the boredom of life at the front, a grim, sardonic humor bubbled up. Here was Capt. Hawkeye Pierce (Alan Alda) making surgical rounds in a gorilla suit; performing a phony appendectomy in order to sideline an inept general; eavesdropping on the sexual exploits of Maj. Hot Lips Houlihan (Loretta Swit), a supposedly prim head nurse. Hawkeye and his pals, confronting death daily, used wisecracks like morphine injections. "I loathe you," rasped one nonadmirer, exasperated at Hawkeye's antics. "I call your loathe and raise two despises," came the retort.

M*A*S*H, with its powerful antiwar message, ran 11 seasons. Some 125 million viewers watched the final episode, a 2½-hour special called "Good-bye, Farewell, and Amen."

In 1975 a TV newsmagazine named *60 Minutes,* which had been limping along for years, received a face-lift. CBS added a third correspondent, Dan Rather, to the Morley Safer–Mike Wallace duo and moved the show to prime time.

It proceeded to take off. Sharply different reportorial styles gave balance and pace: Safer was polished; Wallace, confrontational; Rather, reasonable. The trademark technique of putting the reporters before the camera, on location, lent immediacy and controversy. Safer went to Arizona to uncover a real-estate scam, and federal indictments fol-

Stars of the 1970's, clockwise from top left: the cast of M*A*S*H, Alan Alda sitting; Mary Tyler Moore; Mike Wallace and Harry Reasoner from 60 Minutes; John Belushi and Garret Morris as Coneheads on Saturday Night Live; and at center, Sesame Street's feathery, friendly Big Bird

lowed; Wallace journeyed to the Middle East to interview Jews in Syria; Rather spent time in Florida exposing the finances of a congressman, and a formal House reprimand ensued. In 1979 when Harry Reasoner, a reassuring father figure, added his calm presence, *60 Minutes* went into high gear. It became that rare TV phenomenon: a news program that earned a No. 1 popularity rating.

In 1975, NBC's irreverent *Saturday Night Live* became the most popular offering on late-night TV. For 90 minutes the Not Ready for Prime-Time Players lampooned the great and the would-be great. Chevy Chase satirized a bumbling President Ford; Dan Aykroyd, a cornpone President Carter; and Gilda Radner, the speech mannersims of Barbara Walters. Mock newscasts ("Good eve-ning! I'm Chevy Chase and you're not") alternated with movie parodies. Orson Welles's last words in *Citizen Kane,* viewers learned, were "roast beef on rye," not "Rosebud."

To be sure, some shows still mined tried-and-true nuggets of formula comedy and drama. Teenagers saw their idealized selves in *The Partridge Family* and *The Brady Bunch.* The heartwarming courage of *The Waltons,* a rural Virginia family facing Depression-era hardship, gave inspiration to millions. *Charlie's Angels* and *Happy Days,* both sheer escapism, zoomed to the top in the ratings. Meanwhile, the newly established Public Broadcasting System was treating America to a stream of upscale British imports, including *The Forsyte Saga, Elizabeth R,* and *Upstairs, Downstairs.* Public television also gave children a year-round Christmas present: with Big Bird and Kermit the Frog, *Sesame Street* made it really fun to learn your ABC's.

WOMEN ON THE MOVE

They had come far, but full equality for women remained a long, frustrating march ahead. A cry went up for child care centers, equal employment opportunity, equal pay, and an Equal Rights Amendment.

Demanding full equality, demonstrators parade down New York's Fifth Avenue to celebrate 50 years of say-so at the ballot box.

Barbara Jordan (top) addresses the 1976 Democratic Convention; Congresswoman Millicent Fenwick (middle) represents a New Jersey district; and Shirley Chisholm (above) runs for president in 1972.

It had been a half-century of advances and some setbacks since the day on August 26, 1920, when American women won the right to vote. Now they gathered to mark that event and to rev up for the battles that lay ahead. Militants in Philadelphia put on a karate demonstration. In Miami they smashed crockery. In Syracuse, New York, mothers pushing for state-funded child care lugged their toddlers to a "baby-in" at city hall. "Today is the beginning of a new movement," feminist author Kate Millett told some 10,000 cheering fans at a rally in New York City. "Today is the end of millenniums of oppression."

Yes, a new dawn was surely rising. Congress, responding to the liberated mood of the moment, dusted off an equal rights amendment to the Constitution, which had been languishing in committee since 1923. "Equality of rights under the law shall not be denied or abridged by the United States or by any State on account of sex," the proposal read, and in 1972 Congress passed it overwhelmingly. All that was needed for ERA to become law was formal approval by three-fourths of the states. Other measures sped through Congress: a Child Development Act, an extension of the Equal Employment Opportunity Act of 1972 (to give the Equal Employment Opportunity Commission some muscle), and an Equal Credit Opportunity Act. "This is not a bedroom war," noted Betty Friedan, author of *The Feminine Mystique* (1963) and a founder of the National Organization for Women (NOW), "this is a political movement." And politics seemed to be winning.

Fast Start, Slow Death, for ERA

Then came the cold realities. President Nixon vetoed the Child Development Act, claiming that the day-care centers it authorized might undermine America's family-centered traditions. A hodgepodge of legal decisions supported the Equal Employment Opportunity Act, but their effect was hard to discern. Even though more than half of all adult

Editor Gloria Steinem, showing a gleefully pregnant President Carter on the latest cover of Ms. magazine, expresses disappointment over his first year in office.

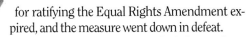

First Ladies Lady Bird Johnson, Rosalynn Carter, and Betty Ford join Bella Abzug to raise a torch at the National Women's Conference in Houston, Texas.

females would join the workforce by 1980, most found themselves restricted to a "pink-collar ghetto" (as Gloria Steinem's *Ms.* magazine put it) of low-wage "women's" jobs, such as typing, cleaning house, waiting tables, selling perfume, and teaching school. For every dollar men earned in 1973, women made only 57 cents, a significant drop from the 63-cents-to-the-dollar ratio recorded 10 years earlier. "We are triumphantly galloping toward tokenism," remarked Steinem of the statistics.

Perhaps the biggest disappointment in the women's rights movement was the roller-coaster course of ERA. On its way to what seemed like certain ratification, the amendment passed quickly through 35 state legislatures. Then, with just three states needed for ratification, progress screeched to a halt. The strident tone of much feminist rhetoric — "Repent Male Chauvinists, Your World Is Coming to an End" was one of the less inflammatory slogans — alarmed mainstream Americans, and the Equal Rights Amendment suddenly became controversial. Opposition rallied around the conservative antifeminist Phyllis Schlafly, a lawyer and mother of six. "I believe that strong nations are built on strong families," Schlafly said, and went on to imply that ERA could bring about tax-funded abortions, homosexual marriages, and more. Would parents find their daughters drafted into the army? Would women be made to share public toilets with men?

The answer was no on all counts, but the damage had already been done. The time limit

From an apron full of buttons to a samplerlike poster (right, above), by 1977 the campaign for women's rights reached fever pitch.

for ratifying the Equal Rights Amendment expired, and the measure went down in defeat.

But on the education and job fronts there were gains for women. The ranks of female executives increased. The number of women attending college rose by 45 percent between 1970 and 1975; in medical school it doubled; in law school it increased fourfold. The nation saw its first female firefighters, airline pilots, railroad engineers, construction workers, and telephone "linepersons." More women went into politics. Nancy Kassebaum of Kansas took a seat in the U.S. Senate, and Connecticut's Ella Grasso became the first elected woman governor of a state. President Carter appointed women to 21 percent of his administration's executive posts.

As women surged into the workforce, they paid a price for their success. Most two-career families required a "superwoman," who, after eight hours of wage-earning toil, was expected to come home, cook dinner, do the laundry, and tuck in the children. "There's a socioeconomic jet lag," declared one California professional woman. "Now we get the jobs all right, all the jobs — at home, with the kids, and at work." Or as Archie Bunker, the never-to-be-reconstructed male chauvinist in TV's *All in the Family,* declared: "All right, Edith, you go right ahead and do your thing . . . but just remember that your thing is eggs over easy and crisp bacon."

In November 1977 women rallied again, some 20,000 strong, at the National Women's Conference in Houston, Texas. Bella Abzug, head of President Carter's National Advisory Committee for Women, gave a speech, and in an interview with *Time* magazine after the conference, she said it all: "The issues aren't going to go away and neither are we."

MILITANT MINORITIES EVERYWHERE

Inspired by the black civil rights movement, all kinds of previously neglected groups — from senior citizens to Americans Indians to homosexuals — began flexing their muscles.

It was like an old black-and-white movie run in reverse. At Wounded Knee, a prairie hamlet in South Dakota, some 200 rifle-toting members of the American Indian Movement (AIM) attacked a trading post, seized 11 hostages, and for 69 days held off a siege by U.S. marshals. The site was significant. Nearly a century earlier, in 1890, the U.S. Cavalry had slaughtered more than 150 Sioux refugees here, women and children included. But now, in 1973, times were different. The AIM attackers, declaring themselves the Independent Oglala Sioux Nation, demanded a review of all Indian treaties and related U.S. government policies. "We have bet our lives that we could change the course of history of . . . Indian America," said Russell Means, an AIM leader.

Indian America was not faring well. Of all the minority groups, Native Americans experienced the highest unemployment (40 percent), the lowest per capita income ($974 a year on large reservations), the worst high-school dropout rate (53 percent), and the lowest standards of housing and sanitation. Alcoholism, tuberculosis, infant mortality, and suicide were epidemic. While some reservations owned rich deposits of coal, oil, and gas, they were being leased under federal supervision to private mining companies at giveaway rates.

Like other beleaguered minorities, Native Americans began protesting. Militants occupied the abandoned federal penitentiary at Alcatraz, an ancient Indian site. Demonstrators marched to Washington on the eve of the 1972 presidential election and barricaded themselves inside the Bureau of Indian Affairs. Gradually history adjusted its course. The Nixon administration returned 48,000 acres of sacred land to the Taos Pueblos; thousands more acres were restored to other tribes.The Sioux won a settlement of more than $100 million for their sacred Black Hills.

One of the most surprisingly militant protests emerged from a minority that up to then had hidden itself in silence. In June of 1969, New York City police raided a Greenwich Village bar, the Stonewall Inn, which catered to homosexuals. The patrons, instead of meekly submitting, fought back with beer bottles and fists. Thus began the gay rights move-

◄

Michelle Morgan takes a quiet bus ride on the first day of voluntary school integration in Milwaukee, Wisconsin. In the Boston area (insets), residents battled forced busing.

ment, which through protest and the ballot box, sought to overturn generations of discrimination and abuse.

The very idea was deeply disturbing to many straight Americans. In Miami, which passed a city ordinance banning discrimination against gays, singer Anita Bryant launched the Save Our Children movement, vowing to stop "this insidious attack on God and His laws." Violence erupted in San Francisco, where a growing gay population had elected a gay city supervisor, Harvey Milk. One November day in 1978, a retired police officer, Dan White, walked into City Hall and emptied the bullets of his .38 revolver into Milk, killing him. Then, for good measure, White stepped into the next office and killed the mayor, George Moscone. In court, White claimed a diet of junk food had rendered him mentally unstable — the notorious "Twinkie defense" — and he was sentenced to seven years in jail.

Maggie Kuhn, founder of the Gray Panthers, gives her organization's militant salute. "The system needs changing" to accommodate old people, she preached.

An understanding mother marches for tolerance during Gay Pride Week in New York City, 1973.

Foot soldiers of the American Indian Movement march on Wounded Knee in 1973, and later to Washington from San Francisco in a five-month, 3,000-mile-longest walk, just to let other Americans know "we are here."

Controversy continued to plague the march to equality of black Americans. The most heated issue was busing, ferrying students outside their school district to achieve racial integration. Several cities tried it, and the Supreme Court okayed it. But a great many Americans resented the idea. In Boston, riots broke out in 1974 when buses carrying black children from Roxbury arrived at schools in predominantly Irish South Boston. Bumper stickers in Louisville, Kentucky, urged drivers to "honk if you oppose busing," and riots erupted there, too. Nationwide, membership in the Ku Klux Klan grew from 5,000 to 10,000 in just two years.

Even so, blacks made significant strides. Despite generally high unemployment, large numbers moved into white-collar, middle-class jobs. More went to college than in the past: one-third of all black high school graduates by 1980. In politics, too, blacks were making their way. Several major cities, including Atlanta and Los Angeles, boasted black mayors. In Washington the Congressional Black Caucus, founded in 1970, was an important voice in the House of Representatives. Presidents Ford and Carter each appointed blacks to Cabinet positions, and Carter named his friend Andrew Young as America's first black delegate to the United Nations. More blacks became judges than ever before.

New Pressures from the Oldest Generation

Some 20 million Americans had reached age 65 when the decade began, and most faced a mandatory, cold-comfort retirement on small fixed incomes. That would change. As the nation's fastest-growing minority, seniors began to make themselves heard. Some joined the militant Gray Panthers, while the mainstream American Association of Retired Persons quadrupled its membership to nearly 12 million. In Congress, 77-year-old Florida Congressman Claude Pepper, hoping to ban forced retirement in corporate America, held hearings. Demanded actor John Wayne, who came to testify, "Which of you is going to step up and put me out to pasture?"

Which, indeed? Congress raised the mandatory retirement age to 70 and, by 1986, would outlaw it altogether. Also, in an effort to combat the terrible effects of inflation, Congress would add a cost adjustment to Social Security benefits, providing something of a cushion for 25 million elderly Americans.

THE LONGEST WALK
TO PROTEST ANTI-INDIAN LEGISLATION
FEBRUARY 11, 1978

PROBING THE SECRETS OF LIFE

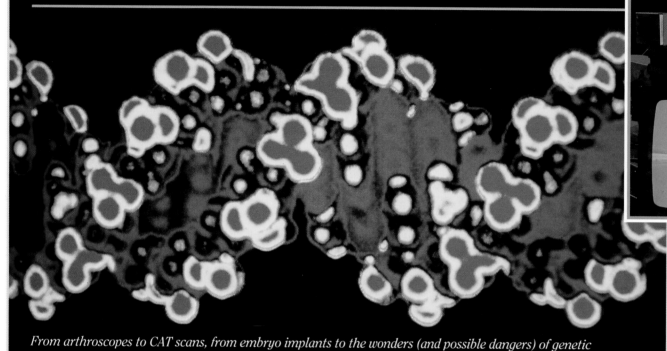

From arthroscopes to CAT scans, from embryo implants to the wonders (and possible dangers) of genetic manipulation, an arsenal of new techniques propelled medical science headlong toward the future.

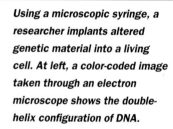

Using a microscopic syringe, a researcher implants altered genetic material into a living cell. At left, a color-coded image taken through an electron microscope shows the double-helix configuration of DNA.

▼ *At age two, test-tube baby Louise Brown was just as normal as she could be.*

S he has a set of lungs like a glassblower," marveled a hospital staffer in Oldham, England, on July 25, 1978. Even if the 5-pound 12-ounce blond, blue-eyed Louise Brown had been delivered without opening her mouth, her birth would have been one of the most resounding in history. She was the world's first test-tube baby.

Blocked fallopian tubes had prevented Louise's mother, Lesley, from conceiving. So surgeons removed an egg from one of Lesley's ovaries, fertilized it in a glass dish with her husband's sperm, and then implanted it in her uterus. Nine months later Louise came squalling into the world. This first in vitro fertilization to result in a full term pregnancy, after 80 previous failures, gave new hope to infertile women everywhere.

The 1971 invention of the silicon chip microprocessor foretold another revolution in medicine. Computers invaded the nation's hospitals to serve as electronic nurses in critical care units. Patients found themselves hooked to an array of electronic monitoring devices, which kept tabs on blood pressure, heartbeat, respiration, kidney function, and the like. A computer could sound an alert for help, or recommend a treatment, or even direct the automatic pumping of needed substances into the patient's body.

The computer was central to another invention, the CAT (computerized axial tomography) scanner. This remarkable machine, for which inventors Allan Cormack and Godfrey Hounsfield won a Nobel Prize, allows doctors a close look at a patient's internal organs without surgery. It takes a series of X-rays, which the computer integrates into a minutely detailed portrait; abnormalities as small as one or two millimeters show up clearly. Other internal viewing techniques soon followed: positron-emission tomography (PET), in which the patient receives an injection of radioactive glucose that helps generate an image; and sonarlike ultrasound, which is used in viewing fetuses in pregnancy and to detect problems such as kidney stones.

One medical advance was prompted not by disease but by a health craze, jogging. Many

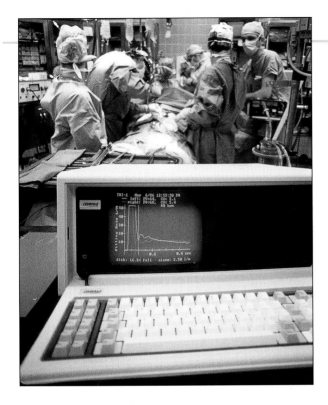

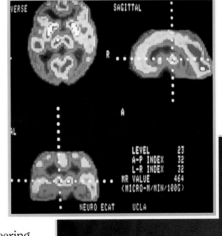

▶

Microelectronic receptors in this artificial forearm will amplify signals from an amputee's remaining muscles, causing motion in the computerized hand.

◀

In a balloon angioplasty, surgeons thread a catheter up a patient's leg toward a clogged artery in his heart. When the catheter reaches the damaged section, a tiny balloon will inflate to dislodge the blockage. A computer in the foreground monitors the procedure.

runners, pounding out their daily miles, found that their knees gave way under the strain. Traditional operations to repair damaged knees required large incisions and could mean months of painful recovery time.

Enter the arthroscope, a new instrument thin enough to slip through a small incision in the knee. Its optical fibers allowed doctors to see right into the joint, and its tiny instruments could perform many types of surgical repair. Patients often returned to work within three to five days.

Other microsurgical techniques were bringing dramatic improvements to patients' lives. Surgeons learned to stitch tiny nerves and blood vessels, to reconnect severed limbs, to probe the eye with diamond-bladed scalpels. A procedure called balloon angioplasty allowed surgeons to ream out clogged coronary arteries without opening the chest.

The surpassing technological achievement of the decade, as important in its way as splitting the atom, was the splicing of genes. With genetic engineering, first accomplished in 1973, scientists could alter a cell's behavior by manipulating its DNA — the hereditary material that controls it. Each strand of DNA contains genes, heredity's building blocks, and by snipping out a particular gene or transplanting a gene from another organism, researchers undertook to custom-tailor life's basic elements. Simple *E. coli* bacteria were transformed into factories for the low-cost manufacture of human insulin (to treat diabetics) and of growth hormone (to overcome hormonal dwarfism).

Bacteria were altered to gobble up oil spills. Plants were engineered to resist disease, drought, frost, and insects. Other research led to tests to determine who might be predisposed to genetic disorders such as Huntington's disease.

Scientists' newfound ability to alter life raised shudders of alarm among many laymen. People worried that researchers, in manipulating DNA, might unwittingly create a virulent killer bacterium that, escaping the laboratory, would sweep the planet. The government set strict controls, but the concerns persisted. "Biologists have become, without wanting it, custodians of great and terrible power," admitted one biologist. "It is idle to pretend otherwise."

Most medical wonders aroused less anxiety. When residents of Old Lyme, Connecticut, developed mysterious arthritic and neurological problems, researchers found the cause to be a bacterium carried by the deer tick; antibiotics lessened the symptoms of Lyme disease. Antibiotics also provided treatment for Legionnaires' disease, a hitherto unknown strain of pneumonia that killed 29 celebrants at an American Legion convention in Philadelphia. And in 1977 a native of Somalia suffered the world's last naturally occurring case of smallpox, a scourge that is for now eradicated.

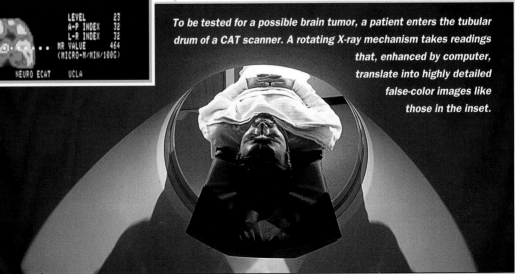

To be tested for a possible brain tumor, a patient enters the tubular drum of a CAT scanner. A rotating X-ray mechanism takes readings that, enhanced by computer, translate into highly detailed false-color images like those in the inset.

385

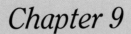

Chapter 9

THE CLOSING YEARS

The Soviet Union dissolves, and America stands preeminent, rich and powerful, with the awesome responsibility of leading the world into the next millennium.

The tools of the Information Age, like this International Maritime Satellite, draw us ever closer together.

OUT OF THE WEST COMES RONALD REAGAN

More than Reagan's robustness and movie-star charm, it was his deep-seated belief in the old-fashioned traditions of patriotism, optimism, and self-sufficiency that stirred many Americans.

◄ Reagan poses with one of the horses at his California ranch in 1979, before launching his bid for the presidency. He presented an image of youthful vigor even though, at age 69, he would be the oldest American ever elected to the presidency.

▲ Standing proud even though he is the smallest, young Ronnie steals the show in this family portrait taken around 1915. Though his family was poor, he was a leader: high school football star, student council president, and summer lifeguard credited with saving 78 people from drowning.

Announcing his candidacy for the presidency in late 1979, Ronald Reagan, onetime actor and former governor of California, would hear from no skeptics concerning America's future. "There are those in our land," he said, "who would have us believe that the United States, like other great civilizations of the past, has reached the zenith of its power. I don't believe that."

It was a time when some Americans might well have believed that their nation was in decline. Inflation was spi-

Lovers on-screen and married off, Ron and Nancy share a tender moment in Hellcats of the Navy, *their only film together.*

◄

In his first adult job, Reagan mans the microphone at an Iowa radio station in 1932.

raling into the double digits, and federal spending seemed to have a life of its own. Overseas, American hostages languished in an Iranian prison despite months of intense negotiating by the Carter administration. And the threat of Soviet expansion always loomed. It seemed as if America the superpower had lost its way. Reagan backers saw their fellow citizens turn to the Republican Party for answers and toward a strong, no-nonsense leader to get the United States back on track. When, at one of the presidential debates, Reagan asked the question "Are you better off than you were four years ago?" few Americans could answer enthusiastically in the affirmative. He won by a landslide.

After delivering his address on Inauguration Day, 1981, Reagan made an electrifying statement. Iran, he announced, was releasing all the hostages. The long-awaited

▲ *A future president plays opposite Pat O'Brien in Knute Rockne — All American in 1940.*

news set the optimistic tone for the change-over to the Reagan presidency.

As Reagan and his wife of almost 30 years, Nancy, swept into the White House, Americans watched with fascination. Gone was the down-home frugality of the Carter administration. The new president and his First Lady were a combination of elegance, graciousness, and easy-going style not seen since the Kennedy administration. Yet Reagan projected the image of a man of the people. He was a self-proclaimed citizen politician.

Ronald Reagan was born on Main Street in Tampico, Illinois. Dutch, as his father had nicknamed him, attended Eureka College near Peoria, where he played football, acted, and became involved in college politics. After graduation he pursued a career as a radio sports announcer, which ultimately led him to Hollywood. Along the way Reagan cultivated an engaging personal style and honed his rhetorical skills, which one day would earn him the moniker the Great Communicator. He also became active in the Screen Actors' Guild, serving as that union's president in the years 1947 to 1952. His next stint, as host of the *General Electric Theater* television series and one of the company's spokesmen, gave Reagan ample opportunity to further fine-tune his innate

▲ *Stepping into the spotlight at the 1981 inaugural ball, Ronald and Nancy Reagan draw a standing ovation.*

Running against Reagan in 1984, Walter Mondale and Geraldine Ferraro (right), the first female vice presidential candidate of a major party, work a Columbus Day crowd. Jesse Jackson (below) campaigns during the Democratic primary.

talent for persuasive public speaking.

Though still a New Deal Democrat through the 1950's, Reagan grew increasingly conservative. By 1962 he was a registered Republican; two years later he supported the ultraconservative Arizonan Barry Goldwater's presidential campaign. Reagan thrilled TV audiences with a powerful speech at the 1964 Republican National Convention, prompting a group of California Republicans to ask him to run for governor. He did so and won easily. The year was 1966, and almost immediately talk of a bid for the presidency began. He would first run for the highest office in 1976, after two terms as governor.

President at last in 1981, Reagan had served only 70 days in office when a would-be assassin's bullet lodged in his chest. His reaction to the brush with death displayed a fortitude rarely seen outside the movies. "Honey, I forgot to duck," he told his wife, quoting boxer Jack Dempsey after his loss to Gene Tunney. Within days Reagan was back in the presidential saddle.

Over his two terms, Reagan became a hero to many Americans. He seemed sincerely concerned with the questions that kept them up at night, and comfortably familiar, right down to his corny jokes and jelly-bean habit. At the

same time, he was tough enough to fire illegally striking air traffic controllers, sending a message that labor unions should henceforth stay in line. As likable on television as he was in person, Reagan was welcome in America's living rooms. He used TV to sell his administration's supply-side economic plan (later called Reaganomics), which proposed to slash federal spending and cut income taxes dramatically. The money freed by this plan, he said, would encourage investments, stimulating economic growth. As a result, profits from the ensuing prosperity would "trickle down" from the upper to the middle and even to the lower classes.

After a short, virulent recession in Reagan's first term, his economic program seemed to work. From late 1982 to 1988, America enjoyed the longest peacetime economic expansion in its history. The economy added more than 17 million new jobs, inflation dropped to single digits, and the gross national product showed the biggest percentage increase in 33 years. But other figures seemed less reassuring. Despite big cuts in social programs, federal spending continued to escalate as the Pentagon's budget soared to offset the perceived Soviet threat. Because of Reagan's massive tax cuts, the government took in less money, and it had to borrow heavily to pay its bills. Once the world's biggest lender, the United States became its largest debtor.

Many Americans also admired Reagan's firm hand in dealing with the Soviets, who were not only beefing up their nuclear arsenal but expanding their influence in countries

Chief Justice Warren Burger escorts Reagan appointee Sandra Day O'Connor, the first female Supreme Court justice.

The Iran-Contra Affair

The worst crisis of the Reagan presidency, as intricate as the plot of a James Bond thriller, erupted in the autumn of 1986. That November reports surfaced that the United States, despite a strict long-standing embargo and a pledge never to pay tribute to terrorists, was secretly selling military equipment to Iran. In return, Iran was supposed to obtain release of American hostages held in Lebanon.

Revelations came thick and fast. Money from the arms sales, it turned out, was being diverted to help Contra rebels battle the leftist Sandinista government in Nicaragua. Back in 1982 Congress had prohibited the use of federal funds for this purpose. Both operations — the Iran arms deal and the Contra aid — were being masterminded by Oliver North, an aide to national security adviser Robert C. McFarlane and his successor John M. Poindexter. Was Reagan himself involved? A seven-year investigation cleared him of wrongdoing.

such as Afghanistan and Angola. Reagan convinced Americans that Soviet expansionism could be stemmed through negotiations combined with a revitalization of the U.S. military. Pouring more than $2 trillion into the Pentagon, the largest peacetime arms buildup in history, the president boosted the size of the armed forces and modernized equipment. And he championed a program to develop weapons that, from their orbit in outer space, would destroy nuclear warheads before they fell to earth: the Star Wars program, opponents dubbed it.

The good news was that the pressure seemed to slow Communist expansionism. The Soviets withdrew from Afghanistan. Their allies, the Cubans, did the same in Angola. But curbing Communist influence wasn't easy. No amount of discreet intervention seemed sufficient to dislodge the leftist Sandinista government from Nicaragua (top of column). In addition, throughout the 1980's, Islamic militants carried out hijackings and terrorist attacks against westerners. Dozens of foreign nationals were taken hostage, tortured, and imprisoned in Lebanon. (The last American captive, journalist Terry Anderson, won release only in 1993.) Despite these distractions, Reagan successfully concluded negotiations with Gorbachev on the Intermediate-Range Nuclear Forces (INF) Treaty in December 1987. The

▼ *Reagan loved the ceremonies of office, from signing autographs for visiting Girl Scouts to giving foreign dignitaries personal tours around Washington, D.C. Here he reviews the White House Honor Guard with Britain's Prime Minister Margaret Thatcher in 1988.*

Reagan confers with National Security Adviser Robert McFarlane (left) and Secretary of State George Shultz aboard Air Force One.

INF Treaty had been 10 years in the making and represented a warming of relations on both sides of the Iron Curtain.

Reagan also had his detractors. Some saw him as a lightweight. "You could walk through Ronald Reagan's deepest thoughts," one critic said, "and not get your ankles wet." Others considered his ideological leanings too far to the right. Poor people and their advocates denounced as a sham the "trickle down" principle implied by Reaganomics: the wealth created at the top never did trickle down, they said. Indeed, each day more Americans fell below the poverty line. Some farmers, confronted with shrinking federal subsidies, faced bankruptcy. "This administration doesn't give a cocklebur for rural America," raged one farm-state senator. Meanwhile, opponents of Reagan's allies on the new religious right began to turn on the president. And civil rights supporters became alienated as Reagan criticized affirmative action and school integration and only reluctantly agreed to renew the Voting Rights Act of 1965.

But many of his adversaries' criticisms seemed not to stick to this popular president, whom Colorado Congresswoman Pat Shroeder had called "Teflon coated." His supporters felt the United States was in many respects "back," just as the Republican campaign ads had promised. Most Americans were happy with a leader who could lick the bad guys, get his programs through Congress with bipartisan approval, and at the end of the day go home to his wife and watch a movie in the White House screening room. When Ronald Reagan left office in 1989, he enjoyed one of the highest presidential approval ratings ever.

FROM GLITZ TO GRUNGE

A lot of people in the 1980's wanted to look like they were rich and powerful, and clever designers were glad to oblige. Then came a crash and a slump and an astonishing inner-city style called hip-hop.

"You ought to do jeans," said a licensing company owner to designer Calvin Klein one night at Studio 54, the late-1970's disco hot spot in New York City. Klein took the advice and created a snug-fitting version of the tradition-al blue jeans. He got Brooke Shields (then, in 1980, a mere 15 years old) to slip them on for a commercial. Many objected to the sexy ads, but before long, a lot of people were paying extravagantly for denims that displayed Calvin Klein's, Gloria Vanderbilt's, and other designers' names on the derrière.

Glamour, wealth, and power — from the elegant First Couple to glitzy nighttime soap operas — were back in style. Business was booming. The rich were out in full force, not only organizing lavish, highly publicized charity functions, but also throwing ex-travagant parties for themselves (billionaire Malcolm Forbes flew some 1,000 of his closest friends to Morocco for his 70th birthday party to the tune of a few million dollars). Fascinated viewers were shown a world where "cham-pagne wishes and caviar dreams" came true in television shows like *Lifestyles of the Rich and Fa-*

▲ *Fashion designer Donna Karan (top) models her own "body-friendly" ensemble. A Giorgio Armani suit (above) was a staple of the corporate climber's power wardrobe.*

Fashion magazines like Harper's Bazaar (with model Linda Evangelista on the cover) and Gentleman's Quarterly, or GQ, defined and reflected style trends. For those who must know what's in and what's out, such magazines wield considerable influence.

mous, and got a glimpse of *haute couture* and the latest in fashion trends from programs like CNN's *Style,* with Elsa Klensch, and MTV's *House of Style.* High-gloss fashion magazines, such as *Vogue* and *Harper's Bazaar,* continued to devote effusive columns to gleaming socialites swathed in sequined couture. Many not-so-wealthy people got caught up in a fever of materialism that found them spending their disposable income on anything that smacked of having it all. Young upwardly mobile couples with large discretionary incomes defined themselves by owning luxury cars and expensive watches. Anything by fashion designer Ralph Lauren, whether it was his knit sport shirts or his bed linens, was *de rigueur* in many households. Those who couldn't afford Lauren settled for imitations of his "country club" effect, a tailored casual look that many associated with the rich at ease.

At the office "power dressing" became an important part of climbing the corporate ladder, and businesswomen, armed with expensive briefcases, went to work in designer suits by Donna Karan. Though her suit jackets were more mod-estly tailored, some suits by

Ralph Lauren remade what men once bought as work and outdoor clothes into fashion statements.

◄ *Exaggerated shoulders, a short jacket, and an above-the-knee skirt added up to a 1980's look.*

With city dwellers snapping up hiking boots and shoes (right) and sturdy jackets (right, below) as if they really needed them, the rugged outdoor look spread like wildfire. Another phenomenon (below) was the sneaker descendant: the high-tech athletic shoe.

Grunge, or lumberjack chic (left), made its way into magazines and onto runways despite its antifashion aura.

other designers had shoulder pads that rivaled a football linebacker's. Businessmen purchased suits and ties by Giorgio Armani, Perry Ellis, and Calvin Klein.

Looking sexy was in, spurring a demand for body-revealing clothing made of clingy stretch fabrics. Formfitting bodysuits and leggings and miniskirts (which had gone underground for some 10 years) motivated the figure-conscious to join health clubs. But even the gym itself was not safe from the reach of fashion: the exercise togs one wore became a matter of style. Everyone from arbitrageurs to inner-city kids fell for athletic shoes, snapping them up at what some felt were exorbitant prices. The passion for upscale casual footwear was matched by a passion for athletic clothes. Between 1979 and 1982 activewear grew from a $2.5-billion to a $4.5-billion annual business. Sweat suits and bicycle shorts became perfectly acceptable street clothes, though many of the "athletes" wearing them were nonexercisers trying to look chic.

The Plain, Simple, Rugged Look

Inevitably, the spendthrift ostentation of the 1980's ran its course. "I think Americans are more concerned with quality of life," said one image consultant about the 1990's. "We were very flashy in the 1980's. And I think we're seeing the pendulum swing back the other way." The October 1987 stock market crash rattled more than a few who had been caught in the web of "godless consumerism." Some cut up their credit cards; others traded in expensive cars for cheaper models. "The strength of fashion now is in its almost total plainness and simplicity," stated one fashion magazine. Shoulder pads disappeared. Party dresses lost their poufs. Designers trotted out moderately priced lines. A poll of 500 adults reported only 7 percent believing that status-symbol products were worth their price. In what some observers have called the We Decade, people seemed to want to slow down. After all the fast-paced scrambling for more, more, more, they were just plain pooped. And there was something else: as baby boomers grew older, settled down, and started families, their priorities began to shift from spending money and time on themselves to spending it on

their families. With a new agenda of simpler living, shoppers began responding to sales pitches that stressed good value and practicality. Sportswear stores and mail-order houses fed a growing demand for a rugged, outdoor look. "For a lot of people trapped in the urban environment, who can't really get to the woods or the mountains, wearing the clothes is a kick," observed one fashion editor.

The outdoor look hit urban streets in a surprising way: inner-city teens appropriated the clothing as part of hip-hop style. Hiking boots and hooded sweatshirts worn with oversized jeans and T-shirts became a uniform that then moved out of the urban centers, such as New York and Los Angeles, and into middle-class suburbs and even onto the high-fashion runway. Because of its associations with gang attire, this hip-hop look made some people nervous, but the style took off anyway. "When you see Giorgio Armani doing pants with the crotch almost down to the knee," said a vice president of a major department store, "it shows you how important it is."

Boots and flannel shirts were the basic elements of the "grunge" look, which was adopted by the twenty-something crowd that some demographers dubbed "baby busters" (in contrast to the older baby boomers). Long, limp hair, torn sweaters, and on the grunge extreme, body piercing comprised what a December 1992 issue of *Business Week* called "slovenly, asexual, antifashion fashion." Grunge nevertheless soon made its way into the style-setting pages of *Vogue* magazine, thus receiving a kind of blessing from fashion moguls. Once again, as had happened so often in America, the establishment had absorbed the antiestablishment by imitation.

◄

Rap group TLC models the hip-hop look which was popular among young people in the city and suburbs in the 1990's.

393

◄ On Black Monday, October 19, 1987, the stock market dropped 22.6 percent, almost double the record set on October 28, 1929.

► In 1989 financier Henry Kravis engineered one of the largest corporate takeovers in American history, $25 billion for RJR Nabisco, and became a hero to the decade's deal makers.

WHEELERS, DEALERS, AND YUPPIES

"Greed is all right.... You can be greedy and still feel good about yourself," Ivan Boesky

assured business-school graduates at the University of California, Berkeley, commencement.

It was one of the most expensive cars that money could buy, not counting the machines that were legal only on the racetrack. The shiny red Ferrari Testarossa (sticker price $90,000) belonged to a young Wall Street financier who had made $12 million trading in stocks. But the trader was so busy making money that he hardly had time to drive.

The Ferrari was typical of the trophies that Wall Street hotshots bought to congratulate themselves on their immense success during the great bull market of the 1980's. In August 1982, stock prices began a long and seemingly endless rise. But oddly enough, the best of times for American corporations were also the worst of times. Financial raiders realized that huge profits could often be made by acquiring companies, breaking them apart, and selling the pieces one at a time. The people who engineered such deals were investment bankers, enthusiastically aided by high-priced law firms. A single deal involving a large corporation could yield multimillion-dollar fees for the banking and law firms and fancy bonuses for the individuals most responsible. In the wings were the specialists in arbitrage, who made money on the sudden fluctuations in stock prices that accompanied a

▲ As Gordon Gekko in the 1987 movie **Wall Street**, actor Michael Douglas projected the ethic of greed that seized the financial world.

Tom Wolfe's scathing novel of 1980's morality, The Bonfire of the Vanities, became a film with (left to right) Tom Hanks, Melanie Griffith, and Bruce Willis.

Traders gape at the latest prices as the stock market plummets in a free fall in October 1987.

takeover. Investing in the stock market had always been a gamble, but in the 1980's Wall Street became one gigantic casino. As long as the market kept going up, it seemed everyone could win, except the workers who lost their jobs when corporations were broken up or restructured.

A horde of aspiring young financial wizards fresh from business school took the wisdom of such idols as Ivan Boesky and Michael Milken (see box, p. 396) to heart and flocked to Wall Street and other financial centers across the country. With profits flowing freely, investment firms offered starting salaries of $80,000 to $110,000, plus signing bonuses. The Wall Street boom, which spilled into many other professions, came as history's blessing for the baby boomers. The generation born after World War II was going to work in an atmosphere of splendid prosperity. In 1984 it was estimated that the 25- to 35-year-old group, which represented 23 percent of the U.S. population, controlled 23 percent of the country's disposable income, an astonishing achievement for men and women at the outset of their careers. Their elders looked in awe and envy at the advent of a new American social phenomenon: the Young Urban Professional, or yuppie.

Yuppies poured into the cities, and, in a process known as gentrification, mom-and-pop businesses were driven out to make way for gourmet shops and upscale restaurants. Opportunistic landlords seized the chance to convert rental apartments into condominiums that sold for six-figure sums. Though many observers and social activists decried gentrification, yuppies brought new life to decaying residential and industrial neighborhoods that the political establishment had written off. The young professionals wanted the best quality money could buy — in houses, food, clothes, and high-tech gadgets of all kinds. But it was with their cars that they really expressed themselves: BMW's, Mercedeses, and other costly, high-performance automobiles became the badges of success. In Atlanta, people interested in purchasing a $32,500 Jaguar had to put their names on a 60-day waiting list.

Polls showed that the yuppies' economic beliefs were close to those of President Ronald Reagan himself: first they

Three High Fliers Who Fell; One Who Didn't

High rollers in the 1980's games of chance, from left to right: Ivan Boesky, Michael Milken, Dennis Levine, and Donald Trump

Two of the biggest players in the drive for greater and greater sums of money were Ivan Boesky and Michael Milken. Boesky, the master of arbitrage, had uncanny luck in guessing before anyone else that a company would be up for grabs. Boesky's forays were often bankrolled by the firm of Drexel Burnham Lambert, whose Beverly Hills, California, office was the domain of Michael Milken. Milken specialized in junk bonds: high-yield lending to finance high-risk ventures. So great was the demand for his financial advice that the limousines of corporate executives clogged the driveway of his home at 6:00 A.M. on Sundays. Neither Milken nor Boesky had any qualms about the astronomical amounts of money they were paid. Boesky satisfied himself that his personal fortune resulted from hard work. "There are no easy ways to make money in the securities market," he declared.

No one seemed a more glowing example of capitalism at its finest than flamboyant Donald Trump, a New York real estate developer who created a vast empire of hotels, apartment towers, and gambling casinos. He was legendary for sweet-talking bankers and crushing competitors as he built up his fortune to $3 billion. He was also very generous in aiding worthy causes. One friend, attempting to explain Trump in the psychological jargon of the era, commented: "No achievement can satisfy what he wants. . . . He is playing out his insecurities on an incredibly large canvas."

As the rich continued to get richer, federal and state authorities began to get wind of abuses in the financial industry. Dennis Levine, a young hotshot Wall Street financier, was convicted of making his $12 million in profits from fraudulent trading. As if to prove that there is no honor among thieves, Levine led authorities right to Ivan Boesky, who, it turned out, was not as clairvoyant as he had seemed: he had been paying cash for corporate secrets. Boesky was hit with the highest fine in American history: $100 million. In an attempt to avoid a long jail term, Boesky began feeding regulators with information about the activities of the king of all traders, Michael Milken.

One of the final echoes of the greed decade began on March 3, 1991, when Michael Milken walked into federal prison in Pleasanton, California, to begin serving his sentence for fraud. He was released in January 1993.

Of all the high fliers, Donald Trump may have been the smartest. Not only did he stay on the right side of the law, but after the stock market crash of 1987, he boasted that he had sold his stocks at their height and was unaffected. Sliding real estate values, however, sent shudders through his far-flung holdings.

▼ *The hero in Jay McInerney's* **Bright Lights, Big City** *regains his sense of self after burning out on the good life.*

wanted to cut government spending (and taxes) and sometime later perhaps do more for the welfare of the poor and the needy. They felt that they deserved their success; after all, they drove themselves to exhaustion to get it, working 100 hours a week if the job demanded it. Leisure time was just an extension of work: eating at posh restaurants, vacationing at exclusive spas, and exercising at swank health clubs provided opportunities to make business contacts (an activity more commonly known as networking). All of this took its toll, however, and one of the expenses that came along with the yuppie lifestyle was the cost of psychotherapy to answer the question "Why am I doing this?"

Despite the size of yuppie salaries, enough never seemed to be enough. The yuppie dream was built on a precarious mountain of debt. Asked why he continued to work at a killing pace, one man replied, "The wife expects a new Jaguar every year, and the three houses aren't paid for yet." In his novel about New York in the 1980's, *The Bonfire of the Vanities*, Tom Wolfe described an investment banker going broke on $1 million a year. Another novel, *Bright Lights, Big City,* by Jay McInerney, captured the spirit of the era with its depiction of the frenetic nightlife of fast-living Manhattanites: a dizzying round of partying and nightclub hopping, fueled by generous doses of cocaine and alcohol. Many readers took the novel as a guide to the "good life," missing its strong undertone of disillusion over the morally bankrupt hedonism of such a lifestyle.

By mid-decade many voices were beginning to question prevailing ethics, finding a pervasive attitude of "rules are for fools." One observer wrote of "the affluent society and the impoverished soul." And there were disquieting signs that many of the era's gains may have been ill-gotten. Even the bible of big business, *Fortune* magazine, declared: "Almost everywhere you look in the business world today . . . you glimpse something loathsome."

In the second half of 1987, the glittering towers of new

wealth were beginning to look as if they rested on shaky foundations. The stock market, which had reached great heights in August, thanks to frenzied speculation, was starting to show signs of weakness. Nervous investors sent the average falling 235 points in the week that ended on Friday, October 16. When brokers reached their Wall Street offices on Monday, October 19, they discovered a mountain of "sell" orders. In Europe and Asia, stock markets were already tumbling. When the New York exchange's trading bell sounded at 9:30 A.M., it unleashed a wave of panic. At the end of the day, the Dow Jones average had plunged 508 points, with 604 million shares traded, ending the five-year bull market.

▲ *One of the hot spots among the limousine-riding, designer-clothes-wearing set was New York City's Palladium, where patrons mingled with like-minded souls on the dance floor.*

◀

The CEO of Chrysler, Lee Iacocca (now retired), was a strong critic of the trend toward mergers and short-term profits.

October 19, 1987, represented "the worst day in the history of the New York Stock Exchange," according to one magazine; it was "the nearest thing to a meltdown that I ever want to see," echoed a financier.

One New York financial firm that had epitomized the high-stakes gambling of the greed decade, Salomon Brothers, laid off 800 employees in a single day. Soon the very magazines that had trumpeted the achievements of the yuppies were running headlines such as "Where Have All the Yuppies Gone?" "Is Greed Dead?" "The New Volunteerism," and "The Simple Life" and opining that "upscale is out; downscale is in."

By the early 1990's the market had stabilized, and the Dow Jones average resumed a mainly upward course. But the high-flying era of the 1980's was gone, and with it went the wilder antics of the yuppies. The spirit of the 1990's had arrived, and Wall Street's hotshots came to the sobering realization that, at least for a while, the party was over.

President Bush works the White House phone to rally support for the 1991 Gulf War against Saddam Hussein. As a young U.S. Navy bomber pilot in World War II (inset, shown with members of his flight crew), Bush flew 58 missions, was shot down over the Pacific, and won the Distinguished Flying Cross.

▼ Almost everyone loved Barbara Bush, a gracious and unpretentious First Lady who wrote the "memoirs" of Millie, the adored White House spaniel.

GEORGE BUSH WINS ABROAD, TRIPS AT HOME

A born aristocrat who saw politics as his civic duty, Bush campaigned like a street fighter. Once in office, he acted forcefully on foreign policy, but at home, facing many domestic problems, he never seemed to hit his stride.

George H. W. Bush, the Republican choice for president in 1988, embodied the old-fashioned virtues of loyalty, fair play, and devotion to duty. The son of Wall Street banker and U.S. Senator Prescott Bush, he learned early to hide his privileged heritage. "I don't want to hear any more about the great 'I Am,'" his mother would admonish. At 18, Bush enlisted in the navy, becoming one of its youngest pilots, and achieved a distinguished record. Then he enrolled at Yale, where he studied economics and was active in sports. After graduating, he left New England for Texas and went into the oil business. In 1951 he cofounded an oil drilling firm.

Only a few careful observers could have detected the driving ambition that spurred this self-effacing man to be president. One was his brother Jonathan: "From an early age his compass has been on the same heading." Following the family tradition of public service, Bush won a seat in

Congress as a representative from Texas, then worked his way up through Republican Party ranks to become vice president under Ronald Reagan. For some, his ambition explained how George Bush could be a gracious aristocrat one moment and a ruthless politician the next.

The prospects for Bush's winning the presidency in 1988 looked promising: he had served alongside an enormously popular president, during which time the economy thrived. The Democrats, with Gov. Michael S. Dukakis of Massachusetts, had a bland candidate who showed little acumen in national politics and whose campaign never seemed to get on track. In the full throes of the race in 1988, Bush launched an all-out attack on his rival. He painted the Democratic candidate as an ultraliberal elitist and pawn of Har-

Democratic presidential candidate Michael Dukakis campaigns with wife, Kitty, at a rally in New York City.

He attended National Security Council briefings on a daily basis, traveled abroad at every opportunity, and developed close personal ties with heads of state the world over. His habit of writing hundreds of notes by hand, and of picking up the overseas phone to chat, established new frontiers in the wielding of American influence. It was this sort of intimate diplomacy that allowed him to bring together 28 countries during the Persian Gulf crisis in 1991, assembling a broad-based military and political alliance that stopped dead the conquest of Kuwait by Iraqi dictator Saddam Hussein (see pp. 412–413).

Bush's domestic policy was a different story. "If it weren't for this deficit looming over everything else," Bush had grumbled early in his presidency, "I'd feel like a spring colt." But loom it did, along with a dreary assortment of other problems. By 1990 the economy was in a deep recession. Corporations, saddled with debt, were laying off workers — "downsizing" was the favored term — and unemployment surged. One American in 10 was on food stamps; 1 in 8 lived in poverty. Real estate prices were skidding, and the savings and loan industry had fallen upon such hard times that an estimated $400 billion in tax money would be needed to bail it out. Racial tensions exploded in the inner cities, with riots in Los Angeles bringing death to 52 people. Meanwhile, the national debt was pushing into the ionosphere. It had doubled twice over in the past decade alone, to a staggering $4 trillion.

Beset by these internal troubles, Bush appeared to do nothing — waiting, it seemed, for the situation to correct itself. Time and again administration officials declared the recession over, only to be proved wrong by yet another set of disappointing economic figures. "Bush doesn't steer," grumbled one critic, "he's floating." Sensing a lack of direction, American voters turned sour; by the eve of the 1992 election, Bush's popularity had sunk to a mere 36 percent.

Midway through his single term, not even a round of golf near the Bush family's summer house in Maine, could make the president forget the nation's mounting domestic troubles.

vard intellectuals, neatly sidestepping his own background and Yale degree. Playing to conservatives, he criticized big government and promised to hold down spending. "Read my lips: no new taxes!" he proclaimed — a promise that would come to haunt him after he was forced to break it as president. Bush won by a landslide.

In office, Bush vowed to uphold the Reagan legacy of laissez-faire government and a strong national defense. Naturally prudent, with long experience in the ways of Washington, he believed he was there to serve, not to pursue new agendas. "People were happy with the status quo," a senior aide explained. Even when Soviet leader Mikhail Gorbachev announced unilateral arms cuts at the United Nations, calling for international cooperation, Bush moved with caution. He liked to quote a personal hero, Yankee catcher Yogi Berra: "I don't want to make the wrong mistake."

Yet Bush was a master at foreign affairs, and when necessary, he could act with lightning speed and decisiveness.

An energetic diplomat, Bush spent much of his time in office conferring with other heads of state. Here (from left) he discusses trade problems with Japanese Prime Minister Kiichi Miyazawa, disarmament with Soviet Premier Mikhail Gorbachev, and the economy with French President François Mitterrand; and he swaps tips on leadership with Russian President Boris Yeltsin.

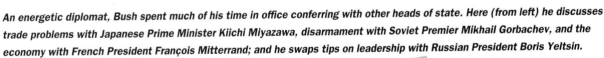

TELEVISION MAKES REALITY PAY

Peter Arnett
Baghdad, Iraq
CNN

Programs featuring clean-living folks with no secrets to hide became rarities on the home screen; they were replaced by a constant stream of real or imaginary people confronting awful problems.

For television's first 30 years, the big three networks controlled the home screen, beaming out soaps and sitcoms, cop shows and westerns, and a hodgepodge of quiz shows, specials, and sports. Their stranglehold loosened in the 1980's, when an upstart fourth national network, Fox Broadcasting, presented its slate of progamming to America's TV audience.

Cable television (more than 60 percent of homes with TV's had cable by 1989) and VCR's (owners leaped in a single decade from 500,000 to more than 11 million) also helped erode the networks' grip on the box. Viewers could now access a huge and often bewildering variety of programs as well as commercial-free movies. Many areas had 30 or more channels, including those devoted to home shopping, weather, around-the-clock news, sports, rock music, and reruns. On a pay-per-view basis, recent films and major sporting events were also available.

Programmers discovered and tapped a seemingly insatiable appetite for news. CNN (Cable News Network) offered two channels of 24-hour TV news, and C-SPAN brought us government officials at work in the hallowed chambers of the U.S. Congress. Communications satellites and the advent of portable video cameras gave new immediacy to "brought-to-you-live" coverage. News now arrived from practically anywhere in the world while it was happening; millions of Americans watched Operation Desert Storm in January 1991 as rockets lit the Baghdad sky. The display of high-tech weaponry in action kept viewers glued to their TV sets.

Real life dramas became a dominant theme of the decade, permeating all types of television fare. Out went the old taboos; in came more graphic sex and violence, private details of ordinary people's lives, and sensationalism. No television genre benefited more, perhaps, than the talk shows, with their intimate format.

Gabfests and Tabloid Shows

For years late-night talk had been dominated by a single host, Johnny Carson. But in the 1980's a bevy of rivals, from Joan Rivers to Arsenio Hall, arose to challenge the veteran. Carson, however, managed to beat them all and stay on top, attracting some 12 million viewers a night with guests such as Bob Hope (who appeared 121 times). After a 30-year stint, Carson made a much-ballyhooed exit in 1992 and was replaced by the affable Jay Leno.

Meanwhile, daytime talk shows thrived. Phil Donahue was their Carson.

Veteran journalist Peter Arnett won praise for staying in the enemy's capital to report on the Persian Gulf War, though he was accused by some of becoming the unwitting instrument of an Iraqi propaganda campaign.

▼ *Late-night TV host Arsenio Hall (right) yucks it up with actor-director Spike Lee (left) and blind singing legend Stevie Wonder.*

Sidekick Ed McMahon (left) plays straight man to Johnny Carson as Johnny does his Carnak the Magnificent routine on NBC's Tonight Show.

When NBC snubbed David Letterman, failing to offer him the *Tonight Show, Dave* jumped to CBS; but NBC retained rights to some comedic bits, calling them "intellectual property."

"Come on, help me out!" he pleaded, dragging studio audiences into debates on issues like incest and abortion. Many critics accused Donahue of sensationalism, but others hailed his candor; reporter David Halberstam called the show "the most important graduate school in America." The first black talk-show star, Oprah Winfrey, went nationwide in 1986. Using a format similar to Donahue's, she quizzed guests on such sensitive topics as AIDS and battered wives. The most outrageous and combative host was Geraldo Rivera, who shocked and titillated huge audiences with investigations into such topics as sex rings, transsexuals, and the contents of Al Capone's secret vault (in which nothing of interest was found).

The Fox network was a pioneer in a new type of television that freely mixed news with entertainment. *A Current Affair*, anchored by Maury Povitch, took its cue from tabloid newspapers like *The National Enquirer*. By paying handsome fees for appearances by people involved in real-life murders and sex scandals — and, even better, to broadcast their home movies — the program gave viewers the voyeuristic pleasure of looking through the peepholes of tightly closed doors.

▶ Rush Limbaugh (left) and Howard Stern (right) heat up the airwaves with their different styles of controversy and candor. Limbaugh specialized in conservative views and contempt for political liberals. Stern dealt in shock, vulgarity, and offensiveness to all.

▼ Along with her engaging style and easy rapport with audiences, gab guru Oprah Winfrey endeared herself to many viewers by shedding 67 pounds, only to regain the weight in a matter of months.

Reality on a Roll

The reality craze spread. Other slice-of-life shows included *Cops, Rescue 911,* and *America's Most Wanted* (which helped law-enforcement officials track down hundreds of fugitive felons). And semibiographical TV movies proliferated, based on subjects torn from the headlines, sometimes before all the facts were known: *The People vs. Jean Harris* (1981); *The Billionaire Boys Club* (1987); *Baby M* (1988); and the tale of the "Long Island Lolita," Amy Fisher, and her relationship with auto body mechanic, Joey Buttafuoco, versions of which aired on all three networks.

Even fictional dramas became more realistic. Characters increased in complexity, and plots unfolded over several episodes rather than being neatly tied up in 30 or 60 minutes. Justice didn't always triumph. The critically acclaimed *Hill Street Blues* told gritty stories about big-city cops fight-

One of the first live-action shows, Cops sent camera crews along as police responded to emergency calls.

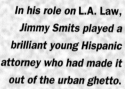

In his role on L.A. Law, Jimmy Smits played a brilliant young Hispanic attorney who had made it out of the urban ghetto.

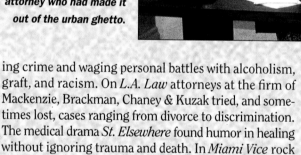

As the compassionate Sgt. Phil Esterhaus on Hill Street Blues, Michael Conrad always ended morning roll calls with "Let's be careful out there."

Bill Cosby played obstetrician Dr. Cliff Huxtable and Phylicia Rashad was his lawyer-wife, Clair, on The Cosby Show.

ing crime and waging personal battles with alcoholism, graft, and racism. On *L.A. Law* attorneys at the firm of Mackenzie, Brackman, Chaney & Kuzak tried, and sometimes lost, cases ranging from divorce to discrimination. The medical drama *St. Elsewhere* found humor in healing without ignoring trauma and death. In *Miami Vice* rock music added a driving beat to the good guy versus bad guy formula as a pair of detectives battled drug lords. Viewers responded by raising actor Don Johnson to star status.

The Cheers gang in 1993 (clockwise from left): George Wendt, Rhea Perlman, Woody Harrelson, Kelsey Grammer, Bebe Neuwirth, John Ratzenberger, Ted Danson, Kirstie Alley

Family Sitcoms

The decade's most popular program, *The Cosby Show*, almost single-handedly revived family sitcoms. At its heart was an affectionate upper-middle-class black American family guided by intelligence, wit, and common sense. "I wanted to give the house back to the parents," said its star, Bill Cosby, who called the shots on every aspect of the show. Audience response was so strong that Cosby's earnings for a single year hit $92 million. In another situation comedy, *Family Ties*, the Keatons were liberal parents who grew up in the 1960's and wrestled with the less idealistic preoccupations of their growing children.

At the other end of the family comedy spectrum was *Roseanne*, featuring an overweight, harried blue-collar mom (played by Roseanne Arnold) who told it like it was. This was not TV's idealized version of family bliss. Like the ravings of Jackie Gleason's Ralph Kramden in *The Honeymooners* more than 30 years before, Roseanne's tough talk and biting put-downs were softened by an underlying love for her spouse and offspring.

Married . . .With Children, however, was a raunchy version of *The Adventures of Ozzie and Harriet.* One episode of the show offended a Michigan housewife so deeply that she attempted to organize an advertiser boycott in protest. But the program's Nielsen rating just shot up higher. Even animators came up with a hit antifamily sitcom. The bratty cartoon figure of Bart Simpson, who tells his father "Eat my shorts," delighted older and younger viewers alike.

Candice Bergen as unwed working mom Murphy Brown

At left, Dynasty stars (left to right) Linda Evans, John Forsythe, and Joan Collins pause in their machinations. At right, Larry Hagman flashes a J. R. Ewing grin.

Other sitcoms looked to the workplace for laughs and relevance. The regulars at Cheers, a Boston pub, won Emmys for more than a decade; and *Murphy Brown* made the lifestyle of a feisty reporter a national issue when the character, played by Candice Bergen, and Vice President Dan Quayle traded gibes over the show's decision to make Murphy a single mother. *The Golden Girls,* hailed as the first hit sitcom to feature an all-female cast, showed there is life, and humor, after age 50, 60, or even 80!

Prime-Time Soaps

On November 21, 1980, the second largest audience in television history — an amazing 450 million fans in 57 coun-

America's favorite dysfunctional family, the Simpsons, gazes in wonder as baby Maggie utters a word.

tries around the world — tuned in to find out "Who Shot J.R.?" on the show *Dallas.* (It was a jilted mistress.) A weekly saga of lust, power, and betrayal in a wealthy Texas oil family, *Dallas* set the pace for prime-time TV soaps, which offered up an addictive array of plot twists, scandalous relationships, greed, and glamour.

Dallas enthralled viewers for 13 years; it was one of the longest-running prime-time series to date. Rapacious J. R. Ewing, played by Larry Hagman, was dubbed the Swine of the Decade by one TV critic. Many envied the villainous J. R. As anthropologist Ashley Montagu observed: "We admire rugged individuals like Mr. Hagman's character precisely because they can get away with it." The *Dallas* craze soon begot *Dynasty,* about the lives of some rich and amoral residents of Denver. The cast, led by John Forsythe and Linda Evans, featured Joan Collins, whose character sleazed her way through orgies of conspicuous consumption and super-heated lust. From 1982 to 1985 *Dynasty* ran neck and neck with *Dallas,* and it boasted cameo performances by former President Gerald Ford and Henry Kissinger.

Toward the end of the 1980's, viewers' interest in the lifestyles of the rich and neurotic seemed to have leveled off. Programs like *thirtysomething, The Wonder Years*, and *Sisters* — tamer dramas about middle-class American families, some of them nostalgic journeys into the past — began to attract large audiences. And a brand-new television world beckoned, promising interactive TV, movies on demand, and an all-in-one computer, telephone, and TV set.

An eccentric FBI agent (Kyle MacLachlan, with costar Sherilyn Fenn) ponders a bizarre murder with supernatural overtones on Twin Peaks, the dark, surreal drama series created for prime-time TV by filmmaker David Lynch.

▶

Firefighters face an impenetrable wall of flame from wildfires that swept through 793,880 acres of Yellowstone National Park in 1988.

▲ In Homestead, Florida, a devastated victim of 1992's Hurricane Andrew clings tightly to what may be the only thing he has left.

▲ Along with the collapse of sections of the Bay Bridge, the 1989 San Francisco earthquake left 62 dead, 3,258 injured, and $5 billion in property damage.

Like the fabled phoenix, a fern rises from the ashes of Mount St. Helens.

WAKE-UP CALLS FROM MOTHER NATURE

While citizens of the earth debated among themselves about how to save the planet from further degradation, they learned anew that nature still has the final word.

It was a startling discovery. Scientists studying the stratosphere over the South Pole in 1983 were amazed to find sharp decreases in ozone, a gas that helps shield the earth from damaging ultraviolet radiation. It was a dramatic warning to humans that abuse of their environment could produce a lethal backlash. Faced with the prospect of an increase in deaths from skin cancer and of untold damage to crops, governments around the world took steps to limit the production of chlorofluorocarbons (CFC's), chemicals believed to hasten the depletion of ozone.

No one could predict if the banning of CFC's would save the ozone layer, and in any case this was just one item in a grim catalog of humanity's sins against the planet. It was especially difficult to find solutions for pollution problems in developing countries, which could not afford to curb industries for the sake of cleaner air and water and of endangered species. At the first Earth Summit, officially called the United Nations Conference on Environment and Development, which was held in Rio de Janeiro in June 1992, Third World nations called on wealthier countries to pay for the preservation of biodiversity, arguing that poor nations could not be made to bear the cost of a cleaner environment, which would benefit all.

By the early 1990's an acre of tropical forest was being cut down every second, adding up to an annual loss of an area larger than the state of Connecticut. The loss of tropical forests was especially worrisome, since these immense concentrations of trees absorb carbon dioxide produced by humans and industry. Scientists monitoring climate patterns warned that increased levels of carbon dioxide and CFC's in the atmosphere could create a greenhouse effect, trapping heat and causing a global rise in temperature. Predictions of the polar ice caps melting and of sea levels rising to swamp coastal cities sparked a fierce debate in the environmental community. Some scientists, pointing to past fluctuations in the earth's temperature, scoffed at these doomsday scenarios. CFC's might actually cool the air, they said, and measurements showed that some glaciers were growing, not melting.

Natural Disasters, Natural Solutions

Doubts about the inevitability of the greenhouse effect did not diminish alarm over the environment. Indeed, it seemed as if Mother Nature were delivering a series of frightening messages that humans were still at her mercy. Hurricanes Hugo and Andrew pummeled the South. In the Northwest, Mount St. Helens blew its top in 1980, killing 57 people and spewing volcanic ash over a vast area. Eleven years later, Mount Pinatubo in the Philippines hurled millions of tons of gases and dust into the air, causing a temporary cooling of the earth and setting the stage for further weakening of the ozone layer. Brush fires in Oakland, California, destroyed more than 3,000 homes and reminded the nation that dream houses can vanish in a nightmare of fire. The Los Angeles earthquake of 1994 brought home, once again, the risks of living in quake-prone areas; and the same month, ice and snow paralyzed much of the country, causing even the federal government to shut down its Washington operations. Perhaps the most sobering of nature's onslaughts came in the summer of 1993, when rains fell almost unceas-

▲ *Some American companies seemed to be learning that what is good for the earth's environment may turn out to be very good for business.*

▲ *Members of Earth First block a dirt road on Bald Mountain, Oregon, to protest excessive logging.*

ingly for two months in the central part of the country, dropping as much as 10 times the normal rainfall. The Mississippi River rose in places to its highest recorded levels, burst through levees, and spread over 13.5 million acres of land. The flood led to 41 deaths, forced some 100,000 people from their homes, and wiped out crops across the Midwest.

By the 1990's most Americans were convinced that sensitivity to the environment was the way to survive into the future. Automobile manufacturers began discussing plans to build a zero-emission electric car. Many localities took steps to divert their flow of trash from landfills to recycling programs. New York City, faced with the necessity of building incinerators to get rid of its trash, embarked on an ambitious recycling program, with mixed results.

In many instances, young people led successful environmental crusades. They put pressure on companies to cease abuses: stopping a fast-food chain from using hard-to-recycle styrofoam packaging, for example, and persuading a tuna company to quit buying from fishermen who snared dolphins in their nets. A lot of these environmental foot soldiers were not even old enough to vote, but their sense of urgency was understandable: they realized all too well that if they remained passive, they would be the ones to inherit the consequences.

◀

The Mississippi River undid decades of flood-control efforts when it rampaged over farms and cities in 1993.

LOOKING FOR HEALTH AND HAPPINESS

As the breakneck pace and materialism of the 1980's took their toll, some people, from celebrities to stockbrokers, turned to New Age therapy as a means of relieving stress and attaining spiritual peace.

As the sun rose on August 16, 1987, hundreds of people who had gathered before the Great Pyramid in Egypt began to chant, beat drums, and raise an unearthly sound from conch shells. They were trying to stave off the end of the world as foretold in an ancient Mayan calendar by providing something they called harmonic convergence. As the new day dawned across the globe, thousands of like-minded souls joined in to create a huge outpouring of noise. If all went well, not only would the earth be saved from destruction but humankind would enter a New Age of peace and harmony.

The collective resonance that rose worldwide was also a cry from the heart. In the midst of the great wealth that piled up in the 1980's, many felt a yawning emptiness in their lives that money, professional achievement, fitness regimes, and conventional religion could not fill. Some people sought meaning and solace in a variety of unconventional ways, all of which came to be lumped under the term *New Age.* "They yearn to get in touch with the soul," explained one philosophy teacher, and to do so, New Agers took many paths, ranging from the serious to the silly: astrology, holistic medicine, crystal healing, meditation, and more.

Through "channeling," some believers claimed to contact the dead and tap the wisdom of the ancients. When a Seattle woman, J. Z. Knight, announced that she had reached Ramtha, a 35,000-year-old warrior and spiritual guide from the lost city of Atlantis, Knight reaped a fortune dispensing Ramtha's wisdom in books and personal appearances. Sedona, Arizona, became a center of New Age spiritualism because it was thought to be a place where mystical magnetic energies emanate from the earth. The pyramids and other Egyptian monuments seemed to hold special allure for New Agers, who made pilgrimages there to chant and meditate, seek ancient truths, be healed of their ailments, and remember experiences from previous lives. "I have met over 130 Nefertitis and Cleopatras," remarked one Egyptian guide, "but I have trouble knowing which one is the real one."

Some New Age gurus offered men and women separate paths to wholeness. Robert Bly, a distinguished poet and author of the

New Age evangelist Shirley MacLaine displays a quartz crystal, used to focus her spiritual powers.

▼ *Devotees of New Age philosophy take part in harmonic convergence at the pyramids at Giza.*

bestseller *Iron John,* led men on a quest for "the primal, powerful, masculine qualities lost in the industrialized 20th century." On wilderness camp-outs Bly's followers beat drums, hunkered down in sweat lodges, revealed their personal problems, and in the process found their lost maleness. As for femaleness, Clarissa Pinkola Estes, a Jungian analyst from Denver, wrote a book to help women, who, she felt, had been cut off from their creative drive. Called *Women Who Run With the Wolves*, the book was a collection of folktales about Wild Woman mythology and, according to Estes, exposed the "ruins of the female underworld." Women also took up the drum. "Drumming is a powerful spiritual tool," said one woman. "It's a direct channel into the rhythms of your body."

One of the high priestesses of the New Age, the actress Shirley MacLaine, wrote a series of bestsellers about her wide-ranging New Age experiences. Her book *Going Within: A Guide for Inner Transformation* describes "techniques of meditation, visualization, color and sound therapy, how to work with crystals, how to work with colored jewelry, acupuncture, acupressure, things that have been helpful to me." Acolytes paid $300 each to hear her speak.

And stock market investors paid $360 a

year for a newsletter published by a New Age astrologist-stockbroker who consulted the stars for his market tips. Skeptics no doubt swallowed their derision when the broker warned his clients to get out of the market — fast! — just days before Wall Street crashed in October 1987.

In medicine some intriguing techniques emerged alongside the quackery. New Agers stirred interest in acupuncture, Japanese shiatsu (finger pressure massage), and reflexology, in which the feet were manipulated to treat other parts of the body. They also promoted homeopathy, an alternative medicine based on the idea that the healing process is sped along by prescribing small amounts of substances that in larger doses would cause symptoms of the diagnosed illness. More dubious was the New Age faith in the medicinal properties of crystals and in aromatherapy, the therapeutic inhaling of plant and flower oils.

Much energy was expended on merely soothing the soul. New Age music, minimalist but melodic, provided a sound track for the mind's meanderings. Accessories such as portable sound-and-light machines promised to induce meditation in the dentist's office and in other stressful surroundings. For a quick fix there were "mind salons" devoted to meditation. Disbelievers strolling through a New Age convention could find a great deal to chuckle at, such as a sign advertising "Brain Waves to Go," but it was hard to dismiss the movement entirely. After all, who could argue that the world lacked peace and harmony.

Yoga in its many forms, among them hatha yoga, shown here, had won legions of adherents by the 1980's as a valuable physical and mental exercise regime and a means of seeking spiritual enlightenment.

Robert Bly took the title of his bestseller from a Brothers Grimm tale about a caged wild man who is freed by a boy. Marianne Williamson (below), author of A Return to Love, taught "spiritual psychotherapy."

#1 NATIONAL BESTSELLER

IRON JOHN

A Book About Men

"Important . . . timely . . . powerful."
—The New York Times

ROBERT BLY

Using an instrument called a Synchro-Energizer and wearing goggles, a high-tech spiritualist seeks the ultimate in meditative tranquillity on a peaceful shore in Cardiff Beach, South Carolina.

▶ *Country music in America took off in the 1980's. Styles ranged from the offbeat twang and poetic lyrics of Lyle Lovett to the reedy warble of veteran Willie Nelson (top inset) to the back-to-basics sound of Randy Travis (bottom inset).*

MUSICAL STYLES GALORE

The variety of music competing for attention was bewildering, approaching the chaotic. And now it wasn't just sound that mattered. Music makers had to appeal to the eyes as well as to the ears.

Good old rock and roll still had power in the 1980's. Tina Turner, who had been perfecting her soulful style throughout the 1960's and 1970's, was still going strong performing her sexy gyrations; and Mick Jagger, who once sneered that he "would rather be dead than sing [his song] 'Satisfaction' at 45," raked in some $80 million during the Rolling Stones 1989 Steel Wheels tour, and in 1994, at the age of 50, embarked on another grueling worldwide tour.

While fans of all ages were enjoying the music of legends such as The Who, Paul Simon, and Eric Clapton, rock and roll itself was expanding to include new styles. On the fringes existed the short-lived punk movement, a music filled with anarchy and destruction that was imported from Great Britain in the late 1970's. Rebellion also infused the power chords and over-the-top antics of the heavy metal bands, from newer groups like Bon Jovi, Metallica, and Guns 'n' Roses, to acts such

as Aerosmith and Ozzy Osbourne, which had gotten their start a decade earlier.

Other strains, collectively called alternative rock, surfaced in the music of the Pretenders, R.E.M., the Police, Elvis Costello, and U2, bands whose members were mostly kids when the Beatles and the Stones were getting started. All the while, rock kept evolving in unexpected directions, among them the highly synthesized, danceable sounds of the Cars, Talking Heads, and Duran Duran.

If the changes in rock were more or less evolutionary, the change in how Americans listened to music was revolutionary. Portable stereo radio-and-audiocassette players, complete with earphones, became the rage. For stunningly loud volume, there were bigger portable cassette players, appropriately nicknamed boom boxes. No longer bound to indoor stereos, music lovers took their favorite tapes almost everywhere. Quite swiftly, play-at-home 45 r.p.m. single records and 33⅓ r.p.m. lp (long playing) record albums be-

◀ *Even by superstar standards, Michael Jackson's fame in the 1980's reached extraordinary proportions.*

Rap Is in the House!

All at once it was everywhere: in suburban malls, in soft-drink commercials, in dictionaries. It was music called rap, full of cryptic chanting and teeth-rattling bass lines, which had sprung up from deep within the inner city to take its place in American culture.

Born in the 1960's of a Jamaican tradition called toasting, rap came to New York City in the early 1970's via DJ Cool Herc, who used two turntables to cut back and forth between songs, blending them into a sound later associated with hip-hop. It soon caught on and spread to the black population of other big cities. Initially the rapper's goal was to whip up the dance crowd, insult rivals, and brag (a tradition with roots in the African-American put-down game "playing the dozens"). The first rap hit, "Rapper's Delight" (1979), by the Sugarhill Gang, was full of playful hyperbole and one-upmanship.

As the 1980's unfolded, rap artists began to embrace serious social issues, such as drug abuse and racism. They also began to play to a wider audience, including many young whites who found the music spoke for them too (Music Television's program *Yo! MTV Raps* has a mostly young white male audience). In rap, white suburban teens seemed to find the rebellious mystique that rock and roll held for their parents a few decades earlier. Although critics, both black and white, charged that hard-core "gangsta" rappers were antisocial and, worse, advocated violence, obscenity, and misogyny, rap groups like Salt 'n' Pepa (above, top) and Arrested Development (above) have shown that rap music can also deliver a positive message of spirituality and nonviolence.

The sultry quartet En Vogue brought back the close harmony and soulful sound of such 1960's groups as the Supremes.

artists. His album *Thriller* won a record eight Grammy awards in 1983. The *Thriller* video, which cost more than $1 million to make, featured Jackson in monster makeup dancing with zombies. It all worked beautifully: at one point Epic Records was selling a million *Thriller* albums a week. The chameleon-like Madonna used MTV to grab attention with songs about issues such as teenage pregnancy and with every sort of look imaginable. Alternately offending and charming her audiences, she succeeded in getting noticed to the tune of a multimillion-dollar annual income.

came endangered species; but records hung on gamely against the competition for years until the noise-free, nearly indestructible compact disc (CD) made them obsolete.

The music video brought another kind of revolution. Sharing space with CNN and HBO on the cable box, Music Television (MTV), which premiered in August 1981, offered film or video renditions of new releases, often starring the singer, 24 hours a day 7 days a week. Entertainers could no longer rely solely on musical talent: how an artist looked on video became as important as how he or she sounded. Pop stars sold themselves as dancers and actors, filming elaborate videos. By 1984, 97 of the top 100 albums, as reported in the music magazine *Billboard,* had promo videos, and artists were writing songs with video technology in mind.

Michael Jackson and videos hit it off splendidly after he broke through MTV's initial resistance to air videos by black

▶

Mick Jagger and Tina Turner turn it loose for the 16-hour African relief benefit, **Live Aid,** *seen by millions via satellite.*

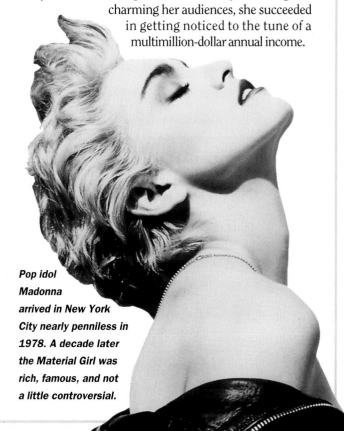

Pop idol Madonna arrived in New York City nearly penniless in 1978. A decade later the Material Girl was rich, famous, and not a little controversial.

Born to a tradition of music (her mother, Cissy Houston, is a gospel singer), Whitney Houston (inset) belts out a tune. Harry Connick, Jr., learned his craft as a teenager from blues and jazz greats James Booker and Ellis Marsalis.

of the queen of soul, Aretha Franklin; and there were new male soul singers, too, like Michael Bolton. Soul's funky progeny, rap music (see box previous page), with artists like Run DMC and LL Cool J, added the vitality of the streets to American music.

Even classical music underwent a renaissance of sorts. Recording companies enthusiastically promoted classical musicians as pop stars (violinists posing in strapless gowns and pianists displaying perfect pectorals) and marketed them to audiences with titles like *A Carnegie Hall Christmas,* featuring opera soprano Kathleen Battle and jazz trumpeter Wynton Marsalis.

Country music — subjected to an urban cowboy makeover in the early 1980's that sometimes left it sounding syrupy and artificial compared to music from the earlier times of Hank Williams and Patsy Cline — boasted a bumper crop of new stars: Randy Travis, Clint Black, Reba McEntire, and Garth Brooks. On their heels came offbeat performers such as Lyle Lovett and k. d. lang. From the country

MTV rapidly became part of American life, replacing radio, to a large extent, as the way to establish new talent in the teen and subteen market. But MTV was not above going after the widest possible audience. For example, noting a rise in popularity of country music, MTV tested a program hosted by honky-tonk star Dwight Yoakam.

With the music business getting more fiercely competitive and complex — as well as more lucrative for the winners and costly for the losers — marketing bigwigs hotly pursued "crossover entertainers" whose music spanned more than one segment of the vast market. One result was a further blurring of the line between "black" and "white" music. Black artists like Michael Jackson, Prince, and Whitney Houston got airtime on stations that drew predominately white listeners. And white entertainers such as Sting, Madonna, Kenny G., and George Michael, began turning up on stations aimed at the urban black audience. Reggae, country, Latino music (as performed by singers like Cuban-born Gloria Estefan), and jazz (for example, the big band orchestrations of Harry Connick, Jr.) also found crossover audiences. Joining them were the heirs and heiresses of earlier musical innovators. Anita Baker and Natalie Cole (daughter of the beloved Nat King Cole who died in his forties at the peak of his fame in 1965) sang in the tradition

Celebrities from Gregory Peck to Cindy Crawford turned out on New Year's, 1993, for Barbra Streisand's first live commercial show in more than 20 years. Receipts for just two nights broke records.

The Three Tenors album of the early 1990's, featuring singers Placido Domingo, Luciano Pavarotti (left), and Jose Carreras, brought opera to a wider listening audience.

Crowd Pleasers and Critical Triumphs

Feline Grizabella sings wistfully of days gone past in the musical Cats.

In looking back at the theatrical year — 1981 or any other — one must always begin by bemoaning the state of the art," said drama critic Frank Rich of *The New York Times*. "Leaden musicals," "star vehicles," and a lack of creativity off-Broadway were a few of the reasons Rich gave for his displeasure with the season of 1981. Nevertheless, Broadway was making money. Out-of-town theatergoers, half-price tickets, and telephone sales had brought the Great White Way its eighth straight profitable season. Musicals were one of the reasons people kept coming, and no one seemed to know how to turn them out better than British composer and wunderkind Andrew Lloyd Webber.

In 1982 Webber, with two hit musicals, *Evita* and *Joseph and the Amazing Technicolor Dreamcoat*, running on Broadway, brought a third to the New York stage: *Cats*. Based on T. S. Eliot's 1939 book *Old Possum's Book of Practical Cats*, it enchanted audiences with its fantastic sets and costumes and hummable theme song, "Memories." Webber's streak of hits continued with *Starlight Express* in 1987 and *The Phantom of the Opera* in 1988. Five years after *Phantom*, Webber turned to Hollywood and chose for his next musical Billy Wilder's legendary film *Sunset Boulevard,* an unsentimental probe into the psyche of an aging screen star as she descends into madness. The Los Angeles debut featured a real screen star, Glenn Close, in the lead role. Like Close, who was no stranger to the footlights, other Hollywood stars felt the need to turn, or return, to the stage, among them Jessica Lange, Gene Hackman, and Al Pacino. Top screen stars had the power to draw audiences, and some fans felt they added a note of glamour.

There was more happening on Broadway, of course, than Andrew Lloyd Webber and Hollywood stars. Chicago playwright David Mamet won a Pulitzer Prize in 1984 for *Glengarry Glen Ross*, a sardonic tale of four hustling real estate agents. August Wilson explored the lives of African-Americans over six decades and five plays, including his Pulitzer Prize–winning *The Piano Lesson* (1989). Wendy Wasserstein won critical acclaim for her two largely autobiographical dramas, *The Heidi Chronicles* (1989) and *The Sisters Rosensweig* (1993). The creators of the 1987 megahit *Les Misérables*, based on the Victor Hugo novel, set their next musical in Vietnam just before the U.S. pulled out. *Miss Saigon* (1991), which opened on Broadway after a to-do over the casting of a white actor as a Eurasian, made a record $37 million in advance sales.

Long, intense, and controversial, playwright Tony Kushner's two-part epic *Angels in America: A Gay Fantasia on National Themes* should have kept theatergoers away. Instead they flocked to the first part, *Millennium Approaches,* which won a Tony award and the Pulitzer Prize.

Opening on Broadway in the spring of 1993, *Millennium* made AIDS a metaphor for the spiritual bankruptcy that seemed to have afflicted 1980's America. A few months later *Perestroika*, the second part of the drama, carried an underlying message of compassion, which Kushner viewed as the way to healing in the next century.

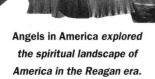

Angels in America *explored the spiritual landscape of America in the Reagan era.*

line-dancing craze to the country music programs, like *Billy Bob's Country Countdown*, that peppered network and cable television, country music was everywhere, its stars in demand as never before. No country singer made friends more quickly in the early 1980's than laid-back Willie Nelson, whose Farm Aid project, begun in 1985, helped relieve down-on-their-luck farmers and flooded-out Midwesterners.

Other performers, too, showed concern for the problems of humanity. "It feels good to be in a house full of people who care," remarked Madonna at an AIDS benefit in New York City in 1987, one of several in which she and other entertainers, including opera legend Leontyne Price and rap star Queen Latifah, participated. Indeed, the quality that musicians and pop stars seemed to share most in an era of wildly different musical styles was a concern for the unfortunate. Many of them worked tirelessly to raise money and public consciousness by staging shows like Live Aid, a rock telethon that reaped millions for African famine relief. Though skeptics charged that the real motive behind celebrity support for worthy causes was to attract more publicity, a great many Americans applauded the fact that, for a time at least, a social conscience was alive and well in music land.

Uncle Sam Polices the World

"One of the fondest expressions around is that we can't be the world's policeman," said Gen. Colin Powell in the early 1990's. "But guess who gets called when suddenly someone needs a cop?"

Suicide was something the U.S. military security officers in Beirut, Lebanon, had not foreseen. On the night of October 23, 1983, a young Lebanese man, connected to terrorist groups intent on driving out foreign troops, crashed a truck full of explosives into the barracks of U.S. marines, who were there at the request of the beleaguered Lebanese government. The blast killed the driver and 241 U.S. troops, a disaster that grimly defined the terrible risks of America's role as the world's primary peacekeeper.

Two days after the Beirut horror, President Reagan, though clearly shaken, went ahead with another military operation. U.S. troops stormed ashore on the Caribbean island of Grenada, where a bloody left-wing coup had ousted a pro-Western government. Cuban soldiers were establishing a base on the island, and 1,000 American students were trapped there. America's invasion of Grenada was

▲ *In Operation Restore Hope, U.S. marines arrive to distribute food in the Somalian interior in December 1992. Civil unrest hindered the humanitarian effort.*

Outside the Vatican Embassy in Panama City, an American soldier awaits the emergence of dictator Manuel Noriega.

◄

Just hours after the suicide bombing of the U.S. military barracks in Beirut, medics gently pull out a survivor.

denounced and derided by some, but Secretary of State George Shultz declared: "We've let the world know that we are going to protect our interests whatever it costs."

Defined since the late 1940's by anticommunism, American interests in the 1980's had expanded to include combating terrorism and the drug trade. On April 28, 1986, U.S. warplanes bombed the compound of the Libyan leader, Muammar al-Qaddafi. President Reagan condemned Qaddafi as the "mad dog of the Middle East" for backing terrorist attacks, including the killing of the marines in Beirut. In December 1989 President Bush sent armed forces to Panama to capture Gen. Manuel Noriega, the anti-American Panamanian dictator. Bush wanted to put Noriega on trial in the United States for drug-trafficking. It was the biggest military operation since Vietnam. Hunted by 24,000 American troops, Noriega took refuge in the Vatican Embassy. U.S. forces surrounded the building but held their fire (while blasting the embassy with music, including the 1970's hit "You're No Good"). Noriega gave up after 11 days.

Despite these successes, the Vietnam ordeal still weighed on the American spirit, creating a reluctance to use military force without clear goals and a good chance at victory. In the summer of 1990, a Middle Eastern dictator assessed America's resolve and decided to test it. The Iraqi leader, Saddam Hussein, invaded Kuwait on August 2. His army, hardened from years of war against Iran, swept aside the small Kuwaiti defense

◄

In Grenada, U.S. troops guard members of the Cuban force sent by Fidel Castro to support the island's Communist regime.

▲ An oil well fire, one of hundreds set by Iraqi troops fleeing the Desert Storm assault, frames an American and his personnel carrier.

Gen. Norman Schwarzkopf (right) and his boss, Gen. Colin Powell (left), chairman of the Joint Chiefs, made Desert Storm work.

forces. The invasion stunned the world, but even more ominous was the possibility that Saddam's war machine might roll south into Saudi Arabia, taking control of much of the world's oil supply.

Saddam's grab of Kuwait presented George Bush with the greatest crisis of his presidency. To do nothing would almost certainly inspire further conquest and other would-be conquerors. To dislodge the Iraqis, however, would require a huge commitment of troops and risk American lives — how many, no one could predict. Realizing that the United States could not and should not handle the task alone, Bush set about constructing a 28-nation alliance to take the field against Saddam.

Troops, supplies, and an armada of aircraft poured into Saudi Arabia, and a massive fleet assembled in the Persian Gulf, all under the command of U.S. general H. Norman Schwarzkopf, a Vietnam combat hero. Pentagon staffers readied plans for tight coordination between ground and air units. Despite the defense experts who talked of the unprecedented power of high-tech U.S. weaponry, there was gnawing fear that America would soon endure a bloodbath in a distant desert.

On the evening of January 16, 1991, the media flashed the news that Iraq was under air attack; Operation Desert Storm had begun. U.S. military sources reported that cruise missiles and "smart bombs" were hitting Iraqi targets with stunning accuracy, even blasting down ventilation shafts.

Stealth bombers, virtually invisible on radar screens, destroyed Iraqi communications. Saddam

remained defiant, so on February 23 General Schwarzkopf ordered his ground troops to invade Iraq and occupied Kuwait. As Allied forces fell upon the Iraqis from the front and the flank, resistance crumbled.

After just 100 hours of ground fighting, President Bush ordered a cease-fire. Fewer than 200 Americans had been killed. Although Saddam remained in power, the Allied campaign had destroyed his capacity to wage war. And for Americans there was an equally important element of the victory, a psychological one. As one army officer put it: "The stigma of Vietnam has been erased."

▼ Cable News Network (CNN) showed how pilots tracked smart bombs right down to impact with Iraqi targets.

Learning the hazards of desert warfare, a U.S. artillery unit sweats out a sudden dust storm in Saudi Arabia.

413

THE WAYS WE TRAVELED

As the century dawned, the locomotive represented the ultimate in power and speed, and the bicycle was the fastest machine most people could afford. Today's nationwide web of highways, bridges, and tunnels was not even a gleam in engineers' eyes. But once the automobile and America embraced each other, things changed. The days of depending on horses, bicycles, and ferries slipped into the past. Speed was one reason for the car's success, but it was more than that: having a personal car meant the freedom to go anyplace a road led, any time, at one's own pace. For many Americans that has always given cars an edge over buses and trains. Just as the automobile shrank distances in our own country, jet passenger service gave us an affordable magic carpet to the world. No longer is international travel the privilege of the leisured rich, sailing on luxury ships. Middle-class families, teachers, and students now roam the globe with the sang-froid of Jules Verne's Phileas Fogg in *Around the World in Eighty Days.*

Bicycles ● 1900's
In ladylike garb, a biker takes a spin. Postmen of the era used bicycles to bring special delivery mail.

Steam Train ● 1905
Summer vacationers meet new arrivals to a resort hotel in the Catskill Mountains.

Horse-Drawn Streetcar ● 1910
Horseless trolleys were just around the corner, but when they came, their styling was a lot like this horsepowered New York City model.

Ford "Woody" ● 1935
The great exodus to the suburbs came after World War II, but well-off city folk had set up country estates long before that. A fixture in their garages was a utility vehicle, or station car, like this classic Ford.

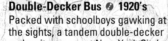

Double-Decker Bus ● 1920's
Packed with schoolboys gawking at the sights, a tandem double-decker makes its way past New York City's Pennsylvania Station.

Ferry ● 1921
Where the Tappan Zee Bridge now crosses, a ferry carries autos over the Hudson River, about 20 miles north of New York City.

Nash Ambassador Six ● 1937
The company offered its bed feature in several sedan models during the Depression.

Yankee Clipper ● 1930's
When Pan American World Airways started the first transatlantic passenger service in 1939, it used this four-engine Boeing B-314, called the Yankee Clipper. Four years earlier Pan American had inaugurated regular transpacific flights.

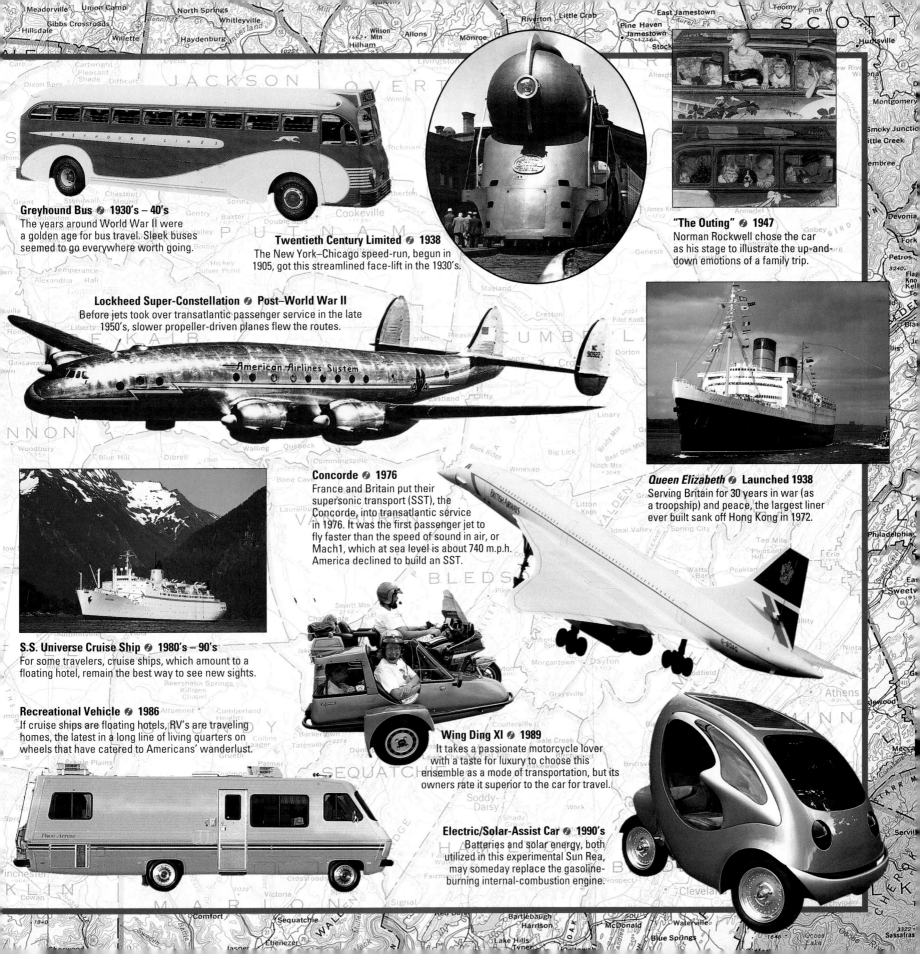

Greyhound Bus ⊘ 1930's – 40's
The years around World War II were a golden age for bus travel. Sleek buses seemed to go everywhere worth going.

Twentieth Century Limited ⊘ 1938
The New York–Chicago speed-run, begun in 1905, got this streamlined face-lift in the 1930's.

"The Outing" ⊘ 1947
Norman Rockwell chose the car as his stage to illustrate the up-and-down emotions of a family trip.

Lockheed Super-Constellation ⊘ Post–World War II
Before jets took over transatlantic passenger service in the late 1950's, slower propeller-driven planes flew the routes.

Concorde ⊘ 1976
France and Britain put their supersonic transport (SST), the Concorde, into transatlantic service in 1976. It was the first passenger jet to fly faster than the speed of sound in air, or Mach1, which at sea level is about 740 m.p.h. America declined to build an SST.

Queen Elizabeth ⊘ Launched 1938
Serving Britain for 30 years in war (as a troopship) and peace, the largest liner ever built sank off Hong Kong in 1972.

S.S. Universe Cruise Ship ⊘ 1980's – 90's
For some travelers, cruise ships, which amount to a floating hotel, remain the best way to see new sights.

Recreational Vehicle ⊘ 1986
If cruise ships are floating hotels, RV's are traveling homes, the latest in a long line of living quarters on wheels that have catered to Americans' wanderlust.

Wing Ding XI ⊘ 1989
It takes a passionate motorcycle lover with a taste for luxury to choose this ensemble as a mode of transportation, but its owners rate it superior to the car for travel.

Electric/Solar-Assist Car ⊘ 1990's
Batteries and solar energy, both utilized in this experimental Sun Rea, may someday replace the gasoline-burning internal-combustion engine.

Milestones on the Road to Tomorrow

Science marched ahead in double time, spewing out inventions along the way. Medicine, robotics, computers, communications, all staged breakthroughs. The space program, though hit by tragedy, reached new heights.

◀

This computerized robot hand, perfected by Japanese scientists in 1984, is deft enough to play a piano melody by Schumann.

One winter night in 1987, someone tried to break into the Bayside Exposition Center in Boston, but the intruder was soon detected by an exceptionally vigilant guard, whose calls for help brought quick reinforcement. The alert guard was neither man nor dog, but a robot. The high-tech world of computer-driven automation, so long imagined in film and fiction, was fast becoming a reality. In medicine, space exploration, communications, agriculture, business, education, and the home, science continued to revolutionize the way we lived. And the pace was accelerating.

Medical advances poured forth from laboratories in the 1980's. Great strides were made in the war against cancer: in 1970 the cure rate for cancer in children was about 10 percent; by 1992, it had reached 66 percent. Delicate, dangerous surgery on the brain and the eye became safer thanks to advances in lasers, using highly focused light, and gamma knives, which directed beams of radiation on the problem area with superb accuracy.

Both wristwatch and beeper, this gadget takes messages from friends or associates who dial the owner's special phone number.

Some of the greatest technical breakthroughs allowed doctors simply to see more clearly. An advance in CAT scan technique, made possible by a computer program, generated three-dimensional pictures of the body's organs at work. With this 3-D approach, doctors could observe a patient's heart beating on a monitor, rotate the picture to allow different angles of view, and zoom in to inspect the heart's internal structure.

Genetic engineering, first achieved in the 1970's, gave medicine a whole new array of tools. By manipulating the genes of bacteria, Swiss scientists created an artificial version of human interferon, a substance that may help to battle some cancers and prevent viral diseases. Other researchers altered the genes of sheep so that the animal's milk contained a human protein that fights emphysema. Genetically modified plants, too, yielded new sources of medicine. Biotech scientists successfully created human monoclonal antibodies from tobacco leaves, opening the door to potential large-scale farming of pharmaceuticals. In one of the most controversial experiments of the 1980's, researchers isolated the gene that makes tomatoes rot. The result was the super tomato, which stays fresh three weeks longer than a regular one. But some consumer advocates raised the alarm, concerned that, while extending a tomato's shelf-life, the genetic alteration might also adversely affect the person who ate one.

Computers became smaller, cheaper, and more powerful, transforming the workplace. The familiar clack of typewriters began to disappear as office workers became computer literate. As high-speed number

Riding piggyback on its huge external fuel tank with attached booster rockets, the space shuttle Columbia (lower right) blasts off from Cape Canaveral on its maiden voyage.

In the nation's worst space disaster, Challenger erupts into a fireball 10 miles above the Atlantic, spewing debris and instantly killing all seven crew members. It was the 25th shuttle launch.

Giving a boost to astronomy, the $1.5-billion Hubble Space Telescope leaves the cargo bay of Discovery for orbit 380 miles above the earth. Ferrying satellites was a basic shuttle mission.

▲ **Marvelously compact, this palm-size video camera with zoom lens and automatic focus records color and sound for playback on TV sets.**

▶

A University of North Carolina researcher tests the interaction of a drug and a protein using 3-D glasses and a robotic arm.

crunching and word processing became commonplace, computer scientists looked toward new frontiers. By the end of the 1980's, computers equipped with voice recognition systems were being put to use in a growing variety of tasks, among them sorting mail, routing collect phone calls, recording stock transactions, and checking credit card purchases.

Despite individual qualms about the quickening pace of life, many Americans began to view high-tech innovations as necessities. It took 20 years to sell the first million television sets in the United States; it took just four and a half years for 1 million people to acquire cellular phones. The portable cellular phone allowed people to conduct business from cars and airplanes or even as they strolled down the street to lunch. Commuters, stuck in traf-

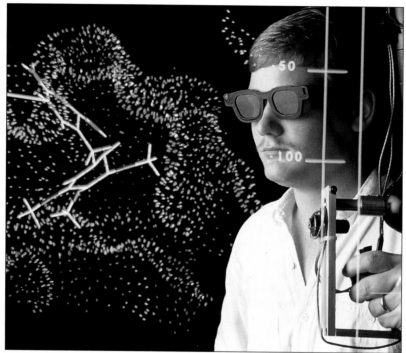

fic, dialed clients, made sales calls, and checked the office.

The fax machine, too, became all the rage. Using existing telephone circuits, it began sending documents whizzing across town, or around the world, at the touch of a few buttons. Productivity soared. But instant communication also exacted a price. People came to feel they were on duty all the time — at home, in the car, on weekends, on vacations. Not surprisingly, leisure time shrank: between 1973

Cellular phones, which transmit conversations via radio waves, became the hottest way to keep in touch after the FCC began awarding licenses by lottery in 1984.

and 1989, it declined by 37 percent, while the average work-week went up from 41 to 47 hours.

Other new devices, ranging from the serious to the silly, appeared in the 1980's. Compact discs, a laser-based sound-reproduction system, quickly gave audio tapes stiff competition and rang the death knell for vinyl records. Microwave ovens, only a curiosity in the 1970's, had by the end of the 1980's found a place in three out of four households in the United States. People came to expect meals in minutes and then meals in seconds. There was the $2,000 chair that played stereo music while giving a massage, the answering machine that responded with the voice of Daffy Duck, and the hand-held computer system that calculated the user's exact geographical location, give or take just 100 feet. By the late 1980's, a 12-ounce palm-size electronic "book," which contained a 1.5-million-word dictionary, was on the market; in standard printed format the dictionary would have weighed 20 pounds.

The diminutive dictionary was nothing compared to other wizardries of microminiaturization. Engineers devised a pressure sensor smaller than the head of a pin that could be inserted in the chambers of the heart. Similar mighty mites may one day manipulate artificial limbs or power microrobots that perform surgery. One scientist envisioned an army of tiny robot submarines that can clean out clogged arteries.

One of the most exciting, and strangest, technologies to emerge in the 1980's was "virtual reality." To experience it, a user dons a helmet equipped with a pair of small television screens connected to a powerful computer, which can generate three-dimensional scenes of almost any kind. The user can walk through an imaginary building, skim over the bottom of the sea, or glide above the surface of a distant planet.

Perhaps the most familiar symbol of technological achievement in these years was the space shuttle, the reusable spacecraft that takes off like a rocket and lands like a plane, on a runway. NASA, the U.S. government space agency, spent $10 billion dollars developing the first shuttle, *Columbia*, which was hailed as the initial step toward building a space station and colonizing space. When three engines and two solid-fuel rockets lifted it from Cape Canaveral in April 1981, a London newspaper trumpeted the event with a one-word headline: "WOW!"

AIDS: Let There Be Hope

The crisis began as a medical oddity. Early in 1981 five young men entered Los Angeles hospitals with an illness caused by an extremely rare parasite, *pneumocystis carinii*. All five were homosexual; all five soon died. Other uncommon ailments began appearing, including a skin cancer, Kaposi's sarcoma, that normally afflicted the elderly. But these victims were young, sexually active gay males, all of whom had lost their natural resistance to a wide spectrum of exotic diseases. Scientists dubbed the condition Acquired Immune Deficiency Syndrome (AIDS), and began searching for a cause.

By the time they reported finding it, in 1984, more than 10,000 Americans had contracted AIDS; almost 9,000 had died from the disease. The circle of disaster widened to include heterosexual men and women, intravenous drug users, and hemophiliacs and other blood-transfusion recipients. Cases were reported in Europe, Latin America, Africa, Asia. Year by year the numbers escalated. By 1992 an estimated 12 million people worldwide had become infected.

The cause was a virus, HIV, that attacks the immune system. Several drugs proved effective in slowing the virus's assault; but a cure, or even a preventive vaccine, remained elusive. Meanwhile, the toll mounted. Screen star Rock Hudson died of AIDS; basketball whiz Magic Johnson tested HIV positive. As the disease touched more and more lives, millions of Americans wore AIDS Awareness Ribbons (above) and prayed for an end to one of the deadliest scourges in medical history.

After orbiting the earth for 54 hours, astronauts John Young and Robert Crippen gently angled the craft downward for reentry. Penetrating the atmosphere at more than 24 times the speed of sound, *Columbia* was flying far faster than any winged vehicle had ever flown and was enduring temperatures of 2300 F° caused by atmospheric friction. Anxiety turned to jubilation as the craft touched down in California "smoother than any airliner," according to Crippen.

Twenty-four additional flights followed in the next five years, and three new shuttles joined the fleet: *Challenger*, *Discovery*, and *Atlantis*. Space flight became almost routine.

Then, in one ghastly moment, catastrophe struck. In January 1986 *Challenger* rose into space carrying a seven-member crew. Just 73 seconds later, it disintegrated in a burst of fire. A rubber seal on a booster rocket had given way, causing the fuel tank to explode. All seven crew members died, including the first schoolteacher in space, Christa McAuliffe, selected from among 11,000 applicants. Millions of Americans, watching on TV, shuddered in horror.

But the space program moved forward. Thirty-two months after the disaster, a redesigned shuttle blasted into orbit. And for all its setbacks, the program was paying dividends in scientific progress. Shuttles launched and retrieved research satellites and enabled lab experiments under gravity-free conditions in fields ranging from agriculture to computer-chip technology. The shuttle also had a role as a vehicle for international good will: on a *Discovery* flight in 1994, a Russian astronaut came along as one of the crew.

▲ **Biosphere 2, an enclosed ecosystem built in the Arizona desert for some $150 million in 1990, was home for two years to a volunteer team that grew its own food, drank recycled water, and breathed recirculated air.**

Computers became steadily smaller, cheaper, and more powerful. This solar-powered laptop, weighing only a few pounds, makes a lengthy writing task an outdoor job.

419

ANd THE WALLS CAME TUMBLING DOWN

"It is possible to suppress, compel, bribe, break or blast — but only for a limited period," declared Soviet premier Mikhail Gorbachev. With that, decades of Communist oppression abruptly ended.

The most dramatic event in half a century of Cold War menace began without hype or fanfare. On November 9, 1989, three weeks after the forced resignation of Communist Party chief Erich Honecker, the new East German government held a press conference. Among the topics was a notice that all border restrictions on crossing into West Germany would be lifted, effective that midnight. No one anticipated what happened next. Tens of thousands of people began gathering by the Berlin Wall. At the stroke of midnight, a joyous, frenzied mob surged through the newly opened checkpoints. Horns honked, trumpets blared, and champagne bubbled over in the streets. "I don't feel like I'm in prison anymore!" shouted one East German. "I just can't believe it!" said another. Twenty-eight miles long and 28 years old, the Berlin Wall had stood since 1961 as the ultimate symbol of Communist oppression. In the blink of an eye, it became part of history's junk heap.

A great tide of freedom was sweeping over Eastern Europe and beyond. Satellite nations bordering the Soviet Union had begun to shake off Communist rule, and in Moscow itself the institutions of Soviet tyranny were lurching toward collapse. The forces of change even reached Communist China, where a free-market economy was tak-

In a frenzy of newly discovered freedom, jubilant Berliners smash away the wall that had divided their city for more than a generation. It happened after Soviet leader Mikhail Gorbachev (inset) launched his glasnost and perestroika policies, unwittingly writing the death warrant for European communism.

ing hold and where a daring grassroots democracy movement rose up to confront the aging leadership. There was no question that years of pressure from the West had taken a toll on the Communist world. Back in 1983 President Ronald Reagan, fearing Soviet power, had called the U.S.S.R. "an evil empire" and ordered up a multibillion-dollar antimissile defense system to be based in space. But the empire mostly crumbled from within.

The person who made it happen was none other than the Soviet Union's top-ranking Communist. Mikhail S. Gorbachev had moved rapidly through party ranks to become,

▲ *In a supreme act of defiance, a lone Chinese demonstrator blocks a Red Army tank column as it nears Tiananmen Square in Beijing. Unlike most 1989 freedom movements, China's ended in tragedy, with the massacre of more than 5,000 civilians.*

at age 54, the first in a new generation of Soviet leaders. Well educated and well traveled, he had seen firsthand the economic successes of the West; he was also painfully familiar with his own country's shortcomings. As secretary of agriculture from 1979 to 1982, he had witnessed four harvests so meager that he did not dare release the production figures. Then, as deputy to two previous heads of state, Yuri Andropov and Konstantin Chernenko, he observed up close the decay and corruption that were eating away at Soviet society. Clearly the time had come for drastic change. Upon Chernenko's death in 1985, Gorbachev outmaneuvered a clique of old-guard hard-liners and got himself elected general secretary. ("This man has a nice smile," said one compatriot, "but he has iron teeth.") Then he set to work.

His first major reform was to fling open the doors of government to public view, ending generations of official secrecy, an act he termed *glasnost.* Henceforth, the U.S.S.R. would enjoy a free press and open discussion of national issues. The second reform, *perestroika,* called for a cellar-to-attic restructuring of the 70-year-old apparatus of Soviet rule. Both initiatives horrified the old guard; *perestroika* was particularly distasteful, since it meant loosening the Communist Party's iron grip on all elements of Soviet society. To be sure, Gorbachev never meant to abolish communism entirely; he merely insisted that the old Marxist system of state ownership and control be brought up to date. Only by making it function more like a Western market-driven

▼ *Union leader Lech Walesa, father of Poland's Solidarity movement, addresses workers in Gdansk. Free elections in 1989 gave his party a sweeping parliamentary majority.*

▼ *Hungarian soldiers cut down barbed-wire fences along the border with Austria, ripping apart the Iron Curtain and opening the first free passage from East to West.*

leaders were gradually being cut loose to succeed or fail on their own. Declared Gorbachev: "Any nation has the right to decide its fate by itself." One by one, the countries of Eastern Europe began to do just that.

For some years Hungary, one of the more progressive satellites, had been experimenting with a consumer-oriented economy known as "goulash communism." The next move was political. In May 1989 Hungary dismantled the barbed wire along its Austrian border, thus becoming the first Communist nation to allow free travel to the West. Refugees poured into Austria by the tens of thousands, looking for a better life. In Poland severe economic troubles forced the nation's military dictator, Gen. Wojciech Jaruzelski, to seek help from the outlawed Solidarity labor union and its leader, Lech Walesa. A few years earlier Walesa, considered a threat to state security, had been thrown in prison. Now, after negotiations in early 1989, Poland became the first Iron Curtain country to form a non-Communist, multiparty parliament. The next year the unthinkable happened: Lech Walesa was elected president.

There was more. In Czechoslovakia thousands of demonstrators gathered in the fall of 1989 demanding freedom. Undaunted by attacks by riot police, the people chanted, "The game is over!" And so it was. A bloodless Velvet Revolution toppled the government, replacing it with one headed by playwright Vaclav Havel, a dissident who had been imprisoned many times for his beliefs. And in Romania, perhaps the most brutal of all the hard-line regimes, the 24-year reign of Nicolae Ceausescu abruptly came to an end, and the dictator and his wife were tried and convicted for commiting genocide. The sentence, death by firing squad, was immediately car-

economy, he reasoned, could the Soviet Union recover from its stagnation.

Determined to boost economic growth, Gorbachev granted a measure of autonomy to the 15 republics that made up the Union of Soviet Socialist Republics. In 1989 he oversaw the creation of a new legislature and the first free elections since 1917. A year later he won approval of a law to end the Communist Party's monopoly on power in the U.S.S.R. But events were running ahead of his control, and the very existence of the U.S.S.R. was coming into doubt.

By the end of 1990 all 15 Soviet republics had declared some form of autonomy. Gorbachev, alarmed that he had given away too much, proposed a Union Treaty that would cede certain powers to the republics while keeping them under the umbrella of the U.S.S.R. But if the pace of change in Gorbachev's view was breathtaking, there were some who wanted change to come even faster, notably Boris Yeltsin, the freely elected president of the Russian Republic. As Gorbachev struggled to mollify the hard-line Communists, Yeltsin publicly quit the Communist Party to dramatize his split with Gorbachev.

Meanwhile, the changes wrought by Gorbachev were noted with wonder in the long-suffering satellite countries of Eastern Europe, and with increasing nervousness by the satellites' old-guard dictators. Accustomed to relying on Moscow for military and economic aid, the Communist

Massed national flags proudly wave over a demonstration in Prague during Czechoslovakia's Velvet Revolution. And a young patriot (inset) bears a portrait of Vaclav Havel, the writer who became the new Czech head of state.

▶

Last of the hard-line dictators, Romania's Nicolae Ceausescu ordered elite troops to fire on demonstrators in December 1989. On Christmas Day he himself was executed.

ried out by soldiers who "could not restrain their hate," according to one witness. An interim president was named the next day. In 1991 the Baltic states of Lithuania, Latvia, and Estonia declared their independence from the Soviet Union.

The world barely had time to catch its breath when an even more astonishing drama began to unfold in Russia itself. In August 1991 Gorbachev was vacationing in his *dacha* by the Black Sea when an unexpected delegation showed up at his door. He grabbed one telephone, then another. No use: the lines were dead. In Moscow, tanks rolled through the streets as elements of the Red Army and the KGB took control. It was a classic coup d'état, launched by hard-line Communists intent on deposing Gorbachev.

Yeltsin put aside his differences with Gorbachev to throw his weight behind the embattled leader. He called on his own loyalists within the military, and they responded by sending troops and armored vehicles to back him up. The nation stood at the edge of civil war. In a show of courage that riveted the world, Yeltsin climbed atop a tank in Red Square and shouted his defiance. Thousands cheered him. The elite Alpha Force of KGB commandos was ordered to storm Yeltsin's residence and kill him, but it refused. Other units stationed outside Moscow refused to

In the coup that fizzled, a crack Soviet tank unit, sent to occupy Moscow in 1991, decks out in flowers and fraternizes with civilians. A year later Russian president Boris Yeltsin (inset) earns a warm welcome during a visit to the United States.

◄

As Soviet communism toppled, so did its icons, such as these statues of Joseph Stalin (foreground) and party leader Mikhail Kalinin, who died in 1946.

▶

Taking advantage of their newly won freedom, factory workers in Minsk, capital of Belarus, mob managers with a litany of grievances.

budge. With the plotters facing a mutiny by the armed forces, the coup unraveled three days after it began.

After 72 hours under house arrest, Gorbachev emerged triumphant. But his victory was short-lived. His reforms were faltering, and the embryonic market economy was in shambles. In the first six months of 1991, the gross national product of the U.S.S.R. fell by 10 percent, prices went up by nearly 50 percent, and the military was still gobbling up half of all industrial production. On Christmas Day, 1991, Gorbachev resigned, turning power over to Yeltsin.

Yeltsin proclaimed his fervent hope of building a new society. "I want our people to live better," he said. It was a wish that both the newly liberated eastern nations and the staunchly capitalist West could heartily applaud.

423

Michael Jordan executes a dunk for the U.S. 1992 Olympic "Dream Team." Arguably the best who ever played, he led the Chicago Bulls to three straight NBA championships before retiring in 1993.

BIG BUCKS, BIG BANGS, IN SPORTS

If sports reflect the ethics of the society in which they are played, there was good news and bad news for America as the 20th century neared the finish line.

It had everything: An impossible dream. Sacrifice and teamwork. Modest young athletes playing for their country, not for personal glory or for the great god money. America in the role of David, and the Soviet Union as Goliath. A danger-fraught journey to an epic confrontation. A mighty upset victory. And then the Americans keeping it all together for one more upset to win the gold medal.

It was, of course, the story of the U.S. hockey team at the 1980 Olympics at Lake Placid, New York. The Americans looked badly overmatched against the Soviet Union and, for that matter, against other European powerhouses like Sweden, Czechoslovakia, and Finland. But in its first game, the U.S. held Sweden to a 2–2 tie and then, astonishingly, beat the Czechs 7–3. Three more wins over less formidable opponents followed, leading to a face-off with the Soviet Union. When the Americans prevailed 4–3 on a wrist-shot goal by Mike Eruzione, all America cheered, and jubilant crowds surged through the frigid Lake Placid streets chanting "U.S.A.! U.S.A.!" Now only Finland's crack squad stood between America and a gold medal. Two days later the U.S. team bested the Finns 4–2, and the 20 young skaters and their coach, Herb Brooks, were America's darlings.

The same 1980 Olympics, though dominated by East Germany and the U.S.S.R., saw another spectacular American feat, by speed skater Eric Heiden. He won five golds, in the 500-, 1,000-, 1,500-, 5,000-, and 10,000-meter races.

Rarely had American sports seemed so pure and wholesome as they did in those days of February 1980. In the years that followed, it seemed to many Americans that sports had lost their last vestige of innocence (if sports ever had any, cynics chimed in) and sunk into a world of acrimonious owner-player disputes, public tantrums, surly behavior, soaring salaries, multimillion-dollar commercial endorsements by athletes, scandals, and outright criminal behavior.

A vicious attack in January 1994 seemed to confirm the view that sports had lost their way. Olympics-bound American figure skater Nancy Kerrigan had just finished a practice session in Detroit, Michigan, when a burly man

Florence Griffith-Joyner seems to take flight on her way to winning one of three golds at the 1988 Olympics in Seoul, South Korea.

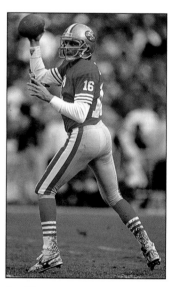

Joe Montana, famous for come-from-behind heroics, won four Super Bowls for San Francisco (1982, 1985, 1989, and 1990).

Spunky 16-year-old Mary Lou Retton won the gold in the all-round gymnastics at the 1984 Los Angeles Olympics.

Wayne Gretzky is the greatest scorer in pro hockey history. In 1978, at age 17, he joined the Edmonton Oilers. He moved to the Los Angeles Kings in 1988.

materialized at the ice rink and swung a club at her leg, apparently intending to deal a crippling blow to her knee. Fortunately his aim was off, and a badly bruised Kerrigan resumed skating a few weeks later. The full horror of the incident soon emerged: it had been planned by people close to Kerrigan's figure-skating rival, Tonya Harding. By eliminating Kerrigan from competition, the plotters hoped to clear the way for Harding to reap the millions of dollars in commercial endorsements and other income that awaited the winner of the Olympic figure-skating gold medal.

Most fine athletes are driven by a fierce will to win, and that led some Americans to raise troubling questions. Did a win-at-any-cost attitude, coupled with the lure of fame and staggering amounts of money, threaten to take the heart and soul out of sports? Might other criminal acts be perpetrated on the behalf of athletes who stood to make fortunes in their chosen sport?

Certainly little doubt remained that sports stars were liberally endowed with feet of clay. Baseball legend Pete Rose, the inspiring "Charlie Hustle," could not resist betting on games when he was manager of the Cincinnati Reds, and was banned for life from the sport he loved. Revelations and rumors of drug and alcohol abuse plagued sports from the biathlon to weight lifting. In 1986 cocaine abuse contributed to the death of University of Maryland basketball star Len Bias, the Boston Celtics number one draft pick, before he got a chance to play in the pros; and the next year the New York Mets pitcher Doc Gooden sought help for cocaine addiction.

These and many more personal tragedies occurred at a time when athletes had never made more money. In 1989 the average yearly pay for a National Basketball Association player reached $750,000 and kept climbing. Three years later, the average major-league baseball player's

salary topped $1 million. At the end of 1993, Dallas Cowboys quarterback Troy Aikman signed an eight-year $50-million contract, which made him the highest-paid professional football player ever. Even so, Aikman's average yearly salary was exceeded by hockey's Wayne Gretzky of the Los Angeles Kings ($8.5 million), baseball's Barry Bonds of the San Francisco Giants ($7.29 million), and basketball's Larry Johnson of the Charlotte Hornets ($7 million). Escalating ticket and concession prices partly funded such stratospheric salaries, but television provided most of the money. Five networks — Fox, NBC, ABC, TNT, and ESPN — paid a total of $4.38 billion to televise National Football League games for four seasons, from 1994 to 1997. Other popular spectator sports also basked in the TV largesse, which translated into whopping paychecks for athletes, as well as lots of money for team owners.

Many fans resented their heroes making millions, but that didn't stop athletes from negotiating fat contracts and endorsements. The players felt that their incomes were justified because athletes have relatively few money-making years, and careers can be cut short by injuries. A 1989 Ball State University study found that 46 percent of all retired National Football League players had been forced to quit due to injuries. And not only contact sports do damage: by her late teens, tennis prodigy Tracy Austin was struggling with a succession of injuries and never again reached top form after winning the U.S. Open in 1981 at the age of 18.

In the end, we ask our sports heroes to give nothing less than their all. That's a tough order, but as long as there are athletes willing to do it — like the eight performers shown on these two pages and hundreds more, known and unknown, past, present, and future — chances are the fans will keep coming.

Greg Louganis shows his gold-medal form. The diver won the springboard and platform events in both the 1984 and 1988 Olympics.

At the 1992 Olympics in France, Californian Kristi Yamaguchi performs her winning original program.

Chris Evert, still intense at 34, sets up at the 1989 U.S. Open. In earlier years she and Martina Navratilova had epic duels.

IN PURSUIT OF PHYSICAL PERFECTION

Whatever it took — sweating at the exercise machines, adopting the eating habits of a monk, going under the surgeon's knife — Americans were determined to realize their ideal bodies.

An exercise enthusiast gets a leg up on the competition with the aid of her personal trainer.

If there was one emblem of the 1980's, an object (aside from the dollar bill) that summed up the spirit of the age, it was the Nautilus machine — a maze of chrome, pulleys, and weights by which legions of exercisers pushed, pulled, sweated, and grunted their way to slimness, strength, and beauty. Some 400,000 Nautilus machines were sold between 1970 and 1984 as exercise became a national obsession. Chanting the slogan "No pain, no gain," fitness addicts put themselves through endless hours of torture (and took pounds off their wallets in the process). Self-improvement has been a cherished American tradition, but in the 1980's the goal was nothing less than physical perfection.

In 10 years, sales of exercise gear went from $5 million to $738 million. The actress Jane Fonda became a fitness maven and sold 1.2 million copies of her exercise videos in just three years.

TV personality Willard Scott with macho movie star Arnold Schwarzenegger, who presided over the opening ceremonies of the 1991 Great American Workout.

The health club was the place to be seen. A far cry from the dank and smelly gymnasiums of the past, these temples of sweat were elaborately high-tech: they were fitted out with exercise bikes, treadmills, ballet barres, and skiing, stair-climbing, and rowing machines. Surrounded by mirrors and hooked up to pulse meters and gadgets to measure blood pressure and oxygen intake, patrons puffed to booming disco music. Those who could afford it built gyms at home to avoid the health-club crowds and beginner's embarrassment. "Who wants to be humiliated," said one well-heeled weakling, "trying to lift 35 pounds when the gorilla next to you is lifting a VW?" Small fortunes were poured into equipping these vest-pocket gyms. Along with the requisite hardware, there were extras like whirlpools and massage therapists. "The home gym threatens to replace the gourmet kitchen as a status symbol," observed one magazine. The ultimate accessory was a personal trainer to bark orders and encouragement.

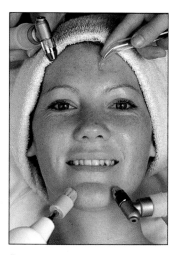

Beauty spas, using state-of-the-art equipment and techniques, offered the latest in facials.

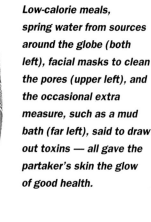

Low-calorie meals, spring water from sources around the globe (both left), facial masks to clean the pores (upper left), and the occasional extra measure, such as a mud bath (far left), said to draw out toxins — all gave the partaker's skin the glow of good health.

A school in Vinton, Iowa, takes steps to reverse the results of a study that showed America's youth is less fit than it was 20 years ago.

The American ideal of beauty underwent a radical change during the decade. "Today, health is beauty," explained the head of a top modeling agency. Models who, in years past, did all they could to preserve the fragile look now sported the legs of boxers and a glint of "serene determination in the eyes." Advertisements featured sleek outlines and rippling muscles to link their products with health. People with waistline problems dove into diet foods, and by 1988 a third of the groceries bought in America were low calorie. Those who wanted total immersion in a healthy regime took "vacations" at expensive spas, which offered exercise classes with names like Body Contouring and Positive Power. Some spas took the idea to its extreme and instituted "boot camp" programs. A place called the Ashram in California, known as the toughest spa in America, charged $1,300 per week for bare-bones accommodations and spartan meals. Guests shared rooms and started their days promptly at 6:30 A.M. with a meditation session. After a glass of orange juice, the sum total of breakfast, they headed off for a 2½-hour hike. One such fitness camp threatened to expel guests who sneaked extra pieces of bread at dinnertime.

To counteract the effects of aging, there was always the knife. In 1986 half a million Americans underwent cosmetic surgery. Vanity was not the only reason: careers were at stake in a society that placed a premium on youthful vigor. "It's the competitive demand to look youthful," said one doctor explaining the boom in cosmetic surgery. One of the specialty's more popular innovations was liposuction, a procedure in which fat was sucked out of the body. It was followed by lipofilling, in which the fat was redeposited elsewhere to form a perfect profile or create a comely curve. By the mid-1980's nearly a quarter of plastic-surgery patients were men. One California salon offered male clients a three-day makeover, involving analysis of skin, nails, and hair, plus a shopping trip with a fashion expert. Retin-A, a drug derived from vitamin A, which stimulates the production of skin cells, was used by some in the belief that it helped correct the damage done by prolonged exposure to the sun. "It's the closest thing we have to a youth cream," said one doctor, although people who used the product sometimes suffered such side effects as skin irritation and scaling.

Excesses aside, the benefits of the fitness craze were undeniable: the incidence of heart disease and stroke dropped in the 1980's, and life expectancy edged upward. More important, people found that fitness could be fun. "We are discovering," said one health writer, "that every human being has a God-given right to move efficiently, gracefully, and joyfully."

Jane Fonda (right) and Richard Simmons (upper right) became gurus of fitness when, like Raquel Welch, Arnold Schwarzenegger, Sandahl Bergman, Marie Osmond, and others, they marketed their expertise through videos (Jane Fonda's Workout and Every Day With Richard Simmons Family Fitness).

427

Moviegoing Gets a Makeover

Certainly the film business has changed over the years, but our passion for movies burns as brightly as ever.

Though most of the old movie palaces are shut, the multiplex and the videocassette have filled the gap.

Listening to the gloomy predictions, many movie lovers in the late 1970's could be forgiven for thinking that the old American ritual of going out to the movies was on its last legs. One-screen movie houses, national fixtures for generations, kept losing customers and shutting down. TV's drain on movie audiences seemed unrelenting, and there was a new threat in the early 1980's: videocassette recorders, user-friendly and increasingly affordable. A new industry was taking off, soon to make movie-video-rental stores as familiar as gas stations. It seemed all too obvious that the future of movies lay in the cozy confines of the home, where you could bring a favorite film from the video store and watch it at your leisure.

Clearly, going out to the movies, the time-honored movie date, and maybe the Hollywood film industry itself, had reached the exit door. That was what the pessimists were saying as the 1980's began, but it didn't happen.

Fast-forward to the mid-1990's. Some of the biggest movie hits of all time, and some of the best loved, had appeared over the past decade and a half. America had a new crop of favorite stars, ranging from Tom Cruise to Geena Davis. Arnold Schwarzenegger had taken action movies to new heights, or depths, in two *Terminators*. Through the efforts of controversial actor-director Spike Lee and others, in films like *Malcolm X* (played by Denzel Washington), African-Americans attained greater influence in Hollywood; and Steven Spielberg turned Alice Walker's novel *The Color Purple,* about a black woman overcoming adversity, into a heart-wrenching film that made a star of Whoopi Goldberg. Director Oliver Stone put forth dark views of American history in *Platoon*, about the Vietnam War, and in *JFK,* dealing with the Kennedy assassination. *Philadelphia* had versatile actor Tom Hanks as an AIDS victim fired by his law firm.

Theaters were selling about a billion tickets a year, or almost 20 million a week. To be sure, ticket sales had hovered around a billion since the mid-1960's, indicating that the percentage of American moviegoers had been declining slightly; but movies were obviously alive and well.

Part of the credit for saving the American institution of moviegoing belongs to a Kansas movie house owner named Stanley H. Durwood, King of the Multiplex, who says he hit upon the idea of

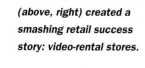

▲ *Videocassettes of movies (above, right) created a smashing retail success story: video-rental stores.*

▼ *Akosua Busia (left) and Desreta Jackson (right) joined Whoopi Goldberg in the 1985 film* The Color Purple.

putting many screens in one theater in 1963. The multiplex took time to catch on, and many fans resented the switch from grand interior spaces to postage-stamp-size viewing rooms; but customers loved having a choice of films. And when multiplexes and malls teamed up, the lure of shopping, dinner, and a movie — all a short walk from free parking — made wonderful sense to millions of Americans.

While the multiplexes attracted substantial numbers of customers, sales of videocassette recorders were going through the roof. In 1982 sales of VCR's reached about 2 million; the next year they doubled. Six years later 58 million American homes had VCR's. By 1993 movies on videocassette were generating $12 billion in annual revenue.

Instead of decimating the ranks of moviegoers, the video boom simply added a movie-watching option. Young people, the great majority of moviegoers, seemed to prefer getting out of the house and seeing a film when it opened, not months later when it showed up in the video store.

Competing for customers, theater operators kept ticket prices low. Adjusted for inflation, a ticket cost about the same in 1993 as it had 10 years earlier. Theaters increasingly looked to their concession stands for profits. "Film exhibitors are mainly in the popcorn business," said a film industry analyst. (That's not surprising when a $2.50 bucket of popcorn typically contains 20 cents' worth of corn.)

Like the little guy who ran the multiplex, Hollywood's big filmmakers also sought new ways to expand profits, and by and large the movie moguls were richly successful. In the 1990's only about 20 percent of industry revenue came from the U.S. box office. Video income accounted for a good chunk of the rest. But two other big profit areas were the foreign market and licensed spin-off products tied in to box office smashes like *Aladdin* and Steven Spielberg's *Jurassic Park*. In 1989 *Batman* grossed $250 million in its first six months, then made twice that much over the next two years from Batman toys, clothes, books, and other licensed merchandise. *Jurassic Park,* based on Michael Crichton's novel about dinosaurs on a murderous romp through a theme park, broke worldwide box office records and raised spin-off merchants' hopes for an even bigger long-term payoff than *Batman*'s.

The whole world seemed to love American films. In fact Hollywood's foreign sales were expected to account for half the industry's revenue by 1997. Unfortunately, according to Don Murray of Mediascope, a film watchdog group, "violent movies . . . sell huge overseas."

Does that mean Hollywood will be turning out even more violence and sex in the years ahead? Not necessarily. Family movies could be the wave of the future. Merchandising tie-ins work best for movies with strong kid appeal, and a study conducted by a California research firm found that PG movies were three times more likely than R movies to surpass the magic $100 million mark at the U.S. box office.

▲ **Multiplexes like this 12-screen theater in East Hartford, Connecticut, all but obliterated old movie houses.**

▲ **Steven Spielberg began his 1980's string of hits with Harrison Ford and a cobra in Raiders of the Lost Ark.**

Kevin Costner, as a U.S. Army officer, searches his soul and joins the Indians in Dances With Wolves.

After Raiders, Spielberg returned to space fantasy and again hit pay dirt with E.T., the Extra-Terrestrial in 1982.

Here Today, Gone Tomorrow

Recreational pursuits zigzagged wildly as the 20th century drew to a close. Cocooning at home was just fine for some, while others threw themselves into thin air and careened down roadless slopes.

I f I die, I die. I told everybody to bring a shovel and a mop, just in case." This intrepid soul was indulging in one of the hottest fads of the 1980's: jumping from a lofty tower with nothing below him but the cold, hard ground, his survival resting on a thick rubber cord, called a bungee, harnessed to his ankles. If all went well, he would zoom earthward at 60 miles an hour for about three seconds, come within five feet of death, and then bounce skyward as the bungee took hold. "It's an indescribable feeling," exclaimed one enthusiast. "It's great. Oh, boy!"

Risk-taking came into vogue with a vengeance in the 1980's as thrill-seekers shot through rapids on rafts, flew into the air on skateboards, and hurtled down rocky trails on mountain bikes. One writer described mountain biking as "a mode of transportation that combines the strenuousness of continuous push-ups with the comfort of falling down a flight of steps in a shopping cart." Other daredevils donned a new kind of roller skate — high-top shoes mounted on a line of rollers (better known under the brand name Rollerblades) — and whizzed along sidewalks and streets at 40 miles per hour. To give the idea a push, the Rollerblade company offered free samples to skate-rental shops along the beaches of Southern California, where the sport quickly caught on. Within three years Rollerblade sales zoomed from $3 million a year to $40 million.

In fads, as in physics, every action has a reaction: while some people were defying death for fun, others turned to gentler sports or curled up with parlor games. Trivial Pursuit hit the living rooms of America in 1982 and kept players pinned to the couch for hours with its 6,000 trivia questions. Indeed, it was one of the favorite modes of "cocooning," the trend of sitting at home and enjoying quiet evenings with family and friends. In general, folks went nutty for games. Pool halls made a comeback as an upscale yuppie pastime. Miniature golf, which had peaked and faded

A bungee jumper (top) launches himself from a hot-air balloon and plunges toward the ground; a sky diver (above) surfs on high-altitude wind currents before releasing his parachute.

Marios, Ninjas, Cabbage Patch Kids, and Barney

Through a landscape beset by hideous creatures, two diminutive fellows, called the Super Mario Brothers, made their determined way, bouncing over dangers and leaping into the imaginations of millions of kids. Created by the Nintendo video game company, the Marios, who were somewhat lacking in conventional charm, became two of the most popular fantasy characters of the 1980's. Even more colorful were four creatures out of the comic books, slick-talking, ninja-kicking, pizza-gobbling crime fighters who, having fallen into radioactive sewage, were mutated from ordinary turtles into human-size talking turtles. The Teenage Mutant Ninja Turtles were featured on television and then starred in a movie that

became a monster hit, grossing $30 million in one week. Turtle products proliferated, accessories to every waking moment in a child's day: clothes, sheets, towels, lunch boxes, toothbrushes, and, of course, toys. At the height of the foursome's popularity, a hamburger chain sold 200,000 Turtle videos each week to avid fans.

Many parents disapproved of the Turtles' violent ways and yearned for the days of the Cabbage Patch Kids, the homely "orphaned" dolls who had been all the rage only a few years before. Then came Barney — a gentle, cuddly purple dinosaur. Barney was so sweet some adults found him cloying. But preschoolers adored the dinosaur and his TV show, *Barney and*

Friends, a half hour of relentless warmth and caring. The show's homey atmosphere, psychologists assured parents, helped compensate for the shrinking extended family. Barney so changed the image of the dinosaur that some children raised on him were no doubt shocked by the portrayal of man-eating Tyrannosaurus rexes and other vicious dinosaurs in the 1993 science fiction movie *Jurassic Park*. (See p. 429.) Through the world of make-believe, children, like their parents, confronted new challenges and risks.

Among recent favorites of America's kids are a lovable, adoptable Cabbage Patch doll (above, left), Barney (above, right), and the Ninja Turtles (right). At top right, a Mario Brother gives the V sign.

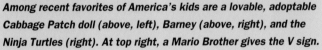

A pair of mountain bikers (left, top) tear full tilt down a slope in Valencia Hills, California. A skateboarder (left) executes a difficult "lip slide" move off the top edge of a skateboard bowl.

in the 1930's, made a reappearance. Manhattanites could putt on a course with a tropical theme: fake flamingos, imitation banana trees, and a 12-foot-tall mechanical alligator that snapped at the fluorescent golf balls aimed its way. Or they could try their skill at real-estate magnate Donald Trump's course in Central Park, which featured replicas of New York landmarks, such as the nearby Plaza Hotel, which he owned, and the Statue of Liberty.

The most popular games of the 1980's were of the electronic video variety, especially those with extraterrestrial themes, such as Asteroids and Space Invaders. "It's a drug," said one 26-year-old addict, ruefully dropping in a quarter for another round. In 1981 alone, players pumped 20 billion

quarters into video games, nearly twice the take of Hollywood films that year and double the profits from all the gambling dens in Las Vegas. An Illinois high school kid put a dent in the industry's earnings by playing for over 16½ hours on a single quarter, scoring 15,963,100 points.

Of all the oddities to capture the public's fancy, not one was odder than the Wacky WallWalker, a gummy glob that when flung onto a wall, slowly flip-flopped its way to the floor. It had all the excitement of watching plants grow; when interest waned, 75 million of them were packed into cereal boxes and the marketer reaped a fortune. He knew exactly what to do next: he cocooned with his computer and wrote *How to Create a Fad and Make a Million Dollars*.

AMERICA STIRS THE MELTING POT

Swept by the mightiest wave of immigration in nearly a century, and by a desire among various groups for greater inclusion, the nation examined some of its most basic premises.

So many undocumented aliens cross the U.S.-Mexican border by night that signs like this one have been posted warning motorists to be on the alert.

Polish citizens line up outside the American Embassy in Warsaw seeking visas permitting them to emigrate to the United States. A boat loaded with Haitian refugees founders in the Atlantic Ocean, and its occupants are rescued and detained at Guantánamo Bay, Cuba. Five children disembark from a jumbo jet in Los Angeles to rejoin parents they haven't seen for four years. A factory worker from China pays a smuggling agent, or "snakehead," $30,000 to be sneaked into the United States.

In the last decades of the 20th century, America experienced one of the heaviest surges of immigration in its history. Between 1983 and 1992, as many as 8.7 million new people came to live in the country, the highest number in any 10-year period since 1910. And this was just the official count: an estimated 5 million more arrived without legal documentation. The newcomers flooded in from Korea and Vietnam, from India and the Philippines, from Ethiopia and Iran, some fleeing poverty, others escaping political oppression or religious persecution, and all seeking a better life. Huge numbers came from the Caribbean. Some 22 percent traveled north across the border from Mexico. Immigrants who hailed from more progressive parts of the world hoped to achieve even greater prosperity for themselves and their children. By 1993 fully 20 million Americans had been born somewhere else.

Wherever the newcomers alighted, they transformed the landscape. Public schools in cities from New York to Los Angeles accommodated students from foreign lands whose native languages and dialects ranged from Tagalog (Philippines) to Lingala (Zaire), Khmer (Cambodia) to Gujarati (In-

A Japanese-American ranches cattle (left, above) in Kamuela on the big island of Hawaii. At an accredited Islamic primary school (left) in Illinois, pupils study Arabic culture along with more traditional subjects.

▶

Their faces reflecting many ethnic roots, new American citizens vow to "support and defend the Constitution" at a naturalization ceremony in the District of Columbia.

dia). Korean-owned grocery stores sprouted on street corners from Brooklyn to San Francisco. Sikhs from northern India drove taxis in Washington, D.C. Chinese of all ages did tai chi chuan exercises in public parks. Clubs opened featuring salsa and other Latino-inspired music. An Islamic mosque rose resplendent in an Ohio cornfield. At Christmas Eve Mass in Lowell, Massachusetts — a 19th-century mill town settled by successive immigrant waves from Ireland,

with people outside their own communities. For such groups, it seemed assimilation would come only gradually, if at all, through the course of generations.

In fact, a movement grew to preserve and strengthen the unique identity of ethnic groups. Under the banner of multiculturalism, revisionists criticized the traditional ideal of the melting pot — an image taken from steelmaking — and favored words such as *mosaic*, *rainbow*, and *salad* to convey the diversity of contemporary American society. They called for modifications in the teaching of American history, giving greater emphasis to the roles of blacks, Hispanics, Asians, Native Americans, and others. Their demands challenged long-standing assumptions and raised troubling questions about the equity of America's social institutions. But some observers worried that multiculturalism threatened to tear apart the very matrix of American society, *pluribus* overwhelming *unum*, as historian Arthur Schlesinger, Jr., suggested. And now and again the multicultural crusade bordered on the absurd: Stanford University students, protesting against a course in Western culture, chanted, "Hey, hey, ho, ho, Western culture's got to go!"

But for much of the world, the United States remained a dreamed-of land, where, in the words of Indian-born American novelist Bharati Mukherjee, "you can rebel against fate or political destiny." As *Time* magazine's Robert Hughes put it: "America is a construction of mind, not of race or inherited class or ancestral territory. . . . America is a collective act of the imagination whose making never ends." And, after all, few nations would expend so much energy on raucous self-examination and reassessment.

Portugal, Greece, and French-speaking Canada — "Silent Night" was regularly sung in Vietnamese.

Many of the recent arrivals, feeling the pressure to assimilate, did their best to fit in. They learned English any way they could: reading newspapers, watching soap operas, listening to their school-age children. One Russian immigrant went so far as to call random 800 numbers just for the chance to practice his language skills. For some, assimilation came through marriage. In 1993 interethnic marriages were three times as common as they had been 20 years earlier. Others clung to their heritage, speaking their native language and neglecting to learn English, and mixing little

▲ *Some Americans have looked into their heritage and adopted certain traditions of their ancestors. Here, American-born blacks dance in honor of a tribal fire god at the Oyotunji African village in the woods of South Carolina.*

Mexican-American girls at a Los Angeles elementary school celebrate Cinco de Mayo wearing authentic native dress.

CLINTON'S TEAM TAKES THE FIELD

A dark horse from Arkansas becomes the first Democratic president in 12 years, promising voters "a new season of American renewal."

Talk about long shots. Just 18 months earlier, back in mid 1991, few Americans had even heard of Bill (William J.) Clinton. Arkansas, where he served as governor, was hardly a bellwether state in national politics. But Clinton was young, smart, and full of energy and ideas. Now, at 46, after one of the most riveting campaigns in years, he was president. Only his idol, John F. Kennedy, had been elected to the White House at a younger age.

The road from Little Rock had as many dips and twists as a roller-coaster. Clinton's national debut, making the nominating speech at the Democratic convention in 1988, cost him; he droned on at such length that nearly everyone stopped listening. But he won respect as an astute strategist when, chairing the Democratic Leadership Council, he outlined a reform program designed to attract middle-class voters. No more "tax and spend," he declared: the new-style Democrats would exercise moderation in all things.

Would they get the chance? With the resounding success of the Persian Gulf War, President George Bush's popularity spurted to a high of 91 percent. No Democratic heavyweight, such as Texas Senator Lloyd Bentsen or Senator Sam Nunn of Georgia, stepped forward to challenge these odds. Clinton, with nothing to lose, did so.

First he had to earn the party nomination. But just before the New Hampshire primary, a pair of sensational

◄

President-elect Bill Clinton visits the Lincoln Memorial with Senator and Mrs. Al Gore and Hillary Rodham Clinton. Inset: Mrs. Clinton speaks on health care reform.

Maverick billionaire H. Ross Perot, having spent $60 million of his own money trying to become president, solicits phone contributions from his supporters.

UNITED WE STAND
AMERICA
P.O. BOX 6
DALLAS, TX 75221

1-800-925-4000

★ ★ ★ ★ ★ ★ ★ ★ ★

UNITED WE STAND
AMERICA, INC.

★ ★ ★ ★ ★ ★ ★ ★ ☆

Senator Al Gore, long a champion of environmental causes, speaks at the Rio de Janeiro Earth Summit in June 1992; a month later he was running for the vice presidency.

disclosures almost sent him crashing. A supermarket tabloid printed the lurid confessions of onetime torch singer Gennifer Flowers, who said she had been his mistress. Clinton denied it, then appeared with his wife, Hillary, on *60 Minutes* to express regret for causing "pain in my marriage." No sooner had he picked himself up than he blundered into a second land mine: a 23-year-old letter suggesting that years earlier, during the Vietnam War, he had cut ethical corners to avoid being drafted. Again Clinton waffled. But he managed to hang on.

A tireless campaigner, Clinton won a fistful of key primaries. Not even the admission that he had tried marijuana seemed to hurt him; after all, he said, he "didn't inhale." As he came into the Democratic Convention, the nomination was his. For his running mate he chose another moderate Southerner, Tennessee Senator Al Gore.

By this time Bush was having problems of his own. The euphoria over Desert Storm had died down, and bitterness over a persistent economic recession mounted. With unemployment at an eight-year high and thousands of middle-class Americans facing pink slips, voters blamed the incumbent. On top of that, Bush seemed unable to control his own party. Conservative columnist Pat Buchanan entered the New Hampshire primary and pulled 37 percent of the vote. And the tone of the Republican Convention, with the right wing of the party seeming to dominate, drove off many moderate Republicans and Reagan Democrats.

What many voters responded to, much to the horror of both Bush and Clinton, was the brash one-liners of H. Ross Perot. A Texas tycoon who had made billions in computer

▶

franchises, Perot joined the race as an independent candidate who promised to roll up his sleeves, "look under the hood," and solve the problems that baffled professional politicians. When critics pointed out that he had no government experience, Perot heartily agreed: "I don't have any experience in running up a $4-trillion debt."

Clinton, too, seized upon the nation's money woes. "The economy, stupid!" read a sign in the Little Rock campaign headquarters, and as a campaign issue, the economy paid off. Voters picked Clinton over Bush by 43 to 38 percent. (Perot, meanwhile, with 19 percent of the vote, made the best showing of any independent candidate since Teddy Roosevelt's Bull Moose campaign of 1912.)

Clinton's inauguration, on a sunny January 20, 1993, marked a shift in generations: he was the first president born after World War II. He came to office with an ambitious set of plans for creating jobs, reducing the deficit, rebuilding the infrastructure, revamping welfare. His top priority, a sweeping reform of the health care system, he delegated to Hillary; the First Lady would play a hands-on role in shaping policy. And though Clinton's record in foreign affairs would prove to be spotty during his first year in office, he was a quick study, not to mention lucky: the day before the inauguration, one of Bush's boldest initiatives caught on when the Israeli parliament lifted a ban on direct talks with the Palestine Liberation Organization, opening the door to a peace settlement. Eight months later the two sides signed an accord at the White House, with Clinton presiding.

With Clinton as stage manager, Israeli Prime Minister Yitzhak Rabin shakes hands with Palestinian leader Yasir Arafat. "Enough of blood and tears," Rabin declared. "Enough!"

Eyes on the Future

Univ. of North Carolina oncologist Julian Rosenman (right) is developing 3-D interactive graphics that can be used to simulate brain surgery.

A headset and instrumented gloves take a NASA researcher into the computer-generated virtual reality of other planets.

Having embarked on the Information Superhighway, we can only guess where it will eventually lead us. Futurists extol the promise of nanotechnology, robotics, and virtual reality, but will such fields improve human life or yield merely toys and time wasters?

Predicting the future has always been a risky business. Back in the 1950's science writers were excited about a car-plane. The "Aerocar" was an idea whose time had come, they felt, and a prototype was actually built. What its backers overlooked was that not many motorists really wanted to learn to be pilots, and highway driving was stressful enough without adding takeoffs and landings. A similar lack of public demand met the two-way picture phone, which has been around since the 1960's.

Today many scientists are predicting that the Information Age will reach full bloom in the 21st century and dramatically change our lives. For that to happen, they say, the digitizing of information must simply continue at its present pace. Digitizing converts things that we are capable of sensing and knowing, such as sights, sounds, and printed text, into bits of energy that can be broadcast through the air on electromagnetic frequencies or sent over communications networks of wires or cables (especially fiber-optic cables, like the one shown at the top of the next page). On the receiving end of this

Tomorrow's homes, like Xanadu (below) in Orlando, Florida, could be built by inflating huge preshaped balloons, then spraying plastic foam over them. Computers maintain Xanadu's internal comfort. MIT's insect-size GNAT robot (right) might do repairs and housework.

digitized information are devices such as TV sets, telephones, and computers — or in the not-too-distant future an all-in-one "box" combining the three, plus a fax machine, a VCR, and other gadgets. A fancy name for this electronic mishmash of communcations networks and terminals is Information Superhighway.

Another name for it is *cyberspace*, a term originated by science fiction writer William Gibson. The amount of information in cyberspace is already vast and is growing exponentially as more people and services add to it. Sometime in the 21st century, the choice of movies for the home viewer may be limited only by the number of films that have *ever* been made. Writers may forgo magazines and books and simply publish on a computer network, and artists and composers may choose between introducing their work in cyberspace or in old-fashioned galleries and concert halls.

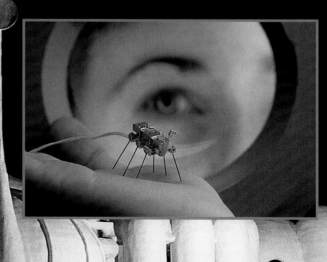

The paving stone for the Information Superhighway is cable made from optical fibers like these, which transmit light rather than electricity and can carry thousands of times more digital information than copper wire can.

Just because a high-tech service or futuristic product exists, however, is no guarantee that it will catch on in a big way. Virtual-reality games were drawing crowds in 1990's amusement arcades, but will they make the leap to favorite home entertainment in the 21st century? Magazines and catalogs with interactive video animation and sound seem to pose a threat to print-on-paper publications. But do a lot of people really want multimedia magazines and catalogs?

Interactive media — TV programs, for example, that allow you to join the cast or win (or lose) money by placing bets — are touted as the wave of the future in home viewing. But how many couch potatoes will choose to interact?

When it comes to driving, most Americans love to interact with their cars, except in stop-and-go traffic. So any "robocar" would have to offer both manual and robot driving. A prototype, designed by the Navigation Laboratory at Carnegie-Mellon University in Pittsburgh, uses a roof camera linked to an inside computer, which scans what's ahead (and behind) and issues driving instructions to the car. Not too far in the future, "robotrucks" could be making streetside garbage pickups and cleaning up toxic-waste dumps. And robocars hooked into electronic traffic movers might make grueling daily commutes, then turn over the controls to the driver in less stressful situations.

Predictions for the 21st Century

Machines no bigger than molecules will become "assemblers," putting together atom by atom everything from new drugs and foods to skyscrapers and workstations on the moon and planets, writes K. Eric Drexler in his book *Engines of Creation: The Coming Era of Nanotechnology.* (*Nano*, a prefix meaning "one billionth," connotes extraordinarily small.)

Increasingly intelligent generations of tiny robots will be produced on "robot breeding farms," according to David H. Freedman, author of *Brainmakers.*

Early in the 21st century, inputting on computers will be done with thought waves, predicts Frank Ogden in *The Last Book You'll Ever Read*, and people will create artistic masterpieces without touching canvas, clay, or any other traditional surface or medium.

Clothes will be as comfortable as "second skins" — made of fabrics that keep you warm in winter, cool in summer, and dry in the rain. As reported in the cutting-edge publication *Mondo 2000,* some designers predict 4-D holographic "cyber-suits" and self-cleaning clothes, using built-in bacteria to eat stains and sweat.

Soon after 2001, antiaging treatments may extend our life span to 100 or more vigorous years, say Marvin Cetron and Owen Davies, authors of *Crystal Globe: The Haves and Have-nots of the New World Order.*

Neurologist Richard M. Restak, M.D., author of *Receptors,* believes that knowledge of the molecular structure of brain tissue and the chemicals that affect it will enable us to have exactly the minds we want.

Cars made of ultralight materials could run on hydrogen, the ultimate clean fuel, whose combustion emits only water and small amounts of nitrogen oxides, writes Marcia D. Lowe of the Worldwatch Institute in *State of the World.*

By 2500 a trillion people could have colonized the solar system, according to Los Alamos National Laboratory physicist Eric Jones and University of Hawaii anthropologist Ben Finney.

Beyond Saturn (above, in a color-enhanced photo from Voyager I *in 1980) lie Uranus, Neptune, and Pluto, and beyond them, the vast mysteries of space. Does space have an end? Is there life out there? Will such questions be answered in the next 100 or even the next 1,000 years?*

▼ *Michael Collins, who piloted the command module for the* Apollo 11 *moon landing, argues that the next goal of the U.S. space program should be to land astronauts on Mars (below, shown at sunset in a picture from the* Viking I *probe of 1976); but probably robots, like the Russian-built experimental Mars Rover (left), will roam the Red Planet first.*

Here are dates, quotes, prices, pictures, charts, and hundreds more facts to help you relive *Our Glorious Century. The nine major sections amplify the book's chapters, and each section covers seven topics: U.S. History & Politics, Everyday Life, Arts & Letters, Entertainment & Sports, Business & Economics, Science & Medicine, and World Political Events.*

◈ Dawn of the 20th Century ◈

U.S. HISTORY & POLITICS

1900

William McKinley, 25th president, reelected with Theodore Roosevelt as vice president; their Republican ticket defeats Democrats William Jennings Bryan and Adlai E. Stevenson

Hawaii becomes U.S. territory

Hurricane devastates Galveston, Texas

U.S. establishes civil government in Puerto Rico

U.S. population is 76 million

1901

McKinley assassinated; Theodore Roosevelt becomes president

Platt Amendment makes Cuba U.S. protectorate

1902

Census Bureau established

Spooner Act authorizes building of Panama Canal

Maryland passes first state workmen's compensation law

Reclamation Act empowers U.S. government to fund irrigation, set aside park land

1903

Panama Canal Treaty signed; U.S. recognizes Panama's

African-American Matthew A. Henson reached the North Pole with Robert E. Peary in 1909.

independence

Muckraking journalists Lincoln Steffens, Ida Tarbell, and others gain national attention as they assail big business and political bosses

U.S. Department of Commerce and Labor established, with George Cortelyou as its first secretary

1904

Theodore Roosevelt, 26th president, wins reelection with Charles W. Fairbanks as vice president; they defeat Democrats Alton B. Parker and Henry G. Davis

Roosevelt Corollary to the Monroe Doctrine declares right of U.S. to intervene in the affairs of Western Hemisphere nations

1905

Roosevelt organizes conference to end Russo-Japanese War

Industrial Workers of the World (IWW or "Wobblies") founded in Chicago as an alternative to the more conservative American Federation of Labor

1906

Earthquake and fire devastate San Francisco

Roosevelt, on first trip outside U.S. by a president in office, visits Canal Zone

U.S. troops occupy Cuba

First national monument, Devil's Tower in Wyoming, dedicated by Roosevelt

1907

U.S. marines land in Honduras to protect U.S. lives and property

Great White Fleet sails around the world

One million immigrants pass through Ellis Island

Oklahoma becomes 46th state

Roosevelt issues executive order prohibiting immigration by unskilled Japanese labor

"The century upon which we have just entered must inevitably be one of tremendous triumph or tremendous failure for the whole human race."

— Vice President Theodore Roosevelt at the 1901 Pan American Exposition

1908

William Howard Taft elected 27th president with James S. Sherman as vice president; they defeat Democrats William Jennings Bryan and John W. Kern

Supreme Court rules industry-wide boycott by labor

constitutes restraint of trade under Sherman Antitrust Act

1909

Civil war in Honduras; U.S. sends troops

U.S. Adm. Robert E. Peary reaches North Pole with Matthew Henson and four Eskimos

Geronimo, Apache Indian chief, dies

National Association for the Advancement of Colored People (NAACP) founded

President Taft sets aside 3 million acres of public land for conservation

1910

U.S. passes Mann Act, prohibiting transportation of women across state lines for immoral purposes

First Socialist elected to Congress

U.S. population is 92 million; 8.7 million immigrants admitted since 1900

1911

Triangle Shirtwaist Co. factory fire in New York City kills 146 workers, brings about reforms in working conditions

Senator Robert M. La Follette of Wisconsin founds National Progressive Republican League

U.S., Japan, Russia, and Britain sign treaty outlawing seal hunting

1912

Woodrow Wilson elected 28th president with Thomas R. Marshall as vice president; they defeat the Progressive ("Bull Moose") ticket of Theodore Roosevelt and Hiram Johnson and the Republican ticket, led by William Howard Taft

New Mexico and Arizona become 47th and 48th states

American statesman Elihu Root wins Nobel Peace Prize

IWW, or "Wobblies," organize strike of 10,000 textile workers in Massachusetts

Titanic hits iceberg and sinks on maiden voyage; more than 1,500 lives lost

U.S. marines sent to Nicaragua

1913

Federal income tax authorized by 16th Amendment

Direct election of U.S. senators decreed by 17th Amendment

EVERYDAY LIFE

1900

Work begins on rapid transit ("subway") system in New York City

First wall-mounted telephone with separate earpiece and mouthpiece

Photostatic copying machine invented

Kodak introduces the Brownie camera

Dance craze: the cakewalk

Connecticut restaurant serves first hamburgers; vendor sells first hot dogs

Paper clip patented

Architect Frank Lloyd Wright gains attention for his prairie-style design of homes

1901

Philadelphia department store installs first escalator

Ragtime becomes popular

Faddists take up Ping-Pong

1902

Spark plug invented

First electrical hearing aid

First animal crackers sold in U.S.

First teddy bear, named for Teddy Roosevelt

Disc brakes fitted to automobiles

First motor scooter

1903

First coast-to-coast crossing by auto, San Francisco to New York

Bottlemaking machine invented

Sanka introduced

1904

Tea bags go on sale

"Typhoid Mary," carrier of disease, identified

Tire chains give traction on icy roads

1905

First neon signs

First Rotary Club founded, in Chicago

Twentieth Century Limited makes express train trip from New York to Chicago in 18 hours

Cullinan diamond found; weighs 3,000 carats

Vick's VapoRub introduced

Autos get bumpers

1906

Light bulbs use tungsten filaments

Alice Roosevelt, the president's daughter, marries Nicholas Longworth in the White House

Stanley Steamer does more than 127 m.p.h.

Jukeboxes

Public relations becomes an occupation

First permanent waves given by London hairdressers

The thermos invented

"Women are growing honester, braver, stronger, more healthful and skillful and able and free, more human in all ways."

— *Charlotte Perkins Gilman,* in Women and Economics, *1898*

1907

Mother's Day proclaimed

First day-care center opens in Rome, directed by physician and educator Maria Montessori

First electric clothes washer

Color photography pioneered

Head of U.S. Forest Service, Gifford Pinchot, begins to use the term *conservation*

Electric vacuum cleaner

Household detergents go on sale

First seaplane

1908

Gyroscopic compass

Silencer for guns invented

Women are wearing narrow sheath skirts and huge Merry Widow hats with dotted veils

First paper cups

Cellophane

Coffee filters

1909

Halley's Comet observed

Lincoln penny replaces Indian-head penny

First hydrofoil

Jigsaw puzzles become popular

First electric toaster

Christmas blizzard (December 25–26) in eastern U.S.; 28 die, $20-million damage

1910

Weekends become a way of life in the U.S.

Electric cooking ranges

The tango sweeps the U.S.

Boy Scouts of America founded

Pajamas replace nightshirts in popularity

V-neck called unhealthy and immoral

First automatic transmissions in automobiles

Bathroom scales

First Father's Day celebration

1911

First transcontinental airplane flight, New York to Pasadena, California

Lincoln Memorial designed

Term *vitamin* coined

Electric self-starters for autos begin to replace cranks

Prototype air conditioners

First rotary eggbeater

Cold cream marketed

Electric frying pans

1912

Girl Guiding in the United States established; becomes Girl Scouts of America

First driver jailed for speeding

SOS in Morse code adopted as international distress signal

1913

Sixty-story Woolworth Building, world's tallest to date, goes up in New York City

Brillo pads become available commercially

First home refrigerator

First modern bra, designed of handkerchiefs, ribbon, and cord

Kewpie dolls sell in the millions

First modern newspaper crossword puzzle

Zippers come into wide use

Couples dance the fox-trot

U.S. Immigrants, by Continent: 1901–90 (in thousands)

Legend:
- Europe
- Canada, Caribbean, & Latin America
- Asia
- Africa

Y-axis: 0, 1000, 2000, 3000, 4000, 5000, 6000, 7000, 8000

X-axis: 1901–1910, 1911–1920, 1921–1930, 1931–1940, 1941–1950, 1951–1960, 1961–1970, 1971–1980, 1981–1990

ARTS & LETTERS

1900

The Wonderful Wizard of Oz, by American author L. Frank Baum

French writer Colette publishes first of her Claudine novels

Red-mopped, button-eyed rag doll Ann became the heroine of the book Raggedy Ann Stories.

British writer and illustrator Beatrix Potter's *The Tale of Peter Rabbit*

American novelist Theodore Dreiser's *Sister Carrie*

Italian composer Giacomo Puccini's opera *Tosca* premieres in Rome

Irish writer and wit Oscar Wilde dies

1901

Up From Slavery, autobiography of American black educator Booker T. Washington, becomes a bestseller

English author Rudyard Kipling's *Kim*

German author Thomas Mann's first novel, *Buddenbrooks*

Spanish-born artist Pablo Picasso begins painting in the style of his Blue Period (1901–04)

Henri Toulouse-Lautrec, French painter of the Paris

cabaret scene, dies

Russian composer and pianist Sergei Rachmaninoff's *Second Piano Concerto*

Russian writer Anton Chekhov's drama *The Three Sisters*

1902

Arthur Conan Doyle's *The Hound of the Baskervilles*

Joseph Conrad's *Heart of Darkness*

French composer Claude Debussy's only complete opera, *Pelléas et Mélisande*

Enrico Caruso makes first gramophone recording

American novelist Owen Wister's *The Virginian*

1903

The Call of the Wild by American writer Jack London

Irish dramatist George Bernard Shaw's *Man and Superman*

Russian Wassily Kandinsky, considered by many the first abstract painter, shows the "Blue Rider"

Irish-born American composer and conductor Victor Herbert's operetta *Babes in Toyland*

First recording of an opera: Italian composer Giuseppe Verdi's *Ernani*

Three famous painters die: American James Whistler and Frenchmen Paul Gauguin and Camille Pissarro

1904

American expatriate Henry James, living in England, publishes *The Golden Bowl*

Controversial American dancer Isadora Duncan, a pioneer of modern dance, visits Russia, wows art critic and ballet producer Sergei Diaghilev

Italian composer Giacomo Puccini's opera *Madame Butterfly*

Irish poet and dramatist J. M. Synge's tragedy *Riders to the Sea*

Russian dramatist Anton Chekhov's *The Cherry Orchard*

1905

Les Fauves artists exhibit at

Salon d'Automne in Paris; first major art movement of the 20th century

Pablo Picasso's Rose Period begins (to about 1906)

Hungarian composer Franz Lehar's operetta *The Merry Widow*

Russian-American Michel Fokine choreographs 3-minute crowd-pleasing solo "The Dying Swan" for legendary ballerina Anna Pavlova

German composer Richard Strauss's opera *Salome*

American photographer Alfred Stieglitz's 291 gallery begins to establish photography as an art form

1906

Albert Schweitzer's *The Quest of the Historical Jesus*

English novelist John

Galsworthy publishes first book in his multivolume *The Forsyte Saga*

American author Upton Sinclair's *The Jungle*

O. Henry (William Sydney Porter) publishes his famous short story "The Gift of the Magi"

French painter Paul Cézanne dies

Children's book series — Bobbsey Twins, Hardy Boys — are launched

1907

Russian dancer Vaslav Nijinsky, still in his teens, makes debut at Maryinski Theatre in St. Petersburg

Irish dramatist J. M. Synge's *The Playboy of the Western World*

Cubism begins in France,

marked by Pablo Picasso's "Demoiselles d'Avignon"

Russian author Maxim Gorki's *The Mother* supports revolutionary spirit

Austrian composer Gustav Mahler's *Symphony No. 8*

American philosopher William James's *Pragmatism*

1908

Ashcan School, mostly realistic painters of city scenes, exhibit in New York City

Austrian-American composer Arnold Schoenberg vexes critics with his atonal *Second String Quartet*

Georges Braque, cofounder with Picasso of cubism, paints "Houses at l'Estaque" in France

French (Romanian-born) Constantin Brancusi, pioneer abstract sculptor, completes "The Kiss"

English novelist E. M. Forster's *A Room With a View*

French painter Maurice Utrillo's White Period (1908–14) explores use of many shades of white in Paris street scenes

English composer Sir Edward Elgar's *Symphony No. 1*

Hungarian composer Béla Bartók's *First String Quartet*

1909

American poet Ezra Pound publishes two collections of poetry, *Personae* and *Exultations*

French painter Henri Matisse's "The Dance"

Russian Sergei Diaghilev's ballet company, Les Ballets Russes, perhaps the best ever assembled, debuts in Paris

Richard Strauss's *Elektra,* with libretto by Austrian poet Hugo von Hofmannsthal, gets mixed reviews because of its dissonant sections

1910

Irish-born American composer Victor Herbert's operetta *Naughty Marietta*

Giacomo Puccini's *La Fanciulla del West (The Girl of the Golden West)* premieres at

Milestones in Radio Technology

1900 R. A. Fessenden sends sound over electro-magnetic waves

1901 Guglielmo Marconi transmits first signal across the Atlantic

1904 John Fleming develops vacuum tube, allowing transmission of speech and music

1906 Lee De Forest invents 3-element vacuum tube, which permits greater amplification of signals; Fessenden pioneers AM radio

1916 David Sarnoff lays groundwork for U.S. broadcasting industry; envisions hundreds of radio stations, millions of radio receivers.

1919 Shortwave transmission

1929 FM radio

1952 Transistor-powered miniature radio sets

the Metropolitan Opera House in New York City, with Arturo Toscanini conducting

Antonio Gaudí, Spanish architect much admired by the surrealists and abstract expressionists, designs one of his last major works, Casa Milá, in Barcelona

Igor Stravinsky writes the music for Sergei Diaghilev's Ballets Russes production of *The Firebird*

First Postimpressionist exhibit opens in London: Paul Cézanne, Vincent van Gogh, Henri Matisse, many others

Three noted Americans die: writer Samuel Clemens (Mark Twain), painter Winslow Homer, philosopher William James

1911

Petrouchka, produced in Paris by Diaghilev's Ballets Russes with music by Igor Stravinsky

Henri Matisse's "The Red Studio"

Richard Strauss's *Der Rosenkavalier,* his most popular opera

Leonardo da Vinci's "Mona Lisa" stolen from the Louvre in Paris; recovered in 1913

English author G. K. Chesterton's first book in a popular series about a mystery-solving priest: *The Innocence of Father Brown*

Georges Braque's "Man With a Guitar," one of the best-known cubist paintings

American novelist Edith Wharton's *Ethan Frome*

1912

American writer Zane Grey's Western novel *Riders of the Purple Sage*

German author Thomas Mann's short novel *Death in Venice*

Italian painter Amedeo Modigliani's "Stone Head"

French composer Maurice Ravel's *Daphnis et Chloë*

1913

O Pioneers! by American writer Willa Cather

American poet Robert Frost's first collection, *A Boy's Will*

First part of French author Marcel Proust's multivolume novel *A la Recherche du Temps Perdu (Remembrance of Things Past)* published

Irish-born British dramatist George Bernard Shaw's *Pygmalion*

English novelist D. H. Lawrence's first major work, *Sons and Lovers*

The Rite of Spring, a Diaghilev ballet with Igor Stravinsky's music, causes first-night audience to riot in Paris

> *"A man who has a million dollars is as well off as if he were rich."*
>
> — *Multimillionaire*
> *John Jacob Astor (1864–1912)*

New York Armory Show in Manhattan gives many Americans their first exposure to modern art; French maverick Marcel Duchamp's "Nude Descending a Staircase" is widely ridiculed; he introduces first mobile

ENTERTAINMENT & SPORTS

1900

Louis Armstrong born in New Orleans

First Davis Cup, international tennis tournament; U.S. beats Britain 3–0

Professional baseball's American League founded

Baseball cards, given away with cigarette packs, introduced

Baseball gets five-sided home plate

Ice hockey games now officially begin with a face-off

Dribbling introduced to basketball

1901

Walt Disney born

Baseball's National League now considers a foul ball a strike (except a foul ball after two strikes); American League adopts same rule in 1903

Boxing becomes legal in England

First American bowling tournament, in Chicago

1903

Thomas A. Edison produces the first western, *The Great Train Robbery,* filmed by E. S. Porter

First World Series between American and National leagues; Boston Red Sox defeat Pittsburgh Pirates 5 games to 3

1904

First Vanderbilt Cup auto race

Ice hockey teams now have six players

Federation of International Football founded; establishes uniform rules for soccer

American Walter Travis captures British amateur golf title

World Series not played, by decision of New York Giants manager, John McGraw, and owner, John Brush, in midseason; Giants win National League pennant, Boston Red Sox are American League champs

1905

Dimple-faced golf ball patented

First nickelodeons open; admission, 5 cents

Public outcry over fatalities in college football will bring about stringent rule changes

Second World Series: New York Giants defeat Philadelphia Athletics 4 games to 1

1906

First French Grand Prix auto race

Thomas Edison's camera-phone synchronizes movie projector and phonograph

Forward pass introduced to football

First film cartoon

Off the shoulder and décolleté, this gown may have turned turn-of-the-century American heads.

Chicago White Sox defeat Chicago Cubs in World Series 4 games to 2

1907

First *Ziegfeld Follies*

First daily comic strip, H. C. (Bud) Fisher's *A. Mutt,* runs in *San Francisco Chronicle;* later becomes *Mutt and Jeff*

American actress Florence Lawrence is first movie celebrity, the Biograph Girl

Film titles replace commentators' running explanations

Cooperstown, New York, hailed as baseball's birthplace

Chicago Cubs defeat Detroit Tigers in World Series 4 games to 0

1908

Baseball outlaws spitball

Jack Johnson first black heavyweight boxing champion

Limit of five personal fouls introduced in basketball to prevent rough play

U.S. wins 15 out of 28 track-and-field gold medals at London Olympic Games

Chicago Cubs defeat Detroit Tigers in World Series 4 games to 1

1909

Mary Pickford featured in *The Gibson Goddess* and other Biograph films

First newsreels

Clay tennis courts make their debut; most games still played on grass

Pittsburgh Pirates defeat Detroit Tigers in World Series 4 games to 3

1910

American driver Barney Oldfield breaks automobile speed record; drives a Benz 133 m.p.h. at Daytona, Florida

William Howard Taft, on baseball's opening day, becomes first president to throw out the first ball

Enrico Caruso sings on an experimental radio broadcast from the Metropolitan Opera in New York City

Philadelphia Athletics defeat the Chicago Cubs in World Series 4 games to 1

1911

Irving Berlin's hit song "Alexander's Ragtime Band"

American composer W. C. Handy's "Memphis Blues"

Treemonisha, a folk opera, completed by black American ragtime composer Scott Joplin

Pitching legend Cy Young retires

WHAT IT COST

Prices: 1900

Daily, Sunday newspapers, 1¢, 3¢

Tailor-made woman's skirt, $4.98

Sheets, pillowcases, 66¢, 14¢

Blankets, $3.75 a pair

Writing paper, 10¢ a lb.

125-piece Limoges dinner set, $30

Men's suits, overcoats, $16, $18

Camera, $1.95

Sheet music, 15¢

Corset, $1.25

European tours, 1 to 4 mos., $145 to $1,100

Women's shoes, $1.50; men's, $2.50

Men's pajamas, $1.45; nightshirt, 48¢

Ladies' suits, $8.75

Dickens's works, 15 vols., $3.75; Thackeray's, 10 vols., $2.35; Macaulay's *England,* 5 vols., 65¢

Rolltop desks, $14 to $150; revolving office chairs, $5.25 to $60

Muffin pan, 20¢; 1-qt. coffee pot, 21¢

Carnegie Hall tickets, 74¢ to $2; B'way theater ticket, $1.50

Gin, 75¢ per bottle; Scotch, 87¢; California red wine, $2.40 per case; French red wine, $5.50 per case

Tea, 75¢ a lb.; strawberry jam, 15¢ a jar; 10 lbs. mackerel, $2.05; can of asparagus, 35¢; can corn, 9¢; can tomatoes, 12¢

Cigar, 5¢

Upright piano, $150; baby grand, $250

3-story Brooklyn brownstones, $9,000; 5-story Riverside Drive (furnished) brownstone, $75,000; 3-story Manhattan brownstone, $18,000

Telephone service, $5 a mo.

Toothbrush, 15¢; man's watch, $2.95; cereal, 8¢ a lb.; soap, 5¢ for 100 cakes; umbrella, $1.49; opera glasses, 98¢

12-gauge shotgun (used), $100

Golfing legend-to-be Bobby Jones wins first title at age 9

Baseball adopts cork-center ball

Jim Thorpe leads Carlisle Indian School football team to victory over Harvard

Philadelphia Athletics defeat New York Giants in World Series 4 games to 2

1912

Hollywood producer-director Mack Sennett's slapstick Keystone Kops

International Lawn Tennis Association founded

Open net introduced in basketball; play no longer stopped to retrieve the ball

Jim Thorpe, outstanding athlete at Stockholm Olympics, is stripped of his medals for playing semipro baseball

Boston Red Sox defeat New York Giants in World Series 4 games to 3

1913

Husband-and-wife team Vernon and Irene Castle get America dancing their castle walk, fox-trot, and other steps

Hollywood becomes center of movie industry

College football players start to wear identifying numbers

Cecil B. DeMille's western *The Squaw Man,* one of first full-length films produced in Hollywood

Underdog Notre Dame football team, using the forward pass, beats Army

Philadelphia Athletics defeat New York Giants in World Series 4 games to 3

BUSINESS & ECONOMICS

1900

U.S. passes Gold Standard Act

Per-capita U.S. annual income: $1,164

International Ladies' Garment Workers' Union founded

High-speed steelmaking invented

Electric ignitions for internal-combustion engines

German aviation pioneer Count Ferdinand von Zeppelin tests his passenger dirigible

1901

Mercury-vapor arc lamp invented

Oil discovered at Spindletop, Texas

U.S. Steel Corporation, first billion-dollar company, organized

1902

First federal action to settle labor dispute

Northern Securities, a railroad monopoly formed the previous year, found in violation of Sherman Antitrust Act

1903

Ford Motor Co. founded

First cable under Pacific Ocean completed; President Roosevelt sends message around world on it

1904

Offset printing

1905

Caterpillar tractors developed

Compressed air used to excavate underwater rail tunnels

Supreme Court rules states may not set maximum working hours

1906

American inventor Lee De Forest, "father of the radio," produces the triode: three-element vacuum tube

Standard Oil of California incorporated

Haloid Co. founded; later becomes Xerox Corp.

Nitrogenous fertilizers increase crop yields

1908

Ford designs first Model T, priced at $850; 15 million will be sold over the next 20 years

General Motors founded

Supreme Court modifies 1905 ruling, now says states may set maximum working hours for women

1909

Bakelite, first plastic, invented

1910

F.W. Woolworth Co. has in excess of 200 stores nationwide

1911

Supreme Court orders dissolution of Standard Oil and American Tobacco companies

Frederick Taylor, efficiency expert, publishes *The Principles of Scientific Management*

1913

Federal Reserve System authorized

SCIENCE & MEDICINE

1900

Palace of Knossos, center of Minoan civilization, discovered by English archeologist Arthur Evans

Radon, a gaseous radioactive element formed when radium decays, discovered by German chemist F. G. Dorn

Quantum theory, dealing with energy transactions at the atomic and molecular level, formulated

First gamma rays observed

Austrian botanist Gregor Mendel's 19th-century work on genetics rediscovered

Austrian psychologist Sigmund Freud publishes *The Interpretation of Dreams*

Third law of thermodynamics postulated: heat flow from a higher to a lower temperature in solids stops at a temperature of absolute zero

William Frederick Cody, or Buffalo Bill, launched his Wild West Show in 1883. It was a hit in both America and Europe until Cody died in 1917.

Ford sets up first moving assembly line, produces 1,000 Model T's daily

John D. Rockefeller starts Rockefeller Foundation with $100-million endowment

R. J. Reynolds pioneers the "American cigarette," a blend of mostly domestic tobaccos

1901

Code of Hammurabi, 18th-century B.C. Babylonian laws, found on tablets

U.S. army surgeon Walter Reed finds yellow fever virus is spread by mosquitoes

A, B, and O blood groups found to exist

Adrenaline isolated

Guglielmo Marconi sends first transatlantic wireless message

White blood cells shown to fight disease

1902

AB blood group discovered

French husband-and-wife chemists Pierre and Marie Curie determine radium's properties

Ivan Pavlov, Russian physiologist, begins study of conditioned reflexes

Chromosomes seen to carry units of heredity

Layered structure of atmosphere observed

1903

The Curies share Nobel Prize in physics

Orville and Wilbur Wright make first flights at Kitty Hawk, North Carolina

Electrocardiograph invented

1904

General theory of radioactivity

Silicones, later widely used in lubricants and other commercial applications, discovered

First working photoelectric cell

1905

Albert Einstein formulates theory of relativity

First successful direct blood transfusion

First artificial joint restores hip movement

Sigmund Freud publishes *Three Essays on the Theory of Sexuality*

French psychologist Alfred Binet devises first intelligence tests

Female XX and male XY chromosomes identified

1906

German bacteriologist August von Wassermann develops syphilis test

Whooping cough bacterium isolated

Earth's interior determined to have a distinct core

Years of Bulls and Bears

Dow Jones Industrial Average — Selected Years 1900–91

High
Low

3000
2400
1800
1200
600
0

1900 1921 1929 1930 1932 1935 1940 1950 1961 1972 1982 1987 1991

1907

Existence of black holes in space postulated

Protozoans implicated in sleeping sickness and malaria

Radioactive decay of uranium used to find geologic age

Cell culture outside the body introduced

1908

Ammonia synthesized

Barium meal technique indicates ulcers on X-rays

Sunspots shown to be magnetic phenomenon

Helium liquefied

1909

Body louse found to transmit typhus

Word *gene* used to describe a factor of heredity

Sigmund Freud lectures in U.S.

1910

Lung disease diagnosed with X-rays

1911

Norwegian polar explorer Roald Amundsen reaches South Pole

Atomic nucleus discovered

Superconductivity discovered

1912

First decompression chamber for underwater divers

Swiss psychologist Carl G. Jung's *The Theory of Psychoanalysis*

Gestalt psychology

Theory of continental drift

U.S. Public Health Service founded

Cosmic radiation discovered

Nuclear transmutation, the conversion of one element into another, demonstrated

"A European war can only end in the ruin of the vanquished and the scarcely less fatal commercial dislocation and exhaustion of the conquerors."

— *Winston Churchill, 1901*

Protons and electrons detected within the atom

1913

Danish scientist Niels Bohr's theory of atomic structure

Diphtheria immunity test

Chlorophyll's composition discovered

Vitamins A and B isolated

Mammographs

Sigmund Freud publishes *Totem and Taboo*

WORLD POLITICAL EVENTS

1900

Boxer Rebellion begins in China

Umberto I of Italy assassinated; Victor Emmanuel III crowned

Boer War: British annex Orange Free State and Transvaal

1901

Queen Victoria dies; Edward VII crowned king of England

Commonwealth of Australia proclaimed

1902

Boer War ends

Aswan Dam on the Nile

1903

Anti-Jewish pogroms in Russia

1904

Russo-Japanese War begins

1905

"Bloody Sunday": Russian troops fire on workers in St. Petersburg; mutiny on battleship *Potemkin*

Sinn Fein, a nationalist political party, organized in Ireland

Sun Yat-sen, Chinese reformer,

founds movement to overthrow Manchu dynasty

1906

French Army officer Alfred Dreyfus, a Jew, exonerated of cowardice in a case involving cover-up and bigotry

Zuider Zee drainage reclaims Netherlands land from the sea

1907

Triple Entente of Britain, France, and Russia formed to counter Triple Alliance of Germany, Italy, and Austria-Hungary

1908

Austria-Hungary annexes Bosnia and Herzegovina

"Young Turks" oust ruling sultan, but lose their dream of a resurgent Ottoman Empire

1910

Edward VII dies; George V crowned king of England

Portugal deposes King Manuel II, proclaims itself a republic

Union of South Africa proclaimed

Japan annexes Korea

Slavery abolished in China

1911

Airplanes deployed offensively in Turkish-Italian conflict

Francisco Madero becomes president of Mexico; executed by rebels two years later

1912

British coal miners, dockworkers, and transport workers go on general strike

Sun Yat-sen and Chiang Kai-shek establish republic in China; emperor abdicates

First Balkan War begins as Montenegro opens hostilities against Ottoman Empire

1913

King George I of Greece assassinated; Constantine I succeeds him

Suffragette Emmeline Pankhurst jailed in London and starts hunger strikes

Second Balkan War begins as Bulgaria attacks Greeks and Serbs

U.S. HISTORY & POLITICS

1914

President Woodrow Wilson declares America's neutrality

Panama Canal opens; civil government established in Canal Zone

Mexican crisis: U.S. marines occupy Veracruz

✠

"A war to end all wars."

— English author H. G. Wells, 1914; phrase quoted by President Woodrow Wilson referring to World War I

✠

Some 10.5 million immigrants from southern and eastern Europe have entered U.S. since 1905

1915

President Wilson addresses Congress, stresses need for military preparedness

Henry Ford charters "peace ship," sails to Norway in attempt to negotiate end to the fighting in Europe

German sympathizer detonates bomb in U.S. Senate building, wounds American financier J. Pierpont Morgan, Jr.

U.S. Coast Guard established

U.S. marines sent to Haiti to protect American lives and property

Supreme Court rules employers may not deny employment on grounds of union membership

Rocky Mountain National Park created

Ku Klux Klan revived in Georgia

1916

Democrats Woodrow Wilson, 28th president, and Thomas R. Marshall, vice president, narrowly reelected over Republican challengers, Charles Evans Hughes and Charles W. Fairbanks; Hughes goes to bed on election night thinking he has won

National Defense Act reorganizes armed forces

Denmark sells U.S. the Virgin Islands for $25 million

Mexican revolutionary Pancho Villa raids Columbus, New Mexico, then returns to Mexico; Gen. John J. Pershing pursues him across border

U.S. troops occupy the Dominican Republic to quell unrest caused by rival factions

Jeannette Rankin, a Montana Republican, elected first U.S. congresswoman

Louis D. Brandeis becomes first Jewish-American named to the Supreme Court

1917

U.S.S. *Housatonic* sunk; Wilson severs diplomatic relations with Germany

U.S. declares war on Germany; General Pershing commands American Expeditionary Forces; U.S. troops in France

Congress passes Selective Service, War Revenue, Espionage, and Trading With the Enemy acts

Congress adopts 14th Amendment (due process)

Puerto Rico becomes U.S. territory

1918

U.S. troops fight at Belleau Wood, St.-Mihiel, Château-Thierry, Aisne-Marne, Meuse-Argonne

Sgt. Alvin York single-handedly captures 132 German soldiers

War ends with signing of armistice on Nov. 11

More than 4 million U.S. troops served in the war; some 350,000 U.S. casualties

Total Allied casualties: about 34 million

President Wilson outlines 14 Points for world peace

In congressional elections Democrats lose control of House and Senate

Socialist Eugene Debs sentenced to 10 years in prison for sedition

U.S. population: 103.5 million

1919

Versailles peace treaty signed

League of Nations founded; Woodrow Wilson presides over first meeting

Isolationists in U.S. Senate balk at ratifying Treaty of Versailles, negotiated by Wilson

Supreme Court upholds 1917 Espionage Act; allows restriction on free speech in wartime

18th Amendment (Prohibition) ratified; Volstead Act passed

American Communist Party formed

✠

"It is a fearful thing to lead this great, peaceful people into war, into the most terrible and disastrous of all wars, civilization itself seeming to be in the balance. But the right is more precious than peace."

— President Woodrow Wilson, April 2, 1917, asking Congress to declare war

✠

President Wilson receives Nobel Peace Prize for advocating a just settlement of World War I and the creation of the League of Nations

---

WHAT IT COST

Prices: 1910

Steinway, $550

Safe deposit box, $5

Buick touring car, $1,400; 30-hp touring car, $2,000; Brush runabout, $485; Ford coupe, $1,050

Campbell's soup, 10¢ a can

Women's nightgowns, 98¢; women's suits, $15 to $25; women's coats, $15 to $20; evening gowns, $37.50

Mink coats, $1,000; Hudson seal coats, $150

Man's shirt, 89¢; celluloid collars, 2 for $25

Men's suits and overcoats, $16 to $32

Can of tomatoes, 6¢;

spinach, 11¢; corn, 9¢; peaches, 16¢; asparagus, 23¢

Bottle of gin, 65¢; bourbon, 68¢;

California red wine, $3.90 a case; French red, $5.75 a case

9-room apartment in New York City, $2,700 per year to rent, $25,000 to buy

7-room Park Avenue apartment, $1,300 per year

7-room Manhattan apartment, $600 per year

9-room Manhattan apartment, $2,400; 7-room on Central Park West, $720

U.S. Unemployment Rate: 1900–90

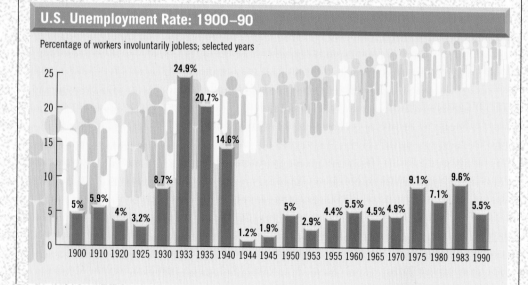

Percentage of workers involuntarily jobless; selected years

Year	Rate
1900	5%
1910	5.9%
1920	4%
1925	3.2%
1930	8.7%
1933	24.9%
1935	20.7%
1940	14.6%
1944	1.2%
1945	1.9%
1950	5%
1953	2.9%
1955	4.4%
1960	5.5%
1965	4.5%
1970	4.9%
1975	9.1%
1980	7.1%
1983	9.6%
1990	5.5%

Massachusetts governor Calvin Coolidge uses National Guard to break Boston police strike

Workers at U.S. Steel strike, demanding union recognition

✠

"England, that nation of shopkeepers, cannot produce soldiers to equal ours."

— *Spokesman for Kaiser Wilhelm*

✠

U.S. Attorney General A. Mitchell Palmer commences Red Scare arrests; seeks to control bombings and other violence

EVERYDAY LIFE

1914

First red and green traffic lights — in Cleveland

Self-service shopping introduced in California; items are arranged alphabetically

First major sewage system using bacteria to decompose waste opens in Manchester, England

Last passenger pigeon dies at Cincinnati Zoo

First live models in U.S. fashion shows

First successful heart surgery — on a dog

Pyrex glassware comes to market

Two-step becomes a popular ballroom dance

1915

Taxicabs in major cities; fare is 5 cents

Lipstick marketed

Nevada establishes quickie-divorce law

1916

First public birth-control clinic opened, by Margaret Sanger

---

in Brooklyn, New York; she is jailed 30 days for creating a public nuisance

Jazz craze spreads

Electric clocks

First supermarket, with self-service and checkout, in Tennessee

U.S. and Canada act to protect migratory birds

Liquid nail polish

Automobile windshield wipers

More states become "dry": Michigan, Montana, Nebraska, South Dakota; number now totals 24

First women's Red Cross uniform

Prototype of agitator washing machines

British "summer time," with clocks pushed an hour ahead, mandated to save energy

French dress designer Coco Chanel makes jersey, a knit

Mid-calf-length skirts with a fur stole and shapeless coat made a fashion statement in 1918.

---

fabric hitherto used in underwear, chic for outerwear

Hetty Green — America's richest woman, worth $100 million — dies

1917

Food freezing introduced commercially

New York State amends its constitution to allow women the vote; women suffragists picketing the White House get jail sentences

Financier Diamond Jim Brady dies

1918

Influenza epidemic will kill more than 25 million worldwide before it runs its course; about 500,000 die in U.S.

Regular airmail service established, New York City to Washington and New York City to Chicago

Ouija boards go on sale

U.S. divided into four time zones; daylight saving time introduced

Stars and Stripes, official armed forces newspaper, starts up

First pop-up toaster patented; not marketed until 1930

Raggedy Ann Stories, popularizing the doll, published by cartoonist Johnny Gruelle

Save-the-Redwoods League organized

The New York Times begins home delivery

Missouri is last state to ratify a compulsory-school-attendance law

1919

U.S. railroad lines total 265,000 miles of track

American Legion organized

First municipal airport — Tucson, Arizona

ARTS & LETTERS

1914

Booth Tarkington, American novelist, publishes *Penrod*

American poet Joyce Kilmer's *Trees and Other Poems;* he is

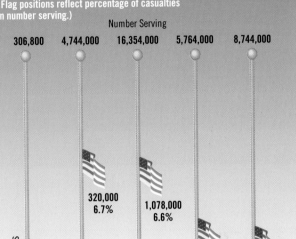

The Human Cost of War

U.S. War Casualties, Killed and Wounded
(Flag positions reflect percentage of casualties in number serving.)

Number Serving

	Spanish-American	World War I	World War II	Korea	Vietnam
Number Serving	306,800	4,744,000	16,354,000	5,764,000	8,744,000
Casualties	4,100 / 1.3%	320,000 / 6.7%	1,078,000 / 6.6%	157,000 / 2.7%	211,300 / 2.4%

---

killed in action in France, 1918

Irish writer James Joyce's *Dubliners* stories and parts of *A Portrait of the Artist as a Young Man* published in the English literary magazine *The Egoist*

✠

"Come on, you S.O.B.'s! Do you want to live forever?"

— *A U.S. marine at the Battle of Belleau Wood*

✠

French painter Georges Braque's "Music"

English composer Ralph Vaughan Williams's *A London Symphony*

American writer Edgar Rice Burroughs's *Tarzan of the Apes*

1915

English novelist Somerset Maugham's *Of Human Bondage*

Dadaist group forms in Zurich, Switzerland, led by, among others, French artist Jean Arp, German poet Hugo Ball, and French poet Tristan Tzara

Ezra Pound begins "The Cantos"

Czech-born Austrian writer Franz Kafka publishes his long story "The Metamorphosis"

English novelist D. H. Lawrence's *The Rainbow* banned for obscenity

Scottish writer John Buchan's thriller *The Thirty-nine Steps*

Marc Chagall, Russian painter living in France, paints "The Birthday"

American poet and novelist Edgar Lee Masters' long verse work *Spoon River Anthology*

1916

American writer Carl Sandburg's *Chicago Poems* celebrate working-class America

Norman Rockwell begins painting covers for *The Saturday Evening Post*

Austrian-born philosopher Martin Buber's *The Spirit of Judaism*

American novelist Theodore Dreiser's *The "Genius"* suppressed by censors

1917

First Pulitzer Prizes: for biography, *Julia Ward Howe*, by Laura E. Richards, Maude H. Elliot, and Florence H. Hall; for history, *With Americans of Past and Present Days*, by J. J. Jusserand

French poet Guillaume Apollinaire coins term *surrealism;* Picasso designs surrealistic sets and costumes for ballet *Parade*

American-born English poet T. S. Eliot's *Prufrock and Other Observations*

Italian sculptor and painter

Amedeo Modigliani's "Crouching Female Nude"

Russian composer Sergei Prokofiev's *Classical Symphony*

Hungarian-born American composer Sigmund Romberg's operetta *Maytime*

1918

First Pulitzer Prizes: for fiction, *His Family*, by Ernest Poole; for drama, *Why Marry?* by Jesse L. Williams; for poetry, *Love Songs,* by Sara Teasdale

American novelist Willa Cather's *My Ántonia*

U.S. Post Office burns issues of the American magazine *Little Review* containing installments of James Joyce's *Ulysses,* judged obscene

English biographer and critic Lytton Strachey's *Eminent Victorians*

German philosopher Oswald Spengler's *Decline of the West*

Spanish painter Juan Gris's cubist "Scottish Girl"

Swiss painter Paul Klee's abstract "Gartenplan"

"Time is a great legalizer, even in the field of morals."

— Journalist H. L. Mencken, A Book of Prefaces (1917)

Norwegian painter Edvard Munch's "Bathing Man"

With publication of his *Poems,* English poet Gerard Manley Hopkins achieves measure of fame almost 30 years after his death

New York Philharmonic Society, in a display of wartime patriotic zeal, bans work of living German composers; Karl Muck, German conductor of Boston Symphony Orchestra, arrested as enemy alien

1919

American writer Sherwood Anderson's collection of related stories *Winesburg, Ohio*

American editor and critic H. L. Mencken's *The American Language*

English writer Thomas Hardy's *Collected Poems*

Austrian-born British expressionist artist and writer Oskar Kokoschka's *The Power of Music*

Bauhaus school of architecture founded by Walter Gropius in Weimar, Germany

French painter Claude Monet's "Nympheas"

English composer Edward Elgar's *Concerto in E Minor for Cello*

German composer Richard Strauss's opera *Die Frau Ohne Schatten*, with the Austrian poet Hugo von Hofmannsthal as librettist

German film *The Cabinet of Dr. Caligari*, directed by Robert Wiene and script by Carl Mayer, landmark in expressionist cinema

American philanthropist A. D. Juilliard dies, leaving $20-million endowment to the music institute that will become the Juilliard School of Music

French-born American composer Edgard Varèse conducts the New York Symphony Orchestra in its first concert of modern music

The Magnificent Ambersons, by Booth Tarkington, wins Pulitzer Prize for fiction

American man of letters Henry Adams's autobiography, *The Education of Henry Adams,* (printed privately, 1906) wins Pulitzer Prize for biography

Already famous, draftee Irving Berlin wrote and sang this tune for a show at his army camp.

ENTERTAINMENT & SPORTS

1914

American Society of Composers, Authors, and Publishers (ASCAP) founded by John Philip Sousa, Victor Herbert, and others to protect musical copyrights

---

"I think that I shall never see A poem lovely as a tree. . . . A tree that may in summer wear A nest of robins in her hair; . . . Poems are made by fools like me, But only God can make a tree."

—"Trees" (1913), by American poet Joyce Kilmer, killed in action in France, 1918

Charlie Chaplin introduces his tramp outfit in *Kid Auto Races at Venice*

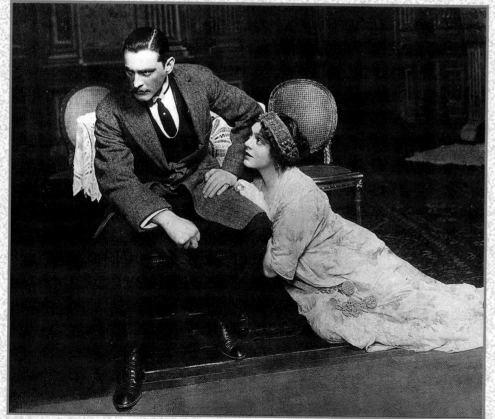

John Barrymore and his older sister, Ethel, do an emotional scene in the prewar Broadway drama Slice of Life. *With their older brother, Lionel, the Barrymores entertained stage and screen audiences for more than 50 years.*

Mack Sennett's *Tillie's Punctured Romance,* with Charlie Chaplin and Marie Dressler

American black composer W. C. Handy's "St. Louis Blues"

Yale Bowl, first of college football super stadiums, opens, seating 80,000

Jack Dempsey starts fighting under the name Kid Blackey

American golfer Walter Hagen, at 21, wins U.S. Open, the first of his 11 major championships (1914–29)

Australia beats U.S. in Davis Cup tennis final

Boston Braves defeat Philadelphia Athletics in World Series 4 games to 0

1915

78-r.p.m. records

American film director D. W. Griffith's *The Birth of a Nation*

Movie serials: *The Perils of Pauline, Ruth of the Rockies, What Happened to Mary?*

Chaplin's *The Tramp*

Douglas Fairbanks stars in *The Lamb*

Welsh composer Ivor Novello writes "Keep the Home Fires Burning," popular wartime song

Jess Willard becomes heavyweight boxing champion, knocking out Jack Johnson in the 26th round

Wimbledon tennis suspended for duration of the war

U.S. Tennis Open moves from Newport, Rhode Island, to Forest Hills, New York

Boston Red Sox defeat Philadelphia Athletics in World Series 4 games to 1

1916

Annual Rose Bowl game begins; Washington State beats Brown 14–0

Professional Golfers' Association (PGA) founded in U.S.

D. W. Griffith's film *Intolerance*

Boston Red Sox defeat Brooklyn Dodgers in World Series 4 games to 1

1917

French actress Sarah Bernhardt, 73, makes her last U.S. tour

Mary Pickford stars in the movie *The Little Princess*

American musical comedy dynamo George M. Cohan writes "Over There"

Charlie Chaplin signs a contract worth $1 million annually

First jazz recordings, by the Original Dixieland Jazz Band, a group of white musicians, include "Tiger Rag," "Clarinet Marmalade," and "Ostrich Walk"

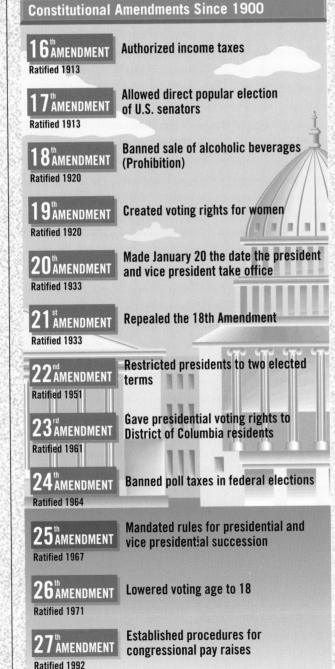

Constitutional Amendments Since 1900

16th AMENDMENT Authorized income taxes
Ratified 1913

17th AMENDMENT Allowed direct popular election of U.S. senators
Ratified 1913

18th AMENDMENT Banned sale of alcoholic beverages (Prohibition)
Ratified 1920

19th AMENDMENT Created voting rights for women
Ratified 1920

20th AMENDMENT Made January 20 the date the president and vice president take office
Ratified 1933

21st AMENDMENT Repealed the 18th Amendment
Ratified 1933

22nd AMENDMENT Restricted presidents to two elected terms
Ratified 1951

23rd AMENDMENT Gave presidential voting rights to District of Columbia residents
Ratified 1961

24th AMENDMENT Banned poll taxes in federal elections
Ratified 1964

25th AMENDMENT Mandated rules for presidential and vice presidential succession
Ratified 1967

26th AMENDMENT Lowered voting age to 18
Ratified 1971

27th AMENDMENT Established procedures for congressional pay raises
Ratified 1992

Keds makes the first tennis footwear

Boston Red Sox pitcher Ernie Shore throws a perfect game against the Washington Senators

First Sunday baseball game is played in New York's Polo Grounds; managers are arrested for breaking the blue law

National Hockey League formed

Seattle Metropolitans defeat the Montreal Canadiens, become first U.S. team to win hockey's Stanley Cup

Chicago White Sox defeat New York Giants in World Series 4 games to 2

1918

Robert LeRoy Ripley begins *Believe It or Not* newspaper cartoon series

Knute Rockne named Notre Dame football coach

Irving Berlin's "Oh! How I Hate to Get Up in the Morning"

George Gershwin's "Swanee"

John L. Sullivan, former heavyweight boxing champion, dies

Jerome Kern's "Rock-a-Bye, Baby"

Boston Red Sox defeat Chicago Cubs in World Series 4 games to 2

1919

Movie giants Charlie Chaplin, Mary Pickford, Douglas Fairbanks, and D. W. Griffith form United Artists to produce and distribute films

Hollywood agrees to submit films to censorship

Jack Dempsey wins world heavyweight boxing crown from Jess Willard

Babe Ruth hits 537-foot home run

Sir Barton is first horse to win the Triple Crown: Kentucky Derby, Preakness, and Belmont Stakes; J. Loftus rides him in all three triumphs

American bandleader Paul Whiteman forms orchestra to play "symphonic jazz"

Mechanical rabbit launches modern greyhound racing

Cincinnati Reds defeat Chicago White Sox in World Series 5 games to 3; in "Black Sox" scandal several Chicago players accused of trying to lose World Series

BUSINESS & ECONOMICS

1914

Federal Trade Commission established

Cadillac develops V-8 engine

Teletypewriter invented

American agronomist George Washington Carver develops soil-replenishment program

✠

"History is more or less bunk."
— Industrialist Henry Ford, 1916

✠

U.S. Circuit Court of Appeals decides airplane patent suit in favor of Wright brothers

1915

First transcontinental telephone call, between Alexander Graham Bell in New York City and Thomas A. Watson in San Francisco

Ford produces its millionth Model T; price is $440

U.S. bankers, led by J. Pierpont Morgan, Jr., float $500-million loan to Britain and France to help their war effort

1916

Trans-Siberian Railroad between Moscow and Vladivostok completed

Dodge introduces first all-steel auto body

1917

Union Carbide founded

Radios used for ground-to-air and air-to-air communication

Liberty Loan Act authorizes bond sales to raise money for the war

War Industries Board sets manufacturing priorities

SCIENCE & MEDICINE

1914

Thyroxine, an amino-acid hormone produced by the thyroid gland, identified

American physicist and inventor Robert Goddard's first rocket experiments; liquid-fuel rockets patented

Interstellar matter, clouds of gas and dust, observed, indicating that space between the stars is not as empty as had been supposed

Guttenberg discontinuity announced: it marks boundary between Earth's core and mantle

1915

Niacin deficiency in diet associated with pellagra

Dysentery bacillus isolated

Albert Einstein completes theory of relativity; remakes physics and astronomy

First carcinogen identified

Disposable scalpel patented

1916

Plastic surgery advances through treatment of war injuries

Vitamins A and B declared essential for growth

American physical chemist Gilbert N. Lewis proposes theory of atomic structure that is later (1919) developed, with colleague Irving Langmuir, into Lewis-Langmuir theory of atomic structure and valence

1917

Vitamin D produced from cod-liver oil

100-inch telescope erected at Mount Wilson, California

Swiss psychologist Carl G. Jung's *Psychology of the Unconscious*

Sigmund Freud completes *Introductory Lectures on Psychoanalysis*

Existence of "black holes" in far space predicted

Rearrangement of chromosomes during meiosis demonstrated

Rocky Mountain Spotted Fever vaccine

1918

British archeologist Leonard Wooley begins Babylonian excavations

✠

> *"Before I built a wall I'd ask to know What I was walling in or walling out."*
>
> —*"Mending Wall" (1914)*, by American poet Robert Frost

✠

German physicist Max Planck, father of quantum theory, wins Nobel Prize

Development of alkyd resins, used in paints for durability, color stability, uniform drying

American astronomer Harlow Shapley determines the size of the Milky Way; places our solar system near the outer

edge of the galaxy

1919

Bees found to communicate through body action

British physicist Ernest Rutherford investigates the structure of the atom

English philosopher and mathematician Bertrand Russell's *Introduction to the Philosophy of Mathematics*

American geneticist Thomas Hunt Morgan's *The Physical Basis of Heredity* summarizes his genetics research on fruit flies

WORLD POLITICAL & WAR EVENTS

1914

Archduke Francis Ferdinand, heir to the Austrian throne, and wife assassinated at Sarajevo

Austria-Hungary declares war on Serbia

European conflicts widen into world war: Germany, Austria-Hungary, and Turkey (Central Powers) oppose Britain, France, and Russia (Allies)

Britain lands troops in France

Battle of the Marne; 1st Battle of Ypres

Trench warfare along entire western front

Pope Pius X dies; Pope Benedict XV elected

Egypt becomes British protectorate

Run on European banks

1915

First German submarine attacks at Le Havre

Italy declares war on Germany

First use of poison gas by Germans, in 2nd Battle of Ypres

German zeppelins raid England

Tetanus in the trenches

German sea-blockade of Britain

Allied landings at Gallipoli, Turkey

Czar Nicholas II takes personal control of Russian army

WHO WENT TO WAR WHEN

After Austria-Hungary declared war on Serbia, World War I spread to include about 30 nations, plus the countries in their empires. The dates indicate when each nation entered the war.

THE ALLIES

July 28, 1914, Serbia
Aug. 1, 1914, Russia
Aug. 3, 1914, France
Aug. 4, 1914, Belgium
Aug. 4, 1914, Great Britain
Aug. 5, 1914, Montenegro
Aug. 23, 1914, Japan
May 23, 1915, Italy
June 3, 1915, San Marino
Mar. 9, 1916, Portugal
Aug. 27, 1916, Romania
Apr. 6, 1917, United States
Apr. 7, 1917, Panama
July 2, 1917, Greece
July 22, 1917, Siam
Aug. 4, 1917, Liberia
Aug. 14, 1917, China
Oct. 26, 1917, Brazil
Apr. 23, 1918, Guatemala
May 8, 1918, Nicaragua
May 23, 1918, Costa Rica
July 12, 1918, Haiti
July 19, 1918, Honduras

THE CENTRAL POWERS

July 28, 1914, Austria-Hungary
Aug. 1, 1914, Germany
Oct. 31, 1914, Ottoman Empire (Turkey)
Oct. 14, 1915, Bulgaria

Douglas Haig becomes British commander in France; Joseph Joffre is French commander

English nurse Edith Cavell executed by Germans, outraging British

Germany builds the Fokker, first plane with interrupter mechanism allowing machine-gun fire between propeller-blade rotations

Britain produces first armored vehicle with tracks,

Children of families laid low by influenza bring food pots to be filled by volunteers in Cincinnati, Ohio. The epidemic peaked in 1918–19. While the flu virus alone seldom killed, it resulted in deadly bacterial infections.

called Little Willie

German aeronautical designer Hugo Junkers makes first all-metal fighter plane

Germans sink *Lusitania*

Reflecting concern that alcohol consumption weakens war effort, France outlaws sale of absinthe; England's George V and the royal household announce they are abstaining from alcohol

---

"Was it for this the clay grew tall? — Oh, what made fatuous sunbeams toil To break earth's sleep at all?"

—"Futility," by English poet Wilfred Owen, killed in action in France, 1918

1916

First zeppelin attack on Paris

Battle of Jutland, between fleets of Britain and Germany, ends in a costly draw

Battles between Italian and

Austrian forces along the Isonzo River in northern Italy rage on

David Lloyd George is British prime minister; Paul von Hindenburg becomes German chief of staff

Battle of Verdun

Allied offensive on the Somme begins

British merchant ship losses during year total 1.5 million tons; ultrasonic machine developed to detect submarines

"Mad monk" Rasputin assassinated in Russia

1917

Revolution in Russia; Czar Nicholas II abdicates

Russian Black Sea fleet mutinies; October Revolution in Petrograd; Bolsheviks V. I. Lenin and Leon Trotsky assume leadership; Russia sues for peace with Germany

U.S. declares war on Germany

Britain's George V orders members of royal family to drop their German titles

First use of massed tanks in battle, by British at Cambrai, France

Mata Hari, charged with spying for the Central Powers, executed by Allies

The streets of St. Petersburg (above), the capital of Russia from 1712 to 1917, were the scene of riot after riot in the 50 turbulent years that culminated in Czar Nicholas II's giving up his throne on March 15, 1917.

Passchendaele (3rd Battle of Ypres) continues slaughter on western front

King Constantine of Greece abdicates; Greece severs relations with Central Powers

Pact of Corfu: Serbia, Montenegro, Slovenia, and Croatia agree to form Yugoslavia

Balfour Declaration calls for Jewish state in Palestine

Sinn Fein, Irish nationalist organization, holds convention in Dublin

Reform in Mexico: universal suffrage, 8-hour day, minimum wage

1918

Former Russian Czar Nicholas II and family secretly executed by Lenin's agents

Germany's Kaiser Wilhelm abdicates

As war ends, Hungary declares independence from Austria; Baltic states of Estonia, Latvia, Lithuania assert independence from Russia; Czechoslovakia created

Bolsheviks form Communist Party under Lenin, move Russian capital to Moscow from Petrograd (called St. Petersburg 1703–1914 and 1991–, Leningrad 1924–91)

Women get suffrage in Britain

1919

Hapsburg dynasty expelled from Austria

Weimar Republic begins in Germany

Eamon de Valera heads

Ireland's Sinn Fein; rebellion breaks out

Benito Mussolini founds Fascist Party in Italy

"I felt like a man standing on a planet that had been suddenly wrenched from its orbit by a demonic hand and that was spinning wildly into the unknown."

— David Lloyd George then chancellor of the exchequer recalling Britain's entering the war

---

Mohandas K. Gandhi begins passive resistance movement in India

Turks exterminate 1.5 million Armenians

Famine in Germany and central Europe

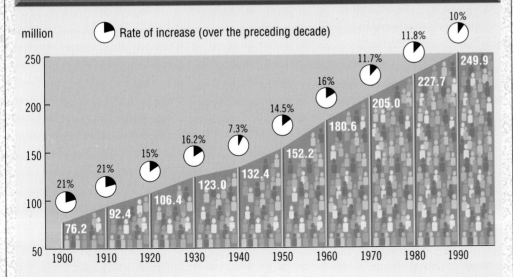

U.S. Population: 1900-90

million   ◗ Rate of increase (over the preceding decade)

Year	Population	Rate of increase
1900	76.2	21%
1910	92.4	21%
1920	106.4	15%
1930	123.0	16.2%
1940	132.4	7.3%
1950	152.2	14.5%
1960	180.6	16%
1970	205.0	11.7%
1980	227.7	11.8%
1990	249.9	10%

U.S. HISTORY & POLITICS

1920

U.S. Senate fails to ratify Treaty of Versailles, containing the commitment to League of Nations desired by President Wilson

Prohibition goes into effect; bootlegging, speakeasies result

19th Amendment (woman suffrage) ratified

League of Women Voters founded

Nationwide Red Scare continues; federal government arrests Communists, anarchists, labor agitators

Bomb blast on Wall Street kills 35 people; anarchists suspected but no arrests are made

Anarchists Nicola Sacco and Bartolomeo Vanzetti indicted for murder

Warren G. Harding elected 29th president; Calvin Coolidge, vice president; their Republican ticket defeats Democrats James M. Cox and Franklin D. Roosevelt

U.S. population: some 106 million; population balance shifts from rural to urban areas

1921

Roaring Twenties beget rapid social change

Sacco and Vanzetti found guilty, later executed

Congress provides for a national budget; sets up General Accounting Office

Quota Act reduces immigration from southern and eastern Europe, gives preference to northern Europe

Veterans Bureau created

Armistice Day (Nov. 11) declared national holiday; Tomb of the Unknown Soldier established at Arlington Cemetery

Ku Klux Klan violence grows in the South

Gen. "Billy" Mitchell demonstrates bombing capabilities of military aircraft

Charles Evans Hughes named secretary of state; Andrew W. Mellon, secretary of the treasury

Four-Power Pacific Treaty: U.S., Britain, France, and Japan recognize spheres of influence

1922

U.S. guarantees Open Door Policy in China

U.S.-British-Japanese treaty limits warships

Congressional elections lessen Republican majority

Congress votes high protectionist tariffs on goods from abroad

Federal Narcotics Control Board established

1923

Warren Harding dies in office (Aug. 2); Calvin Coolidge becomes president

Senate investigates Teapot Dome scandal; Harding administration officials implicated in illegal granting of oil-field leases; criminal prosecutions follow

◆

"If you don't say anything, you won't be called on to repeat it."

— *President Calvin Coolidge*

◆

KKK membership estimated at 2 million; conclave in Indiana draws 200,000 members; attacks grow on blacks, Jews, Catholics, immigrants; KKK terrorism in Oklahoma brings about martial law

U.S. troops begin final withdrawal from Germany

Coolidge addresses Congress; radio carries presidential message for first time

On June 13, 1927, Charles A. Lindbergh gets a ticker tape parade in New York City, 24 days after he took off on his solo transatlantic flight.

1924

Financier (later Coolidge's vice president) Charles Dawes puts forth plan to reduce German reparations and stabilize German currency; Dawes's plan accepted by Germany and the Allies

Calvin Coolidge elected 30th president; his vice president is Charles G. Dawes; they defeat Democratic ticket of John W. Davis and Charles W. Bryan

J. Edgar Hoover named director of the Bureau of Investigation, later renamed Federal Bureau of Investigation

Congress gives citizenship to Native Americans

Immigration laws further limit immigrants, exclude Japanese

First woman governor elected: Nellie Taylor Ross of Wyoming

Soldiers' bonus bill passes over Coolidge veto

Pan-American Treaty signed; provides for arbitration to settle Western Hemisphere disputes

1925

John Scopes "monkey trial" tests Tennessee law prohibiting the teaching of evolution; matches Clarence Darrow for defense vs. William Jennings Bryan for the prosecution; teacher Scopes is convicted, then acquitted on technicality

Florida law requires daily Bible reading in public schools

U.S. troops restore order in Panama

1926

U.S. Supreme Court rules 1867 Tenure of Office Act unconstitutional; president now may dismiss Cabinet officers and executive appointees without Senate approval

Marines sent to Nicaragua

Army Air Force founded

1927

Charles Lindbergh makes first solo transatlantic nonstop flight; pilots his monoplane, *The Spirit of St. Louis,* from New York to Paris in 33 hours 29 minutes; "Lucky Lindy" becomes national hero

Federal Board of Radio Control, later the Federal Communications Commission, established

Supreme Court rules Texas law forbidding blacks to vote in primaries is unconstitutional

1928

U.S. joins 64 countries in signing Kellogg-Briand Pact, outlawing war

Alien Property Act provides $300 million to compensate Germans for property seized in U.S. during war

Herbert C. Hoover elected 31st president; Charles Curtis, vice president; their Republican ticket defeats Democrats Alfred E. Smith, first Catholic nominated for presidency, and Joseph T. Robinson

1929

"Black Thursday" (October 24) in U.S.; stock prices fall; market then steadies briefly before plummeting on October 29, signaling start of worldwide Great Depression

St. Valentine's Day Massacre in Chicago; six mobsters machine-gunned by rival gang

President Hoover appoints commission to investigate the spread of crime under Prohibition

EVERYDAY LIFE

1920

First transcontinental airmail route: New York to San Francisco

First commercial radio station: KDKA in Pittsburgh

Canned horse meat for dog food introduced

Jantzen makes one-piece elasticized swimsuit

U.S.S.R. first country to legalize abortion

Band-Aid adhesive strips

1921

French fashion-setter Coco Chanel introduces Chanel No. 5

Polygraph (lie detector) test invented

Knee-length skirts turn heads

Eskimo Pie ice-cream bars

Betty Crocker character introduced

Movie actor Fatty Arbuckle sex-and-sadism scandal rocks Hollywood

First Miss America Pageant, Atlantic City, New Jersey

Cultured pearls perfected

First public lending library for recordings opens in Detroit

1922

First mechanized telephone switchboard, in New York City

Self-winding watch invented

Reader's Digest is founded by Lila and DeWitt Wallace in basement apartment in Greenwich Village section of New York City

> *"The victor belongs to the spoils."*
>
> — *F. Scott Fitzgerald, in* The Beautiful and Damned *(1922)*

Ship-to-shore radio service

A 21-ton meteorite lands near Blackstone, Virginia; creates 400-foot-wide crater

Scripps-Howard becomes first U.S. newspaper chain

First transcontinental flight in less than 24 hours: Lt. James Doolittle flies from California to Florida in 23 hours 35 minutes

Cable Act passed: U.S. women no longer lose their citizenship if they marry aliens

First shopping mall with unified architecture and management: Country Club Plaza, Kansas City, Missouri

Emily Post's *Etiquette,* the first of her books on proper social behavior and good manners

1923

The treasures of Egyptian pharaoh Tutankhamen's tomb, discovered the year before, give rise to a King Tut craze

First antiknock gasoline

Sedans become more popular than open cars

Mah-jongg becomes a fad

Milky Way candy bar

Dance marathons

Henry R. Luce and Briton Hadden start *Time* magazine

1924

First U.S. gay rights organization formed

Americans own 2.5 million radios

First around-the-world flight; U.S. Army pilots make the trip in 175 days

First disposable handkerchiefs, Celluwipes; later renamed Kleenex

First Popsicles

Flagpole sitting

First crossword puzzle books

Women's "knickers" are shortened, become "panties"

1925

The New Yorker magazine begins publication

First international radio broadcast: London to Maine

First electric phonograph

Flashbulb prototype introduced

Dry ice (solidified carbon dioxide) used for refrigeration

Electric coffee percolators

National spelling bees begin

The Charleston becomes a dance rage

Flapper fashions are in vogue: cloche hats, waistlessness, above-the-knee dresses

1926

Increase in air traffic results in

Congress passing first U.S. law to regulate aviation, the Air Commerce Act

First public demonstration of TV

Book of the Month Club starts

Magician Harry Houdini dies

Miniature golf craze

1927

Wall-mounted can openers

First underwater color photographs, published in *National Geographic*

Couples dance the fox-trot

Commercial transatlantic telephone service begins, between New York and London

Al Capone's fortune estimated at $105 million

Holland Tunnel, first underwater vehicular tunnel, opens; creates auto link between New York and New Jersey under the Hudson River

1928

Adhesive tape

Rolleiflex, double-lens reflex camera, introduced

First transatlantic television transmission

1929

FM radio

Birdseye company markets frozen food

Foam rubber

U.S. issues new, smaller-sized paper currency

Jimmy Doolittle makes first "blind" (by-instruments-only) plane flight

First air-conditioned rail passenger car

ARTS & LETTERS

1920

First Dada Fair, in Berlin; at dadaist exhibit in Cologne, visitors are allowed to smash paintings

F. Scott Fitzgerald publishes his first novel, *This Side of Paradise*

American novelist Sinclair Lewis's *Main Street*

French writer Colette's novel *Chéri* explores an affair between a woman and a younger man

The Outline of History, an account of humankind's development, by Englishman

H. G. Wells, who also wrote fiction and science fiction

English abstract painter Ben Nicholson's "Sunflowers"

Spanish painter Juan Gris's "Book and Newspaper"

French composer Maurice Ravel's ballet music *La Valse*

American novelist Edith Wharton's *The Age of Innocence*

American dramatist Eugene O'Neill's *The Emperor Jones*

1921

American novelist John Dos Passos's *Three Soldiers*

English writer D. H. Lawrence's novel *Women in Love*

English biographer and critic Lytton Strachey's *Queen Victoria*

Italian-born English writer Rafael Sabatini's historical novel *Scaramouche*

French painter Fernand Léger's "Three Women"

French painter Georges Braque's "Still Life With Guitar"

Two masterpieces by 18th-century English painters, Thomas Gainsborough's "Blue Boy" and Sir Joshua Reynold's "Portrait of Mrs. Siddons," sold for total of 200,000 pounds

Italian tenor Enrico Caruso dies in Naples

Russian composer Sergei Prokofiev's opera *The Love for Three Oranges* debuts in Chicago

Russian-born American composer Igor Stravinsky's *Symphony for Wind Instruments*

Hungarian-born American composer Sigmund Romberg's operetta *Blossom Time,* based on the music of Franz Schubert

1922

American-born English poet T. S. Eliot's *The Waste Land*

American novelist Sinclair Lewis's *Babbitt*

American playwright Anne Nichols's *Abie's Irish Rose* debuts on Broadway, starting

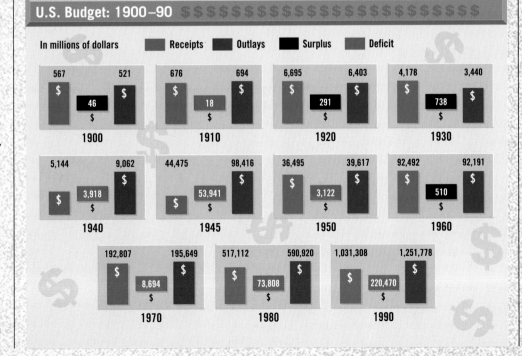

U.S. Budget: 1900–90

In millions of dollars — Receipts — Outlays — Surplus — Deficit

Year	Receipts	Surplus/Deficit	Outlays
1900	567	46 (Surplus)	521
1910	676	18 (Surplus)	694
1920	6,695	291 (Surplus)	6,403
1930	4,178	738 (Surplus)	3,440
1940	5,144	3,918 (Deficit)	9,062
1945	44,475	53,941 (Deficit)	98,416
1950	36,495	3,122 (Deficit)	39,617
1960	92,492	510 (Surplus)	92,191
1970	192,807	8,694 (Deficit)	195,649
1980	517,112	73,808 (Deficit)	590,920
1990	1,031,308	220,470 (Deficit)	1,251,778

a run of 2,327 performances

American dramatist Eugene O'Neill's *Anna Christie*

American actress and singer Lillian Russell dies

1923

American poet Robert Frost's collection *New Hampshire*

American dramatist Philip Barry's *You and I*

American dramatist Elmer Rice's *The Adding Machine*

Irish writer James Joyce's *Ulysses*

French writer Marcel Proust dies

English poet A. E. Housman's *Last Poems*

German expressionist Max Beckmann's woodcut "Charnel House"

Italian composer Ottorino Respighi's *Concerto Gregoriano*

German-born American composer Paul Hindemith's song cycle *Das Marienleben*

Russian Marc Chagall, living in France, paints "Love Idyll"

British painter Augustus John's portrait of English novelist and poet Thomas Hardy

◆

"[Flapper] Jane isn't wearing much this summer: one dress, one step-in, two stockings, two shoes. No petticoat; no brassiere; of course, no corset."

— Journalist Bruce Bliven

◆

French painter Maurice de Vlaminck's "Village in Northern France"

Finnish composer Jean Sibelius's *Symphony No. 6*

Austrian-born American composer Arnold

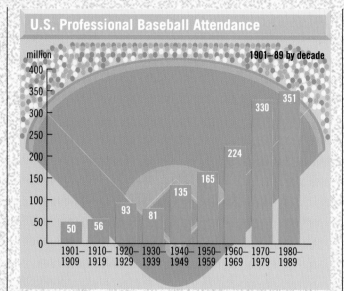

U.S. Professional Baseball Attendance

million — 1901–89 by decade

Decade	Million
1901–1909	50
1910–1919	56
1920–1929	93
1930–1939	81
1940–1949	135
1950–1959	165
1960–1969	224
1970–1979	330
1980–1989	351

Schoenberg's *Piano Suite*, first work based solely on 12-tone system

American painter John Marin's "Sunset"

1924

German writer Thomas Mann's novel *The Magic Mountain*

English novelist E. M. Forster's *A Passage to India*

Surrealism in art and poetry: Salvador Dali, Max Ernst, and Guillaume Apollinaire

Irish dramatist Sean O'Casey's *Juno and the Paycock*

English writer P. G. Wodehouse's comic character Jeeves, the quintessential English butler, achieves fame on both sides of the Atlantic

Spanish painter Joan Miro's "Catalan Landscape"

American composer Rudolf Friml's *Rose Marie*

German composer Richard Strauss's *Intermezzo*

Robert Frost wins the first of his four Pulitzer Prizes for poetry (1924, 1931, 1937, 1943)

American writer Lewis Mumford's *Sticks and Stones*

1925

American novelist Theodore Dreiser's *An American Tragedy*

American writer F. Scott Fitzgerald's *The Great Gatsby*

American poet Ezra Pound publishes *A Draft of XVI Cantos*

Czech-born Franz Kafka's novel *The Trial*, written in German, published posthumously

Spanish painter and sculptor Pablo Picasso's "Three Dancers"

French painter Georges Rouault's "The Apprentice"

Russian composer Dmitri Shostakovich's *Symphony No. 1*

American writer John Erskine's humorous novel *The Private Life of Helen of Troy*

American novelist Sinclair Lewis's *Arrowsmith*

1926

American writer Ernest Hemingway's novel *The Sun Also Rises*

British archeologist, soldier, and writer T. E. Lawrence's *The Seven Pillars of Wisdom*

English poet and dramatist A. A. Milne's *Winnie-the-Pooh*

English historian G. M. Trevelyan's *History of England*

British sculptor Henry Moore's "Draped, Reclining Figure"

Norwegian painter Edvard Munch's "The Red House"

Italian composer Giacomo Puccini's unfinished opera *Turandot* debuts posthumously at La Scala in Milan, under Italian conductor Arturo Toscanini

Hungarian-born American composer Sigmund Romberg's operetta *The Desert Song*

1927

American novelist Willa Cather's *Death Comes for the Archbishop*

Sinclair Lewis's novel *Elmer Gantry*

English author Virginia Woolf's novel *To the Lighthouse*

American novelist B. Traven's *The Treasure of the Sierra Madre*

American artist Edward Hopper's "Manhattan Bridge"

American dancer Isadora Duncan's autobiography *My Life;* she dies in accident

1928

American painter Georgia O'Keeffe's "Nightwave"

American painter John Sloan's "Sixth Avenue and Third Street"

English novelist and critic Aldous Huxley's *Point Counterpoint*

D. H. Lawrence's *Lady Chatterley's Lover*

English writer Evelyn Waugh's *Decline and Fall*

French painter Georges Braque's "Still Life With Jug"

English composer William Walton's *Viola Concerto*

American dramatists Ben Hecht and Charles MacArthur's *The Front Page* opens on Broadway

1929

English author and critic Virginia Woolf's long essay "A Room of One's Own," about obstacles facing a woman writer

American novelist Thomas Wolfe's *Look Homeward, Angel*

German writer Erich Maria Remarque's pacifist novel of World War I, *All Quiet on the Western Front*

American novelist William Faulkner's *The Sound and the Fury*

Ernest Hemingway's *A Farewell to Arms*

American dramatist Elmer Rice's *Street Scene*

American painter Lyonel Feininger's "Sailing Boats"

◆

"Four be the things I am wiser to know: Idleness, sorrow, a friend, and a foe. Four be the things I'd been better without: Love, curiosity, freckles, and doubt."

— Dorothy Parker, in *Enough Rope* (1926)

◆

American painter Grant Wood's "Woman With Plants"

Museum of Modern Art opens in New York City

ENTERTAINMENT & SPORTS

1920

Baseball Hall of Fame established in Cooperstown, New York

Bill Tilden becomes first American to win men's tennis singles title at Wimbledon

Boston Red Sox sell Babe Ruth to New York Yankees for $125,000

Super horse Man o' War retires after winning 20 of 21 races

Water skiing gets popular

American composer Jerome Kern writes the music for the hit Broadway show *Sally*

Swashbuckling American actor Douglas Fairbanks in Hollywood film *The Mark of Zorro*

American dancer and choreographer Martha Graham makes her professional debut as a lead dancer in the modern ballet *Xochitl* after studying at the Denishawn School of Dancing under Ruth St. Denis and Ted Shawn

Cleveland Indians batter Roy Chapman killed by spitball; pitch outlawed in major-league baseball the next year

American bandleader Paul Whiteman's "Whispering" and (flip side) "The Japanese Sandman" first record to sell a million copies

Cleveland Indians defeat Brooklyn Dodgers in World Series 5 games to 2

1921

Graham McNamee makes the first broadcast of a baseball game, from the New York Giants stadium, the Polo Grounds

Rin Tin Tin in Hollywood debut

The Kid, with Charlie Chaplin as star, writer, and director

When Rudolph Valentino died at age 31 in 1926 in New York City, fans backed up 11 blocks to view "The Sheik's" body at the undertaker's.

American film director D. W. Griffith's *Dream Street*

New York Giants defeat New York Yankees in World Series 5 games to 3

1922

Irving Berlin's "April Showers"

Brother-sister song-and-dance team of Fred and Adele Astaire appear on Broadway in *For Goodness Sake*

Louis Armstrong leaves New Orleans, joins King Oliver's band in Chicago

American explorer and filmmaker Robert Flaherty's *Nanook of the North,* an early documentary on Eskimo life

French director Maurice Tourneur's American film *Last of the Mohicans,* based on American writer James Fenimore Cooper's 1826 novel

Comedian Will Rogers begins writing a weekly column for *The New York Times;* his homespun, wry humor will make him one of the most popular men in America

New York Giants defeat New York Yankees in World Series for second year in a row, 4 games to 0

1923

American film director and producer Cecil B. DeMille's *The Ten Commandments*

King Oliver and Jelly Roll Morton make jazz recordings

American actor Lon Chaney appears as Quasimodo in *The Hunchback of Notre Dame,* continues playing monsters in *The Phantom of the Opera* (1925) and other movies

Popular tunes: "Tea for Two," "Yes, We Have No Bananas," "I Want to Be Happy"

Jack Dempsey, knocked out of the ring by Luis Firpo, climbs back in and retains his world heavyweight title

New York Yankees defeat New York Giants in World Series 4 games to 3

1924

American composer George Gershwin's pioneering symphonic jazz composition *Rhapsody in Blue* premieres, played by Paul Whiteman's orchestra with Gershwin at piano

Fred and Adele Astaire in George Gershwin's Broadway musical *Lady Be Good*

St. Louis Cardinal Rogers Hornsby has batting average of .424, still highest in modern baseball era

America's Walter Hagen wins British Open golf title for second time

Douglas Fairbanks stars in *The Thief of Bagdad*

Hollywood film comedian Buster Keaton's *The Navigator*

Brothers George and Ira Gershwin write songs "Lady Be Good," "Fascinating Rhythm," "The Man I Love"

Washington Senators defeat New York Giants in World Series 4 games to 3

1925

Hollywood film director King Vidor's *The Big Parade*

Dance instructor Arthur Murray offered printed instructions to "become popular over night."

Hit song: "Show Me the Way to Go Home"

Charlie Chaplin's *The Gold Rush*

First air-conditioned theaters, in New York City

Grantland Rice starts picking All-American college football players in *Collier's Weekly* magazine

Bill Tilden wins U.S. men's singles tennis title

Pittsburgh Pirates defeat Washington Senators in World Series 4 games to 3

1926

Gene Tunney takes the heavyweight boxing title from Jack Dempsey

Film idol Rudolph Valentino dies; in the crush of 100,000 mourners at his New York City funeral, many are injured and get first aid in the funeral home

John Barrymore stars in the film *Don Juan*

Jazz great Duke Ellington begins recording

Songs: "One Alone," "I Found a Million-Dollar Baby in the Five-and-Ten-Cent Store," "Bye, Bye, Blackbird"

St. Louis Cardinals defeat New York Yankees in World Series 4 games to 3

1927

H.O.D. Segrave drives automobile some 204 m.p.h. at Daytona Beach, Florida; first time a motor vehicle exceeds 200 m.p.h.

Babe Ruth hits 60 home runs

Harlem Globetrotters professional basketball team organized

Johnny Weissmuller, American swimmer who later stars in *Tarzan* movies, sets 100-yard-freestyle world record

American performer Al Jolson stars in *The Jazz Singer,* first movie talkie

Swedish actress Greta Garbo's Hollywood film *Flesh and the Devil*

Broadway musical *Funny Face:* music and lyrics by George and Ira Gershwin, starring Fred and Adele Astaire

Jerome Kern and Oscar Hammerstein's innovative musical drama *Show Boat*

Richard Rodgers and Lorenz Hart's Broadway musical *A Connecticut Yankee*

◆

"Honey, I just forgot to duck."

— Jack Dempsey to his wife after losing the heavyweight title to Gene Tunney, September 1926

◆

New York Yankees defeat Pittsburgh Pirates in World Series 4 games to 0

1928

Baseball's Ty Cobb retires with lifetime .367 batting average

Walt Disney's Mickey Mouse shorts gain wide popularity

Eddie Cantor stars in Broadway musical *Whoopee*

Hit songs: "Bill," "Makin' Whoopee," "You're the Cream in My Coffee"

New York Yankees defeat St. Louis Cardinals in World Series 4 games to 0

1929

Hollywood sees its future in talkies; slow fade-out of silent films begins

The Marx Brothers' first movie, *Cocoanuts,* is based on their 1925 Broadway show of the same name

Gypsy Rose Lee attracts notice with her burlesque act

American singer, actor, and composer Hoagy Carmichael's song "Star Dust"

First Academy Awards (Oscars): for acting to Janet Gaynor and Emil Jannings, for best picture to *Wings*

◆

"Kissing your hand may make you feel very very good but a diamond and sapphire bracelet lasts forever."

— *Anita Loos, in* Gentlemen Prefer Blondes *(1925)*

◆

First of Hollywood's lavish musicals: *The Broadway Melody*

Cole Porter's Broadway musical *Fifty Million Frenchmen*

Hit songs: "Tiptoe through the Tulips," "Singin' in the Rain"

American golfer Bobby Jones wins U.S. Open

Georgia Tech beats California 8–7 in the Rose Bowl

Philadelphia Athletics defeat the Chicago Cubs in World Series 4 games to 1

BUSINESS & ECONOMICS

1920

Federal Power Commission created

1922

U.S. puts high protectionist tariffs on goods from abroad

Shell Oil Company incorporates

Labor unrest: nationwide strikes by coal miners, rail workers

U.S. announces typical budget, with a surplus: revenues of $4.9 billion, expenditures of $4.1 billion

1923

Bulldozer invented; prototype of future earthmoving machines

Oklahoma regulates oil fields to discourage excess production; regulations become model for other oil-producing states

Nevada and Montana initiate old-age pensions

Continuous hot-strip rolling for steel developed

1924

Ford's 10-millionth auto comes off the assembly line

Leica produces the first 35mm camera, prototype for many others

U.S. leads industrialized countries in working days lost because of strikes

1925

First analog computer

Privately owned airlines begin to carry U.S. airmail

Chrysler Corporation's Caterpillar tractor unit established

1926

Scottish inventor John Logie Baird transmits recognizable TV images

Begun in 1926, the Chrysler Building in New York City was not finished until after the Crash.

Continuous casting method for nonferrous metals developed

Aerial crop dusting with insecticides improves harvests

1927

Prototype color motion pictures

First teleprinters

1928

General Mills founded

Boeing Corporation, North American Aviation established

First working robot

Record day of trading on the New York Stock Exchange: 6.6 million shares

Short-term interest rates hit record high: 10 percent

1929

German dirigible *Graf Zeppelin* flies around world in 20 days 4 hours 14 minutes; future of lighter-than-air travel seems bright

Empire State Building construction begins

Brylcreem, a nongummy hair cream, marketed in Britain

October 29th stock market crash: U.S. securities plummet $2 billion in value

SCIENCE & MEDICINE

1920

Structure of the Milky Way defined

Sigmund Freud publishes *General Introduction to Psychoanalysis*

Existence of neutrons within atoms postulated

1921

German psychiatrist Hermann Rorschach introduces inkblot test for investigating mental illness

Vitamin E discovered

Vitamin D found to prevent rickets

White corpuscles isolated from the blood

1922

King Tut's tomb discovered

A "father of space travel" (with American Robert Goddard), Romanian-born German scientist Hermann Oberth presents his dissertation on long-range, liquid-propelled rockets, "The Rocket Into Interplanetary Space," to Heidelberg University, and it is rejected as foolishness

1923

Bacterium that causes scarlet fever isolated

Sigmund Freud publishes *The Ego and the Id*

Vladimir Zworykin develops the iconoscope, prototype of later TV tubes

Earth's magnetism studied

Relationship of a star's radiance to its mass calibrated

1925

Dog teams deliver antidiphtheria serum to Nome, Alaska, during epidemic

Height of ionosphere measured

Quantum mechanics, dealing with the structure of the atom and the movement of sub-atomic particles, advances with the work of French physicist Louis de Broglie, German physicist Werner Heisenberg, and Austrian physicist Erwin Schrodinger

First successful experiments with hydroponics

1926

Vitamin B isolated

WHAT IT COST

Prices: 1920

Daily, Sunday newspapers, 2¢, 5¢

Portable phonograph, $22.49; double-faced 10" records, 85¢

Men's suits, $47.50; overcoats, $50; pajamas, $4.75; silk shirts, $5.90 to $9.75; percale shirts, $1.95

Ladies' "frocks," $30 to $75; skirt, $17.50; ladies' pumps, $6.75 to $12.20

Mink coats, $1,250 to $5,000; Hudson seal coats, $300

Man's derby, $10; neckties, $1.10

Misses' suits with fur collars, $59.50

Man's watch, $9.50

Wardrobe trunks, $22.50, $34.75, $45

Thomas Gainsborough painting, $2,100; Joshua Reynolds, $15,000; George Romney, $4,550

Restaurant lunch, $1; B'way ticket, 75¢ to $2.50; Carnegie Hall recital, 50¢ to $2

Washington, D.C., hotel room with bath, $3.50 (European plan), $2 (American plan)

West End Ave. 3-room, 1-bath apartment, $1,320 to $1,800 yearly; 2, 3, & 4 rooms on West 75th, $2,500 to $4,500

8-room Westchester house (New Rochelle), $20,000 to buy; similar house in New Jersey, $8,500; Long Island houses offered for $7,500

Sofa and armchair, $275; 10-piece dining room suite (6 chairs), $249 to $545; 4-piece bedroom suite, $173.50 to $445

106-piece china set, $65

Canned vegetables, 19¢; canned fruits, 34¢

Chandler touring car, $1,895; sedan, $2,895; limousine, $3,395

Novel, $1.75; biography, $4

Console phonograph (in cabinet), $225

Studebaker, $1,785

Town houses: $25,000 to $75,000 in Manhattan, $5,500 to $8,500 in the Bronx

10-room house on 2 acres on North Shore of Long Island, $18,500

New method of capturing atmospheric nitrogen results in cheaper agricultural fertilizers

Americans Richard Byrd and Floyd Bennett fly to the North Pole and back from Spitsbergen island, northern Norway

X-rays found to cause genetic mutations

Speed of light measured by German-born American physicist A. A. Michelson

1927

First tetanus shots for humans

1928

Coming of Age in Samoa, by American anthropologist Margaret Mead, published

◆

"Life is a foreign language; all men mispronounce it."

— American journalist and literary critic Christopher Morley, in Thunder on the Left, 1925

◆

Improved tests for pregnancy, involving injecting women's urine into experimental animals, such as mice, rabbits, and rats

Geiger counter, for detecting radioactivity, invented

Iron lung invented

Vitamin C discovered

British bacteriologist Alexander Fleming discovers penicillin

American physiologist and physician George Papanicolaou develops Pap smear to detect uterine cancer

1929

Relationship of high blood pressure to heart disease explored

Sex hormone estrone identified

Nerve impulses measured

WORLD POLITICAL EVENTS

1920

The Hague becomes the seat of the International Court of Justice

Civil war ends in Russia

Adolph Hitler reorganizes German Workers' Party under his leadership

Government of Ireland Act: Southern and Northern Ireland to have separate parliaments

Free City of Danzig, mandated by Treaty of Versailles, established under League of Nations

Poland, with France's help, invades Communist Russia and occupies the Ukraine and western Belorussia

Treaty of Sèvres recognizes Armenian independence after years of war with Turkey; but Communist Russia then takes over eastern Armenia, and Russia and the Turks eventually divide up Armenia between them

Mohandas K. Gandhi leads campaign for Indian independence from Britain

Japan gets former German colonies in Pacific

British East Africa renamed Kenya; becomes crown colony

Joan of Arc canonized

Famine in China

Alvaro Obregon elected president of Mexico

1921

Germany assessed some $32 billion in reparations for World War I; German mark plunges in value, inflation soars; Hitler organizes Nazi Party

Takashi Hara, Japanese premier, assassinated; Crown Prince Hirohito becomes prince regent

Sweden abolishes capital punishment

1922

Germany cedes Upper Silesia to Poland

Mussolini marches on Rome; forms Fascist government

Pope Pius XI elected by College of Cardinals

Britain gives Egypt independence

Irish Free State established

Turkey proclaimed a republic by its first president, Kemal Ataturk

British-controlled Indian government gives Gandhi 6-year prison sentence for civil disobedience

Communist Russia reorganizes itself into the Union of Soviet Socialist Republics

1923

Hitler leads Nazi storm troopers in Beer Hall Putsch (revolt), an attempt to overthrow the Bavarian state government in Munich; it fails; Hitler jailed for 9 months and writes *Mein Kampf (My Struggle)*

Russian-born Jewish scientist and statesman Chaim Weizmann becomes president of Zionist World Organization

Tokyo-Yokohama earthquake kills 120,000

1924

Lenin, U.S.S.R. premier, dies; Stalin emerges as Soviet strongman; Leon Trotsky's influence wanes

Stanley Baldwin becomes British prime minister; Winston Churchill, chancellor of the exchequer

1925

Locarno Pact: Germany agrees not to maintain or build fortifications in the Rhineland

Hitler reorganizes Nazi Party; publishes first volume of *Mein Kampf*

Boundaries between Irish Free State and Northern Ireland defined

Pahlavi dynasty founded in Iran, ending the 131-year Kajar dynasty; new leader is former army officer Reza Khan, who becomes Reza Shah Pahlavi

Sun Yat-sen, head of China's Nationalist Party, dies

Teachers' Pay

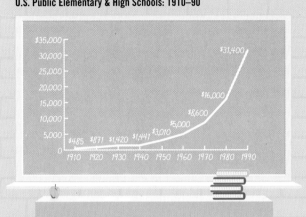

Average Annual Teaching Salary, U.S. Public Elementary & High Schools: 1910–90

Britain passes Unemployment Insurance Act, aimed at giving jobless some relief

Japan grants general men's suffrage in a move toward greater democratization

1926

Hitler Youth organization established; Joseph Goebbels becomes Nazi Party leader in Berlin, signaling Hitler's expansion from his power base in Bavaria

Stalin exiles Trotsky from the Soviet Union

General strike cripples Britain

Republic of Lebanon founded

French-Spanish forces subdue the fiercely independent Berber tribes, known as the Riffs, in Morocco

Ibn Saud declared king of Saudi Arabia

Hirohito is emperor of Japan

Mexico nationalizes Catholic Church property

1927

"Black Friday" in Germany; economy in ruins

Rioting in Austria

Civil war in China

1928

President Obregon of Mexico assassinated

First five-year economic plan begins in U.S.S.R.; many more will follow

Chiang Kai-shek becomes president of China

1929

Hitler appoints Heinrich Himmler reichsfuehrer SS, head of the black-uniformed elite security forces called the Schutzstaffel

Arabs and Jews clash in Palestine

◆

"The Italian proletariat needs a blood bath for its force to be renewed."

— Benito Mussolini in 1920

◆

Lateran Treaty, signed in Rome by Cardinal Gasparri for Pius XI and by Mussolini for King Victor Emmanuel III, creates independent Vatican City and recognizes Roman Catholicism as Italy's only state religion

U.S. HISTORY & POLITICS

1930

U.S. Depression deepens: 4.5 million unemployed, 1,300 bank failures

Smoot-Hawley Act raises tariffs, restricts trade; worldwide depression under way

> *"I am convinced we have seen the worst."*
>
> — President Herbert Hoover, 1930

President Hoover, hoping to stimulate economy, asks Congress for $100-million public works program

Republicans, who have controlled both houses of Congress since 1918, lose majority in House

U.S., Britain, and Japan continue limitation on naval armaments

U.S. Federal Bureau of Prisons established

Supreme Court rules liquor purchases do not violate 18th Amendment, which restricts liquor manufacture and sales

U.S. population: 123 million

1931

U.S. unemployment at 9 million, bank closings total 2,300

Over Hoover's veto, Congress increases the money World War I veterans can withdraw under the "bonus bill" of 1924; full cash payments finally authorized in 1936

Hoover, acknowledging world economic crisis, suggests one-year moratorium on war reparations

Hattie T. Caraway, an Arkansas Democrat, first woman appointed to U.S. Senate; elected the following year

"The Star-Spangled Banner" becomes the official national anthem

Social worker Jane Addams and educator Nicholas Murray Butler, both Americans, share the Nobel Peace Prize

1932

Franklin Delano Roosevelt elected 32nd president; John Nance Garner, vice president; they defeat Republicans Herbert Hoover and Charles Curtis

FDR coins the term *New Deal*

U.S. unemployment reaches 13.7 million

Jobless veterans march on Washington; U.S. troops, led by Gen. Douglas MacArthur, disperse them

U.S. and Canada agree to build the St. Lawrence Seaway

Lindbergh baby kidnapped; later found dead

1933

FDR temporarily shuts down all U.S. banks; gives first "fireside chats"; calls special session of Congress

Congress passes flurry of New Deal legislation, including Farm Credit Act and National Industrial Recovery Act (NIRA); the latter creates the National Recovery Administration (NRA)

Both 20th Amendment, setting presidential inauguration on Jan. 20, and 21st Amendment, repealing Prohibition, ratified

U.S. drops gold standard

Frances Perkins appointed secretary of labor; first woman Cabinet member

Ranger, first U.S. aircraft carrier, launched

1934

Congress continues to pass New Deal legislation

FDR initiates Good Neighbor Policy in Latin America

1935

Social Security Act becomes law; Rural Electrification Authority (REA) and Works Progress Administration (WPA) set up

U.S. senator Huey Long of Louisiana assassinated

Organized Labor's Ups and Downs

U.S. Union Membership As a percentage of the workforce, 1930–90

1930 11.6%
1940 26.9%
1950 31.5%
1960 31.4%
1970 27.3%
1980 21.9%
1990 16.1%

Supreme Court rules National Industrial Recovery Act is unconstitutional

1936

FDR and Garner reelected with huge majority, defeating Alfred M. Landon and W. Franklin Knox; Democrats dominate Congress

Congress passes Neutrality Act

Supreme Court rules against Agricultural Adjustment Act

Bruno Hauptmann, convicted of Lindbergh baby kidnapping and murder, executed

1937

FDR attempt to "pack" the Supreme Court by adding six justices defeated

1938

Reflecting U.S.-German tensions, both nations recall their ambassadors

U.S. House of Representatives establishes Committee on Un-American Activities

Supreme Court upholds "equality" of education for blacks and black petitioner's right to be admitted to University of Missouri Law School

1939

FDR asks Congress for defense budget of $1.3 billion; total budget is $9 billion

U.S. Supreme Court rules sit-down strikes illegal

FDR appoints William O. Douglas and Felix Frankfurter to the Supreme Court

EVERYDAY LIFE

1930

Apple sellers set up stands on city street corners

Hydraulic brakes, balloon tires, and self-starters now common on American cars

U.S. transcontinental air service on 3-engine, 12-passenger Ford monoplanes

Pundits proclaim that technological advances will transform America into a technocracy, or government by technical wizards

Coin-operated jukeboxes

Homemaking listed by U.S. government as an occupation

Al Capone arrested for income tax evasion

Betty Boop makes her debut in Max Fleischer's cartoon "Dizzy Dishes"

1931

Nevada legalizes gambling; casinos in Reno and Las Vegas hope to attract respectable tourists

In New York City, Empire State Building, world's tallest, opens; George Washington Bridge completed; Rockefeller Center construction begins

Dick Tracy comic strip debuts

Alka-Seltzer

Episcopal Church decides formally to permit remarriage after divorce

> *"Better the occasional faults of a government that lives in a spirit of charity than the constant omissions of a government frozen in the ice of its own indifference."*
>
> — President Franklin D. Roosevelt, accepting renomination in June 1936

1932

Amelia Earhart becomes first woman to fly solo across the Atlantic

Hoovervilles, breadlines, and soup kitchens multiply

Federal gasoline tax: 1 cent per gallon

RCA demonstrates TV picture

3 Musketeers candy bars

1933

World's Fair in Chicago

René Lacoste's cotton tennis shirt, *Le Crocodile*

Republican Fiorello La Guardia wins New York City mayoral election

First solo around-the-world flight; Wiley Post does it in 7 days 18 hours

Ritz crackers, 7-Up, Spam introduced

Alcatraz, maximum-security prison on island in San Francisco Bay, opens

Violence erupts as coal miners strike in Pennsylvania; governor calls out the National Guard

Earthquakes in Los Angeles

1934

Nylon developed

Dionne quintuplets, first known to have lived past earliest infancy, born in Ontario, Canada, to Elzire and Oliva Dionne; Annette, Émilie (the first to die, of an epileptic seizure, at age 20), Yvonne, Marie, and Cécile all lived into adulthood

John Dillinger, Public Enemy No. 1, killed by FBI agents

Congress establishes death penalty for kidnapping across state lines

Diesel locomotives in passenger-train service

Drought worsens in the Great Plains; wind storms cause black blizzards of top soil

Union Pacific train goes from New York City to Los Angeles in 57 hours

1935

Agriculture officials seek to control Great Plains "Dust Bowl" erosion; Soil Conservation Service set up

First acrylics: Lucite, Plexiglas

Pan Am World Airways begins transpacific service: San Francisco to Manila in the Philippines

Will Rogers dies in Alaska plane crash with his friend, aviator Wiley Post

By the 1930's drive-up, carryout establishments like this teapot-topped ice cream parlor in Hollywood were sprouting up everywhere in America.

Rumba latest dance craze

Alcoholics Anonymous organized

European cars offer front-wheel drive

First canned beer

Fluorescent lighting demonstrated

1936

Dale Carnegie's self-help book, *How to Win Friends and Influence People*

Exodus from Dust Bowl region reaches peak

Life magazine begins publication

Two luxury ocean liners go into service: France's *Normandie* and Britain's *Queen Mary*

Waring blender, early electric food blender, promoted by popular bandleader Fred Waring

17-year locusts appear in the Northeast

Boulder (later renamed Hoover) Dam, on Colorado River between Arizona and Nevada, provides Southwest with hydroelectric power; forms Lake Mead

First low-income government housing units, in Greenbelt, Maryland; Public Works Administration constructs two-story apartment building

1937

San Francisco's Golden Gate Bridge opens

German dirigible *Hindenburg* explodes in Lakehurst, New Jersey; disaster reported live on national radio

Howard Hughes sets new transcontinental flying record: 7 hours 28 minutes

Aviatrix Amelia Earhart disappears while flying over the Pacific in an attempt to circle the globe

Xerography invented

Polyurethane, polystyrene

First cellophane tape on sale

First grocery carts

1938

Teflon

Some 20,000 TV sets in use in New York City area

British ocean liner *Queen Elizabeth* launched

Howard Hughes circumnavigates world in

3 days 9 hours 17 minutes

Hurricane devastates New England

Orson Welles's radio version of H. G. Wells's *War of the Worlds* terrifies listeners, who believe Martians have actually invaded America

Ballpoint pen patented

First commercial use of nylon: toothbrush bristles

1939

World's Fair opens in New York City

Goldfish swallowing

Roller-skate dancing the rage; women skaters popularize full skirts with matching bloomers

Cigarette manufacturers, fearful war will cut European paper supplies, develop domestic substitute

ARTS & LETTERS

1930

American writer Sinclair Lewis becomes first American to win Nobel Prize for literature

English actor and dramatist Noël Coward's comedy *Private Lives*

American writer William Faulkner's *As I Lay Dying*

German expressionist painter Max Beckmann's "Self Portrait With Saxophone"

Hungarian composer Béla Bartók's vocal work *Cantata Profana: The Nine Enchanted Stags*

American writer Dashiell Hammett's *The Maltese Falcon,* with the hard-boiled detective character Sam Spade

American playwright Marc Connelly's religious drama *The Green Pastures,* with an all-black cast

American writer Katherine Anne Porter's short-story collection *Flowering Judas*

American painter Grant Wood's "American Gothic"

German-born American composer and violist Paul Hindemith's *Concerto for Viola and Chamber Orchestra*

1931

American novelist Pearl Buck's *The Good Earth*

French painter Pierre Bonnard's "The Breakfast Room"

Spanish surrealistic painter Salvador Dali's "The Persistence of Memory"

French painter Henri Matisse's "The Dance" murals

Australian soprano Nellie Melba and Russian ballerina Anna Pavlova die

English composer William Walton's oratorio *Belshazzar's Feast*

American writer William Faulkner's novel *Sanctuary*

"There are three things which I shall never forget about America — the Rocky Mountains, the Statue of Liberty, and Amos 'n' Andy."

— George Bernard Shaw, 1933

German philosopher Oswald Spengler's *Mankind and Technology*

American philosopher and educator John Dewey's *Philosophy and Civilization*

RCA-Victor releases first LP recording: Beethoven's *Fifth Symphony*

1932

American writer Ernest Hemingway's *Death in the Afternoon,* on bullfighting

American popular historian and philosopher Will Durant starts writing his multivolume *The Story of Civilization*

American writer William Faulkner's *Light in August*

Lithuanian-born American painter Ben Shahn's "Sacco and Vanzetti"

American composer Samuel Barber's *Overture to School for Scandal*

English writer Aldous Huxley's novel *Brave New World*

Sir Thomas Beecham establishes London Philharmonic Orchestra

American sculptor Alexander Calder shows his stabiles (stationary works) and mobiles (moving sculptures)

English painter Ben Nicholson's "Black Swans"

American architect Frank Lloyd Wright publishes both *An Autobiography* and *The Disappearing City;* founds the Taliesin Fellowship, a training program for architects and artists in Wisconsin and Arizona

American composer John Philip Sousa dies

American poet Archibald MacLeish's *Conquistador*

1933

American writer Gertrude Stein's *The Autobiography of Alice B. Toklas*

American writer Erskine Caldwell's novel *God's Little Acre*

"Mellon pulled the whistle /
Hoover rang the bell /
Wall Street gave the signal/
And the country went to hell."

— *Depression doggerel*

American historical novelist Hervey Allen's *Anthony Adverse*

Exiled Russian Communist leader Leon Trotsky's three-volume *The History of the Russian Revolution*

French writer and art historian André Malraux's *La Condition*

WHAT IT COST

Prices: 1930

Hudson seal fur coats, $150 and $295

Women's shoes, $14 and $16.50; suede handbag, $22.50

Women's suits, $45; lace frocks, $49.95; negligees, $29.50; corsets, $5 and $10

Men's suits, $39.50; shirts, $1.65; shoes, $11.20 to $12.80

Men's overcoats, $37.50, $47.50, $57.50

Boy's 2-trouser suit, $28.50

Gladstone bag, $19.50

Radio, $158; Atwater Kent radio, $109

Plane fare NY–LA round-trip, $159.92 (reduction of $107.51)

NY hotel room with bath, $3 for single occupant, $4 for double, $18 and $21 weekly respectively

Bath towels, 48¢

Vacuum cleaner, $52.50 new, $17.95 rebuilt

10-piece Hepplewhite dining room suite (6 chairs), $490

Movie tickets, 10–75 ¢

Cruise to Bermuda, $70; 14-day West Indies cruise, $140

Chevrolet roadster, $495; coupe, $565; sedan, $675

16-ft. motorboat, $945

NY apartments: 2-room East 54 St., $66 monthly; 3-room East 93 St., $1,100 yearly; Tudor City 3-room, 1-bath, $127 monthly; 6-room, 3-bath, $237

Humaine (*Man's Fate,* 1934 English translation)

English novelist James Hilton's *Lost Horizon;* a Hollywood film version made in 1937

Tobacco Road, a play by Jack Kirkland based on Erskine Caldwell's 1932 novel, opens on Broadway

American composer Aaron Copland's *The Short Symphony*

Russian-born American choreographer George Balanchine and patron Lincoln Kirstein establish the School of American Ballet

1934

American writer F. Scott Fitzgerald's *Tender Is the Night*

English composer Benjamin Britten's *Fantasy Quartet*

British author Robert Graves's historical novel *I, Claudius*

English novelist James Hilton's *Goodbye, Mr. Chips*

Russian composer, pianist, and conductor Sergei Rachmaninoff's *Rhapsody on a Theme of Paganini*

American writer John O'Hara's

novel *Appointment in Samarra*

Orchestral version of Paul Hindemith's *Mathis der Maler* causes uproar in Berlin; Nazis ban it, denounce Hindemith as a "spiritual non-Aryan"

1935

American novelist Thomas Wolfe's *Of Time and the River*

American writer Clarence Day's *Life With Father;* in 1939 a successful Broadway play

American-born British poet and critic T. S. Eliot's verse drama *Murder in the Cathedral*

Swedish theologian Karl Barth's *Credo*

Russian composer Sergei Prokofiev's ballet music *Romeo and Juliet*

John Steinbeck's novel *Tortilla Flat*

English firm Penguin Books' paperbound books catch on, presage the paperback revolution in book publishing

American dramatist Clifford Odets's *Waiting for Lefty*

1936

Margaret Mitchell's *Gone With the Wind*

American dramatist Eugene O'Neill wins Nobel Prize for literature

Final book in writer John Dos Passos' *U.S.A.* trilogy published

Dutch painter Piet Mondrian's "Composition in Red and Blue"

American composer Samuel Barber's *Symphony No. 1*

Welsh poet Dylan Thomas's *Twenty-Five Poems*

American writer Walter Edmonds's historical novel *Drums Along the Mohawk*

American journalist John Gunther's *Inside Europe*

American poet Robert Frost's collection *A Further Range*

1937

American literary critic Van Wyck Brooks's *The Flowering of New England*

Ernest Hemingway's novel *To Have and Have Not*

American historical novelist Kenneth Roberts's *Northwest Passage*

Spanish painter and sculptor Pablo Picasso's "Guernica"

Spanish painter Joan Miro's "Still Life With Old Shoe"

French painter Georges Braque's "Woman With a Mandolin"

Russian composer Dmitri Shostakovich's *Symphony No. 5*

American writer John P. Marquand's novel *The Late George Apley*

John Steinbeck's novel *Of Mice and Men*

1938

American playwright Thornton Wilder's *Our Town*

American composer Aaron Copland's ballet score *Billy the Kid*

Spanish-born American philosopher George Santayana's *The Realm of Truth*

American writer Carl Van Doren's biography *Benjamin Franklin*

British novelist Graham Greene's *Brighton Rock*

French painter Raoul Dufy's "Regatta"

Italian-born American composer Gian Carlo Menotti's first performed opera, *Amelia Goes to the Ball*

German composer Richard Strauss's opera *Daphne*

"Leaping lizards!
Who said
business is bad?"

— *Cartoon figure Little Orphan Annie*

Robert Sherwood's play *Abe Lincoln in Illinois*

American writer Marjorie Kinnan Rawlings's *The Yearling*

George S. Kaufman and Moss Hart's *The Man Who Came to Dinner* opens on Broadway

American writer Pearl S. Buck wins Nobel Prize

1939

John Steinbeck's *The Grapes of Wrath*

Welsh writer Richard Llewellyn's novel *How Green Was My Valley*

American-born British sculptor Jacob Epstein's "Adam"

Irish poet and dramatist W. B. Yeats dies

British sculptor Henry Moore's "Reclining Figure"

French painter Maurice Utrillo's "La Tour Saint Jacques"

American primitive painter Anna Mary Robertson Moses ("Grandma Moses") wins acclaim

---

ENTERTAINMENT & SPORTS

1930

Hell's Angels, produced by Howard Hughes, makes Jean Harlow a star

Radio detective program *The Shadow* premieres

Marx Brothers' film *Animal Crackers*

Hit songs: "I Got Rhythm," "Embraceable You," "Walkin' My Baby Back Home"

Germany's Max Schmeling wins world heavyweight boxing title

German-born American actress Marlene Dietrich stars in the film *Blue Angel*

Thoroughbred Gallant Fox takes horse racing's Triple Crown; jockey Earl Sande rides him home in the Kentucky Derby, Preakness, and Belmont Stakes races

Bobby Jones becomes first golfer to achieve a Grand Slam by winning all four major titles: U.S. Amateur and Open, British Amateur and Open

Philadelphia Athletics defeat St. Louis Cardinals in World Series 4 games to 2

1931

Charlie Chaplin writes, directs, and stars in *City Lights*

James Cagney and Jean Harlow in *Public Enemy*

Radio program *Little Orphan Annie* premieres

"When women go wrong, men go right after them."

— Mae West, in She Done Him Wrong (1933)

Boris Karloff in the movie *Frankenstein* plays his specialty, a monster

The first movie in full technicolor: Walt Disney's cartoon *Flowers and Trees*

George S. Kaufman and Morris Ryskind's satirical Broadway show *Of Thee I Sing,* with songs by George Gershwin

Notre Dame football coach Knute Rockne dies in plane crash

Hit songs: "Goodnight, Sweetheart," "When the Moon Comes Over the Mountain"

Ellsworth Vines, Helen Wills Moody win U.S. men's, women's tennis singles titles

St. Louis Cardinals defeat Philadelphia Athletics in World Series 4 games to 3

1932

American movie director and producer Cecil B. DeMille's *Sign of the Cross* continues his line of religious spectaculars

Greta Garbo, John and Lionel Barrymore, Joan Crawford, and Wallace Beery in Hollywood's *Grand Hotel*

Cole Porter's Broadway musical *The Gay Divorce* with Fred Astaire

Katharine Hepburn's first movie, *A Bill of Divorcement,* makes her a Hollywood star after successful Broadway roles

Jack Sharkey takes world heavyweight boxing title from Max Schmeling

Olympic Games in Los Angeles draw 1,400 athletes from 37 countries

New York Yankees defeat Chicago Cubs in World Series 4 games to 0

1933

Greta Garbo in the movie *Queen Christina*

King Kong, with Fay Wray in the hands of the big special-effects gorilla

Radio program *The Lone Ranger* premieres

Ruby Keeler, Dick Powell, and Ginger Rogers in the movie musical *42nd Street,* with dances choreographed by Busby Berkeley

Italian boxer Primo Carnera wins world heavyweight title

Busby Berkeley's innovative Hollywood musical *Gold Diggers of 1933*

Mae West stars with Cary Grant in *She Done Him Wrong;* speaks the famous line "Come up and see me sometime"

Jimmy and Tommy Dorsey form

one of the swing era's most popular orchestras

Radio City Music Hall opens in New York City; boasts world's largest movie screen: 70 feet wide by 40 feet tall

Katharine Hepburn in the movie *Little Women*

Hit songs: "Easter Parade," "Stormy Weather"

First baseball All-Star game

New York Giants defeat Washington Senators in World Series 4 games to 1

1934

Movie director Frank Capra's *It Happened One Night,* with Clark Gable and Claudette Colbert, wins five major Academy Awards

Shirley Temple sings "On the Good Ship Lollipop" in the film *Bright Eyes*

Fred Astaire and Ginger Rogers dance in the movie musical *The Gay Divorcée*

William Powell and Myrna Loy star in the movie *The Thin Man,* first in their lighthearted detective series

Cole Porter's Broadway musical *Anything Goes* debuts with

Ethel Merman

Benny Goodman organizes his swing band

Joe Louis wins his first professional fight

"I zigged when I should have zagged."

— Jack Roper after being knocked out by Joe Louis, 1939

New York's Madison Square Garden pioneers college basketball doubleheaders

St. Louis Cardinals defeat Detroit Tigers in World Series 4 games to 3

1935

George Gershwin's Broadway musical drama *Porgy and Bess*

Greta Garbo stars in the film *Anna Karenina*

British film director Alfred Hitchcock's suspense

thriller *The 39 Steps*

American film director John Ford's *The Informer* wins him his first Academy Award

Marx Brothers' *A Night at the Opera*

Fred Astaire and Ginger Rogers in Hollywood musical *Top Hat*

Jeanette MacDonald and Nelson Eddy in Hollywood version of Victor Herbert's 1910 operetta *Naughty Marietta*

Clark Gable, Charles Laughton in the film *Mutiny on the Bounty*

Hit songs: "Begin the Beguine," "I Got Plenty o' Nuthin'," "It Ain't Necessarily So"

Radio program *Fibber McGee and Molly* premieres

First night baseball game, in Cincinnati

Omaha, ridden by jockey W. Sanders, becomes third Triple Crown winner

College football's Heisman Trophy, awarded to season's outstanding player, established; first winner is University of Chicago running back Jay Berwanger

Two of the most popular film comedians of the 1930's, Mae West and W. C. Fields (born William Claude Dukenfield), finally get together in their first and only joint movie, My Little Chickadee, released in 1940.

Sex symbol Jean Harlow (born Harlean Carpentier) was just 26 when she died of uremic poisoning in 1937 after making more than 20 movies.

Detroit Tigers defeat Chicago Cubs in World Series 4 games to 2

1936

American black athlete Jesse Owens wins four gold medals at Olympic Games in Berlin

Charlie Chaplin's film *Modern Times*

Broadway musical *On Your Toes;* music and lyrics by Richard Rodgers and Lorenz Hart

New York Yankees defeat New York Giants in World Series 4 games to 2

1937

Walt Disney's first full-length animated film, *Snow White and the Seven Dwarfs*

Radio soap opera *Stella Dallas* premieres

Ventriloquist Edgar Bergen with his dummy Charlie McCarthy

quickly rises to become the country's top-rated radio program

Richard Rodgers and Lorenz Hart's Broadway musical *Babes in Arms*

Harold Rome's Broadway musical revue *Pins and Needles,* performed by ILGWU workers, starts run of more than 1,100 consecutive performances

French director and writer Jean Renoir's film *Grand Illusion*

Hit songs: "A Foggy Day in London Town," "I've Got My Love to Keep Me Warm," "Bei Mir Bist Du Schoen"

Joe Louis beats James J. Braddock, becomes world heavyweight boxing champion

War Admiral, ridden by jockey C. Kurtsinger, becomes the fourth horse to win the Triple Crown

U.S. beats Britain in Davis Cup tennis

New York Yankees beat New York Giants in World Series for second year in a row, 4 games to 1

1938

Swing innovator Glenn Miller forms his band

Benny Goodman and his orchestra play jazz concert at New York City's Carnegie Hall

Ella Fitzgerald writes (with bandleader Chick Webb) and sings "A-Tisket, A-Tasket," which becomes a national hit

Spencer Tracy and Mickey Rooney star in *Boys' Town*

Errol Flynn and Olivia de Havilland in the movie *The Adventures of Robin Hood*

Baseball Hall of Fame opens in Cooperstown, New York

Henry Fonda and Bette Davis in the film drama *Jezebel*

Leslie Howard in the British film version of *Pygmalion,* George Bernard Shaw's 1913 play

> *"You're the Nile,*
> *You're the*
> *tower of Pisa,*
> *You're the smile*
> *On the*
> *Mona Lisa. . . ."*
>
> — Cole Porter,
> Anything Goes (1934)

British suspense-film master Alfred Hitchcock directs *The Lady Vanishes*

America's Don Budge becomes first to achieve tennis Grand Slam, winning all four major titles in one year: Australian, French, British, and U.S.

Jockey Eddie Arcaro wins his first Kentucky Derby riding a horse named Lawrin

New York Yankees defeat Chicago Cubs in World Series 4 games to 0

1939

David O. Selznick's film version of Margaret Mitchell's novel *Gone With the Wind;* Clark Gable and Vivien Leigh star

Swedish actress Ingrid Bergman's first American film, a remake of *Intermezzo*

Judy Garland stars in *The Wizard of Oz*

John Ford's film *Stagecoach,* starring John Wayne

Greta Garbo stars in the film *Ninotchka*

James Stewart in Frank Capra's film *Mr. Smith Goes to Washington*

Gary Cooper stars in the film *Beau Geste*

Hit songs: "Roll Out the Barrel," "The Last Time I Saw Paris," and in Germany, "Lili Marlene"

First televised major-league baseball game: W2XBS telecasts Cincinnati Reds versus Brooklyn Dodgers at Ebbets Field in Brooklyn

Little League baseball founded

New York Yankees defeat Cincinnati Reds in World Series 4 games to 0

Baseball player Lou Gehrig sets record for consecutive games played: 2,130; retires suffering from fatal disease

BUSINESS & ECONOMICS

1930

Stock market doldrums continue

Great Atlantic and Pacific Tea Co. (A&P) becomes world's largest retailer

King Kullen "warehouse grocery" opens in Jamaica, New York; offers one-stop, self-service shopping, free parking

1931

Synthetic rubber

American inventor Thomas A. Edison dies

1932

Federal Reserve System reorganized

Reconstruction Finance

Corporation established

Glass-Steagall Act authorizes easing credit, selling off gold reserves as Depression-fighting measures

1933

Federal Deposit Insurance Corporation established

> *"Bankers are*
> *just like*
> *anybody else,*
> *except richer."*
>
> — Ogden Nash,
> I'm a Stranger Here Myself (1938)

Federal Securities Act

National Labor Board

1934

Export-Import Bank founded

Muzak Company supplies background music in the workplace

Federal Housing Administration helps mortgage-seekers

Radar demonstrated

1935

Wagner Act requires employers to accept collective bargaining

1936

Douglas DC-3 goes into service; becomes aviation's workhorse

Unemployment insurance begins; funded by 1-percent payroll tax

Sit-down strike at General Motors plant in Flint, Michigan, forces management to recognize United Automobile Workers

Robinson-Patman Act prohibits chain stores from selling at or below cost to drive out local competition

Walsh-Healy Act requires companies with government contracts to pay employees minimum wage, observe 40-hour workweek

Oil discovered in Saudi Arabia

1937

U.S. Steel Corporation, under threat of a sit-down strike, recognizes United Steel Workers; confrontation between Republic Steel workers and police ends with 10 demonstrators killed

1939

U.S. economy in upswing

United Mine Workers strike; win concessions

First jet airplane flight, in Germany

Russian-born American aeronautical engineer Igor Sikorsky builds and flies a direct-lift helicopter

Two U.S. aircraft builders, Northrop Aircraft and McDonnell-Douglas, founded

SCIENCE & MEDICINE

1930

Planet Pluto discovered

Antityphus serum

Yellow-fever vaccine

Electromechanical analog computer

Bathysphere used to explore ocean floor

Sigmund Freud's *Civilization and Its Discontents* published

Adler Planetarium, first in the U.S., opens in Chicago

1931

Vitamin A isolated

Cyclotron invented

Heavy water, with a heavy isotope of hydrogen called deuterium, separated from ordinary water; later used in regulating nuclear chain reactions

First electron microscope

First clinical use of penicillin

Sex hormone androsterone isolated

1932

Auguste Piccard ascends to altitude of 17.5 miles in a balloon

First example of antimatter: positrons (positive electrons)

1933

Insulin shock therapy developed for psychoses

Sodium pentathol used for anesthesia

Swiss psychologist Carl Jung's book *Psychology and Religion*

Vitamin B$_2$ isolated

Cosmic rays thought to be evidence of massive explosion creating the universe 10 billion years before

1934

Sex hormone progesterone identified

1935

Lobotomy, surgical cutting of brain's frontal lobe, used to treat mental illness

U-235, isotope of uranium, discovered; later used as a nuclear fuel

Sulfa drugs for streptococcal infections

1936

Oxygen tents for severe breathing difficulties

Austrian psychologist Sigmund Freud's *Autobiography*

Earth's inner core confirmed

1937

Insulin to control diabetes

> *"The most beautiful thing we can experience is the mysterious. It is the source of all true art and science."*
>
> — *Albert Einstein,* What I Believe (1930)

First blood bank

National Cancer Institute established

Electroshock therapy for schizophrenia

1938

Swiss chemists first manufacture LSD

Living coelacanth caught off the coast of Africa; primitive fish thought to have become extinct 60 million years ago

Uranium atom split

Vitamins E and B$_6$ discovered

1939

Rh factor identified in human blood

Vitamin K isolated

Nuclear fission: uranium bombarded by neutrons

WORLD POLITICAL EVENTS

1930

Nazi Party scores heavy gains in German elections

Mahatma Gandhi, continuing to preach nonviolence, leads 200-mile march demanding Indian independence from Britain

Revolutions in Argentina and Brazil

Emperor Haile Selassie begins reign in Ethiopia

Osachi Hamaguchi, Japanese prime minister, shot by right-wing assassin, later dies of wounds

1931

Oswald Mosley forms a fascist party in Britain

Japan occupies Manchuria

1932

Nazis win majority in German Reichstag elections; Adolph Hitler, Austrian-born, becomes German citizen

Famine in U.S.S.R.; second five-year plan begins

Japan accused of pricing goods under cost to gain market share

1933

Adolph Hitler appointed German chancellor; Reichstag fire in Berlin further bolsters Nazis; Hitler given dictatorial authority

Germany begins to rearm; Joseph Goebbels named minister of propaganda, Hermann Goering, Prussian prime minister

Germany and Japan quit the League of Nations

Stalin purges opposition in U.S.S.R.; restores diplomatic relations with the U.S.

1934

Hitler takes title of "fuehrer," meets Mussolini in Venice, solidifies power in "Night of the Long Knives"

Japan renounces naval arms treaties that limit size of its navy and ships

Mao Tse-tung starts "Long March," a retreat to Shanghai, which saves his Red Chinese Army

U.S.S.R. joins the League of Nations

1935

Germany absorbs the Saar; adopts compulsory military service

Italy invades Ethiopia

Stalin stages "show trials," effectively purging Soviet Union of Communist leaders he did not trust

1936

Civil war erupts in Spain

Britain's George V dies; Edward VIII succeeds him, despite rumors of his relationship with American divorcée Wallis Simpson; Edward abdicates in order to marry Mrs. Simpson and is succeeded by his brother George VI

Germany occupies Rhineland; German elections give Hitler 99 percent of vote

Creation of the Axis: Hitler and Mussolini pledge a joint foreign policy for Germany and Italy; Germany signs anti-Communist agreement with Japan

1937

Neville Chamberlain becomes British prime minister; pursues appeasement of Hitler

Japan invades China; Chiang Kai-shek's Nationalists join

with Mao's Communists to meet the threat

1938

Germany annexes Austria

Winston Churchill leads anti-appeasement movement in Britain; France calls up reservists

Spanish Nationalists bomb Barcelona

> *"I have found it impossible to carry the heavy burden of responsibility and to discharge my duties as King as I would wish to do without the help and support of the woman I love."*
>
> — *Edward, duke of Windsor, in December 1936 after his abdication*

Chinese Nationalists retreat to Chungking, new capital

1939

German invasion of Poland triggers World War II; Britain and France declare war; FDR declares U.S. neutral

Germany annexes Danzig, absorbs Czechoslovakia; Hitler signs alliance with Italy, nonaggression pact with U.S.S.R.

Britain evacuates women and children from London; issues gas masks to Londoners

British Expeditionary Force arrives in France to fight German invasion

U.S.S.R. invades Finland and eastern Poland

Spanish Civil War ends as Franco captures Madrid

Pope Pius XII elected by College of Cardinals

U.S. HISTORY & POLITICS

1940

Congress passes Selective Service Act, first peacetime draft

U.S. authorizes sale of surplus war matériel to Britain

Alien Registration Act passed; affects 5 million aliens living in U.S.

U.S. permits sale of arms to South America; tells Germany that attempts to take over French and Dutch colonies in the Western Hemisphere will not be tolerated

$3 million; no individual may contribute more than $5,000

FDR reelected for third term; first and only president elected for more than two terms; his new vice president is Henry A. Wallace; they defeat Republicans Wendell L. Willkie and Charles L. McNary

U.S. population: some 132 million; 7.3-percent increase is lowest 10-year increase since record keeping began

1941

U.S. makes lend-lease agreement with Britain; freezes Germany's assets in America

Supreme Court

House of Representatives votes 203 to 202 to extend draftees' army service for 18 months; FDR then signs this Selective Service extension

First use of paratroopers: in war games in Louisiana

California antimigrant law, aimed at keeping Okies out of state, ruled unconstitutional

FDR and British prime minister Winston Churchill confer at sea off Newfoundland coast; sign Atlantic Charter, joint statement of peace aims

Japanese-U.S. relations reach impasse; at end of November

U.S. declares war on Japan; Jeannette Rankin casts only dissenting vote in Congress; Axis powers declare war on America

U.S. outlaws discrimination against blacks in defense industry

National Defense Mediation Board formed to avert strikes by defense workers

1942

U.S. moves Japanese-Americans from West Coast to inland detention camps

Douglas MacArthur named commander in chief of Allied forces in the Far East

FBI captures German saboteurs put ashore in New York and Florida

1943

Winston Churchill and FDR confer in Casablanca on conduct of war

FDR and Churchill meet with Chiang Kai-shek in Cairo and with Stalin in Tehran

Pentagon building, new home for the War Department, completed in Arlington, Virginia

Enrico Fermi and Robert Oppenheimer are among the scientists on the atom bomb (Manhattan Project) research and development team at Los Alamos, New Mexico, under the command of Brig. Gen. Leslie R. Groves

U.S. Supreme Court rules that requiring students to salute the flag is unconstitutional

Anti-Strike Act forbidding job actions in war industries passes over FDR's veto

Construction begins in Washington State of two reactors to produce plutonium for atom bombs

1944

Congress establishes rank of five-star General of the Army

Dumbarton Oaks, a mansion in the Georgetown section of Washington, D.C., hosts

conference of Chinese, Soviet, British, and U.S. officials that lays plans for United Nations

FDR, with running mate, Harry S. Truman, wins fourth term, defeating Republican challengers, Thomas E. Dewey and John W. Bricker

"Our planes were destroyed on the ground! On the ground!"

— President Franklin D. Roosevelt, stunned by the Japanese attack on Pearl Harbor, December 7, 1941

1945

United Nations charter signed at ceremonies in San Francisco

Big Three Conference: FDR, Churchill, and Stalin confer at Yalta, a resort town on the Black Sea in the Crimean region of the Ukraine, Soviet Union

Franklin Roosevelt dies; Vice President Harry S. Truman succeeds him

U.S. tests first atom bomb, in Alamogordo, New Mexico

Truman, Churchill (replaced midway by new British prime minister, Clement Attlee), and Stalin meet at Potsdam, Germany, to discuss policies after the war

MAJOR MILITARY ACTIONS OF WORLD WAR II

1940

Germany invades France, Belgium, Holland, Luxembourg, Denmark, Norway

Some 380,000 British and other Allied troops evacuated from Dunkirk

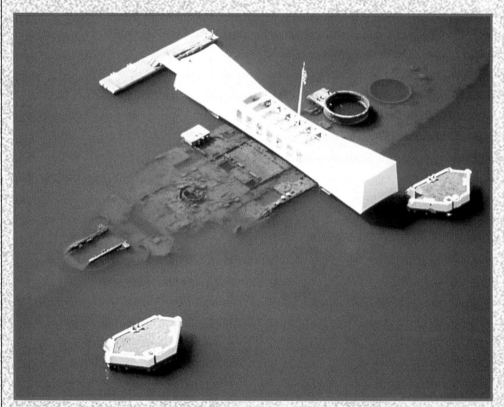

Dedicated in 1962, the gleaming white Arizona Memorial lies over the sunken hulk of the battleship U.S.S. Arizona, the tomb of about 1,000 marines and navy men who went down with the ship on December 7, 1941.

U.S. sells destroyers to Britain

U.S. 1940 political campaign: limited television coverage of Democratic and Republican conventions, election returns

Presidential campaign expenditures restricted to

U.S. Office of Scientific Research and Development (OSRD) set up; oversees work on atom bomb and other projects

FDR names Robert H. Jackson and James F. Byrnes to

U.S. War and Navy departments warn Pacific commanders of possibility of Japanese attacks

December 7: Japanese bomb Pearl Harbor; U.S. fleet suffers major losses, carriers escape

The zany antics of Portuguese-born "Brazilian bombshell" Carmen Miranda delighted GI's and civilians alike in wartime Hollywood musicals.

Germans enter Paris

Blitz of London — night bombing by planes of the Luftwaffe (German Air Force) — begins, continues into 1941

RAF (Royal Air Force of Britain) counters Blitz with night bombing of Germany

"Sighted sub, sank same."

— *U.S. Navy pilot Donald F. Mason, reporting sinking of German submarine with depth charges, January 28, 1942*

Battle of Britain: RAF sweeps the skies over England; prevents a German invasion

Germany steps up U-boat attacks

British 8th Army goes on offensive in North Africa

1941

German general Rommel assumes command of Axis forces in North Africa

Germans land in Crete

German super battleship *Bismarck* sunk in North Atlantic after repeated torpedoing and bombardment by British ships

Germany invades U.S.S.R., making huge gains; enters the Ukraine; reaches outskirts of Leningrad and Moscow

Soviets launch counter-offensive against German invaders

Pearl Harbor

British battleship *Prince of Wales* and battle cruiser *Repulse* sunk by Japanese torpedo planes near Singapore

Japanese invade Philippines

Hong Kong surrenders

1942

Japan invades Dutch East Indies, Burma, Singapore; Philippines fall; Japanese troops force American and Filipino prisoners of war to take infamous Bataan Death March

Jimmy Doolittle bombs Toyko

In Battle of the Coral Sea, U.S. naval and air forces halt Japanese drive to Port Moresby, New Guinea; both sides suffer severe losses

U.S. wins Battle of Midway, first major engagement fought entirely by carrier-based forces

Rommel battles with British field marshal Montgomery at El Alamein; U.S. troops land in North Africa; Rommel pushed back

British-led troops in Burma take the offensive against Japanese, with mixed results

Britain steps up bombing attacks on Germany

French fleet scuttled in Toulon

1943

Island-hopping in the Pacific: U.S. takes Guadalcanal in the Solomons, lands in New Guinea, captures Tarawa in the Gilberts

German forces defeated with huge losses at Stalingrad

Dwight Eisenhower assumes command of Allied North African forces; U.S. and British troops unify; Tunis and Bizerte fall; Germany's African army surrenders

Allies land in Sicily, then Italy; U.S. 7th Army under Gen. George S. Patton, Jr., takes Palermo and Naples

Nonstop Allied bombing of Germany commences

RAF smashes Berlin; U.S. bombers hit Romanian oil fields at Ploesti

1944

U.S. 5th Army in Italy attacks at Cassino

Allied landings at Anzio, 33 miles south of Rome

Allies take Rome, June 4

June 6: D-Day in Normandy: Allies land greatest invasion force in history; Eisenhower is supreme commander

British capture Florence, Italy

British airborne assault on Arnhem, Netherlands, fails

Germans now retreating on two fronts: from U.S. and Allied forces in the west, from Soviet forces in the east

Allies liberate Paris at end of August, cross German frontier

Battle of the Bulge, last major German offensive on the western front, begins in December, ends in January 1945 with German defeat

Russians attack in the Ukraine, rout Germans at Minsk, enter Brest Litovsk

Soviet forces occupy Hungary and Yugoslavia

Island-hopping in Pacific continues: Americans take Guam in the Marianas

U.S. naval and air forces win Battle of Leyte Gulf; American troops under Douglas MacArthur land in Philippines

1945

U.S. and British troops cross the Rhine River at Remagen, move deeper into Germany

U.S. forces capture Manila, capital of the Philippines, occupied by the Japanese since 1942

Soviet forces take Warsaw, Krakow, Budapest; reach Oder River

U.S. troops take Iwo Jima and Okinawa

"Wars are not 'acts of God.' They are made by man. . . . What man has made, man can change."

— *Frederick M. Vinson, future chief justice of the Supreme Court, at Arlington Cemetery, Memorial Day, 1945*

Allies triumphant in Burma

Soviet army enters Berlin; meets U.S. troops

U.S. drops atom bombs on two Japanese cities, Hiroshima and Nagasaki

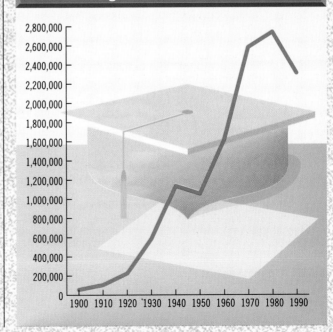

U.S. Public High School Graduates: 1900–90

EVERYDAY LIFE

1940

War in Europe results in mass migration of artists, composers, writers, and scientists to America

Oglethorpe University in Georgia puts bottle of beer, encyclopedia, movie fan magazine, and hundreds of similar artifacts in "Crypt of Civilization" time capsule, to be opened in 8113

Electronic flash for camera marketed

Dances: the jitterbug, conga line, lindy hop, kangaroo jump

Life expectancy is 64; it was 49 in 1900

Nylon stockings in; silk stockings on the way out

Tacoma (Washington) Narrows Bridge collapses in high winds; design flaw blamed

Kings Canyon National Park created in California

First 160 miles of Pennsylvania Turnpike open

Earl Tupper invents Tupperware

1941

U.S. savings bonds and stamps

Rationing of auto tires starts

M&M candies — for GI's

"Comin' In on a Wing and a Prayer."

— Title of a song written by Harold Adamson in 1943

Regular TV broadcasting, though number of receivers is very small

Dacron, a synthetic polyester textile fiber, introduced

Greta Garbo chooses seclusion

Mt. Rushmore National Monument completed: faces

Simplicity prevailed in wartime fashions, as in this 1942 dress worn by actress Brenda Marshall.

more than 50 feet high of Washington, Jefferson, Lincoln, and Teddy Roosevelt carved out of granite cliff in Black Hills of South Dakota

Grand Coulee Dam, on Columbia River in Washington, completed

Cheerios on sale

Slumber parties popular with teenage girls

Aerosol can invented

Lincoln Continental, American luxury car, makes untimely debut as war threatens

Le Pavillon, legendary French restaurant, opens in New York City

1942

GI's get free mailing privileges

Women enlist for noncombat military service in WAACS (Women's Auxiliary Army Corps), WAVES (Women Appointed for Voluntary Emergency Service), WAFS (Women's Auxiliary Ferrying Squadron), SPARS (*Semper Paratus* Always Ready Service), and Women's Reserve of the Marine Corps

"Look at an infantryman's eyes, and you can tell how much war he has seen."

— Bill Mauldin, cartoon caption in Up Front (1944)

U.S. lowers draft age to 18

Supreme Court rules Nevada divorces are legal in other states

Coconut Grove nightclub fire in Boston kills hundreds; fire doors fail

Rents frozen for the duration of the war

Employment shortage; more women go to work

1943

FDR orders 48-hour workweek in areas of labor shortage; time-and-a-half pay for hours over 40

Income tax withholding on wages introduced

Baggy, pleated, double-breasted zoot suits become antiestablishment symbols

Rationing continues to tighten on many kinds of food and also on shoes

Wage and price freeze

Salvage drives collect scrap for the war effort

Polio epidemic kills hundreds, cripples thousands

Scrabble

1944

GI Bill of Rights signed

First eye bank

First nightly national TV newscast

Ringling Brothers and Barnum & Bailey Circus fire kills 163 persons in Hartford, Connecticut

Black markets grow; estimated illegal annual gross is $1 billion

Inflation rampant

1945

B-25 bomber crashes into the Empire State Building at the 78th and 79th floors; 13 die

Silly Putty developed

Water fluoridation introduced

ARTS & LETTERS

1940

American writer and journalist Ernest Hemingway's novel *For Whom the Bell Tolls*, about the Spanish Civil War

American black author Richard Wright's novel *Native Son*

American philosopher, educator, and editor Mortimer Adler's *How to Read a Book*

British novelist Graham Greene's *The Power and the Glory*

Hungarian-born British writer Arthur Koestler's novel *Darkness at Noon*

German expressionist painter and printmaker Max Beckmann's "Circus Caravan"

American writer Carl Sandburg wins Pulitzer Prize for *Abraham Lincoln: The War Years*, his biography of Lincoln, which Sandburg began writing in 1920

American writer Carson McCullers's novel *The Heart Is a Lonely Hunter*

English writer Eric Ambler's *Journey Into Fear*, one of his many novels dealing with international espionage and crime

American writers Elliott Nugent and James Thurber's Broadway comedy *The Male Animal*

Electronics Hits Home

Percentage of U.S. Households With Telephones, Radios, TV's: 1920–90

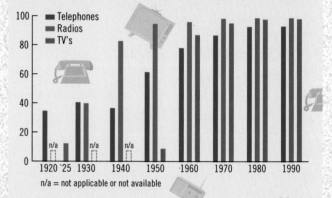

n/a = not applicable or not available

Numbers of U.S. Telephones, Radios, TV's: 1920–90 (in millions)

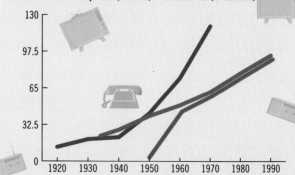

WHAT IT COST

Prices: 1940

Daily, Sunday newspapers, 3¢, 10¢

Mink coats, $1,500 to $1,900; Persian coats, $295 to $595

Woman's dinner dress, $49.99; print dresses, $35; woman's hat, $10

Women's suits, $15; coats, $19.95 to $39.95

Corsets, $7.95 to $9.95

Skis, $12.94

Men's shoes, $7.95 to $9.95; shirts, $1.85 to $3.85

Men's suits, $20 to $29.50; overcoats, $35 to $85

Hotel weekend in Asbury Park, NJ, $5.50 per person inc. meals

Scotch, $2.89 a bot.; gin, 99¢; rye, $1.39; French red wine, 83¢ a bot., $4.79 for 6 bots.

Radio consoles, $39.95

Hudson 6 Sedan, $793

Radio-phonograph, $69.95

B'way ticket, 55¢ to $3.30

10-piece dining room set, $895; sofa and two armchairs, $169

26-oz. bot. tomato juice, 17¢

Spin-dry washers, $59.95

Man's pipe, $1

Soap, 2½¢ a cake

Upright piano, $365; refrigerators, $119.95 to $189.50

Elizabeth Arden skin cream, $1 to $6; Arden lipstick, rouge, eye shadow kit, $4

Carnegie Hall tickets, 75¢ to $2.75

15 days in Mexico, all inclusive, $278.70

4-room apartment on West 72 St., New York City, $105 mo.; 3-room on East 74 St., $1,200 yearly

---

European composers now in the U.S. include Béla Bartók (Hungarian), Paul Hindemith (German), Arnold Schoenberg (Austrian), Igor Stravinsky (Russian), Kurt Weill (German)

French painter Édouard Vuillard and Swiss painter Paul Klee die

1941

Scottish physician and novelist A. J. Cronin's *The Keys of the Kingdom*

American author James Agee and American photographer Walker Evans's text-and-picture book about Alabama sharecroppers, *Let Us Now Praise Famous Men*

National Gallery of Art opens in Washington, D.C.

German dramatist Bertolt Brecht's *Mother Courage and Her Children*, with music by Paul Dessau, performed in Zurich, Switzerland

English actor and dramatist Noël Coward's *Blithe Spirit*

American painter Edward

Hopper's "Nighthawks"

1942

American religious educator and writer Lloyd C. Douglas's *The Robe*

A private in the U.S. Army, Marion Hargrove, writes humorously about his experiences in the wartime bestseller *See Here, Private Hargrove*

American writer William Faulkner's novel *Go Down, Moses*

American journalist William Shirer's *Berlin Diary: The Journal of a Foreign Correspondent*

English poet laureate John Masefield's tribute to those responsible for the successful evacuation of Dunkirk, *The Nine Days of Wonder*

American theologian Reinhold Niebuhr's *The Nature and Destiny of Man*

British sculptor Henry Moore's drawings of Londoners during the Blitz

English composer Benjamin Britten's *Violin Concerto*

Russian composer Dmitri Shostakovich's *Symphony No. 7*, composed during the Germans' siege of Leningrad

American author Thornton Wilder's Broadway play *The Skin of Our Teeth*

American journalist William L. White's bestseller *They Were Expendable*, about PT-boat action against the Japanese in the Pacific

American-born English poet T. S. Eliot's *Four Quartets*

French novelist Albert Camus's *The Stranger*

English novelist C. S. Lewis's *The Screwtape Letters*

French painter Georges Braque's "Patience"

French painter Pierre Bonnard's "Blue Bird"

American writer Philip Wylie's wide-ranging attack on American values and institutions, *Generation of Vipers*

American composer Aaron Copland and American choreographer Agnes de Mille team up on the ballet *Rodeo*

"*Books cannot be killed by fire. People die, but books never die. No man and no force can abolish memory. . . . In this war, we know, books are weapons.*"

— Franklin D. Roosevelt, to the American Booksellers Association, 1942

1943

American writer William Saroyan's *The Human Comedy*

American novelist Betty Smith's *A Tree Grows in Brooklyn*

American poet Robert Frost's collection *A Witness Tree*

French dramatist, novelist, and philosopher Jean-Paul Sartre's *Being and Nothingness* sets out his basic views on existentialism

Dutch painter Piet Mondrian's "Broadway Boogie Woogie"

English sculptor Henry Moore's "Madonna and Child"

Russian-born French painter Marc Chagall's "The Juggler"

American war correspondent Richard Tregaskis's fighter's-eye view of the first major U.S. landing in the Pacific, *Guadalcanal Diary;* becomes a Hollywood movie the same year

American war correspondent Ernie Pyle's *Here Is Your War*, a collection of his frontline dispatches that were popular with soldiers and civilians alike

American flying ace and writer Robert L. Scott, Jr.'s, *God Is My Co-Pilot*, a firsthand account of the China-Burma air war

American abstract expressionist painter Jackson Pollack's first one-man exhibit, at a New York City gallery

American regionalist painter Thomas Hart Benton's "July Hay"

American poet Stephen Vincent Benét's unfinished verse epic *Western Star*, published posthumously

1944

English novelist W. Somerset Maugham's *The Razor's Edge*

American novelist John Hersey's *A Bell for Adano*

French painter Georges Rouault's "Homo, Homini, Lupus"

Russian composer Sergei Prokofiev's vocal work *War and Peace*

British novelist Joyce Cary's *The Horse's Mouth*

American novelist Charles Jackson's *The Lost Weekend*

Danish author Isak (Karen

Christence) Dinesen's *Winter Tales*

American author and social critic Lewis Mumford's *The Condition of Man*

1945

American dramatist Tennessee Williams's *The Glass Menagerie* opens on Broadway

English author George Orwell's novel *Animal Farm*

Austrian-born Israeli philosopher Martin Buber's *For the Sake of Heaven*

Broadway stars ran the Stage Door Canteen for GI's, and in 1943 this movie told the story.

American-born British sculptor Jacob Epstein's "Lucifer"

Russian-born American abstract painter Max Weber's "Brass-band"

German composer Richard Strauss's instrumental work *Metamorphoses*

Russian composer Sergei Prokofiev's ballet score *Cinderella*

English writer Evelyn Waugh's novel *Brideshead Revisited*

American novelist Sinclair Lewis's *Cass Timberlane*

ENTERTAINMENT & SPORTS

1940

Charlie Chaplin plays both the Tramp and a Hitler figure in Chaplin's first talking picture, *The Great Dictator*

Welsh playwright Emlyn Williams's *The Corn Is Green* opens on Broadway

American director John Ford's film *The Grapes of Wrath*, starring Henry Fonda

Walt Disney's animated film *Fantasia* uses a sound track by the Philadelphia Orchestra, conducted by Leopold Stokowski

Katharine Hepburn, Cary Grant, and James Stewart in the movie *The Philadelphia Story*

Bing Crosby, Bob Hope, and Dorothy Lamour make the first of seven "Road" films, *Road to Singapore*

British film director Alfred Hitchcock's *Rebecca*

Gaslight, Hollywood remake of a British film, stars Swedish-born Ingrid Bergman and French actor Charles Boyer

Jazz musician Duke Ellington's reputation as a serious composer grows

Richard Rodgers and Lorenz Hart's Broadway musical *Pal Joey*

Hit songs: "The Last Time I Saw Paris," "Oh, Johnny," "When You Wish Upon a Star," "Blueberry Hill"

Popular radio shows: *The Shadow, Fibber McGee and Molly, The Jack Benny Show, Gangbusters*

U.S. tennis men's singles title won by W. Donald McNeill; women's singles title, by Alice Marble

Southern California beats Tennessee in the Rose Bowl 14–0

Cincinnati Reds defeat Detroit Tigers in World Series 4 games to 3

1941

Orson Welles in the title role of the movie masterpiece *Citizen Kane,* which he also directed and produced

American film director John Ford's *How Green Was My Valley*

Humphrey Bogart plays hard-boiled private eye Sam Spade in Hollywood's *The Maltese Falcon,* directed by John Huston

Walt Disney's *Dumbo*

Hit songs: "Deep in the Heart of Texas," "Chattanooga Choo Choo," "White Cliffs of Dover," "Boogie Woogie Bugle Boy"

Long-running radio show *Duffy's Tavern* premieres

First baseball helmets, to protect against pitched balls, tested by Brooklyn Dodgers

Whirlaway, ridden by jockey Eddie Arcaro, wins horse racing's Triple Crown: Kentucky Derby, Preakness, and Belmont Stakes

Lou (Iron Horse) Gehrig dies; New York Yankee played in 2,130 consecutive games, 1925–39

> *"There are no atheists in the foxholes."*
>
> — Sermon by Father William T. Cummings, serving as a chaplain on Bataan, the Philippines, 1942

New York Yankees Joe DiMaggio sets long-standing record of hitting safely in 56 consecutive games

New York Yankees defeat Brooklyn Dodgers in World Series 4 games to 1

1942

Walt Disney's *Bambi*

Humphrey Bogart and Ingrid Bergman in *Casablanca*

British actress Greer Garson in Hollywood's *Mrs. Miniver*

Bing Crosby and Fred Astaire in Hollywood musical *Holiday Inn*

Hit songs: "White Christmas," "Praise the Lord and Pass the Ammunition," "That Old Black Magic," "I Left My Heart at the Stage Door Canteen," "Paper Doll"

St. Louis Cardinals defeat New York Yankees in World Series 4 games to 1

1943

Richard Rodgers and Oscar Hammerstein's music and lyrics for Broadway musical

Oklahoma!, their first collaboration, with choreography by Agnes de Mille

Alfred Hitchcock's *Shadow of a Doubt*

Broadway musical *One Touch of Venus,* with music by Kurt Weill and lyrics by Ogden Nash, stars Mary Martin

Hit songs: "Oh, What a Beautiful Morning," "I'll Be Seeing You (in All the Old Familiar Places)," "Mairzy Doats"

Count Fleet wins Kentucky Derby, Preakness, and Belmont Stakes to take horse racing's Triple Crown; Johnny Longden the jockey

New York Yankees defeat St. Louis Cardinals in World Series 4 games to 1

1944

Lawrence Olivier is director and star of British film version of Shakespeare's *Henry V*

Alfred Hitchcock's *Lifeboat*

Bing Crosby and Barry Fitzgerald in *Going My Way*

Otto Preminger directs Gene Tierney and Dana Andrews in suspenseful Hollywood mystery *Laura*

Hit songs: "Don't Fence Me In," "Rum and Coca-Cola," "Accentuate the Positive"

Professional sports hard-pressed to find draft-exempt players; teams have many old and very young players, such as Cincinnati Reds 15-year-old pitcher Joe Nuxhall

Intracity World Series, last to be played entirely in one stadium: St. Louis Cardinals beat the St. Louis Browns 4 games to 2

1945

John Wayne in film version of William L. White's 1942 book *They Were Expendable*

Ray Milland and Jane Wyman in *The Lost Weekend,* based on Charles Jackson's novel published the year before

American musicians Dizzy Gillespie, Charlie Parker, and Thelonious Monk establish bebop as new direction for jazz

Pvt. Joe Louis says_

"We're going to do our part ...and we'll win because we're on God's side"

Heavyweight champ from 1937 to 1949, Louis donated his money, time, and name to the war effort.

Richard Rodgers and Oscar Hammerstein's *Carousel*

Open City — an Italian semidocumentary directed by Roberto Rossellini, script by Sergei Amidei and Federico Fellini, and featuring Anna Magnani — films suffering in wake of war as Germans retreat

Popular radio shows: *The Green Hornet, Superman, The Red Skelton Show, Inner Sanctum, Allen's Alley*

New York Yankees sold for $2.8 million

Jockey Eddie Arcaro wins his third Kentucky Derby

Detroit Tigers defeat Chicago Cubs in World Series 4 games to 3

BUSINESS & ECONOMICS

1940

Supreme Court rules California and Alabama laws that ban picketing are illegal

1941

U.S. embargoes oil shipments to Japan

Office of Price Administration and Civilian Supply set up; becomes Office of Price Administration (OPA) in 1942

Hasselblad develops first single-lens reflex camera with interchangeable lenses

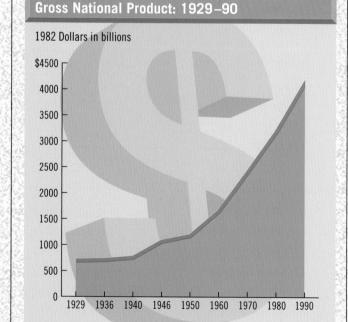

Gross National Product: 1929–90

1982 Dollars in billions

$4500	
4000	
3500	
3000	
2500	
2000	
1500	
1000	
500	
0	1929 1936 1940 1946 1950 1960 1970 1980 1990

Union Pacific puts world's largest steam locomotive in service: the 6,000-horsepower Big Boy

Quality Inns, a motel chain, founded

1942

War Production Board orders halt of nonessential building

1943

First Liberty cargo ships launched

Striking miners cut off coal production: U.S. takes over the mines

World's longest oil pipeline opens; the "Big Inch" stretches from Texas to Pennsylvania

1944

International Monetary Fund established

War Production Board allows manufacturers to increase output of consumer goods

1945

World Bank founded

Federal Communications Commission (FCC) allots 13 channels for TV broadcasting

SCIENCE & MEDICINE

1940

Penicillin developed as antibiotic

Cyclotron for atomic research goes into operation at the University of California

Freeze-drying of food

First vaccine against leprosy

1941

Element plutonium discovered by a team of American scientists led by Glenn Seaborg; it will be used in atomic reactors and weapons

Sulfadiazine becomes most widely used sulfa drug, effective against many types of infections

1942

First U.S. jet plane, Bell XP-59, flown

Italian-born American physicist Enrico Fermi achieves the first nuclear chain reaction, in an atomic pile at the University of Chicago

German scientists develop V-2 rocket

First electronic digital calculator

DDT, considered a miracle pesticide, is marketed

Aqua-Lung designed

Dexedrine, central nervous system stimulant, produced

1943

ACTH, a naturally occurring hormone produced by the pituitary gland, isolated

Streptomycin, an antibiotic that fights bacterial infection, developed

Army doctors prevent venereal disease with sulfathiazole

Silicones

1944

Quinine, important in fighting malaria and previously obtainable only from the bark of cinchona trees, synthesized

DNA, building block of heredity in living things, isolated

First atom bomb, equivalent to 20,000 tons of TNT, tested in desert at Alamogordo, New Mexico; its explosive power comes from plutonium

Scarlet fever successfully treated with penicillin

Science: The Endless Frontier

— Title of a book by Vannevar Bush, chairman of the U.S. Office of Scientific Research and Development, 1945

1945

Rocket-testing range established at White Sands, New Mexico

Dr. Benjamin Spock's *The Common Sense Book of Baby and Child Care* is published

WORLD POLITICAL EVENTS

1940

Italy declares war on Britain and France

Winston Churchill becomes British prime minister; gives "blood, toil, tears, and sweat" speech

Slacks fit women's wartime can-do spirit; and Broadway's Natalie Schafer showed them off in style.

France's premier, Marshal Henri Philippe Pétain, signs armistice with Germany, overruling many of his countrymen; Pétain then heads collaborationist Vichy government

Britain allies herself with Polish government-in-exile and with Free French under Charles de Gaulle

Rationing begins in Britain

Japan joins with Germany and Italy in a military and economic pact

Exiled Soviet leader Leon

Trotsky assassinated by Stalin's agents in Mexico

1941

Rudolf Hess, a trusted lieutenant of Hitler's, flies to Scotland, apparently intending to negotiate peace; he is jailed by British, later sentenced to life imprisonment for war crimes

1942

Gestapo head Reinhard Heydrich assassinated by British-trained Czech partisans; in reprisal, Nazis kill thousands

Nazis begin mass murder of Jews in gas chambers

1943

Italy surrenders to Allies, later declares war on Germany

1944

German army officers fail in attempt to assassinate Hitler

Germany's "desert fox," Field Marshal Erwin Rommel, commits suicide

Civil war in Greece, after Germans withdraw, between Communists and royalists

1945

V-2 rocket attacks on Britain cease

German army in Italy surrenders

Concentration camps liberated

Hitler commits suicide; Mussolini murdered by Italian partisans

Germany capitulates; V-E Day: May 8

Japan gives up (August 14); surrender signed on U.S. battleship *Missouri* in Tokyo Bay (September 2, V-J Day)

Douglas MacArthur heads Allied occupation of Japan; his administration lasts until 1951

Vietnam, led by Ho Chi Minh, unilaterally declares independence from France

Germany cut into four zones of military occupation, with Great Britain, France, the Soviet Union, and the United States each controlling a

sector; Berlin similarly divided into four zones

Churchill overwhelmingly rejected by British voters; Clement Attlee succeeds him as prime minister

Vidkun Quisling, Norwegian wartime leader who collaborated with the Nazis, executed for high treason

World War II dead: some 50 million, including 10 million victims of Nazi concentration camps

Nationalists and Communists fight to control China

"We shall fight on the beaches . . . we shall fight in the fields and in the streets . . . we shall never surrender."

— British Prime Minister Winston Churchill, after the evacuation from Dunkirk, June 4, 1940

Arab League, a loose alliance of Arab nations, founded to advance Arab unity; its original members are Egypt, Iraq, Lebanon, Saudi Arabia, Syria, Transjordan, and Yemen

Nuremberg trials of Nazi war criminals begin

Marshal Tito heads Communist regime in Yugoslavia

Charles de Gaulle, Free French leader, elected president of liberated France's provisional government

Europe impoverished; black markets flourish

War in Indochina looms as French seek to reassert control of their former colonial holdings in Southeast Asia (Vietnam, Laos, and Cambodia)

U.S. HISTORY & POLITICS

1946

U.N. General Assembly holds first meeting in London; Norway's Trygve Lie elected secretary-general; John D. Rockefeller, Jr., gives $8.5 million for U.N. center in New York City

U.S. grants independence to Philippines

U.S. troops will remain in South Korea until 1949, when Soviets leave North Korea

U.S. establishes Atomic Energy Commission

Wartime spy agency OSS (Office of Strategic Services) becomes CIA (Central Intelligence Agency)

U.S. conducts nuclear weapons tests in the Pacific

1947

Congress approves aid to Greece and Turkey; policy to resist Communist aggression becomes the Truman Doctrine

●

"Our policy is directed not against any country or doctrine but against hunger, poverty, desperation, and chaos."

— George C. Marshall, address at Harvard University on the European Recovery Program, June 5, 1947

●

Gen. George Marshall named secretary of state; calls for European Recovery Program

Department of Defense and National Security Council established

House Un-American Activities Committee (HUAC) charges

"Hollywood Ten" with contempt; they are sentenced to jail terms

Truman launches loyalty program to investigate all federal employees

U.N. grants U.S. trusteeship over Micronesia

Supreme Court rules public school busing of parochial school students is constitutional

John F. Kennedy married socialite Jacqueline Bouvier in 1953 in as glamorous a ceremony as patrician Newport, Rhode Island, had ever seen.

Philippines gives U.S. 99-year leases on military bases

1948

Alger Hiss indicted for perjury after denying he passed secret State Department documents through Whittaker Chambers to the Soviets

Congress approves European Recovery Program, known as Marshall Plan: $17 billion to Europe

Organization of American States established

Truman, by executive order, bans segregation in the armed forces

Supreme Court rules that state or federal courts may not enforce "restrictive covenants" preventing owners from selling real estate to minorities

Court rules the use of public

school facilities to provide religious instruction for children during the school day is unconstitutional, violating the separation of church and state

Democrat incumbent Harry S. Truman, 33rd president, and his running mate, Alben W. Barkley, defeat Republicans Thomas E. Dewey and Earl Warren and two third-party challengers: the States Rights'

candidate, Strom Thurmond, and the Progressive Party's Henry A. Wallace

1949

NATO (North Atlantic Treaty Organization) formed by U.S., Canada, and 10 Western European countries

U.S. withdraws troops from Korea

1950

Two Puerto Rican nationalists make unsuccessful attempt to assassinate Truman

North Korean troops invade South Korea; U.N. sends forces to repel aggression under Gen. Douglas MacArthur; Chinese troops join conflict

U.S. recognizes Bao Dai in Vietnam; sends $15 million to French to put down Ho Chi

Minh; by 1954 total reaches $2.5 billion

Truman orders development of the hydrogen bomb

Alger Hiss convicted of perjury

Senator Joseph McCarthy warns of Communists in the State Department; begins his committee hearings

U.S. Army takes over railroads to prevent general strike

American diplomat Ralph Bunche wins the Nobel Peace Prize for negotiating an end to the Arab-Israeli war; he is the first black to win the award

Truman signs bill for some $88 million in economic aid to the Navajos and Hopis; some $31 million awarded to Utes as compensation for tribal lands

Total U.S. population: 151 million; California becomes second most populous state, rising from fifth; New York City called world's most densely packed urban area, with some 88,000 persons per square mile

1951

Japanese peace treaty formally ends World War II

Fighting continues in Korea; General MacArthur relieved of command

22nd Amendment goes into effect, limiting a president to two terms in office

Senator Estes Kefauver investigates organized crime

Korean War cease-fire talks commence

1952

Puerto Rico becomes a U.S. commonwealth

Republican vice presidential nominee, Richard M. Nixon, makes his "Checkers" speech

U.S. explodes first hydrogen bomb on atoll in the Marshall Islands

Congress passes McCarran-Walter Immigration Act over Truman's veto, continuing 1924 quota system

Japan agrees to U.S. military bases on its territory

Dwight David Eisenhower elected 34th president with running mate, Richard Milhous Nixon; the first Republican ticket to win since 1928; they defeat Democrats Adlai E. Stevenson and John J. Sparkman

1953

Julius and Ethel Rosenberg, found guilty of atomic espionage two years before, executed at Sing Sing prison in Ossining, New York

George Marshall wins Nobel Peace Prize for his European Recovery Program

Korean War ends; armistice signed at Panmunjom

●

"We must not confuse dissent with disloyalty."

— Edward R. Murrow, on his See It Now broadcast about Senator Joseph McCarthy, March 7, 1954

●

Department of Health, Education, and Welfare created

Eisenhower appoints Earl Warren, governor of California, chief justice of the Supreme Court

Eisenhower orders the dismissal of any federal employee who takes the Fifth Amendment during congressional hearings

Refugee Relief Act increases immigration quotas for refugees from Communist countries

1954

Senator McCarthy, in televised hearings, seeks to prove Communist infiltration of the U.S. military; his conduct draws Senate condemnation

Secretary of State John Foster Dulles hardens U.S. policy against the Soviets

U.S. and Canada agree to build DEW radar line: early-warning system against aircraft and missile attacks

Five members of Congress wounded when backers of Puerto Rican independence open fire from Capitol visitors' gallery

Supreme Court, in *Brown* v. *Board of Education of Topeka*, calls for an end to "separate but equal" public schools

Nautilus, first atomic-powered submarine, launched

Congress passes legislation adding "under God" to the Pledge of Allegiance

U.S. backs coup to overthrow the government in Guatemala

Eisenhower signs legislation to permit the sharing of atomic knowledge and fuel with friendly nations

1955

Ngo Dinh Diem, premier of South Vietnam, rejects unification elections, claiming North Vietnam would not conduct fair elections; U.S. supports him and sends military advisers to train South Vietnamese army

Senator Joseph McCarthy (above) squared off against special army counsel Joseph N. Welch in the Army-McCarthy hearings.

Eisenhower suffers heart attack; stock market suffers $14-billion paper loss

Rosa Parks refuses to give up seat in "whites only" bus section in Montgomery, Alabama; Dr. Martin Luther King, Jr., leads bus boycott

---

> *"Get together a half-dozen like-minded Americans and pretty soon you'll have an association . . . and a fund-raising campaign."*
>
> — *Frederick Lewis Allen,*
> Big Change *(1952)*

1956

Southern congressmen urge resisting desegregation of schools "by all lawful means"

Agricultural (Soil Bank) Act pays U.S. farmers $750 million annually to reduce acreage under cultivation

Supreme Court rules that firing a public employee for taking the Fifth Amendment is unconstitutional

Dwight David Eisenhower, 34th president, and Richard Milhous Nixon win reelection, defeating Democrats Adlai E. Stevenson and Estes Kefauver; first Republicans reelected since William McKinley ticket in 1900

1957

Eisenhower Doctrine proposes broad-based aid to nations in the Middle East resisting Soviet aggression

Congress passes Civil Rights Act, establishing a federal Civil Rights Commission and a civil rights division in the attorney general's office

Arkansas governor Orval Faubus calls up National Guard to keep black students out of Central High in Little Rock; Eisenhower sends federal troops to enforce desegregation

Martin Luther King, Jr., forms Southern Christian Leadership Conference

Supreme Court rules First

Amendment freedom of the press extends to publications deemed obscene, if they meet certain standards

1958

Vice President Nixon, on goodwill trip to South America, jeered by demonstrators

National Aeronautics and Space Administration (NASA) established

Arkansas governor Faubus blocks desegregation by closing some public schools, reopening them as private facilities

National Defense Education Act supports science and language education and provides loans to students going into teaching

Supreme Court rules State Department cannot deny a citizen a passport because it finds his opinions or membership in an organization objectionable

1959

Alaska, Hawaii become 49th, 50th states

Vice President Richard Nixon and Soviet premier Nikita Khrushchev stage "Kitchen Debate" in Moscow

NASA selects its first seven astronauts

Supreme Court holds state and federal governments can prosecute the same person for the same crime

U.S. launches first ballistic-missile submarine

Supreme Court rules Little Rock school closings unlawful

Soviet premier Nikita Khrushchev makes unprecedented U.S. tour

---

EVERYDAY LIFE

1946

Wartime price controls lifted on most consumer goods

A-bomb tests at Bikini atoll in the Pacific inspire creation of the bikini swimsuit

Fulbright Scholarship program set up

1947

Parisian designer Christian Dior's "New Look": V necklines, ruffles, tiny waists, midi length, flouncy skirts

Millions of veterans attending college on the GI Bill of Rights

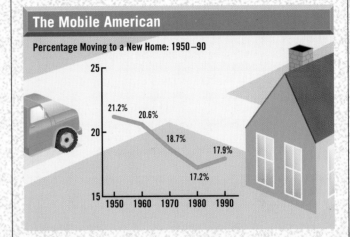

The Mobile American

Percentage Moving to a New Home: 1950–90

Year	Percentage
1950	21.2%
1960	20.6%
1970	18.7%
1980	17.2%
1990	17.9%

Flying saucer sightings reported around the country

Slinky toy introduced

Florida Everglades designated a national park

1948

Selective Service Act continues military draft

Trumpeter Miles Davis introduces cool jazz

> *"A good gulp of hot whiskey at bedtime — it's not very scientific, but it helps."*
>
> — *Alexander Fleming, discoverer of penicillin, on treating the common cold, March 1954*

First electronically controlled elevators

CBS begins nightly TV newscast

1949

U.S. president's salary raised to $100,000; vice

---

president's, to $30,000

Cost of living drops; GM workers accept pay cut, car prices are down

Levittown, Long Island, New York, the first prefab suburban community, is completed

1950

National Council of Churches established

Minimum wage raised from 40 to 75 cents per hour

Brink's robbery: 7 men in Halloween masks steal $1.5 million in cash and checks

Estimated number of television sets: 3.1 million

Prefab fallout shelters for sale

Prepackaging of meat in supermarkets becomes common

1951

Massive flooding of Mississippi River valley causes over $1 billion in losses

Fluoridated water shown to reduce tooth decay

First transcontinental TV broadcast: Edward R. Murrow's *See It Now*

Direct long-distance dialing

Saddle shoes, poodle skirts, and crinolines the rage

1952

Revised Standard Version of the Bible

American clergyman Norman Vincent Peale's inspirational and self-help book *The Power of Positive Thinking*

WHAT IT COST

Prices: 1950

Daily, Sunday newspapers, 3 ¢, 15 ¢	Metropolitan Opera tickets, $2.50 to $20; B'way play, $1.20 to $4.80
Eliz. Arden hand cream, $1	
Women's jackets, $22.95; skirts, $12.95	Novel, $4
	Women's suits, $25; shoes, $8.99
Men's suits, $95 to $115	
Schrafft's dinners, N.Y.C. $1.90	TV-radio-phonograph console, $349.95
Ranch mink, $2,400; Persian, $900; fur-trimmed coat, $106	35mm camera, $192.50
Blouses, $6.95 to $10.95	Upright piano, $560
Man's bathrobe, $15.95	Cigar, 10 ¢
Plymouth sedan, $1,758; convertible, $2,111; Austin, $1,345	Sofa and two chairs, $279; 4-piece mahogany bedroom set, $203
Scotch, (bot.) $4.29; bourbon, $4.05	Cowhide two-suiter, $29.95
	Nylons, 3 pr. for $4.50
Men's shoes, $14.95	2-bedroom house in Bethpage, NY, $8,990
NY–Rome round trip (off-season), $485.40; NY–London, $385; NY–Paris, $407	NYC Fifth Ave. 6-room co-op, $19,250

Pocket-size transistor radios

Bwana Devil, first 3-D movie, draws big crowds

Panty raids

1953

Sir Edmund Hillary and Tenzing Norkay make the first ascent of Mt. Everest

Hugh Hefner launches *Playboy* magazine

First noncommercial television station begins broadcasting from Houston, Texas

Color telecasts begin

1954

The Reverend Billy Graham holds revival meetings in U.S., England, and Germany

Plastic contact lenses available

Air Force Academy founded

Hurricanes Carol, Edna, and Hazel cause millions of dollars in damage

TV dinners gain popularity

Comic book publishers, enjoying record sales, respond to complaints about violence and vulgarity by promising self-censorship

Davy Crockett TV show sets off craze for coonskin caps

Pianist Liberace a TV sensation

1955

Kermit the Frog debuts on TV show *Sam and Friends*

Eisenhower gives first televised presidential news conference

College fashions: straight skirts, matching pastel sweaters, circle pins, for women; the button-down Ivy League look for men

Unemployment reaches record 65 million; minimum wage raised to $1 per hour

Disneyland opens in Anaheim, California

Ray Kroc opens his first McDonald's in Des Plaines, Illinois

Kentucky Fried Chicken opens

1956

Ringling Brothers and Barnum & Bailey presents last show under the Big Top tent

Best-selling book *The Search for Bridey Murphy* sets off reincarnation craze

Interstate Commerce Commission bans segregation on buses and trains crossing state lines

Bermuda shorts popular with men and women

Stainless-steel razor blades

Battery-powered wristwatches

The Huntley-Brinkley Report, nightly TV news show with Chet Huntley and David Brinkley, debuts on NBC

U.S. adopts "In God We Trust" as national motto

1957

Mayflower II re-creates original voyage from Plymouth, England

George (Mad Bomber) Metesky arrested for planting 32 bombs in New York City area, ending a 16-year search

Frisbee fad

Drive-in movie theaters peak in popularity

1958

Hula Hoops: 100 million sold

"Beat" clothes: sandals, baggy sweaters, khaki pants

John Birch Society founded

1959

Collegians stuffing themselves into phone booths is a fad

First Barbie dolls marketed

◼

"An atheist is a man who has no invisible means of support."

— Fulton Sheen, auxiliary bishop of New York, December 1955

◼

House of Representatives investigates rigged TV quiz shows

Average family watches television 5 hours a day

U.S. postmaster general bans English novelist D. H. Lawrence's 1928 book *Lady Chatterley's Lover* from the mails

TV cowboy shows spur sales of kids' boots, ten-gallon hats, and lassos

ARTS & LETTERS

1946

American novelist John Hersey's *Hiroshima*

American playwright Eugene O'Neill's *The Iceman Cometh*

French painter Fernand Léger's "Composition with Branch"

Russian-born American choreographer George Balanchine's ballet *Nightshadow*

American poet and novelist Robert Penn Warren's *All the King's Men*

1947

American playwright Arthur Miller's *All My Sons*

Holocaust victim Anne Frank's *The Diary of a Young Girl* published in German, five years later in English

American playwright Tennessee Williams's *A Streetcar Named Desire*

American journalist John Gunther's *Inside U.S.A.*

French novelist Albert Camus's *The Plague*

English sculptor Henry Moore's "Three Standing Figures"

Austrian painter Oskar Kokoschka's "Das Matterhorn"

Armenian-born American painter Arshile Gorky's "Agony"

American novelist William Faulkner wins Nobel Prize

1948

South African novelist Alan Paton's *Cry, the Beloved Country*

American novelist James Michener's *Tales of the South Pacific*

Dwight D. Eisenhower's *Crusade in Europe*

American novelist Norman Mailer's *The Naked and the Dead*

English novelist Graham Greene's *The Heart of the Matter*

American clergyman and novelist Lloyd C. Douglas's *The Big Fisherman*

American painter Andrew Wyeth's "Christina's World"

The sleek, angular styles of some 1950's fashions were softened with long bows and gloves.

American abstract expressionist artist Jackson Pollock's "Composition No. 1"

English composer Benjamin Britten's *Beggar's Opera*

1949

German-born American theologian Paul Tillich's *The Shaking of the Foundations*

English poet and dramatist T. S. Eliot's verse play *The Cocktail Party*

American novelist A. B. Guthrie, Jr.'s, *The Way West*

American playwright Arthur Miller's *Death of a Salesman*

English novelist George Orwell's satiric *1984*

French painter Marc Chagall's "Red Sun"

1950

American novelist John Hersey's *The Wall*

Swiss sculptor Alberto Giacometti's "Seven Figures and a Head"

American playwright Carson McCullers's *The Member of the Wedding*

1951

American novelist J. D. Salinger's *The Catcher in the Rye*

American novelist James Jones's *From Here to Eternity*

American marine biologist and writer Rachel Carson's *The Sea Around Us*

American novelist William Faulkner's *Requiem for a Nun*

American novelist Herman Wouk's *The Caine Mutiny*

Spanish painter Salvador Dali's "Christ of St. John of the Cross"

Russian-born American composer Igor Stravinsky's opera *The Rake's Progress*

English composer Benjamin Britten's opera *Billy Budd*

Dutch-born American painter Willem de Kooning's "Woman"

1952

Irish-born French dramatist Samuel Beckett's *Waiting for Godot*

Black American novelist Ralph Ellison's *Invisible Man*

American novelist Ernest Hemingway's *The Old Man and the Sea*

American novelist John Steinbeck's *East of Eden*

American novelist Bernard Malamud's *The Natural*

French painter Georges Rouault's "End of Autumn"

French painter Raoul Dufy's "The Pink Violin"

French painter Fernand Léger completes murals for U.N. building in New York City

1953

Black American novelist James Baldwin's *Go Tell It on the Mountain*

●

"From birth to age 18, a girl needs good parents. From 18 to 35, she needs good looks. From 35 to 55, she needs a good personality. From 55 on, she needs good cash."

— Sophie Tucker, in 1953 at age 69

●

Canadian-born American novelist Saul Bellow's *The Adventures of Augie March*

American playwright Arthur Miller's *The Crucible*

American playwright William Inge's *Picnic*

Russian-born French painter Marc Chagall's "Eiffel Tower"

Purchasing Power of the Dollar: 1950–90

(1982 = $1)

$4.15				
	$3.37			
		$2.57		
			$1.22 $1	$0.77
1950	1960	1970	1980 '82	1990

1954

American historian Bruce Catton's *A Stillness at Appomattox*

French modernist painter Jean Dubuffet's "Les Vagabonds"

English composer Benjamin Britten's opera *Turn of the Screw*

Austrian-born American composer Arnold Schoenberg's opera *Moses and Aaron*

1955

American Shakespeare Festival opens

English novelist William Golding's *Lord of the Flies*

American playwright Tennessee Williams's *Cat on a Hot Tin Roof*

American playwright William Inge's *Bus Stop*

American novelist Sloan Wilson's *The Man in the Gray Flannel Suit*

American Patrick Dennis's Broadway comedy *Auntie Mame*

Marian Anderson becomes first black American to sing at the Metropolitan Opera

Russian-born American novelist Vladimir Nabokov's *Lolita* published in France, three years later in America

English novelist Graham Greene's *The Quiet American*

1956

Beat poet Allen Ginsberg's *Howl and Other Poems*

American novelist Grace Metalious's *Peyton Place*

American composer Lejaren Hiller produces *Illiac Suite*, the first major piece of computer-generated music

Greek-born American singer Maria Callas makes her debut at the Metropolitan Opera in Vincenzo Bellini's *Norma*

British prime minister Winston Churchill's first of four volumes of *A History of the English-Speaking Peoples*

American sociologist William H. Whyte's *The Organization Man*

1957

Russian Boris Pasternak's *Dr. Zhivago*, denied publication in the Soviet Union, published in Italy

English playwright John Osborne's *Look Back in Anger*

Some of the prefab houses built in Levittown, such as this model priced at under $8,000, were reserved for returning veterans and their families.

American playwright Eugene O'Neill's *Long Day's Journey Into Night*

Beat novelist Jack Kerouac's *On the Road*

English novelist John Braine's *Room at the Top*

American writer John Cheever's novel *The Wapshot Chronicle*

American novelist Leon Uris's *Exodus*

American sociologist Vance Packard's *The Hidden Persuaders*

English composer William Walton's *Concerto for Cello and Orchestra*

1958

American novelist Truman Capote's *Breakfast at Tiffany's*

American poet Archibald MacLeish's verse drama *J.B.*

American economist John Kenneth Galbraith's *The Affluent Society*

Guggenheim Museum, designed by Frank Lloyd Wright, opens in New York City

Soviets force Boris Pasternak

to refuse the Nobel Prize

English playwright Harold Pinter's *The Birthday Party*

English sculptor Henry Moore's "Reclining Figure"

American pianist Van Cliburn wins Tchaikovsky competition in Moscow

1959

American novelist Philip Roth's *Good-bye Columbus*

American novelist William Faulkner completes trilogy that includes *The Hamlet* (1940), *The Town* (1957), and *The Mansion* (1959)

American sociologist Vance Packard's *The Status Seekers*

American novelist James Michener's *Hawaii*

ENTERTAINMENT & SPORTS

1946

American film director William Wyler's *The Best Years of Our Lives*, about homecoming GI's

American film director Frank Capra's *It's a Wonderful Life*, with James Stewart

Humphrey Bogart and Lauren Bacall in director Howard Hawks's screen version of mystery writer Raymond Chandler's *The Big Sleep*

English director Alfred Hitchcock's *Notorious*, with Ingrid Bergman and Cary Grant

Americans Alan Jay Lerner and Frederick Loewe's Broadway musical *Brigadoon*

American songwriter Irving Berlin's Broadway musical *Annie Get Your Gun*

Hit songs: "Chiquita Banana," "To Each His Own," "Come Rain or Come Shine," "Doin' What Comes Natur'lly," "Full Moon and Empty Arms"

The National Basketball Association is founded

A "nuclear" family made up of mannequins is posed around the dinner table inside a frame house about two miles away from ground zero just before an atom bomb test conducted in Nevada on March 17, 1953.

St. Louis Cardinals defeat Boston Red Sox in World Series 4 games to 3

1947

Turkish-born American director Elia Kazan's *Gentleman's Agreement*

Hit songs: "Almost Like Being in Love," "Open the Door, Richard," "Woody Woodpecker," "How Are Things in Glocca Morra?"

Jackie Robinson, first black in major league baseball, plays for the Brooklyn Dodgers; named Rookie of the Year

On TV: *Kraft Theater, Howdy Doody, Meet the Press*

Thor Heyerdahl sails *Kon-Tiki* raft from Peru to Polynesia in 101 days

Power-server Jack Kramer

takes his second U.S. men's singles tennis title in a row

New York Yankees defeat Brooklyn Dodgers in World Series (first widely televised) 4 games to 3

1948

British film director Michael Powell's *The Red Shoes*

American film director Jules Dassin's *Naked City*

American songwriter Cole Porter's Broadway musical *Kiss Me, Kate*

On TV: Ed Sullivan's *The Toast of the Town*, Milton Berle's *Texaco Star Theater, Philco Playhouse, Ford Theater, Ted Mack's Amateur Hour*

Hit songs: "Buttons and Bows," "It's a Most Unusual Day," "A — You're Adorable," "So in Love," "Enjoy Yourself — It's Later Than You Think"

Olympic Games held in London

Thoroughbred Citation, ridden by Eddie Arcaro, wins horse racing's Triple Crown

Cleveland Indians defeat Boston Braves in World Series 4 games to 2

1949

Italian director Vittorio de Sica's *The Bicycle Thief*

Americans Richard Rodgers and Oscar Hammerstein's Broadway musical *South Pacific*

British film director Carol Reed's classic thriller *The Third Man*

On TV: *The Lone Ranger, The Perry Como Show, Arthur Godfrey and His Friends, Hopalong Cassidy*

Hit songs: "Some Enchanted Evening," "Let's Take an Old-Fashioned Walk," "My Foolish Heart," "Dear Hearts and Gentle People"

Joe Louis retires; Ezzard Charles captures heavyweight boxing crown

American tennis star Pancho Gonzales takes second straight U.S. men's title

New York Yankees defeat Brooklyn Dodgers in World Series 4 games to 1

1950

Hollywood film director Joseph Mankiewicz's *All About Eve*, with Bette Davis and Anne Baxter

American film director Billy Wilder's *Sunset Boulevard*, with Gloria Swanson and William Holden

On TV: *The George Burns and Gracie Allen Show, Your Hit Parade, The Jack Benny Show, What's My Line?*

Composers Frank Loesser and Abe Burrows's Broadway musical *Guys and Dolls*

Hit songs: "Good Night, Irene," "Third Man Theme," "Mule Train," "Mona Lisa"

American cartoonist Charles Schultz creates the comic strip *Peanuts*

New York Yankees defeat Philadelphia Phillies in World Series 4 games to 0

1951

Film director Elia Kazan's version of *A Streetcar Named Desire*, with Marlon Brando

Humphrey Bogart and Katharine Hepburn in director John Huston's *The African Queen*

A Place in the Sun, with Elizabeth Taylor and Montgomery Clift

An American in Paris, with Gene Kelly and Leslie Caron

Japanese film director Akira Kurosawa's *Rashomon*

Americans Richard Rodgers and Oscar Hammerstein's Broadway musical *The King and I*

Hit songs: "Tennessee Waltz," "How High the Moon," "Too Young," "Because of You"

●

"I refuse to endanger the health of my children in a house with less than three bathrooms."

— Film actress Myrna Loy, Mr. Blandings Builds His Dream House (1947)

●

On TV: *I Love Lucy, The Red Skelton Show*

Jersey Joe Walcott wins heavyweight boxing title

New York Yankees defeat New York Giants in World Series 4 games to 2

1952

Fredric March in screen version of Arthur Miller's *Death of a Salesman*

Grace Kelly and Gary Cooper in *High Noon*, directed by Fred Zinnemann

Gene Kelly, Debbie Reynolds, and Donald O'Connor in *Singin' in the Rain*

On TV: *The Today Show, Dragnet, This Is Your Life, The Adventures of Ozzie and Harriet*

Hit songs: "Cry," "Blue Tango," "Any Time," "Kiss of Fire"

Olympic Games held in Helsinki

Rocky Marciano KO's Jersey Joe Walcott to win heavyweight boxing title

Jockey Eddie Arcaro wins his fifth Kentucky Derby

New York Yankees defeat Brooklyn Dodgers in World Series 4 games to 3

1953

Roman Holiday, with Audrey Hepburn and Gregory Peck

From Here to Eternity, directed by Fred Zinnemann, starring Burt Lancaster, Deborah Kerr, Frank Sinatra, and Montgomery Clift

On TV: *My Little Margie, Our Miss Brooks, Person to Person, Captain Kangaroo*

Hit songs: "Song From the Moulin Rouge," "Till I Waltz Again With You," "April in Portugal," "Vaya con Dios"

American tennis star Maureen (Little Mo) Connolly wins women's Grand Slam

New York Yankees defeat Brooklyn Dodgers in World Series 4 games to 2

1954

English director Alfred Hitchcock's *Rear Window*, with James Stewart and Grace Kelly

American director Elia Kazan's film *On the Waterfront*, with Marlon Brando

Japanese director Akira Kurosawa's *Seven Samurai*

Italian director Federico Fellini's *La Strada*

On TV: *Disneyland, Make Room for Daddy*, Groucho Marx's *You Bet Your Life*

Hit songs: "Little Things Mean a Lot," "Hey There," "Young at Heart," "Sh—Boom"

Roger Bannister breaks the 4-minute barrier for the mile: 3 minutes, 59.4 seconds

New York Giants defeat Cleveland Indians in World Series 4 games to 0

1955

Hollywood's film version of *Mister Roberts*, with Henry Fonda and Jack Lemmon

American actor James Dean stars in *East of Eden* and *Rebel Without a Cause*

The Blackboard Jungle, with Glenn Ford and Sidney Poitier, has Bill Haley and the Comets' hit song "Rock Around the Clock" on its sound track

French director Henri Georges Clouzot's *Diabolique*

Hit songs: "Maybellene," "Ballad of Davy Crockett," "Cherry Pink and Apple

Blossom White," "Yellow Rose of Texas," "Ain't That a Shame"

On TV: *Gunsmoke, Beat the Clock, The Mickey Mouse Club, The Honeymooners*

Brooklyn Dodgers defeat New York Yankees in World Series 4 games to 3

1956

Elvis Presley performs on Ed Sullivan's television program

Hollywood epic *Giant;* James Dean's last film

Producer Mike Todd's *Around the World in 80 Days*

Americans Alan Jay Lerner and Frederick Loewe's Broadway musical *My Fair Lady*

On TV: *The $64,000 Challenge, Wyatt Earp*

Hit songs: "Heartbreak Hotel," "Don't Be Cruel," "Great Pretender," "My Prayer," "Wayward Wind," "Love Me Tender," "Whatever Will Be, Will Be"

Rocky Marciano retires unbeaten; Floyd Patterson KO's Archie Moore to win heavyweight boxing championship

New York Yankees defeat Brooklyn Dodgers in World Series 4 games to 3

1957

English director David Lean's *The Bridge on the River Kwai,* with Alec Guinness and William Holden

American director Sidney Lumet's *Twelve Angry Men*

Swedish director Ingmar Bergman's *The Seventh Seal*

American composer Leonard Bernstein's Broadway musical *West Side Story*

On TV: *The Jack Parr Show, Leave It to Beaver, American Bandstand, Alfred Hitchcock Presents*

Hit songs: "Tammy," "Love Letters in the Sand," "It's Not for Me to Say," "Young Love," "Chances Are," "That'll Be the Day," "Whole Lotta Shakin' Goin' On" "Wake Up, Little Susie"

Brooklyn Dodgers move to Los

Movie actor James Dean became a heartthrob to legions of teenage girls in movies like East of Eden.

Angeles; New York Giants move to San Francisco

Bobby Fischer, age 13, hailed as chess genius

Milwaukee Braves defeat New York Yankees in World Series 4 games to 3

1958

Screen version of Tennessee Williams's play *Cat on a Hot Tin Roof,* with Elizabeth Taylor and Paul Newman

On TV: *Lawrence Welk, Playhouse 90, Maverick, The Pat Boone Show*

Hit songs: "Volare," "It's All in the Game," "All I Have to Do Is Dream," "Bird Dog," "At the Hop," "Peggy Sue"

Golfer Arnold Palmer wins his first Masters Tournament

U.S. beats England for yachting's America's Cup

New York Yankees defeat Milwaukee Braves in World Series 4 games to 3

1959

Marilyn Monroe, Tony Curtis, and Jack Lemmon in *Some LIke It Hot*

Ben Hur, with Charlton Heston and Stephen Boyd

French director Jean-Luc Godard's *Breathless*

French director François Truffaut's *The 400 Blows*

Hit songs: "Mack the Knife," "Battle of New Orleans," "Venus," "Lonely Boy," "There Goes My Baby," "Sixteen Candles"

On TV: *Bonanza, Rawhide, General Electric Theater, Perry Mason*

Sweden's Ingemar Johansson wins world heavyweight boxing title, defeating Floyd Patterson

Boston Celtics win first of eight straight NBA championships.

Los Angeles Dodgers defeat Chicago White Sox in World Series 4 games to 2

BUSINESS & ECONOMICS

1946

Workers in steel, coal, auto industries strike for higher pay; Truman's threat to draft railroad workers brings pact

First nationwide survey of consumer attitudes

1947

Congress passes Taft-Hartley Act, which sets limits on union practices, such as closed shops

1948

United Auto Workers (UAW) wins first escalator clause from management, basing wages on cost of living

New York's Idlewild (later Kennedy) Airport opens

1949

Congress of Industrial Organizations (CIO) expels 11 unions as Communist

Cost of living drops; UAW takes pay cut; car prices fall

First Volkswagen sold in U.S.

1950

First regional shopping center, with central pedestrian mall, opens in Seattle

Diner's Club introduces the first multiuse credit card, accepted in lieu of cash in 27 restaurants

U.S. produces two-thirds of world's cars and trucks

General Motors' earnings top $600 million, largest ever for a U.S. corporation

1951

Trading stamps catch on as a sales incentive

Atomic Energy Commission (AEC) builds first nuclear reactor

UNIVAC, first commercially practical computer, debuts

AT&T has a record 1 million stockholders

"What is good for the country is good for General Motors, and what's good for General Motors is good for the country."

— *Charles E. Wilson, testifying before Senate Armed Forces Committee, 1952*

1952

Truman seizes steel mills to end strike; Supreme Court rules action unconstitutional

Federal Communications Commission (FCC) assigns some 2,000 new TV stations

George Meany heads American Federation of Labor (AFL); Walter Reuther becomes president of the Congress of Industrial Organizations (CIO)

1953

Tidelands Oil Act: states get offshore oil rights

U.S. College Graduates: 1900–90

■ Total number of graduates ■ Female graduates ■ Male graduates

	1900	1910	1920	1930	1940	1950	1960	1970	1980	1990
Female total	5,237	8,437	16,642	48,869	76,954	103,217	136,187	343,060	456,000	558,000
%	19.1 / 80.9	22.7 / 77.3	34.2 / 65.8	39.9 / 60.1	41.3 / 58.7	23.9 / 76.1	35.0 / 65.0	41.5 / 58.5	49.0 / 51.0	53.5 / 46.5
Male total	22,173	28,762	31,980	73,615	109,546	328,841	252,996	484,174	474,000	485,000

27,410 ... 1,043,000

Sources: Statistical Abstract; Historical Abstracts

Philadelphia-born actress Grace Kelly, star of 10 films between 1951 and 1956, weds Prince Rainier III of Monaco in a lavish royal ceremony.

Small Business Administration created

IBM's first commercial computers

1954

Premium gasoline introduced

Atomic-generated electricity will one day be "too cheap to meter," says Lewis Strauss, chairman of the Atomic Energy Commission

Major tax reform introduced with passage of Internal Revenue Code

1955

Container ships revolutionize cargo shipping

AFL and CIO unions, with a total of 15 million members, merge under George Meany

1956

Congress authorizes 41,000-mile

interstate highway system

TV videocassette recorder demonstrated by Ampex

1957

Pan Am is first to use a U.S. jetliner, a Boeing 707, on a commercial flight

AFL-CIO expels Teamsters Union, whose leader, Jimmy Hoffa, faces corruption charges

Ford introduces the Edsel

1958

Aluminum car engine developed

Pan Am begins transatlantic jet service

U.S. Federal Aviation Agency established

American Express launches credit card

1959

Computers with transistors

instead of vacuum tubes are marketed

COBOL: first computer programming language for business use

SCIENCE & MEDICINE

1946

ENIAC, often called the first computer, unveiled

Mayo Clinic reports that the antibiotic streptomycin checks tuberculosis

Sun found to emit radio waves

1947

Dead Sea Scrolls found near Qumran, in region of Jordan later occupied by Israel

Edwin Land invents Polaroid instant-picture camera

Mumps vaccine developed

Polio virus is isolated

1948

Peter Goldmark perfects long-playing record: 33⅓ r.p.m.

U.N. establishes World Health Organization

Cesium atomic clocks: accurate to 1 second in 1,000 years

Dr. Alfred Kinsey's *Sexual Behavior in the Human Male*

200-inch mirror telescope dedicated on Mount Palomar, California

Britain adopts national health plan

William Shockley and associates at Bell Labs invent the transistor

1949

American Cancer Society takes stand against cigarette smoking

Cortisone, believed effective in treating rheumatoid arthritis, is manufactured

1950

Antihistamines available to alleviate colds and allergies

First embryo transplants in cattle

New elements created by the Berkeley cyclotron: Berkelium 97 and Californium 98

1951

Researchers generate electricity from nuclear fuel

1952

Polio epidemic strikes over 50,000

In Denmark first sex-change operation: George Jorgenson becomes Christine Jorgenson

Amniocentesis introduced

First artificial-heart-valve implant; electric shock first used to restart human heart

Galaxies found to be twice as far away as previously thought

New element: Einsteinium 99

1953

Heart-lung machine used for the first time during surgery

Breeder reactors, which make their own fuel as they run

American pilot Chuck Yeager, in rocket-powered Bell X-1A, hits a record Mach 2.5, or 2.5 times the speed of sound

● ━

"Science is the search for truth — it is not a game in which one tries to beat his opponent, to do harm to others."

— Linus C. Pauling,
No More War! *(1958)*

━ ●

American scientist James D. Watson and English scientist Francis H. C. Crick build model of double-helix deoxyribonucleic acid (DNA)

New element: Fermium 100

Dr. Alfred Kinsey's *Sexual Behavior in the Human Female*

1954

Virologist Jonas Salk's polio vaccine tested on public

Astronomers, observing blue-

green area on Mars, postulate theory of extraterrestrial life

FORTRAN: first computer programming language

First images of atoms produced by newly invented ion microscope

First successful kidney transplant

1955

National Hurricane Center established in Miami, Florida

First widespread testing of a birth control pill

First optical fibers

New element: Mendelevium 101

1956

Kidney machines

Human growth hormone isolated

Neutrinos, particles without mass or charge, discovered

1957

Interferon, a family of virus-fighting proteins, discovered

First nuclear power plant, in Shippingport, Pennsylvania

Soviets launch first man-made satellites: *Sputniks I* and *II*

DNA synthesized

Soviet nuclear-waste facility explodes, contaminating 100 square miles in southern Urals

1958

Measles vaccine developed

Explorer I, first U.S. earth satellite, detects Van Allen radiation belt

Ultrasound for examining fetuses in the womb

Pacemaker to regulate heartbeats invented

New element: Nobelium 102

1959

Explorer VI, U.S. satellite, transmits first TV pictures of Earth from space

British paleontologist Louis Leakey discovers the remains of a human who lived 1.75 million years ago

Soviet *Lunik II* is first man-made object to strike the Moon

WORLD POLITICAL EVENTS

1946

Civil war in China between Nationalists and Communists

Italy votes to become republic; Umberto II abdicates

Churchill makes his "Iron Curtain" speech in Fulton, Missouri; Cold War begins

Top Nazis put on trial in Nuremberg, Germany; tribunal sentences Goering and 11 others to death

Japanese war criminals go on trial; 7 are sentenced to hang, 16 to life imprisonment

1947

Princess Elizabeth, heiress to British throne, marries Philip, duke of Edinburgh

Britain nationalizes coal mines, communications, and electrical industry

Both Arabs and Jews reject British proposal to divide Palestine; U.N. suggests alternate partition plan

India gains independence from Britain; Jawaharlal Nehru prime minister

A South Korean boy dons GI boots and a poster left over from Dwight Eisenhower's visit in late 1952.

1948

U.S.S.R. sets up European satellite nations; stages coup d'état in Czechoslovakia

Berlin Airlift begins after U.S.S.R. blockades roads and rails from the West

> *"Whether you like it or not, history is on our side. We will bury you!"*
>
> — Nikita Khrushchev, referring to capitalist nations, at a reception held in the Polish Embassy, Moscow, 1956

Israel becomes a nation with David Ben-Gurion as prime minister and Chaim Weizmann as president; war erupts with the Arab League; 400,000 Palestinian refugees flee from Israel to nearby Arab countries, creating the long-standing Palestinian homeland problem

Korea is divided into North and South

Mohandas K. Gandhi assassinated in India

1949

Germany is divided into East and West

Berlin blockade lifted by Soviets

Republic of Ireland cuts ties with Great Britain and declares independence

Communists under Mao Tse-tung win mainland China; Nationalists under Chiang Kai-shek flee to Taiwan

Israel admitted to U.N.; capital moved to Jerusalem

U.S.S.R. tests atom bomb

1950

China invades Tibet; claims sovereignty

U.S.S.R. and China begin aiding Communist leader Ho Chi Minh's Democratic Republic of Vietnam

German-born British scientist Klaus Fuchs jailed for giving atomic secrets to U.S.S.R.

1951

Conservative Party wins British election; Churchill once again prime minister

Eamon De Valera prime minister of Ireland

1952

Anti-British riots in Egypt; King Farouk abdicates

Britain's George VI dies; his daughter Elizabeth II's reign begins

Mau Mau terrorism in Kenya against British

1953

Joseph Stalin dies, succeeded by Georgy Malenkov; Nikita Khrushchev becomes head of the Communist Party Central Committee

Norway's Dag Hammarskjold elected U.N. secretary-general

U.S.S.R. explodes hydrogen bomb

1954

Ho Chi Minh defeats French at Dien Bien Phu; conference in Geneva grants independence to Laos and Cambodia, and approves a temporary split of Vietnam into North and South

Col. Gamal Abdel Nasser comes to power in Egypt

1955

First summit conference since World War II convenes in Geneva; Eisenhower's "open skies" proposal rejected by Soviets

European Communist countries join Warsaw Pact; West Germany joins NATO

Anthony Eden is British prime minister, replacing Churchill

Nikolai Bulganin succeeds Georgy Malenkov as Soviet premier

Argentine dictator Juan Domingo Perón deposed

1956

Israel invades Sinai Peninsula; Anglo-French forces occupy

the Suez Canal, then withdraw; all parties agree to cease-fire; U.N. force takes over the canal

Khrushchev denounces Stalin's policies at 20th Soviet Communist Party Conference

Ghana gains independence

Anti-Communist Hungarian revolution suppressed by Soviet troops

U.S. Church Membership: 1937–93

Percentage of people polled who consider themselves members of Christian or Jewish faith

U.S. Church Attendance: 1939–93

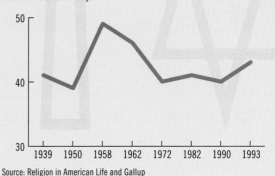

Percentage of people polled who report attending a church or synagogue service in the last 7 days

Source: Religion in American Life and Gallup

Fidel Castro begins guerrilla campaign to oust Cuban dictator Fulgencio Batista

Golda Meir becomes prime minister of Israel

1957

Israel withdraws from Sinai

Britain's prime minister Anthony Eden resigns; Harold Macmillan succeeds him

Soviets test intercontinental

ballistic missile (ICBM)

European Common Market founded

1958

Nikita Khrushchev becomes Soviet premier

Algerians revolt against French rule; Charles de Gaulle becomes president of France

Chinese Communists shell

Quemoy and Matsu, offshore islands held by Nationalist Chinese

Pope John XXIII elected

1959

Pope John XXIII calls Vatican Council II, first since 1870

China suppresses Tibetan revolt; Dalai Lama flees

Castro overthrows Batista, becomes Cuban premier

U.S. HISTORY & POLITICS

1960

Cuban premier Fidel Castro confiscates American property; U.S. declares embargo on Cuban exports

U-2 spy plane shot down over U.S.S.R.; U.S. pilot Francis Gary Powers imprisoned, later exchanged for convicted Soviet spy Rudolf Abel

U.S. flag adds stars for Alaska and Hawaii, making 50 stars

Lunch-counter sit-ins begin in Greensboro, North Carolina to protest local practice of not serving black customers

Presidential candidates John F. Kennedy and Richard M. Nixon debate on national TV

U.S. population: 179,323,000

John F. Kennedy and Texas senator Lyndon Johnson defeat Republicans Richard M. Nixon and U.N. ambassador Henry Cabot Lodge, Jr., to win 35th presidency and vice presidency

1961

U.S. severs ties with Cuba

Kennedy establishes Peace Corps, a volunteer group that helps developing countries improve living conditions

Bay of Pigs invasion: U.S.-backed attempt to foment an uprising against Cuba's Fidel Castro fails

JFK proposes 10-year space program with goal of "landing a man on the Moon in this decade"

Congress of Racial Equality (CORE) sponsors "Freedom Riders"

23rd Amendment grants residents of the District of Columbia the right to vote in presidential elections

Supreme Court rules in *Mapp* v. *Ohio* that illegally obtained evidence is not admissible in state or federal courts

Skyjacking made a federal crime punishable by death

1962

James Meredith becomes first black student at University of Mississippi after federal troops quell rioting

President Kennedy names Byron R. White and Arthur J. Goldberg III to Supreme Court

For a week in October 1962, the world held its breath wondering if the Cuban missile crisis meant nuclear war.

Cuban missile crisis: JFK imposes a naval blockade on Cuba and demands removal of Soviet ballistic missiles from Cuban bases; Khrushchev refuses, then backs down in exchange for U.S. pledge not to attack Cuba

Testing of nuclear weapons moved underground

1963

In *Gideon* v.*Wainright*, Supreme Court rules accused criminals have right to court-appointed counsel in state felony cases

Mass protests against segregation in Birmingham, Alabama

JFK visits Berlin Wall; makes "*Ich bin ein Berliner*" speech before West German crowd

Hotline linking U.S. and Moscow established; first used during 1967 Six-Day War

Black activist Medgar Evers of the National Association for the Advancement of Colored

People (NAACP) slain in Mississippi

Supreme Court bans mandatory prayer and Bible reading in public schools

U.S. and U.S.S.R. sign Limited Nuclear Test Ban Treaty

More than 200,000 gather in Washington, D.C., for civil rights march; Martin Luther King, Jr., gives his "I have a dream" oration

Clean Air Act passed

Nov. 22: JFK assassinated in Dallas; Vice President Lyndon Johnson assumes the presidency; Lee Harvey Oswald, arrested as the gunman, shot by Dallas nightclub owner Jack Ruby two days later

Warren Commission set up to investigate JFK assassination

Cape Canaveral renamed Cape Kennedy in honor of JFK

1964

24th Amendment, eliminating poll tax, ratified

Jack Ruby convicted for murdering Lee Harvey Oswald

Gen. Douglas MacArthur dies at the age of 84

Three civil rights volunteers for the black voter registration drive found murdered in Mississippi

Civil Rights Act of 1964 passed

North Vietnam attacks U.S. Navy ships in Gulf of Tonkin; LBJ orders bombing of North Vietnam; first U.S. antiwar demonstrations

Warren Commission finds no evidence of conspiracy in JFK assassination; 888-page report cites Oswald as the sole triggerman

Martin Luther King, Jr., wins Nobel Peace Prize

National Wilderness Preservation System created to protect and preserve over 9 million acres of land, including national parks and wildlife refuges

Lyndon Johnson, incumbent 36th president, elected with

Minnesota senator Hubert Humphrey as vice president; they defeat Republican Arizona senator Barry Goldwater and running mate, New York representative William E. Miller

Office of Criminal Justice set up to improve justice system

1965

First U.S. ground combat troops land in Vietnam; U.S. forces grow to 184,300

Malcolm X, Black Muslim leader, fatally shot in Harlem

Mutilating or destroying a draft card becomes federal crime

Martin Luther King, Jr., leads over 3,000 on 54-mile march from Selma to Montgomery

Project Head Start begins; provides education, social services, and medicine to disadvantaged children and their families

Race rioting devastates Los Angeles's Watts district

Medicare, government health insurance program for people 65 and over, enacted into law

President Johnson appoints Abe Fortas to Supreme Court; Fortas resigns four years later

"Let us never negotiate out of fear, but never fear to negotiate."

— *President John F. Kennedy, in his Inaugural Address, January 20, 1961*

Voting Rights Act outlaws voter registration tests and puts voter registration under federal supervision

Water Quality Act passed

Quota system, putting limits on immigration according to national origin, abolished

1966

Vietnam: U.S. bombs Hanoi and Haiphong, supports the South Vietnamese government of Gen. Nguyen Cao Ky; U.S. defense secretary Robert McNamara reports that neither air war nor "pacification program" is succeeding; U.S. forces grow to some 400,000

Supreme Court establishes Miranda warnings to ensure rights of accused criminals

Department of Transportation created

U.S. B-52 bomber collides in midair with a fuel-resupply plane over Spain; unarmed H-bomb dislodged and falls into Atlantic but is later recovered by midget sub

National Organization for Women (NOW) founded by Betty Friedan and others

Clean Waters Restoration Act passed

1967

25th Amendment authorizes U.S. president to nominate vice president if office is unoccupied; also, upon the removal of the president from office or his death or resignation, the amendment specifies the vice president shall become president

Thurgood Marshall becomes first black Supreme Court justice

Congress establishes Corporation for Public Broadcasting

Race riots erupt in Detroit; death toll reaches 40, with 2,000 injured

Anti-Vietnam war protests grow; some 75,000 protesters march on the Pentagon

1968

Vietnam: U.S. forces total some 500,000; Vietcong stage Tet Offensive

North Koreans seize U.S. intelligence ship *Pueblo* and its crew in Sea of Japan, claiming violation of territorial waters

LBJ announces he will not seek reelection; proposes peace talks with North Vietnam and partial halt to bombing

"The Negro says 'Now.' Others say 'Never.' The voice of responsible Americans says . . . 'Together.' There is no other way."

— *Vice President Lyndon Johnson, May 1963*

Martin Luther King, Jr., assassinated by James Earl Ray in Memphis; riots break out in over 100 cities; Ray pleads guilty, sentenced to 99 years in prison

Group of Columbia University students, mostly members of Students for a Democratic Society (SDS), seizes five university buildings during Vietnam War protest

Senator Robert F. Kennedy, Jr., assassinated by Sirhan Sirhan in Los Angeles after celebrating victory in California presidential primary

Antiwar demonstrators clash with police in Chicago during

Democratic Convention

Congress passes 1968 Civil Rights Act, forbidding discrimination in housing

Shirley Chisholm becomes first black woman elected to Congress

American Indian Movement (AIM) founded in Minneapolis

Feminists crash Miss America Pageant, tossing bras and steno pads into "freedom trash cans" and proclaiming "Women's Liberation"

Richard Nixon elected 37th president, with Maryland governor Spiro Agnew as his vice president, defeating Democrats Hubert Humphrey, vice president under LBJ, and his running mate, Maine senator Edmund Muskie, and American Independent candidates, George Wallace and Curtis LeMay

1969

Vietnam War: U.S. forces peak at 543,000 in April; My Lai massacre raises issue of U.S. atrocities; expanded Paris peace talks include Vietcong; Nixon announces troop withdrawal: by year's end 75,000 Americans return home; U.S. looks to South Vietnam to play greater role in the fighting; bombing of Cambodia continues; North Vietnamese leader, Ho Chi Minh, dies; 250,000 antiwar demonstrators march on Washington

Senator Edward Kennedy drives his car off bridge on Chappaquiddick Island; he escapes injury but companion, Mary Jo Kopechne, drowns

Nixon appoints Warren Burger as Supreme Court chief justice, succeeding Earl Warren, who retires

EVERYDAY LIFE

1960

Federal law passed to prevent quiz-show rigging

Restaurateur Roy Kroc owns and operates 228 McDonald's restaurants; plans to open 100 new ones every year

Oral contraceptives available

Hurricane Donna ravages Atlantic coast, claims 30 lives

Accused kidnapper and rapist Caryl Chessman executed in San Quentin, Texas, after 12 years of appeals

High rate of heart fatalities among middle-aged men attributed to cigarette smoking

Aluminum cans for beverages and food begin to appear

85 million TV sets in use

1961

FCC (Federal Communications Commission) chairman Newton N. Minow calls TV a "vast wasteland"

First electric toothbrushes, named Broxodents, introduced by Squibb

Jackie Kennedy look: bouffant hairdos, pillbox hats, and gloves; also two-piece suits by Oleg Cassini

1962

Seattle World's Fair, with 607-foot Space Needle, opens

Diet colas Tab and Diet Rite appear in supermarkets

Walter Cronkite becomes anchor of *CBS Evening News;* remains for 20 years

1963

Kodak introduces Instamatic camera with film cartridge; Polaroid color camera goes on sale

Tranquilizer Valium produced by Roche Labs

First Trimline push-button telephones

Pentel invents and markets felt-tip pens

1964

Surgeon general cites health hazards of cigarette smoking; Federal Trade Commission calls for warnings on cigarette packages

New York World's Fair: visitors see Michelangelo's "Pietà," on loan from the Vatican; General Motors' Futurama is most popular attraction

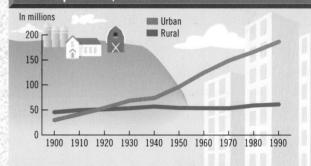

Spectacular jewel heist from New York's American Museum of Natural History; perpetrators, led by Murph the Surf, return most of loot in exchange for lenient sentences

American psychologist Eric Berne's book *Games People Play* encourages many to analyze their own and others' social interactions

Austrian fashion designer Rudi Gernreich rocks the fashion world with his topless bathing suit, the "monokini"; French designer André Courrèges favors short white boots, short skirts, and trapezoidal lines, topped off with dark sunglasses; British designer Mary Quant takes everything to new mod heights

1965

U.S. mints clad coins made of alloys of copper and nickel to replace higher-silver-content

dollars, half-dollars, quarters, dimes

Young men's hair getting shaggier while young women sport the Sassoon look: short, smooth, swingy bobs with bangs

Miniskirt introduced

1966

The New York Herald Tribune folds

Winston becomes bestselling cigarette; for first time filter brands surpass nonfilters

Truman Capote throws "black and white ball" at New York

City's Plaza Hotel and invites 500 of "just my real friends"

National Association of Broadcasters instructs disc jockeys to screen records for obscene or hidden meanings

1967

Albert de Salvo, the Boston Strangler, sentenced to life imprisonment

British model, Twiggy, comes to New York City and wows Americans in her short skirts, jumpsuits, and boots

100-millionth telephone installed in U.S.

1968

Jacqueline Kennedy marries Greek shipping magnate Aristotle Onassis

American social scientist Paul Ehrlich, in *The Population Bomb*, predicts famine will cause the death of billions of

At the Lincoln Memorial on August 28, 1963, Martin Luther King, Jr., began his famous speech: "I say to you today . . . I still have a dream."

people between 1970 and 1985

Afro hairdos and loose-fitting robes in colorful fabrics become popular among black people

First quartz watches cost $1,000

1969

The Saturday Evening Post suspends publication

The Condon Report, a U.S. government-sponsored study of Unidentified Flying Objects headed by physicist E. U. Condon, rejects the idea that beings from outer space have visited Earth

Granny dresses, floor-length maxicoats, clogs, tie-dyed fabrics

Pesticide DDT banned in residential areas

Commune leader Charles Manson and followers murder pregnant actress Sharon Tate and four others in Los Angeles

ARTS & LETTERS

1960

American journalist William Shirer's *The Rise and Fall of the Third Reich*

American author John Updike's *Rabbit, Run*

American artist Jasper Johns's "Painted Bronze (Beer Cans)"

American writer Harper Lee's novel *To Kill a Mockingbird*

Russian-born violinist Isaac Stern begins campaign to save Carnegie Hall in New York City from the wrecking ball

American Ballet Theatre tours the U.S.S.R.; first U.S. dance company ever to do so

1961

American journalist Theodore H. White's *The Making of the President: 1960*

American novelist Joseph Heller's *Catch-22*

Black American author James Baldwin's *Nobody Knows My Name*

American writer J. D. Salinger's novel *Franny and Zooey*

In 1965, with the Vietnam War already dividing Americans, this Washington, D.C., coin shop owner displayed her feelings on draft evasion.

American playwright Tennessee Williams's *The Night of the Iguana*

British playwright Robert Bolt's *A Man for All Seasons*

World-renowned Spanish cellist Pablo Casals, 84, plays at a White House state dinner

American opera singers Joan Sutherland and Leontyne Price make their debuts at the Metropolitan Opera in New York City

Ballet dancer Rudolf Nureyev defects from the U.S.S.R.

"Today nothing is out because everything is in. Every costume from every era. . . . Nowadays the doorman doesn't know who to let in."

— Marshall McLuhan, 1968

1962

American novelist William Faulkner's *The Reivers*

American author John Steinbeck's *Travels With Charley: In Search of America*

Russian-born American author Vladimir Nabokov's *Pale Fire*

American writer Ken Kesey's novel *One Flew Over the Cuckoo's Nest*

German writer Günter Grass's *The Tin Drum* is published in America

American playwright Edward Albee's *Who's Afraid of Virginia Woolf?*

American artist Andy Warhol's "Marilyn Monroe" and "Green Coca-Cola Bottles"

The first building in the Lincoln Center for the Performing Arts complex, Avery Fisher Hall, opens in New York City

American artist Frank Stella's "Jasper's Dilemma"

American composer William Schuman's *Symphony No. 8* performed for the first time in New York City; Schuman named president of Lincoln Center

1963

German-born American political theorist Hannah Arendt's *Eichmann in Jerusalem: A Report on the Banality of Evil*

American artist Robert Rauschenberg's "Estate"

American composer Samuel Barber wins Pulitzer Prize for *Piano Concerto No. 1*

Russian writer Alexander Solzhenitsyn's novel *One Day in the Life of Ivan Denisovitch*

American feminist Betty Friedan

criticizes the myth of the happy homemaker in her book *The Feminine Mystique*

British novelist John Le Carré's *The Spy Who Came In From the Cold*

American poet Sylvia Plath's novel *The Bell Jar*

American playwright Neil Simon's *Barefoot in the Park*

Pop art — in which everyday objects are used as subject matter or in the work itself — is given a major showing in New York City's Guggenheim Museum; works by Andy Warhol, Jasper Johns, Robert Rauschenberg, and Roy Lichtenstein exhibited

Russian-born dancer Rudolf Nureyev and British dancer Margot Fonteyn electrify audiences as ballet partners at the Royal Ballet in London

War Requiem, by English composer Benjamin Britten, is widely lauded

1964

American writer Saul Bellow's novel *Herzog*

Los Angeles County Museum of Art opens

American historian Richard Hofstadter's *Anti-Intellectualism in American Life*

American writer Ernest Hemingway's *A Moveable Feast* published posthumously

American playwright Frank Gilroy's *The Subject Was Roses*

American artist Helen Frankenthaler's "Interior Landscape"

Russian-born French artist Marc Chagall finishes stained-glass panel for U.N. building in New York City in memory of Nobel Peace Prize winner and U.N. secretary-general Dag Hammarskjold

Los Angeles Music Center for the Performing Arts opens; 28-year-old Indian-born conductor Zubin Mehta leads the Los Angeles Philharmonic for full week of festivities

1965

National Foundation on the Arts and Humanities established

American historian Arthur Schlesinger, Jr.'s, *The Thousand Days: John F. Kennedy in the White House*

U.S. Professional Football Attendance

1934–92 (selected years)

Number of Regular-Season Games

1934	1940	1950	1960	1970	1980	1990	1992
60	50	78	78	182	224	224	224

American sculptor Louise Nevelson's "An American Tribute to the British People"

American playwright Neil Simon's *The Odd Couple*

American artist George Segal's "The Diner"

Bestsellers: British spy novelist Ian Fleming's *Thunderball,* Robin Moore's *The Green Berets,* Arthur Hailey's *Hotel*

Op Art tours the U.S. in The Museum of Modern Art show, "The Responsive Eye"

American composer and conductor Leonard Bernstein and the New York Philharmonic begin a two-year retrospective program of 20th-century music

1966

New Metropolitan Opera House, adorned with immense Marc Chagall murals, opens at New York's Lincoln Center with an all-star cast and top ticket price of $250; Samuel Barber's opera *Antony and Cleopatra* performed

Whitney Museum opens in New York City

American writer William Manchester's *The Death of a President*

American writer Bernard Malamud's novel *The Fixer*

American writer Jacqueline Susann's *Valley of the Dolls*

British playwright James Goldman's *The Lion in Winter*

U.S. joins in effort to save temples and statues in Abu Simbel, Egypt, from rising waters of Lake Nasser

Floods in northern Italy damage priceless Venetian and Florentine art treasures

1967

American writer William Styron's *The Confessions of Nat Turner*

British ethnologist Desmond Morris's popular account of human evolution and behavior, *The Naked Ape*

American playwright Eugene O'Neill's *More Stately Mansions* opens on Broadway

American avant-garde composers John Cage and Lejaren Hiller collaborate on *HPSCHD,* scored for 59 amplified channels and 7 harpsichords

Indian-born conductor Zubin Mehta begins a world tour with the Los Angeles Philharmonic

1968

American playwright Neil Simon's *Plaza Suite*

Black American activist Eldridge Cleaver's *Soul on Ice*

American writer Tom Wolfe's novel *The Electric Kool-Aid Acid Test*

The Temple of Dendur arrives from Egypt in 661 pieces to be reconstructed in The Metropolitan Museum of Art

"Liberty without learning is always in peril and learning without liberty is always in vain."

— John F. Kennedy, Vanderbilt University, 1963

American composer Philip Glass's *Piece in the Shape of a Square* is performed for first time in New York City

1969

American writer Philip Roth's novel *Portnoy's Complaint*

American writer Kurt Vonnegut's novel *Slaughterhouse Five*

American writer Mario Puzo's bestselling *The Godfather*

New York governor Nelson Rockefeller donates his collection of primitive art to The Metropolitan Museum of Art

ENTERTAINMENT & SPORTS

1960

Camelot — with songs by lyricist Alan Jay Lerner and composer Frederick Loewe and starring Richard Burton, Julie Andrews, and Robert Goulet — opens on Broadway

British film director Alfred Hitchcock's *Psycho*

Butterfield 8 with Elizabeth Taylor

French film director François Truffaut's *Shoot the Piano Player*

Hit songs: "Theme From *A Summer Place,*" "Never on Sunday," "Itsy Bitsy Teenie Weenie Yellow Polkadot Bikini"

Italian director Federico Fellini's *La Dolce Vita,* with Marcello Mastroianni

Montreal Canadiens win professional hockey's Stanley Cup for fifth straight year

American rock-and-roll star Chubby Checker popularizes hit dance the twist on Dick Clark's *American Bandstand*

The Fantasticks, starring Jerry Orbach, opens; becomes longest-running musical to date

Twenty-year-old folk singer and composer Bob Dylan ("Blowin' in the Wind," "The Times They Are A-Changin'," "Like a Rolling Stone") comes to New York, sings in Greenwich Village clubs

Black American entrepreneur Berry Gordy establishes Motown Records

On TV: *Route 66, My Three Sons, The Andy Griffith Show,* and first prime-time cartoon, *The Flintstones*

Black American sprinter Wilma Rudolph wins three gold medals at the Olympics held in Rome

Arnold Palmer wins U.S. Open golf championship

Pittsburgh Pirates defeat New York Yankees in World Series 4 games to 3

Ebbets Field, former home of the

Brooklyn Dodgers, torn down

1961

American composer and lyricist Frank Loesser's musical *How to Succeed in Business Without Really Trying*

Audrey Hepburn and George Peppard star in film version of Truman Capote's *Breakfast at Tiffany's*

Clark Gable, Marilyn Monroe in *The Misfits,* the last film for both of them

On TV: *Dr. Kildare, Bonanza, The Dick Van Dyke Show, Wide World of Sports*

Roger Maris of New York Yankees hits 61 homers in 162 games; tops Babe Ruth's total of 60-homers in 154 games

New York Yankees defeat Cincinnati Reds in World Series 4 games to 1

1962

American film director John Frankenheimer's political suspense thriller *The Manchurian Candidate*

American actresses Bette Davis

and Joan Crawford star in Robert Aldrich's *Whatever Happened to Baby Jane?*

American movie actress Marilyn Monroe dies; death ruled suicide

British director David Lean's *Lawrence of Arabia*

British actor Sean Connery plays first James Bond role in *Dr. No*

American director Stanley Kubrick's movie version of Vladimir Nabokov's novel *Lolita*

Hit songs: "Blowin' in the Wind," "Walk On By," "Locomotion"

The Tonight Show with Johnny Carson premieres

Musical *Stop the World — I Want to Get Off,* with British actor Anthony Newley, opens on Broadway

Black American boxer Sonny Liston knocks out Floyd Patterson to become world heavyweight champion

Jackie Robinson is first black American inducted into the Baseball Hall of Fame

---

WHAT IT COST

Prices: 1960

Daily, Sunday newspapers, 5¢, 25¢

Men's suits, $60 to $108; overcoats, $63.85 to $99.50; raincoats with zip-out linings, $49.50

Women's suits, $26 to $70; blouses, $9 to $29; dresses, $30 to $38; girdle, $8.99; women's shoes, $8.99

Man's electric hairbrush and scalp massager, $9.95

Steak dinner, $2.65; turkey dinner, $2.95

Cruises to West Indies and South America, from $345 (13 days)

AM-FM radio, $79.95

Leg of lamb, 59¢ a lb.; 10 lbs. potatoes, 39¢; 2 bags carrots, 19¢; string beans, 19¢ a lb.;

blueberry pie, 59¢

B'way play, $2.90 to $6.90

B'way musical, $4.60 to $9.40

Hillman sedan, $1,735

Hardcover novel, $5.75

Tiffany heart-shaped diamond ring, $5,350; 2-k diamond ring, $995

Woman's 14-k gold watch, $39.95

5-piece bedroom set, $598

9-piece dining set, $988

Automatic washer, $199; vacuum cleaner, $49.95

Briar pipe, $1.39

LP record, $2.98

23" console TV, $245

4-bedroom, 2-story colonial, $27,990; other houses, $18,990 to $21,990 — all NY suburbs

Jack Nicklaus wins the U.S. Open

Basketball center Wilt Chamberlain scores a record 100 points in a single game for the Philadelphia Warriors

New York Yankees defeat San Francisco Giants in World Series 4 games to 3

1963

American cartoonist Charles M. Schulz's Peanuts book *Happiness Is a Warm Puppy* is a bestseller

Roger Maris connects at Yankee Stadium for his 61st home run of the season on October 1, 1961.

British- born film director Alfred Hitchcock's thriller *The Birds*

American film director Stanley Kubrick's *Dr. Strangelove*

Rock-and-roll sensations the Beatles top the charts in Britain

Hit songs: "Puff (The Magic Dragon)," "If I Had a Hammer," "The Times They Are a-Changin' "

American chef Julia Child makes *boeuf bourguignon* on TV; her cooking demonstrations give French cuisine a boost in American kitchens

Stan "the Man" Musial retires after 22 seasons of baseball as a St. Louis Cardinal; his lifetime batting average is .331

Pro Football Hall of Fame is established

Los Angeles Dodgers defeat New York Yankees in World Series 4 games to 0

1964

Hit songs: The Beatles' "I Want to Hold Your Hand," Roy Orbison's "Oh, Pretty Woman," Supremes' "Baby Love"

Hit musicals: *Hello, Dolly; Fiddler on the Roof; Funny Girl*

In discotheques, go-go girls dance the frug, monkey, watusi, funky chicken

On TV: *Peyton Place, The Munsters, Gilligan's Island, The Man From U.N.C.L.E., Flipper*

The Beatles tour the U.S., appear on the Ed Sullivan show; make their acting debut in *A Hard Day's Night;* their second film, *Help!,* appears a year later, and the animated feature *Yellow Submarine* appears in 1968

Anthony Quinn stars in *Zorba the Greek*

Elizabeth Taylor divorces singer Eddie Fisher; 10 days later marries Richard Burton, her costar in *Cleopatra*

Julie Andrews and Dick Van Dyke star in film *Mary Poppins*

Don Schollander wins four gold medals in the 100-, and 400-meter freestyles, and two relays at the Tokyo Olympics

Cassius Clay (later Muhammad Ali) knocks out Sonny Liston to win heavyweight boxing title

St. Louis Cardinals defeat New York Yankees in World Series 4 games to 3

1965

Singer Nat King Cole dies

British rock group the Rolling Stones come on strong with hit single "(I Can't Get No) Satisfaction"; mod husband-and-wife duo Sonny and Cher strike it big with "I Got You, Babe"; Beach Boys' "Help Me, Rhonda" is a hit

The Sound of Music, movie musical starring Julie Andrews, captivates almost everyone

On TV: *Get Smart, Green Acres, I Spy, I Dream of Jeannie*

American film director Sidney

"This is the greatest week in the history of the world since the Creation."

— President Richard M. Nixon, after the Moon landing, July 1969

Lumet's *The Pawnbroker,* with Rod Steiger

Sandy Koufax of the Los Angeles Dodgers pitches the last of his four no-hitters, a perfect game

Houston Astrodome, first roofed stadium, opens

Man of La Mancha opens on Broadway

Los Angeles Dodgers defeat Minnesota Twins in World Series 4 games to 3

1966

Elizabeth Taylor and Richard Burton star in *Who's Afraid of Virginia Woolf?*

British actor Michael Caine plays the title role in the movie *Alfie,* about an incorrigible womanizer

French film director Jean-Luc Godard's masterpiece *Masculin-Féminin*

Hit songs: "Born Free," "The Sounds of Silence," "Winchester Cathedral," "Good Vibrations"

Walt Disney dies

America's Jim Ryun sets world record for the mile: 3 min. 50 sec.

Cabaret opens on Broadway with Joel Grey and German actress Lotte Lenya; *Mame* opens with Angela Lansbury and Beatrice Arthur

First black coach of a professional sports team: Bill Russell of basketball's Boston Celtics

On TV: *Star Trek, The Dating Game, The Smothers Brothers' Comedy Hour, Mission Impossible, Batman*

Sandy Koufax retires from the Los Angeles Dodgers after winning an unprecedented third Cy Young award

Baltimore Orioles defeat Los Angeles Dodgers in World Series 4 games to 0

1967

Bonnie and Clyde, with Warren Beatty and Faye Dunaway

Mike Nichols's *The Graduate,* with music by Simon and Garfunkel, stars Dustin Hoffman and Anne Bancroft

Aretha Franklin tops the charts with "You Make Me Feel (Like a Natural Woman)"; other hit songs: "To Sir With Love," "Windy," The Beatles' "Penny Lane," The Doors' "Light My Fire"

The Phil Donahue Show premieres on TV

First Super Bowl: Green Bay Packers defeat Kansas City Chiefs 35–10

Miniskirts were barely a year old when this Paris model displayed her silvery kidskin outfit in 1966.

American tennis player Billie Jean King reigns as top women's player

You're a Good Man, Charlie Brown opens on Broadway

St. Louis Cardinals defeat Boston Red Sox in World Series 4 games to 3

1968

Motion Picture Association establishes voluntary G, M, R, and X rating system

Stanley Kubrick's *2001: A Space Odyssey*

French-born Polish director Roman Polanski's witchcraft film *Rosemary's Baby,* with Mia Farrow

American director Mel Brooks's *The Producers*

The Smothers Brothers' show is canceled after they criticize CBS for censoring antiwar folk singer Joan Baez

Hit songs: "Mrs. Robinson," "Sittin' on the Dock of the Bay," O. C. Smith's "Little Green Apples"

On TV: *60 Minutes, Julia, Rowan and Martin's Laugh-In, The Mod Squad, The Dick Cavett Show*

Soap operas start expanding from 15 minutes to half-hour formats

Super Bowl II: Green Bay Packers beat Oakland Raiders 33–14

U.S. wins Davis Cup; Australia loses trophy after four straight triumphs

The musical *Hair,* nudity and all, moves from Joseph Papp's Public Theater to Broadway

Baltimore Colts quarterback Johnny Unitas is all-time passing leader: 2,261 completions for 33,340 yards and 252 touchdowns

Peggy Fleming wins the gold in women's figure skating at the Olympics in Grenoble, France

Detroit Tigers beat St. Louis Cardinals in World Series 4 games to 3

1969

Paul Newman and Robert Redford in *Butch Cassidy and the Sundance Kid*

Easy Rider, with Peter Fonda, Jack Nicholson, and Dennis Hopper

Oh! Calcutta! nude musical, opens on Broadway

Willie Mays of the San Francisco Giants hits his 600th home run

Hit songs: "Raindrops Keep Fallin' on My Head," "A Boy Named Sue," "Aquarius/Let the Sunshine In," "Sugar, Sugar"

Baseball's two major leagues are split into east and west divisions; division winners at end of season meet each other in play-offs for league pennant; winners of play-offs meet in World Series

Super Bowl III: New York Jets, led by quarterback Joe Namath, defeat the Baltimore Colts 16–7

Premiere of *Sesame Street* on public television

"Can't grown-ups understand? This music makes us go. It's what's happening!"

— *Los Angeles teenager, on rock and roll, 1965*

Some 400,000 gather on a 600-acre dairy farm in Bethel, New York, for the Woodstock Music Festival

Underdog New York Mets amaze the baseball world by winning the National League pennant, then defeating the Baltimore Orioles in the World Series 4 games to 1

BUSINESS & ECONOMICS

1960

Federal, state, and local income taxes reach an average of 25 percent of earnings

---

Chrysler's De Soto line is discontinued after 32 years

President Eisenhower predicts a $2-million budget surplus, stating that "1960 promises to be the most prosperous year in our history"

1961

Minimum wage raised to $1.15 per hour; will rise to $1.25 by 1963

Texas Instruments patents silicon chip

Maraging steel, an alloy 10 times stronger than normal steel, introduced; finds use in making rockets and missiles

1962

American Airlines introduces computerized reservations

American labor leader Cesar Chavez forms the National Farm Workers Association (NFWA)

Federal employees gain right to organize and employ collective bargaining, but not to strike

The AFL-CIO pushes for a 35-hour workweek

1963

Equal Pay Act passed requiring equal pay for equal work in industries engaged in commerce

Federal government earmarks some $2 billion for student loans and improvement of U.S. college facilities

AFL-CIO president George Meany calls automation a "curse to society"

1964

Boeing's 727 airliner debuts

First fully automated factory: Sara Lee plant in Deerfield, Illinois

Chesapeake Bay Bridge-Tunnel, 23 miles long, completed; Verrazano-Narrows Bridge, world's longest single-span suspension bridge (4,260 ft.) to date, opens

Jimmy Hoffa, Teamsters Union president, convicted on corruption charges; is fined

---

A Shrinking Share for American Carmakers

U.S. Percentage of World Auto Production, 1950–91

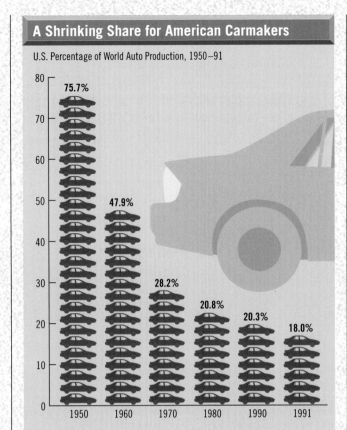

- 1950: 75.7%
- 1960: 47.9%
- 1970: 28.2%
- 1980: 20.8%
- 1990: 20.3%
- 1991: 18.0%

$10,000 and sentenced to eight years in prison; beginning in 1967, serves four years until President Richard Nixon commutes his sentence

National Commission on Technology, Automation, and Economic Progress is set up to study the effect of automation on jobs

1965

Use of pure oxygen to reduce impurities in steelmaking is developed; open-hearth method declines

International Telephone and Telegraph (ITT) acquires the American Broadcasting Company (ABC) in major communications merger

Stock tickers are connected to computers for instant printout of transactions

Vehicle Air Pollution and Control Act regulates auto emissions

---

Major power blackout in northeastern United States and parts of Canada affects 30 million people; causes rethinking of nation's energy policies

American labor leader Cesar Chavez organizes strikes and nationwide boycotts to win contracts from California grape growers

1966

Consumer advocate Ralph Nader's book *Unsafe at Any Speed* cites General Motors' sports car Corvair as dangerous

LBJ signs the Traffic Safety Act, requiring car safety standards

1967

Muriel Siebert is first woman to buy a seat on New York Stock Exchange

Public Broadcasting Service created to provide financial

---

support for educational and noncommercial television and radio broadcasting

Henry J. Kaiser, construction mogul, dies; led work on Hoover Dam (1936), San Francisco–Oakland Bay Bridge (1936), and Grand Coulee Dam (1942)

Major oil deposits are discovered in Alaska

1968

U.S. requires antipollution devices on cars

Trading volume on N.Y. Stock Exchange tops 16.4 million shares for first time since 1929

Merger of New York Central and Pennsylvania railroads, largest corporate merger to date, creates Penn Central, with 21,000 miles of track

The United Auto Workers (UAW) splits from the AFL-CIO and forms the Alliance for Labor Action with the Teamsters Union

Direct U.S.-U.S.S.R. commercial flights begin; Soviet Aeroflot lands at Kennedy Airport the same day U.S. jet takes off for Moscow

John Hancock Building completed in Chicago; at 1,127 feet, tallest multiuse structure in world

1969

The Peter Principle, a book by Laurence J. Peter and Raymond Hull, proposes that company employees rise to the level of their incompetence

Chevron Corporation offshore oil-well spill near Santa Barbara fouls California's coast, triggers public outrage

Environmental Policy Act mandates "environmental impact" statements for all federal projects

British-French Concorde supersonic airliner (SST) makes maiden flight

Railroad conductors, switchmen, firemen, engineers, and trainmen join in one railroad union

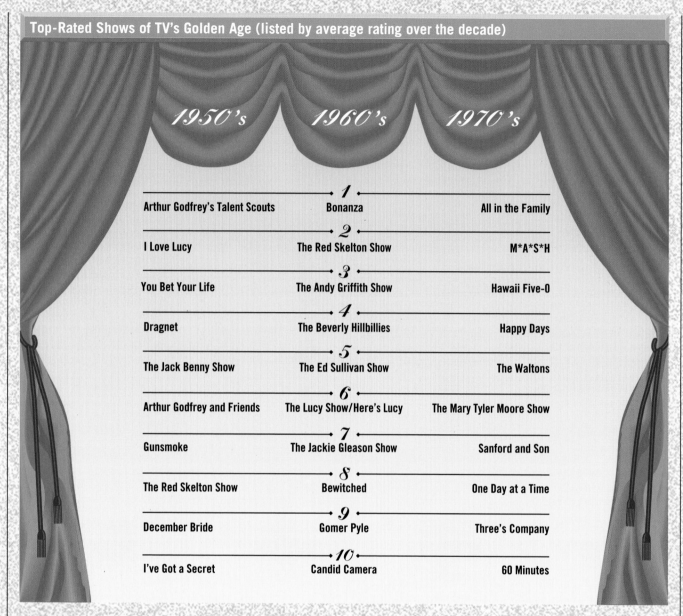

Top-Rated Shows of TV's Golden Age (listed by average rating over the decade)

1950's — 1960's — 1970's

	1950's	1960's	1970's
1	Arthur Godfrey's Talent Scouts	Bonanza	All in the Family
2	I Love Lucy	The Red Skelton Show	M*A*S*H
3	You Bet Your Life	The Andy Griffith Show	Hawaii Five-O
4	Dragnet	The Beverly Hillbillies	Happy Days
5	The Jack Benny Show	The Ed Sullivan Show	The Waltons
6	Arthur Godfrey and Friends	The Lucy Show/Here's Lucy	The Mary Tyler Moore Show
7	Gunsmoke	The Jackie Gleason Show	Sanford and Son
8	The Red Skelton Show	Bewitched	One Day at a Time
9	December Bride	Gomer Pyle	Three's Company
10	I've Got a Secret	Candid Camera	60 Minutes

SCIENCE & MEDICINE

1960

First laser, high-intensity light beam, developed by American scientist Theodore Maimen; first laser eye surgery performed two years later

Term *bionics* used by American scientist J. E. Steel to describe creating devices and machines modeled on living organisms and their parts

Nuclear submarine *Triton* cruises underwater around the world

Pioneer 5 orbits sun, sends back radio signals

Team led by anthropologists Mary and Louis Leakey finds first *Homo habilis* fossils at Olduvai Gorge, Tanzania; human ancestor estimated to be 1.6 to 1.9 million years old

First underwater firing of Polaris, an intermediate range ballistic missile (IRBM) with nuclear warhead

Bathyscaphe *Trieste*, a navigable underwater ship for deep-sea exploration, descends 38,800 feet to the bottom of the Mariana Trench in the Pacific

1961

Yuri Gagarin, Russian cosmonaut, is first man in space

Astronaut Alan Shepard, Jr., America's first man in space, takes 15-minute suborbital flight

Earth found to be not a perfect sphere but a slightly irregular ellipsoid, based on information from Vanguard satellites

Oral polio vaccine, developed by Russian-born American immunologist Albert Sabin, becomes available

Chimpanzee is transported 155 miles into space in successful Project Mercury suborbital test flight

The element Lawrencium is discovered by scientist Albert Ghiorso and his team

First intercontinental ballistic missile (ICBM) fired; travels 4,200 miles

1962

John H. Glenn, Jr., first American in orbit, circles Earth three times; Scott Carpenter and Wally Schirra follow with orbital flights

American scientist James Watson and British scientists Francis Crick and Maurice Wilkins share Nobel Prize for physiology or medicine

Dr. Frances O. Kelsey leads successful effort to ban thalidomide after babies with deformities are born to mothers who used the sedative

Satellite *Telstar 1* carries out communications tests

IBM introduces disk storage system for computers

Savannah, first nuclear-power surface ship, puts to sea

Mariner II launched to probe Venus

U.S. marine biologist and conservationist Rachel Carson publishes *Silent Spring*, a warning about the damage pesticides cause to the environment

1963

Russia's Valentina Tereshkova is first woman in space

Astronaut L. Gordon Cooper completes 22 orbits around the Earth in last of Mercury series; first American to stay in space for over 24 hours

Nobel Peace Prize awarded to American chemist Dr. Linus C. Pauling; first person to hold two unshared prizes (Nobel Prize for chemistry in 1954 was his first)

First successful microcomputer, the PDP-8, is introduced by Digital Equipment Corporation

First quasar (quasi-stellar radiation source) identified; most distant object known

A home video recorder is demonstrated in London

1964

American physicists Murray Gell-Mann and George Zweig propose quark theory positing that subatomic particles, including neutrons and protons, are made up of even smaller particles

IBM word processor that corrects and stores typing

Ranger VII produces close-up photos of Moon

Home kidney dialysis for diabetics

Green Revolution: new rice strain bolsters food supply in underdeveloped countries

TV transmission via stationary satellite used to relay Tokyo Olympic Games to North America

1965

U.S. astronaut Edward White takes "space walks"

Mariner IV transmits close-up pictures of Mars

Measles vaccine

Environmental studies introduced in U.S. schools

World's first working commercial communications satellite, *Early Bird*

1966

First successful artificial heart pump implanted in a patient at Methodist Hospital, Houston, Texas

First direct-dial transatlantic phone call

Surveyor I soft-lands on Moon; sends back more than 11,000 photos of lunar surface

American physician William Masters and his research associate, Virginia Johnson, publish *Human Sexual Response*

Boreholes cut into Greenland glacier date ice layers; bottom layer is more than 150,000 years old

1967

Launch pad fire at Cape Kennedy, Florida, kills Apollo astronauts Virgil I. (Gus) Grissom, Edward H. White II, and Roger B. Chaffee

Dolby device invented; filters out background noise in audio recordings

American surgeon René Favalero introduces coronary artery bypass operation

Cholesterol named a factor in heart disease

South African surgeon Dr. Christiaan Barnard performs first human heart transplant

operation

The grizzly bear, bald eagle, and Florida manatee are put on the endangered species list

1968

Apollo 8: first manned flight around Moon

Geneticist James Watson's *The Double Helix*, about the discovery of the structure of DNA, is a bestseller

Theory of plate tectonics introduced by American scientists; explains origin of mountain chains, distribution of earthquakes and volcanoes, development of ocean basins

Vaccine against meningitis

1969

Composition of hemoglobin in human blood determined

Cyclamates, used in artificial sweeteners, banned because of possible harmful effects

American engineer invents first microprocessor, the Intel 4004

> *"We have always said that in our war with the Arabs we had a secret weapon — no alternative."*
>
> — *Golda Meir, prime minister of Israel, October 3, 1969*

Bubble memory invented: computers now can retain data when turned off

The element Hahnium discovered by scientist Albert Ghiorso and his team

Astronaut Neil A. Armstrong becomes first man to walk on the Moon; his *Apollo 11* crewmates are Edwin E. (Buzz) Aldrin, Jr., and Michael Collins; 100 million viewers worldwide watch live TV broadcast from Moon

The **Apollo 11** *lunar landing, on July 20, 1969, was followed by five more landings, ending with the* **Apollo 17** *mission in December 1972.*

WORLD POLITICAL EVENTS

1960

Soviet premier Nikita Khrushchev visits U.N. General Assembly in New York; pounds shoe in anger

Organization of American States (OAS) accuses Dominican Republic's President Rafael Trujillo of assassination attempt on Venezuela's President Romulo Betancourt; Trujillo resigns

Belgian Congo gains independence, followed by nearly 20 other European colonies in the 1960's

Israelis capture Nazi Adolf Eichmann in Argentina; he is convicted of war crimes in 1961 and hanged in 1962

Organization of Petroleum Exporting Countries (OPEC) is founded by third-world oil-producing countries to oversee production and prices

South Vietnam established

1961

East German authorities erect Berlin Wall

U.S.S.R. resumes nuclear testing

U.N. secretary-general Dag Hammarskjold killed in air crash in the Congo

U Thant of Burma is named third U.N. secretary-general

1962

East and West Pakistan established

Pope John XXIII convenes Vatican Council II to renew Roman Catholic doctrine and religious life

Rebel French Army officers, opposed to a free Algeria, fire on President Charles de Gaulle's car near Paris; Algeria gains independence

1963

South Vietnamese government overthrown in coup; Ngo Dinh Diem assassinated

Pope John XXIII dies; Pope Paul VI succeeds him

Profumo crisis in Britain: cabinet officer John Profumo forced to resign in sex scandal involving call girls Christine Keeler and Mandy Rice-Davies; Profumo's friend Stephen Ward, called a procurer, commits suicide

1964

Khrushchev ousted as Soviet premier; replaced by Alexei Kosygin, who shares power with Leonid Brezhnev

Yasir Arafat leads Arab Al Fatah guerrillas against Israelis

Jawaharlal Nehru, India's first prime minister, dies

Emerging African nations: Kenya, Tanzania, Zambia

1965

Winston Churchill dies

Pope Paul VI visits United States

Civil war erupts in Dominican Republic; LBJ sends U.S. troops

Rhodesia declares independence from Britain

1966

Cultural Revolution in China; Red Guards formed

France withdraws almost completely from NATO military affairs; NATO headquarters moved from Paris to Brussels the next year

Prime Minister Hendrik Verwoerd of South Africa assassinated; John Vorster succeeds him

Indira Gandhi, Nehru's daughter, becomes prime minister of India

Svetlana Alliluyeva, Soviet dictator Joseph Stalin's daughter, defects to West

1967

Arab-Israeli Six-Day War: responding to attacks by its Arab neighbors, Israel occupies territories within Egypt, Jordan, and Syria; occupies all of Jerusalem

Ché Guevara, Cuban revolutionary leader, killed in Bolivia

French president de Gaulle calls for a "free Quebec"

1968

Clashes between Catholics and Protestants in Northern Ireland escalate

Alexander Dubcek's democratic reforms in Czechoslovakia culminate in Prague Spring; Soviet and Warsaw Pact troops crush dissent; Dubcek arrested

1969

Strategic Arms Limitation Talks (SALT) held in Helsinki, Finland; U.S. and U.S.S.R. have preliminary discussions about limiting nuclear arms

France's President de Gaulle resigns; Georges Pompidou succeeds him

Soviets and Chinese clash in Manchuria

Yasir Arafat heads Palestine Liberation Organization; Golda Meir is prime minister in Israel

Willy Brandt becomes West German chancellor

U.S. HISTORY & POLITICS

1970

U.S. and South Vietnamese forces attack North Vietnamese military bases in Cambodia

National Security Adviser Henry Kissinger begins secret peace talks with Hanoi

Bearing the seals of the 13 original states under a 50-star flag, a float glides past the Library of Congress on America's 200th, July 4, 1976.

National Guard troops, called out to quell student demonstrations, panic and open fire, killing four antiwar protesters at Kent State University in Ohio; hundreds of colleges close in sympathy

Chicago 7 found not guilty of rioting at the 1968 Democratic National Convention

First Earth Day

EPA (Environmental Protection Agency) created to unify America's efforts to combat pollution

President Nixon appoints Harry Blackmun to the Supreme Court

U.S. population: 203 million

1971

Vietnam: Lt. William Calley, Jr., found guilty of murder for My Lai massacre; U.S. forces fight in Cambodia and Laos, bomb and mine North Vietnamese targets; U.S. troops down to 140,000

The New York Times publishes the Pentagon Papers, classified Defense Department documents detailing decisions that led to deeper U.S. involvement in Vietnam; papers were supplied by former Defense aide Daniel Ellsberg, who is indicted for theft and espionage; charges against him later dismissed

26th Amendment ratified:

18-year-olds can vote

Supreme Court upholds busing to integrate public schools

William Rehnquist and Lewis Powell named associate justices of the Supreme Court

1972

Vietnam: war drags on; Paris peace talks, begun between U.S. and North Vietnam (later including Vietcong) in May 1968, continue

Nixon visits China; U.S.-China joint communiqué pledges normalization of relations; Nixon becomes first U.S. president to visit Moscow

Watergate break-in: police arrest five men inside Democratic National Committee headquarters in Washington, D.C.; cover-up by members of Nixon's staff begins

Equal Employment Opportunity Act requires equal hiring practices for both sexes

George Wallace, Alabama governor and a third-party candidate in 1968 presidential election, shot by deranged gunman Arthur Bremer and paralyzed from waist down; Wallace withdraws from 1972 presidential race

President Richard Nixon and Vice President Spiro Agnew reelected, winning 60.7 percent of the popular vote and 520 electoral votes; they defeat George McGovern and Sargent Shriver

1973

Vietnam cease-fire signed in Paris; last American troops leave Vietnam; prisoners of war released in Hanoi; sporadic fighting continues between North and South Vietnam

Vice President Agnew resigns: accused of income tax evasion; Gerald Ford named vice president

American Indian Movement (AIM) protesters occupy village of Wounded Knee, South Dakota, where in 1890 U.S. Cavalry killed more than 150 Sioux

Watergate scandal: Senate committee holds TV hearings; former White House counsel John Dean implicates Nixon and others; presidential advisers John Ehrlichman and H. R. Haldeman and former Attorney General John Mitchell eventually indicted and go to jail; "Saturday night massacre": Watergate special prosecutor Archibald Cox fired; Attorney General Elliot Richardson resigns; White House releases tapes of discussions between Nixon and staff after Watergate break-in; tapes have gaps

Supreme Court rules on *Roe* v. *Wade:* says states may not interfere with a woman's right to abortion in the first trimester (three months) of pregnancy; in second trimester, states may regulate or prohibit abortion in the interests of the woman's health

1974

Watergate: House Judiciary Committee votes to impeach Nixon, who then resigns; Gerald Ford becomes 38th president; Nelson Rockefeller, vice president

President Ford pardons Nixon unconditionally for federal crimes, possible federal crimes, committed in Watergate cover-up

Ford grants limited amnesty to Vietnam war draft dodgers and deserters

1975

Vietcong and North Vietnamese triumph in South Vietnam, take Saigon; last Americans evacuated; Vietnam will become one country in 1976

Two assassination attempts made on President Ford in California by Lynette (Squeaky) Fromme, a disciple of Charles Manson, and Sara Jane Moore, associated with antigovernment groups

---

> *"What did the president know and when did he know it?"*
>
> — Senator Howard Baker, at the Watergate hearings, June 1973

America's *Apollo 18* links up with Soviets' *Soyuz 19;* astronauts and cosmonauts hold joint news conference from space

1976

U.S. celebrates Bicentennial; millions watch "tall ships" enter New York Harbor

U.S-Soviet treaty limiting underground testing of nuclear warheads

Legionnaires' disease kills 29 in Philadelphia

Jimmy Carter elected 39th president with Walter Mondale as vice president; they defeat Gerald Ford and Robert Dole

1977

Carter pardons most Vietnam draft evaders; lifts bans on travel to Cuba, Vietnam, Cambodia

Human rights becomes cornerstone of Carter's foreign policy

Carter declares a national energy crisis; Congress adopts Carter's proposal to establish a Department of Energy

Senate subcommittee reveals that Lockheed Aircraft Corporation paid out $22 million in bribes to sell its planes abroad

1978

Carter arranges Camp David talks on Mideast peace between Egypt's Anwar Sadat and Israel's Menachem Begin

U.S. agrees to give up Panama Canal by year 2000

Supreme Court rules University of California Medical School has violated white student Allan Bakke's civil rights by denying him acceptance because of school's racial quotas, designed to increase school's minority enrollment; Court orders the medical school to admit Bakke

1979

Carter administration reels under *stagflation* (stagnant economic growth, high inflation), caused in part by surge in oil prices

Three Mile Island nuclear reactor in Pennsylvania suffers near-meltdown; accident casts doubt on future of nuclear energy as an alternative to fossil fuels

Worst air disaster to date in U.S. history: 275 die in Chicago DC-10 crash; all DC-10's are grounded to check for possible accident-causing design flaws

EVERYDAY LIFE

1970

American chemist and two-time Nobel Prize winner Linus Pauling advocates huge doses of vitamin C to combat colds and flu

Women in the U.S. Army achieve rank of general: Anna Mae Hays and Elizabeth P. Hoisington promoted from colonel

Health foods gain favor with health-conscious Americans

The Beatles break up

1971

Charles Manson and three codefendants convicted of Tate-LaBianca murders

TV stops accepting cigarette advertising

California adopts nation's first standards reducing lead emissions in gasoline

Hot pants, shag haircuts, and midi skirts arrive on the scene

1972

All-volunteer army replaces military draft

Ms. magazine, focusing on changing aspirations of women, founded; *Life* magazine suspends regular publication

Hurricane Agnes hits eastern U.S. killing 118

First woman admiral in the U.S. Navy: Alene B. Duerk

First woman rabbi ordained

> *"It occurred to me when I was 13 and wearing white gloves and Mary Janes and going to dancing school, that no one should have to dance backwards all their lives."*
>
> — *Feminist Jill Ruckelshaus, 1973*

Pocket calculators hit the market with hefty price tags starting at $100; prices to be driven down in following years by calculator glut

1973

Gasoline shortages precipitate energy crisis

Airline passengers screened in an effort to halt rash of skyjackings

Sears Tower is completed in Chicago; at 1,454 feet it is tallest building in the world to date

"Gatsby" look is popular, inspired by new film version of *The Great Gatsby*

1974

Heiress Patricia Hearst kidnapped; later joins radical Symbionese Liberation Army; captured by FBI agents in 1975 and convicted for robbery in 1976; released in 1979, after President Carter commuted her sentence, having served 22 months in prison

Mikhail Baryshnikov, Soviet ballet star, defects to Canada

"Streaking," running naked at public events, is ubiquitous prank

Smog effects: up to 4,000 deaths and 1 million lost workdays annually attributed to tailpipe exhaust, according to EPA

Speed limit is set at 55 m.p.h. to conserve gas

1975

Four women are ordained Episcopal priests in Washington

Teamster leader Jimmy Hoffa disappears

Energy crisis continues

Pet rocks and mood rings are popular fads

Van McCoy's number one single, "The Hustle," starts dance craze of the same name

1976

Women get Rhodes Scholarships for the first time

Barbara Walters becomes first woman news anchor, makes $1-million deal

Rev. Sun Myung Moon's Unification Church accused of brainwashing its members by parents of "Moonies"

Parents of comatose Karen Ann Quinlan win right to turn off respirator

Billionaire Howard Hughes dies a recluse

Swine flu is cited as a danger by the Center for Disease Control

Shere Hite's *The Hite Report: A Nationwide Study of Female Sexuality* is a bestseller

Fashion notes: designer Diane von Furstenberg's jersey wrap dresses; ethnic chic; wedge haircuts inspired by Olympic gold medalist Dorothy Hamill are popular

Concorde supersonic transport begins commercial run between Washington, D.C., and Europe

1977

Blackout in New York City leaves 9 million without electricity for up to 25 hours; looting results in 3,700 arrests

National Women's Conference held in Houston

Elvis Presley dies in Memphis, Tennessee, at age 42

Convicted murderer Gary Gilmore refuses to appeal his death sentence; executed by firing squad in Utah; first capital punishment in U.S. since 1967

Daredevil George Willig scales 110-story World Trade Center tower

Disco nightclub, Studio 54, opens in Manhattan

Transcendental meditation, yoga, Eastern religious movements captivate many Americans

WHAT IT COST

Prices: 1970

Women's print dresses, $32; coat dresses, $80

Mink coats, $1,190 to $1,490

Sheets & pillowcases, $5 to $10

Convertible couches, $249 to $539

B'way musical tickets, $4.50 to $12

35mm camera, $115

Stereo LP, $3.49

Stereo system, $119.95

4-piece bedroom set, $743

3-piece living room set, $399

Rental car, 5-day business week, $43 incl. mileage

Leased Cadillac, $225 mo.; Chevrolet, $148 mo.;

Triumph Spitfire (sports 2-seater), $2,395

2-bedroom East Side N.Y.C. apartment, $555 a mo.

Five Most Inflationary Years Since 1960

U.S. Consumer Price Index, Percentage Changes

ALL ITEMS

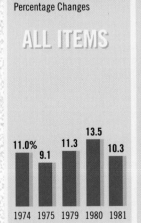

1974	1975	1979	1980	1981
11.0%	9.1	11.3	13.5	10.3

ENERGY

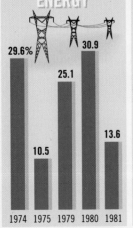

1974	1975	1979	1980	1981
29.6%	10.5	25.1	30.9	13.6

FOOD

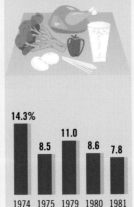

1974	1975	1979	1980	1981
14.3%	8.5	11.0	8.6	7.8

HOUSING

1974	1975	1979	1980	1981
9.6%	9.9	13.9	17.6	11.7

TRANSPORT

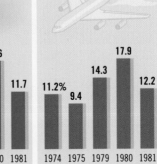

1974	1975	1979	1980	1981
11.2%	9.4	14.3	17.9	12.2

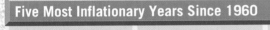

Diane Keaton character in movie *Annie Hall* inspires new look: floppy hats, long skirts, large glasses, clunky boots

1978

California voters affirm Proposition 13 to reduce property taxes; start of nationwide grassroots taxpayers' rebellion

First woman general in the U.S. Marine Corps: Margaret A. Brewer

Mass suicide in Guyana: some 900 Americans kill themselves on orders of their cult leader, Jim Jones, who also dies

Love Canal area, near Niagara Falls, New York, evacuated because of toxic waste contamination

Jim Fixx's *The Complete Book of Running* is a bestseller

The last Volkswagen Beetle is made in Germany

1979

Sony Walkman introduced

The Complete Scarsdale Medical Diet and *The Pritikin Program for Diet and Exercise* become bestsellers

Soaring inflation, worst since 1946, creates great anxiety; investors flee to gold, driving price above $500 an ounce

Roller disco skating becomes popular pastime

ARTS & LETTERS

1970

American writer Saul Bellow's novel *Mr. Sammler's Planet*

American writer James Dickey's *Deliverance*, later made into a film starring Jon Voight and Burt Reynolds

British playwright Anthony Shaffer's thriller *Sleuth* opens on Broadway; later (1972) a Hollywood movie

American playwright Neil Simon's *Last of the Red-Hot Lovers* opens on Broadway

American painter Alice Neel's "Andy Warhol"

American designer Buckminster Fuller receives award from American Institute of Architects for his geodesic domes — large, lightweight, prefabricated structures

1971

English novelist and essayist E. M. Forster's *Maurice*, written in 1914, published after author's death in 1970

American writer Erich Segal's bestselling tale of young lovers facing fatal illness, *Love Story*

American novelist Herman Wouk's *The Winds of War*

"Dare to be naive."

— Buckminster Fuller, 1975

Russian novelist Alexander Solzhenitsyn's *August 1914*, about the Russian defeat by the Germans at Tannenberg early in World War I

Conceptual art, more concerned with making statements (on such topics as feminism and personal identity) than with creating pleasing art, briefly captivates art circles

American artist Nancy Graves's "Pacific Ocean Floor, 150 Miles Out"

American composer Leonard Bernstein's *Mass*, specially commissioned for the occasion, is performed at the opening of the John F. Kennedy Center for the Performing Arts in Washington, D.C.

1972

Treemonisha, a ragtime opera written by Scott Joplin (1868–1917) in 1911 and performed just once in New York City's Harlem, is revived in Atlanta, Georgia

American journalist Frances FitzGerald's *Fire in the Lake: The Vietnamese and the Americans in Vietnam*

American composer Aaron Copland's *Three Latin-American Sketches*

American painter Andrew Wyeth's "Bale"

American regionalist painter Thomas Hart Benton's "Turn of the Century Joplin"

Michelangelo's "Pietà," in St. Peter's basilica in Rome, is damaged by a maniac with a hammer

1973

American novelist Thomas

In 1970 Howard Cosell (above) and "Dandy Don" Meredith launched **Monday Night Football.**

Pynchon's *Gravity's Rainbow*

American journalist David Halberstam's *The Best and the Brightest*

American poet Robert Lowell's collection *The Dolphin*

Russian novelist Alexander Solzhenitsyn publishes the first of his three-volume (1973–76) *The Gulag Archipelago;* Soviet authorities strip him of his citizenship, and he settles in U.S. in 1976

American sculptor Duane Hanson's "Janitor" and other hypernaturalistic pieces

American painter Alfred Leslie's "A View of Sunderland From Mt. Sugarloaf"

American painter Jim Dine's "Untitled Tool Series"

American painter Helen Frankenthaler's "Nature Abhors a Vacuum"

English composer Benjamin Britten's opera *Death in Venice*

American composer Walter Piston's orchestral work *Fantasia* performed

1974

Tinker, Tailor, Soldier, Spy, newest spy novel by English writer John Le Carré (pen name of David John Moore Cornwell) is bestseller

American novelist Erica Jong's *Fear of Flying*

American author Robert Pirsig's *Zen and the Art of Motorcycle Maintenance*

American writer Annie Dillard's reflections of a year living

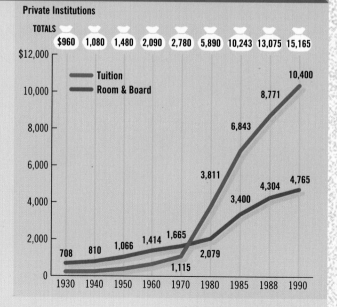

Average Four-Year College Costs, Public and Private

Public Institutions

TOTALS

| $730 | 830 | 1,070 | 1,400 | 1,840 | 2,488 | 3,899 | 4,618 | 5,289 |

- Tuition
- Room & Board

Room & Board: $659, 748, 932, 1,221, 1,487, 1,648, 2,513, 2,892, 3,283

Tuition: $71, 82, 138, 179, 353, 840, 1,386, 1,726, 2,006

| 1930 | 1940 | 1950 | 1960 | 1970 | 1980 | 1985 | 1988 | 1990 |

Private Institutions

TOTALS

| $960 | 1,080 | 1,480 | 2,090 | 2,780 | 5,890 | 10,243 | 13,075 | 15,165 |

- Tuition
- Room & Board

Room & Board: 708, 810, 1,066, 1,414, 1,665, 2,079, 3,400, 4,304, 4,765

Tuition: (1,115), 3,811, 6,843, 8,771, 10,400

| 1930 | 1940 | 1950 | 1960 | 1970 | 1980 | 1985 | 1988 | 1990 |

close to nature in a Virginia valley, *Pilgrim at Tinker Creek*

American journalists Carl Bernstein and Bob Woodward's *All the President's Men*, an account of the Watergate scandal

English-born American poet W. H. Auden's collection *Thank You, Fog: Last Poems*, published the year after Auden's death

British playwright Peter Shaffer's *Equus* opens on Broadway

American painter Chuck Close's "Robert/104,072"

American sculptor Alexander Calder's "Universe" mounted in Chicago's Sears Tower

1975

American writer E. L. Doctorow's novel *Ragtime*

British novelist Richard Adams's *Watership Down*, about a community of humanlike rabbits that faces crisis and tragedy

American novelist Robert Stone's *Dog Soldiers*, mixing drugs and the Vietnam War

British playwright Tom Stoppard's *Travesties* opens on Broadway

American New Realism painter Richard Estes' "Central Savings"

French composer Hector Berlioz's nearly 140-year-old opera *Benvenuto Cellini* has its first American performance

American soprano Beverly Sills debuts at the Metropolitan Opera in New York City

1976

American writer Alex Haley combines fact and fiction in his book *Roots: The Saga of an American Family* to tell of his search for his African forebears

British novelist Paul Scott's *The Raj Quartet,* about India under British rule

American painter Audrey Flack's still life "Queen," combining, like many other notable works of the period, traditional painting and photography

American painter Jennifer Bartlett completes her 158-foot-long work, "Rhapsody," which contains 988 foot-square metal units depicting variations on themes such as trees, mountains, oceans, and houses

American composer Philip Glass and artist Robert Wilson's collaborative opera *Einstein on the Beach*

1977

Australian novelist Colleen McCullogh's *The Thorn Birds*

American writer Joan Didion's *A Book of Common Prayer*

American playwright David Mamet's *American Buffalo*

Greek-born American painter Lucas Samaras's "Reconstruction # 28"

American artist Nicholas Africano's "The Cruel Discussion"

American poet James Merrill's complex, intellectually far-ranging verse work *Divine Comedies*

"Future shock . . . the shattering stress and disorientation that we induce in individuals by subjecting them to too much change in too short a time."

— *Alvin Toffler in* Future Shock *(1970)*

English author and scholar J.R.R. Tolkien's *The Silmarillion* — a story begun in 1917 of his fantasy world called Middle-Earth and finished, after Tolkien's death in 1973 by his son Christopher — is published

Polish composer Henryk Gorecki's *Symphony No. 3,* completed the year before,

premieres at Royan, France; dealing with the suffering of World War II, the symphony achieves worldwide fame in the early 1990's

1978

American writer William Manchester's *American Caesar: Douglas MacArthur 1880–1964*

American author James Michener's *Chesapeake;* like many of his books, a study of a region's history and people

American painter Neil Jenney begins his oil on wood "North America Abstracted," finished in 1980

1979

Former Secretary of State Henry Kissinger's memoir *The White House Years*

American writer Tom Wolfe's *The Right Stuff*, about America's first group of astronauts

American historian and social critic Christopher Lasch's *The Culture of Narcissism* portrays Americans as self-absorbed, celebrity dazzled, and guilt ridden

English writer John Le Carré's *Smiley's People*, one of his several novels featuring British secret service agent George Smiley

---

ENTERTAINMENT & SPORTS

1970

Company opens on Broadway, first of several collaborations by composer-lyricist Stephen Sondheim and producer-director Harold Prince

American cartoonist Garry Trudeau's comic strip *Doonesbury* debuts

The Mary Tyler Moore Show, The Partridge Family, The Odd Couple, and *The Flip Wilson Show* are among the premieres on TV

Number one singles: Jackson 5's "I Want You Back," "ABC"; Simon and Garfunkel's "Bridge Over Troubled

Waters"; Carpenters' "Close to You"

Kansas City Chiefs (AFL) defeat Minnesota Vikings (NFL) 23 to 7 in Super Bowl IV at Tulane Stadium, New Orleans, Louisiana

Monday Night Football, featuring games between professional teams, premieres; announcers are Howard Cosell and Don Meredith

Arthur Ashe lifts the victory cup after defeating Jimmy Connors to win Wimbledon's singles in 1975.

Merger of National Football League (NFL) and American Football League (AFL), negotiated in 1966, takes effect; National Football League now has two divisions: National Football Conference (NFC) and American Football Conference (AFC)

U.S. yacht *Intrepid* wins the America's Cup

Baltimore Orioles defeat Cincinnati Reds in World Series 4 games to 1

1971

Broadway musical *Follies,*

music and lyrics by Stephen Sondheim, produced and directed by Harold Prince

American movie director Stanley Kubrick's *A Clockwork Orange*, based on the 1962 novel by English author Anthony Burgess

George C. Scott's performance in *Patton* wins him an Oscar

New on TV: *All in the Family, Columbo, The Sonny and Cher Comedy Hour;* and from the British Broadcasting Corporation: *Masterpiece Theatre*

Bestselling album: Carol King's *Tapestry;* hit singles: "One Bad Apple," "Joy to the World," "Maggie May," "Theme From Shaft"

Baltimore Colts (AFC) defeat Dallas Cowboys (NFC) 16 to 13 in Super Bowl V at Orange Bowl Stadium, Miami, Florida

Billie Jean King, tennis star, becomes first woman athlete to capture $100,000 a year in prize money for competition

Returning to boxing after being stripped of his heavyweight title in 1967 for refusing military service, Muhammad Ali loses to Joe Frazier, who keeps the world heavyweight title

Pittsburgh Pirates defeat Baltimore Orioles in World Series 4 games to 3

1972

Liza Minnelli and Joel Grey in Hollywood musical *Cabaret*

American director Francis Ford Coppola's movie *The Godfather*

Marlon Brando in the steamy, controversial *Last Tango in Paris*

Broadway musical *Jesus Christ Superstar;* later becomes a Hollywood movie (1973)

Swedish film director Ingmar Bergman's *Cries and Whispers*

*M*A*S*H* premieres on TV

Hit singles: "I Am Woman," "American Pie," "Let's Stay Together," "Candy Man"

Dallas Cowboys (NFC) defeat Miami Dolphins (AFC)

24 to 3 in Super Bowl VI at Tulane Stadium, New Orleans, Louisiana

Professional baseball players strike; start of season delayed 13 days

American swimmer Mark Spitz wins 7 gold medals at the 1972 Olympics in Munich

Bobby Fischer captures world chess title from Boris Spassky of the Soviet Union

Oakland A's defeat Cincinnati Reds in World Series 4 games to 3

1973

Composer-lyricist Stephen Sondheim and producer-director Harold Prince's *A Little Night Music* opens on Broadway

New York City judge rules pornographic film *Deep Throat* obscene and bans it; film goes on to make $30 million

French director François Truffaut's *Day for Night*

Paul Newman and Robert Redford in *The Sting*

American film director George Lucas's *American Graffiti*

Top songs: "Tie a Yellow Ribbon," "You're So Vain," "Killing Me Softly With His Song," "Rocky Mountain High"

Miami Dolphins (AFC) defeat Washington Redskins (NFC) 14 to 7 in Super Bowl VII at The Coliseum, Los Angeles, California

American League introduces Designated Hitter (DH) to bat for pitcher: DH only hits, does not play a field position; pitcher only pitches, does not bat

Secretariat wins horse racing's Triple Crown; first such feat since 1948

Oakland A's defeat New York Mets in World Series 4 games to 3

1974

Polish director Roman Polanski's Hollywood movie *Chinatown*, starring Jack Nicholson

British import *Upstairs, Downstairs* debuts on TV; *The Autobiography of Miss Jane Pittman* wins an Emmy

Barbra Streisand's "The Way We Were," Hues Corporation's "Rock the Boat" are number-one hits

Miami Dolphins (AFC) defeat Minnesota Vikings (NFC) 24 to 7 in Super Bowl VIII at Rice Stadium, Houston, Texas

Muhammad Ali regains world heavyweight boxing title by

knocking out George Foreman

Hank Aaron tops Babe Ruth's lifetime mark of 714 home runs; he will reach 755 before retiring after the 1976 season

Frank Robinson of the Cleveland Indians becomes first black to manage a major league team, the Cleveland Indians

Oakland A's defeat Los Angeles Dodgers in World Series 4 games to 1

1975

American movie director Steven Spielberg's *Jaws*

Robert Altman's film *Nashville*

One Flew Over the Cuckoo's Nest wins Academy Awards for best picture; best director, Milos Forman; best actor, Jack Nicholson; and best actress, Louise Fletcher

A Chorus Line opens on Broadway

British-made film *The Rocky Horror Picture Show* lampoons old monster movies, wins cult following

On TV: *Saturday Night Live*

Pittsburgh Steelers (AFC) defeat Minnesota Vikings (NFC) 16 to 6 in Super Bowl IX at Tulane Stadium, New Orleans, Louisiana

Golfer Jack Nicklaus wins fifth Masters title

Arthur Ashe, the first black man to attain number one ranking in tennis (1968), defeats heavily favored fellow American Jimmy Connors to win the Wimbledon singles tennis championship

> *"I'm as mad as hell, and I'm not going to take it anymore."*
>
> — From the movie Network (*1976*)

Casey Stengel dies at 85, former player (1912–25) and manager (Brooklyn Dodgers, Boston Braves, New York Yankees, New York Mets) whose clowning, colorful double-talk, and winning teams made him a baseball legend

Cincinnati Reds defeat Boston Red Sox in World Series 4 games to 3

1976

Sylvester Stallone in the first of the *Rocky* movies

Taxi Driver, with Robert de Niro as a bitter Vietnam veteran

Dustin Hoffman and Robert Redford in the film version of Woodward and Bernstein's book *All the President's Men*

John Wayne's last film, *The Shootist;* he dies at 72 three years later

British rock star Peter Frampton's album *Frampton Comes Alive* goes gold

Pittsburgh Steelers (AFC) defeat Dallas Cowboys (NFC) 21 to 17 in Super Bowl X at Orange Bowl Stadium, Miami, Florida

Jimmy Connors wins U.S. Open men's tennis singles title; Chris Evert wins women's singles

14-year-old Romanian gymnast Nadia Comaneci scores unprecedented perfect 10's at the Montreal Olympics

Cincinnati Reds sweep New York Yankees in World Series 4 games to 0

1977

Star Wars, American director George Lucas's hit sci-fi film starring Harrison Ford

Close Encounters of the Third Kind, a Hollywood sci-fi fantasy about nice aliens befriending selected earthlings, directed by Steven Spielberg

Annie Hall, with Woody Allen as director, actor, and coauthor, also stars Diane Keaton

Saturday Night Fever, with John Travolta, lifts disco dancing to a new level of popularity

Broadway musical *Annie*, based on Harold Gray's comic strip *Little Orphan Annie*, which debuted in 1924

Fleetwood Mac releases hit album *Rumors*

Punk rock, typified by loud, simplistic music and anarchic themes, finds a niche

On TV: *Roots* miniseries, based on Alex Haley's 1976 book, captures huge audience, estimated at more than 100 million viewers

Oakland Raiders (AFC) defeat Minnesota Vikings (NFC) 32 to 14 in Super Bowl XI at Rose Bowl, Pasadena, California

Brazilian superstar Pelé (Edson Arantes do Nascimento), the greatest soccer player of his era, retires after playing his last three years with the New York Cosmos

Canadian ice hockey great Gordie Howe, at age 49 playing for the New England Whalers, scores his 1,000th professional goal; he retires at 52 in 1980

Baseball speedster Lou Brock of the St. Louis Cardinals passes Ty Cobb's nearly 50-year-old record of 892 career steals; Brock reaches 938 before retiring after 1979 season

New York Yankees defeat Los Angeles Dodgers in World Series 4 games to 2

A College Inflation Index

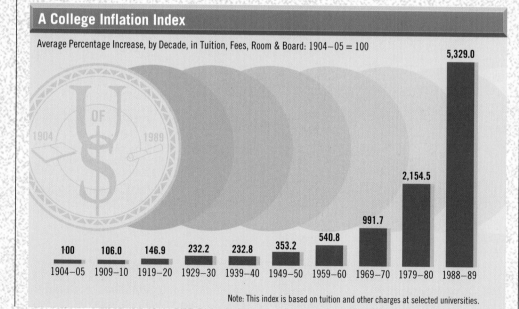

Average Percentage Increase, by Decade, in Tuition, Fees, Room & Board: 1904–05 = 100

1904–05	1909–10	1919–20	1929–30	1939–40	1949–50	1959–60	1969–70	1979–80	1988–89
100	106.0	146.9	232.2	232.8	353.2	540.8	991.7	2,154.5	5,329.0

Note: This index is based on tuition and other charges at selected universities.

1978

Vietnam films: *The Deer Hunter* with Robert de Niro and *Coming Home* with Jon Voight and Jane Fonda

Hollywood musical *Grease*, with John Travolta and Olivia Newton-John, wows the younger set

Swedish film director Ingmar Bergman's *Autumn Sonata,* with Swedish-born American actress Ingrid Bergman and Liv Ullmann

Ain't Misbehavin', a musical tribute to jazz pianist, entertainer, and composer Fats Waller (1904–43), opens on Broadway

On TV, a banner year for prime-time premieres: *Dallas, Fantasy Island, The Incredible Hulk, Mork and Mindy, Taxi;* also the TV news magazine *20/20*

Hit songs: Billy Joel's "Just the Way You Are"; Bee Gees' "Stayin' Alive," "Night Fever"; Rolling Stones' "Miss You"

Dallas Cowboys (NFC) defeat Denver Broncos (AFC) 27 to 10 in Super Bowl XII at Louisiana Superdome, New Orleans

Muhammad Ali beats Leon Spinks; becomes first boxer to capture the heavyweight crown three times

Chris Evert wins fourth straight U.S. Open tennis singles title

New York Yankees defeat Los Angeles Dodgers in World Series 4 games to 2

1979

Director Francis Ford Coppola's dark vision of the Vietnam War, *Apocalypse Now*

China Syndrome, Hollywood drama about an accident and cover-up at a nuclear power plant, stars Jane Fonda and Jack Lemmon

Hollywood's *Kramer vs. Kramer,* with Meryl Streep and Dustin Hoffman, dramatizes a bitter child-custody battle

Pittsburgh Steelers (AFC) defeat Dallas Cowboys (NFC) 35 to 31 in Super Bowl XIII at Orange Bowl, Miami, Florida

Pittsburgh Pirates defeat Baltimore Orioles in World Series 4 games to 3

BUSINESS & ECONOMICS

1970

OSHA (Occupational Safety and Health Administation) established by U.S. Congress to promote a safe and healthful working environment

First jumbo jet: Boeing 747

One of world's most sought-after stamps, 1856 British Guiana one penny, fetches $280,000; same stamp will sell for $935,000 ten years later

1971

President Nixon orders wage and price freeze; U.S. dollar devalued by 8.75 percent

Amtrak, a semipublic corporation created by the U.S. Congress in 1970, takes over intercity passenger trains

Rolls-Royce, Britain's prestigious carmaker, files for bankruptcy while continuing to make luxury cars

1972

U.S. GNP (gross national product) reaches $1 trillion

"There's no such thing as a free lunch."

— attributed to American economist Milton Friedman, 1974

Dow Jones stock index tops 1,000 for first time

Standard Oil changes name to Exxon

1973

New York City's World Trade Center opens; taller of nearly identical twin towers is 1,368 feet high

Congress approves trans-Alaska pipeline, linking Alaska's North Slope oil fields and Valdez tanker terminal; set to open in 1977

Nuclear power: orders are placed for 41 reactors; eventually 32 will be canceled

U.S. devalues dollar for second time in three years

A year after the oil crisis of 1973, this gas station was up-front with its customers: they could fill their tanks, but it would not be cheap.

1974

U.S. wage and price freezes end

U.S. oil companies' average profits increase in first half of year by more than 90 percent, incensing Americans struggling with high prices and low supplies of gasoline and fuel oil

AT&T establishes a homosexual antidiscrimination policy

Worldwide inflation; U.S. stock market sinks

1975

First Women's Bank opens

U.S. unemployment reaches 9.2 percent

U.S. senator William Proxmire of Wisconsin initiates Golden Fleece Awards for companies or government agencies he finds profligate in wasting public money

1976

American-born oil tycoon J. Paul Getty dies at 84

Tanker disaster off Massachusetts coast spills million of gallons of oil

Genentech founded; first biotechnology company to develop new products through genetic engineering

1977

Laker Airlines, British carrier, offers bargain-basement fares between New York and London, starts trend to low-cost, no-frills air travel

U.S. Congress tightens auto pollution rules over carmakers' objections

Bethlehem Steel reports losses of $477 million

1978

President Carter invokes Taft-Hartley Act to end 110-day coal strike

Strikes shut down New York City newspapers

Minimum wage rises from $2.65 to $2.90 an hour; average women's wages are 59 percent of men's

Five American Cyanamid women employees agree to voluntary sterilization; normally company bars women of reproductive age from working in jobs exposing them to lead

U.S. GNP (gross national product) reaches $2 trillion, having doubled in six years

1979

U.S. Steel closes 15 plants, lays off 13,000 workers

Minnesota Mining and Manufacturing Company (3M) introduces Post-it notes, which soon become ubiquitous in home and office

Fresh round of OPEC crude-oil price hikes; spot fuel shortages; meanwhile, U.S. automakers resist downsizing cars

Congress approves $1.5-billion loan guarantee to financially troubled Chrysler Corporation

SCIENCE & MEDICINE

1970

Lasers find increasing use in communications, industry, military devices, medicine, and science

First nerve transplant

Artificial gene synthesized

L-dopa approved for treating Parkinson's disease

Floppy disks for storage of computer data are introduced

1971

Vitamin B_{12} synthesized

Phosphates in detergents found to cause water pollution

U.S. Food and Drug Administration (FDA) warns use of DES (diethylstilbestrol) by pregnant women can cause cancer and birth defects in offspring

Astronomers discover two previously undetected galaxies next to Milky Way

1972

CAT (computerized axial tomography) scan introduced, giving 3-D images of internal body

Artificial satellites begin photographing Earth's surface

Brain pacemaker for epileptics

1973

Nuclear magnetic resonance (NMR) helps scientists explore molecular structure and aids doctors in studying and diagnosing abnormalities and diseases

U.S. space station program: astronauts of *Skylab 2* return to Earth after 28-day mission involving rendezvous with previously launched, unmanned *Skylab 1*

DNA molecules cut and joined by using enzymes; recombinant DNA produces chimera, or hybrid tissues

1974

Freon, a fluorocarbon propellant released into atmosphere from aerosol sprays, suspected of depleting Earth's ozone layer

Mariner 10, unmanned U.S. spacecraft launched in 1973, sends data and photos from flybys of Venus and Mercury

1975

620-million-year-old marine worm is oldest fossil yet found within U.S.

Astronomers detect galaxy 10 times larger than the Milky Way

1976

Lyme disease, transmitted by tick bites, first identified in Old Lyme, Connecticut

Artificial gene, implanted in human cell, functions normally

Oil-eating microbes and algae developed as possible aid in fighting pollution

1977

Voyager 1 and *Voyager 2* unmanned spacecraft launched, will later transmit discoveries about Jupiter and Saturn, including newly discovered moons of both planets; *Voyager 2* eventually travels on past Uranus and Neptune

Balloon angioplasty allows repair of obstructed arteries

Brains of schizophrenics found to have chemical imbalances

Austrian-born American psychologist Bruno Bettelheim's *The Uses of Enchantment: The Meaning and Importance of Fairy Tales*

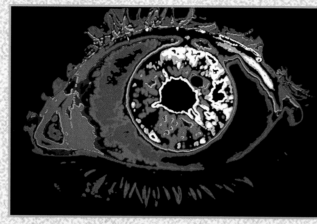

Scientists and doctors in the 1970's pioneered new ways of seeing without visible light. Here infrared light reveals hemorrhages in the eye.

1978

First test-tube baby, Louise Joy Brown, conceived outside the mother's body, born in England to Lesley and John Brown

Scientists discover a moon orbiting Pluto

1979

Black hole found in center of Milky Way

U.S. surgeon general affirms that cigarettes cause heart disease, cancer, and other illnesses

WORLD POLITICAL EVENTS

1970

Anwar Sadat becomes president of Egypt

Edward Heath is elected British prime minister

Chileans elect Marxist Salvador Allende Gossens president

General, and former president of France, Charles de Gaulle, dies at age 79

Assassination attempts: on Pope Paul VI and on Jordan's King Hussein

1971

People's Republic of China (mainland China, under Communist rule) admitted to U.N.; Taiwan ousted

East Pakistan becomes the independent nation of Bangladesh

Maj. Gen. Idi Amin takes control of East African republic of Uganda

1972

"Bloody Sunday" Derry massacre in Northern Ireland; Britain imposes direct rule

Arab terrorists kill 2 Israelis and take 9 others hostage at Munich Olympics; all 9 Israeli hostages, a West German policeman, and 5 terrorists later killed in shoot-out

1973

Chile's President Salvador Allende Gossens dies during military takeover; allegedly a suicide

After 18-year exile, Juan Perón elected president of Argentina

Yom Kippur War: Egypt and Syria attack Israel in October; cease-fire in November

Under the banner of OPEC (Organization of Petroleum Exporting Countries), Arab nations, protesting support for Israel, embargo oil shipments to U.S., Western Europe, Japan; crude-oil prices soar from $2 to as high as $34 a barrel by decade's end

1974

Generalissimo Francisco Franco, dictator of Spain for 35 years, steps down at 81, turning nation over to Prince Juan Carlos de Borbón

Emperor Haile Selassie of

Ethiopia deposed after 58 years

Mexico announces discovery of vast oil reserve

1975

Khmer Rouge take power in Cambodia; accelerate reign of terror

Communist Pathet Lao rule in Laos

Civil war in Lebanon involves Christians, Muslims, and PLO (Palestine Liberation Organization) guerrillas

Suez Canal, closed since 1967 Arab-Israeli war, reopens

Portugal grants Angola independence after years of civil war

Chiang Kai-shek, president of Taiwan and longtime leader of Chinese Nationalists, dies

Eamon de Valera, a former prime minister and president of Ireland, dies

1976

Israeli commandos rescue hostages held by pro-Palestinian skyjackers at Entebbe, Uganda

China's Mao Tse-tung and Chou En-lai die; "Gang of Four," including Mao's widow, attempt unsuccessful coup

Military junta takes over in Argentina

Blacks in South Africa riot against apartheid

Venezuela nationalizes its oil industry, kicking out American and other foreign companies

1977

Nicaragua's Roman Catholic bishops charge President Anastasio Somoza with atrocities against civilians in Somoza's escalating conflict with left-wing Sandinista Front of National Liberation

Menachem Begin becomes Israel's new premier when his Likud Party bests the Labor Party of Shimon Peres

1978

Rioting in Iran against rule of shah (Mohammad Reza Pahlavi); Muslim religious

leader, Ayatollah Ruholla Khomeini, unites opposition to shah

Italian Red Brigades kidnap and kill former Italian premier Aldo Moro

Pope Paul VI dies; his successor, John Paul I, dies within the year and is succeeded by John Paul II, formerly Poland's Cardinal (Karol) Wojtyla, who is the first non-Italian elected pope in 456 years

1979

U.S.S.R. invades Afghanistan

Shah of Iran ousted after 28 years of rule by followers of Ayatollah Khomeini; Iranian mob storms American Embassy in Tehran, holds 66 Americans hostage

> *"Human rights is the soul of our foreign policy, because human rights is the very soul of our sense of nationhood."*
>
> — *President Jimmy Carter, December 6, 1978, commemorating the 30th anniversary of the U.N. Declaration of Human Rights*

Sandinistas take control in Nicaragua; Somoza flees

Margaret Thatcher is Britain's first woman prime minister

Irish Republican Army (IRA), a terrorist group dedicated to ending British rule of Northern Ireland, assassinates Britain's revered Earl Mountbatten by blowing up his yacht in the Irish Sea

Anthony Blunt, former curator of the queen's art collection, admits spying for the Soviet Union against Britain and its allies

U.S. HISTORY & POLITICS

1980

President Carter orders U.S. grain embargo of U.S.S.R. after the Soviets invade Afghanistan

FBI agents posing as Arab businessmen offer bribes in exchange for political favors in two-year sting operation; Operation Abscam leads to indictment of 30 public officials, including seven congressmen and a senator

U.S. breaks diplomatic relations with Iran; attempt to rescue 53 American hostages in Iran via helicopter ends in failure

Equal Employment Opportunity Commission establishes regulations forbidding sexual harassment of employees by their superiors

Mariel boat lift brings more than 100,000 Cubans to U.S.; fears aroused that some are criminals or mentally ill

Mount St. Helens erupts in southwestern Washington; some 57 people are killed, and ash spreads 120 miles

Carter signs draft registration measure; 4 million men age 19 and 20 are required to register

Supreme Court rules in *Richmond Newspapers* v. *Virginia* that conditions must be extreme for press and public to be barred from attending criminal trials

U.S. population is 226,542,203

> *"I really can't express with words what it's like to be back in America again. I just wish there were 52 more with me."*
>
> — *Richard Queen, hostage, upon being released for health reasons after 250 days of captivity in Iran in July 1980*

Ronald Reagan elected 40th president as he and running mate, George Bush, win 489 of 538 electoral votes; defeat incumbents Jimmy Carter and Walter Mondale with almost 51 percent of the popular vote; Independent John B. Anderson gets 6.6 percent

1981

Iran frees American hostages after 444 days in captivity; U.S. agrees to release Iranian funds, and Iran agrees to repay U.S. bank loans

President Reagan wounded in assassination attempt; John Hinckley, Jr., later charged with attempted murder, found not guilty by reason of insanity

Reagan lifts grain embargo on the Soviet Union

U.S. Navy jets down two Libyan fighters over Gulf of Sidra after being fired upon; Libyans call U.S. naval maneuvers in gulf an act of aggression

Reagan fires striking air-traffic controllers after they defy a return-to-work order

Arizona appellate court judge Sandra Day O'Connor, 51, becomes first female Supreme Court justice

1982

More than 600,000 march in New York City peace rally to protest nuclear arms buildup

1965 Voting Rights Act is extended 25 years

The Vietnam War Memorial in Washington, D.C., is dedicated; designed by Yale architecture student Maya Lin and inscribed with more than 57,000 names of Americans killed or missing in Vietnam

The proposed Equal Rights Amendment (ERA) runs out of time, ratified by only 35 of the 38 states required

1983

Reagan presents Strategic Defense Initiative (SDI); high-tech shield would protect U.S. against nuclear missiles

Martin Luther King, Jr., is first American since George Washington to have his birthday declared a national holiday

Environmental Protection Agency (EPA) scandals: Anne McGill Burford, EPA administrator, resigns after revelation she offered public lands for private development; Interior Secretary James Watt resigns under fire

Terrorist bombs blow up U.S. Embassy in Beirut; extremist drives explosives-laden truck into U.S. barracks in suicide mission, kills 241 U.S. troops

Prime Minister Maurice Bishop of Grenada is ousted in left-wing coup; U.S. sends more than 3,000 troops to restore

The U. S. Naval Academy class of 1980 made history: it included 55 proud young women like this one.

order, evacuate American medical students

Congressional committee states that internment of Japanese-Americans during World War II was a "grave injustice" caused by hysteria and bigotry

1984

California Wilderness Act bans road construction and logging in many unspoiled areas of the state

Congress passes Boland Amendment outlawing military aid to Nicaraguan Contras

In "journey of peace" Reagan

How Americans Eat

Per Capita Consumption of Various Foods (in pounds per year), 1910–90

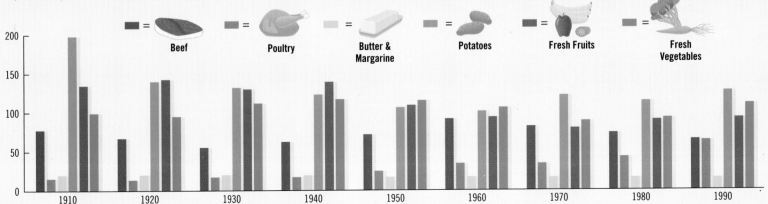

■ = Beef ■ = Poultry ■ = Butter & Margarine ■ = Potatoes ■ = Fresh Fruits ■ = Fresh Vegetables

WHAT IT COST

Prices: 1990

Daily, Sunday newspapers, 40¢/$1.25	$200; $11 each hardback; $5 each paperback
Tailor-made woman's skirt, $150 (wool, lined)	Macaulay's *History of England*, 6 vols. $220
Sheets, pillow cases, $25–$75 (single bed)	Rolltop desk, $2,499 (reproduction, oak)
Blankets, $19.99–$34.99 (single bed)	Revolving office chair, $100–$500
Writing paper, $17.99 (100 sheets, with envelopes)	Muffin pan, $6.99 (12-muffin holder)
125-piece Limoges dinner set, $3,000	1-quart coffee pot, $12.99
Men's suits, $295–$895; overcoats, $595–$895 (prestige store, top of the line)	Carnegie Hall ticket, $10–$40
	Broadway musical ticket, $35–$65
Camera (35mm, autofocus), $90	Gin (bottle), $9.49; Scotch $16.99
Sheet music, $3.50 (single sheets)	California red wine (case), $59.94
Corset, $12 (Macy's)	French red wine (case), $38.94
European tours, 1–4 months, $2,000–$8,000	Tea, $5.98 per pound (name brand)
Women's shoes, $95–$255 (top label)	Strawberry jam, $1.99 (jar)
	Mackerel (10 lb.), $25
Men's pajamas, $55–$125 (prestige store, all cotton, top of the line)	Canned asparagus, $1.99 (15 oz.)
	Canned corn, 59¢
	Canned tomatoes, 79¢
Ladies' suits, $260–$320 (prestige line)	Top line cigar, $3
	Upright piano, $2,200–$7,000
Dickens' works, 21 vols.,	Baby grand piano, $5,000–$25,000

visits China, his first trip to a Communist country

Castro releases some two dozen U.S. prisoners; takes back about 2,700 criminals and mental patients included in 1980 Mariel boat lifts

Reagan and Bush reelected, routing Democrats Walter Mondale and New York congresswoman Geraldine Ferraro, first female vice-presidential candidate of a major party

1985

President Reagan goes to Germany to honor victims of the Holocaust and mark 40th anniversary of U.S-West German reconciliation; decision to visit Bitburg

military graves, where some SS Waffen officers are buried, stirs controversy

Congress votes sanctions against South Africa with anti-Apartheid Act

Reagan has surgery for colon cancer; resumes duties a week later

Hurricanes Elena, Gloria, Juan, and Kate cause some $2.5 billion in damage

1986

Iran-Contra scandal: National Security Adviser John Poindexter, his aide Oliver North, and others implicated in secret plan to sell arms to Iran in exchange for help in freeing U.S. hostages in

Lebanon; profits from arms sales are used to supply arms to Contras fighting Sandinista regime in Nicaragua

Supreme Court upholds affirmative action hiring quotas set for minorities and women

Reagan names William Rehnquist chief justice to the Supreme Court

Reagan halts trade to Libya; Libya fires on U.S. planes; in retaliation for Libyan attack on disco frequented by GI's in West Germany, U.S. bombs Qaddafi headquarters in Tripoli, killing 15 civilians

Congress approves $100 million military and humanitarian aid to Contras

Holocaust survivor and author Elie Wiesel wins Nobel Peace Prize

Immigration-law reforms offer amnesty to aliens, mandate criminal prosecution of employers who hire illegal aliens

After a presidential commission estimates 20 million people use marijuana monthly, 5 million use cocaine, and 500,000 heroin, federal workers in jobs considered "sensitive" become subject to random drug testing

1987

U.S. grants Kuwaiti tankers in Persian Gulf naval protection from Iraq; Iraqi missile hits U.S.S. *Stark* and kills 37 Americans; Saddam Hussein apologizes

The Supreme Court rules that states may require all-male private clubs to admit women

Senate rejects Reagan's Supreme Court nominee Robert Bork; Douglas Ginsburg withdraws his name from Supreme Court consideration after revelations that he had tried marijuana in the past

Iran-Contra update: former CIA Dir. William Casey, 74, dies leaving unanswered questions about involvement in secret dealings; Oliver North tells Congress his covert actions were justified

for national security and authorized by his superiors; Poindexter backs up North, adds he acted on his own authority, without consulting the president; congressional committee states that president bears "ultimate responsibility"

Earthquake measuring 6.1 on the Richter scale hits Los Angeles; 6 killed, 100 injured

1988

Panamanian strongman Gen. Manuel Noriega indicted by U.S. grand jury on international drug trafficking charges; U.S. imposes sanctions on Panama, civil disorder ensues

U.S. cruiser *Vincennes* downs Iranian airliner, mistaking it for a warplane, 290 die; U.S. offers reparations to survivors

Fierce fires in Yellowstone Park

George H. W. Bush, with Indiana Sen. J. Danforth Quayle as his running mate, elected 41st president, defeating Massachusetts Gov. Michael Dukakis and Texas Sen. Lloyd Bentsen with 53.9 percent of the popular vote

Terrorist bomb blows up Pan American flight 103 over Lockerbie, Scotland, killing 70

"Government is not the solution, it's the problem."

— *President Ronald Reagan, inaugural address, 1981*

1989

Supreme Court rules 5–4 that flag burning is protected by the Constitution

Earthquake measuring 7.1 on the Richter scale hits San Francisco Bay area; highways and sections of the Bay Bridge collapse; some 62 people are killed; damage runs into billions

Explosion on the battleship *Iowa*

kills 47; a controversial navy probe implicates a sailor; accusations later withdrawn

Gen. Colin Powell becomes first black chairman of Joint Chiefs of Staff

U.S. invades Panama; Manuel Noriega surrenders; later tried and convicted in Florida court of drug trafficking, money laundering, racketeering

President Bush and Soviet leader Gorbachev hold shipboard summit off Malta

Iran-Contra update: Robert McFarlane sentenced to two years probation and fined $20,000; Oliver North convicted on three charges, acquitted on nine; convictions later overturned on appeal

Exxon Valdez oil tanker spill in Alaska is largest in history: 11 million gallons foul coast

1990

Middle East crisis: Iraq's Saddam Hussein invades Kuwait; U.S. oil supplies imperiled; U.N. General Assembly imposes sanctions; U.S. organizes Operation Desert Shield

Supreme Court Justice William Brennan resigns; David Souter appointed

Bush signs Americans With Disabilities Act; prohibits discrimination against disabled persons; new protection for employees with AIDS is provided

Iran-Contra update: John Poindexter convicted on five felony counts; sentenced to six-month prison term for lying to Congress

Supreme Court rules that a person has the right to refuse life-sustaining treatment

U.S. population is 248,709,873

1991

Operation Desert Storm begins with air war; high-tech bombs and missiles hit Iraqi targets; later U.S. and U.N. tank forces rout enemy on ground; 100,000 Iraqi troops surrender, some 100,000 Iraqis are killed; Iraq sues for peace, though Saddam Hussein remains in power

Last American hostage in Lebanon, Terry A. Anderson, freed by Islamic terrorists after six years in captivity

Ex-Grand Wizard of the Ku Klux Klan David Dukes defeated in runoff for Louisiana governor

Civil Rights Act of 1991, making it easier for workers to seek damages in job discrimination cases, signed by Bush

Supreme Court Justice Thurgood Marshall retires; Bush's nominee Clarence Thomas accused by University of Oklahoma Law School professor Anita Hill of having sexually harassed her 10 years earlier; after hearing before Senate Judiciary Committee, Thomas wins Senate confirmation

1992

Iran-Contra update: President Bush pardons Reagan administration officials involved in Iran-Contra affair, including former Defense Secretary Caspar W. Weinberger

Massive riots sparked in Los Angeles after four white police officers are acquitted on all charges but one in 1991 beating of black motorist Rodney King; 58 people are killed, $1 billion worth of damage; two officers are later

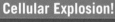

Cellular Explosion!

U.S. Cellular-Phone Customers: 1987–93

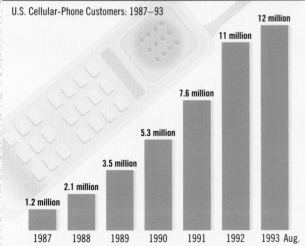

In mid-1993, 9,500 new cellular-phone subscribers were signing up every day.

found guilty of violating King's civil rights

Hurricane Andrew hits South Florida and Louisiana; 13 people killed, some 250,000 left homeless; world's costliest insured loss from a natural disaster

"I have come to the definite conclusion that if the United States is indeed the great melting pot, the Negro either didn't get in the pot or he didn't get melted down."

— Supreme Court Justice
Thurgood Marshall in 1987

27th Amendment, first proposed in 1789, ratified; bars Congress from enacting midterm pay raises for itself

Arkansas Gov. Bill Clinton elected 42nd president, with Tennessee Sen. Albert Gore

as his running mate; they defeat Republican incumbents George Bush and Dan Quayle and third-party slate of H. Ross Perot and Adm. James Bond Stockdale

U.S. marines land in Mogadishu, Somalia, as part of Operation Restore Hope; U.S.-led U.N. effort to relieve famine meets resistance from hostile Somali warlords; Clinton sends additional forces after more than a dozen Americans are killed; U.S. gives U.N. control of operation in May 1993

1993

President Bush and Russian President Boris Yeltsin sign second Strategic Arms Reduction Treaty (START II); U.S. and Russian arsenals to be cut by two-thirds

Florida state attorney Janet Reno becomes first female U.S. attorney general after two other Clinton nominees are rejected

First Lady Hillary Rodham Clinton heads commission on U.S. health care system reform; outlines the proposed program before congressional committees

First direct U.S. involvement in the former Yugoslav republic, effort to parachute relief supplies to Moslem towns in eastern Bosnia-Herzegovina, has mixed success: Bosnian Moslems praise effort; Serbs step up their attacks

Explosion rocks World Trade Center in New York City, killing five; 15 suspects are indicted, including Islamic Sheik Omar Abdel Rahman; plan to bomb other sites in New York comes to light

Four federal agents are killed and more than a dozen are wounded in raid on religious cult compound in Waco, Texas; 51-day standoff ends when compound is burned to the ground; more than 80 cult members, including leader, David Koresh, die

Hundreds of thousands of gays march on Washington, D.C., for equal rights and end of discrimination against them

Dedicated in 1993, the Vietnam Women's Memorial in Washington, D.C., pays special tribute to the women who served in the Vietnam war.

Holocaust Memorial Museum opens in Washington, D.C., to honor the 6 million Jews and millions of others killed by Nazis in World War II

Supreme Court Justice Byron White retires; U.S. Court of Appeals Judge for the District of Columbia, Ruth Bader Ginsburg, replaces him

Floods hit the Midwest as Mississippi River and its tributaries break through levees; many die, 100,000 are left homeless

1994

Earthquake measuring 6.7 on the Richter scale hits Los Angeles, killing 67, causing $20 billion in damage

CIA official Aldrich Hazen Ames and his wife accused of spying for eight years on behalf of the Soviet Union and betraying U.S. double agents

U.S. pulls out of Somalia

Questions resurface about President and Mrs. Clinton's investment in the Whitewater Development Corporation, an Arkansas real estate venture tied to a failed savings and loan association

EVERYDAY LIFE

1980

Game of the year: Rubick's Cube, with 43.2 quintillion possibile combinations

U.S. service academies graduate their first women: Annapolis (55); West Point (62); Air Force (97)

Hotel fire in Las Vegas kills 84, injures 700

Low-calorie, low-cholesterol foods begin to be marketed

Designer jeans by Calvin Klein, Gloria Vanderbilt, and others are fashion craze; preppy look, including blazers, kilts, cardigans, and buttoned-down shirts, are popular among college crowd

Ted Turner's Cable News Network (CNN) offers round-the-clock news coverage

1981

Storybook wedding: Britain's Prince Charles marries Lady Diana Spencer; 700 million watch ceremony on TV

Nutrasweet, a sugar substitute, is introduced

Jean Harris, school headmistress, convicted of

murdering Scarsdale diet doctor Herman Tarnower

Cost of a first-class postage stamp goes up to 20 cents

Nintendo markets Pac-Man video game, which becomes an arcade craze

1982

World's Fair in Knoxville, Tennessee

A national daily newspaper, *USA Today*, debuts

Sun Myung Moon's Unification Church marries more than 2,000 couples in mass ceremony; separately, jury convicts Moon of income tax evasion

Tylenol terror: tamperer puts cyanide in over-the-counter medication; seven people die

EPCOT Center, $800-million Disney futuristic theme park, opens in Orlando, Florida

Over 500,000 protesters march in New York City against nuclear arms

San Francisco becomes first U.S. city to ban handguns

MTV on more than 250 cable stations

Jane Fonda's workout videos become huge success

1983

First compact discs (CD's) marketed

First black woman, Vanessa Williams, is crowned Miss America; her title later taken away for having posed nude for magazines in the past

Cabbage Patch dolls

Cajun cuisine, sushi bars, gourmet popcorn, and homemade pasta become eating trends

"Flashdance" look, inspired by actress Jennifer Beals in movie of the same name, makes off-the-shoulder sweatshirts, headbands, leg warmers popular among young people

The word *yuppie*, meaning young urban professional, comes into use

PeoplExpress no-frills airline offers inexpensive flights

Prince Charles, heir to the British throne, married kindergarten teacher Lady Diana Spencer on July 29, 1981, at St. Paul's Cathedral, London.

1984

New York passes the nation's first mandatory seat belt law

World's Fair in New Orleans

Gunman kills 21 at McDonald's in San Ysidro, California

New York real estate magnate Donald Trump builds 39-story, 614-room casino in Atlantic City, New Jersey

Motion Picture Association of America introduces new movie rating: PG-13, film off-limits to children under 13 unless accompanied by an adult

Hugely successful board game Trivial Pursuit introduced

1985

Wreckage of the *Titanic* is discovered on ocean floor after 73 years

Live Aid concert raises more than $450 million for African famine relief

Crack, smokable crystallized cocaine, creates a new drug menace

The shoulder pad makes a comeback in women's wear

New Coke is marketed; consumer complaints cause Coca-Cola Company to bring back original product under the name Coca-Cola Classic

Pop star Madonna wears undergarments as outerwear and sets a new style

1986

Nancy Reagan launches "Just Say No" antidrug campaign

New York City hosts Statue of Liberty centennial celebration

Britain's Prince Andrew and Sarah (Fergie) Ferguson wed

A fourth major television network, Fox, begins telecasts

The last of the Playboy clubs close in New York City, Chicago, and Los Angeles

Hands Across America campaign raises $100 million for the homeless and poor

1987

"Baby M" case: surrogate mother Mary Beth Whitehead denied custody of child to which she gave birth

Jim Bakker's TV ministry brought down after sexual and financial scandals come to light

Eighteen-month-old Jessica McClure falls down abandoned well in Midland, Texas; millions watch rescue broadcast live on TV

Duchess of Windsor's jewelry fetches $50.3 million in estate sale

Miniskirts make a comeback

Smoking is restricted in public buildings, schools, and restaurants in 40 states and hundreds of cities

Fuji markets the Quicksnap disposable camera; Acuvue disposable contact lenses are introduced

The term *couch potato* enters the vocabulary: a person who spends a lot of time lounging around, often in front of the TV

1988

Computer hacker releases virus that infects 6,000 systems

Fax machine sales hit 1 million

"They're like — whooah! — bigger than any man!"

— A 10-year-old Michigan boy, explaining why he likes dinosaurs, 1993

McDonald's switches from nonbiodegradable to recyclable packaging

Latest rage: Nintendo home video games

Teens favor ragged jeans

ripped open at knees

Retin-A, an acne medicine, becomes a hot commodity when it is found to help repair damaged skin

1989

Digital audiotape recorders appear on the market

Oat bran becomes popular when studies show it may reduce cholesterol

Cartoon characters called Teenage Mutant Ninja Turtles are big hit among young audiences

Aunt Jemima gets a makeover: she is slimmed down, a neat hairdo replaces her bandanna, and she is given earrings and modern clothes

1990

200 million celebrate 20th anniversary of Earth Day

Illegal social club goes up in flames in Bronx, New York, when jealous boyfriend sets fire to it; 87 killed

New highs for suburban living: 115 million people, 46.2 percent of the population

Jeffrey Dahmer arrested in Milwaukee, Wisconsin, and charged with multiple murders

Ellis Island, entry point for millions of immigrants to the U.S., restored and opened as a museum

1991

Postal rate for first-class mail increases to 29 cents

Grunge chic and hip-hop styles become popular with teens

1992

A Florida court permits a child to choose his adoptive parents over his birth parents; press calls it "divorcing" one's parents

Environmental Protection Agency declares second-hand smoke to be a known carcinogen

1993

Pope John Paul II visits Denver, Colorado, celebrates World Youth Day, and reaffirms church's position against abortion and birth control

New guidelines for food labels require that amounts of fat, sodium, cholesterol, protein, and carbohydrate be printed on packaging; terms such as "light" and "low fat" must meet certain criteria

Britain's Prince Charles and Princess Diana separate

ARTS & LETTERS

1980

Retrospective of works by Spanish artist Pablo Picasso at the Museum of Modern Art; some 1,000 works displayed

In the 1980's this hand-held TV set reflected the rapid pace of electronic miniaturization.

American painter Jasper Johns's "Dancers on a Plate"

American Wing opens at the Metropolitan Museum of Art

American novelist James Michener's *The Covenant*

American novelist Joyce Carol Oates's *Bellefleur*

American novelist Walker Percy's *The Second Coming*

1981

Indian novelist and critic Salman Rushdie's *Midnight's Children*

South African novelist Nadine Gordimer's *July's People*

American writer John Updike's novel *Rabbit Is Rich*

British import *The Life and Adventures of Nicholas Nickleby* opens on Broadway at a record $100 per ticket

1982

Black American novelist Alice Walker's *The Color Purple*

American dramatist Harvey Fierstein's *Torch Song Trilogy* opens on Broadway

Library of America begins publishing quality editions of works by major American authors

J. Paul Getty Museum in Malibu, California, gets $1.1-billion bequest from oil magnate Getty, making it best-endowed museum in U.S.

1983

Journalist Seymour Hersh's *The Price of Power: Kissinger in the Nixon White House*

Environmental artist Javacheff Christo wraps 11 islands in Biscayne Bay, Florida, with pink polypropylene at a cost of $3 million

British novelist John le Carré's *The Little Drummer Girl*

American novelist William Kennedy's *Ironweed*

Magazine *Vanity Fair* is reintroduced after 47 years

1984

American novelist Norman Mailer's *Tough Guys Don't Dance*

American historian Daniel Boorstin's *The Discoverers*

American historian Barbara Tuchman's *March of Folly*

American dramatist David Mamet's *Glengarry Glen Ross*

New York City's Museum of Modern Art reopens after four years of renovations

1985

Record auction price for an old master painting: $10.5 million for Andrea Mantegna's "Adoration of the Magi"

American novelist Anne Tyler's *Accidental Tourist*

American novelist E. L. Doctorow's *World's Fair*

American novelist Tom Clancy's *The Hunt for Red October*

"It may be that the deep necessity of art is the examination of self-deception."

— Artist Robert Motherwell, 1985

1986

Robert Penn Warren named first U.S. poet laureate

American painter Andrew Wyeth's "Helga" series of paintings are shown

American artist Jasper Johns's "Out the Window" sells for $3.6 million

American choreographer and dancer Martha Graham's dance company celebrates its 60th anniversary

Canadian writer Margaret Atwood's futuristic novel *The Handmaid's Tale*

American novelist Tom Clancy's *Red Storm Rising*

1987

$53.9 million paid for "Irises" painted by Dutch artist Vincent van Gogh

American writer Tom Wolfe's novel *The Bonfire of the Vanities*

Black American novelist Toni Morrison's *Beloved*

American lawyer and novelist Scott Turow's *Presumed Innocent*

American journalist Randy Shilts's *And the Band Played On: Politics, People, and the AIDS Epidemic*

Black American dramatist August Wilson's *Fences* opens on Broadway

American conservative Allan Bloom attacks cultural relativism in *The Closing of the American Mind*

1988

German-born historian and author Peter Gay's *Freud: A Life for Our Times*

Colombian novelist Gabriel García Márquez's *Love in the Time of Cholera*

American historian James McPherson's *Battle Cry of Freedom: The Civil War Era*

American writer Don DeLillo's novel *Libra*

American writer Robert Fulghum's *All I Really Need to Know I Learned in Kindergarten*

American playwright David Henry Hwang's *M. Butterfly* opens on Broadway

1989

Record price for 20th-century painting: $47.8 million for a self-portrait by Pablo Picasso

Record price for work by a living artist: $20.68 million for "Interchange" by Dutch-born

American painter Willem de Kooning

British writer John le Carré's spy novel *The Russia House*

Indian novelist and critic Salman Rushdie's *Satanic Verses* creates furor in Islamic world, where many consider the book blasphemous; the Ayatollah Khomeini of Iran offers a $1-million bounty for the killing of Rushdie, who goes into hiding

American novelist E. L. Doctorow's *Billy Bathgate*

American novelist Amy Tan's *The Joy Luck Club*

American dramatist Wendy Wasserstein's *The Heidi Chronicles* opens

1990

$100-million art heist at Isabella

U.S. Consumer Price Index

1913–92 (All Urban Consumers; 1982–84 = 100)

Year	CPI
1913	9.9
1920	20.0
1929	17.1
1930	16.7
1931	15.2
1935	13.7
1940	14.0
1950	24.1
1960	29.6
1970	38.8
1975	53.8
1980	82.4
1982-84	100.0
1985	107.6
1990	130.7
1992	136.2

Stewart Gardner Museum in Boston

$82.5 million paid for Vincent van Gogh's "Portrait of Dr. Gachet"

American writer John Updike's *Rabbit at Rest,* in which protagonist of previous novels, Rabbit Angstrom, dies

American lawyer and novelist Scott Turow's *Burden of Proof*

1991

American writer Anne Tyler's novel *Saint Maybe*

Publisher and former ambassador to Britain Walter Annenberg will leave his $1-billion art collection to the Metropolitan Museum of Art

"Somewhere out in this audience may even be someone who will one day follow in my footsteps, and preside over the White House as the President's spouse. I wish him well!"

— *Barbara Bush, Wellesley College commencement, 1990*

1992

Black American novelist Toni Morrison's *Jazz*

American novelist Michael Crichton's thriller *Rising Sun*

Black American novelist Alice Walker's *Possessing the Secret of Joy*

American author David McCullough's *Truman*

First woman U.S. poet laureate: Mona van Duyn

1993

American journalist David Halberstam's *The Fifties*

American historian Gordon S. Wood's *The Radicalism of the American Revolution*

ENTERTAINMENT & SPORTS

1980

American director Martin Scorsese's *Raging Bull,* with Robert DeNiro

Film version of Judith Guest's 1976 novel *Ordinary People* is directed by Robert Redford

Coal Miner's Daughter, with Sissy Spacek

Former Beatle John Lennon shot and killed by fan

83 million watch *Dallas* to find out "who shot J.R."

On TV: CBS news anchor Walter Cronkite retires, Dan Rather replaces him; Ted Koppel's *Nightline* debuts on ABC

Pittsburgh Steelers (AFC) defeat Los Angeles Rams (NFC) 31 to 19 in Super Bowl XIV at the Rose Bowl, Pasadena, California

U.S. and 53 other nations and territories boycott Moscow Summer Olympics to protest Soviet invasion of Afghanistan

U.S. hockey team upsets U.S.S.R., then defeats Finnish team to win gold medal at Winter Olympics in Lake Placid, New York; speed skater Eric Heiden wins 5 golds

Sweden's Bjorn Borg wins fifth straight men's singles tennis title at Wimbledon

World Series: Philadelphia Phillies defeat Kansas City Royals 4 games to 2

1981

On Golden Pond, with Katharine Hepburn, Henry Fonda, and Jane Fonda

Director Steven Spielberg's *Raiders of the Lost Ark*

British director Hugh Hudson's *Chariots of Fire*

Musical *Cats* opens on Broadway

On TV: *Hill Street Blues, Dynasty, Falcon Crest*

Oakland Raiders (AFC) defeat Philadelphia Eagles (NFC) 27 to 10 in Super Bowl XV at

In his 1988 book A Brief History of Time, British physicist Stephen Hawking elucidated cosmology.

the Superdome, New Orleans, Louisiana

Britain's Sebastian Coe sets world record for the mile: 3 min., 48.4 sec.

World Series: Los Angeles Dodgers defeat New York Yankees 4 games to 2

1982

Director Steven Spielberg's *E.T. The Extra-Terrestrial*

British director Richard Attenborough's *Gandhi,* with Ben Kingsley

Tootsie, with Dustin Hoffman and Jessica Lange

Sophie's Choice, with Meryl Streep and Kevin Kline

On TV: *Cagney & Lacey, Cheers, St. Elsewhere, Family Ties*

Michael Jackson's hit album *Thriller*

Graceland, Elvis Presley's estate, opens to public

San Francisco 49ers (NFC) defeat Cincinnati Bengals (AFC) 26 to 21 in Super Bowl XVI at the Silverdome, Pontiac, Michigan

World Series: St. Louis Cardinals defeat Milwaukee Brewers 4 games to 3

1983

The Big Chill, with Glenn Close, William Hurt, and Kevin Kline, written and directed by

Lawrence Kasdan

The Year of Living Dangerously, with Mel Gibson, Linda Hunt, and Sigourney Weaver

Director James Brooks's *Terms of Endearment,* with Shirley MacLaine and Jack Nicholson

Australian director Bruce Beresford's *Tender Mercies,* with Robert Duvall

On TV: Epic series make it big with *The Thorn Birds* and *The Winds of War*

TV movie "The Day After" paints grim picture of America after a nuclear attack

Final regular *M*A*S*H* episode watched by more than 120 million viewers, said to be the largest audience for any nonsports TV program

Tom Brokaw named news anchor at NBC; Peter Jennings at ABC

Washington Redskins (NFC) defeat Miami Dolphins (AFC) 27 to 17 in Super Bowl XVII at the Rose Bowl, Pasadena, California

National Hockey League: New York Islanders capture fourth straight Stanley Cup

Jimmy Connors wins U.S. Open men's singles tennis title for fifth time

Ricky Henderson of the Oakland A's steals a record 130 bases

World Series: Baltimore Orioles defeat Philadelphia Phillies 4 games to 1

1984

Czech-born film director Milos Forman's *Amadeus*

American director Steven Spielberg's *Indiana Jones and the Temple of Doom*

British film director David Lean's *A Passage to India,* based on E. M. Forster's novel, with Peggy Ashcroft and Alec Guinness

Arnold Schwarzenegger in *The Terminator*

On TV: *The Bill Cosby Show, Murder, She Wrote*

Michael Jackson wins record 8 Grammys; *Thriller* album sells 37 million copies

Summer Olympic Games held

in Los Angeles; Carl Lewis wins four golds in track events, Mary Lou Retton five golds in gymnastics; Greg Louganis 2 golds in diving

Winter Olympics in Sarajevo, Yugoslavia; Brian Boitano takes gold in men's figure skating

Los Angeles Raiders (AFC) defeat Washington Redskins (NFC) 38 to 9 in Super Bowl XVIII at Tampa Stadium, Tampa, Florida

Martina Navratilova wins Grand Slam in women's tennis; takes fifth Wimbledon singles title

World Series: Detroit Tigers defeat San Diego Padres 4 games to 1

1985

American film director Sydney Pollack's *Out of Africa,* with Robert Redford and Meryl Streep

Japanese film director Akira Kurosawa's *Ran*

The Trip to Bountiful, with Geraldine Page

Radio host Garrison Keillor's *Lake Wobegon Days*

On TV: *The Golden Girls*

"We Are the World," top-selling single record, wins Grammy

Bruce Springsteen's *Born in the U.S.A.* is top-selling album: 15 million

San Francisco 49ers (NFC) defeat Miami Dolphins (AFC) 38 to 16 in Super Bowl XIX at Stanford Stadium, Palo Alto, California

Cincinnati Reds' Pete Rose makes 4,192nd hit; breaks Ty Cobb's record for most hits in the major leagues

Houston Astros' Nolan Ryan strikes out 4,000th batter

World Series: Kansas City Royals defeat St. Louis Cardinals 4 games to 3

1986

Writer-director Woody Allen's *Hannah and Her Sisters,* with Michael Caine and Mia Farrow

American film director Martin Scorsese's *The Color of Money,* with Paul Newman and Tom Cruise

British film director James Ivory's *A Room With a View*

American director Oliver Stone's *Platoon*

Top Gun, with Tom Cruise

Children of a Lesser God, with Marlee Matlin

On TV: *L.A. Law, Matlock, A Current Affair; The Oprah Winfrey Show* goes national

Chicago Bears (NFC) defeat New England Patriots (AFC) 46 to 10 in Super Bowl XX at the Superdome, New Orleans, Louisiana

World Series: New York Mets defeat Boston Red Sox 4 games to 3

1987

Italian director Bernardo Bertolucci's *The Last Emperor*

Broadcast News, written and directed by James L. Brooks

Fatal Attraction, with Michael Douglas and Glenn Close

Wall Street, with Michael Douglas and Charlie Sheen

On TV: *A Different World, Beauty and the Beast, Jake and the Fat Man*

Les Misérables opens on Broadway

Madonna has 10 straight top-10 singles

Michael Jackson's album *Bad* sells 25 million copies

New York Giants (NFC) defeat Denver Broncos (AFC) 39 to 20 in Super Bowl XXI at the Rose Bowl, Pasadena, California

New York Yankee Don Mattingly hits six grand-slam home runs in single season

World Series: Minnesota Twins defeat St. Louis Cardinals 4 games to 3

1988

American film director Barry Levinson's *Rain Man*, with Dustin Hoffman

Dangerous Liaisons, with Glenn Close and John Malkovich

The Accused, with Jodie Foster

Bull Durham, with Kevin Costner and Susan Sarandon

On TV: *thirtysomething, Murphy Brown, Roseanne*

Phantom of the Opera opens on Broadway

Summer Olympics in Seoul, South Korea: swimmer Matt Biondi wins 5 golds, Janet Evans 3; Jackie Joyner-Kersee wins Heptathlon; Canadian Ben Johnson stripped of gold in 100m race when he tests positive for steroids

---

"Ninety feet between bases is perhaps as close as man has ever gotten to perfection."

— Red Smith on baseball, 1981

United States garners 6 medals in Winter Olympics held in Calgary, Alberta, Canada

Washington Redskins (NFC) defeat Denver Broncos (AFC) 42 to 10 in Super Bowl XXII at San Diego Stadium, San Diego, California

World Series: Los Angeles Dodgers defeat Oakland A's 4 games to 1

1989

American film director Oliver Stone's *Born on the Fourth of July*, with Tom Cruise

Driving Miss Daisy, with Jessica Tandy and Morgan Freeman

American film director Edward Zwick's *Glory*

Black American actor and director Spike Lee's *Do the Right Thing*

Batman, with Michael Keaton and Jack Nicholson

My Left Foot, with Daniel Day-Lewis

On TV: *Life Goes On, Coach;* Special: *Lonesome Dove*

San Francisco 49ers (NFC) defeat Cincinnati Bengals (AFC) 20 to 16 in Super Bowl XXIII at Joe Robbie Stadium in Miami, Florida

Pete Rose banned for life from baseball for gambling, later sentenced for income tax evasion

World Series: Oakland A's defeat San Francisco Giants 4 games to 0

1990

American broadcast journalist and writer Charles Kuralt's book *A Life on the Road*

American film director Martin Scorsese's *Goodfellas*

Kevin Costner stars in and directs *Dances with Wolves*

Reversal of Fortune, with Jeremy Irons and Glenn Close

Misery, with James Caan and Kathy Bates

Ghost, with Whoopi Goldberg, Demi Moore, and Patrick Swayze

On TV: *The Simpsons, Hard Copy, Cops, Seinfeld, Northern Exposure;* Special: *Twin Peaks*

A Chorus Line closes after a record 6,137 performances on Broadway

San Francisco 49ers (NFC) defeat Denver Broncos (AFC) 55 to 10 in Super Bowl XXIV at the Superdome, New Orleans, Louisiana

World Series: Cincinnati Reds defeat Oakland A's 4 games to 0

1991

American film director Jonathan Demme's *The Silence of the Lambs*, with Anthony Hopkins and Jodie Foster

American director Oliver Stone's *J.F.K.*

Disney animated feature *Beauty and the Beast*

On TV: *Homefront, Home Improvement*

Michael Jackson signs most lucrative entertainment contract ever, with Sony Corporation

New York Giants (NFC) defeat Buffalo Bills (AFC) 20 to 19 in Super Bowl XXV at Tampa Stadium, Tampa, Florida

Los Angeles Lakers basketball star "Magic" Johnson announces he is HIV positive and retires from regular play

World Series: Minnesota Twins defeat Atlanta Braves 4 games to 3

1992

Director-actor Clint Eastwood's western *Unforgiven*

Aladdin, Disney's animated tale from the Arabian Nights

American playwright Tony Kushner's two-part *Angels in America* opens on Broadway

Johnny Carson retires from *The Tonight Show,* comedian Jay Leno replaces him

On TV: *Melrose Place, Martin, Picket Fences*

A 1993 arm injury ended 46-year-old Nolan Ryan's career, after 324 wins and 5,714 strikeouts.

Radio talk-show host Rush Limbaugh's book *The Way Things Ought to Be*

Michael Jordan leads the Chicago Bulls to third straight NBA title

Dream Team, made up of stars from the National Basketball Association, takes the gold at the Summer Olympics in Barcelona, Spain

U.S. wins 11 medals at the Winter Olympic Games in Albertville, France

Washington Redskins (NFC) defeat Buffalo Bills (AFC)

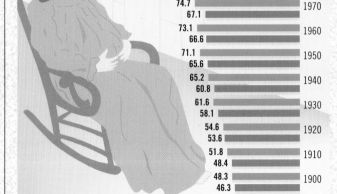

American Longevity, Years of Life Expected at Birth

Years of Life Expected at Birth: 1900–2010

Female Male

Year	Female	Male
2010	♀ 81.3	♂ 74.4
2000	80.4	73.5
1990	78.8	72.0
1980	77.5	70.0
1970	74.7	67.1
1960	73.1	66.6
1950	71.1	65.6
1940	65.2	60.8
1930	61.6	58.1
1920	54.6	53.6
1910	51.8	48.4
1900	48.3	46.3

37 to 24 in Super Bowl XXVI at the Metrodome in Minneapolis, Minnesota

World Series: Toronto Blue Jays defeat Atlanta Braves 4 games to 2

1993

American film director Martin Scorsese's *The Age of Innocence,* based on Edith Wharton's novel

American director Steven Spielberg's *Jurassic Park* and *Schindler's List*

The Piano with Holly Hunter and Harvey Keitel; *The Firm,* with Tom Cruise and Gene Hackman; *Philadelphia,* with Tom Hanks;*The Fugitive,* with Harrison Ford

On TV: *NYPD Blue, Lois and Clark, Frasier*

Chicago Bulls basketball superstar Michael Jordan announces his retirement

"If, in fact, the great ride is over, I don't know how the skills of investment manipulation will translate to anything else."

— Tom Wolfe, author of The Bonfire of the Vanities, 1987

Dallas Cowboys (NFC) defeat Buffalo Bills (AFC) 52 to 17 in Super Bowl XXVII at the Rose Bowl, Pasadena, California

Tennis star Monica Seles stabbed and seriously injured by spectator at a tournament in Hamburg, Germany

Football coach Don Shula of the Miami Dolphins surpasses Chicago Bears great George Halas's NFL record of 324 career victories

Tennis great Arthur Ashe dies of complications from AIDS contracted through a

Big screen televisions, with VCR's and stereo hookups, turn homes into private screening rooms to watch the latest release or a favorite classic.

transfusion of tainted blood

World Series: Toronto Blue Jays defeat Philadelphia Phillies 4 games to 2

1994

Baseball's two major leagues are split into three divisions; each league's three division winners, plus a runner-up, enter play-offs at end of season; play-off winners meet in World Series

BUSINESS & ECONOMICS

1980

Banking industry deregulated

Congress levies special tax on chemical and petroleum industries; resulting Superfund will be used to clean up toxic wastes

Honda announces it will build an auto assembly plant in Ohio

Chrysler reports largest loss ever by U.S. carmaker; avoids bankruptcy with $1.5-billion federally guaranteed loan

Dow Jones ends year at 960.58

National debt at $908.5 billion

1981

HDTV (High Definition Television) developed

General Motors reports worst loss in 60 years; Chrysler loses $1.7 billion

First computerized trading on stock exchange

IBM personal computer (PC) goes on sale

Dow Jones ends year at 875.00

1982

U.S. unemployment highest in 42 years

Dun & Bradstreet reports more than 20,000 companies filed for bankruptcy

First decline in Consumer Price Index in nearly 17 years

Court order breaks up AT&T

$6-billion merger: U.S. Steel and Marathon Oil

U.S. savings and loan institutions lose $4.6 billion

Coca-Cola agrees to buy Columbia Pictures

Compaq markets IBM PC clones

Union Pacific, Missouri Pacific, and Western Pacific railroads merge

Dow Jones ends year at 1046.54

1983

Reagan's tax cuts take effect; seven years of low-inflation growth begin

Weirton Steel employees buy the company to prevent plant closing

Continental Airlines files for bankruptcy

OPEC countries drop oil prices to $29 per barrel, a $5 cut

IBM cleared of antitrust violation charges

Popular cable channel MTV helps to revive record industry

General Motors and Japanese automaker Toyota announce a joint venture to build cars in U.S.

Dow Jones ends year at 1258.64

1984

Texaco buys Getty Oil for $I billion

Congress passes Gramm-Rudman Act to curb federal deficit

Average price of a single-family home tops $100,000

More than 70 banks fail; highest rate since the Great Depression

Record trade deficit of $123.3 billion

Dow Jones ends year at 1211.57

National debt at $1.564 trillion

1985

Capital Cities acquires ABC network for $3.43 billion

Australian entrepreneur Rupert Murdoch buys seven TV stations and 20th Century-Fox; plans to start Fox TV network

R. J. Reynolds buys Nabisco for $4.9 billion

General Electric buys RCA for $6.2 billion

Record fatalities in civilian air travel: over 2,000 die worldwide in crashes

EPA begins ban on leaded gasoline

1986

Arbitrageur Ivan Boesky caught in insider trading scandal; agrees to pay $100 million fine and name other lawbreakers

$39 billion in merger deals as "merger mania" continues

Dow Jones ends year at 1546.67

1987

AT&T digitizes all long-distance facilities

Clean Water Act passes; costs for enforcement will run in the hundreds of millions

Stock market plunges more than 500 points in a single day

Record trade deficit: $170 billion

Dow Jones ends year at 1938.83

1988

Drexel Burnham Lambert pleads guilty to Securities and

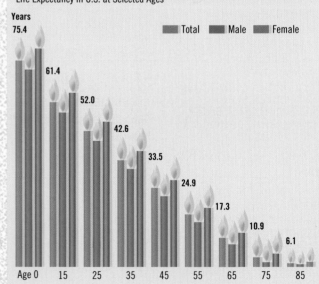

Still Years to Go at 85

Life Expectancy in U.S. at Selected Ages

Years

Total ▪ Male ▪ Female

75.4, 61.4, 52.0, 42.6, 33.5, 24.9, 17.3, 10.9, 6.1

Age 0 · 15 · 25 · 35 · 45 · 55 · 65 · 75 · 85

Exchange Commission violations, including insider trading; later declares bankruptcy

Kohlberg Kravis Roberts buys RJR-Nabisco for $25 billion

Bill Cosby donates $20 million to Spelman College in Atlanta

Dow Jones ends year at 2168.57

National debt at $2.601 trillion

1989

Congress passes legislation to bail out the savings and loan industry; cost is estimated at some $400 billion

Junk-bond broker Michael Milken charged with fraud; later Milken pays $600 million fine, is sentenced to jail term

Eastern Airlines declares bankruptcy

Warner Communications and Time-Life merge in $11.7-billion deal, making Time Warner largest communications company in U.S.

Dow Jones ends year at 2753.20

1990

Greyhound's 6,300 bus drivers go on strike

Biggest Japanese purchase of U.S. company: Matsushita buys Music Corporation of America for $6.6 billion

Exxon indicted for environmental violations in *Exxon Valdez* oil spill; later, Exxon agrees to billion-dollar cleanup

McDonald's opens in Moscow

Drexel Burnham Lambert closes as a result of scandals and heavy losses

Federated Department Stores, Allied Stores, Ames Department Stores, Circle K, and Southland Corporation file for bankruptcy

Dow Jones ends year at 2633.66

1991

Pan Am files for bankruptcy

BCCI (Bank of Credit and Commerce International) scandal: fraud charged in seven countries

General Motors announces closing of 21 North American plants and loss of 74,000 jobs over four years

IBM's first loss ever: $1.73 billion in first quarter

Per capita income lags behind inflation for first time since 1982

British publishing magnate Robert Maxwell found dead in waters off Canary Islands; his empire collapses because of financial irregularities

Dow Jones ends year at 3168.83

1992

Retailing woes continue: R. H. Macy files for bankruptcy

> *"A few years ago, there was only a handful of people who could bid $1 million. Today you have unlimited billions . . ."*
>
> — *Dealer Richard Feigen on the art auction boom, 1986*

Charles Keating and two associates are fined $1.9 billion for bilking investors in savings and loan scandal

Health care costs hit $838.5 billion, or 14 percent of total economic output

U.S. unemployment hits 7.8 percent in June, highest in eight years

U.S. savings bonds purchases of $17.66 billion top previous high of $12.38 billion in 1944

Dow Jones ends year at 3301.11

National debt at $4.003 trillion

1993

AT&T offers $12.6 billion for McCaw Cellular Communications, nation's largest cellular phone company

Mattel agrees to buy rival toymaker Fisher-Price in stock swap worth $1.1 billion

Viacom bids $8.2 billion for Paramount Communications

IBM announces $8.9-billion downsizing charge

Dow Jones ends year at 3754.09

SCIENCE & MEDICINE

1980

Hepatitis B vaccine

Superabsorbent tampons taken off the market when their use is connected to some incidents of toxic shock syndrome

Sonar device breaks up kidney stones, supplants surgery for kidney stones in many cases

Aegyptopithecus, thought to be oldest primate fossil, found in Egypt

Voyager I completes first successful flyby of Saturn; discovers a 15th moon of Saturn

1981

Autoimmune deficiency syndrome (AIDS): newly named disease kills 269 Americans

Largest known star discovered; R136A's mass is 2,500 times greater than that of sun

First commercial MRI (magnetic resonance imaging) unit; it produces detailed images of internal body tissues

Auto, factory, and power plant emissions said to be culprits in the formation of acid rain

First flight of *Columbia*, a reusable spacecraft called the space shuttle

1982

First artificial heart implant; patient Barney Clark survives 112 days

Halley's Comet observed by astronomers, first time since 1909–11; makes closest approach to sun in 1986 as it continues on its orbit that will bring it back in view in about 77 years

1983

AIDS research given number-one priority by U.S. Public Health Service

First successful human embryo transplant

First synthetic chromosome created

Sally K. Ride, first American female astronaut, crew member of the space shuttle *Challenger*

1984

First successful fetus surgery

Genetic fingerprinting based on DNA code discovered

Two more rings found around Saturn

First baby born from frozen embryo

Baboon heart is transplanted to 15-day-old baby; she survives for 20 days

1985

Blood test to detect AIDS becomes available

Single optical fiber carries 300,000 phone calls

Laser used to clear arteries

Scientists confirm progressive depletion of ozone layer above Antarctica

1986

Experts forecast AIDS cases and deaths will increase tenfold in next five years

Chernobyl nuclear-reactor disaster in U.S.S.R.: hundreds of square miles affected by fallout

First triple transplant (heart, lung, liver)

First growth-inhibiting gene discovered

Space shuttle *Challenger* explodes just after liftoff; schoolteacher Christa McAuliffe and the other six crew members are killed

1987

Congress authorizes the Superconducting Super Collider, a huge atomic research tool capable of accelerating particles to extremely high energies

Coelacanths, so-called living fossil fish, observed in depths of Indian Ocean

Dinosaur egg found

First undisturbed site occupied by the Clovis people, first humans in America, discovered in state of Washington

1988

International treaty to reduce chlorofluorocarbon emissions

Homo sapiens fossils found in Israel dating back 92,000 years

British theoretical physicist Stephen Hawking's book, *A Brief History of Time: From the Big Bang to Black Holes,* is a surprise bestseller

The personal computer, with nearly infinite uses, becomes the workhorse of busy offices.

1989

Genetic indicator for cystic fibrosis discovered

Voyager 2 makes first flyby of Neptune and discovers a third moon of Neptune

Deer ticks found to carry Lyme disease

1990

Cancer therapy using genetically altered cells

Well preserved fossil skeleton of *Tyrannosaurus rex* found in South Dakota

A tiny golden calf sculpture dating from second millennium B.C. found in Israel

Powerful Hubble telescope put into orbit; fails to operate successfully but is repaired in

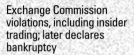

late 1993 by space-walking astronauts aboard the space shuttle *Endeavor*

1991

Cholera reappears in America after 100-year absence

Taxol, drug derived from yew tree, approved for trials in treatment of ovarian and breast cancer

Biosphere 2 begins; scientists live in artificial ecosystem

1992

FDA questions safety of silicon-gel breast implants

50th U.S. space shuttle mission: *Endeavor* crew includes first married couple in space

Twelve million people worldwide dead of AIDS

1993

Department of Energy Secretary Hazel R. O'Leary declassifies documents relating to effects of radiation on human subjects tested during the Cold War by U.S. agencies and military services

"The more we tried to build humanlike machines, the more we admired what a human is."

— David Nitzan of SRI International on the development of robots, 1988

Congress, reversing its 1987 approval, votes to kill the Superconducting Super Collider and spend $640 million to shut it down

Lou Gehrig's disease gene found

FDA approves a drug to treat multiple sclerosis

Princeton University's Dr. Andrew Wiles claims to have found proof for French mathematician Pierre de Fermat's "last theorem," sought for more than 350 years

1994

Heterosexual transmission accounts for 9 percent of new AIDS cases, up from less than 2 percent in 1985

Astronomers find proof of existence of planets outside of our solar system; the Sun and orbiting bodies are no longer considered unique in the universe

WORLD POLITICAL EVENTS

1980

Former prime minister of India Indira Gandhi wins election and returns to power

Rhodesia becomes the independent state of Zimbabwe

Yugoslav leader Marshal Tito dies at age 87 after 35 years in power

Deposed shah of Iran, Mohammad Reza Pahlavi, 60, dies in exile in an Egyptian military hospital

Shipyard workers in Gdansk, Poland, strike to protest rising price of meat; electrician Lech Walesa emerges as leader of labor movement that becomes known as Solidarity, first independent labor union allowed in a Soviet satellite

Assassins open fire on exiled Nicaraguan dictator Anastasio Somoza's car in Paraguay; Somoza, his driver, and his financial adviser are killed

Christian Democrat José Napoléon Duarte is elected president of El Salvador; first civilian president in 49 years

1981

Pope John Paul II is shot and wounded; would-be assassin Mehmet Ali Agca arrested, tried, and sentenced to life imprisonment; pope later hears Agca's confession and absolves him

François Mitterrand is first Socialist to be elected president of France

Irish Republican Army (IRA) member Robert (Bobby) Sands, 27, dies after a 66-day

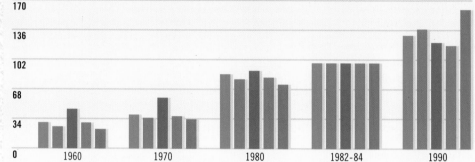

U.S. Consumer Price Index, Selected Items

■ = Food ■ = Housing ■ = Apparel ■ = Transport ■ = Medical

170 · 136 · 102 · 68 · 34 · 0

1960 · 1970 · 1980 · 1982-84 · 1990

hunger strike in prison in Belfast, Ireland

Egypt's President Anwar Sadat, 62, is assassinated in Cairo by Islamic extremists; Vice President Hosni Mubarak succeeds him; Sadat's peace treaty with Israel stands

Israeli statesman and war hero Moshe Dayan dies at age 66

China's Communist Party denounces former leader Mao Tse-tung's policies; Mao's widow, Jiang Qing, given suspended death sentence and imprisoned

1982

Argentina invades the British Falkland Islands; Britain blockades Argentina and sinks its sole cruiser, killing 320; U.S. backs Britain; after almost a month of fighting, 1,000 Argentine troops surrender to Britain's 243-man force

Israel withdraws from Sinai and returns it to Egypt, abiding by 1978 Camp David accord

Poland outlaws Solidarity labor union

Leonid Brezhnev, Communist Party secretary for 17 years, dies at 75; KGB head Yuri Andropov, 68, succeeds him

Israeli land, sea, and air forces invade southern Lebanon in effort to wipe out PLO strongholds; PLO is evacuated

as multinational peacekeeping force moves in

1983

Klaus Barbie, Nazi Gestapo "Butcher of Lyons," is extradited from Bolivia to France; he is found guilty of war crimes and sentenced in 1987 to life imprisonment

NATO ministers affirm decision to deploy intermediate range nuclear forces (INF) if U.S.-Soviet arms talks fail; Green Movement mounts protests in Western Europe

Korean Airlines Boeing 747 en route from New York to Seoul shot down by Soviet missile for violating Soviet air space in North Pacific; all 269 passengers and crew killed

Conservative Margaret Thatcher becomes British prime minister; Labor Party support falls to postwar low

Israeli Prime Minister Menachem Begin resigns; Foreign Minister Yitzhak Shamir succeeds him

After 16 years in office, Canadian Prime Minister Pierre Elliott Trudeau resigns; replaced by Progressive Conservative Brian Mulroney

Syria shoots down U.S. plane, navy pilot is captured; Rev. Jesse Jackson wins pilot's release in 1984

Poland's Solidarity leader Lech Walesa wins Nobel Peace Prize

Benigno Aquino, returning from exile to Philippines to continue opposing Ferdinand Marcos, is murdered; 1 million mourners attend Aquino's funeral

1984

Soviet leader Yuri Andropov, 69, dies; Politburo member Konstantin Chernenko, 72, becomes General Secretary of Communist Party Central Committee

U.S.S.R. and 14 other nations, professing fear of anti-Soviet actions, boycott Summer Olympics in Los Angeles

British agree to leave Hong Kong in 1997

Bishop Desmond Tutu of South Africa wins Nobel Peace Prize for antiapartheid efforts

Indian troops retake Golden Temple in Amritzar after Sikh extremists seize it; 800 Sikhs, 200 soldiers die; Indira Gandhi, 66, assassinated by her Sikh bodyguards; 1,000 are killed in anti-Sikh riots; Gandhi's son Rajiv becomes prime minister

1985

Israel begins pullout from Lebanon

Shiite terrorists hijack TWA jet, beat and kill American sailor, take other American passengers prisoner and hold them hostage in Beirut; terrorists release hostages after Israelis free Arab prisoners

Remains of Nazi war criminal Dr. Joseph Mengele, buried in Brazil, are identified

Earthquake measuring 7.8 on Richter scale hits Mexico City; more than 5,000 perish

Members of the Palestinian Liberation Front seize cruise ship *Achille Lauro,* murder Leon Klinghoffer, wheelchair-confined American

Colombian volcano erupts, 25,000 are killed or missing

U.N. marks 40th anniversary

Soviet General Secretary Chernenko dies; Mikhail Sergeyevich Gorbachev comes to power in U.S.S.R. and asks for economic reforms; Reagan and Gorbachev meet, agree to renew cultural ties, hasten arms control

Terrorists attack El Al Airlines counters in Rome and Vienna, killing and wounding dozens; Israel retaliates against PLO headquarters in Tunis, kills Palestinian leaders and bodyguards

1986

Austrian presidential candidate and former U.N. head Kurt Waldheim is accused of hiding his Nazi past

President Ferdinand Marcos of the Philippines is deposed, and he and his family are given refuge in Hawaii; Corazon Aquino, widow of slain opposition leader Benigno Aquino, becomes president

120 nations call for antiapartheid trade sanctions against South Africa

Haitian dictator Jean-Claude "Baby Doc" Duvalier deposed, flees to France

1987

Reagan and Mikhail Gorbachev sign treaty to eliminate medium-range intermediate

nuclear weapons from U.S. and Soviet arsenals

Soviet leader Gorbachev initiates policy of *glasnost,* or openness

West German Mathias Rust, 19, flies small plane undetected into Moscow; Soviet defense minister is fired

"[This is] the clearest opportunity to reduce the risk of war since the dawn of the nuclear age."

— Secretary of State James Baker speaking of Gorbachev's reforms, 1989

Margaret Thatcher voted into office as British prime minister for third time

Costa Rican President Oscar Arias's Central American Peace Plan is signed; Arias receives Nobel Peace Prize

South Korea holds first direct presidential election; ruling party is reelected

338 of 452 defendants in Sicilian Mafia trial are convicted and sentenced to prison

1988

Vietnam sets withdrawal from Cambodia; 50,000 troops to leave by end of year, remainder by end of 1990

Voters remove Chilean dictator Augusto Pinochet Ugarte from office

Earthquake strikes Armenia; over 55,000 are killed

Cease-fire signed between Nicaraguan Sandinistas and Contras

Benazir Bhutto becomes prime minister of Pakistan, first woman to head any Moslem state

Iran and Iraq declare peace, both sides claiming victory

1989

Communist regimes crumble in Eastern Europe: Solidarity wins first free Polish elections in 40 years; the next year Lech Walesa becomes president of Poland; Berlin Wall comes down; Romanians overthrow and execute Nicolae Ceausescu; Velvet Revolution in Czechoslovakia ends with playwright Vaclav Havel elected president

Tiananmen Square reform protests in China bring government crackdown; some 5,000 die

Japan's Emperor Hirohito dies after 62-year reign

1990

West and East Germany reunite after 45 years

Soviet republics, led by Lithuania, Armenia, and Georgia, agitate for independence

Elections in Nicaragua: Sandinistas ousted in free elections; Violeta Chamorro becomes president

South African President F.W. de Klerk and African National Congress (ANC) leader Nelson Mandela shake hands at a luncheon in Philadelphia.

South Africa, in conciliatory move, frees antiapartheid leader Nelson Mandela after decades of imprisonment

Margaret Thatcher resigns as British prime minister; John Major, chancellor of the exchequer under Thatcher, succeeds her

Charter of Paris signed by 34 nations; brings formal end to Cold War

Hungary ends Communist rule by electing a centrist coalition government; Yugoslav republics of Croatia and Slovenia declare independence; non-Communist regimes take hold in Albania, Bulgaria, Romania

1991

Hard-line Communists attempt coup against Gorbachev; Russian Republic President Boris Yeltsin calls for general strike; coup defeated; Soviet Union breaks up as republics declare independence; Gorbachev resigns

Rajiv Gandhi, son of Indira, assassinated while campaigning for prime ministership of India

South African President Frederik W. de Klerk proposes dismantling of apartheid

Arab-Israeli peace talks commence in Madrid, Spain

Haiti's Jean-Bertrand Aristide,

first democratically elected president, is deposed; thousands of Haitians seek asylum in the U.S.

Mt. Pinatubo, a volcano in the Philippines, erupts

1992

British Prime Minister John

Major narrowly reelected

Earth Summit in Rio de Janeiro: largest gathering of world leaders to date; agreements signed on endangered species, environmental law, and global warming

White South Africans vote to end white rule by 1994

In the former Yugoslavia, bloody civil war erupts between the Serbs, Croats, and Moslems in Bosnia; U.S. offers "full weight of American diplomacy" to bring peace

1993

New South African constitution to be written; President F. W. de Klerk and African National Congress leader Nelson Mandela jointly win Nobel Peace Prize

Czechoslovakia peacefully splits into two states: the Czech Republic and Slovakia

In Russia, power struggle between President Boris Yeltsin and parliament; Yeltsin survives vote on impeachment, dissolves parliament; former parliament members revolt and are put down by troops loyal to Yeltsin

Israel and the PLO sign peace accords; Yitzhak Rabin and Yasir Arafat shake hands at White House

1994

U.S. drops 19-year ban on trade with Vietnam, seen as a potentially lucrative market for American goods and services

Jewish settler slaughters more than 36 Muslims as they pray inside a shrine in the West Bank town of Hebron; this, along with retaliatory attacks by Muslims, imperils Arab-Israeli peace accord signed a few months earlier

Millions vote in Ukraine's first free elections as an independent republic; 118 Communists among those winning seats in 450-member Parliament

First fully free elections in post-apartheid South Africa bring Nelson Mandela to power

Credits

2 *middle left (flagship)* Lake County (IL) Museum/Curt Teich Postcard Archives; *"Peace" and "Pearl Harbor" buttons* Hake's Americana & Collectibles; *remainder* Private Collection. **3** *top (5&10¢ store) and middle (amusement park)* Lake County (IL) Museum/Curt Teich Postcard Archives; *remainder* Private Collection. **7** *top* Library of Congress; *bottom* FPG International. **8** ©Equitable Life Assurance of the USA; *bottom* Library of Congress. **9** *top* National Archives; *bottom* Archive Photos/Camerique. **10** *top* James H. Karales/Peter Arnold, Inc.; *bottom* Wally McNamee/Woodfin Camp & Associates. **11** Rob Matheson/The Stock Market. **12-13** Library of Congress. **14** *left* Brown Brothers; *right* The Lewis W. Hine Collection, The New York Public Library. **14-15** Library of Congress. **15** *left* Library of Congress; *right* From the collection of David R. Phillips. **16** *top* Chicago Historical Society; *bottom (l. to r.)* Library of Congress; National Archives; The Bettmann Archive; Culver Pictures. **17** *top left* Library of Congress; *top right* The Bettmann Archive; *bottom (l. to r.)* Museum of American Political Life/Photographed by Sally Andersen-Bruce; The Bettmann Archive; UPI/Bettmann. **18** *left* Library of Congress; *right* Culver Pictures. **19** *top right* Collection of William L. Simon; *remainder* The Bettmann Archive. **20** *left* The Bettmann Archive; *middle* Culver Pictures; *right* Brown Brothers. **21** *top left* Culver Pictures; *bottom right* The Bettmann Archive; *remainder* Library of Congress. **22** *top* Culver Pictures; *bottom* The Bettmann Archive. **23** *top left* Theodore Roosevelt Collection/Harvard College Library; *top right* Culver Pictures; *bottom* Brown Brothers. **24** *background* Library of Congress; *left* The Bettmann Archive; *right* Knight Library, University of Oregon. **24-25** From the collection of David R. Phillips. **25** *top* Library of Congress; *remainder* The Bettmann Archive. **26** *box: left* Brown Brothers; *top right* Culver Pictures; *middle right* UPI/Bettmann; *bottom right* Pach/Bettmann; *far right* Library of Congress; *bottom* Culver Pictures. **27** *left* California Museum of Photography/Keystone-Mast Collection/University of California, Riverside; *right* The Texas Collection, Baylor University, Waco, Texas; *bottom* From the collection of the Minnesota Historical Society. **28** *top* Culver Pictures; *bottom left* Courtesy National Automotive History Collection, Detroit Public Library; *bottom right* Brown Brothers. **28-29** *background* The Bettmann Archive. **29** *both* Brown Brothers. **30** *top* The Bettmann Archive; *center (both)* Library of Congress. **30-31** *bottom (l.to r.)* Culver Pictures; The Bettmann Archive; Brown Brothers. **31** *upper left and upper right* Culver Pictures; *middle right* Seaver Center for Western History Research, Natural History Museum of Los Angeles County. **32** *left* From the Bostwick-Frohardt Collection, owned by KMTV and on permanent loan to Western Heritage Museum, Omaha, Nebraska; *middle* The Bettmann Archive; *right* Frank Driggs Collection. **32-33** *top* The Bettmann Archive. **33** *right* New York Public Library Picture Collection; *remainder* Library of Congress/Photographed by M. Rudolf Vetter. **34** *bottom* From the collection of David R. Phillips; *remainder* The Bettmann Archive. **35** *left (top to bottom)* The Bettmann Archive; Private Collection; The International Museum of Photography at George Eastman House; *remainder* Library of Congress. **36** *clockwise from top left:* "His Master's Voice" is a registered trademark of the General Electric Company/Culver Pictures; Morton International, Inc.; Courtesy of the Dial Corp.; National Archives; The "Sailor Jack & Bingo" logo is a registered trademark and is reproduced with the permission of Borden, Inc.; Advertisement courtesy of the Faultless Starch-Bon Ami Company/The Bettmann Archive; Uniroyal Goodrich Licensing Services, Inc./Collection of Ruth Kravette, Authentic Old Ads, Jericho, NY; Used with permission of General Mills, Inc.; Flexible Flyer is the trademark of the Roadmaster Corporation, Olney, Illinois. **37** *clockwise from top left:* "Simple Simon and Pieman" logo courtesy of Franchise Associates, Inc.; Courtesy of Motorola Museum of Electronics; Coca-Cola is a registered trademark of The Coca-Cola Company; A registered trademark of Schering-Plough HealthCare Products, Inc., USA/Reproduced with permission of Schering-Plough Healthcare Products, Inc., the trademark owner; Xerox 9400 duplicator ad ©1977, Xerox Corporation; ©Revlon, Inc.; Eveready Battery Company, Inc.; The USDA Forest Service, the State Foresters, the Ad Council and Foote, Cone & Belding; Fruit of The Loom, Inc.; Courtesy of Clairol, Inc.; *center* Peter Max, 1972/Courtesy ViaMax, New York. **38** *top right* Brown Brothers; *bottom left* Courtesy of The Adirondack Museum; *remainder* Culver Pictures. **39** *top left* Bettmann/Hulton; *top right* Culver Pictures; *bottom* Brown Brothers. **40** *left* Culver Pictures; *remainder* The Bettmann Archive. **41** *"Heidelberg Belt"* Original poster from the Lindan Historical Collection of Electrotherapy and Unusual Healing Devices, Cleveland, OH; Published by the Museum of Questionable Medical Devices, Minneapolis, MN; *"Iron Bitters"* From the collection of Romy Charlesworth; *"Warburg's Tincture" and "Dr. Shoop's Tablets"* Smithsonian Institution; *bottom left* The Bettmann Archive; *bottom right* The Granger Collection, New York. **42** *left (top to bottom)* Culver Pictures; Collection of Theodore Robinson, Richboro, PA; Brown Brothers; *top right* The Granger Collection, New York; **42-43** *bottom* Brown Brothers. **43** *clockwise from top:* The Bettmann Archive; The Granger Collection, New York; Library of Congress; Culver Pictures. **44** *upper left and upper right* Culver Pictures; inset Courtesy Department Library Services, American Museum of Natural History; *bottom right* The Bettmann Archive. **44-45** *background* Courtesy Department Library Services, American Museum of Natural History. **45** *left* UPI/Bettmann; *right (ship)* Culver Pictures; *(figure)* Bettmann/Hulton. **46** *top left* Private Collection/Photographed by Steven Mays; *bottom left* Brown Brothers; *top right* Chicago Historical Society; *bottom right* Library of Congress. **47** *top* National Archives; *circle* Brown Brothers; *remainder* The Bettmann Archive. **48** *left* The Bettmann Archive; *bottom middle* Library of Congress; *buttons* Sophia Smith Collection/Photographed by Mark Sexton. **49** *left* Brown Brothers; *right* The Cousley Historical Collections/Photographed by Steven Mays. **50** *top left* J. Messerschmidt/Bruce Coleman Inc.; *bottom left* Library of Congress; *top right* The Bettmann Archive; *bottom right* Culver Pictures. **51** *left* Theodore Roosevelt Collection, Harvard College Library; *top right* The Bettmann Archive; *bottom right* Culver Pictures. **52** *top left* The Bettmann Archive; *middle left and bottom left* Culver Pictures; *bottom grouping (l. to r.)* Library of Congress; Culver Pictures; Library of Congress; *bottom right* The Bettmann Archive. **53** *top center and bottom center* The Bettmann Archive; *remainder* UPI/Bettmann. **54** *top grouping* Culver Pictures; *bottom* The Bettmann Archive; *remainder* US Department of the Interior, National Park Service, Edison National Historic Site. **55** *top* Brown Brothers; *bottom* Culver Pictures. **56** *left* Philadelphia Museum of Art/Louise and Walter Arensberg Collection; *center* Yale Collection of American Literature, Beinecke Rare Book and Manuscript Library, Yale University; *right* Library of Congress. **57** *bottom right* Brown Brothers; *remainder* Culver Pictures. **58** *left (grouping)* Collection of William L. Simon; *center* Brown Brothers. **59** *top left* The Bettmann Archive; *top middle* Frank Driggs Collection; *top right* Collection of William L. Simon; *bottom* Museum of The City of New York, The Theater Collection. **60** *top left* Culver Pictures; *top right (page)* The Bettmann Archive; *(photo)* Library of Congress; *bottom left* Henry W. and Albert A. Berg Collection, The New York Public Library; *bottom right* The Bettmann Archive. **61** *top grouping (Collier's)* The Bettmann Archive; *(remainder)* Culver Pictures; *bottom* Culver Pictures; *bottom right* The Bettmann Archive. **62-63** FPG International. **64** *bottom left* The Hulton-Deutsch Collection, London; *remainder* The Granger Collection, New York. **65** *top* The Granger Collection, New York; *bottom left* Brown Brothers; *bottom right* National Archives. **66** *top middle* Süddeutscher Verlag; *bottom* UPI/Bettmann; *remainder* Imperial War Museum, London. **67** *top* New York Public Library Picture Collection; *bottom* Imperial War Museum, London. **68** *top (l. to r.)* Imperial War Museum, London; Culver Pictures; Edward Vebell Collection/Photographed by Steven Mays; *bottom* Musée d'Histoire Contemporaine. **68-69** *bottom* Bayerisches Armeemuseum, Germany. **69** *top* Culver Pictures; *middle left* Brown Brothers; *top right* National Archives of Canada; *remainder* Imperial War Museum, London. **70** *all* Imperial War Museum, London. **70-71** *bottom (background)* Imperial War Museum, London. **71** *bottom left* National Archives; *top right* Bruce Bairnsfather Estate, Courtesy of A.E. Johnson Artists' Agents; *remainder* Imperial War Museum, London. **72** *top to bottom:* Culver Pictures; National Archives; Ullstein Bilderdienst, Germany; Popperfoto, London. **72-73** *background* Imperial War Museum, London. **73** *both* Imperial War Museum, London. **74** *top left* Brown Brothers; *top right* Collection of William L. Simon; *bottom* UPI/Bettmann. **75** *left (all)* Edward Vebell Collection; *top right* The Bettmann Archive; *bottom right* National Archives. **76** *top (all)* Sovfoto; *bottom* National Archives. **76-77** *bottom* Robert Hunt Library. **77** *top right* UPI/Bettmann; *center* Edward Vebell Collection; *remainder* Novosti from Sovfoto. **78** *left* Imperial War Museum, London; *right* Hulton Picture Company. **79** *top left* Illustrated London News; *medal* Edward Vebell Collection/Photographed by Steven Mays; *top right* Private Collection; *bottom* UPI/Bettmann. **80** *clockwise from top left:* The Cousley Historical Collections/Photographed by Richard Levy; The Cousley Historical Collections/Photographed by Richard Levy; The Nancy Drew Game™ photograph is used with permission from Hasbro, Inc.; David Galt/Games & Names, New York, NY; Steven Mays/"The Encyclopedia of Collectibles" for Time-Life Books, courtesy Rebus, Inc., NY; David Galt/Games & Names, New York, NY; Steven Mays/"The Encyclopedia of Collectibles" for Time-Life Books, courtesy Rebus, Inc., NY; center Monopoly® is a registered trademark of Tonka Corporation ©1936, 1992 Parker Brothers, a subsidiary of Tonka Corporation. All rights reserved. Used with permission. **81** *clockwise from top left:* The Cousley Historical Collections/Photographed by Richard Levy; Milton Bradley Company, a division of Hasbro, Inc., all rights reserved; The Cousley Historical Collections/Photographed by Richard Levy; Milton Bradley Company, a division of Hasbro, Inc.; Nintendo of America, Inc.; Nintendo of America, Inc.; Milton Bradley Company, a division of Hasbro, Inc.; Milton Bradley Company, a division of Hasbro, Inc., all rights reserved. Used with permission; The Cousley Historical Collections/Photographed by Richard Levy; Milton Bradley Company, a division of Hasbro, Inc., all rights reserved; *center* The Cousley Historical Collections/Photographed by Richard Levy. **82** *(l. to r.)* National Archives; The Granger Collection, New York; *remainder* Stock Montage, Inc. **83** *top left* Culver Pictures; *top right* State Archives of Michigan; *bottom* National Archives; *poster grouping (center)* Smithsonian Institution; *(top left)* The Granger Collection, New York; *(top right)* Imperial War Museum, London/Photographed by Angelo Hornak, London; *(bottom left)* Culver Pictures; *(bottom right)* Library of Congress. **84** *top right* Collection of William L. Simon; *remainder* Edward Vebell Collection. **85** *top* Collection of William L. Simon; *remainder* National Archives. **88** *top* National Archives; *bottom* Sygma. **89** *top left* Brown Brothers; *top middle* West Point Museum, United States Military Academy, West Point, New York; *top right* Library of Congress; *bottom* National Archives. **90** *right* The New Jersey Historical Society; *remainder* National Archives. **91** *top* State Historical Society of Wisconsin; *bottom* National Archives. **92** *top left* Movie Still Archives; *bottom left* Frank Driggs Collection; *bottom right* UPI/Bettmann; *sheet music* Collection of William L. Simon. **93** *top* Brown Brothers; *remainder* Culver Pictures. **94** *helmets* Edward Vebell Collection/Photographed by Steven Mays; *remainder* National Archives. **95** *top middle* Harry S. Truman Library; *top right* Imperial War Museum, London; *remainder* National Archives. **96** *top left* From "Memoirs of the Harvard Dead" by M.A. DeWolfe Howe, Harvard University Press, reprinted by permission; *bottom left* Robert Hunt Library; *top right* National Archives; *middle right* Imperial War Museum, London. **97** *top* Brown Brothers; *bottom* National Archives; inset Popperfoto. **98** *top right* Edward Vebell Collection; *remainder* National Archives. **99** *top left* National Archives; *top right* Brown Brothers; *bottom* Edward Vebell Collection/Photographed by Steven Mays. **100-101** ©Equitable Life Assurance of the USA. **102** *top* National Archives; *bottom* Library of Congress. **103** *left* E.T. Archive; *top right* National Archives; *bottom right* Globe Photos. **104** *left and top* The Bettmann Archive. **105** *top* Museum of The City of New York, L1226.3G/Permanent deposit of the Public Works Art Project, through the Whitney Museum of American Art; *bottom middle* The Cousley Historical Collections/Photographed by Steven Mays; *remainder* The Bettmann Archive. **106** *top* UPI/Bettmann; *bottom* Photography Collection, Harry Ransom Humanities Research Center, The University of Texas at Austin. **107** *bottom* Museum of The City of New York, L1226.3G/Permanent deposit of the Public Works Art Project, through the Whitney Museum of American Art; *remainder* UPI/Bettmann. **108** *top left* Memphis Commercial Appeal; *bottom left* Smithsonian Institution; *bottom middle* Steven Laschever; *top right and middle right* UPI/Bettmann; *bottom right* Stock Montage, Inc. **109** *top* UPI/Bettmann; *bottom* Ohio Historical Society. **110** *left* Ohio Historical Society; *middle* University of Hartford, Museum of American Political Life; *right* Culver Pictures. **111** *bottom* UPI/Bettmann; *remainder* Brown Brothers. **112** *clockwise from top* Library of Congress; Brown Brothers; Library of Congress; Rudolph Vetter; Rudolph Vetter; Museum of American Political Life/Photographed by Sally Andersen-Bruce; Culver Pictures. **113** *top left and bottom left* AP/Wide World Photos; *top middle* Steven Laschever; *top right* Library of Congress; *bottom right* UPI/Bettmann. **114** *top* UPI/Bettmann; *middle* National Archives; *bottom* Courtesy of Edmund H. Harvey, Jr. **115** *left* Courtesy United Airlines; *center (stickers)* Smithsonian Institution; *top right* Culver Pictures; *bottom right* Collection of William L. Simon. **116** *top* Brown Brothers; *bottom middle* The Cousley Historical Collections/Photographed by Steven Mays; *bottom right* The Bettmann Archive; *remainder* National Baseball Library, Cooperstown, NY. **117** *top left and bottom right* UPI/Bettmann; *top middle* Culver Pictures; *remainder* Brown Brothers. **118** *top left* Culver Pictures; *top right* Cover-drawing by Rea Irvin ©1925, 1953 The New Yorker Magazine, Inc.; *remainder* The Bettmann Archive. **119** *top left* Brown Brothers; *top right* UPI/Bettmann; *bottom left* Reader's Digest; *bottom middle* Brown Brothers; *Scopes Trial page (left)* Brown Brothers; *(middle)* The Bettmann Archive; *(right)* UPI/Bettmann. **120** *both* Brown Brothers. **121** *top left* ® & ©1994 Tribune Media Services, Inc., All rights reserved; *bottom left and bottom right* The Cousley Historical Collections/Photographed by Steven Mays; *remainder* Piggly Wiggly Corporation. **122** *center* Culver Pictures; *bottom right* UPI/Bettmann; *remainder* The Bettmann Archive. **123** *top left* Culver Pictures; *bottom left* Courtesy of Illustration House, Inc., New York City; *top middle* Brown Brothers; *top right* The Bettman Archive; *bottom right* Library of Congress. **124** *top left* The Bettmann Archive; *middle left* Private Collection; *bottom left* Culver Pictures; *right* Brown Brothers. **125** *top left* UPI/Bettmann; *top middle* The Cousley Historical Collections/Photographed by Steven Mays; *top right* Culver Pictures; *bottom* The Bettmann Archive. **126** *top left (Sheik)* Sy Seidman Collection/Culver Pictures; *(Nellie)* Private Collection; *center* Brown Brothers; *top right* Frank Driggs Collection; *bottom left* Private Collection and Collection of William L. Simon/Photographed by Richard Levy. **127** *top to bottom* Frank Driggs Collection; Michael Ochs Archives/Venice, CA; The Bettmann Archive; UPI/Bettmann Newsphotos. **128** *top left and top right* Culver Pictures; *stars* The Bettmann Archive; *remainder* Brown Brothers. **129** *top left* Movie Still

Archives; *top right* Edwin Bower Hesser/The Kobal Collection; *remainder* Culver Pictures. **130** *left* The Bettmann Archive; *middle* Henry Ford Museum & Greenfield Village, Dearborn, Michigan/Photographed by Ted Spiegel; *right* Springer/Bettmann Film Archive. **131** *bottom right* Culver Pictures; *remainder* Brown Brothers. **132** *left* Brown Brothers; *inset* National Automobile Museum Library. **133** *top left* The Bettmann Archive; *top right* Automobile Quarterly/Photographed by Nicky Wright; *middle right* American Automobile Manufacturer's Association; *bottom* Culver Pictures. **134** *left (top to bottom)* SuperStock; ©1988 Cindy Lewis, All rights reserved; Richard Spiegelman. *right (top to bottom)* SuperStock; Richard Spiegelman; ©1989 Cindy Lewis, All rights reserved; ©1992 Cindy Lewis, All rights reserved. **135** *clockwise from top left* ©1986 Cindy Lewis, All rights reserved; ©1982 Cindy Lewis, All rights reserved; ©1991 Cindy Lewis, All rights reserved; Automobile Quarterly; Ford Motor Company; ©1992 Cindy Lewis, All rights reserved; ©1990 Cindy Lewis, All rights reserved; Automobile Quarterly; *center (top)* ©1986 Cindy Lewis, All rights reserved; *(bottom)* ©1991 Cindy Lewis, All rights reserved. **136** *top left* The Granger Collection, New York; *bottom left* Brown Brothers; *remainder* The Bettmann Archive. **137** *top* Culver Pictures; *bottom left* The Bettmann Archive; *bottom right* ©Al Hirschfeld. Drawing reproduced by special arrangement with Hirschfeld's exclusive representative, The Margo Feiden Galleries Ltd., New York. **138** *top right* Brown Brothers; *bottom left* FPG International; *remainder* The Bettmann Archive. **139** *top left grouping: (top)* ©1928 by Simon & Schuster Inc., Reprinted by permission of Pocket Books, a division of Simon & Schuster Inc.; *(left)* The Bettmann Archive; *(right)* UPI/Bettmann Newsphotos; *top right* NASA; *bottom* Lee Boltin Picture Library. **140** *background* The Bettmann Archive; *top right* International Museum of Photography at George Eastman House; *bottom left* The Bettmann Archive; *bottom right* Brown Brothers. **141** *Bartons* Culver Pictures; *right* The Hall of History Foundation, Schenectady, New York; *remainder* The Bettmann Archive. **142** Brown Brothers; *inset* Culver Pictures. **143** *top right* Culver Pictures; *remainder* Brown Brothers; **144** *top* Museum of American Political Life/University of Hartford; *middle* Culver Pictures; *bottom* The Bettmann Archive. **145** *top left* Florida State Archives; *top right* UPI/Bettmann; *center* Culver Pictures; *bottom right* Brown Brothers. **146-147** Library of Congress. **148** *left* UPI/Bettmann; *right* Underwood & Underwood Collection/The Bettmann Archive. **149** *left* Culver Pictures; *right* Collection of William L. Simon. **150** *bottom right* Museum of The City of New York; *remainder* The Bettmann Archive. **151** *top left* Brown Brothers; *box (clockwise from top)* Reprinted with permission Macmillan Publishing Company from "Gone With The Wind" by Margaret Mitchell ©1936 by Macmillan Publishing Company; UPI/Bettmann; Culver Pictures; From "The Grapes of Wrath" by John Steinbeck, ©1939, renewed ©1967 by John Steinbeck, Used by permission of Viking Penguin, a division of Penguin Books USA Inc./Photography courtesy of the Henry W. and Albert A. Berg Collection, The New York Public Library; UPI/Bettmann; Culver Pictures. **152** Culver Pictures. **153** National Archives; *insets* Library of Congress. **154** *top left* Museum of American Political Life, University of Hartford/Photographed by Steven Laschever; *grouping (top)* The Cousley Historical Collections; *(middle)* Culver Pictures; *(bottom)* Franklin D. Roosevelt Library/©1933, 1961 Peter Arno. **155** *left* Culver Pictures; *right* UPI/Bettmann. **156** *bottom* Brown Brothers. **157** *left* Sherman Grinberg Film Library, Inc./Courtesy of the Franklin D. Roosevelt Library; *center* UPI/Bettmann; *right* The Bettmann Archive. **158** *top left* Library of Congress; *bottom left* UPI/Bettmann; *right* National Museum of American Art, Washington, DC/Art Resource, NY. **159** *top right* National Archives; *remainder* Culver Pictures. **160** *background* Culver Pictures; *clockwise from top* The Kobal Collection; The Kobal Collection; Culver Pictures; Smithsonian Institution; Lester Glassner Collection/Neal Peters. **161** *background* Culver Pictures; *clockwise from top (Astaire & Rogers)* The Kobal Collection; Photofest; Lester Glassner Collection/Neal Peters; Culver Pictures; ©The Walt Disney Company. **162** *top left* Fred Cook Collection; *bottom left* UPI/Bettmann; *bottom middle* The Bettmann Archive; *bottom right* Culver Pictures. **162-163** *background* Frank Driggs Collection. **163** *box (left)* Culver Pictures; *(right)* Fred Cook Collection; *(Ellington)* The Bettmann Archive; *(Goodman)* Culver Pictures; *remainder* Frank Driggs Collection. **164** *top* Culver Pictures; *bottom left* Chicago Playing Card Collector, Inc.; *bottom right* UPI/Bettmann. **165** *top left* Naismith Memorial Basketball Hall of Fame; *top right and bottom right* UPI/Bettmann; *oval* UPI/Bettmann Newsphotos; *remainder* AP/Wide World Photos. **166** *top right (poster)* New York Public Library; *(actors)* Culver Pictures; *remainder* Museum of The City of New York/The Theater Collection. **167** *top left* New York Public Library; *top right* Culver Pictures; *remainder* Museum of The City of New York/The Theater Collection. **168** *top left* Brown Brothers; *top right* The Cousley Historical Collections; *bottom* UPI/Bettmann. **169** *top left* AP/Wide World Photos; *grouping (top)* UPI/Bettmann Newsphotos; *(bottom left)* ©1935 Oklahoma Publishing Company, reprinted with permission; *(bottom right)* UPI/Bettmann; *remainder* The Bettmann Archive. **170** *top left* The Bettmann Archive; *bottom left* UPI/Bettmann; *remainder* Brown Brothers. **171** *top* Hake's Americana & Collectibles; *bottom left* UPI/Bettmann; *bottom middle* Brown Brothers; *bottom right* Hake's Americana & Collectibles/Photographed by Richard Levy. **172** *background* Archives of Labor and Urban Affairs/Wayne State University; *both insets* UPI/Bettmann. **173** *top* Culver Pictures; *bottom* UPI/Bettmann. **174** *bottom left* Museum of American Political Life, University of Hartford/Photographed by Steven Laschever; *remainder* UPI/Bettmann. **175** *top left* Library of Congress; *top right* The Cousley Historical Collections/Photographed by Steven Mays; *bottom* Brown Brothers. **176** *top* The Bettmann Archive; *bottom left* AP/Wide World Photos; *bottom right* Brown Brothers. **177** *both* UPI/Bettmann. **178** *background* Brown Brothers; *car* UPI/Bettmann; *box (top)* Brown Brothers; *(bottom)* UPI/Bettmann. **179** *top left* Brown Brothers; *top right* Smithsonian Institution; *center (top to bottom)* Hake's Americana & Collectibles; Archives Unit, University of Liverpool; Brown Brothers. **180** *middle left* Courtesy of Edith Bel Geddes; *middle right* Brown Brothers; *remainder* UPI/Bettmann. **181** *clockwise from top right* Culver Pictures; Hake's Americana & Collectibles; Courtesy of Western Pennsylvania Conservancy; The Frank Lloyd Wright Archives; Angelo Hornak, London; The Brooklyn Museum/Gift of The Walter Foundation. **182** *clockwise from top right* Library of Congress; Moulin Studio Archives, San Francisco; The Bettmann Archive; Culver Pictures; *circle* H. Armstrong Roberts. **183** *clockwise from top left* Moulin Studio Archives, San Francisco; New York Public Library Picture Collection; Collection of The Queens Museum of Art, New York/Gift of Bob Golby; Scenic Art, Inc.; Private Collection; Ted Spiegel; *center* Private Collection. **184** *top* UPI/Bettmann; *bottom left* AP/Wide World Photos; *bottom middle* UPI/Bettmann; *bottom right* Brown Brothers. **185** *top* UPI/Bettmann; *middle* Paul Dorsey/Life Magazine ©1938 Time Warner Inc.; *bottom* Library of Congress. **186** *left* AP/Wide World Photos; *center (both)* Library of Congress; *right* FPG International. **187** *top* Bundesarchiv; *bottom* UPI/Bettmann; *inset* National Archives. **188-189** National Archives. **190** *left* Roger Schall; *inset* National Archives. **191** *bottom right* Novosti Photo Library; *remainder* Imperial War Museum, London. **192** *top left* National Archives; *top right* Joe Lyndhurst; *bottom* UPI/Bettmann. **193** *top left* Imperial War Museum, London; *inset* Bettmann/Hulton; *bottom left* Robert Hunt Library; *bottom right* Robert Capa/Magnum. **194** *top left* UPI/Bettmann Newsphotos. **194-195** *bottom* National Archives. **195** *left* UPI/Bettmann Newsphotos; *right* AP/Wide World Photos. **196** *left* UPI/Bettmann; *right* AP/Wide World Photos. **197** *top* The Cousley Historical Collections/Photographed by James McInnis; *bottom* National Archives. **198** UPI/Bettmann. **199** *top left* National Archives; *top right (roof)* Marc Riboud/Magnum; *middle right* from The Lords of Japan, pg. 10 by Henry Wiencek, Tree Communications, Stonehenge Press; *bottom right* National Archives; *bottom center* Joe Lyndhurst. **200** *left* National Archives; *right* Imperial War Museum, London. **200-201** *background* SuperStock. **201** *box (both)* National Archives; *bottom left* Roger Viollet; *bottom right* Imperial War Museum, London. **202** *top* Jack Novak/Photri; *bottom* Sovfoto. **202-203** *background* Smithsonian Institution. **203** *left* Sovfoto; *right* ITAR-TASS/Sovfoto. **204** *top left* National Archives; *top right* Jack Novak/Photri; *inset* Smithsonian Institution. **204-205** *bottom* AP/Wide World Photos. **205** *top* US Marine Corps; *bottom* National Archives. **206** *top to bottom* National Archives; National Archives; Roger Schall; AP/Wide World Photos; National Archives. **207** *top* Imperial War Museum, London; *middle* Sovfoto; *bottom* Imperial War Museum, London. **208** *top to bottom* National Archives; National Archives; US Marine Corps. **209** *all* National Archives. **210** *top left* National Archives; *bottom left* Ewing Krainin; *bottom middle* Culver Pictures; *bottom right* Joe Lyndhurst. **211** *top left* John Phillips/Photo Researchers, Inc.; *top middle & right* ©1944 Bill Mauldin, reprinted with permission of Bill Mauldin; *middle right* Culver Pictures; *bottom* ©1944 George Baker. **212** *left* UPI/Bettmann; *right* US Army. **213** *top & bottom left* UPI/Bettmann Newsphotos; *top middle & right* Library of Congress. **214** *top* National Archives Trust Fund Board; *bottom* Library of Congress. **215** *top left* Bildarchiv Preussischer Kulturbesitz, Berlin; *top right* Eddie Adams/Sygma; *bottom* UPI/Bettmann. **216** *left grouping* Erich Lessing/Art Resource, N.Y.; *center* UPI/Bettmann; *top right* National Archives; *bottom* UPI/Bettmann. **217** *top left* UPI/Bettmann; *remainder* National Archives. **218** *top left* Franklin Roosevelt Library; *top right* Norman Rockwell Trust; *center* National Archives; *bottom* US Naval Historical Center. **219** *top left* AP/Wide World Photos; *center* The Bettmann Archive; *bottom* UPI/Bettmann Newsphotos. **220** *left* National Archives; *middle* AP/Wide World Photos; *right* Michigan Historical Commission. **221** *page* AP/Wide World Photos; *inset* National Archives. **222** *both* National Archives. **223** *top* Bundesarchiv; *bottom* National Archives. **224** *all* National Archives. **225** *top left* AP/Wide World Photos; *bottom center grouping* Submarine Force Library and Museum, Groton, CT; *remainder* National Archives. **226-227** *all* National Archives. **228** *top left* James McInnis; *remainder* Charles Silliman. **228-229** *background* US Army. **229** *top* National Archives; *bottom* UPI/Bettmann. **230** *bottom right* Photri; *remainder* National Archives. **231** *left* UPI/Bettmann Newsphotos; *top right* Smithsonian Institution; *remainder* National Archives. **232** *top left* UPI/Bettmann; *bottom left* AP/Wide World Photos; *remainder* Library of Congress. **233** *top left* Frank Driggs Collection; *top right* Lester Glassner Collection/Neal Peters; *bottom left and middle* Courtesy of Carol Nehring; *bottom right* AP/Wide World Photos. **234** *top left* Library of Congress; *bottom* Printed by permission of the Norman Rockwell Family Trust ©1942 The Norman Rockwell Family Trust. **234-235** Brown Brothers. **235** *top* Frank Driggs Collection; *bottom left* Performing Arts Research Center/New York Public Library At Lincoln Center; *bottom middle* The Bettmann Archive; *bottom right* Culver Pictures. **236** *left* Photoworld; *top right* ©The Walt Disney Company: *bottom right* The Bettmann Archive; *remainder* The Cousley Historical Collections. **237** *center right* National Baseball Hall of Fame; *top right* National Archives; *bottom left (both)* Culver Pictures; *bottom middle* Smithsonian Institution; *bottom right* UPI/Bettmann Newsphotos; *remainder* UPI/Bettmann. **238** *top middle* The Kobal Collection; *top right & center right* Photofest; *bottom left* Culver Pictures; *bottom right* Springer/Bettmann Archive; *remainder* Movie Still Archives. **239** *top (circle & sailors)* Culver Pictures; *(Patton)* Photofest; *center left (Robert Taylor)* MGM/Frank Tanner; *center middle (oval)* Neal Peters Collection; *center right & bottom right* Photofest; *bottom left* Culver Pictures; *remainder* Movie Still Archives. **240** *top* UPI/Bettmann; *bottom* AP/Wide World Photos. **241** *top left (oval)* Ed Clark, Life Mag azine ©Time Warner, Inc.; *top right* The Bettmann Archive; *bottom left* Smithsonian Institution; *bottom right* UPI/Bettmann. **242** *left* AP/Wide World Photos; *bottom* National Archives. **243** *left* The Bettmann Archive; *right* Alfred Eisenstaedt, Life Magazine ©Time Warner, Inc. **244-245** Archive Photos/Camerique. **246** *both* UPI/Bettmann. **246-247** *background* United Nations; *bottom* Brown Brothers. **247** *left* National Archives; *right* AP/Wide World Photos. **248** *left* UPI/Bettmann; *center* Jack Novak/Photri; *right* Brown Brothers. **249** *top left* UPI/Bettmann; *top right* H. Cartier-Bresson/Magnum; *bottom right* Culver Pictures; *inset* State Historical Society of Missouri, Columbia. **250** *top left* Tim Street-Porter; *top right* FPG International; *bottom right* H. Armstrong Roberts; *inset* UPI/Bettmann. **251** *top left* Ernst Haas/Magnum; *top middle* AP/Wide World Photos; *top right* The Bettmann Archive; *bottom left* UPI/Bettmann Newsphotos; *bottom right* Brown Brothers. **252** *left* The Kansas City Star; *right* David Harris. **253** *left* Culver Pictures; *right* UPI/Bettmann. **254** *top right* The Cousley Historical Collections/Photographed by Steven Mays; *bottom right* Harry S. Truman Library; *bottom left* Stock Montage. **255** *top left* UPI/Bettmann; *top right* UPI/Bettmann Newsphotos; *middle right* Culver Pictures; *bottom right* The Bettmann Archive. **256** *left* Culver Pictures; *right* UPI/Bettmann. **257** *both* UPI/Bettmann. **258** *left* Culver Pictures; *middle* The Bettmann Archive; *right* UPI/Bettmann. **259** *top left* George Rodger/Magnum; *remainder* The Bettmann Archive. **260** *left* Archive Photos; *right* Eve Arnold/Magnum. **260-261** Archive Photos. **261** *top* Photofest; *bottom* J.R. Eyerman/Life Magazine ©1953 Time, Inc. **262** *bottom* Photofest; *right* Howard Frank. **263** *top left* Motion Picture and TV Photo Archive; *top right and bottom right* Photofest; *bottom left and middle* Movie Still Archives. **264** *top left* Neal Peters Collection; *top right* Photofest; *remainder* Movie Still Archives. **265** *top left* Photofest/©Walt Disney Productions; *top middle* Movie Still Archives; *bottom right* Globe Photos; *remainder* Photofest. **266** *left* Magnum; *inset* Brown Brothers. **267** *top left* The Bettmann Archive; *top middle* UPI/Bettmann; *top right* Brown Brothers; *bottom* Movie Still Archives. **268** UPI/Bettmann Newsphotos. **269** *top left* UPI/Bettmann; *top right* National Archives; *bottom* The Bettmann Archive. **270** *top and middle left* The Cousley Historical Collections/Photographed by Steven Mays; *right* UPI/Bettmann; *bottom left* The Cousley Historical Collections. **271** *top left* Hake's Americana & Collectibles; *remainder* AP/Wide World Photos. **272** *background* Dennis Stock/Magnum; *top* UPI/Bettmann; *bottom left* Elliot Erwin/Magnum; *bottom right* The Bettmann Archive. **273** *top right* ©1953 Marvin Koner/Black Star; *bottom left and right* UPI/Bettmann. **274** *bottom right (Wood)* Cincinnati Art Museum, The Edwin and Virginia Irwin Memorial, ©1994 Estate of Grant Wood/VAGA, New York; *remainder (clockwise from top)* The Cleveland Museum of Art; Columbus Museum of Art, Ohio; Art Resource, N.Y.; The University of Arizona Museum of Art; Art Resource, N.Y. **275** *center* Collection of the Brandywine River Museum, gift of Harry G. Haskell ©Andrew Wyeth; *remainder from top center* The Phillips Collection, Washington D.C.; Hirshhorn Museum and Sculpture Garden, Smithsonian Institution, Gift of Joseph H. Hirshhorn, 1972/Photographed by Lee Stalsworth; National Museum of American Art/Art Resource, N.Y.; Janet Fish; National Gallery of Art, Washington; Krannert Art Museum and Kinkead Pavilion, University of Illinois, Champaign/Photographed by Wilmer Zehr, ©1994 Estate of Stuart Davis/VAGA, New York; "Composition," 1955 by Willem de Kooning, Solomon R. Guggenheim Museum, New York/Photographed by David Heald ©The Solomon R. Guggenheim Foundation, New York. **276** US Air Force Photo; *inset left* Cornell Capa/Magnum; *inset right* Francis Laping/Black Star. **277** *top (all)* UPI/Bettmann; *bottom* The Bettmann Archive. **278** *top both* UPI/Bettmann; *bottom* AP/Wide World Photos. **279** *top middle* Dan Weiner, Courtesy of Sandra Weiner; *bottom* Bob Henriques/Magnum; *right* Karsh/Woodfin Camp & Associates. **280** *left* The Bettmann Archive; *middle top* UPI/Bettmann News-photos; *middle bottom* Brown Brothers; *right* UPI/Bettmann. **281** *top left* UPI/Bettmann Newsphotos; *top middle and right* UPI/Bettmann; *bottom* The Bettmann Archive. **282** *left* The Bettmann Archive; *top right* Hake's Americana & Collectibles/Photographed by Steven Mays; *bottom right* Burt Glinn/Magnum. **283** *left* FPG International; *top right* Private Collection/Photographed by Steven Mays, by permission of Little, Brown and Company; *middle right* Private Collection/Photographed by James McInnis, by permission of Simon and Schuster; *bottom right* ©Dennis Hallinan/FPG International. **284** *bottom left* BMI/Michael Ochs Archives/Venice, CA; *middle* Charles Trainor/Globe Photos; *top right* By permission of MCA Records/Photographed by Richard Levy; *middle* Kevin Jordan Collection/Photographed by Richard Levy, by permission of MCA Records; *bottom right* Michael Ochs Archives/Venice, CA. **285** *top left* Kevin Jordan Collection/Photographed by Richard Levy, by permission of Ace Records, Ltd.; *bottom left* Frank Driggs Collection; *middle* Bob Martin/Globe Photos; *inset* By permission of MCA Records/Photographed by Richard Levy; *bottom right* Michael Ochs Archives/Venice, CA. **286** *top left and right* Photofest; *bottom left* Movie Still Archives. **287** *bottom left* Photofest; *remainder* Archive Photos. **288** *left (top three)* Museum of The City of New York/The Theater Collection; *left bottom* Frank Driggs Collection/Photographed by James McInnis; *top right* New York Public Library; *bottom right* Museum of The City of New York/The Theater Collection. **289** *inset* Archive Photos; *remainder* Museum of The City of New York//The Theater Collection. **290** *top right* By permission of The Detroit Free Press; *top left* TASS/Sovfoto; *bottom* RIA-Novosti/Sovfoto. **291** *left* Denis Gifford Collection; *right* National Archives; *top inset* Brown Brothers; *bottom inset* NASA. **292** *top left* Eastfoto; *bottom left* UPI/Bettmann; *right* Culver Pictures. **293** *left* Gillhausen/Black Star; *top right* UPI/Bettmann; *bottom right* MTI/Eastfoto. **294** Courtesy of Edmund H. Harvey, Jr./Photographed by Richard Levy. **295** *middle* Photri; *remainder* Sovfoto. **296** *left* UPI/Bettmann; *top right* Motorola; *bottom right* Dan Mc-

Coy/Rainbow. **297** *top left and center* March of Dimes Birth Defects Foundation; *bottom left* From "The Double Helix" by James D. Watson, Atheneum Press, New York, 1968, pg. 215; *bottom right* AP/Wide World Photos. **298** *top* Elliot Erwitt/Magnum; *bottom* National Archives. 298-299 *top* Chrysler Corporation; background*(highway cloverleaf)* The Bettmann Archive. **299** *top* Volkswagen of America, Inc.; *bottom* The Bettmann Archive. **300** *top left* Eve Arnold/Magnum; *top right* Movie Still Archives; *bottom* UPI/Bettmann Newsphotos. **301** *top left* UPI/Bettmann; *top right* Michael Ochs Archives/Venice, CA; *bottom* Burt Glinn/Magnum. **302-303** James H. Karales/Peter Arnold, Inc. **304** UPI/Bettmann. **305** *top left* Karsh/Woodfin Camp & Associates; *top right* John F. Kennedy Library; *bottom* both J. Scherachel/Life Magazine ©Time Warner, Inc. **306** *top* UPI/Bettmann; *bottom* Paul Conklin. **307** *top left* UPI/Bettmann Newsphotos; *top right* Fred Ward/Black Star; *bottom* The Mark Shaw Collection/Photo Researchers, Inc. **308** *right* Fotokhronika/Tass/Sovfoto; *remainder* UPI/Bettmann. **309** *left* New China Pictures/Eastfoto; *right* Volker Krämer/Stern/Black Star. **310** Bob Henriques/Magnum; *inset* Semyon Raskin/Magnum. **311** *top* Rene Burri/Magnum; *bottom* UPI/Bettmann. **312** *left* The Cousley Historical Collections/Photographed by James McInnis; *right* UPI/Bettmann; *bottom* Fred Ward/Black Star. **313** *left* Bettmann Newsphotos; *top right* Gene Daniels/Black Star; *bottom right* UPI/Bettmann. **314** *all* UPI/Bettmann. **315** *both* Yoichi R. Okamoto/LBJ Library Collection. **316** *left* Flip Schulke/Black Star; *right* Bob Adelman/Magnum. **317** *top left* UPI/Bettmann; *top right* Flip Schulke/Martin Luther King, Jr. Picture Collection/Black Star; *bottom left* Fred Ward/Black Star; *bottom right* ©1963 Charles Moore/Black Star. **318** *top left* ©1969 John Launois/Black Star; *top right* Bob Fitch/Black Star; *bottom inset* Hicks/FPG International; *bottom* Charles Moore/Black Star. **318-319** Deelan Haun/Black Star. **319** *top* Bob Adelman/Magnum; *bottom* Leonard Freed/Magnum. **320** *top* Photri; *bottom left* ITAR-TASS/Sovfoto; *bottom right* Hake's Americana & Collectibles/Photographed by James McInnis. **321** *all* Photri. **322** *middle right* Fred Ward/Black Star; *remainder* NASA. **323** *top* Photri; *bottom left* Karsh/Woodfin Camp & Associates; *bottom right* Howard Sochurek. **324** *center* ©1993 Cindy Lewis, All rights reserved; *bottom right* Photofest; *remainder* Michael Ochs Archives/Venice, CA. **325** *top* Photos courtesy of Mattel, Inc.; *bottom left* Laufer/Globe Photos; *bottom right* Scheler/Black Star. **326** *left* Kevin Jordan Collection/Photographed by Richard Levy, by permission of Motown Records; *middle right* Jim Britt/Michael Ochs Archives/Venice, CA.; *remainder* Lester Glassner Collection/Neal Peters. **326-327** *background* Photofest. **327** *left* Photofest; *top middle* Photofest; *center* Frederic Lewis/Archive Photos; *bottom middle* Steve Paley/Michael Ochs Archives, Venice, CA; *right* Kevin Jordan Collection/Photographed by Richard Levy, by permission of MCA Records. **328** *left* AP/Wide World Photos; *middle* UPI/Bettmann; *right* AP/Wide World Photos. **329** *bottom right* Michael Sullivan/Black Star; *remainder* AP/Wide World Photos. **330** *banana split and turkey* L. Fritz/H. Armstrong Roberts; *Jell-O* H. Armstrong Roberts; *Dagwood* Karen Leeds/The Stock Market; *remainder* James McInnis. **331** *coke* The Coca-Cola Company; *ice cream cone* L. Fritz/H. Armstrong Roberts; *spinach ad* The Granger Collection, New York; *TV dinner* Victor Scocozza/FPG International; *fries* Rick Osentowski/Envision; *hot dogs* Brent Bear/H. Armstrong Roberts; *hamburger* R. Kord/H. Armstrong Roberts; *remainder* James McInnis. **332** *left* Roy Cummings/Camera 5; *middle* David Steen/Camera Press, London; *right* Camera 5. **333** *top left* James H. Karales; *top right* William Claxton/Visages; *bottom left* Carl Shiraishi; *bottom right* Archive Photos. **334** *top* Movie Still Archives; *bottom left* CBS, Inc.; *bottom right* Photofest. **335** *top left* Photofest; *remainder* Lester Glassner Collection/Neal Peters. **336** *top left* Museum of The City of New York/The Theater Collection; *inset* Collection of Richard Seidel/Photographed by James McInnis; *bottom left* Photofest; *right* Bernd Uhlig. **337** *top left* Sygma; *top right* Sam Siegel; *bottom* Dennis Stock/Magnum. **338** *top right* Peter Max; *remainder* Lisa Law. **339** *top left and bottom left* From *Aquarian Odyssey* ©Don Snyder; *middle left and bottom background* Lisa Law; *buttons* Hake's Americana & Collectibles/Photographed by James McInnis; *bottom right* Herb Green/Michael Ochs Archives/Venice, CA. **340** *top* Larry Burrows/Life Magazine ©Time Warner, Inc.; *inset* Yoichi R. Okamoto; *bottom* AP/Wide World Photos. **341** *top* Larry Burrows/Life Magazine ©Time Warner, Inc.; *bottom* Vietnam News Agency. **342** *top* Co Rentmeester/Time Warner, Inc.; *left inset* UPI/Bettmann; *middle inset* AP/Wide World Photos; *right inset* Larry Burrows/Life Magazine ©Time Warner, Inc; *bottom* National Archives. **343** *top* Jack Kightlinger/LBJ Library Collection; *center* Catherine Leroy/SIPA Press; *right* AP/Wide World Photos; *bottom* AP/Wide World Photos. **344** *top left* The Andy Warhol Foundation for the Visual Arts, Inc./Art Resource, N.Y.; *bottom left* Burt Glinn/Magnum; *top right* Fred Stein/Black Star; *bottom right* Collection of Richard Fox/Photographed by James McInnis. **345** *top left* Collection of Richard Fox/Photographed by James McInnis; *middle left* Fred W. McDarrah; *bottom left* Scala/Art Resource, N.Y.; *top right* Roy Lichtenstein; *bottom right* Charles Moore/Black Star. **346** *top left* UPI/Bettmann; *top right* Nacio Jan Brown/Black Star; *bottom* John Launois/Black Star. **347** *top left* Bernard Gotfryd/Woodfin Camp & Associates; *bottom right* Hiroji Kubota/Magnum; *remainder* Nacio Jan Brown/Black Star. **348** *top left* UPI/Bettmann Newsphotos; *center* UPI/Bettmann. **348-349** UPI/Bettmann. **349** *top left* Sally Anderson-Bruce; *top right* Bob Fitch/Black Star; *buttons* Hake's Americana & Collectibles/Photographed by James McInnis; *bottom* Paul Fusco/Magnum. **350** *left* Wally McNamee/The Washington Post; *right* Bill Eppridge/Time Warner, Inc. **351** *top left* Claus Meyer/Black Star; *bottom right* Archive Photos; *remainder* Burt Glinn/Magnum. **352-353** Wally McNamee/Woodfin Camp & Associates. **354** UPI/Bettmann; *inset* Fred Ward/Black Star. **355** *left* AP/Wide World Photos; *center* Michael Abramson/Liaison Agency; *right* UPI/Bettmann Newsphotos. **356** *top* Bettmann; *middle* AP/Wide World Photos; *bottom* US Air Force. **357** *left* UPI/Bettmann; *top right* Reuters/Bettmann; *bottom right* Demylder/Gamma Liaison. **358** *right* J.P. Laffont/Sygma; *crooks (l. to r.)* UPI/Bettmann Newsphotos; J.P. Laffont/Sygma; UPI/Bettmann; UPI/Bettmann; UPI/Bettmann; UPI/Bettmann; Fred Ward/Black Star. **359** *top left* J.P. Laffont/Sygma; *bottom left* David Burnett/Contact Press Images; *bottom middle* AP/Wide World Photos; *bottom right* David Burnett/Contact Press Images. **360** *top left* Eric Hartmann/Magnum; *top right* Hake's Americana & Collectibles/Photographed by James McInnis; *bottom left* Keith Gunner/Bruce Coleman Inc.; *bottom right* Jeff Foott. **360-361** *background* NASA. **361** *top left* Hake's Americana & Collectibles/Photographed by James McInnis; *top right* Camilla Smith/Rainbow; *bottom left* UPI/Bettmann; *bottom right* Bernard Gotfryd/Woodfin Camp & Associates. **362** *top* Dennis Brack/Black Star; *bottom left* Coco McCoy/Rainbow; *bottom right* Associated Press/Time Picture Syndication. **363** *top* John McGrail Photography, Inc.; *bottom* George Herben/Woodfin Camp & Associates. **364** *top left* Harold Krieger/New York Magazine; *top right* Sandy Solmon/Globe Photos; *remainder* Paul Fusco/Magnum. **365** *top* Andy Levin; *bottom left* Bill Stanton/Magnum; *bottom right* Globe Photos. **366** *top left* James McInnis; *top right* Photofest; *bottom left* Leee Childers/Neal Peters; *bottom right* Ormond Gigli/Time Magazine. **367** *left* Montgomery Ward; *top middle* Al Freni; *remainder* James McInnis. **368** *clockwise from top left* The Cousley Historical Collections/Photographed by James McInnis; Ellis Herwig/Stock, Boston; Philip Gould; Doug Wilson/Black Star; Costa Manos/Magnum. **368-369** *(ships)* Kenneth Garrett/Woodfin Camp & Associates. **369** *clockwise from top* Wally McNamee/Woodfin Camp & Associates; Wally McNamee/Woodfin Camp & Associates; Salvatore C. DiMarco, Jr.; Richard Howard; Wally McNamee/Woodfin Camp & Associates. **370** *left* Fred Ward/Black Star; *right* Hake's Americana & Collectibles/Photographed by James McInnis. **371** *left* Elizabeth Sunflower/Contact Press Images; *top right* The Cousley Historical Collections/Photographed by James McInnis; *bottom right* Arthur Grace/Sygma. **372** Black Star. **373** *left* O. Franken/Sygma; *top inset* Ledru/Sygma; *bottom inset* C. Spengler/Sygma; *right* James Andanson/Sygma. **374** *top and bottom left* Photofest; *bottom right* Frank Driggs Collection. **374-375** Michael Ochs Archives/Venice, CA. **375** *top left and bottom left* Photofest; *top right* Kevin Jordan Collection/Photographed by James McInnis; *middle right* Brian D. McLaughlin/Michael Ochs Archives/Venice, CA.; *bottom right* Michael Ochs Archives/Venice, CA. **376** *top left and bottom left* Movie Still Archives; *top right* Stefani Kong/Sygma; *bottom right* Lester Glassner Collection/Neal Peters. **376-377** *background* James McInnis. **377** *both* Movie Still Archives. **378** *both* Movie Still Archives. **379** *top left* Photofest; *top right* Thomas Arma/Photofest; *bottom right* Howard Frank/Personality Photos, Inc.; *remainder* Movie Still Archives. **380** *left (top to bottom)* Library of Congress; Robert McElroy/Woodfin Camp & Associates; Paul Fusco/Magnum; *right* Werner Wolff/Black Star; *pendant* The Cousley Historical Collections/Photographed by James McInnis. **381** *top left* UPI/Bettmann; *top right* Diana Mara Henry; *top center* Library of Congress; *bottom center* Abigail Heyman. **382** *bottom* Brent Jones; *remainder* Alex Webb/Magnum. **383** *top left* Julie Jensen; *top right* Charles Gatewood/Magnum; *bottom* Michael Abramson/Black Star; *inset* Wally McNamee/Woodfin Camp & Associates. **384** *top left* Howard Sochurek; *top right* John Marmaras/Woodfin Camp & Associates; *bottom* Lester Sloan/Woodfin Camp & Associates. **385** *top left* Jim Olive/Peter Arnold, Inc.; *top right* Dan McCoy/Black Star; *bottom left* Gould/DeAnza/Peter Arnold, Inc.; *bottom right* Howard Sochurek/John Hillelson Agency. **386-387** Rob Matheson/The Stock Market. **388** *left* Ronald Reagan Library/National Archives; *right* The Bettmann Archive. **389** *top* Ronald Reagan Library/National Archives; *bottom* Photofest; *left* The Bettmann Archive; *right* Movie Still Archives. **390** *top* Ronald Reagan Library/National Archives; *bottom left* D. Goldberg/Sygma; *bottom middle* Gianfranco Gorgoni/Contact Press Images; *bottom right* Fred Ward/Black Star. **391** *both* Ronald Reagan Library/National Archives. **392** *top left* Erica Lansner/Photoreporters; *bottom left* Dan Lecca/GQ Magazine; *magazines* Courtesy of Harper's Bazaar, Photography by Patrick Demarchelier, and GQ Magazine, Photography by Wayne Maser; *center* Karl Lagerfeld; *bottom right* Theo Westenberger/Gamma Liaison. **393** *left* Luigi Cazzaniga; *center top & middle* Courtesy of Timberland, Inc.; *bottom* Karl Lagerfeld; *top left* L. Norovitch/Gamma Liaison. **394** *left* Susan Meiselas/Magnum; *right* ©1987 Twentieth Century Fox Film Corp. **394-395** Jonathan Levine/Onyx. **395** *left* DPA Photoreporters; *right* Andrew Popper. **396** *top (l. to r.)* Joyce Ravid/Onyx; UPI/Bettmann; AP/Wide World Photos; Rick Maiman/Sygma; *bottom* Random House Inc. **397** *top left* James Colburn/Photoreporters; *top right* John Roca/LGI; *bottom* Enrico Ferorelli. **398** *top left* John Ficara/Sygma; *top right* The White House; *bottom* Courtesy of the Bush Presidential Materials Project. **399** *top left* Steve Liss/Time Magazine; *top right* Larry Downing/Woodfin Camp & Associates; *bottom (l. to r.)* Jeffrey Markowitz/Sygma; P. LeSegretian/Sygma; D. Aubert/Sygma; Jeffrey Markowitz/Sygma. **400** *top* Turner Broadcasting; *bottom left* Paramount Pictures/EC; *bottom right* Chris Haston, NBC/Globe Photos. **401** *top left* NBC/Globe Photos; *top middle* Kimberly Butler/LGI; *top right* Paul Morse/LGI; *bottom left* Karen Kuehn/Matrix; *bottom right* Barry Slobin/Motion Picture & TV Photo Archive. **402** *top left* NBC/Globe Photos; *top middle* Motion Picture & TV Photo Archive; *top right* Courtesy of NBC, Inc.; *bottom right*Courtesy of CBS, Inc.; *bottom left* Everett Collection/Paramount Pictures. **403** *top left* Neal Peters Collection; *bottom left* Motion Picture & TV Photo Archive; *center* ©CBS Inc.; *bottom right* Capital Cities/ABC Inc. **404** *top left* Lannis Waters/Sygma; *top right* Craig Fujii/The Seattle Times; *bottom left* George Nikitin/Sygma; *bottom right* Harald Sund. **405** *top right* David Goss/Impact Visuals; *center* Martha Stanitz; *bottom* Les Stone/Sygma. **406** Ken Regan/Camera 5; *bottom* Elkoussy/Sygma. **407** *top left* Vintage Books, a division of Random House; *top right* Alon Reininger/Contact Press Images; *bottom left* Lynn Goldsmith/LGI; *bottom right* Peter Menzel. **408** *left* Ken Regan/Camera 5; *top* ©David Gahr; *inset* Neal Peters Collection; *oval* Alan Silfen/Outline. **409** *top left* Michael Benabib/Retna Pictures; *middle left* Alice Arnold/LGI Photo Agency; *bottom left* J.L. Atlan/Sygma; *top right* Bruce Malone/Retna Pictures; *bottom right* Herb Ritts/Warner Brothers Records. **410** *top left* ©David Gahr; *top right* Ross-Marino/Sygma; *bottom left* Globe Photos; *bottom right* Paul Valesco/Wide World Photos. **411** *top left* Martha Swope; *top right* Marc Thibodeau/Merle Frimark; *bottom right* Playbill, Inc.; *bottom center* Boneau/Bryan-Brown. **412** *top left* A. Tannenbaum/Sygma; *top right* Betty Press/Woodfin Camp & Associates; *bottom left* Peter Jordan/Network Matrix; *bottom right* J. Langevin/Sygma. **413** *top left* J. Langevin/Sygma; *bottom left* Sygma;*top right* Kenneth Jarecke/Contact Press Images; *bottom right* ©1991 Cable News Network, Inc., All Rights Reserved. **414** *top right and center* The Bettmann Archive; remainder *(clockwise from top left)* The Bettmann Archive; Culver Pictures; M. Theriot/H. Armstrong Roberts; Pan American World Airways; FPG International; Library of Congress. **415** *Wing Ding* J.P. Laffont/Sygma; *remainder (clockwise from top left)* FPG International; UPI/Bettmann; Norman Rockwell Paintings Trust; Dick Davis/Photo Researchers, Inc.; Tony Stone Worldwide; Bob Abraham/The Stock Market; Bill Varie/The Image Bank; Renee Lynn/Photo Researchers; Renee Lynn/Photo Researchers, Inc.; Library of Congress. **416** *top* Gregory Heisler/The Image Bank; *bottom* Lizzie Himmel. **417** Schneeberger, Johnson & Peritore/National Geographic Society; *left inset* Michelle McDonald Picture Group; *right inset* Photri. **418** *top left* Panasonic Company/Division of Matsushita Electric Corporation of America; *bottom left* Craig Blankenhorn/Black Star; *right* Peter Menzel. **419** *top left* Richard Pan/The Image Bank; *top right* Peter Menzel; *bottom* Jeffrey Aaronson/Network Aspen. **420** *top* Alexandra Avakian/Woodfin Camp & Associates; *bottom* Francis Apesteguy/Gamma-Liaison. **421** *top* S. Franklin/Magnum; *bottom left* Wesolowski/Sygma; *bottom right* Eric Bouvet/Gamma-Liaison. **422** *left* Peter Turnley/Black Star; *center* J. Groch/Sygma; *right* B. Bisson/Sygma. **423** *top left* Peter Turnley/Black Star; *top right* Deborah Copaken/Contact Press Images; *bottom left* Alexandra Avakian/Contact Press Images; *bottom right* Yuri Ivanon/Time Picture Syndication. **424** *left* Al Tielemans/Duomo; *top right and bottom right* David Madison/Duomo. **425** *top left* Steve Powell/Allsport; *top right* Michael Layton/Duomo; *center* Rick Steart/Allsport; *bottom left* Tony Duffy/Allsport; *bottom right* Focus On Sports. **426** *top left* Tony Stone Worldwide; *oval* James Colburn/Photoreporters, Inc.; *bottom (l. to r.)* Mark Sennet/Visages; Steven Mark Needham/Envision; *(bottles)* Michael A. Keller/The Stock Market; *top right* Thomas Del Brase; *bottom right* Al Satterwhite/The Image Bank. **427** *top* Tobey Sanford; *middle right* Ray Fairall/Photoreporters; *bottom right* Douglas Dubler/LGI. **428** *top left* Robert McElroy/Woodfin Camp & Associates; *top right* James McInnis; *bottom* Everett Collection/Warner Brothers, Inc. **429** *bottom* Globe Photos; *top right* James McInnis; middle *right and bottom* inset The Kobal Collection. **430** *top left* Tim Davis/David Madison Photography; *middle left* Vandystadt/Allsport; *top right* Mike Powell/Allsport; *bottom* William R. Sallaz/Duomo. **431** *top right* Nintendo of America, Inc.; *bottom left* Jacques Chenet/Woodfin Camp & Associates; *bottom middle* Lisa Rose/Globe Photos; *bottom right* Photoreporters, Inc. **432** *top left* Mike Yamashita/Woodfin Camp & Associates; *bottom left* Steve Liss/Time Magazine; *top right* Steven Rubin/J.B. Pictures for Time. **432-433** *bottom* US News & World Report. **433** *top left* Steve Liss/Time Magazine; *bottom right* James Balog/Black Star. **434** *left* John Ficara/Sygma; *top right* Robert F. Kusel/Sygma; *bottom right* Glenn James/Sygma. **435** *left* Carlos Humberto/Contact Press Images; *center* Houghton Mifflin Company; *right* Reuters/Bettmann. **436** *top left and bottom right* Peter Menzel; *top right* NASA/Photo Researchers, Inc.; *bottom left* Kevin Fleming. **437** *top left* Adam Hart-Davis/Science Photo Library; *top right* SuperStock; *bottom left* Peter Menzel; *bottom right* Photri. **438** The Bettmann Archive. **440** Collection of the Museum of American Folk Art, New York, Gift of Anne Baxter Klee. **441** Culver Pictures. **442** Culver Pictures. **445** The Bettmann Archive. **446** *both* Culver Pictures. **448** The Bettmann Archive. **449** Library of Congress. **450** The Granger Collection, New York. **453** *left* UPI/Bettmann Newsphotos; *right* Culver Pictures. **454** Pete Saloutos/The Stock Market. **457** UPI/Bettmann. **459** Movie Still Archives. **460** Photofest. **462** Owen/Black Star. **463** Lester Glasner Collection/Neal Peters. **464** UPI/Bettmann Newsphotos. **465** New York Public Library/Theater Collection. **466** George C. Marshall Research Foundation. **467** UPI/Bettmann Newsphotos. **468** The Bettmann Archive. **469** AP/Wide World Photos. **470** The Bettmann Archive. **471** ©1949 New York Newsday. **472** UPI/Bettmann. **473** Movie Still Archives. **474** Neal Peters Collection. **475** UPI/Bettmann. **476** New York Daily News. **477** AP/Wide World Photos. **478** Wayne Miller/Magnum. **480** *left* UPI/Bettmann; *right* UPI/Bettmann Newsphotos. **483** NASA. **484** Wally McNamee/Woodfin Camp & Associates. **486** UPI/Bettmann. **487** Focus On Sports, Inc. **489** Ellen Pines Sheffield/Woodfin Camp & Associates. **490** Howard Sochurek/Woodfin Camp & Associates. **491** US Naval Academy. **493** Dirck Halstead/Gamma Liaison. **494** Sygma Paris. **495** Geltzer & Company; *inset(ballgame)* David Madison/Duomo. **496** David Gamble/Sygma. **497** AP/Wide World Photos. **498** Mitsubishi; Movie Still Archives. **499** Camerique/H. Armstrong Roberts. **501** AP/Wide World Photos.

Efforts have been made to reach the holder of the copyright for each picture. In several cases, these sources have been untraceable, for which we offer our apologies.

INDEX

*Page numbers in **bold** type refer to illustrations and captions; those in brackets [ ], to charts.*